The Rise of "The Rest"

D0881696

THE RISE OF "THE REST"

Challenges to the West from Late-Industrializing Economies

ALICE H. AMSDEN

OXFORD
UNIVERSITY PRESS

OXFORD
UNIVERSITY PRESS

Oxford   New York
Auckland   Bangkok   Buenos Aires   Cape Town   Chennai
Dar es Salaam   Delhi   Hong Kong   Istanbul   Karachi   Kolkata
Kuala Lumpur   Madrid   Melbourne   Mexico City   Mumbai   Nairobi
São Paulo   Shanghai   Taipei   Tokyo   Toronto

Copyright © 2001 by Oxford University Press

First issued as an Oxford University Press paperback, 2004

Published by Oxford University Press, Inc.
198 Madison Avenue, New York, New York 10016

Oxford is a registered trademark of Oxford University Press.

Library of Congress Cataloging-in-Publication Data

Amsden, Alice H. (Alice Hoffenberg)
    The rise of "the rest" : challenges to the west from late-industrializing economies /
Alice H. Amsden.
        p. cm.
    Includes bibliographical references.
    ISBN 0-19-513969-0; 0-19-517059-8 (pbk)
        1. Industrialization—Developing countries—History.   2. Competition, International.
    I. Title.

HC59.7 .A7784 2000
338.9'009172'4—dc21   00-039947

9 8 7 6 5 4 3 2 1

Printed in the United States of America
on acid-free paper

Preface

Market behavior is premised on the idea of "scarcity"—it is the essence of value. It is, therefore, curious that leading theories of economic development treat knowledge as a free good. In the theory that underpins policy prescriptions for free trade, knowledge falls like manna from heaven. In the "new" growth theories of the 1980s, knowledge in a given country is the quintessential "public" good whose use by one individual or firm does not diminish its availability to others.

Yet knowledge is possibly the most precious of all assets. The knowledge needed to compete in world markets, as distinct from factual information, comprises unique skills, sui generis capabilities, novel product concepts and idiosyncratic production systems. Because knowledge is proprietary and firm-specific, it is anything but universally available and free. It is the key to economic development, which involves a transformation from wealth-creation centered on primary product-based assets to wealth-creation centered on knowledge-based assets.

This book examines how latecomers caught up in an environment in which knowledge was difficult to access and constituted an entry barrier of incumbent firms. It analyzes the general properties of "pure learning," or industrializing "late," on the initial basis of technologies that were already commercialized by firms from other countries. The market behavior of economies that industrialized during the First and Second Industrial Revolutions with the aid of radically new technologies, and the market behavior of economies that industrialized in the absence of any original production techniques or products, turns out to be distinct, necessitating different policies, institutions, and theories in order for economic development to succeed.

Many people helped with this study. I am grateful for suggestions, comments or other forms of aid from Bjorn Beckman, Brenda Blais, Connie Chang, Wan-Wen Chu, Daniel Chudnovsky, Joel Clark, Carissa Climaco, John Coatsworth, Josh Cohen, Diane Davis, Carter Eckert, Zdenek Drabek, Yoon-Dae Euh, Peter Evans, Giovanni Federico, Duncan Foley, Roberto Frenkel, David Friend, Pankaj Ghemawat, Stephen Haber, Maria Innes Barbero, Devesh Kapur, Maryellen Kelley, Duncan Kincaid, Emine Kiray, Sanjaya Lall, Thomas Tunghao Lee, Liz Leeds, Choon Heng Leong, Youngil Lim, Yeo Lin, the late Qiwen Lu, Brooke Malkin, Daniel Malkin, Sunil Mani, Stephen Marglin, Sunshik Min, Antonio Morales, Mauricio Mesquita Moreira, Juan Carlos Moreno, Mona Mourshed, O Wonchol, PK O'Brien, Arturo O'Connell, Peter Perdue, Tom Rawski, Jaime Ros, Bish Sanyal, John Schrag, Martin Schulz, Helen Shapiro, Ajit Singh, Andres Solimano, Edward Steinfeld, Frances Stewart, Akira Suehira, Lance Taylor, Peter Temin, David Unger, Nick von Tunzelmann, and Kathy Yuan.

Unpublished data were kindly provided to me by Nancy Birdsall, Jorge Mario De Soto Romero, R. Deininger, Masataka Fujita, Anwarul Hoda, Angus Maddison, and Wang Tzyy-po.

A grant from the Social Science Research Council made it possible to work with Joana Andrade and Dulcie Monteiro-Filha on the performance standards set by BNDES, Brazil's development bank, over a 25 year period. The first-class research of these people is greatfully acknowledged. Information on China's automobile industry is based on a field trip to the First Auto Works, Beijing Jeep and first tier parts suppliers in June 1997 with Dong-Yi Liu, Tom Rawski and Yu-Xin Zhang, sponsored by the Chinese Academy of Social Science. Yeong Bon Lee performed outstanding work in estimating the off-line sources of finance for Japan's and Korea's bureaucracies reported in Chapter 6. Working with Hyun-Dae Cho on a paper about Korea's technology policies in the 1990s helped me to formulate my ideas about technology policy more generally.

Jon Clark, my research assistant, deserves special thanks for being cool, calm, clever and amusing.

For their stimulating ideas and extensive criticisms, I bow deeply to Duncan Kennedy, Lex Kelso, Michael Piore, José António Ocampo, the late Raymond Vernon, Alfred Chandler, Joel Mokyr, and Takashi Hikino.

Cambridge, Massachusetts   A. H. A.
May 2000

Contents

The Rise of "The Rest"

1

Industrializing Late

After World War II a handful of countries outside the North Atlantic—*"the rest"*—rose to the ranks of world-class competitors in a wide range of mid-technology industries. National incomes soared at unprecedented rates and per capita incomes doubled within decades. How industrialization among these prime latecomers succeeded, why it followed a unique and novel path, and what some countries did to advance farther than others are the questions this book addresses. By the end of the century, hubris from economic success had led "the rest" to overexpand and fall into debt. But it gave every sign of continuing to nibble away at the North Atlantic's bread-and-butter manufacturing, just as the North Atlantic's multinational companies continued to jostle to enter its financial markets, to sell to its consumers, and to buy the assets of its up-and-coming firms. In 1965 "the rest" supplied less than one-twentieth of world manufacturing output. By 1995 it supplied nearly one-fifth (see table 1.1).

Among backward countries a great divide had already appeared by the end of World War II in the form of *manufacturing experience*. "The rest"—comprising China, India, Indonesia, South Korea, Malaysia, Taiwan, and Thailand in Asia; Argentina, Brazil, Chile, and Mexico in Latin America; and Turkey in the Middle East—had acquired enough manufacturing experience in the production of silk, cotton textiles, foodstuffs, and light consumer goods to move into mid-technology and later high-technology sectors. *"The remainder,"* which comprised countries that had been less exposed to modern factory life in the prewar period, failed thereafter to achieve anywhere near "the rest's" industrial diversification. The dividing line between the two sets of countries was not absolute, as noted later, but countries without robust manufacturing experience tended to fall further behind, and the developing world became

1

Table 1.1. "The Rest's" Share in World Population, World GDP, and World Manufacturing Output, 1965–1995

Share	1965 (%)	1995 (%)
With China		
Population	47.5	49.5
GDP	7.0	14.1
GDP in manufacturing	4.9	17.4
Without China		
Population	33.1	35.7
GDP	6.3	11.6
GDP in manufacturing	4.3	12.9

Sources: Data for countries in "the rest" and world totals for GDP and population are adapted from Hill (1996). Data for manufacturing GDP were derived using DRI/McGraw Hill GDP data multiplied by the proportions of manufacturing in GDP found in UNIDO (1997) and various years and World Bank (1976) and various years, except for Taiwan, which was taken from Republic of China (1996) and various years. Data for China in 1965 are estimates. Proportions of manufacturing in total world value added (1965 and 1995) were used as proxies for proportions of manufacturing in total world output and were taken from World Bank (1982 and 1987).

divided between those that were excluded from modern world industry and those that were redefining its terms.

The rise of "the rest" was one of the phenomenal changes in the last half of the twentieth century. For the first time in history, backward countries industrialized *without proprietary innovations*. They caught up in industries requiring large amounts of technological capabilities without initially having advanced technological capabilities of their own. Late industrialization was a case of *pure learning*, meaning a total initial dependence on other countries' commercialized technology to establish modern industries. This dependence lent catching up its distinctive norms.

Knowledge-Based Assets

Economic development is a process of moving from a set of assets based on primary products, exploited by unskilled labor, to a set of assets based on knowledge, exploited by skilled labor. The transformation involves attracting capital, human and physical, out of rent seeking, commerce, and "agriculture" (broadly defined), and into manufacturing, the heart of modern economic growth. It is in the manufacturing sector that knowledge-based assets have been nurtured and most intensively used. The greater such assets, the easier the shift from primary product production to industrial production (and later to the supply of modern services).

A "knowledge-based asset" is a set of skills that allows its owner to produce and distribute a product at or above prevailing market prices (or below market costs). The requisite skills are both managerial and technological in nature. They are science-based or artisan and are embodied in an individual or firm, depending on the scale of the physical plant and the complexity of the production process. Three generic technological capabilities that nurture knowledge-based assets may be distinguished: *production capabilities* (the skills necessary to transform inputs into outputs); *project execution capabilities* (the skills necessary to expand capacity); and *innovation* capabilities (the skills necessary to design entirely new products and processes) (see table 1.2).

Knowledge is a special input because it is difficult to access, whether by "making" or "buying." Unlike information, which is factual, knowledge is conceptual; it involves combinations of facts that interact in intangible ways. Perfect information is conceivable—with enough time and money, a firm may learn all the extant facts pertaining to its business. Perfect knowledge is inconceivable because knowledge is firm-specific and kept proprietary as best as possible to earn technological rents.

Most theories and policy prescriptions related to economic development, however, fall closer analytically to the accessible rather than inaccessible end of the cognition spectrum, which we may define at one extreme by perfectly accessible information (say, a stylized fact) and at the other extreme by wholly inaccessible knowledge (the combination of tacit and implicit ideas that form a firm-specific concept). In the Heckscher-Ohlin-Samuelson trade theory, which still governs policy debates on economic openness, perfect knowledge ("technology") is a key assumption that renders firms in all countries in the same industry equally productive, which then leaves an uncompetitive country with only one efficient policy choice: adjust prices (reduce wages) rather than develop know-how (subsidize learning), which by assumption is already at the world frontier. In "new" growth models, business entities do not exist at all, and so proprietary, firm-specific knowledge cannot constitute an entry barrier; information is a free good in any given economy, and the diffusion of information globally, which guides international growth rates, becomes mostly a matter of investing in education (rather than, for example, in firm formation). In the "new institutional economics," the process of economic development is conceived as a movement towards increasingly perfect information, markets, and, thus, minimal "transactions cost"—rather than a process of developing knowledge-based assets to reduce production costs and enhance market position (see chapter 10). In theories where market imperfections are rooted in "information failures," the inaccessible end of the cognition spectrum is more relevant, but even in such cases (see, for example,

Table 1.2. Technological Capabilities

Production capability[1]

Production management—to oversee operation of established facilities
Production engineering[2]—to provide information required to optimize operation of established facilities, including the following:
  1. Raw material control: to sort and grade inputs, seek improved inputs
  2. Production scheduling: to coordinate production processes across products and facilities
  3. Quality control: to monitor conformance with product standards and to upgrade them
  4. Trouble-shooting to overcome problems encountered in course of operation
  5. Adaptations of processes and products: to respond to changing circumstances and increase productivity
  6. Repair and maintenance of physical capital, according to regular schedule and when needed

Project execution (investment capability)

Personnel training—to impart skills and abilities of all kinds
Preinvestment feasibility studies—to identify possible projects and ascertain prospects for viability under alternative design concepts
Project execution—to establish or expand facilities, including the following:
  1. Project management: to organize and oversee activities involved in project execution
  2. Project engineering: to provide information needed to make technology operational in particular setting, including the following:
     a. Detailed studies (to make tentative choices among design alternatives)
     b. Basic engineering (to supply core technology in terms of process flows, material and energy balances, specifications of principal equipment, plant layout)
     c. Detailed engineering (to supply peripheral technology in terms of complete specifications for all physical capital, architectural) and engineering plans, construction and equipment installation specifications)
  3. Procurement (to choose, coordinate, and supervise hardware suppliers and construction contractors)
  4. Embodiment in physical capital (to accomplish site preparation, construction, plant erection, manufacture of machinery and equipment)
  5. Start-up of operations (to attain predetermined norms innovation capability).

Innovation capability

The skills necessary to create new products or processes, the type of skills depending on the novelty of the new techology.
  1. *Pure science*: the search for intrinsic knowledge
  2. *Basic research*: the search for radically new technology
  3. *Applied research*: the search for differentiated products
  4. *Exploratory research*: the search for refinements of differentiated products
  5. *Advanced development*: the search for the optimum manufacturability of refined differentiated products

1. Activities listed refer to the operation of manufacturing plants, but similar activities pertain to the operation of other types of productive facilities as well.
2. This usage of the term departs from conventional usage in that the term is used far more broadly to include all of the engineering activities related to the operation of existing facilities. In this usage, the term encompasses product design and manufacturing engineering as these terms are generally used in reference to industrial production. See the entries under these headings in the *McGraw-Hill Encyclopedia of Science and Technology* (New York: McGraw-Hill Book Company, 1977).

Sources: Adapted from Westphal et al. (1985) and Amsden et al. (2000).

Stiglitz 1989), the examples chosen to illustrate problems of under-development typically relate to information, not knowledge (financial markets, for instance, supposedly fail in poor countries because they lack enough information about inexperienced borrowers). Government policies to further development also remain riveted on education and firm-neutral infrastructure (World Bank 1998–99). Where government policy is sanctioned by economists to go beyond public goods, as in patenting, it is designed to overcome the advanced-economy problem of *too free* knowledge, which supposedly leads to underinvestment, rather than the backward-economy problem of too few knowledge-based assets, which leads to the inability of these countries to compete at world prices even in industries that suit their capital and labor endowments, such as textiles, steel, chemicals, automobiles, and heavy electrical equipment, depending on the development stage.

The nature of technology itself makes knowledge difficult to acquire. Because the properties of a technology cannot necessarily be fully documented, process optimization and product specification remain an art.[1] The managerial skills that comprise such an art are themselves tacit rather than explicit. Technological capabilities that create new products and novel production techniques are part of a firm's "invisible" assets (Itami 1987). Such assets allow a firm to sell below competitors' costs and above their quality standards. Because knowledge-based assets are proprietary, intangible and hence difficult to copy, they lead to above-normal profits and earn their owners monopoly rents (Wernerfelt 1984).

Given such "entrepreneurial" or "technological" rents, there is a great reluctance on the part of a firm to sell or lease its cutting edge intangible assets. Rather than sell them, their value may be maximized if kept proprietary and exploited inside the firm (Hymer 1976). The secrecy of these assets is typically protected by law, as in disclosure restrictions on former employees. Even if such assets are offered for sale, as they are in technology transfers, diffusion from one enterprise to another enterprise may be highly imperfect (see chapter 3 for the prewar period) and dependent on an advanced level of skills on a *buyer's* part. Whatever is sold may comprise merely the codified part of a technology. The knowledge about how a production process works, and how to improve that process, may never be divulged.

Given imperfect knowledge, productivity and quality tend to vary sharply across firms in the same industry—a fortiori across firms in the same industry in different countries. The price of land, labor, and capital no longer uniquely determines competitiveness. The market mechanism loses status as its sole arbiter, deferring instead to institutions that nurture productivity. Because a poor country's lower wages may prove inadequate against a rich country's higher productivity, the model of "comparative advantage" no longer behaves predictably: latecomers cannot necessarily industrialize simply by specializing in a low-technology industry. Even in such an industry, demand may favor skilled incumbents (economic historians continue to debate, therefore, how Japan, for example, triumphed before World War II over the lower-wage textile industries of China and India, as examined in chapter 2).[2]

Under such unfavorable conditions and uncertainty as to how to proceed, latecomer governments face a choice. They may either do nothing at all, relying instead on a market-driven realignment of their exchange rate, which is tantamount to a cut in their real wages, or they may intervene and try to raise productivity by means that are not necessarily entirely clear. This choice is illustrated in figure 1.1. A movement from A to B constitutes a wage cut. A movement from A to C constitutes a productivity increase. The great advantage of the former is that it is automatic. If a country cannot compete against imports, eventually the value of its exchange rate will fall, entailing a decline in real wages.[3] Nevertheless, wage cuts are no guarantee that either skills will rise or that total costs will fall sufficiently. In the long run falling wages in a poor country may be no match for rising productivity in a rich one, as shown by the fate of the handloom weavers before World War I (see chapter 2). The advantage of subsidizing learning, by contrast, is that industrialization receives a jump start that may be sustainable. The great disadvantage is that the engine of growth may overheat from "government failure."

The North Atlantic emulators of England never faced quite such a drastic choice because they industrialized in tandem with an extraordinary wave of

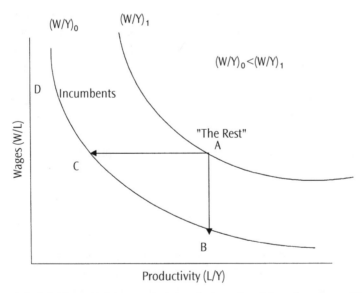

Figure 1.1. Subsidizing learning or cutting real wages. L = labor; Y = output; W/L = real wage per worker; W/Y = unit labor costs. Unit labor cost loci are rectangular hyperbolas, the product of real wage and labor-output ratio. They, therefore, are constants.

technological change, referred to as the Second Industrial Revolution. Unlike investors in "the rest," the imaginations of investors in the North Atlantic were fired by expectations of huge riches from new technologies, which unlocked the finance and human capital necessary for a "three-pronged" investment: in manufacturing plants with minimum efficient scale; in managerial and technological capabilities; and in marketing (Chandler Jr. 1990). The United States may have been backward after the Napoleonic Wars by British standards, but Eli Whitney's cotton gin proved the epochal breakthrough necessary to create a leading manufacturing sector for the flagging American economy. In France, ominous competition from Britain in the textile industry was foiled by world-renowned Parisian fashion designs and brilliantly colored fabrics made possible by a precocious science-based chemical sector (see chapter 2). Even Sweden, Northern Europe's laggard, accelerated its industrialization after the 1860s with inventions that became the origin of blue-ribbon multinational firms: the telephone (L. M. Ericcson 1876); the separator (Alfa Laval 1879); electrical equipment (ASEA 1890); and bearings (SKF 1907) (Hikino and Amsden 1994).[4] Japan, the pioneer of the late industrialization model, faced formidable entry barriers into world markets, but had richer assets than those of "the rest" at a comparable development stage—rich enough to colonize its neighbors, Korea, Taiwan, and Manchuria. Step-by-step Japan entered the orbit of modern industry by innovating new ways to produce traditional products, initially silk (invented in China)[5] and cotton textiles (modernized in India before Japan).

Whatever the dislocations of World War II, the knowledge-driven entry barriers of the North Atlantic and Japan reappeared with the coming of peace. Japan's lead in textiles, bicycles, and other low-tech sectors was sustained by labor-market imperfections. Japan may have had higher *average* wages than other Asian countries, but at the bottom end of the skill scale its wages remained relatively competitive. Labor-intensive industries (the "informal" sector) typically employed part time and female workers, and the wage gap between such workers in Japan and its neighbors was smaller than the wage gap between them in more capital-intensive and skill-intensive industries (the "formal" sector) (see table 1.3). In the mid- and high-technology industries in which the North Atlantic predominated, Schumpeterian "gales of creative destruction" did not, contrary to theory, blow entry barriers down (Schumpeter 1942). The same multinational companies whose innovations had secured them market power in the late nineteenth century were still exercising that power over nascent companies in "the rest" in the late twentieth century: Hoechst, Bayer, Dow, and DuPont in chemicals; Dunlop, Pirelli, Goodyear, and Firestone in tires; Ford, Fiat, General Motors, and Mercedes in automobiles; Siemens, Philips, Westinghouse, and General Electric in electronics; John Deere, DEMAG, Escher-Wyss, and Olivetti in machinery; and Anaconda, Arbed, Krupp, and Nippon Steel in primary metals (Chandler Jr. 1990).

Table 1.3. Daily Earnings in East Asia, 1968

Country (1968)	Formal Sector (US $)[1]	Informal Sector (US $)[2]
Japan	6.5	1.08
Taiwan	1.6	0.61–0.76
Korea	1.6	0.37–0.40
W. Malaysia	na	1.08
Thailand	1.4	0.5

1. Average daily earnings, male and female. Daily wage estimated from monthly earnings and hours. Local currencies converted into dollars using existing exchange rates. (ILO 1970).
2. Minimum daily wages (unskilled male workers). (Chomchai 1973).

"The rest" thus continued to face the same policy choice (see figure 1.1) it had faced for over a century. By the 1950s, however, most latecomers also faced a skill gap with the North Atlantic and Japan that had greatly widened (see table 1.4, which measures the gap by per capita income). In response to an inability to compete, governments in "the rest" swallowed traditional medicine and applied downward pressure on wages. Martial law in Korea and Taiwan, for example, prevented the formation of trade unions. But for the first time, governments also opted *en masse* for an interventionist, institutional solution.

A New Control Mechanism

To compensate for its skill deficit, "the rest" rose by devising an unorthodox, original economic model. This model qualifies as new because it was governed by an innovative *control mechanism*. A control mechanism is a set of institutions that imposes discipline on economic behavior.[6] The control mechanism of "the rest" revolved around the principle of *reciprocity*. Subsidies ("intermediate assets") were allocated to make manufacturing profitable—to facilitate the flow of resources from primary product assets to knowledge-based assets—but did not become giveaways. Recipients of subsidies were subjected to *monitorable performance standards that were redistributive in nature and results-oriented*. The reciprocal control mechanism of "the rest" thus transformed the inefficiency and venality associated with government intervention into collective good, just as the "invisible hand" of the North Atlantic's market-driven control mechanism transformed the chaos and selfishness of market forces into general well-being (Mandeville 1714 [repr. 1924]). The reciprocal control mechanism of the North Atlantic minimized market

Table 1.4. Per Capita GDP by Region, 1870–1992 (1990 International Dollars)

Region[1]	1870	1913	1950	1973	1995
(a) North Atlantic Economies[2]	2,238	3,957	5,676	12,412	17,761
(b) Latin America	760	1,439	2,487	4,387	5,031
(c) Asia	582	689	708	1,701	3,267
(d) Africa	450	575	830	1,311	1,221
(e) The rest[3]	717	913	1,074	2,245	7,122
Argentina	1,311	3,797	4,987	7,970	8,130
Brazil	740	839	1,673	3,913	5,279
Chile	na	2,653	3,827	5,028	8,794
Mexico	710	1,467	2,085	4,189	5,093
India	558	663	597	853	1,537
Indonesia	657	917	874	1,538	3,393
South Korea	na	948	876	2,840	11,868
Taiwan	na	794	922	3,669	13,028
Thailand	717	846	848	1,750	6,491
Malaysia	na	na	na	na	7,808
Turkey	na	979	1,299	2,739	na
(b)/(a)	.34	.36	.44	.35	.28
(c)/(a)	.26	.17	.12	.14	.18
(d)/(a)	.20	.15	.15	.11	.07
(e)/(a)	.32	.23	.19	.18	.42

1. Regional averages are computed by summing the GDP for a whole region and then dividing by the region's total population.
2. North Atlantic economies are a simple average of 14 European countries plus Australia, New Zealand, Canada, and the United States.
3. "The rest" excludes China.

Sources: Country averages except for 1995 adapted from Maddison (1995). Data for 1995 were kindly provided by Angus Maddison and are unpublished.

failure. The reciprocal control mechanism of "the rest" minimized government failure.

A control mechanism involves a *sensor*, to detect the "givens" in the process to be controlled; an *assessor*, to compare what is happening with what should happen; an *effector*, to change behavior; and a *communications network*, to transmit information between all functions.[7] In "the rest," the exogenous givens that *industrial* policy makers took were the prices determined by *macroeconomic* policy makers, such as the exchange rate, the general interest rate, the tax rate, and sometimes even the tariff rate (determined historically by finance ministries to generate revenues). Industrial policy makers were thus largely *price takers*. They were economic engineers whose job was to make manufacturing industry profitable and to circumvent any difficulty posed to industrialization by prevailing prices, whether such prices were politically, technocratically, *or market* determined.

Given prevailing prices, the first of "the rest's" engineering experiments set prices *as though* free markets obtained. The rationale was to allow manufacturers to buy their imported inputs, and sell their final outputs, at world prices. Toward this end, some countries created free trade ("export processing") zones. The theory behind such zones was that "the rest's" manufacturers were intrinsically profitable at world prices given their low wages. To industrialize, it was necessary simply to "get the prices 'right'." Free trade zones were a step in this direction because manufacturers were detached from prevailing exchange rate distortions except for their purchases of local inputs, mostly labor. All imported inputs were freed of duties, a major concession in the face of large international price distortions. In exchange for duty-free imports, firms had to export 100 percent of their output.

Despite this experiment in liberalism (which occurred in East Asia in the 1950s and 1960s), few firms except those in the most labor-intensive industries took advantage of duty-free concessions to locate in free trade zones. Other industries, including cotton textiles, could not export all (or any) of their output at world prices because they were *not* competitive at such prices. Productivity was below world norms and lower wages did not compensate except in the most labor-intensive sectors, which were profitable even before World War II.

Development planners, therefore, went one step further. They offered duty drawbacks on imported inputs that were embodied in exports; 100 percent exporting was no longer necessary. Again, the result was mixed: labor-intensive manufacturing flourished (often under foreign ownership), but the manufacturing sector did not diversify.

Therefore, economic engineering went even further. Greater subsidies were offered to the textile industry and prospective mid-technology manufacturers; effectively, a deliberate attempt was made to *"get the prices 'wrong'"*—to rig them in order to make manufacturing activity profitable. At the same time, one key principle of earlier experiments was retained and reinforced, the *principle of reciprocity*: a subsidy (such as duty-free imports) was to be tied to a performance standard (such as 100 percent exporting).

In the cotton textile industry, for example, the privilege of selling in the protected domestic market was made conditional on the fulfillment of export targets. Later, other industries had to match imports with an equivalent value of exports (or comply with some sort of "trade balancing" arrangement). In automobile assembly and consumer electronics, the right to sell locally under tariff protection was tied to the "localization" of parts and components manufacture. A condition for receiving the soft loans of development banks was the employment of nonfamilial professionals in responsible positions, such as chief financial officer and quality control engineer, as examined in chapter 6 with respect to Brazil. Development bank credit for heavy industries committed borrowers to contributing their own capital (under debt-equity ratio requirements) and constructing plants of minimum efficient scale. In India, price controls in the pharmaceutical industry encouraged cost-saving innovation and exporting in exchange for loose foreign patent laws. In Korea, a lucrative license to establish a general trading company depended on exports meeting criteria related to value, geographical diversity, and product complexity. As industries in "the rest" upscaled, performance standards shifted to research and development (R&D). Chinese "science and technology enterprises" were granted a special legal status in exchange for performance standards with respect to technically trained employment and new products in total sales. Small Taiwanese firms were "cherry-picked" to locate in science parks that obliged them to spend a certain percentage of their sales on R&D and employ advanced production techniques.

Starting in the late 1950s, then, the allocation of subsidies in all countries in "the rest" except one—Argentina—was systematized. It was circumscribed and crisscrossed by a dense network of relatively transparent rules and requirements that were reciprocal in nature. In theory, the problem of moral hazard arose, as firms got too large for governments to allow to fail. In practice, governments might not allow national leaders to fail, but they *did* allow their *owners* to go bankrupt, leaving production capacity intact but transferring ownership rights to other entities, thereby reducing the risk of moral hazard (for Korea, see Amsden and Euh 1995). Corruption was the scourge of late industrialization. Within the jurisdiction governed by a reciprocal control mechanism, however, corruption was arguably minimized (as illustrated below by Thailand). Nor was corruption patently evident in times of great financial instability, as one would expect if it were of fundamental importance. The foreign debt crises that shook Latin America starting in 1982 and East Asia starting in 1997 were caused by the developmental state's tendencies to overexpand (see chapter 9). Latin America's protracted stagnation probably owed more to the developmental state's failure to create a new "leading sector" than to its corrupt practices. Corruption throughout "the rest" was endemic historically, and it is unclear if it increased or decreased after World War II, or after liberalization in the 1980s. Overall, corruption probably dampened growth, to a degree that varied by country, but given "the rest's" reciprocal control mechanism, did not derail it. Corruption may be regarded as a perverse performance standard, but one that is unmonitorable and, hence, of indeterminate size.[8]

"The rest" rose, therefore, in conjunction with "getting the control mechanism 'right' " rather than "getting the prices 'right.' " Over a century of sluggish development was reversed and unprecedented manufacturing expansion ensued. Growth rates of manufacturing output and manufacturing output per capita grew faster for decades *outside* the North Atlantic than inside it. Between 1960 and 1980, "the rest's" real annual growth rate of manufacturing output averaged 9 percent (see table 1.5). Exports in most countries grew annually in the two-digit range *for nearly 50 years* (see chapter 7). Between 1950 and 1973 per capita incomes doubled in some countries and quadrupled in others. In Asia, including India, they again either almost doubled or rose by an even larger factor between 1973 and 1995 (see table 1.4). Increases in per capita income were especially striking in light of rapid population growth (see table 1.6), which went hand-in-hand with high rates of urbanization (see table 1.7).

Table 1.5. Real Annual Average Growth Rates of Manufacturing Output (O) and Manufacturing Output per Employee (O/E), 1960–1995

Country	1960–70 (%)		1970–80 (%)		1980–90 (%)		1990–95 (%)		1960–95 (%)	
	O	O/E	O	O/E	O	O/E	O	O/E	O	O/E
Argentina	5.4	na	0.9	4.6	−1.4	−3.1	11.6	13.8	2.1	3.4
Brazil	8.0	na	9.0	2.2	0.1	1.6	25.2	24.3	8.5	6.4
Chile	9.4	na	1.8	3.4	2.9	−1.1	10.4	7.2	5.5	2.4
China	na	na	8.4	3.7	9.6	8.9	13.5	13.2	9.9	7.7
India	3.1	na	4.0	−0.1	7.4	7.0	2.3	−0.6	4.5	2.6
Indonesia	6.4	na	14.2	9.9	7.4	−1.7	15.1	4.5	10.1	4.2
Korea	17.7	na	16.0	8.4	12.0	5.8	10.9	10.7	14.6	7.8
Malaysia	10.9	na	11.8	4.3	9.5	5.0	19.8	9.5	12.0	5.6
Mexico	9.7	na	7.2	3.9	2.2	3.1	8.4	11.1	6.6	5.0
Taiwan	15.0	na	12.6	3.7	7.2	4.9	4.8	5.6	10.6	4.5
Thailand	9.1	na	10.1	−2.1	9.6	1.3	13.2	9.1	10.1	1.5
Turkey	8.1	na	5.1	1.5	7.1	4.9	4.7	5.8	6.5	3.7
Average for "the rest"	9.7	na	9.1	3.5	6.8	3.6	11.7	9.1	9.0	4.7
Canada	4.7	na	3.6	2.3	2.2	2.0	0.0	2.1	3.0	2.1
France	6.9	na	3.8	4.8	1.0	2.4	1.7	4.3	3.6	3.8
Germany	7.7	na	2.1	3.9	1.3	1.5	3.7	5.0	3.7	3.2
Italy	8.2	na	4.2	4.0	2.8	4.8	2.3	1.5	4.7	3.9
U.K.	2.9	na	0.0	2.0	1.2	4.2	0.1	3.2	1.2	3.1
U.S.	4.2	na	5.0	2.3	3.6	4.8	2.9	3.2	4.1	3.5
Average for the N. Atlantic	5.8	na	3.1	3.2	2.0	3.3	1.8	3.2	3.4	3.3
Japan	15.2	na	5.3	6.0	5.8	5.3	6.3	7.6	8.4	6.1

Notes: Statistics for each column represent averages of real annual growth rates for the years included in the column heading. Real variables were calculated using the wholesale price index in International Monetary Fund (various years).

Sources: All Taiwan data taken from Republic of China (various years). Data for gross domestic manufacturing output and output per employee for years up to 1990 are taken from World Bank (various years). All subsequent data taken from UNIDO (various years).

Table 1.6. Population by Country (in Thousands), 1850–1995

Country	1850	1900	1930	1950	1980	1995
Argentina	1,100	4,693	11,900	17,150	28,237	34,600
Brazil	7,234	17,984	33,570	51,941	118,518	157,800
Chile	1,443	2,974	4,370	6,082	11,145	14,300
Mexico	7,662	13,607	17,175	27,376	69,655	93,700
Turkey	na	11,900	14,930	20,809	44,737	61,644
China	412,000	400,000	489,000	546,815	981,235	1,218,800
India	187,657	235,729	278,620	359,000	679,000	930,600
Indonesia	22,977	42,746	60,600	79,043	147,490	198,400
South Korea	na	8,772	13,670	20,557	38,124	44,900
Taiwan	na	2,864	4,615	7,882	17,642	21,146
Thailand	5,230	7,320	12,395	19,442	46,700	60,200
France	36,350	40,598	41,610	41,836	53,880	58,100
Germany	19,952	31,666	40,810	49,983	61,566	81,700
U.K.	25,601	38,426	45,865	50,363	56,314	58,600
U.S.	23,352	76,391	123,670	152,271	227,757	263,082
Japan	32,000	44,103	64,200	83,563	116,800	125,030

Sources: All data except for 1995 from Maddison (1995). Data for 1995 from *1996 Almanac* (Boston: Houghton Mifflin).

Table 1.7. Population by City (in Thousands), 1850–1990

City	1850	1900	1950	1970	1990
Berlin	424	1,884	3,336	3,208	3,454
Chicago	30	1,699	3,621	3,369	2,784
London	2,362	4,537	3,348	2,772	6,670
Madrid	271	540	1,618	3,146	2,910
Moscow	369	1,039	4,537	6,942	8,747
New York	516	3,437	7,892	7,896	7,323
Paris	1,053	2,714	2,850	2,591	2,152
Rome	176	425	1,652	2,782	2,800
Tokyo	596	1,440	5,385	8,841	8,112
Bangkok	160	587	605	1,867	5,876
Beijing	1,649	1,700	2,768	7,500	5,700
Bombay	644	776	2,839	5,971	12,916*
Buenos Aires	178	663	2,981	2,972	2,961
Istanbul	900	874	983	2,136	6,620
Jakarta	54	115	1,861	4,579	8,259
Mexico City	210	345	2,235	2,903	19,479*
Rio de Janeiro	266	811	2,377	4,252	5,615
Santiago	115	256	1,350	2,662	4,385
Sao Paulo	31	240	2,017	5,925	10,099
Seoul	90	201	1,446	5,443	10,628

Notes: The actual year and the indicated year for a population figure may diverge.
*Indicates population for the greater metropolitan area.

Sources: Data other than for 1990 adapted from Showers (1979). Data for 1990 adapted from *1996 Almanac* (Boston: Houghton Mifflin).

Globalization and National Ownership

While all countries in "the rest" succeeded in building mid-technology industries, some went further than others in becoming knowledge-based economies. China, India, Korea, and Taiwan began to invest heavily in their own proprietary national skills, which helped them to sustain national ownership of business enterprises in mid-technology industries and invade high-technology sectors based on "national leaders." By contrast, Argentina and Mexico, and to a lesser extent Brazil and Turkey, increased their dependence for future growth on foreign know-how. In these countries, foreign investment predominated but local expenditures on science and technology by foreign investors were virtually nil. Instead, by the year 2000 a long-term strategy had emerged—by design or default—that featured foreign licenses and spillovers from foreign investment as the engine of growth. The long-run technology strategy of Malaysia, Indonesia, and Thailand still remained unclear in 2000 given the relative youthfulness of these countries' industrial sectors. In Chile, developmental machinery had been retired as early as 1973. After harsh downward pressure had been applied on wages, long-term growth came to depend on continuing to exploit minerals (copper) and on engineering new "boutique" agro-industries.

The "make" or "buy" technology choice within "the rest" was not black and white. All countries continued to "buy" large quantities of foreign technology, and every country had to invest in some adaptive engineering in order to make foreign technology work. Moreover, "the rest" in general had become more international. In step with globalization, national enterprises had invested overseas in production and distribution. They had formed joint ventures and "strategic alliances" with foreign firms at home. Nevertheless, a division had emerged within "the rest" between "integrationists" and "independents," between countries that sought to clone themselves to foreign investors as a national growth strategy (epitomized by Mexico's affiliation to the North Atlantic Free Trade Agreement [NAFTA]) and countries that sought to create national*ist* innovation systems to champion "national leaders" with their own proprietary knowledge-based skills.

The difference between the two approaches, each credible and rational, depended on the two most important forces influencing the transition from primary product asset formation to knowledge-based asset formation: history—the *type* of manufacturing experience a country had acquired in the early stage of this transition; and income distribution—how equally resources were divided *within* the primary sector.

Manufacturing Experience

We classify countries as being in "the rest" or "the remainder" depending on their manufacturing experience. Nevertheless, the set of countries with and without manufacturing experience at the end of World War II was not cut-and-dry. We arbitrarily define experience so as to exclude countries whose manufacturing sectors were overwhelmingly engaged in processing a single primary product—for example, sugar refining in Cuba, petroleum refining in Venezuela, and cotton spinning and weaving in Egypt and Pakistan.[9] We also exclude countries by virtue of their special size or unique historical experience.[10]

Analytically, however, experience and inexperience are distinct; without such experience, developmental machinery is more likely to forsake capital accumulation and degenerate into "rent seeking"—personal enrichment through a redistribution of existing assets. Past manufacturing experience creates relatively high expectations on the part of potential investors that future manufacturing activity will succeed, which, as suggested above, provides an incentive to use resources to expand manufacturing capacity rather than to achieve immediate self-enrichment. Manufacturing experience also creates the qualified managers and engineers necessary to implement investment plans. After World War II, this elite was instrumental in establishing and operating the reciprocal control mechanisms of the developmental state and the most recalcitrant institution to emerge in prewar years: the nationally owned, professionally managed firm (see chapter 8).

Prewar manufacturing experience fell into three nonexclusive categories: *pre-modern; émigré,* and *colonial* (see table 1.8). The first type, pre-modern, emerged from artisan handicrafts and was of longest standing. It was found mainly in China, India, the Ottoman Empire, and Mexico.[11] The second type of experience, émigré, arose from the know-how transferred by permanent or quasi-permanent emigrants. Émigrés from China were critical in the industrialization of Indonesia, Taiwan, Thailand, and Malaysia (Malaysia also had a large émigré Indian population). Emigration to the manufacturing industries of Turkey and Latin America came mostly from North Atlantic countries and represented the influence of foreign *individuals* before the arrival of foreign *firms* (which began operating in Latin America only around the 1920s, as noted in chapter 3). The third type of manufacturing experience was colonial, or the know-how and organizations that emerged through formal colonial ties. Colonial transfers (ignoring "neocolonial" influences) were either from the North Atlantic (as in India) or, in the case of Manchuria (China), Korea, and Taiwan, from Japan.

As thus conceived, manufacturing experience is not simply a stock of knowledge. It is a stock of knowledge that passes through *a specific historical and institutional filter.* The distinction between émigré and colonial experi-

Table 1.8. Source of Pre-Second World War Manufacturing Experience

Country	Pre-Modern	Émigré	Colonial
Argentina		N.A.	
Brazil		N.A.	
Chile		N.A.	
China	x		N.A., J.
India	x		N.A.
Indonesia		C.	N.A.
Korea			J.
Malaysia		C., I.	N.A.
Mexico	x	N.A.	
Taiwan		C.	J.
Thailand		C.	
Ottoman Empire (Turkey)	x	N.A.	N.A.

Notes: x indicates presence of experience. N.A. = North Atlantic; J = Japan; I = India; C = China.

ence may be hypothesized to differentiate a wide range of practices among latecomers, not least of all their long-run technology strategy—whether to "make" or "buy." Countries that invested heavily in national firms and national skills—China, India, Korea, and Taiwan—*all* had *colonial* manufacturing experience. Countries that were magnets for foreign direct investment and slow to invest in advanced skills (or inept at doing so)—Argentina, Brazil, Chile, Mexico, and Turkey—*all* had North Atlantic *émigré* experience.

Following World War II and the rise of radical independence movements and decolonization, countries with colonial manufacturing experience were able to nationalize, expropriate, or acquire foreign-owned business enterprises. Nationally owned enterprises could thereby seize "second-mover" advantage in expanding industries with large economies of scale (Amsden & Chu, 2003). Countries with North Atlantic émigré experience, by contrast, had no comparable discontinuity (Turkey's history was slightly more complicated than Latin America's, as discussed in chapter 3). Countries with North Atlantic émigré experience also tended to have a larger stock of foreign investment because their prewar manufacturing experience had gone furthest and hence their domestic markets had become relatively large and an attraction to foreign investors. Consequently, nascent national enterprises tended to be *"crowded out"* by multinational firms (see chapter 8).

Thus, the *depth* of prewar manufacturing experience distinguished "the rest" and "the remainder." The *type* of prewar manufacturing experience distinguished countries *within* "the rest." The greater the continuity before and after World War II in the transmission of knowledge, and the greater the *discontinuity* in the ownership of foreign firms, the greater the basis for the rise of national leaders and national skill formation.

The Policy Paradox of Income Distribution

The primary sectors of "the rest" were highly diverse—in terms of what they produced, how production was organized (although family ownership predominated except in mining), and whether or not resources were equally distributed.[12] Equality of land distribution among countries in "the rest" varied widely (see table 1.9). Assuming that data for 1960 are accurate,

Table 1.9. Distribution of Land, Income, and Education, Various Years

Country	Land (Gini) 1960	Income (Ratio[1]) 1975–83	Income (Gini) 1986–95	Education[4] (% High School) 1960	Education[5] (Coeff. of Var.) 1960
Argentina	0.86	na	na	3.0	0.24
Brazil	0.83	27.7	0.6	2.0	0.48
Chile	na	na	0.57	2.1	0.29
China	na	na	0.42	na	na
India	0.58	10.1	0.3	0.0	0.86
Indonesia[2]	0.55	11.9	0.34	0.1	0.87
S. Korea[3]	0.35	4.9	na	2.6	0.65
Malaysia	0.75	na	0.48	1.5	0.65
Mexico	0.62	15.4	0.5	1.4	0.51
Taiwan	0.45	4.3	na	4.2	0.51
Thailand	0.46	11.2	0.46	0.6	0.60
Turkey	0.6	na	na	0.7	0.68
Japan	0.41	4.0	na	6.3	0.20
France	0.52	na	0.37	2.1	0.19
Germany	0.54	na	0.28	1.8	0.19
U.K.	0.72	na	0.33	1.8	0.08
U.S.A.	0.71	10.7	0.4	6.5	0.06

1. Ratio by which the income of the top fifth of the population exceeds that of the bottom fifth.
2. Rural population only.
3. Urban population only.
4. Percentage of population that achieved a high school education (completed or uncompleted).
5. Coefficient of variation is standard deviation divided by the population-weighted mean years of schooling in population.

Sources: Land ginis: data kindly supplied by R. Deininger, World Bank. Income ratio: all countries except Taiwan and Indonesia: United Nations and Department of International Economic and Social Affairs (1985); Taiwan: Li (1988); Indonesia: Gelb and associates (1988). Income Ginis: World Bank (various years). Education: data kindly supplied by Nancy Birdsall, Carnegie Foundation. U.S.A.: calculated from Bureau of Census data.

then countries with the most unequal land distributions were Argentina, Brazil, and Malaysia (Gini coefficients of 0.7 or above). Countries with the most equal land distributions were Korea, Taiwan, and Thailand (Gini coefficients below 0.5). Postwar land reform in Japan, Korea, and Taiwan had created some of the world's most equally distributed economies (nationalizations in Malaysia after 1960 reduced inequalities as well). Other measures of equality (the income Gini and the income ratio of the top fifth of the population to the bottom fifth) show essentially the same distributional pattern as land Ginis, but two differences stand out: more *inequality* in Mexico and more equality in India (India's income Gini coefficient in the late 1980s/early 1990s was only 0.3). Comparable data for China are generally unavailable, but land distribution even after economic reform (beginning in 1978) was almost certainly highly equal. Data on land distribution for Chile are also missing, but Chile's income Gini, at almost 0.6, indicates that inequality was very high.

Countries that invested heavily in national firms and national skills—China, India, Korea and Taiwan—*all* had relatively equal income distributions. A national economy may be regarded as an organic whole. The greater income inequality (by social class, race, religion, or region), the more that organic whole is fractured, and the more difficult it is to mobilize support for national business enterprises and firm-specific national skills. After World War II, greater equality induced a relatively large flow of resources from primary product production to manufacturing and also resolved a *policy paradox* in industry's favor.

First, the flow of resources from agriculture to manufacturing may be expected to depend on relative rates of return, and an unequal distribution of natural resources tends to create Ricardian quasi-rents. These rents make it more difficult for manufacturing to compete for resources, especially in the absence of knowledge-based assets that create offsetting entrepreneurial manufacturing rents. With quasi-rents in the primary sector, subsidies have to be higher than otherwise to make manufacturing relatively profitable, and performance standards, being a cost to recipients of intermediate assets, become more difficult to apply.

Large absolute concentrations of resources in the primary sector also entail relatively large *absorptive capacities* of human capital. Assuming family ownership of productive units in all sectors (however large each individual unit might be), then a rich family's educated progeny is more likely to remain in the primary sector or to divide its time between sectors when natural resources are skewed in its favor. With large concentrations of natural resources, and fixed entry costs to learn about manufacturing, the *core competencies* of investors from the primary (and tertiary) sector are unlikely to be squarely in manufacturing, as exemplified by Brazil.

Second, subsidies may be allocated by government to either a relatively large number of firms (*diffusion*) or to a relatively small number of "national leaders" (*concentration*). The major instruments used to diffuse or concentrate subsidies are the same whatever the country: industrial licensing (which influences how many firms are allowed to operate in any given industry); and performance standards with respect to debt-to-equity ratio ceilings (which influence firm size) and profit distribution (which influence firm structure). Paradoxically, countries in "the rest" with relatively equal existing income distributions followed the concentration approach whereas countries with relatively *un*equal income distributions followed the diffusion approach (see chapter 8).

The association between income *in*equality and diffusionist policies is paradoxical because, if governments (especially authoritarian governments) are regarded as a handmaiden of the rich and powerful, then a concentration of subsidies is expected when existing income distribution is highly skewed. With the exception of India, moreover, governments in "the rest" tended to be authoritarian in the early postwar years. Late industrialization largely unfolded against a backdrop of undemocratic politics. Nevertheless, the developmental state of late industrialization tended to be increasingly technocratic, with a view toward long-term growth as well as an ear toward vested interests. Assuming that the probability of social unrest rises with inequality, and assuming further that technocrats are risk averse, then within the boundaries of a technocratic reciprocal control mechanism, policies of diffusion and existing income inequality may be expected to go hand-in-hand.

There is a broad consensus among political economists that income distribution has a major bearing on economic development, an intuition that is largely born out by statistical tests. Uncertainty exists only over the channels through which distribution transmits its effects on economic behavior. In late industrialization, income distribution may be hypothesized to affect: the degree to which national firms establish their core competencies inside or outside manufacturing and the degree to which industrial policies concentrate or diffuse intermediate assets in order to diversify industry. The greater inequality, the more diffusionist the policies and, hence, the greater the difficulty of creating national leaders with proprietary, cutting-edge skills.

Institution-Building

Like clockwork, reciprocal control mechanisms began to be constructed in the late 1950s or early 1960s everywhere in "the rest" except Argentina. In Thailand, a coup brought a general to power with pro–private business sympathies. A Promotion of Industrial Investment Act in 1960 created a Board of Investment that quickly began fomenting manufacturing activity, as examined shortly. In Malaysia, a Pioneer Industry Ordinance of 1958 sparked industrial promotion which then intensified after race riots erupted in 1969 (Hoffmann and Tan Siew 1980 and Rasiah 1995). In Indonesia, a new military government that came to power in 1966 under General Soeharto started the long road to industrialization using many institutions established by former President Sukarno.[13] In Korea, industrialization accelerated after a coup by Young Turks in 1961 and the rise to power of an arch-developmentalist, Park Chung Hee (Cole and Lyman 1971). In Taiwan, the Third Development Plan (1961–64) emphasized the need to promote heavy industry, and with the formation of an Industrial Development Bureau in 1970, major investment projects accelerated (Wade 1990). In India, Parliament passed an Industrial Policy Resolution in 1956 that triggered intense efforts to restructure existing industries and, mostly, to diversify into new basic manufacturing sectors (Sandesara 1992). In Turkey, a 1960 coup led to the establishment of a State Planning Office and the start of Turkish postwar industrial expansion (Keyder 1987). In Brazil, a "basic-industries approach was part of a pervasive ideology of economic development and modernization that influenced government allocations from the late 1940s and reached its culmination in the 'Target Plan' (Programa de Metas) whose projects were formulated in the early 1950s and implemented in 1957–61 under President Kubitschek" (Leff 1968, p. 46). In Chile, the reconstitution of a development corporation in 1961 (CORFO) was the fillip behind more intensive industrial promotion (Mamalakis 1976). In Mexico, the new presidency of Miguel Alemán made industrialization his only economic goal and along with a "new group" of progressive industrialists, launched a vigorous plan to bolster manufacturing activity (Mosk 1950). Even China, with an entirely different internal control mechanism at the time, intensified its attempts at industrialization in 1958 with a Great Leap Forward.

The synchronization of institution-building in different countries, on different continents, suggests a "moment in history" at play. It was a euphoric moment defined by the "winds of change" of decolonization and a rise in the ideology of development planning.[14] It was also a desperate moment defined by rising brain drain of the highly educated (see table 1.10) and dwindling opportunities for overseas migration by "unlimited" labor supplies (see table 1.11). Moreover, when one country began introducing developmental machinery, other countries in close proximity followed suit: The industrial promotion systems of Malaysia, Indonesia, and Thailand, for example, were introduced at roughly the same time and closely resembled one another.

Table 1.10. Non-Return Rates among Foreign Male Students[1] in the United States

Country	Students (1964)	% Non-Return (1969)
Argentina	521	21.6
Brazil	528	8.2
Chile	387	13.3
China	1,716	38.3
India	6,136	7.2
Indonesia	635	2.8
Korea	2,067	11.0
Mexico	1,145	18.8
Taiwan	3,426	11.7
Thailand	1,168	3.6

1. Absolute number of students in 1964. Non-return rates apply to five years after graduation.

Source: Adapted from Myers (1972).

In the immediate postwar years, for the government *not* to intervene would have seemed strange. Thus, gross domestic capital formation started to rise, if cyclically (see table 1.12), and government's share in gross investment attained high levels (see table 1.13), with foreign direct investment accounting for only a small share of capital formation (see table 1.14).

We briefly review the developmental institutions created by *Thailand*, a case of relative minimalism as far as government intervention is concerned (World Bank 1993). In later chapters, we analyze control mechanisms thematically rather than from the perspective of a single country. A country overview,

Table 1.11. Estimated Voluntary World Migration Movements, 1815–1980

	1815–1914	1919–39	1945–80
(a) Total voluntary migrants (est.)	82,100,000	13,919,000	24,750,000
(b) Years in era	100	21	36
(c) Avg. voluntary migrants/year (est.)	821,000	662,810	687,500
(d) Population, median year (millions)	1,240	2,000	3,200
(e) Yearly voluntary migrants per million world inhabitants [(c)/(d)]	660	330	215

Sources: Data are compiled from a number of different sources that are not necessarily complimentary. Figures for number of voluntary migrants for each of the three periods listed are adapted from Segal (1993). World population statistics adapted from Woytinsky and Woytinsky (1953). Segal lists major voluntary migration movements by sending country for each era and includes estimates for the number of migrants within each movement. We aggregated his estimates for each era listed. Segal does not purport to account for every migrant or even every significant movement of migrants. Furthermore, some estimates are not listed. Therefore, they almost certainly understate total flows for each era.

Table 1.12. Gross Domestic Capital Formation as a Percentage of Gross Domestic Product

Country	1950 (%)	1960–64 (%)	1965–69 (%)	1970–74 (%)	1975–79 (%)	1980–84 (%)	1985–89 (%)	1990–95 (%)
Argentina	19	14.0	20.2	20.1	25.4	22.3	18.3	17.0
Brazil	17	na	24.2	20.6	22.6	20.4	21.2	20.0
Chile	16	14.2	15.9	14.4	15.4	15.7	16.5	22.7
India	13	17.5	17.9	15.5	19.1	19.6	21.1	22.2
Indonesia	7	14.3	8.3	na	na	25.6	25.2	29.0
Korea	13	13.9	23.0	22.9	27.9	29.7	29.1	36.2
Malaysia	12	15.2	15.6	23.1	25.1	34.3	26.5	34.5
Mexico	17	17.8	19.6	19.1	21.4	21.9	19.1	19.8
Taiwan	14	19.0	23.6	29.1	30.0	26.9	20.6	23.6
Thailand	14	21.2	23.8	23.1	24.5	28.0	29.2	39.9
Turkey	14	15.5	16.3	21.1	23.4	19.5	22.8	22.7
Coefficient of variation	22.5	15.4	25.5	20.3	17.7	22.6	18.9	29.4

Sources: All data for Taiwan taken from Republic of China (1996). All other data taken directly from International Monetary Fund (various years).

Table 1.13. Percentage of Public Share in Gross Domestic Capital Formation, 1960–1996

Country	1960–64	1965–69	1970–74	1975–79	1980–84	1985–89	1990–96
Argentina	na	na	37.6	41.9	24.5	28.4	15.7
Brazil	25.3	29.1	28.7	35.8	37.3	32.3	23.5
Chile	na	na	62.1	50.4	37.6	45.7	22.1
India	46.0	41.5	41.2	45.0	48.6	47.9	29.6
Indonesia	na	na	na	na	43.8	33.2	34.7
Korea	27.4	23.8	24.3	21.9	24.5	22.2	24.0
Malaysia	27.8	38.5	31.4	37.9	46.1	41.1	33.8
Mexico	58.0	33.8	33.7	40.7	41.7	29.8	21.6
Taiwan	40.9	36.4	38.5	49.2	47.4	38.3	49.2*
Thailand	31.3	33.0	25.4	28.2	30.0	22.6	19.5
Turkey	49.8	53.1	41.9	47.8	56.7	52.3	25.7

*1990–94 only

Sources: All data for Taiwan taken from Republic of China (1996). All other data for 1970 and after adapted from Glen (1998). Data for the 1960s come from the following: Brazil (various years), Chandhok (1996), Bank of Korea (various years), Malaysia (various years), Mexico (1994), Thailand (various years), Turkey (various years).

from the mouths of former high-ranking government officials, gives some sense of the depth and breadth of controls.[15]

Thailand's Reciprocal Control Mechanism

Thailand's control mechanism was managed by a civil service that emerged out of a 1932 political movement whose reforms led to civil servants being

Table 1.14. Net Foreign Direct Investment as a Percentage of Gross Domestic Capital Formation, 1960–1995

Country	1960–64	1965–69	1970–74	1975–79	1980–84	1985–89	1990–95
Argentina	1.0	0.5	0.2	1.2	2.0	4.4	9.2
Brazil	na	7.6	5.7	4.2	3.8	2.0	2.0
Chile	−1.3	3.0	−7.0	3.9	7.8	4.6	8.7
India	na	0.0	0.0	0.0	0.1	0.4	1.0
Indonesia	na	0.3	na	na	25.6	25.2	28.3
Korea	0.2	0.6	2.7	0.8	0.3	1.5	0.8
Malaysia	na	10.2	12.3	12.5	11.9	8.7	20.2
Mexico	3.5	4.4	4.1	3.4	3.2	7.1	13.7
Taiwan	4.4	−4.9	1.5	1.0	0.8	1.7	1.4
Thailand	1.7	3.7	3.5	1.3	2.7	3.6	4.2
Turkey	2.1	0.9	1.6	0.5	0.6	1.7	2.2

Sources: All data for Taiwan taken from Republic of China (1996). All other data taken directly from International Monetary Fund (various years).

selected by academic merit. Given an academic meritocracy, the Thai civil service became very well-educated in a society where social status came to depend on higher education. In 1963 as much as one-third of Thai students studying abroad were government officials taking a leave of absence (Evers and Silcock 1967). Thailand's Board of Investment (BOI), the overseer of industrial promotion, claimed that until the 1990s, it had never faced a short-age of well-trained engineers despite low school enrollments. Because in the early phase of industrialization most Thai manufacturing firms were first-generation family-owned, government officials tended to be better educated than private entrepreneurs.[16] Whatever the balance, the BOI attracted the brightest talent after World War II, as did elite bureaucracies in Meiji Japan and other countries in "the rest" (Daito 1986).

Deviation from the principle of academic merit in Thailand came mainly at the hands of overseas education and American foreign aid:

> Only just before World War II were holders of foreign degrees given specific recognition as technical experts within the Thai civil service structure, but from the beginning these degrees gave access to opportunity and rapid pro-motion. . . . The academic merit system was further undermined by the in-creasing impact of American education after World War II. . . . [Applicants to new training courses were] mainly jointly nominated by Thai officials and American advisers. . . . Paradoxically the new system made it much easier for those who enjoyed the proper patronage to secure an overseas degree (Evers and Silcock 1967, pp. 86–87).

A permanent opposition to the developmental policies of the Thai civil service arose in the form of American-trained economists.[17] Officials in the Board of Investment complained of constant criticism from the 'pure econo-mists' in the Prime Minister's Office who "misunderstood the real world." 'Pure economists' countercharged that private enterprise would have grown strong without BOI support; that power bred corruption; and that the BOI's methods of 'picking winners' were arbitrary. The BOI responded by appointing its critics as advisers.

Coverage   A very large number of investment projects in Thailand grew up under the BOI's wing. A survey of Thailand's big businesses in the 1990s estimated that around 70 percent of the manufacturing firms belonging to the largest industrial groups had received benefits and had fulfilled perfor-mance standards under contract with the BOI (Suehiro 1993). According to the BOI's own estimates, it was involved in roughly 90 percent of Thailand's major manufacturing projects covering both the private and public sectors and foreign and local firms, with investments totaling around $14 billion by 1990. Given Thailand's thin industrial base, and BOI's relatively small staff, an official with the BOI for 23 years (1968–1991) *knew every major investor personally*. In 1990, 70 percent of the BOI's professional staff were engineers and only 100 engineers were employed in total.

A coup d'état in 1958 had brought to power a prime minister interested in promoting private enterprise. Before the Sarit regime, state-owned enterprise was paramount partly in reaction to a fear of Chinese economic domination (see chapter 8). As it became clearer that manufacturing activity under the BOI's direction could generate profits, the government became more committed to industrialization, and as commitment to industrialization from top political leaders strengthened, industrial promotion expanded and development flourished despite militarism and corruption (for comparable cause and effect in Taiwan, see Amsden 1985). *"Everyone was nervous that rapid growth would end"*, and success itself helped keep corruption in check, at least through the early fast-growth years.

Thailand's real annual average growth rate of manufacturing output jumped from 5.6 percent in the preplan period before 1960 to 9.1 percent in 1960–70 and 10.1 percent in 1970–80 (see table 1.5). The share of manufacturing in GDP rose from 12.5 percent in 1960 to 18.3 percent in 1975 (see chapter 5). The BOI's pervasive influence thus went hand in hand with sustained manufacturing expansion.

New Rules   The BOI gave tax breaks, tariff protection (in consultation with the Ministry of Finance), subsidized credit (reserved for national firms by a development bank, the Industrial Finance Corporation of Thailand), entry restrictions (in consultation with the Ministry of Industry), and special benefits for foreign firms (permission to own land and to import labor). These benefits were exchanged for performance standards related to export targets, local content requirements, debt-equity ratio ceilings, national ownership floors, operating scale minima, investment time-table obligations, regional location criteria, and eventually product quality specifications and environmental rules. The government specifically promoted technology transfers from multinational firms by making the support of such firms contingent on their hiring local managers. The Foreigners' Occupation Control Law restricted the number of working visas issued to foreign personnel, thereby initiating the replacement of foreign managers and engineers with Thais.

In the 1960s, Thailand's corporate income tax was as high as 30 percent and its import duties on inputs for finished manufactures were pervasive; import duties were a major source of government revenue since before the eighteenth century. Despite Thailand's reputation for "openness," import duties around the time of the Third National Economic and Social Development Plan (1972–76) averaged 30–40 percent and 60 percent on luxuries. In 1983, the average nominal tariff was 31 percent in "open" Thailand compared with 24 percent in "fortress" Korea (James et al. 1987). Therefore, the right to a reduction or exemption of import duties was a rich reward. To protect local industry, however, duty exemptions were only given for machinery and other inputs NOT made in Thailand (variants of this 'Law of Similars' existed throughout "the rest," the first instance possibly dating to the 1930s in Brazil). Board of Investment staff argued that "tax benefits under the Investment Promotion Law were the beginning of business prosperity in this country."

All BOI projects followed the same procedure no matter who initiated them (missions abroad to court potential investors were usually BOI initiated). Proposals were first subject to *Project Analysis* by engineers, who checked technical feasibility and capacity fit with related industries, and economists, who checked conformance with policy criteria specified in five-year plans (discussed in chapter 6). Viable proposals were then sent to a *Decision Committee* with members from the BOI and private industry, and if an affirmative decision were reached, proposals went to a *Privileges Committee* to review the benefits package involved. As a way to reduce corruption, Decision Committee meetings on major projects were open to all concerned ministries, and approved projects, no matter what their size, had to have a detailed *Return Statement* indicating the rationale for their acceptance. After approval, inspectors monitored performance (for instance, they checked to see if specified technologies had been bought and machinery had been installed). On average, the BOI annually withdrew benefits from 7 percent of its clients for noncompliance with agreed terms.

Performance standards attached to tax breaks were designed to create new capacity in "targeted" industries based on modern as opposed to second-hand equipment. Existing firms that expanded their own capacity through acquisition of an existing firm or extension of an existing plant facility did not qualify (although new plants of existing firms did quality). Additional performance standards were negotiated when projects were being screened. In the case of *prescreened projects*, performance criteria were laid down by the BOI. Cotton textile manufacturers, for example, had to export 50 percent of their output after the first energy crisis (1973) to qualify for new or continued support; this applied equally to foreign and national firms. Given this 50 percent floor (which was arrived at after "detailed study"), a textile firm was selected for promotion depending on how competitive its proposal was in terms of the additional performance standards it promised.

In the case of *guided projects*, the BOI divided all industries into three classifications with varying benefits lasting for a finite duration. This procedure was criticized by economists, so the BOI went to a case-by-case decision rule. This procedure was unworkable, so in 1977 the BOI went back to a three-way classification but used new criteria to select the industries for the largest privileges, such as *export-intensity* and *regional location* rather than capital- or labor-intensity. On average, only 15 percent of applications were rejected, but only companies that fit BOI criteria tended to apply.

In the case of *big projects*, the BOI and potential clients engaged in intense bargaining. Major sticking points were the number of entrants in an industry the BOI would promote (and the Ministry of Industry would license) and the amount of "own-capital" firms would supply (which influenced a firm's debt/equity ratio). In the case of colored television picture tubes, for example, considerations of scale economy led the BOI to offer privileges to only one player. Players in big projects were selected in a transparent process involving all ministers with economic portfolios.

Economists criticized the BOI in its early years of operation for being too generous in allocating benefits:

> the BOI has been extremely promiscuous in giving away promotion certificates. It has never seriously asked the question: what industry NOT to promote. Like a woman out on a shopping spree (to be fair to the ladies, let me point out that all Secretaries-General of the BOI have been male) it has issued promotion certificates, regardless of whether they are mass consumption items (textiles) or luxury goods consumed by relatively few people (refrigerators and air conditioners), regardless of the minimum scale of operation (motor cars), regardless of the actual intentions of those who asked for and got the promotion certificates (petrochemicals), regardless of whether the industry is already firmly established and thus new investments in that industry would not be as risky as in the beginning (hotels and textile mills in the late 1960's, cement) and regardless of efficiency (fertilizers). (Siamwalla 1975, p. 38)

The BOI may or may not have been *indiscriminate* in its support of inappropriate industries, but in the early 1960s the virtue of promiscuity was to trigger a broad-based growth momentum. This, in turn, ensured the BOI's popularity and support from top politicians and business leaders.

Disequilibria At critical turning points before the 1990s (defined by exogenous shocks, big new projects, or more foreign competition), the BOI responded by altering the scope and nature of support. Tariffs were the business of the Ministry of Finance, but a key section of a general tariff law gave the BOI power to impose *surcharges* on existing tariffs. When Thai industry faltered after the second energy crisis (1979), twenty product groups were subjected to import surcharges ranging from 10 percent to 40 percent on top of existing duties (Narongchai and Ajanant 1983). Likewise extraordinary measures were taken in order to build major industries. In the case of automobiles, one of the most problematic industries in the BOI's portfolio, from 1978–90 the BOI banned imports of small cars (below 2,400 cylinders) and limited the number of brands and models of automobiles that could be assembled or produced locally. A diesel engine project related to motor vehicles, and competitively bid on by three Thai-Japanese joint ventures, typified the BOI's non-bureaucratic side. On the issue of number of entrants to produce diesel engines in Thailand, the BOI's technical staff "fought hard" for a limit of one, at most two, but was overruled by the BOI's governing board, which wanted more competition and licensed "no more than three firms." On the issue of using Thailand's casting capacity to make engine blocks, the BOI supported local Thai casters against the Japanese claims of poor quality but in exchange forced Thai casters to subcontract work to smaller Thai suppliers. Finally, on the issue of exports, the BOI got an export commitment from Japanese contenders (who had initially demanded export *restrictions*) by making bidding among them more cut throat (Doner 1991).

All the BOI's daring-cum-bureaucratism may have reflected "culture" at work, but not necessarily Thai culture. Developmental bureaucracies throughout "the rest" exhibited similar behavior in disequilibria. The culture among latecomers at the time was "getting the job done," rather than "getting the prices 'right.' "

It is to how the job got done that attention is now turned.

I

SINKING BEHIND, 1850–CIRCA 1950

2

The Handloom Weavers' Bones

The fierce competition triggered after 1815 by Britain's technological revolution in textiles created havoc and ultimately four defensive strategies among textile-producing countries. At the *high end* of the capabilities scale, France exploited its traditional artisanship in hand spinning and hand weaving, and the United States adopted a mass production system similar to England's, but produced coarse rather than fine fabrics (Temin 1988).[1] At the *low end* of the capabilities scale, Mexico followed the United States into mass production. China, India, and the Ottoman Empire tried to imitate France while simultaneously struggling to produce industrial yarn and cloth for mass consumption.

Despite superficial similarities, the history of "the rest's" prewar textile industries could not have been more different from those of France, the United States or Japan. The latter innovated their way out of trouble whereas the former did not. Whatever the strategy—mass production or artisan—and whatever the degree of economic openness—protectionist (as in Mexico and Brazil) or free trade (as in China, India, and the Ottoman Empire)—the textile industries of "the rest" failed to become dynamic world players until after World War II.

This chapter begins to explore the reasons behind "the rest's" failure. To convey the extent of its skill deficit, the capabilities of France, the United States, and Japan are examined to the extent necessary to establish a benchmark.

Artisanal Assets: France

Descriptions of France's obstacles to economic development after the Napoleonic Wars read very much like those of India or Latin America:[2] an archaic class structure, an infantile banking system, an unfavorable set of commercial laws, low demand, cheap labor that delayed mechanization, expensive foreign machinery, and, compared to Britain, relatively expensive coal and capital, fewer engineers, smaller plants, inferior equipment, fewer technical improvements, meager ancillary services in industrial districts, worse infrastructure, and thus higher costs of production. Supposedly the continent was faced with a problem of backwardness "just like that of today's underdeveloped countries" (Crouzet 1972, p. 101).

Nevertheless, by 1815 France was already at the world technological frontier in certain fields that were scientifically advanced for their time. Moreover, France already had a *diversified* industrial base. Industry in 1815 is estimated to have accounted for roughly 20 percent of national income (Kuznets 1966), whereas immediately after World War II, China, India, and the Ottoman Empire had still not achieved even half that proportion, assuming roughly similar national accounting conventions (see chapter 5). France "had to *transform* existing industries, to 'modernize' them by the large-scale introduction of the new techniques which had been invented and perfected in England, [but] it did not need to build up completely new industries from scratch" (Crouzet 1972, p. 101). A revisionist historiography began to argue that France was never really backward.[3]

By 1851, at the Great Exhibition of industrial works in London's Crystal Palace, French manufacturers demonstrated innovativeness in new "science-based" technologies such as machinery (in the form of a turbine water wheel), photography (such as the Daguerreotype), and dyes for textiles ("It is a universally admitted fact that, for some of the more delicate chemical preparations, such as vegetable alkaloids, the productions of the French manufacturer excel those of other nations") (Great Exhibition of the Works of All Nations 1968). In traditional "Parisian industries" such as silk textiles, clothing, shoes, leather ware, jewelry, silverware, furniture, tapestries, glass, and precision instruments, French capabilities were unrivaled. Not all French handicrafts, including textiles, were quickly modernized. Parisian fashion industries, for example, remained "unregenerate in their lack of mechanisation and factory organisation" yet also remained "a pillar of French exports" (Pollard 1990, p. 36). Nevertheless, France had the entrepreneurial and artisanal skills to adapt old products to new tastes. It had accumulated enough mechanical skills to develop the most modern types of machinery to reduce production costs.

In Alsace, for example, as early as 1815–30 water frames and hand mules were replaced by power-driven mules in spinning, and there was a decisive shift from handlooms to powerlooms in weaving. "The readiness of the Alsatian manufacturer to invest in up-to-date equipment owed much to the development of a creative local machine-construction industry" (Landes 1969, pp. 160–61). Artisan production flourished even in a relatively backward district such as Troyes, where, as elsewhere in France, "the handloom weaving industry never recovered from the crisis of the 1780s" but where "the transition to steam power and mechanisation did not begin in earnest until the 1870s." Given its history of high-quality manufacture (in 1782 the Inspector of Manufactures noted that Troyes relied on its "high quality" rather than low prices in order to compete), Troyes began to specialize in hosiery and then diversified into knitted gloves, mittens, trousers, drawers, waist-coats, camisoles, petticoats, dresses, shirts, vests and bathing suits. Specialization was made possible by the introduction of a circular knitting frame that "boosted productivity in the industry without altering its essentially artisan character" (Heywood 1981, pp. 559–61).[4]

As the twentieth century approached and France belatedly entered the Second Industrial Revolution, its industries became increasingly like those of Germany and the United States in terms of their capital-intensity and large-scale business enterprises. Still, France's manufacturing experience allegedly lent these industries and organizations a specific slant. For one, "French industry had a strategy of niches, aiming at quality products rather than cheap products and partly reflecting the heterogeneity of the national market. The fact that a number of innovations were devised by individual inventors (photo, automobile, aviation, cinema, radio) reflects the French emphasis on quality" (Fridenson 1997). For another, although French big business clustered in the same set of industries that gave rise to big business elsewhere, it was neither as large nor as numerous as the giants of the United States and Germany, and it tended to exhibit more personal than managerial capitalism (Smith 1993).

Thus, France was not so far behind England at the time of the Napoleonic wars to prevent it from transforming its pre-capitalist artisan skills into market empowering assets. No developing country had nearly as many assets to compete.

Survival Costs: China, India, and the Ottoman Empire

Just as a revisionist literature challenged the idea of France's backwardness, so too a revisionist literature emerged in the 1970s to challenge conventional history about backwardness in countries that eventually formed "the rest." The debate about India was over British imperialism.[5] In China it concerned the Treaty ports and the contribution of the "comprador."[6] In the Ottoman Empire it centered on the staying power of traditional skills.[7] In Latin America it involved the significance of linkages from primary product exports to manufacturing and the quality of industrialization under autarchy during the two world wars and Great Depression.[8] Common to most country studies was the contention that foreign influence was more benign than previously imagined. It was also alleged, with fresh evidence, that despite inefficiencies, obsolete technology, old capital stock and limited diversification, manufacturing growth before World War II had been faster than once acknowledged.[9] In the case of countries with pre-modern manufacturing experience, mainly China, India and the Ottoman Empire, there was also the specific claim that, contrary to Karl Marx's allegation, *the bones of handloom weavers had not bleached the periphery's plains.*

In fact, after international opening and before the much-delayed rise of industrial textile production, the Chinese, Indian and Ottoman handloom weaver survived British competition. Given an estimated productivity differential of mechanized to handloom spinning of over 40:1 but of mechanized to handloom weaving in the vicinity of less than 10:1 (Chao 1975), imports of spun yarn typically ruined hand spinners. Imported yarn, however, was used by handloom weavers to make cloth for the domestic market. Technically, then, Marx was wrong and the revisionists won the day. Nevertheless, their victory was pyrrhic. Because artisans in "the rest" competed on the basis of low wages rather than high skills, *they survived by being pauperized rather than by being innovative,* as in France. 'Economic openness' worked against them through two channels: domestic demand declined for artisan luxuries (see Gadgil 1959 for India); and competitive imports rose. There was a pervasive inability to use existing commercial and technical skills to innovate around foreign competition, in contradiction to the United States and France.

Table 2.1 summarizes some of the shaky evidence. In the case of the Ottoman Empire, the least developed of "the rest's" major pre-modern industrial economies, by the eighteenth century Ottoman handicrafts had already begun to cater mainly to lower-end domestic consumers and by the nineteenth century textile exports had become nil (Faroqhi 1994; Genc 1994, p. 67). What becomes evident thereafter is the rising relative importance of both yarn and cloth imports, and the late appearance of domestic industrial yarn and cloth production (not until the 1880s and 1900s respectively). At the time of World War I, imports of cotton cloth accounted for more than three-fourths of total consumption, and the Ottoman Empire had become Britain's third best trading partner (Pamuk 1986) and (Inalcik 1987). A monotonic decline in *total* textile employment is indicated in table 2.2. Not until the appearance of domestic industrial production after 1882 does employment begin to rise.

The pattern in India is similar, although the loss of the domestic market to imports before the rise of domestic industrial production is less severe and the appearance of mechanized textile production comes much sooner. Throughout the nineteenth century India's imports of yarn increase while mechanized yarn production awaits the founding of the first modern Indian textile mill in 1854. As for cloth, after 1850 the implied share of imports in

Table 2.1. Estimates of Textile Output and Trade—France, Ottoman Empire, India, China, and Mexico, 1790–1924

	Yarn				Cloth		
Years	Exports	Imports	Handloom	Industrial	Exports	Imports	Handloom
France (in tons)							
1781–90		0	3,742		0	772	2,315
1803–12		0	7,496		441	1,102	4,630
1815–24		0	17,637		1,102	0	11,905
1825–34	110	0	31,747		1,984	0	22,267
1835–44	210	110	46,517		4,079	0	37,148
1845–54	210	0	62,942		7,165	110	45,966
Ottoman Empire (in tons)							
1820–22							
I	0	150	11,550	0	0	450	11,550
II	0	150	12,900	0	0	450	12,900
III	0	150	14,250	0	0	450	14,250
1840–42							
I	0	2,650	8,250	0	0	4,100	8,250
II	0	2,650	9,750	0	0	4,100	9,750
III	0	2,650	11,250	0	0	4,100	11,250
1870–72	0	7,750	3,000	0	0	17,300	3,000
1880–82	0	6,500	2,000	500	0	24,700	2,000
1909–11	0	12,550	1,000	5,000	0	49,350	1,000
India[1] (yarn in million lb.; cloth in million sq. yd.)							
1790					50		
1820		3				26	
1840	0.6	17			26	199	
1870	6.0	34			14	1,189	
1880–84	43.0	42	150	151	36	1,766	1,000
1900–1904	234.0	28	110	532	120	1,992	1,286
1920–24	67.0	48	70	679	195	1,387	1,468
China[2] (yarn in million lb.; cloth in million sq. yd.)							
1810					544		
1820					302		
1875	12.4	632.3	0			457	1,637
1905	304.3	393.3	90.2			509	1,981
1919	178.5	333.6	297.6			787	1,798
1931	−76.0	173.3	966.9			300	1,815
Mexico[3] (yarn in tons; cloth in million sq. yd.)							
1807	0				0	7.0	
1817	0				0	0.7	
1827	0				0	22.0	
1837	0				0		
1843	0			3,867	0		
	0			327	0		

Table 2.1. (*continued*)

Years	Yarn				Cloth		
	Exports	Imports	Handloom	Industrial	Exports	Imports	Handloom
1854	0			3,346	0		
	0			2,843			
1856	0				0	41.9	
1870	0				0		
1872	0				0	40.8	
1877–78	0			2,753	0		

Notes: Rough estimates only. Blank spaces indicate that data are not available.
1. Implied share of imports in Indian cloth consumption is around 50 percent. This share is disputed in other sources, which claim a share at the turn of the century of imports of around 75 percent. See, for example, Chandavarkar (1994).
2. Imports for China are net of exports.
3. Mexico: varas = 36 English inches; piece of manta = 32 yars = 26.75 meters divided by .836 = one yard (see Thomson 1989, p. xiv, for conversion).

Sources: Adapted from: France: Markovitch (1966), as cited in Heywood (1977); Ottoman Empire: Pamuk (1986); India, other than exports: Twomey (1983); India's and China's exports: Twomey (1983); China, other than exports: Reynolds (1975); Mexico, imports: Herrera Canales (1977); Mexico, yarn and cloth: Thomson (1991) and Roberto Sandoval Z, as cited in Cardoso (1987), p. 152.

total estimated consumption is around 50 percent, although some say 75 percent is more accurate.[10] From 1896–97 to 1898–99 imports account for 60 percent of total cloth consumption, handloom weavers' output accounts for 30 percent, and mills' share accounts for only 9 percent (Mehta 1953). Starting from 1800 the number of Indian handicraft workers declined in absolute number (see table 2.2).

Handloomed cloth in China fared better than in India, and allegedly accounted for almost 80 percent of total cloth consumption as late as 1905 (see table 2.1).[11] Nevertheless, "imported yarn met around 70 percent of Chinese demand (for machine-made yarn around 1908), and under pressure from imports the local spinning industry remained depressed" (Kuwahara 1986, p. 120). Conjectures also suggest an absolute employment decrease in China's textile sector in this period.[12]

What is unclear from any of the direct evidence presented by revisionist accounts is how handloom weavers competed *at all* against British cloth imports, which were both low in price and high in quality (measured by consistency, color, touch, and weight). The favored hypothesis is that handloom weavers catered to a special market segment that imports could not or would not reach, as in China (the same arguments are made for India, the Ottoman Empire and Mexico):

The performance of the handicraft weaving sector . . . is a remarkable one, and suggests the existence of a strong and partially discrete market, espe-

Table 2.2. Estimates of Employment in the Textile Industry—
Ottoman Empire and India, 1800–1929

Year	Spinning	Weaving	Total
Ottoman Empire[1]			
1820–22	215,000	65,250	280,250
1840–42	162,500	62,000	224,500
1870–72	50,000	53,750	103,750
1880–82	33,300	45,000	78,300
1909–11	16,650	87,759	104,409
India[2] (in millions)			
1800 (high est.)	4.5	1.8	6.3
1800 (low est.)	2.8	1.1	3.9
1850	4.2	1.8	6
1880	1.5	1	2.5
1913	0.9	1.5	2.4
1929	0.6	1.7	2.3

1. Estimates only. Represents full-time employment.
2. Estimates only. Represents handicraft-textile employment.

Sources: For Ottoman Empire, adapted from Pamuk (1986); for India, adapted from Twomey (1983).

cially in the rural interior of China, for the generally heavier and longer-wearing handicraft product. Domestic mill cloth and imported goods were not perfect substitutes for the handicraft cloth (Feuerwerker 1970, p. 374).[13]

Nevertheless, while imported and mill cloth may not have been *perfect* substitutes for handicraft cloth, they must have been fairly close substitutes among "the rest's" price-sensitive, impoverished consumers. Consumer preferences, therefore, may not be an entirely satisfactory explanation for how handweavers survived.

Another possibility is that their productivity rose in the nineteenth century because technology was *not* stagnant. Three technological advances in hand-loom weaving were known to have occurred: the *improved wooden loom* (locally engineered through learning-by-doing); the *iron-gear loom* (invented in Japan); and the *Jacquard loom* (invented in the first decade of the nineteenth century in France). In the case of China, the insight for the improvement in the wooden loom came from factory production, so such an advance could not have increased productivity in the nineteenth century because factory production had not yet emerged by that time. The iron-gear loom was imported from Japan in 1906 "but it did not come into wide use until the Chinese modified the foot pedals to accommodate the bound feet of the Chinese women" (Chao 1975, pp. 185–87). Thus, neither could this loom have contributed to higher productivity during the nineteenth and early twentieth century. As for the Jacquard loom, it, too, was imported into China in 1906 by a Japanese textile expert, who instructed students in Tientsin in a state-sponsored school. But not only was this loom not present in China in the nineteenth century, it also did not increase speed but simply permitted greater variety of native cloth (Chao 1975, pp. 185–87). Technological change in handloom weaving in the nineteenth century was thus relatively stagnant in China and presumably elsewhere, as most accounts make no mention of new techniques.

Still another possibility (assuming high price substitution between imported and domestic handwoven cloth) is that handloom weavers competed against imports by lowering their own costs, that is, by maintaining parity with (or undercutting) imported cloth prices—which were falling steeply in the nineteenth century—through reductions in production costs (we assume inputs are limited to yarn and labor). Since the prices of *both* imported yarn and cloth were declining in the nineteenth century, in order for handloom weavers to compete without lowering their own remuneration (whatever the economic arrangement under which they worked), the price of imported yarn would have to have fallen more than that of imported cloth (by an amount related to the share of yarn in total costs). These precise calculations are not possible to make,[14] but over the long run it is likely that the price of imported (and hence domestic) cloth fell by *more* than the price of imported yarn:

> Generally speaking, the fall in price of yarn was caused by the innovation in the spinning process in Britain, while the decline in price of cloth was caused by the innovation in the weaving as well as spinning process. It follows that, from the long-range point of view, the fall in price of cloth per piece was greater than the fall in price of the yarn required for one piece of cloth. It is clear then that the remuneration for weaving per piece became less, while on the other hand, it is most probable that the productivity of labour of traditional handicrafts did not rise significantly. The only way to cover the decrease in remuneration per piece was to work harder and for more and more hours. (Matsui 1968, pp. 20–21)

Considering India, "*we have grounds for supposing that the Indian handloom weavers became worse off economically or fewer in number*" (Matsui 1968, p. 21, emphasis added).

It is highly unlikely, however, that the supply of handloom weavers fell. As yarn imports rose, and as unemployed hand spinners turned to hand weaving, the number of potential entrants into weaving probably rose substantially. Hence, domestic prices and profit margins of hand weavers became subject to severe downward pressure. In the Ottoman Empire "the export industries [such as silk and carpet weaving] shared with many domestically targeted sectors [such as cotton textiles] a reliance on cheap labor, that *generally suffered a decline in real wages*" (Quataert 1994, pp. 89–90, emphasis added). In China, textile manufacturing was being relocated to lower wage areas. Whereas location was once determined by proximity to cotton-growing areas, "the new hand weaving centers possessed *more surplus labor than other places*" (Chao 1977, p. 187, emphasis added).[15]

Thus, hand weaving in the nineteenth century appears to have competed against imports, if at all, by cutting the price of both yarn *and labor*. If some dynamic entrepreneurial response to lower wages was supposed to follow, it is not obvious that it ever did. The response to British competition of artisans in France and artisans in China, India, and the Ottoman Empire could not have been more distinct.

American Comparative *Dis*advantage

The American textile industry before the arrival of the British mechanic Samuel Slater in 1789 was largely confined to household spinning of wool and linen using manual or water power. Modern textile manufacture awaited the know-how that Slater brought with him from England, but soon the industry became the first to exhibit large-scale production units. Capital became more concentrated in manufacturing as profitability from commerce declined. Because artisans lacked the necessary capital, finance was undertaken by merchants: "The low or nonexistent profits in foreign trade from 1807 to 1815 *and the promise during these years of high returns in domestic enterprise*, brought Appletons, Cabots, Lawrences, Lowells, and other leaders of the merchant aristocracy into textile manufacture" (Cochran 1972, p. 80, emphasis added). With this concentration of capital came a new organization of textile manufacture—the Waltham system—which, in turn, increased productivity and presumably profitability: "The new form was more purely American than its predecessor, which had used English machinery and English type of labor. It was, in fact, the prototype of the big modern corporation, organized for mass production and integrating all processes from the raw material through the finished product under one management and, as far as possible, in one plant" (Ware 1931, p. 60).

The Boston Manufacturing Company, established in 1813 at Waltham, Massachusetts, became the first company to be organized in this new way. A sample of six large multiplant firms, including this company, tended to exhibit "remarkably higher" productivity in the period 1820–59 than the average of the entire industry (Davis and Stettler 1966, p. 230).

By the decade between 1814 and 1824, the American cotton textile industry was no longer merely a borrower of British production processes. A big breakthrough came with the power loom, invented by Paul Moody for

Francis Cabot Lowell. Other major innovations included the Waltham dresser, the double speeder and filling frame, the self-acting loom temple, and pickers and openers (Gibb 1950). There followed a series of midi-innovations in the form of the cap spinner and an imperfect ring spinner, the self-acting mule, and improvements in roving frames. Mechanical problems inherent in the English gear drive had multiplied in the United States due to poor copying, and these problems limited operating speeds. Then the innovation of the belt drive greatly increased spindle speed. With virtually no capital investment, output per spindle rose by almost 50 percent (Davis and Stettler 1966).[16]

Thus, starting with Eli Whitney's cotton gin in 1793, innovations are what helped the American textile industry prosper behind tariff barriers in a large and expanding domestic market. Throughout the nineteenth century, "both wage rates and returns to capital in the form of interest were higher in the United States than in Great Britain" (North 1965, p. 675–76). If the United States was to become a manufacturing nation, it faced the same choice that most learners face (portrayed in figure 1.1): "it had either to narrow these [wage] differentials or indeed to improve its productivity." Unlike what happened to the handicraft sector in "the rest," however, "success in American manufacturing came about . . . not by reducing the price of productive factors below that in competitive producing areas, but by improving productivity so substantially that it more than made up for this difference" (North 1965, pp. 675–76). In the American textile industry, not even an extraordinary rate of innovation raised productivity to the point where unit labor costs equaled or fell below those of England. But given tariff protection (discussed later), this did not seem to deter investments in the textile industry or weaken the growth impulses that the textile industry transmitted to the rest of the American economy.

Mexico's "Adaptive" Response[17]

Experience in manufacturing textiles (woolens) was longer in Mexico than in the United States. Accounts exist of lively manufacturing activity in Spanish colonial Mexico dating at least to the eighteenth century (Thomson 1989). This historical experience, however, failed to help Mexico's *modern* textile industry significantly, either because artisan activity did not involve a sophisticated division of labor or the adaptive skills of the modern sector were weak.[18] Finance was not necessarily the principle problem; private finance, often from speculators in raw cotton, initially turned out to be abundant for Mexico's early cotton textile ventures.[19] Instead, low productivity contributed to low profitability and, hence, low specialization, which then made capital shy.

Mexico's modern textile companies were often owned and managed by foreigners or were jointly owned by foreigners and second-generation foreigners ("Creoles"). Merchants from France, Spain, England, and the United States figured among the most prominent proprietors of spinning mills (Potash 1983). Allegedly the skills of foreign technicians "were quickly passed on to Mexican technicians who proved well matched to the task of servicing, repairing and even building imitations of foreign textile machinery." After an economic slowdown in 1842, "the technological demands of the industrial sector remained fairly modest and could easily be serviced by a small group of immigrant technicians, combined with the technical dexterity of the Mexican artisan." Thus, it has been argued that "early republican Mexico faced few insurmountable technical obstacles" (Thomson 1991, pp. 294–95). In this view the cost problems of Mexico's cotton mills were due to the high prices of raw cotton and transportation, both politically determined (raw cotton producers blocked cheap imports of raw cotton while state investments in infrastructure were nil until railroad development).[20]

This conclusion about technology, however, is consistently contradicted by scraps of qualitative evidence, such as the case of La Constancia, Mexico's oldest spinning mill built in 1836. After the death in 1846 of its owner Esteban de Antuñano, Mexico's industrial "visionary," a major war between Mexico and the United States cut communications between the two countries. Despite a decade of technology transfer and learning, La Constancia's new manager was apparently unable to replace a broken drive wheel until 1849, which kept all spindles inoperative for three years (Thomson 1989). In the case of Miraflores, the integrated spinning and weaving mill of the Martinez del Río family in Mexico City, there is no indication that the owners made any attempt to absorb, let alone improve, foreign knowledge of how to set up a textile plant or run it. The resident manager of Miraflores was a Scot, whose duties included the supervision of operations, the management of new installations and constructions, and the verification of accounting procedures. "The Scot had a free hand in running the factory. The partners had little technical training pertinent to textile manufacturing and, as a matter of principle, they preferred to limit themselves to matters of finance and to stay out of production" (Walker 1986, p. 141).

This hands-off strategy almost always resulted in bad management. The acrimonious debate among industrialists over free or controlled raw cotton imports featured countercharges of bad management as the fundamental cause of the textile industry's woes. In one case industrialists were described as being "grossly ignorant . . . they are precisely the ones whose factories are found to be inefficient (mal economizados), and who seem to base all their hopes in keeping themselves going on the closure or ruin of other factories, or on the monopolists." In the case of other industrialists, "the small profits they received were due to the way they managed their factories, and by the ruinous deals they made at the time they were founded," not least of all the hiring of foreign managers at exorbitant cost (Thomson 1989 pp. 261; 255–56, my translation). Data on productivity are scarce, but what exists for 1845–54 (in the form of spindles per worker) suggests stagnation (Potash 1983).

Given the threat to profit margins posed by gross inefficiencies in production, entrepreneurs spread their energies thin. They speculated in Mexican and non-Mexican public debt and diversified into industries other than textiles, without investing either in skill formation at the industry-level or in organizational capabilities to manage across product lines, as did postwar diversified business groups. Besides *La Constancia, La Economía* ("The Cost-Efficient"), and other textile mills, the financial portfolio of Mexico's leading industrialist, Antuñano, included investments in cotton cultivation and ginning, textile merchandising, factories to produce glass, porcelain, paper and iron, as well as a wheat-growing hacienda (Thomson 1989). The Martinez del Río family, a leading Panamanian textile proprietor in Mexico City, invested more of its assets in the 1850s in government paper of various sorts (stocks, bonds, debt) and stocks and shares in *non*family businesses than in family businesses, only one of which was textiles.[21]

Although no modern textile mill in Mexico allegedly arose out of traditional woolen cloth-producing *obrajes*, there was an intimate relationship between mechanized spinning mills and handloom weaving mills (which largely met the same fate as the hand weaving sector in China, India, and the Ottoman Empire) (Thomson 1991). The inner-city shopkeepers, merchants, and manufacturers of Puebla, which accounted for between 32 percent and 38 percent of total Mexican yarn production from 1843–52, did not "entertain visions of sustained industrialization." Instead, they "saw their role as one of using available modern spinning technology to renew and increase their economic control over the weaving artisanate whom they supplied with yarn and whose cloth they marketed." They differed from their pre-Independence counterparts in becoming owners of spinning factories and sometimes large weaving establishments as well. Like their predecessors, however, they "*continued to use credit links with independent weavers as the principal means of controlling and profiting from cotton manufacture*" (Thomson 1989, pp. 257–58).[22] This suggests that investments in modern technological capabilities were small because it was more lucrative for entrepreneurs to manipulate prices of raw cotton and handloomed cloth behind tariff barriers than to aspire to becoming internationally competitive in either cloth or yarn. Tariff protection, however, was vulnerable to smuggling, so even production for the home market was a tepid affair.

Protectionism

After the Napoleonic wars, all countries with premodern industries, whether in the North Atlantic or "the rest," turned to tariffs for protection. Due to colonial rule, however, tariff rates in the early nineteenth century became negligible in China, India, and the Ottoman Empire, whereas they reached 35–45 percent in the United States and a slightly higher range in England (see table 2.3).[23] Starting in the 1830s, tariffs in Mexico fluctuated widely by decade and were undermined by smuggling, but were closer on average to rates in the United States than other countries in "the rest" with premodern textile experience.

Three questions arise about tariffs in this period: How necessary were they?; How long did they last?; and How effective were they?

In the case of Europe, it has been argued that immediately after the Napoleonic Wars "protection was absolutely necessary to the survival of most Continental industries" (Crouzet 1972, p. 101). It is unclear how necessary protection was in France, but in the textile industry tariffs were certainly in effect for a long time and succeeded in meeting their goals: "The cotton industry in particular was almost immune from foreign competition on its domestic market, with outright prohibitions imposed on imports of cotton yarns, cloths and knitwear in 1793. These survived largely intact until 1860. . . . In the meantime, the French cotton industry experienced a period of sustained growth" (Heywood 1981, pp. 554–54) and (Heywood 1977).[24] As early as 1830, cotton textiles accounted for over 10 percent of France's exports (Woodruff 1966). Between 1781 and 1854 France imported virtually no yarn or cloth (see table 2.1).

Tariffs were necessary for the Mexican textile industry to stay afloat. They were also of long duration and of minimal effectiveness, both in keeping out imports and in promoting domestic learning. According to one estimate, "manufacturers were never remotely competitive with their overseas competitors." Domestic prices were estimated to exceed international prices by a factor of at least two in the 1830s, when Mexico's textile industry first got protection, through the 1890s, when protection was renewed (Walker 1986, p. 162). In 1872 as much as 52 percent of Mexico's imports were still accounted for by textiles (Herrera Canales 1977).[25]

In the United States, a textile tariff was introduced in 1816. This sparked a long debate starting with a passage in Frank Taussig's 1892 classic, *The Tariff History of the United States*, which stated that while protection was initially justified on infant industry grounds, it soon became redundant: "almost certainly by 1832, the industry had reached a firm position, in which it was able to meet foreign competition on equal terms" (Taussig 1892, p. 136).[26] This conclusion, however, was subsequently challenged, both by a direct comparison of British and American costs and prices (Harley 1992) and by econ-

Table 2.3. Average Tariff Rates on Imported Goods—Selected Countries, 1820–1970

Years	Average Tariff Rates (%)	Years	Average Tariff Rates (%)
China		Mexico[g]	
1843–1922	5.0	1913	33.7
1929–38	8.0	1929	18.4
		1937	17.0
		1948	11.1
India		1960	20.1[h]
circa 1800	3.5	1970	17.7
1862–1894	5.0		
1913	4.0		
1925	14.0	U.K.	
1937	28.9	1820	45.0–55.0
1955	30.4	1875	0.0
		1913	0.0
		1925	5.0
Ottoman Empire[a]		1931	na
1838–62	5.0	1950	23.0
1862–1902	8.0		
1907–14	11.0		
		U.S.	
		1820	35.0–45.0
Brazil		1875	40.0–50.0
1851–70	26.5	1913	44.0
1881–90	39.0	1925	37.0
1890–99	27.0	1931	48.0
1900–1914	42.0	1950	14.0
1945–50	14.4		
1960–65	85		
1967–70	37.0	France	
		1820	na
		1875	12.0–15.0
Argentina		1913	20.0
1913	26.0	1925	21.0
1925	26.0	1931	30.0
1927	23.8	1950	18.0
1945–50	12.2[b]		
1962	148.8[c]		
1969	36.0[d]	Germany	
		1820	8.0–12.0
		1875	4.0–6.0
Chile		1913	13.0
1913	na	1925	20.0
1925–27	27.5[e]	1931	21.0
1932	35.0	1950	26.0
1955	39.1		
1961	89.0[f]		
1967–70	na		

Table 2.3. (*continued*)

Years	Average Tariff Rates (%)
Japan	
1820	na
1875	5.0
1913	19.8
1925	22.6
1931	23.8
1950	na

a. Turkey.
b. Ad valorem tariff.
c. Maximum value.
d. Nominal protection.
e. Before 1928, basic tariff.
f. Nominal protection.
g. The entries for 1929, 1937, and 1948 represent coefficient of custom duties. The coefficient of custom duties is the quotient, at current values, of customs duties and total imports.
h. Nominal protection.

Sources: Data for Argentina, Brazil, Chile, and Mexico for 1925 and later (unless otherwise noted below) adapted from Ground (1988, p. 196). Measures "nominal tariff" rates: an average of available rates on consumer, intermediate, and capital goods. Data for India (1937 and 1955) and Chile (1945–1950) adapted from Maizels (1963, p. 141). Measures "average ad valorem rates of import duty on a sample of manufactured goods in selected countries." Data for Turkey adapted from Issawi (1966, pp. 38–40). These were blanket tariff rates established by law. Rates from 1838 to 1902 were set according to the Anglo-Turkish Commercial Convention of 1838 (subsequently renegotiated in 1862). This pact also called for a blanket duty on exports of 12 percent. Data for Brazil for the years 1890–1924 adapted from Leff (1982, p. 175). Measures "import duties as a percentage of the value of Brazilian Imports." Data for India for the years 1913 and 1925 and for Argentina (1913) taken from Lewis (1949, p. 48). Measure "average tariff levels." Data for Brazil for 1851 to 1890 adapted from Leff (1982, pp. 74, 175). Measures "import duties as a percentage of the value of imports." Data for India for the nineteenth century adapted from Lewis (1970, p. 328). Measures "average tariff levels." Data for 1913 for Mexico, China, U.K., U.S., France, Germany, and Japan (1875) adapted from Bairoch (1993, pp. 37, 40). Other data for Japan are from Yamazawa (1975). They exhibit large standard deviations about the mean. Data for China and Mexico measure "import duties as a percent of special imports." All other data measure "average tariff rates on manufactured products." Data for China adapted from Wright (1966). The figure for 1843–1929 is the nominal ad valorem rate set according to international agreements. Not until the period 1922–1929 was the 5-percent rate levied across the board. Prior to that time, schedules varied depending on the good being traded and as a result according to Wright "[A]n effective ad valorem rate of 5 seldom, if ever existed" (p. 590). The figure for 1929–1938 represents the estimated annual collection of import duties as a percentage of the total value of imports (calculated based on the estimates and schedules provided in the New National Tariff instituted February 1, 1929).

ometric inference.[27] Even after controlling for different fabrics, the American cotton textile industry "failed to achieve technological parity with Britain in the ante-bellum years. Removal of the tariff would have placed almost all American cotton textile producers, including the famous Waltham and Lowell mills, under severe pressure. Few would have survived the introduction of free trade" (Harley 1992).

The counterfactual question has also been posed of whether or not China, India, and the Ottoman Empire could have prospered more had tariffs been higher. While this question is impossible to answer, the Mexican evidence suggests that "the rest's" skill deficits were too deep and too wide to be repaired with a single policy instrument such as tariffs; hence the broadside assault on such deficiencies after World War II.[28]

Skill Deficits

The breadth of skill deficits in "the rest's" textile industries may be assessed in terms of the three generic skills introduced in chapter 1: *production, project execution,* and *innovation* (see table 1.2). The deficits of the cotton textile industry spanned all three.

With respect to skills to execute new projects, "the rest's" demand forecasting was often inaccurate, its financial planning was nonexistent, and technology acquisition was bungled, all of which increased start-up costs.[29] A Brazilian cotton mill that was established in 1853 with 2,500 spindles, 100 looms and cotton ginning equipment "suffered at the outset mishaps, circumstances and events which slowed down its progress and forced the owners to lose part of their capital. Imperfect machinery brought the first mishap, the result of bad faith of the machine shop. The second mishap was the poor planning and construction of the transmission belts—they were damaged and had to be repaired. The last mishap (still affecting its prosperity) is the absence of energetic administration" (Stein 1957, p. 42). Even India's jewel, the Empress Mill, "had a few teething troubles and the company's performance was far from satisfactory initially. Consequently, the value of the shares began to fall" (Tripathi 1990, p. 59). Due to bureaucracy, China's Shanghai Cotton Cloth Mill had a gestation period of thirteen years (Feuerwerker 1958)! After plants were erected, profitability suffered from ill-conceived operations management and administrative practices; poor training, maintenance, and repair; and mismanaged labor relations, all of which increased operating costs and reduced quality further. In one Indian textile mill visited by a foreign expert as late as the 1930s: "Much of the machinery is old and some of it of an obsolete type, but most of it would be good enough if it were kept clean and in repair. But on the spinning and drawing frames I saw any number of rollers with felts worn uneven, matted and dirty, and out of line; in very bad condition indeed" (Moser 1930, p. 102). In Brazil, few enterprises knew their unit costs, and it was reported *as late as 1945* that "rare are the textile mills that have systematic cost accounting" (Stein 1955).

The textile mills of the North Atlantic and Japan were not necessarily paragons of efficiency. In Japan's pre-1880's cotton mills, faulty mill design due to the incompetence of local engineers resulted in additional costly construction work. Water was adopted as the motive force, but it was too weak to drive the machinery (Nakaoka 1991). Nevertheless, by the 1920s, a comparison of efficiency in Chinese cotton mills and Japanese cotton mills operating in China (C-mills and J-mills, respectively) shows a large productivity gap in Japan's favor.[30] The playing field was level for capital goods. Both types of companies bought their equipment from the same foreign suppliers; in 1927–32 the top five textile machinery sellers in C-mills and in J-mills were identical (Kuwahara 1986). C-mills and J-mills were also well-matched in other respects; Japan, in fact, was China's main teacher. Chinese companies enjoyed a demand-side advantage in the form of the militant boycotts that erupted in the interwar period against buying foreign goods, which provided Chinese mills with a form of protection. J-mills suffered further from the usual costs of distant operations, but they had the upper hand in skills and distribution.[31] Nevertheless, when the Great Depression provoked cutthroat competition in the Chinese cotton industry, many Chinese mills went bankrupt or experienced dull performance whereas most local Japanese mills grew steadily and were profitable from the start, accounting by 1930 for approximately 40 percent of China's spindles (Kuwahara 1986).

Table 2.4 shows differences in production costs in C-mills and J-mills in 1935 (based on a sample of forty-three firms). Production costs (mill expenses) are net of raw material costs, which were estimated to be as high as 88 percent of production costs depending on the yarn count (Chao 1975). The most significant cost difference related to labor, followed at a distance by machine repairs. Since J-mills paid higher wages than C-mills, the higher labor costs of C-mills stemmed from lower productivity. Table 2.5 gives an array of productivity estimates for 1935. J-firms out-performed C-firms across the board: in yarn per spindle per hour, yarn per worker hour, and in number of spindles and looms a worker operated. Differences in productivity were related to organization, technology, management, labor relations, and distribution. These proprietary knowledge-based assets, individually and collectively, were not easy for an outsider to decipher and duplicate.[32]

Japan's companies reduced the coordination problems of operating overseas by sending large numbers of directors, middle managers, and production workers from Japan to China (and, when a J-mill was starting, sending key workers from China to Japan for training). Japanese textile mills had been

Table 2.4. Production Cost of 20 Count Cotton Yarn in China, 1935

	Chinese-Owned Mills	Japanese-Owned Mills
Labor costs	10.7	6.3
Salaries	1.2	0.6
Power and coal	5.5	4.8
Machine repairs supplies	1.8	0.6
	1.7	0.5
Packing	1.5	1.2
Transportation	0.2	0.2
Miscellaneous	1.5	0.5
Total	24.5	15.1

Source: Adapted from Kuwahara (1991).

improving their practices since the 1890s, when they first tried to export to China. Ultimately, they "improved the efficiency of mill operation based on statistical data" (Kuwahara 1992, p. 151). They prepared a process chart of the mixing ratio of raw cottons appropriate to the projected yarn count, the draft ratio of sliver, setting the gauge span, the speed of spindles, and the twisting of sliver and yarn on the basis of home-mill practices. The fact that key managerial and technical positions in J-mills were occupied by Japanese employees limited the possibilities of technology transfer to C-mills.

Chinese mills were characterized by the contract system (labor relations—from recruitment, to training, to job performance, to dismissal—were handled by independent bosses) and nepotism (the bosses were often personally related

Table 2.5. Cross-Country Comparison of Productivity, Cotton Textiles, 1929

Country	Yarn per Hour	Spindles per Operative	Yarn per Worker Hour	Looms per Operative
U.S. South	4.5	1,120	5,000	na
U.K.	5.0	600	3,000	3.6–4.0
Japan	5.4	400	2,100	5.5–5.8[1]
Japanese mills in China	4.5–5.5	200–400	1,000–1,100	3.0
Chinese mills	3.0–4.0	165–240	600–700	2.0
Brazil (1921)	na	na	na	2.0–3.0
India (1927)[2]	na	160–180	na	2.0
Mexico (1909)	na	na	na	2.0–3.0

1. Excluding automatic looms.
2. Only Bombay.

Sources: Lu (1993), except for Brazil (Pearse 1921), India (Rutnagu 1927) and Mexico (Clark 1909).

to the mill's owner). By contrast, J-mills emphasized worker training and paternalism, which succeeded in reducing labor turnover. C-mills' average job duration was measured in months whereas J-mills' average job duration was measured in one to three years.

Machine performance depended on the engineering ability of individual firms. Repair, maintenance, the adjustment of machines to a variety of raw cottons and room temperatures, remodeling machines through replacement with the most up-to-date parts were all major engineering challenges in cotton factories. Nevertheless, "it was difficult for the engineers and experienced workers of other firms to imitate and command expertise accumulated in one company; much know-how, such as the twisting rate of the sliver during the drawing process and preliminary spinning process, was kept secret. This know-how created the differences in quality and productivity of cotton yarn among the firms" (Kuwahara 1992, pp. 156–157).

Thus, the skill deficits of "the rest" were multifaceted, involving not simply an inability to innovate new products and processes but also an inability to produce at world standards of efficiency and an inability to execute investment decisions. Those responsible ranged from shop-floor production workers to middle managers to individual owners. The problems behind "the rest's" backwardness were as broad as they were deep.

Conclusion

It is interesting that the United States textile industry was rarely competitive at world prices during the *200 years* spanning 1800 to 2000. It survived behind trade barriers of one sort (tariffs) or another (voluntary export restraints). Yet up until the American Civil War in the 1860s, textiles comprised American manufacturing's "leading sector."

Equally stunning is the fact that over much of the same time period, but without tariffs or other forms of protection, the textile industries of China, India, and (to a lesser extent) the Ottoman Empire *did* become competitive at world prices. Yet at least before World War II, they never became as developmental as their counterparts in the American or French textile industries. British competition in "the rest" swiftly destroyed handloom spinning while handloom weaving hung on through wage cuts. When industrial yarn and cloth production finally emerged, it was upstaged by Japanese mills, which soon became the world's most efficient producers, taking 40 percent of China's domestic textile market through foreign investments and knocking out India's exports to China.

Nor does it seem reasonable to conclude that because the textile industries of "the rest" grew only slowly before World War II under market forces, they did not enjoy comparative advantage. *Ex ante*, a country's comparative advantage can never be known, but there were early signs of the textile industry's impending success. At the end of the American Revolutionary War, the U.S. textile industry was threatened by exports of "Indies" (from India) and "Nankeens" (from China) (Ware 1931). At the Crystal Palace Exhibition in London, one visitor favorably compared the textiles of India with those of France: "The Indians are the French of the Orient for their industrial genius (*genie industriel*)."[33] There are thus grounds for believing that textiles were an appropriate industry in India and China to develop, one that would be highly successful in world markets. Soon, however, Indian and Chinese textile exports sharply declined (see table 2.1).

Despite a revisionist literature that romanticizes the handloom weaver and resuscitates his (India) or her (China and the Ottoman Empire) bones from the bleached plains where Karl Marx left them, "the rest's" artisans were tragic figures. They competed by cutting their own wages and retreating to geographically inaccessible low-income regional markets. There is no evidence of "flexibility" or inventiveness on their part, traits typically attributed in the 1990s to small-scale firms. The most important prewar industry, cotton textiles, did not inspire hope that "the rest" could develop a viable alternative to modern mass production along the lines developed by France.

Japan, with only modest protection until the interwar period, ultimately triumphed in both cotton textiles and silk by pioneering a new approach to manufacturing, as examined in the next chapter in the case of silk. Without a comparable set of skills, "the rest's" prewar textile industries merely stumbled along. Protectionism, as practiced in Mexico, proved inadequate in the absence of more comprehensive supports and a disciplinary control mechanism to stimulate economic growth. That only came later.

3

Tribulations of Technology Transfer

In theory, technology transfer should enable a backward country to achieve world productivity norms. In practice, because technology is 'tacit' and never completely codifiable, the best technology transfer rarely achieves productivity parity between buyer and seller.[1] The more tacit a technology is, the more difficult it is to transfer. Given any level of tacitness, the more monopolistic the power of the seller and the lower the skills and organizational capabilities of the buyer, the worse the transfer. Transfer may be most perfect through the medium of direct foreign investment, but such investment does not necessarily arrive when it is needed.[2] If it arrives too early, it may "crowd out" national firms (see chapter 8).

A shyness of foreign investors left "the rest" with a serious skill deficit that grew over time relative to that of the North Atlantic and Japan. The tacitness problem arose early because of the sectoral composition of "the rest's" manufacturing output. Whatever the source of manufacturing experience, all countries tended to share the same sequential industry mix. By the 1930s or much earlier, food processing (including tobacco and beverages) dominated at around 30–40 percent of total manufacturing output (especially the refining of sugar, brewing of beer, and milling of flour). Next in importance were textiles and apparel (cotton and silk).[3] Then came cement, paper, matches, and, after the turn of the century, steel. These are all natural resource-based industries.[4] Because the specific properties of a natural resource vary by location, a successful technology transfer requires substantial investments in local learning and adaptation.

Japan set a benchmark for learners that began with technology transfer. Japan started to industrialize rapidly only in the 1890s, about the same time as China and slightly after Brazil, India, and Mexico.[5] Japan's first Western-style raw silk factory using imported equipment was founded by the Maebashi local government as late as 1870 (the first modern Chinese silk filature, founded by a silk merchant, made its appearance in Shanghai in 1881 [Eng 1984]). Japan's pioneering firm in cotton textiles, the Osaka Cotton Spinning Company, was established with the assistance of foreign engineers in May 1882 (Miyamoto 1988) (the first modern cotton spinning mill appeared in China in 1890). Given Japan's engineering capabilities and basic knowledge, its absorption of foreign know-how was more proactive, systematic, and thoroughgoing, as analyzed below in the case of the silk industry.

Technology Transfer

A technology transfer was always a necessary condition for late industrialization but almost never a sufficient one. Transfers were especially problematic before World War II, when transportation and communication were relatively poor and "the rest" was in an early phase of industrial transformation. Therefore, the process of technology transfer was probably less satisfactory in the period 1850–1950 than in the next fifty years.

Before the 1910s, foreign "firms" were less likely to establish manufacturing operations in "the rest" then were foreign "individuals." Not a single Lancashire textile-based company before 1910 operated as a multinational enterprise in China, India, Turkey, Mexico, or Brazil.[6] The performance of an individual, moreover, was not necessarily comparable to that of a firm: "British individuals abroad are not equivalent to British managers, who can draw on the home company's on-going experience and remain part of a business organization with knowledge of all facets of the business operations. Likewise, British trading companies that provided managerial supervision (management contracts) are not identical to a managerial organization that grows from an operating parent enterprise's experience in textile manufacturing" (Wilkins 1987, p. 121). The same weaknesses were true of the French, Spanish, and American individuals who, as noted in the last chapter, dominated Mexico's modern textile industry beginning in the 1830s. Italian immigrants often became entrepreneurs in Argentina, but a subsidiary of an Italian multinational, Pirelli, was first established in Argentina only in 1917 (Ines Barbero 1990). This was the same year that Ford Motor Company began assembling cars in Argentina (Diaz Alejandro 1970). Because individuals were not part of ongoing business organizations, their know-how was not necessarily up-to-date. British engineers in India's cotton mills, for example, often followed technological developments in Lancashire with a considerable time lag (Kiyokawa 1983). Not infrequently, foreign know-how bordered on the sham. In the 1880s, several Anglo-Brazilian sugar factories were promoted by railroad contractors and were universally a failure: "Contemporary opinion was unanimous in regarding the direction of these companies as deplorable," although the financial success of some *Brazilian* sugar factories suggested that it was possible to run them successfully (Graham 1968, p. 153).[7] Even the big trading companies, which preceded the multinationals, were not especially effective in their technology transfer. In China, two British silk mills were brought into being by prominent British trading companies, Jardine, Matheson & Company and Kungping Company, but "owing to poor management these filatures all failed within a few years" (Lieu 1936, p. 34).

Sometimes the effectiveness of the foreign technicians was constrained by cultural and social disparities. In the case of the Ottoman Empire in the 1850s, "Christian Europeans simply were not the most effective role models and were unpersuasive as opinion leaders, even in those instances when they knew the language. Their advice often was ignored. In many cases, the hired technicians believed their job was to run the equipment and not necessarily to teach new skills. The enormous wage differentials between foreign and Ottoman workers that were typical contributed to poor relations between the two groups" (Quataert 1992, p. 32). In Brazil before the abolition of slavery in 1888, the St. John del Rey gold mining company "simply adapted to local conditions. The British management of the St. John, for example, desperately wanted to employ free Brazilian labor and could not. They turned reluctantly [but profitably] to slave labor," which extended the life of slavery and delayed the rise of modern industry (Eakin 1989, 266–67).

When foreign firms finally superseded foreign individuals as technology providers in "the rest," they were more likely to enter a foreign market to enjoy an ongoing process rather than to be a first-mover and act as a catalyst for industrial expansion.[8] "Direct British investment in Brazilian manufacturing grew with Brazil's over-all industrial power", it did not lead it. Thus, "the British were not the cause of Brazilian industrialization. [Indeed], the activities of some of them tended to hinder that process. But others worked shoulder-to-shoulder with Brazilians to bring it about" (Graham 1968, p. 142). In the case of Mexican railways, "local companies constructed a total of 226 kilometers of track before North American capital arrived to construct the country's two major arteries" (Coatsworth 1981, p. 38).[9] Ultimately, American and European multinationals invested heavily in the manufacturing industries of Latin America, particularly in consumer goods, but when they did so in large numbers beginning in the 1910s or 1920s, many modern industries had already been founded (Phelps 1936). Most Latin American cigarette firms were established in the early years of the twentieth century and some in the 1890s. They grew rapidly in Argentina, Brazil, Chile, and Mexico. In these markets, the largest in the region, British-American Tobacco gained a beachhead either just prior to or after the First World War frequently by acquiring a local firm (Shepherd 1989). The founders of Argentina's meat packing industry included one British firm as well as two native-owned firms, which were taken over in 1907 by American packers (Crossley and Greenhill 1977).

The Corning Glassworks and the Pittsburgh Glass Company bought controlling interest in Argentina's financially strapped Cristalerías Rigolleau Company in 1942, thereby acquiring "an old and prestigious firm that already enjoyed a commanding position in its field and established connections with both suppliers and buyers" (Lewis 1990, p. 51).

In China, except for a couple of unsuccessful attempts, no textile mill owned by a Westerner was established until 1914 whereas modern Chinese mills began appearing in the 1890s (Chao 1975). Some Japanese investments in China's cotton mills involved big *zaibatsu* as opposed to individuals, but whoever the investor, it took over existing Chinese mills; the Chinese themselves were the trailblazers (Koh 1966). Foreign firms invested in Chinese industries other than textiles, but such firms initially tended to be very small, with no notable names of multinational manufacturers among them (Allen and Donnithorne 1954).[10] Foreign individuals in India were responsible for starting the jute industry, a major nineteenth-century exporter. The initiative for railroad construction also came from foreigners. But Indians took the lead in creating the cotton textile, power generation, shipping, construction, sugar, iron and steel, engineering, agricultural implements, and later chemical, automobile, and aircraft industries (Agarwala 1986). Initially, London would not allow India to develop its own steel industry for fear that it would displace British steel exports to India. When such exports were challenged by German steel, a domestic steel industry became acceptable. The British "must have thought that the abolition of the irksome prospecting laws would induce English entrepreneurs to set up steel plants in India. However, only one Englishman made a feeble attempt to enter the field," and India's first steel mill was built by a prominent Indian entrepreneurial family, the Tatas (Tripathi and Mehta 1990, p. 61).

In Turkey, the "foreigners" who often established modern production facilities were really émigrés who had lived in the Ottoman Empire for generations. For example, the largest textile factory built in Izmir before 1912–13 was owned by a descendent of old French and English commercial families active in the Izmir region since the late eighteenth and early nineteenth centuries (Clark 1969). Ironically, foreign investment in Turkey became real only after native non-Muslims were driven out of the country after World War I by nationalists who hoped to create a larger economic role for native Muslim capitalists. Instead, foreign investors filled the breech and eventually accounted for 63 percent of manufacturing output (Keyder 1994).

As in "the rest," so too in Japan: foreign investors were not the first-movers. As late as the period from 1896 to World War I, "when the Japanese had already demonstrated their general progressive drive and their specific industrial aptitudes, direct foreign investments in manufacturing began to appear" (Reubens 1955, p. 220).[11]

In theory, foreign firms are desirable because they provide "spillovers" (discussed in chapter 9) and a positive role model: "One cannot go into the Chinese-owned (textile) mills in China (circa 1930) without realizing the influence of the Japanese-owned mills" (Moser 1930, p. 66). Nevertheless, foreign role models may crush domestic competition. In China's cigarette industry, British American Tobacco (BAT), a giant multinational, and Nanyang, a local firm, competed head-on in the 1910s for China's growing market. Chien Chao-nan, the owner of Nanyang, put a deposit on a warehouse in the foreign concession area of Shanghai to begin production (Nanyang had accumulated experience producing cigarettes in Hong Kong using Japanese technology). "The very next day a BAT comprador tried to buy the building," which started a vehement argument that only ended when one of BAT's own compradors (a Cantonese like Chien) "defended Nanyang's position and urged BAT's management not to force Chien to surrender his rights to the building." Chien installed 119 American cigarette-making machines and later bought the site (Cochran 1980, p. 74).[12] In another case in the 1890s, entrepreneurs who attempted to manufacture textiles in the Ottoman Empire for local consumption (in Egypt) were brought to bankruptcy by the pressure of lobbyists for Manchester textile interests. The British ambassador first attempted to block the mill's construction with administrative delays but then, to insure his own reappointment against threats from English textile manufacturers, acted more vigorously in getting the local government to impose high production taxes on the mill. Construction was halted (Clark 1969).

Using a foreign firm as a benchmark was especially important in industries whose technology was changing rapidly, such as textiles (in the late nineteenth century the spinning ring was displacing the mule and automatic looms were gaining ground). In these industries, an engineering orientation on the part of management was essential to keep abreast of technological change. Yet technological expertise was not necessarily a characteristic of foreign investors. Japan's first major steel works received technical assistance from Germany in 1897, but "the German engineers did not work as hard as the Yawata Works had expected. They lacked the basic knowledge and abilities to lead Japanese engineers and foremen." This was in spite of the fact that the chief engineer, Mr. Toppe, earned a very high salary—*twice as much as the Prime Minister of Japan!* Yawata reached the conclusion that "the German engineers who came to the Far East (at the turn of the century) were hardly first rate" (Yonekura 1994, p. 43).[13] In Mexico, financing of industry "fell to a relatively small clique of (European) merchant-financiers who, because of their backgrounds in commerce and money-lending, were more adept at rigging the market and manipulating government policy than at streamlining production methods or innovating new processes or techniques" (Haber 1989, p. 5). Foreign firms accounted for roughly 20 percent of output in India's textile industry, but they were hardly exemplary models. As table 3.1 indicates, few directors either in European-owned mills or Indian-owned mills had a technical background; mercantile backgrounds were the norm in both cases.

Follow-up investments by technology buyers were necessary to adopt and modify foreign imports and to absorb foreign know-how. This was especially so in "the rest" because most of the industries being opened there before World War I were heavily raw material-based, as noted earlier, and local investments were necessary to adapt foreign techniques to local processing specifications. British-American Tobacco, for example, invested heavily in training Chinese farmers to grow American-type tobacco (Cochran 1980). The scholar-comprador Cheng Kuan-ying organized, developed, and then managed the Shanghai Cotton Cloth Mill beginning in 1879. To determine whether foreign machinery could actually process China's raw cotton, Cheng contacted a fellow-Cantonese in the United States and asked him to engage a technical expert to investigate the matter. The American, A. W. Danforth, came to Shanghai and expressed doubts about the suitability of the shorter fibers of Chinese cotton for machining. Cheng then sent Danforth back to the United States with some samples of raw Chinese cotton, and the resulting cloth was found to be equal in quality to American cloth (Hao 1970). (Production was delayed, however, because Cheng allegedly concentrated power in his own hands and "tended to treat the company's funds as his own" [Feuerwerker 1958, p. 212].) In the case of steel making, cost and quality are highly sensitive to the right choice and combination of raw materials, which cannot be determined simply by a mathematical formula. "They require patient and careful full-scale experimentation, which means years of painstaking effort to determine the best combinations."[14] Thus, Japan's Yawata Steel Works was in big trouble initially because "the blast furnace designed by a German engineer was too large for the soft and low-quality Japanese coke. Because of the high pressure and friction of the large furnace, the Japanese coke was crushed into powder and prevented air circulation and down flow of iron ore and flux" (Yonekura 1994, p. 44).[15]

Table 3.1. Background of Indian Factory Directors (Cotton Textiles), 1913 and 1925

Directors	1913		1925	
	Total	Technically Trained	Total	Technically Trained
European	30	4	24	2
Indian	132	8	151	9

Source: Adapted from Kiyokawa (1983).

Just as teaching in technology transfers was far from ideal, learning was also imperfect due to insufficient local investments to absorb foreign know-how. In 1890 as much as 60 percent of all technical personnel in the middle management of Bombay textile mills was European. As late as the 1920s, roughly one third of all such managers remained foreign (Kiyokawa 1983). Insufficient learning by Indians to dispense with the services of foreign advisers had apparently occurred. The Mexican textile industry may have started in the 1830s, but in the 1890s "foreign visitors commented that plants were managed by an Englishman with sound Lancashire experience or by men trained in the Manchester district of England. In 1896 a new plant in Torreon brought in forty skilled workers from France" (Keremitsis 1987, p. 197). One of Brazil's largest cotton mills, America Fabril, was started by two merchants and an industrialist in 1878. But as late as 1921, its managing director was a Yorkshireman and more than forty English foremen were engaged in various departments (Pearse 1929). A visitor to Sao Paulo in 1930 "found foreign technicians very numerous; one sees them everywhere" (Dean 1969, p. 177). The Shanghai Cotton Cloth Mill, as noted earlier, first used the American A. W. Danforth as a consultant. Later, after a fire, Danforth "was entrusted with the technical responsibility for erecting a plant, purchasing machinery, and organizing production for the new Hua-sheng Mill" (Feuerwerker 1958, p. 221). Apparently, local managers in the first plant expansion had not acquired the capabilities (or trust) to undertake these tasks themselves in the second plant expansion. Contrariwise, between 1914 and 1922, China witnessed an increase in its spindles and looms of over 300 percent, and most of the mills in this period were able to save money and hire Chinese engineers rather than foreign technicians (Chao 1975). Similarly, in 1900 the British-owned Rio Flour Mills in Brazil reported that through a training program many Brazilians had learned the trade so that "all our millers, engineers, and other skilled workmen, with the exception of less than half a dozen, and all our ordinary workman to the number of about 250, are natives of, or permanently settled in the country" (Graham 1968, p. 139). The Osaka Spinning Company began to produce yarn in 1883 and, "as always, an English engineer came to direct the installation of the spinning machines. A foreign engineer working at the mint in Osaka came to help with the installation of the steam engines. But a Japanese engineer also joined in, so the installation did not completely depend on foreign engineers. The age of complete dependence on foreigners was passing" (Chokki 1979, p. 149).

As machinery development in the North Atlantic became more sophisticated, machinery procurement in "the rest" became more difficult; buying the right machine became an art. Japan's earliest spinning mills "acquired their technical knowledge through foreign engineers who had been sent to Japan to install the equipment and give technical advice." The Osaka Spinning Company, however, set a precedent by sending an engineer to England to learn for himself. When he returned to Japan, he published a book on *How to Spin* that diffused information throughout the industry. Later, the engineer became the president of the highly profitable Osaka Spinning Company (Chokki 1979, pp. 148–49). In the latter half of the 1880s, all Japan's major cotton mills "became careful about the selection of machines, and sent technical advisors to England in order to investigate various kinds before purchasing" (Takamura 1982, p. 285). The Brazilian proprietor in 1925, by contrast, demonstrated "little knowledge of and less interest in the manufacture of cloth." Production details were left to foremen "whose sole recommendation was a routine apprenticeship of ten or fifteen years as workmen." Entrepreneurs "felt that cotton mills were run on the principle of feeding in raw cotton at one end and getting out cloth at the other," and that "the knottiest problem of a textile enterprise was 'to order machinery'." Machinery was ordered by sitting down with a foreign sales representative and discussing the appropriate product to buy (Stein 1955, p. 117; see also Birchal 1999).

Some of the most successful industries, even if minor in overall size, acquired their technology simply through reverse engineering (copying) and studying foreign blueprints. They thrived by catering to small, specialized (often monopolistic) market niches, operating with low inventories and simple cost accounting systems. All this, plus transport costs, made foreign machinery uncompetitive. In Chile, "several large engineering works were in operation in Valparaiso by the end of the century manufacturing [in fact, only assembling] locomotives, railway rolling stock, marine engines, mining machinery, bridges and every other kind of engineering work; the mining machinery was reported to be 'of a very high class' " (Platt 1973, p. 232). In the case of Brazil's light engineering sector in the period 1930–45, which produced customized products with labor-intensive techniques, some entrepreneurs were Italian immigrants who learned their trade in Brazil while others were Brazilian-born (the same story applies to Argentina). Whatever their origin, they imbibed an "industrial mentality" at the Institute for Technological Research at the São Paulo Polytechnic Institute. Requirements for administrative and technical manpower were met locally (Leff 1968).

Nevertheless, the Polytechnic in São Paulo graduated mainly civil, not production, engineers. By 1945 it had supplied a total of only four hundred engineers whose degrees were of interest to industry. Industrialists did not lobby the government for more technical education nor did they fund a private technical school because it was cheaper for them to hire foreign technicians (Dean 1969). Technical training everywhere in "the rest" was practically nonexistent.[16] Despite its vast mineral wealth, Brazil did not have a school of mines until 1875 (Rippy 1947). In China, an expert study found that the total need for technicians in eighty-two Chinese mills in the mid-1930s was estimated to be 4,000 persons, yet only 500 employed by those firms had received some professional training in China or abroad. As late as the 1930s, only one college in China was graduating textile engineers (Chao 1975, p. 154). Even in India, the first real institute for technical education, the Victoria Jubilee Technical Institute in Bombay, was not established until the 1880s (with private money). A conference convened in India by Viceroy Curson to expand technical schooling at the turn of the century received a "pathetic" response from local governments and was not pursued further (Kiyokawa 1983, p. 21).[17]

The neglect of technical education in "the rest" was matched by a neglect of general education. Not surprising, the limited available data indicate that by comparison with the North Atlantic and Japan at a (roughly) comparable period of development, school enrollment, mean years of schooling, and adult literacy rates were much lower in "the rest" (see tables 3.2, 3.3, and 3.4). By 1950 mean years of schooling in "the rest" were not even half of what they were in the North Atlantic in 1913. Adult illiteracy in Argentina and India was higher than what it was in the North Atlantic by a large order of magnitude. All this contrasts with early Meiji Japan, which founded a college

Table 3.2. Mean Years of Schooling—North Atlantic and "the Rest," 1820–1992

	1820	1870	1913	1950	1973	1992
Argentina				4.8	7.0	10.7
Brazil				2.1	3.8	6.4
Chile				5.5	8.0	10.9
Mexico				2.6	5.2	8.2
India				1.4	2.6	5.6
Korea				3.4	6.8	13.6
Taiwan				3.6	7.4	13.8
Average				3.3	5.8	9.9
Belgium				9.8	12.0	15.2
France			7.0	9.6	11.7	16.0
Germany			8.4	10.4	11.6	12.2
Italy				5.5	7.6	11.2
Netherlands			6.4	8.1	10.3	13.3
Sweden				9.5	10.4	14.2
U.K.	2.0	4.4	8.8	10.8	11.7	14.1
Portugal				2.5	4.6	9.1
Spain				5.1	6.3	11.5
U.S.	1.8	3.9	7.9	11.3	14.6	18.0
Average	1.9	4.2	7.7	8.3	10.1	13.5

Notes: Data provided for persons aged 15–64. Blank spaces indicate data were unavailable.

Source: Data adapted from Maddison (1995). Maddison has weighted each level of schooling. Years of primary schooling receive a weight of 1, years of secondary schooling are multiplied by a factor of 1.4, and years of postsecondary schooling are multiplied by a factor of 2.

"The rest" only includes countries for which Maddison provides data. There are no corresponding data for China, Indonesia, Malaysia, Thailand, or Turkey.

Table 3.3. Adult Rates (%) of Illiteracy—Selected Countries, 1850–1990

Country	1850[a]	1900[b]	1950[c]	1970	1980	1990
Germany[d]	20	12	na	1	1	1
Sweden	10	na	na	1	1	1
Austrian Empire[e]	43	23	na	1	1	1
Belgium	48	19	3	1	1	1
U.K.[f]	32	na	na	3	1	1
France	43	17	4	1	1	1
Italy	78	48	14	6	4	3
Spain	75	56	18	6	7	4
U.S.	20	11	3	1	1	1
Argentina	na	54	14	7	6	5
Brazil	na	na	51	34	26	18
Chile	na	na	20	11	9	7
China	na	na	na	na	35	22
India	na	95	83	66	59	52
Indonesia	na	na	na	43	33	18
Korea	na	na	23	12	6	4
Malaysia	na	na	62	42	30	22
Mexico	na	na	43	26	17	12
Taiwan	na	na	na	na	na	na
Thailand	na	na	48	21	12	7
Turkey	na	na	68	49	34	19

[a] Germany 1849, Austria 1851, Belgium 1856, U.K. 1851, France 1851, Spain 1857, Italy est., U.S. 1870.
[b] Argentina 1895, India 1901, France 1901, Italy 1901, Germany 1871.
[c] Argentina 1947, Chile 1952, Korea 1955, Malaysia 1947, Thailand 1947, France 1946, Italy 1951. Data for Mexico refer to the total population over six years of age. U.S. and Argentina data refer to the population over fourteen years of age. All other data refer to the population over fifteen years of age.
[d] Data for 1850 and 1900 are for Prussia.
[e] Data for 1850 and 1900 are for the Austrian Empire.
[f] Data for 1850 and 1900 are for England and Wales only.

Sources: Data for 1850 and 1900 (for all countries other than India, Argentina, and U.S.) adapted from Cipolla (1969). Data for 1850 measure those who could not read. Both 1850 and 1900 data for these countries refer to total population over ten years of age. Data for Argentina for 1900 adapted from Randall (1977; refers to the population six years of age or older). Data for India for 1850 and 1900 adapted from Lal (1988). Data for the United States for 1850 and 1900 adapted from West (1975, p. 42). This data refer to the total population over ten years of age. Data for 1950 were adapted from UNESCO (1972). Data for 1950 refer to the total population over fifteen years of age. Data for 1970 for Germany, Sweden, Austria, Belgium, U.K., France, and U.S. adapted from World Bank (1976, 1994). All other 1970 data taken from UNESCO (1993). All 1970 data refer to the total population over fifteen years of age (except Malaysia which refers to the population over ten years of age). Data for 1980 for Germany, Sweden, Austria, Belgium, U.K., France, and U.S. adapted from World Bank (1985). All other 1980 data taken from UNESCO (1993). All data refer to the total population over fifteen years of age. Data from 1990 for Germany, Sweden, Austria, Belgium, U.K., France, and the U.S. are adapted from World Bank (1995). All other 1990 data adapted from UNESCO (1993). All 1990 data refer to the total population over fifteen years of age.

Table 3.4. Literate Population in Selected Countries, 1869–1951

Year	Literate Population (% of Total)	Year	Literate Population (% of Total)
India		Mexico	
1901	5	1910	23
1911	6	1921	29
1921	7	1930	33
1931	10	1943	55
1941	16	1950	57
1951	17		
		Chile	
Argentina		1943	76
1869	22		
1895	46		
1929	75	China	
1943	85	1930	30
Brazil		Turkey	
1877	14	1927	10
1942	50	1940	20
		1950	33

Notes: Argentina: 1869 and 1895 figures represent percentages of the total population six years of age or older; 1929 figure represents total population over fourteen years of age. Turkey: All data for population six years of age or older. China: Represents male population seven years of age or older. Mexico: 1921 data represents the population five years of age or older; 1910, 1930, and 1950 data represent the population six years of age or older.

Sources: All Indian data adapted from Lal (1988, p. 134). All data for 1942–43 adapted from Hughlett (1946, p. 347). Argentine data for the 19th century adapted from Randall (1977, vol. 2). Data for Turkey adapted from Hale (1981, p. 67). Nineteenth-century data for Brazil adapted from Graham (1968). Data for China adapted from Rawski (1989, p. 58). All Mexican data (other than 1943) adapted from Wilkie (1970).

of engineering in 1877, vigorously promoted universal primary schooling, and created an elitist university system (students enrolled in higher education rose from 12,000 in 1895 to 127,000 thirty years later) (Kawabe and Daito 1993). Simultaneously, the recruitment and private training of middle managers by big business also improved (Daito 1986).

By way of conclusion, there is virtually no case of a major investment in "the rest's" early industrial history being undertaken without *some* foreign technology transfer, if only copying. Even the Indian textile industry, with its reputation for indigenous pioneering, started modern operations with a mill in Bombay in 1854 that was partially English-owned, using techniques and personnel from Lancashire (Mehta 1953). China's first successful chemical works were founded around World War I by Chinese, but the entrepreneurs involved were educated in Tokyo, Kyoto, and Berlin (Rawski 1980). Yet due to weaknesses on both the supply and demand sides, technology transfer was a highly imperfect process. This conclusion is based on anecdotal evidence, but no reason suggests such evidence is unrepresentative of the experience of the great majority of "the rest's" technology transfers between 1850 and 1950.

The North Atlantic Contrast

Flaws inherent in technology transfer also afflicted the North Atlantic. "Right up to 1850 and 1860, continental centres frequently failed to achieve British productivity and economy even when using apparently similar equipment" (Pollard 1981, p. 182).[18] But the technology acquisition process of the two sets of learners differed. First, because most countries in "the rest" were geographically isolated from the centers of advanced learning, first Great Britain and then other North Atlantic countries, and international transportation and communication were expensive and slow before, say, 1920, "the rest" rarely experienced the mode of technology transfer that North Atlantic countries experienced which were located closer to Britain: not just receiving teachers at home but also *sending students abroad*. When, for example, Norwegian textile entrepreneurs in the early second half of the nineteenth century began to look to Britain for its supply of equipment, "this led to a series of visits to Britain by virtually all the important Norwegian textile entrepreneurs in search of information and the new technology" (Bruland 1989, p. 61). By 1870 almost one-third of entrepreneurs in the Rhineland and Westphalia were estimated to have visited Britain on business or to study business (Kocka 1978). The visit of Norwegian and German entrepreneurs was only part of a "grand tour" of foreigners to England: "Prussian, Bavarian, Hanoverian nobles, Russian princes and counts, French marquises, and a medley of Swedes, Danes, Portuguese and Spanish notables pushed their way into Birmingham button factories, swooped elegantly round chemical works, paper mills, munitions foundries or shipyards, and reported their findings back to their ministers at home" (Robinson 1975, p. 3, as cited in Bruland 1989, p. 62).

The disadvantages of learning only by receiving teachers from afar are obvious. One is that learning through an intermediary may be unreliable; firsthand observation is better. Another is that the curious student is denied the opportunity of search activity. Yet there is scant evidence before, say, 1910 that firms in "the rest" sent emissaries to technology suppliers in the North Atlantic. Typical of "the rest" in this period was the way China got its technology for its first steel mill, Han-yeh-ping, established in 1896. That the Chinese director of the mill "should have felt fully able to instruct the Chinese Minister in London about the kinds of equipment to be purchased is only an example of the omnipotence that every Confucian official claimed" (Feuerwerker 1964, p. 95). The exceptions that support the rule involved unusually well managed companies. To acquire technology for the Tata group's steel mill, Jamshedji Tata, the founder of the group, traveled to the United States in 1907 for four months and conferred with steel experts in Cleveland and Birmingham (he was described by the American press as the "J. P. Morgan of the East Indies") (Fraser 1919, p. 20). Japan, unlike "the rest", sent engineers overseas starting with textile manufacturing, as noted earlier. Later, Japan's first steel mill, the Yawata Works, sent a team to a German company for six months (Yonekura 1994). Ironically, this same German company was the technology supplier to Japan's and China's major steel works; the chief engineer in both cases was the incompetent Mr. Toppe. The Japanese ultimately fired him; the Chinese, by contrast, never appear to have learned of his third-rate skills (Yonekura [1994] and Feuerwerker [1964]).

After World War II, when the costs of learning became cheaper with new and better modes of transportation, communication, and education, technology acquisition by "the rest" increasingly took the form of sending students, workers, engineers, and managers overseas to learn. An excellent example is South Korea's Pohang Iron and Steel Mill (POSCO), which sent hundreds of production and nonproduction workers abroad for hands-on training (Amsden 1989). Before World War II, comparable training was a serious lapse in "the rest's" education.

Second, the freshness of learning is greatest when it is ongoing. In the case of Norwegian textile firms, "visits to England for the inspection and purchase of equipment were not necessarily confined to the setting-up period, but continued to be made in order to keep up with technical developments and to purchase further equipment" (Bruland 1989, pp. 65–66). While firms in "the rest" often bought the latest equipment, in some industries capacity utilization was so low that equipment purchases by the same firm were infrequent, especially since bankruptcy rates tended to be very high (see chapter 4). Thus, "it is perhaps an exaggeration to state that the transfer of technology which provided the basis for modern industry in twentieth-century China was a single-shot affair, but it does appear that later infusions were slower and smaller than the initial dosage" (Feuerwerker 1967, p. 313).

Third, "the rest's" backward skills and low level of literacy and education made it more difficult—and expensive—to absorb foreign know-how. The relative expense can be gauged by the length of time a foreign expert stayed at a client's company and the salary she was paid. The aggregate picture for British workers in Norway is one of short stays and high turnover (Bruland 1989). By contrast, the anecdotal picture painted earlier for "the rest" is one of quasi-permanent foreign managers and long-duration workers.

Even assuming equal lengths of stay, technical assistants were much more expensive for "the rest" than for the North Atlantic. Spinners in Norway in 1861 earned 34.2 Norwegian shillings while British female spinners in Norway earned 49 shillings, or 1.4 more (Bruland 1989). But assuming conservatively that a British worker got twice what she got at home when she worked in "the rest," then she would earn eight times what an Indian worker earned and ten times what a Chinese worker earned (given that in 1933 the wages per week of a spinner were estimated to be around 71 shillings in the United States, forty shillings in the United Kingdom, twelve shillings in Japan, ten shillings in India, and eight shillings in China, where 1£ = 20 shillings) (Mehta 1953, p. 144). This large wage differential was likely to cause social problems, as it did in the Ottoman Empire, as well as to place a huge financial burden on firms. Moreover, assuming that when locals eventually replaced foreigners in supervisory and managerial positions their salaries were not readjusted downward, then the artificial wage gap between production- and nonproduction employees became huge.

Fourth, the scale of efficient operation was rising steadily throughout the nineteenth century. Thus, because "the rest" industrialized later than the North Atlantic, it had to contend with greater problems of scale. Costs of finance, labor relations, and learning, moreover, do not necessarily change linearly with larger scale.

Finally, the list of capabilities that "the rest" was lacking was far longer than that of the North Atlantic. In addition to not having proprietary technology, "the rest" had few established firms. Not only did countries in "the rest" have to import foreign know-how, they also had to create de novo the organizations to implement that know-how. Even in Norway, without a history of handicraft textile production, the textile companies that acquired British technology were ongoing companies from one or another background (Bruland 1989).

Beyond Technology Transfer: The Silk Industry

Despite being the inventor of silk and despite a seven-fold rise in silk output between 1870 and 1928, the Chinese silk industry sustained an extraordinary reversal at the hands of Japan. From 1859–61 China accounted for 50.6 percent of world raw silk exports while Japan accounted for only 6.7 percent (see table 3.5). Between 1927–29 China's share had fallen to 21.9 percent whereas Japan's share had jumped to 67.2 percent (Federico 1994, p. 53). By 1929 Japan's largest single industry was silk reeling, more important than even cotton yarn (Yamazaki 1988).[19] Raw silk exports are estimated to have financed no less than 40 percent of Japan's imports of machinery and raw materials between 1870 and 1930.[20] Silk manufacture was "a training school for Japanese industrialization" (Hemmi 1970).[21]

Table 3.5. Export Shares in Silk (%)—Selected Countries, 1859–1938

Country	1859–61	1873–75	1905–7	1911–13	1927–29	1936–38
Italy	26.5	30.9	32.8	19.2	10.3	6.2
China	50.6	53.1	33.9	35.4	21.9	10.7
Japan	6.7	8.3	27.0	41.5	67.2	83.1
Turkey	7.6	4.1	4.8	3.2	0.3	0.0
Other	8.6	3.7	1.5	0.7	0.2	0.0

Source: Adapted from Federico (1994), p. 53.

Both China and Japan modernized their traditional silk industries by importing technology from Italy, including the design of steam filatures. Japan,
however, excelled relative to China in raising productivity and quality further.
Productivity in Chinese silk manufacture stagnated (measured by the number
of reels per basin). It is estimated that China's productivity at the beginning
of World War I was lower than Italy's productivity calculated at the time of
its technology transfer to China (Federico 1994). The economic success of
Japan's silk industry extended beyond adding improvements to imported technologies.[22] After studying foreign practices, Japan redefined silk manufacture
as a business in response to an industry-wide crisis.

Silkworm disease (pebrine) appeared in France in 1854 and soon spread
throughout the world. It devastated the French silk reeling industry and left
France a major importer of raw silk to be woven into fabric. The American
silk weaving industry emerged after the Civil War behind a protective tariff
never lower than 45 percent and became an even larger importer than France
of raw silk (Federico 1994). Both the European and American silk weaving
industries preferred silk reeled in steam filatures over silk reeled by hand
because the more mechanically spun product was considered superior in reg-
ularity, winding, cleanliness, and elasticity. Japan's strength ultimately became that of producing machine-reeled raw silk of consistent, medium-grade
quality in large, reliable quantities for the fast-growing American market. By
1909 Japan had overtaken China as the world's leading raw silk exporter
despite the fact that at the high end Chinese silk was superior to Japanese
silk and despite the fact that in the 1870s and 1880s American buyers had
complained that Japanese silk was irregular and inferior (and that Chinese
business practices were dishonest) (Li 1981).

One factor behind China's fall was the spread of pebrine disease. Feeble
government efforts to eradicate it by forcing peasants to follow a painstaking
method devised by Louis Pasteur had failed (Eng 1984). By the 1920s,

it was estimated that the silkworm egg sheets sold on the market were 75
to 95 percent diseased. In Japan and France, one ounce of eggs would yield

110–133 pounds of cocoons, whereas in China one ounce would yield 15–25 pounds. The failure to check this disease was the most critical technological factor in the decline of the Chinese silk industry in the twentieth century. (Li 1981, p. 23)

The erratic supply of eggs raised costs at subsequent stages of production because raw materials were a very high percentage of total costs. At the turn of the century, raw materials accounted for roughly 80 percent of the value of final output (Federico 1994). In 1933 the value of raw material as a percentage of output value was estimated to be higher in Shanghai steam filatures (raw silk reeling) than in any other Shanghai industry (twelve in total) except cotton textiles and flour milling (see table 3.6).

In countries that maintained a supply of healthy silkworm eggs (the Ottoman Empire and Japan), government regulation was instrumental. In theory, private collective action could have substituted for government coordination (Aoki et al. 1997). In practice, government regulation contained an element of coercion that was necessary to force compliance. In the case of Turkey, the residents of Bursa (near Izmir), whose silk manufacture dated to the Byzantine era, banded together and at great cost imported healthy eggs for breeding. Despite initial success, the temptation of high profits led some raisers to engage in "fraudulent practices," which resulted in diseased eggs and inferior raw silk. The residents' efforts could not overcome "corruption, indifference, and lack of capital" and silk raising at Bursa "appeared doomed."

Table 3.6. Twelve Leading Industries in Shanghai, 1931–1933

	Number of Factories		Average Number of workers per Factory		Value of Raw Material (as % of Output) in 1933
	1931	1933	1931	1933	1933
Foundries	35	20	22	36	44.0
Machinery industry	289	160	36	68	44.0
Chemical industry	60	78	128	118	55.0
Matches	3	4	473	402	68.0
Cotton spinning	27	29	2240	2083	75.0
Cotton weaving	61	69	102	129	88.0
Steam filatures	66	49	611	607	82.0
Silk weaving	251	115	40	85	63.0
Knitted goods	96	52	80	136	70.0
Rubber goods	29	41	233	269	38.0
Wheat flour	14	15	160	168	83.0
Cigarettes	44	45	312	388	40.0

Source: Adapted from Lieu (1936, pp. 383-85).

Their knight in shining armor came to the rescue in the form of the imperial Ottoman Public Debt Administration, which was formed in 1881 by European bondholders of the huge Ottoman debt. To raise revenue, the Debt Administration promoted silk production by reviving a silk research station, establishing a model silkworm nursery, upgrading production standards, and—whatever debt holders' ideological commitment to free trade—imposing import duties on silkworm eggs entering Turkey in order to protect local egg growers. Between 1880 and 1908, raw silk exports from Bursa (mainly to France) rose threefold (Quataert 1983, p. 485).[23]

The role of the government in the silk industry in Japan was at least as comprehensive as that of the Debt Administration in the Ottoman Empire. From the late nineteenth century, it was illegal in Japan for individual households to breed their own eggs; special farmers were licensed to raise eggs and only these could be used in sericulture (Li 1981, p. 24). In addition, as soon as the Meiji government came to power it established inspection offices to ensure quality control and founded research stations to study silkworm diseases (comparable stations appeared in China only in the 1920s, depending on the region) (Hemmi 1970). It has been estimated that between one third and one half of Japan's raw silk growth in the period 1870–1929 was due to the increased availability of inputs (Federico 1994).

The Japanese government also created model silk reeling filatures. These went bankrupt, but technology transfer to the private sector was marked. The Tomioka Filature,[24] the first Western-style silk plant in Japan, was sold to the Mitsui family and then became the Katakura Silk Manufacturing Company, one of the largest and most profitable in the country. The Miyamada model factory inspired a joint management company (Nakayama-sha) whose technology spread throughout the Suwa region (Togo 1997).

In terms of capital, it was made available to the silk-reeling industry by government-controlled financial institutions. With the backing of the Yokohama Specie Bank (est. 1880) and the Bank of Japan (est. 1882), commercial banks were able to assist wholesalers in making loans to silk reelers (Japan's development banks are discussed in chapter 6). By 1917, 94.7 percent of all filatures could afford to use steam rather than charcoal or firewood, up from only 36.7 percent in 1892 (Ono 1986).

Japanese entrepreneurs also managed to overcome organizational problems that had been a source of inefficiency in silk manufacture for generations. Stages in the silk production process, being discrete and decentralized, gave rise historically to a large number of brokers who insured against risk by buffering one production stage from another. But middlemen also myopically shied away from responsibility for the whole process. In China, "those who engaged in the silk business did not necessarily have a long-term stake in improving the quality of the product. They simply invested their funds hoping to get a quick and high return" (Li 1981, p. 154).[25] The nature of ownership and control, in particular, contributed to low quality and poor management.[26] In the case of filatures, they typically involved partnerships for only one year. Cantonese filaturists rented from the clans, gentry, and landlords who had built "wild chicken" filatures as a form of real estate speculation. The stock company was the typical organizational form, but most investors preferred to spread their capital thin in several ventures rather than concentrate it in one filature, with profits tending to be redistributed rather than reinvested. "The separation of ownership and management considerably lessened the capitalization requirement for operating a filature and made entry into the industry easier, since fixed capital for construction of buildings and machinery had been borne by the leasors or former owners. At the same time, this structural change not only accentuated the lack of horizontal integration of the industry, but also encouraged speculation, promoted instability and discouraged technical renovation and expansion of the plants" (Eng 1984, p. 362). Because of a shortage of credit, rising land values, and escalating construction costs in Shanghai in the late 1920s, 89 percent of filaturists rented their plant and equipment.[27]

Bigger business units with greater market power evolved in Japan in response to problems of short-termism, speculation, and decentralized control over the production process. The number of middlemen fell, partially through the formation of rural producer cooperatives but especially through the strengthening of general trading companies (which also controlled China's overseas silk trade). Large, vertically integrated manufacturing companies also emerged. While Japanese filatures generally remained small, after 1910 two vertically integrated companies dominated the machine-reeling production stage (Katakura in Nagano and Gunze in Kansai), which increased management control over the whole production process and set a benchmark for the rest of the industry. In 1929, in terms of net profits, the Katakura Silk Manufacturing Company ranked thirteenth among Japan's top fifty industrial and service enterprises (Yamazaki 1988).

By way of summary, the Japanese silk industry was the first to introduce a new pattern of production that involved more government and bigger business: government limited entry at the beginning of the production process for purposes of quality control; it financed research; it contributed to organization-building by investing in model factories; and it created development banks to finance new production equipment. This enabled private enterprise to undertake the three-pronged investment analyzed more fully in the next chapter. Vertically integrated silk manufacturers emerged in Japan to control the entire output chain, and managerial hierarchies became devoted to motivating labor and monitoring productivity. General trading companies, an extension of Japan's diversified business groups, established the distribution channels necessary to procure raw materials and dispose finished products at highly competitive prices. Technology transfer was thus only the beginning of an intensive learning process, even in a traditional, low-tech industry such as silk.

Conclusion

Every latecomer must learn from an established master. But not all learners are equal. As anecdotal evidence on prewar technology transfer suggests, the more backward the learner, the more difficult the transfer. This tendency perpetuates divergence in income between rich countries and poor countries attempting to catch up with the world technological frontier.

Technology transfer to "the rest" before World War II had its moments of mutual gain and cooperation. But it also suffered from weak absorptive skills on the demand side and geographical distance, high costs, incompetence, and ill-will on the supply side. Foreign investors—first individuals and then firms—typically arrived on the scene after an industry had already been started. They may have raised productivity and quality in the firms they acquired, but usually they did not serve as a catalyst for industrial diversification. No matter how open the economy of a technology buyer, technology transfer proved unreliable as a means to equalize productivity internationally. Ultimately, additional means were necessary—and were mobilized—to narrow the gap.

4

Three-Pronged Investment

“ “T he rest" followed a 'low road' to industrial development between 1850 and 1950 for lack of proprietary technology
and related know-how and skills. Although manufacturing experience accumulated, and the growth rate of output may even have increased,[1] "the rest"
could not industrialize fast enough just to keep pace with the North Atlantic.[2]
Few firms had been able to make the "three-pronged investment" to which
(Chandler Jr. 1990) attributes the success of the modern business enterprise:
in up-to-date machinery and plants of optimal scale; in managerial hierarchies and technological skills; and in distribution networks. Each qualification
is examined below to understand why progress in "the rest" was so halting.

The profit motive drove the sojourn down the low road insofar as *government's role was minimal* except in the steel industry, which emerged only after
1900.[3] Tariffs, where they existed, were designed as much for purposes of
revenue as for industrialization (for average tariffs in selected countries between 1820 and 1970, see table 2.3). Discriminatory tariffs in England
against India's manufactured exports did not approximate conditions of free
trade. But critics of the Raj's policies have focused on the absence of domestic
protective tariffs rather than on the presence of discriminatory external tariffs
as the more serious constraint on industrial expansion (see, for example,
Bagchi 1972). Protection in Latin America was largely confined to textiles,
but even in the textile industry, protection was intermittent and undermined
by smuggling (see the discussion of Mexico in chapter 2). China and the
Ottoman Empire experienced an "imperialism of free trade," or forced market
opening by European powers (Gallagher and Robinson 1953); their tariffs
were nil. Government policies in India, Latin America, China, and the Ottoman Empire before World War I, therefore, provide a laboratory to study the
effects of liberalism on attempts to industrialize without world-class skills.

Without new products or processes that might have fired the imaginations of wealthy investors, a long struggle had to be waged in order to attract capital into manufacturing. Minimalist manufacturing skills with respect to management and technology meant that manufacturing investments were perceived as being risky and unprofitable (or only profitable if monopolies were formed) relative to money-lending or investments outside the manufacturing sphere. Capital may or may not have been "scarce"—attractive investment opportunities seemed to bring capital out of the woodwork in countries with premodern manufacturing experience. Competing uses, however, stood in the way of industry for available funds. Given the "shyness" of capital, countries in "the rest" made few investments in the assets required in order to grow. Therefore, bankruptcy rates in manufacturing were high (usually neglected in measured profit rates), contributing to a business climate of speculation, venality, and fraud long before the rise of cronyism and the developmental state.

Prong One: Large-Scale Production Units

Before World War II, the accumulation of skills and the growth of firms both lagged and undermined one another. Without modern firms, skills were slow to develop, and without cutting-edge skills, modern firms were slow to form.

"The rest's" *small-scale firms* tended not to be dynamic agents of industrial change, in contradistinction to the developmental role they played in England during the First Industrial Revolution, the socially progressive role they played in Europe's "industrial districts" after World War II (Piore and Sabel 1984), and the innovative role they played in the United States in the 1990s. In India, small firms before World War II operated "cotton gins and presses, rice and oil mills, jute presses, open-pan processes of sugar manufacture, and small powerloom or handloom factories," but they "did not start an industrial revolution" or "pioneer any new methods of production or any new industries" (Bagchi 1972, p. 442). In the case of hand-weaving, as we saw earlier, they did not even generate enough incremental technical improvements to survive other than by cutting their own real rates of return.

In Shanghai in the 1930s, small firms competed on the basis of flexibility and being able to change their process and product quickly in response to shifts in demand (as was also the case of small-scale firms after World War II in Taiwan, where many Shanghai firms migrated). Shanghai enterprises

> expected to make money in a short period of time; therefore, they did not want to invest too much capital in their business. When they made some money, they were ready to clear out at any time. Hence, they preferred to

rent their factory buildings, machinery, and electric power. Anything that will lower the cost of production and make it unnecessary to invest large sums of money is always welcome to them. (Lieu 1936, pp. 103–4)

Although small-scale firms in Shanghai in the 1930s minimized costs and were "flexible," they did little to contribute to skill formation.

In Latin America, a study in 1946 noted that "the most striking feature of the manufacturing and processing industries throughout Latin America is the fairly large number of relatively small establishments. Even in Argentina and Brazil, the average number of employees in a plant is, respectively only 16.0 (1944) and 16.2 (1942)," compared with 42.76 (1939) in the United States. According to a 1939 Argentine industrial census, out of 53,907 enterprises, only 420 had payrolls of over 200 people in a single plant. Moreover, "the majority of small Latin American plants are poorly equipped. They lack modern, low-cost methods of production and distribution. Obsolete manufacturing procedures represent high costs of manufacturing" (Hughlett 1946, p. 48).[4]

Without proprietary technology, firms in "the rest" never managed to grow on a par with leading enterprises in smaller European countries which, like countries in "the rest," suffered from low domestic demand. Some of the North Atlantic's biggest firms in the nineteenth century emerged in the smallest countries (Daems [1986] and Schroter [1997]). They did so by innovating their way into foreign markets: "Skilled industries with a high labour content were becoming an important element in world trade. From these specialisations emerged great manufacturers in the small countries—Sulzer, Brown Boveri, Escher Wyss in Switzerland, de Laval in Sweden, Burmeister in Denmark, Carel in Belgium, Werkspoor and Philips in the Netherlands" (Saul 1982, p. 125). In Switzerland, Geigy (1864), CIBA (1884), Sandoz (1886), and Hoffmann-La Roche (1894) innovated new products in aniline dyes and pharmaceuticals, and on the basis of these innovations established multinational firms (Fritzsche 1996).[5]

"The rest's" inability to generate even remotely comparable innovations meant that imports flooded its domestic markets (as in textiles) and manufactures remained only a small share of its total exports, despite the rapid rise of manufactures in world trade. By 1926 the share of manufactures in total exports was estimated to be as high as 43 percent in Japan, 37 percent in the United States but only 19 percent in India and 3 percent in Mexico (see table 4.1). In 1928 manufactured products were estimated to account for only 16.5 percent of China's total exports (Hsiao 1974). The products that figured prominently in this "manufacturing" share, moreover, were raw material-based, and included hides, bean cake, bean oil, groundnut oil, wheat flour, pig iron, tin ingots, and cigarettes. Despite the prominence of the cotton textile industry in China and India, cotton textile exports as a share of total

Table 4.1. Manufactures as a Share (%) of Exports—Selected Countries, 1899–1959

Years	Manufacturing Share	Years	Manufacturing Share
Mexico		Japan	
1909–10	2	1899	22
1926	1	1913	31
1940	3	1929	43
1945	na	1955	64
1950	7	1959	74
India		U.S.	
1899	8	1899	18
1913	13	1913	21
1929	19	1929	37
1955	31	1955	48
1959	34	1959	48

Sources: Data for Mexico adapted from Reynolds (1970, p. 205). All other data adapted from Maizels (1963, p. 64).

exports were almost nil (see tables 4.2 and 4.3).[6] Latin America's exports from 1850 to at least 1950 were overwhelmingly comprised of raw or pro-cessed primary products (for Argentina, see Diaz Alejandro [1970]). Brazil exported some cotton manufactures during World War II to neighboring countries, but this ceased when war ended (Wythe 1955). Thus, even if Latin America's primary product exports "crowded-in" manufacturing invest-ments, as revisionist historians allege, they did not "crowd-in" *manufactured* exports (see Cardenas et al. [2000] and Cortes Conde [1992]). Without ex-

Table 4.2. China's Export Composition, 1868–1928

Product	1868	1898	1928
Raw cotton	0.8	0.0	3.4
Raw silk	36.8	28.0	15.7*
Tea	55.4	18.1	3.7
Cotton manufactures	0.0	0.0	3.8
Silk manufactures	3.0	6.7	2.7*
Sub-total	96.0%	52.8%	29.3%
Others	4.0	47.2	70.7
Total	100%	100%	100%

Notes: China's trade data for the pre–World War I period are unreliable (Murphey 1977).
*Breakdown of exports for raw and manufactured silk is estimated from Hsiao (1974).

Sources: Adapted from Latham (1978 and 1981).

Table 4.3. India's Export Composition, 1870–1929

Product	1870	1900	1924/25–1928/29
Raw cotton	36.4	10.7	21.0
Raw jute	4.3	8.6	9.1
Rice	7.1	13.2	9.9
Wheat	0.2	3.8	1.3
Tea	2.0	7.4	8.7
Cotton manufactures	2.2	1.2	2.8
Jute manufactures	0.4	6.6	16.2
Sub-total	52.6%	51.5%	69.0%
Other	47.4	48.5	31.0
Total	100%	100%	100%

Source: Adapted from Latham (1979 and 1981).

ports, the scale necessary to build world-class firms in small countries was missing.

Exchange rate movements in the last quarter of the nineteenth century were fairly supportive of exporting. For countries on the silver standard (China, Chile, India, Japan, Korea, Malaya, Mexico, and Thailand), the price of silver relative to gold fell almost steadily between 1873–94, implying a devaluation by roughly 50 percent over these two decades (Nugent 1973). Still, manufactured exports stagnated, thereby stunting the growth of large-scale firms.

Given domestic and foreign demand, the scope for large-scale business enterprise is greater the more concentrated the domestic market. By 1907 Japan's so-called "Big Six" spinning enterprises were among the most efficient in the world and the most oligopolistic. They accounted for 61 percent of all spindles, a higher level of concentration than in spinning industries throughout "the rest," which were nonetheless fairly concentrated (Kuwahara 1986, p. 108).[7] But whereas high industry concentration, large firm size, and efficiency converged in Japan's textile industry, they diverged in the textile industries of "the rest," as in other industries. Following a merger movement in Mexico after 1900, high rates of concentration were endemic in the cement, brewing, soap, and explosives industries, but performance was abysmal (Haber 1989). The exception that proved the rule (that high concentration and good performance complement one another only in the presence of cutting-edge skills) was in the Mexican glass industry. One firm, Vidriera Monterrey, secured a national monopoly based on an original automated glass-bottle blowing process; Vidriera Monterrey evolved into one of Mexico's most dynamic business groups, Vitro, SA, maintaining a reputation for excellence down through the 1990s (see chapter 8).

Thus, in the absence of skill formation, firms in "the rest" remained small, and without an increase in firm size, investments in skills remained negligible.[8] The average factory in Argentina, the country in "the rest" with the highest per capita income, was smaller in 1946 than in 1941. World War II "mainly encouraged the proliferation of many small-scale, poorly capitalized, and technologically backward firms" (Lewis 1990, p. 39). In the 1920s and 1930s, when industrial output was expanding in Brazil, both industrial concentration and average firm size tended *to decline* (Dean 1969). Indian data on average firm size showed no increase over time in spinning, despite rising scale economies in spinning at the world frontier (Kuwahara 1986). The number of spindles per mill was 24.3 in 1879–80 and 25.1 in 1943–44. Looms per mill rose from only 2.3 to 5 (Chand 1949).

Firms in "the rest" even failed to maintain parity in size with North Atlantic firms. Using the average number of workers per factory in Shanghai as a rough measure of firm size by industry (see table 3.6), it is clear that cotton spinning had the greatest concentration of large-scale firms, followed by silk weaving and, more distantly, by cigarettes and matches. Yet when one compares the size of leading textile enterprises in "the rest" and the North Atlantic, "the rest's" businesses are tiny. Table 4.4a–b examines the first, second, and tenth largest cotton spinning mills in different countries circa the turn of the century and at the end of the 1920s. True enough, over time firm size increased in both Brazil and India (the two countries with intertemporal data). But firm size was considerably smaller in Brazil, India, and Mexico than in the United States and Japan, and over time the gap between the two sets of countries tended to widen.

Prong One (Continued): Capital Investment

A global culture of "modernism" gripped leading firms in "the rest" in the fifty years spanning 1890–1939, which overlapped with the North Atlantic's Second Industrial Revolution. This culture emphasized capital formation, modern technology, and the latest managerial techniques.

The modernist ethos of the times was evident in China's Nanyang Cigarette Company, which emerged around the turn of the century and survived war, revolution, and reform to remain a major cigarette manufacturer in China in the 1990s, as noted earlier. Nanyang was extremely precocious in its building of a managerial elite. Chien Chao-nan, one of two brothers who owned Nanyang, convinced family members in the 1910s that to compete against British American Tobacco they had to become more like it and hire trained salaried managers, a radical departure from past practice. Earlier, outsiders had sat

Table 4.4a. Largest Cotton-Spinning Firms by Country, circa 1897

Firms*	Spindles (in Thousands)
U.S. (1897)	
1. Knight	388.9
2. Amoskeag	290.0
10. Boot	153.0
Japan (1897)	
1. Kanegafuchi	81.8
2. MIE	56.8
3. Naniwa	26.0
India (1897)	
1. Maneckji Petit	131.1
2. J. Sassoon	90.1
10. Swadeshi	50.8
Mexico (1909)	
1. CIDOSA	70.7
2. Manufactura	47.9
5. Antonio Abad	25.9
Brazil (1909)	
1. Allianca	56.4
2. Confianza	42.8
10. Pernam.	31.0

*1st, 2nd, 10th largest generally provided.

Sources: For U.S., Japan, and India: Yonekawa (1982); for Mexico and Brazil (1909): Clark(1909).

on Nanyang's board of directors, but only after a long family feud were they appointed to high supervisory posts. In very tangible and transparent ways, "they contributed directly to Nanyang's commercial success during the post World War I golden age by their innovations in finance, manufacturing, marketing, and purchasing" (Cochran 1980, p. 151).

Nanyang was also one of the first Chinese companies to introduce principles of scientific management. It assigned the task of improving its manufacturing system to a young Chinese man who had studied business administration at the Massachusetts Institute of Technology in the late 1910s. "The

Table 4.4b. Largest Cotton-Spinning Firms by
Country, circa 1928

Firms	Spindles (in Thousands)
U.S. (1928)	
1. Amoskeag	790
2. Lockwood Green	571
10. BBR & Knight	237.4
Japan (1928)	
1. Dainippon	896.7
2. Toyo	859.9
10. Wakayama	138.8
India (1928)	
1. Madura	335.6
2. United Sassoon	245.2
10. Shopurgi Bro.	97.3
China (1929)	
1. Shenxin	310.5
2. Yong'an	213.2
7. Jinhua	33.6
10. na	
Brazil (1919)	
1. Amer. Fabril	85.3
2. Matarazzo	60.0
10. Belge-Bres.	23.9

* 1st, 2nd, 10th largest generally provided.

Sources: For U.S., Japan, and India: Yonekawa (1982); for Brazil
(1919): Pearse (1921); for China: Lu (1993).

approach to business management which most impressed the Chinese M.I.T.
undergraduates was that of the American efficiency expert, Frederick Winslow Taylor, whose classic book, *The Principles of Scientific Management*, was
available to them in Chinese" (Cochran 1980, p. 153).[9]

A faith in modern technology is illustrated by an anecdote about Nanyang
in 1916, when its expansion created financial problems and disagreement
between its two owners. Chien Chao-nan had ordered twelve new American
cigarette manufacturing machines. His brother feared insolvency and can-
celed the order. Furious, Chien allegedly agonized: "What shall we do! What

shall we do! Whoever works in the manufacturing business must have far-sighted vision and cannot be so niggardly about insignificant amounts of money" (Cochran 1980, pp. 79–80).

Pioneers of the cotton mill industry of Bombay supposedly "started with the choicest of British made machinery" (Rutnagur 1927, p. 49). Jamshedji Tata introduced ring spinning in the 1880s at around the same time that the process was introduced in Manchester (Agarwala 1986). A prestigious delegation to Brazil in 1921 commented: "we visited, during our tour, a large number of cotton mills and were impressed with the modern mill architecture (and) the first-class machinery" (Pearse 1921, p. 29). The high-speed ring spinning frame was developed in the early nineteenth century and became widely used in New England by 1868. Supposedly "the ring frame then conquered the industry of Asia, that of Japan during 1889 and that of India during the 1900s. The new factory industry of China established in 1890 was based exclusively upon ring spinning, like the contemporary industries of Brazil and Mexico" (Farnie 1991, p. 154).

The ethos of modernism notwithstanding, in addition to a failure to invest in the technological capabilities necessary to generate the demand on which large-scale firms depended, "the rest" was slow in reality to make the investments necessary to modernize its capital equipment. Gross fixed capital formation was extremely low in "the rest," at least in the very few countries for which data (of questionable reliability) are available. It was only one-half or one-fourth of what it was in the North Atlantic and Japan, suggesting that asset formation was extremely slow. As indicated in table 4.5, in the period

Table 4.5. Gross Fixed Domestic Investment (% of GDP)—Selected Countries, 1870–1938

Country	1870–89	1890–1913	1914–38
France	12.8	13.9	16.1[a]
Germany	na	na	12.9[b]
U.K.	8.4	8.5	7.8
U.S.	16.3	15.9	14.2
Japan	12.6[c]	14.4	16.2
India	4.5	5.6	7.0
Korea	na	4.9[d]	7.0
Taiwan	na	8.7[e]	15.6

Notes: Current market prices.
[a] 1922–1938
[b] 1925–1938
[c] 1885–1889
[d] 1911–1913
[e] 1903–1913

Source: Adapted from Maddison (1991, p. 9).

1870–89, gross fixed domestic investment (GFDI) as a share of GDP was approximately 13 percent in France and Japan but only 5 percent in India.[10] In 1890–1913 it was still about 14 percent in France and Japan and around 5 percent in India and Korea. By 1914–38 it had risen to around 16 percent in France and Japan and 7 percent in India and Korea.[11] "The rest's" share and the North Atlantic's share of gross fixed investment in GDP remained more or less in constant relative proportions to each other; convergence was nil, assuming the data are accurate.

Nor does capital-intensity measured at the industry level appear to have kept abreast with that in the North Atlantic. Data are available for cotton spinning using spindles per worker as a proxy for capital-intensity (see table 4.6). This ratio jumped sharply in Japan between 1929 and 1938 because labor became more expensive as wages rose and night work was outlawed for women and children (the major source of labor in Japan's cotton mills). By contrast, spindles per worker stayed more or less constant from 1900 to 1938 in Brazil, India, and Mexico, which suggests that "the rest" was not investing in more advanced equipment comparable to that of Japan. In terms of absolute number of spindles per worker, the ratio was about the same in Brazil, Mexico, and India. Yet Brazil and Mexico had higher wages than India, so if they wanted to compete against India in world markets, they needed a higher ratio (productivity level). For their part, Indian mills were slower to introduce ring spinning technology than Japan, their major competitor. The percentage of ring spindles in total spindles in 1913 was estimated to be 97.7 percent in Japan, 86.9 percent in the United States, 72.5 percent in India, and 18.7 percent in England (India's teacher) (Takamura 1982).[12]

Numerous reasons underpinned the slow introduction of machinery in "the rest," not least of all stagnating wages. Determining the movement of wages during the nineteenth and early twentieth centuries in most countries is empirical guesswork, especially since wages varied sharply by industry, region, gender, age, and even factory. Still, if there was once a shortage of labor (as there clearly was during early railway construction in Brazil [Mattoon 1977], Mexico [Ficker 1995], and India [Kerr 1995]), then it had vanished by the turn of the century or earlier in countries with premodern or émigré sources of manufacturing experience. A labor shortage was superseded by an "unlimited" labor supply save in isolated locales (Lewis 1954).[13] In competitive industries, therefore, given labor abundance, the movement of average wages around a *flat or falling trend* depended largely on demand fluctuations, productivity, labor organization, and labor relations. In Argentina, Brazil, and Mexico, paternalism was the supposed answer to labor unrest. In India and China, most large companies subcontracted the management of labor to outside "jobbers" or "bosses."[14]

It was estimated that in the Mexican textile industry, "by the end of the Porfiriato (1910), the average worker had less buying power than in 1877"

Table 4.6. Investment in Cotton Manufacture, International Comparison, 1900, 1913, 1929, 1938

Country	1900	1913	1929	1938
Japan				
Mills	80	152	245	272
Spindles	1,268	2,415	6,347	12,550
Workers	56	108	160	151
Spindles/worker	23	22	40	83
Brazil				
Mills	110	240	395	355
Spindles	735	1,513	2,651	2,696
Workers	39	82	124	116
Spindles/worker	19	18	21	23
China (total)				
Mills	12	31	120	na
Spindles	417	1009	3,638	4,300
Workers	na	na	242	na
Spindles/worker	na	na	15	na
Chinese only				
Mills	7	22	74	na
Spindles	259	544	2,088	na
Workers	na	na	155	na
Spindles/worker	na	na	13	na
India				
Mills	192	271	339	380
Spindles	5,118[1]	6,780[1]	9,506	10,020
Workers	185	260	403	438
Spindles/worker	28	26	24	23
Mexico				
Mills	134	118	145	137
Spindles	589	753	839	832
Workers	28	33	40	34
Spindles/worker	21	23	21	25

Notes: Spindles and workers in thousands. The data for spindles are not strictly comparable because for some countries they may refer to active spindles and for other countries they may refer to total spindles. Generally the data for China are subject to a wide margin of error. The China total includes Chinese-owned mills, Japanese-owned mills and mills owned by other nationalities, mostly British. The data are not always for the year specified but are the closest available.
1. Bombay only

Sources: United States: Woytinsky and Woytinsky (1953, p. 1072). Japan, 1900: Clark (1914, p. 40); 1913–28: Moser (1930, pp. 50–51); 1938: Woytinsky and Woytinsky (1953, p. 1067). Brazil: Stein (1938 and 1957), Woytinsky and Woytinsky (1953, p. 1067). China, 1900–1928: Moser (1930, pp. 87–88; 1938), Woytinsky and Woytinsky (1953, p. 1067). India, 1900–1913: Chandavarkar (1994, p. 250; 1929–1938), Koh (1966, #251, p. 369). Mexico: Haber (1989).

(Keremitsis 1987, p. 188 and Gomez-Galvarriato, 2000). In Argentina, there was a continuous outbreak of strikes between 1907–1929, during which time the real salaries of the strikers are estimated to have first fallen and then risen, reaching only a slightly higher level in 1930 than twenty years earlier (Dorfman 1970, p. 269). Wages in the Bombay textile industry up to 1914 were "remarkably stable" and rose only slowly, if at all (depending on job classification) (Mehta 1953). Between 1926 and 1937, wages fell steeply, depending on the occupation. Similarly in the Calcutta jute mills, average monthly money wages between 1900 and 1939 (in rupees) rose from only 12.0 to 19.6. Real wages in Shanghai's cotton mills in the period 1910 to 1930 were also stable or declining. Only in the 1930s, amidst massive strikes and political mobilization, did they increase. The same pattern of stagnant real wages tended to characterize China's coal mining industry (Rawski 1989),[15] while Beijing's real wage index (1913 = 100) showed a slight decline for laborers (114 in 1900 to 112 in 1925) and a steep decline for coolies (130 in 1900 and 108 in 1925) (Lieu 1928).

Stagnant or declining wages led to unrest, strikes, and low productivity.[16] At the same time, it constituted a disincentive for firms to invest in machinery.

After the Napoleonic Wars low wages by English standards on the European continent also deterred investment (Landes 1969), but an innovative machinery sector brought down machinery costs radically and hence resistance to capital formation. In "the rest," local machinery builders also reduced capital costs, although by a different method. Instead of innovating new models, they ingeniously *copied* foreign designs. Copies were of a lower quality than foreign makes due to inferior raw materials, but sold at a fraction of foreign prices.[17] Inexpensive machinery found its best markets in the informal sector and in the repair and maintenance shops of large-scale firms. Cheap machinery also appeared on the market in the form of secondhand equipment from bankrupted firms. By the end of the 1930s, China's machinery building industry had advanced to the point where a leading firm became involved in export markets (Rawski 1975).[18]

Nevertheless, the main equipment of modern business enterprises continued to be imported from abroad, as illustrated by the railroads, and tended to be more expensive than in countries of origin, contributing further to sluggish investment rates in "the rest." The financial difficulties of importing machinery during the Great Depression,[19] and the geopolitical difficulties of importing it during the two World Wars, added to the obsolescence of "the rest's" capital stock. At the end of World War II, not just technology and skills but also the age of capital equipment were far behind the world frontier.

Prong Two: Modern Management and the Railroads

Railroads were among the first big businesses, and starting in the second half of the nineteenth century, they appeared in both the North Atlantic and "the rest" (see table 4.7). Potentially, they were incubators for the capital and modern management systems necessary to diversify into new industries. This potential, while realized throughout most of the North Atlantic, was largely (although not entirely) wasted in "the rest."

Where railroads were constructed, typically they constituted the single most important economic activity at the time, in terms of capital formation and employment. British exports of capital between 1865 and 1914 averaged £90,400,000 per annum in the transportation sector compared with only £12,300 in agriculture and extractive industries, its second most important use (Davis and Huttenback 1986).[20] Railroads were the first modern business enterprise because

> the capital required to build a railroad was far more than that required to purchase a plantation, a textile mill, or even a fleet of ships. Therefore, a single entrepreneur, family or small group of associates was rarely able to own a railroad. Nor could the many stockholders or their representatives manage it. The administrative tasks were too numerous, too varied, and too complex. They required special skills and training which could only be commanded by a full-time salaried manager. (Chandler Jr. 1977, p. 87)

Railroads were also midwife to other big businesses through backward linkages. Britain's North Atlantic emulators began to produce domestically the inputs Britain formerly supplied to them: locomotives, coke-smelted pig iron, rails (puddled and rolled iron), and later steel, all in large-scale business units. Moreover, the managerial innovations within the railroad system were a model for replication by other industries, especially in the United states:

> As the first modern business enterprises, the railroads became the administrative model for comparable enterprises when they appeared in other forms of transportation as well as in the production and distribution of goods. The railroads were highly visible; the American businessmen could easily see how they operated. . . . every businessman who produced or distributed goods in volume had to work closely with railroad managers. (Chandler Jr. 1977, p. 188)

Thus, even if average firm size in "the rest" was relatively small, the railway mania that gripped Argentina, Brazil, Chile, China, India, and Mexico created the potential to groom big businesses and, hence, salaried managers with professional expertise. Technology transfer in the case of railroads was relatively transparent and competitive.

Table 4.7. Railroads (Kilometers of Track), 1870–1950

Kilometers by Country	1870	1913	1950
U.K.	21,500	32,600	31,350
U.S.	85,200	402,000	360,150
Germany	18,900	63,400	36,900
France	15,500	40,800	41,300
Japan	0	10,600	27,400
Argentina	730	33,500	42,900
Brazil	750	24,600	36,700
Chile	700	8,100	8,500
China	0	9,850	22,200
India	7,700	55,800	54,800
Indonesia	80	5,000	6,600
Mexico	350	20,500	23,300
Thailand	0	950	1,800
Turkey	200	5,450	7,700

Source: Adapted from Maddison (1995).

The transition from family-owned and-managed firms to joint stock companies with salaried managers was slow even in Europe; it appeared at the earliest only toward the end of the nineteenth century (Kobayashi and Morikawa 1986 and Church 1994). "The rest," however, experienced a delay not only in this transition. It also failed to exploit other derivative benefits from railroad building as a consequence of its scarcity of skills. Hence, managerial resources arose much later in "the rest" than in Europe or even Japan, although Japan's railroad construction started relatively late (see table 4.7). The modernism of the Nanyang Cigarette Company cited earlier was the exception to the general rule.

For one, the backward linkages from railroads to heavy industry never materialized on a par with European latecomers—Germany, for instance. Within a matter of ten or twenty years and with the aid of tariffs, Germany had successfully import-substituted almost all locomotives and iron rails used on Prussian railways (Fremdling 1983). In China, by contrast, the only partially successful attempt to give reality to the slogan that railroads should be built "without borrowing foreign funds and without using foreign iron" was a 19-mile rail link built in 1894 to an iron mine" (Huenemann 1984, p. 46). In the 1930s, all China's 139 new locomotives were still being procured from abroad (Chang 1943). Although China's experience with railroads was more fraught with problems of backwardness and imperialism than other latecomers' experience, import substitution in India, Argentina, Brazil, and Mexico barely progressed either.[21] In Brazil, engineers in Sao Paulo experimented with products from the province's iron mine and foundry, but discovered that their quality was inferior to that of Britain. When steel replaced iron as the principal material for rails, Brazil could not compete internationally (as examined below). In the 1860s the first steam engines were shipped to Brazil from England; in the 1920s Brazil was still importing locomotives from General Electric, although there was some locomotive assembly in both Brazil and Chile (for Chile see chapter 3). As late as 1968, Brazil was still importing locomotives and just establishing policies to import substitute them (Mattoon 1977).

The fact that finance for railroads always came from overseas (whether self-finance was possible is examined later) typically meant that foreigners also appointed top managers who, in turn, made decisions about whom to hire and where to source materials. Nevertheless, while Meiji Japan also borrowed abroad to build its first railways, it decoupled finance from technology (as Japan's disciples were to do after the World War II), borrowing capital from a bank and buying technology from an independent source, which gave the Japanese government more control over import substitution and the localization of top managers (Ramseyer and Rosenbluth 1995). By contrast, while the "Mexicanization" of most of the workforce on Mexico's most important rail line had almost been complete by 1914, top functionaries remained foreign (Ficker 1995). On India's railroads, Europeans and Indians interfaced around 1900 only at the point in the managerial hierarchy where contractors were responsible for overseeing labor (Kerr 1995).

Despite all this, the learning of production skills as well as project execution capabilities due to railroad construction was considerable. Foreign general inspectors on minor railroad lines began to be replaced by Brazilians at the turn of the century, aided by the establishment of a civil engineering college, noted earlier, and engineering clubs (Mattoon 1977). In China, the Hsinning Railway in the southern Kwangtung province was organized around 1914 by a Chinese-American and was financed, constructed, and operated entirely by Chinese (Hsu 1915, reprint 1968). Moreover, the skills acquired by government regulators were considerable, depending on the country. The East India Company and later the Raj attempted to monitor every major railroad construction and operation, and "the Government of India exercised extensively its rights of supervision and direction." A major form of supervision was "access to virtually all the accounts, proceedings, minutes, papers, etc. of the Railway company and to appoint, ex officio, a member of the Railway Company's Board with 'a right of veto in all proceedings whatsoever, at Boards of the said Directors' " (Kerr 1995, p. 19). Precisely the same mechanism, appointment of a government representative to a company's board of directors, was adopted after World War II by the Indian government to monitor development bank loans (see chapter 6).

Nevertheless, as late as the interwar period, there was gross ignorance about fundamental managerial principles even in some latecomer countries' major railroads, and central regulation was weak. According to China's Minister of Railways from 1935–37, China lacked a centralized and accurate system of accounting as well as rational procedures for the management of stores and materials (Chang 1943). Moreover, foreign ownership and control of railroads introduced a large 'moral hazard' into the entire business environment. Cheating, fraud, and corruption were rife in almost all major railway projects, encouraged by *'the guarantee'*—that foreign investors would receive a prespecified rate of interest (ranging in "the rest" from 5 percent to 7 percent) on their invested capital regardless of actual profitability. " 'The whole history of Indian railways', maintained a state official before the 1884 Select Committee, 'has been one long and unsuccessful attempt to get them constructed without a guarantee' " (Macpherson 1955–66, p. 185). Guarantees were the rule in almost all countries outside the United States (Davis and Huttenback 1982, p. 344 n. 35), but did the most damage where costs were least easily monitored, as in "the rest," where virtually all inputs were sourced from abroad.[22] Thus, not only did the railroad boom in "the rest" fail for the most part to generate a corps of well-trained and experienced local salaried managers, but it also provided endless bad examples of fraudulent business deals.

The rise of salaried managers in "the rest" awaited the emergence of foreign firms and diversified business groups. The latter overcame the problems of small scale in a single sector by diversifying into many different industries, thereby creating heavy overall demand for managerial expertise (see chapter 8). India's "management agency" system was a premonition of this, but in its early incarnation did not perform well (as examined in a later section). Instead, Japan led the way insofar as the zaibatsu retained *family ownership* but adopted *professional control* (see chapter 8) (Morikawa 1986 and Morikawa 1992). Only after World War II did countries in "the rest" accrue sufficient managerial resources in business *and* government in the form of project execution skills to insure that major investments in heavy industry which, like the railways, used foreign capital and technology, maximized domestic backward linkages and minimized foreign currency costs.

Prong Three: Distribution

Distribution costs were decisive for competitiveness especially in certain consumer goods industries. Nanyang, China's cigarette manufacturer, was at a persistent disadvantage vis-à-vis British American Tobacco because it could not match its huge advertising expenditures (Cochran 1980). In the Chinese tea industry, luring the British tea drinker away from British-owned Indian tea brands was also beyond the resources of Chinese producers (Rawski 1989).

In Latin America, typically even the largest manufacturers sold their output to importers, who then sold this output to wholesale distributors. Textile firms suffered from being in the grip of cotton brokers on the one hand and wholesalers on the other. Therefore, some Brazilian sales directors of smaller mills introduced organizational innovations to loosen this grip, such as different handling procedures and packaging. Some opened their own retail stores for direct sales.

> That the large mills of Rio and Sao Paulo did not follow in the path of the smaller mills of the interior may have been caused by the close integration of the largest cloth merchant houses with some of the mills. In some cases, cloth merchants were also directors of cotton mills; in others, they closely supervised management by occupying positions on the key auditing committees which, in turn, supervised the managing directors; in still others, mills and merchants dovetailed their actions because years of selling through one wholesale house sufficed to establish effective liaison. (Stein 1957, p. 122)

In Mexico, the linkage between manufacturing and distribution was so close that even after World War II, all the larger department and dry goods stores in Mexico City owned and operated cotton mills. "The industry is thoroughly integrated along vertical lines" (Mosk 1950, p. 123).

The Indian and Chinese textile industries also used distributors when selling locally, but omitted importers. Both forms of distribution were comparable to North Atlantic practice as late as 1914: "The specialist marketing function integrated with production in a corporate structure was slow to develop in countries, notably Britain, France and Italy, where centuries of internal and overseas trade had built up a network of wholesaling factors and merchants, through whom, for much of the nineteenth century, most producers distributed their goods" (Church 1994, p. 133).

The Japanese textile industry developed a system of distribution that fell between one of integrated production and selling within the firm, and totally disintegrated selling using (arms-length) distributors. The Japanese Cotton Mills Association (Boseki Rengokai) was not just a cartel but also an association to integrate vertically the operations of procuring raw cotton, making textile goods, and exporting. This integration helped cut costs by eliminating intermediaries. The Boseki Rengokai used three major importers to procure raw cotton and these importers had representatives in all cotton growing areas of the world, which allowed them to buy the best cotton at the lowest price. This helped Japanese mills to maximize returns to "cotton mixing," where for any given quality standard of yarn, the lowest-cost raw cotton is used. Boseki Rengokai also had an agreement with the Japan Steamship Company that reduced transportation costs (Odell 1916).[23] Neither India, China, Brazil, nor Mexico had the organizational capabilities or global scope to replicate this system.[24] Thus, although empirical evidence about distribution in "the rest" is extremely limited, it seems likely that firms did not invest much in building their own distribution capacities. Nor did they create large trading companies on the Japanese model,[25] which played an important role in the success of Japan's two leading sectors, cotton textiles and silk.

Finance

While "the rest's" investment rates were unmistakably low, it is unclear if they were low in manufacturing due to a *scarcity* of capital (a deficit between the total absolute supply of savings and the demand for savings) or a *shyness* of capital (a deficit between supply and demand due to an unwillingness of savers to lend). If a country runs a persistent surplus in its balance of payments such that savings exceed investment, then capital shyness may be said to exist (Das 1962 and Bagchi 1972). Alternatively, one may think of shyness in terms of the excess product a country either does or can produce above some specified measure of the subsistence needs of its population (Riskin 1975).

The total absolute supply of capital in "the rest" appeared to be greatest in those economies with the largest populations and longest premodern manufacturing experiences (China and India). Capital shyness in these countries was also great. Hence, it is in these countries that one may examine the hypothesis that the root cause of shyness was an absence of skills, and that the effect of shyness was undercapitalization and defensive financial practices that further undermined investor confidence.

India ran a surplus in its balance of payments (merchandise and bullion) for the period 1835–1946 (Banerjee 1963; Maddison 1971). As early as the 1840s, there was also substantial qualitative evidence that when profitable opportunities arose, capital appeared:

> The early mills were not exceptionally costly ventures by local standards. A company could get into operation in Bombay for an investment of Rs. 500,000 to Rs. 1 million or about £50,000 to £100,000 at prevailing exchange rates.[26] This covered cost of land, buildings, equipment and inventory. Many other types of enterprise projected in the same period involved sums as great or greater. Shares were issued in units of Rs.2,500 or, more typically, Rs.5,000. These were not amounts intended to attract the small investor. Yet *the number of people in Bombay with sums to risk in promising enterprises was sufficiently great* so that when the Oriental mill was floated in 1854 with paid-up capital of Rs.1,250,000 divided into 500 shares of Rs.2,500, *no one was permitted to subscribe for more than four shares.* (Morris 1983, p. 575)

According to a partner of Tata Sons and Company, "The public in India, especially in Bombay are ever ready to put their money in mill concerns started by individuals or firms who have a reputation for honesty and efficiency, and who have a good deal of mill experience" (Chandavarkar 1994, p. 67 and 243). With a successful business in textiles, Tata was able to raise money from the private sector in 1907 for a large steel mill. "The total Capital of the new Company was subscribed by the Indian public in a remarkably short space of a few weeks, the number of shareholders being about 7,000" (Fraser 1919, p. 77).

China's potential economic surplus in 1933 was also estimated to be very large, possibly more than 25 percent of GNP (Riskin 1975).[27] Assuming that the magnitude of surplus is a function of wealth, then a large surplus is not surprising given evidence of China's material well-being at an earlier period in history.[28] A British sea captain who traveled from Hainan to Canton in 1819 noted: "Scarcely any people can be supposed to enjoy a more happy or contented life. . . . People of the poorest sort here are better clothed than the same class of persons even in England. . . . We have seen nothing in the shape of a beggar." Other Western accounts also allegedly emphasized the absence of poverty, high productivity, and extensive and vigorous commercial life, not just in Canton but in other provinces as well (Murphey 1977, p. 163). Supposedly a "comparison of nineteenth-century China's economic situation with Meiji Japan's indicates that at least with respect to per capita agricultural product, and possibly even total income per capita, the Chinese were not worse off" (Riskin 1975, pp. 81–82). Given the scale of compradors' operations, "contrary to the generally held view, an important reason for China's relatively slow economic development in the nineteenth century was not the scarcity of capital, because large amounts of Chinese funds were readily available" (Hao 1970, p. 348). The Chee Hsin Cement Company, for example, allegedly had no trouble raising capital after the turn of the century. Its 29 shareholders held diversified portfolios, with interests in other industries, commerce, and banking (Feuerwerker 1967). More significant, it has been estimated that "the Chinese economy could have afforded the modest degree of capital formation involved in building the railroads that were constructed with foreign financing, but both private capitalists and public officials had other priorities—a situation for which imperialism was partially, but not entirely, responsible" (Huenemann 1984, p. 131).

Nevertheless, even if capital was lodged in the woodwork, extricating it required investment opportunities with high expected returns and low risks. Reliable data for "the rest" are scarce on prewar profit rates, especially for the long run,[29] although wartime returns were generally very high.[30] Nor with insufficient evidence can it be determined if manufacturing earned more or less than alternative investments, which were represented in China by trade and money-lending.[31] What is clear is that bankruptcies and divestments in "the rest" were high even among large, modern manufacturing firms. Of thirty-one Chinese-owned mills that operated before 1911, all but one changed hands at least once (of the five foreign mills, none changed hands). Between 1923 and 1931,[32] nineteen units were reorganized, five units were taken over by creditors, eleven units were bankrupt, and seventeen units were sold to others" (Chao 1975, p. 126). In India, only five of the pioneering textile firms of the nineteenth century survived until World War I. Out of a total of ninety-seven mills erected in Bombay between 1855 and 1925, twelve were burnt down or else were closed and dismantled, sixteen transferred their managing agencies voluntarily and forty-five went into liquidation and were reconstructed under other names (Rutnagur 1927, p. 37).[33] High bankruptcy rates afflicted other industries in India no less than textiles. The number of joint stock companies increased steadily after the beginning of the twentieth century, but between 1921 and 1935, paid-up capital did not register much of a rise. "This was due to the fact that there occurred a very large number of company failures, with the result that *the Indian investor, habitually shy, became shyer still*" (Das 1962, p. 161, emphasis added).[34]

Japan's cotton textile industry also had high turnover initially: between 1893 and 1911 there were eighty new starts and eighty-three dissolutions, which is an even higher ratio than existed in the Chinese textile industry between 1912 and 1930, with sixty-eight starts and twenty-two dissolutions (although the respective time periods and development phases differed). Speculation and fraud were also familiar figures in Japanese textile mills (cotton and silk), as noted below. Nevertheless, Japan's labor-intensive industries ultimately broke the vicious circle surrounding capital shyness, and this breakthrough may be attributed to Japan's relatively high productivity. Given a large productivity advantage (which we observed in the case of Japanese textile firms operating in China [see chapter 2]), profitability was also relatively high. Profit rates were higher for Japanese textile companies operating in China than for Chinese companies (which in turn earned higher profits than Western-owned mills) (Kuwahara 1992). In turn, high profits and high rates of capitalization went hand-in-hand ("It is a significant fact that while there are in the whole of China nearly twice as many Chinese mills as those of Japanese ownership, the total capital invested in this industry by the Chinese is merely a little over half of the amount invested by the Japanese" [King and Lieu 1929, p. 6].) Given sufficient investment resources, not least of all from Japan's newly founded development banks (see chapter 2), large-scale manufacturers were able to survive. Ultimately, the number of firms in Japan's textile industry bottomed out and the "oligopolistic system" began, whereupon profitability became more robust and liquidations diminished (Kuwahara 1986; Kuwahara 1992; and Yonekawa 1982).[35]

Fattening Profits

Firms in "the rest," by contrast, speculated in fixed assets (examined later) and engaged in dubious financial practices in order to raise capital.[36] They guaranteed dividends (as noted earlier with respect to railroads), and they made inadequate allowance for depreciation. All told, they were seriously undercapitalized, which further lowered their chances of survival.

The *kuan-tu shang-pan* in China, or bureaucrat-owned, merchant-managed enterprises,[37] borrowed short-term at high interest rates, guaranteed dividend payments without regard to earnings, and made inadequate provision for depreciation and insurance. Guaranteed dividends (*kuan-li*) were subtracted from gross income before the profit-and-loss account was created. To attract merchant capital, guaranteed dividends were usually 8 or 10 percent on the subscribed capital and constituted part of the operating expenses of the company. If a firm's profits were inadequate or if a firm was operating at a loss, the *kuan-li* was taken from the capital or additional funds were borrowed (Feuerwerker 1958, p. 18). Guaranteed dividends in relatively large-scale enterprises persisted in China until at least the 1930s.

The severe undercapitalization of Chinese firms may have arisen because there was no incentive under a fixed dividend *kuan-li* system to maintain a high equity ratio. Whatever the cause, because Chinese entrepreneurs tended deliberately to build excessively large plants relative to their limited equity capital, they had to borrow short-term at very high interest rates to meet their financial needs. Often their needs went unmet, and they were seriously short of working capital, which was fatal in the silk and textile industries in which raw materials were 70 to 80 percent of production costs (Chao 1975).

Underbudgeting for depreciation allowances was another way to inflate reported profits. This was routinely done by China's largest cement mill, Chee Hsin, whose lower overhead costs than comparable cement mills in the North Atlantic "were typical of Chinese manufacturing firms. In part they were the product of a strikingly low allowance for depreciation," on the order of 2.84 percent of gross revenues over the period 1908–39. In a capital-intensive industry such as cement, this allowance was "a ridiculously inadequate figure." In fact, underbudgeting for depreciation wasn't such an irrational strategy on the part of Chee Hsin because domestic demand for cement was growing slowly due to deteriorating political conditions and a slowdown in construction. Chee Hsin enjoyed almost a regional monopoly until the 1930s, and so despite its obsolescent equipment and partially because of its artificially low overhead, it showed high gross profits—26.35 percent of gross revenues from 1908–39. Under these circumstances, "entrepreneurship (became) a matter of getting the largest possible share of a limited pie rather than continually seeking new ways to produce a bigger and better one" (Feuerwerker 1967, p. 325–26).

To raise capital and employ managing directors, India developed a unique institution called the "management agency" system. Agents were paid commissions regardless of company performance, a form of guaranteed dividend. This was a disincentive to good performance and an invitation to corruption.

The origins of the agency system are obscure,[38] but most likely in the initial stages of industrialization, before the rise of wealthy entrepreneurial families, the requisite capital for a project had to be raised from a small group of prosperous but busy merchants, most of whom were not related to each other through any family. "Such a situation would make it desirable to place the management of a company in the hands of a person or firm possessing business reputation but willing to undertake the responsibility only if the remuneration was high and guaranteed for a long period" (Rungta 1970, p. 228).[39]

Eventually, such firms became controlled by a single family, and the system became similar to the Japanese *zaibatsu* (family-owned diversified business group) (Tripathi 1982; Gadgil 1959). The modus operandi of the zaibatsu system in India was that a rich family would launch a company and allot controlling interests to family members and friends. Simultaneously, the controlling shareholders would form a managing agency firm (typically a sole proprietorship or partnership) to which the management of the new firm(s) was entrusted. The remuneration of the managing agency was usually fixed in terms of a certain percentage of annual sales or production—whatever the mill's performance.

Abuse crept in because there was no control over agents. Whereas the managing directors of Lancashire mills worked under the control of a board of directors, nonfamily shareholders under an agency system had very little voice in management.[40] According to one report in the *Indian Textile Journal* of November 1899:

> We cannot alter Japanese and Chinese competition, we cannot control the monsoon, we cannot even apparently do much to improve (cotton) cultivation, and competition with Manchester in the higher counts of yarn and finer fabrics is fraught with many impediments. But the glutted market in the Far East is entirely our own making, our miserable mismanagement is our own (and) our rapacious dishonesty is our own. (Rutnagur 1927, p. 51)

Markets were glutted because managing agents were interested only in their own commission, which was pegged to production, so they continued to produce at full steam even when the demand for their goods was steeply falling. "The result was that not only did the high profit vanish, but the companies began to operate at a loss" (Rungta 1970, p. 232).

Without oversight, corruption became pervasive, as observed in Bombay in the 1870s:

Cotton was purchased by uneducated selectors who were no judges of staple or of value and whose honesty was more than doubtful; it was weighed by corrupt weighers who were bribed for excess weight. Coals were purchased which were defective in quality or weight or both and the cotton was manufactured by machinery that was loaded with surreptitious commissions and maintained with stores in which the teeth of the shark had made heavy marks. The factory pay sheet was charged with useless or fictitious employees, and the employees themselves paid bribes to the jobbers and overlookers. The Board of Directors was faked, the auditors were chosen for the amiability of their disposition, and lavish office expenses and lawyer's fees added dignity to the business. Every canon of honest trading and manufacturing seemed to have been turned upside down, and the whole when considered together gave one the impression that the industry existed for no other purpose than to support a gigantic system of swindling. (Rutnagur 1927, pp. 50–51)

Thus, while the management agency system started as an expedient means to raise capital and circumvent a scarcity of managerial talent, it ended as a disastrous way to build skills.

Speculation

A shortage of market empowering assets in "the rest's" manufacturing sector was a natural breeding ground for speculative behavior because it diminished investors' expectations of making large manufacturing profits. Instead, speculation became regarded as an option with low opportunity costs.[41] In industries based on the processing of a natural resource, speculation in the raw material sometimes took precedence over maximizing returns to manufacturing. The Silk Association of America wrote about the international market in 1911: "Silk is not sold to-day purely on the basis of supply and demand, but has become to a large extent a speculative article. Hence, the trade at large is at a loss how to protect itself against the gambling spirit which has been infused into the trading in this most valuable commodity" (Li 1981, p. 88).

In the 1920s, speculating in raw cotton was common in New York and Liverpool, but speculation by cotton manufactures in Japan and China was special because very large quantities of cotton were bought ahead of demand and none of such purchases was hedged.[42] Regarding China, where locally grown cotton was bought and sold speculatively in Shanghai, the general secretary of the International Federation of Cotton and Allied Textile Industries stated: "it will be readily understood that the business of cotton spinning is only of secondary importance under such conditions; it will depend upon the luck or otherwise in the purchase of the raw material whether the mill makes a profit or a loss" (Pearse 1929). If advanced purchases were for cotton unsuitable to existing fashions, then there was a costly inventory build-up. Or product quality suffered on account of mills spinning warehoused cotton rather than cotton appropriate to what was in demand.[43]

In addition to speculating in cotton, coal, and jute, India's managing agents also sometimes speculated in the stocks of their own companies, taking profits in one and losses in another to maximize their own commissions. Moreover, the whole relationship between distribution and manufacture in cotton textiles, where the merchant ultimately diversified into production, was such that a speculative element arose. When Indian merchants were squeezed out of the raw cotton export trade by large North Atlantic (and later Japanese) traders, they continued to buy Indian cotton locally and invested their capital in spinning mills. By investing in industry, they gained considerable flexibility in their operations. They could buy raw cotton when prices were low and sell when prices rose. If the cotton trade remained depressed, they could switch stocks intended for export to the manufacture of yarn. Rather than build warehouses to store their yarn, they could deploy their cotton in its best short-term use and adjust their operations to the uncertainties of the market (Bombay employed daily labor right through World War II). While clever, even *"the aggressive and successful merchants were not motivated by the urge to embark upon a process of cumulative technological development, but rather by an anxiety to hedge their bets, to diversify and to survive"* (Chandavarkar 1985, pp. 647–48, emphasis added).[44]

The "Little Push" into Heavy Industry: Iron and Steel

The modern, labor-intensive industries addicted to speculation and financial mismanagement never really broke these habits until after World War II, when loans from development banks partially overcame problems of under-capitalization, and performance standards mitigated against specualtion. Instead, what appeared in "the rest" before the war was the growth of large-scale firms in industries requiring high enough thresholds of capital to make mismanagement extremely costly. The wherewithal to enter such industries initially came from: (a) "national leaders" in labor-intensive sectors that had accumulated capital and project execution experience and (b) government support.

Five premodern and émigré countries within "the rest" built integrated steel works before 1945 (see table 4.8). Two proved to be successes (Brazil and India), two were disappointments (Mexico and Turkey), and a fifth was a fiasco (China). Why these five countries—among all developing countries—got to the point of even erecting a modern steel complex relates to two ad-

Table 4.8. "The Rest's" Early Integrated Steel Mills, 1894–1941

Country	Works	Ownership	Established	Steel Capacity[1]
Brazil	Volta Redonda (CSN)	state	1941	270,000
China	Han-Yeh-Ping	mixed	1894	50,000[2]
India	Tata (TISCO)	private	1907	100,000
Mexico	Fundidora	private	1900	90,000
Turkey	Karabuk	state	1939	150,000
Japan	Yawata	state	1901	150,000

1. In tons. Design capacity. Design capacity may be misleading because often original designs were altered or were expected to be reached in stages. The Volta Redondo works is named Companhia Siderurgica Nacional (CSN). The Tata works' name is Tata Iron and Steel Company (TISCO). Fundidora refers to La Fundidora de Fierro y Acero de Monterrey.
2. There are no data on steel ouput at Han-yeh-ping until 1907. An output of 50,000 tons was reached in 1910 and was only exceeded in 1914.

Sources: Adapted from Baer (1969) for Brazil; Feuerwerker (1964) for China; Morris (1983) for India; Hershlag (1968) for Turkey; and Yonekura (1994) for Japan.

vantages: their raw material endowment and accumulated finance and manufacturing experience in the form of managerial skills.

The countries that had succeeded in developing a textile industry also tended to be the countries that succeeded in developing an integrated iron and steel industry. There is no example in "the rest" (including the colonial learners discussed in the next chapter) of a country popping up out of nowhere and becoming a leading steel supplier overnight.[45] The transfer of experience from cotton textiles to steel was very direct in at least three cases. In China, the merchant Sheng Hsuan-Huai, who was behind the founding of the first textile mill, was also behind the founding of the first steel mill (Feuerwerker 1958). In Mexico, Carlos Prieto, a merchant-financeer with diversified holdings, including textiles, acquired control of Mexico's first integrated steel monopoly (Haber 1989). The Tata group in India, which made its fortune in textiles, used the profits and organization it derived from textiles to diversify into steel (and when steel demand collapsed in the 1920s, subsidies from textiles sustained it) (Morris 1983). Moreover, firms' success in manufacturing steel derived from their knowledge acquired as steel importers. Information in India about manufacturing and marketing came from within the Tata group: "The family firm, Tata and Sons and Company, was one of the largest iron and steel importers and dealers in India. It knew the local market intimately. It also had offices in China and Japan where it expected to find an important demand for both steel and foundry iron" (India was a major exporter of iron ore to Japan) (Morris 1983, p. 589). As for Brazil, "Volta Redonda once had a monopoly position as the country's sole importer (of steel)," which helped to forecast market trends (Baer 1969, p. 129). There were fewer organizational linkages between textiles and steel in Japan, Brazil, and Turkey because the first major steel works in these countries were state-owned. Nevertheless, governments typically managed production units in other industries such as alcohol distilling, salt, and coal mining.

All five steel manufacturing countries in "the rest" also had experience smelting iron before trying their hands at steel.[46] Brazil's first pig iron producer, Esperança, began operations in 1891. Brazil supposedly had about seventy small shops producing roughly two thousand tons of pig iron at the turn of the century. Numerous small iron and steel plants also appeared in the 1920s, having originated in other industries (Baer 1969; Rady 1973). In the case of China, the Tayeh (iron ore) and P'inghsiang mines had been developed before an integrated steel complex was started around them (the railroad to Tayeh, noted earlier, was designed to facilitate the production of steel which, in turn, was supposed to supply rails for the railroads) (Feuerwerker 1964). In nineteenth-century India, modern iron making was widespread in several regions, especially Bengal. In 1889, the Bengal Iron and Steel Company, mentioned earlier, employed about 500 persons in its smelting works and 1,000 in its foundries (Chaudhuri 1964). American investors established an iron smelter in Mexico in 1881 under the name of the Iron Mountain Company. It used fairly modern techniques of ore reduction. Other, smaller operations also appeared. Descriptions of Turkey beginning in the 1840s make reference to iron foundries with furnaces and forges (Clark 1974). True enough, 'the rest's" early iron making facilities may not have provided a direct technology transfer to integrated steel making given differences in the size of operating equipment. But they were part of a buildup of skills and a community of firms.

Despite manufacturing experience and despite the fact that the technology for steel making was already mature by the time it appeared in "the rest," operating at full capacity with a positive profit rate was a big challenge. Compared with earlier industries, steel making involved much larger-scale facilities and equipment. More raw materials (mainly coal, coke, and iron ore) were involved whose physical properties varied by geographical location. Optimizing the returns from such natural resources required trial and error, as noted earlier. Because costs of transportation for finishing were high, plant location decisions were multivariate and project execution skills to plan investments were critical. Entry also required fast ramp-up, thereby precluding evolutionary learning, and continuous process production meant that distribution and production had to be carefully coupled and coordinated.[47]

Failure at steel making struck in China because the owners of China's first mill, Han-yeh-ping, were over their heads when they initiated their investment, not fully aware of the costs and planning involved. Poor management began with the disregard of foreign technical advice and the wrong location decision for the plant, which was situated too far from available deposits of coal and iron ore. The start-up of operations was seriously delayed, which meant government guarantees to buy a certain number of steel rails were forfeited. To modernize production facilities more capital became necessary, but the company's poor reputation made raising finance problematic. Short-term debt was incurred and Han-yeh-ping's financial structure deteriorated. In exchange for loans, the company sold coal and iron ore to Japan's newly founded Yawata Steel Works at a fixed, long-term price (Feuerwerker 1964). Eventually, all of Han-yeh-ping, and not just its iron ore and coal divisions, fell under Japanese control (Yonekura 1994). By 1916 Han-yeh-ping had become an accomplice to Japan's expansionism in the Pacific, including China itself.

Turkey's first integrated steel mill, Karabük, was part of the state owned Sümer Development Bank, and was a product of technical assistance from the German firm Krupp in 1932–33. Political rivalry between Germany and Britain ultimately left a British engineering firm, H. A. Brassert, in charge of the project. Limited information suggests that the Turkish military was responsible for locating the plant in a remote inland region for defense reasons, far from coal deposits and 600 miles overland from iron ore.[48] But poor foreign technical assistance did not make matters better: "the German advisers and later the British who executed the plan cannot be excused from a large degree of responsibility for the defects of the plant. There was an element of gigantomania in the striving for magnitude of the project (Karabuk's capacity was about equal to that of Yawata), with too little thought for raw materials, the complementarity of the various parts of the plant and the most urgent demand for simpler semi-finished goods, tools and agricultural equipment" (Hershlag 1968, p. 105). In 1950 only two out of three blast furnaces as well as two out of four open hearth furnaces were reported to be functioning. Although output was growing, Karabük was operating at undercapacity despite being heavily protected and enjoying a domestic monopoly (Singer 1977).

By contrast, both Brazil's Volta Redonda steel works (CSN), a state enterprise also with high tariff protection, and the Tata steel works (TISCO), a private Indian venture without tariff protection (except in the 1920s), had good records.[49] An economist concluded in 1969 "it seems reasonably clear that Brazil's steel industry is competitive in the comparative cost sense, without any recourse to external benefits or—at this time—infant industry arguments." Volta Redonda, with one-quarter of Brazil's total steel output in the early 1960s, was so efficient that no adjustment had to be made for its advanced age in calculating the performance of the whole Brazilian steel industry (Baer 1969, p. 151). TISCO also grew rapidly—each year by 8 percent on average for its first three decades (from 100,000 tons of finished steel in

1912 to 800,000 tons of finished steel in 1939, when it supplied three-quarters of India's steel consumption). A Rand study noted that TISCO was "one of the largest steel mills in the British Empire as well as one of the lowest cost producers in the world" (Johnson 1966, p. 12).

The success of both companies—Volta Redonda and TISCO—involved rich raw iron reserves, adequate capitalization, and heavy investments in project execution skills. Both undertook extensive preparations in choosing the optimal plant site and in selecting the optimal process design (from U.S.-based Arthur G. McKee & Company in the case of Brazil and U.K.-based Julian Kennedy, Sahlin and Company in the case of India). Neither project was realized without long preparation. In the case of TISCO "planning and design had been done so well that by the time the first World War broke out the enterprise had gone beyond its initial teething difficulties. But it had taken the Tata organization many years and millions of rupees to go from initial conception to the beginning of production" (Morris 1983, pp. 591–2).[50]

Second, both TISCO and CSN invested heavily in management capabilities and worker training. The Brazilian government was the main stockholder of CSN but the American EXIMBANK was the largest lender and stipulated that "management would include Brazilian administrators and engineers trained in the United States." At the time of construction, some 55 American experts and 127 Brazilian engineers were employed. Workers were recruited from the best schools and trained on- and off-the-job (Rady, 1973, pp. 145, 201). In 1919 TISCO set up a technical institute to train Indians who would eventually replace foreign personnel, whose number peaked at 229 in 1924, almost twenty years after TISCO started operating. Not until 1936 was the first Indian appointed general manager and not until World War II was TISCO fully Indianized.[51] Behind both sets of managers, moreover, was a strong motivation. TISCO was a *swadeshi* (Indian national) enterprise and Volta Redonda was a national showcase.

In sum, we can say that the early steel mills in "the rest" that succeeded did so because they made the three-pronged investment analyzed earlier. All five mills, both successes and failures, invested in large-scale plants (maybe too large in Turkey and too small in China). But only the successes also invested heavily in managerial hierarchies—to plan the project and run the plant—and distribution.

Nevertheless, the three-pronged investment in steel made by countries in "the rest" was much different from the type made by leading companies in the North Atlantic. It involved a role for the government, whether as owner (in Brazil, Turkey, and Japan) or trouble shooter (in India).[52] "During the planning and construction phases (of TISCO), the Tatas received extensive and official assistance—geological surveys, reduced transport costs, eased access to land and water rights, simplified import arrangements for construction materials, and an agreement that the state would buy 20,000 tons of steel rails annually for ten years at import prices" (Morris 1983, p. 589).[53]

The three-pronged investment also involved a greater role for the diversified business group. In TISCO's case, as already noted, a sister affiliate in textiles served as a cash cow for the original investment in steel, and Tata's trading arm provided market information about steel demand. In addition, when TISCO was about to fail after World War I, the Tata group bailed it out: "it was unthinkable for the Tatas to let the founder's most prized legacy languish" (Tripathi and Mehta 1990, p. 66). One of the founder's sons pledged part of his personal fortune to get a bank loan and all the Tatas pressured the government for higher tariffs. After World War II, the major agents supporting the three-pronged investment were the same agents that appeared before the war in the steel industry: government and diversified groups.

Conclusion

Without novel products or world-class skills, "the rest" took a long and halting journey down a low road to industrialization. Devoid of innovative assets, firms lacked credibility with potential investors. Without capital, it was difficult to undertake the three-pronged investment necessary to compete in modern industries: in large-scale plants and up-do-date equipment, in technological capabilities and management teams, and in distribution. Nor did small-scale firms circumvent the need for such investments by modernizing artisan production systems and substituting them for mass production. The extent to which this happened appears to have been negligible. Small-scale firms before World War II, and for most of the postwar period, did not act as an agent of late industrial development. Instead, due to the relative unattractiveness of investing in manufacturing without proprietary skills, high bankruptcy rates and low rates of return prevailed, and these encouraged imprudent financial practices, speculation, cheating, and fraud. The relatively liberal economic system that prevailed throughout "the rest" before World War II, therefore, was embroiled in its own forms of corruption.

After almost one hundred years, there was no obvious, endogenous, organic solution to "the rest's" economic predicament. It was in this context of industrial growth without industrialization that the developmental state was born.

5

Manufacturing Experience Matters

Countries in "the rest" that industrialized rapidly after World War II had accumulated manufacturing experience in the prewar period. This differentiated them from countries in "the remainder." Path dependence was such that no economy emerged from the blue as an industrial competitor. Whatever other types of "leap-frogging" occurred in late industrialization, this was not one of them. In the previous chapter, we analyzed how premodern artisanship and North Atlantic emigration affected the accumulation of manufacturing experience. In this chapter we look at how colonial rule and Chinese emigration affected it. We focus on Malaysia, Indonesia, Taiwan, Thailand (with no formal colonial ties,)[1] and Korea (with no Chinese emigration). We then sum up the strengths and weaknesses of different types of manufacturing experience for "the rest" as a whole.

If manufacturing performance in a given period depends on the accumulation of prior experience in *manufacturing* as opposed to other types of economic activity, then this should manifest itself statistically. To test for this, aggregate cross-country data may be used to estimate two regression equations covering twenty-nine countries[2] in which the dependent variable is *per capita manufacturing output in 1994* ($PCMAN_{94}$).[3] In one equation, the independent variable is per capita GDP in 1950 ($PCGDP_{50}$). In this equation, the adjusted R^2 is only 0.35, suggesting that only 35 percent of the cross-country variation in per capita manufacturing output in 1994 can be explained by variations in per capita *income* in 1950, a proxy for general economic activity (see figure 5.1). In the second equation, the independent variable is per capita manufacturing output in 1950 ($PCMAN_{50}$). The adjusted R^2 in this equation is 0.75, or more than double the first adjusted R^2. Thus, 75 percent of the variation in manufacturing output per capita in 1994 may be explained by variations in per capita *manufacturing* output in 1950. Assuming the data are

Figure 5.1. Regression for Manufacturing Experience

Manufacturing Output per Capita, 1994, As a Function of:

Regression	Constant	GDP per Cap., 1950	Mfg. Output per Cap., 1950	Adj. R-square
1. n = 29*	92.4 (1.4)	0.11 (4.0)		0.35
2. n = 29*	45.9 (1.2)		0.95 (9.1)	0.75

*Countries include Nigeria, Kenya, Burma, Pakistan, India, Ceylon, UAR, Guatemala, Honduras, Jordan, Indonesia, Philippines, Paraguay, Panama, Morocco, Colombia, El Salvador, Ecuador, Trinidad and Tobago, Peru, Venezuela, Costa Rica, Mexico, Brazil, Chile, Turkey, Barbados, South Africa, and Argentina. Countries were selected according to the availability of data. Korea and Taiwan were omitted as outliers. Dependent variable: manufacturing output per capita, 1994, in current dollars (UNIDO 1997). Figures in parentheses are t-statistics. GDP per capita, 1950, is measured in 1990 international dollars (Maddison 1995). Manufacturing output per capita, 1950, is estimated by multiplying the share of manufacturing in GDP by GDP and then dividing by population (United Nations 1963).

accurate and the sample is random, manufacturing experience appears to hold some special power over subsequent manufacturing per capita output that general economic activity lacks.

We now try to understand this specificity.

The Elements of Manufacturing Experience

Japan's mobilization for war and invasion of Manchuria in the 1930s provided a lightning rod for the industrialization of its neighbors, colonies and noncolonies alike. Foreign investments in manufacturing began in Southeast Asia around the time of World War I, but manufacturing activity accelerated in the 1930s. Japan hastily adopted industrial policies to promote manufacturing for war preparation in its colonies, Korea and Taiwan, thereby planting the seeds for their highly successful postwar industrial promotion systems. Colonial governments in Indonesia and Malaysia responded to Japan's threats with defensive investments, including protectionism against Japanese exports.[4] A bloodless coup d'état in Thailand in 1932 ushered in a period of nationalist development initially in collaboration with Japan. While "economic policy stayed liberal in most (Southeast Asian) colonies throughout the late nineteenth and early twentieth centuries" (they had never been liberal in Japanese colonies), economic policy was already somewhat protectionist when growth resumed in the late 1930s following the Great Depression (Lindblad 1998, p. 19).

Korea

The abhorrence with which Koreans held the experience of Japanese colonialism created a nationalistic historiography after independence that belittled the long-term contributions of Japan's occupation to Korean industrial growth.[5] A newer revisionist scholarship, however, suggests that the industrial development of Korea under Japanese rule was deep and greater than hitherto acknowledged.[6]

Industrialization advanced in Korea starting with World War I and accelerated with the Manchurian Incident in 1931. As Western economies at the time of World War I could no longer supply their Asian markets, and as Japanese factories filled the breech, Japan's domestic production capacity became insufficient to meet its own colonies' demand for goods and services. Thus, a 1911 Corporation Law that restricted colonial investments in industries that competed with Japanese home industries was relaxed. Korea's industrial development around this time, while not phenomenal, was characteristic of what was to come later. First, both old and new Japanese *zaibatsu* (business groups) were a major factor in Korean industrialization. The Mitsui group, for example, invested in the Chosen Textile Corporation (1917), the Chosen Rawsilk Thread Corporation (1919), the Namboku Cotton Ginning Corporation (1919), and the Onoda Cement mill (1917). Big business groups thus made an early appearance in Korea's industrial expansion, partly because of the relative importance of heavy industries. By 1939, large factories (with more than 200 workers) accounted for about 1 percent of the total number of factories but produced about two-thirds of output by value (Suh 1978).[7] Second, while Japanese investments were of much larger scale than Korean investments, the large Korean-owned corporation made an early appearance as well, in both silk (the Chosun Silk Mill, 1919) and cotton textiles. The Kyongsong Textile Corporation (originally founded in 1911 and reorganized in 1919 as the Kyungsung Spinning and Weaving Company) was established with the specific ideal of promoting national development, and large Korean landowners and leading Korean business people were initially owners (management problems ultimately led to the same familial pattern of ownership and control as elsewhere in "the rest," as noted in chapter 4). Third, while turn-of-the-century small-scale investments were concentrated in food processing (especially rice milling), new, larger investments covered multiple industries, including iron and steel (the largest investment was by the Mitsubishi group in 1917), mining, shipbuilding, cotton ginning, food processing, silk, lumber, brewing, dye manufacturing, medicines, flour, cement, sugar, and cotton spinning and weaving.

Industry mostly stagnated in the 1920s, but hydroelectric power investments in the northern part of the country by a new Japanese zaibatsu (the flag-bearer was the Japan Nitrogen Fertilizer Corporation, Nihon Chisso) eventually led to the creation by 1937 of the Korean Nitrogen Fertilizer Corporation (Chosen Chisso) and a big electrical-chemical industrial complex. Growth was slow, but between 1922 and 1930 the number of factories with more than 50 employees increased from 89 to 230, and among them were 49 factories that were Korean-owned. By 1930 over one-third of all workers were employed in factories with more than 100 employees (ignoring the large numbers of Korean migrants working in Japan). The total number of factory workers in 1930 was estimated at just over 100,000, distributed among food processing (32.2 percent of workers), textiles (19 percent), chemicals (17.5 percent), ceramics (6 percent), and other industries (Park 1985, p. 42). In that year, Korea's population was roughly 13.6 million and the population of Seoul is surmised as having been 355,000 (see tables 1.6 and 1.7). Korea's lag behind Japan may be very roughly estimated as follows: the percentage of factory workers in total population in Korea (101,000/13.6mil) in 1930 was 0.75 percent. The comparable percentage in Japan (1.68mil/64.2mil) was 2.6 percent, or roughly 3.5 times greater.[8]

Japan's takeover of Manchuria presented the second opportunity for Korean industrialization, as Korea was regarded in Tokyo as the bridge between China and Japan. The Korean business community enthusiastically welcomed Japan's expansionism as good for profits. During this time another major characteristic of Korean industry emerged: heavy government direction (Kohli 1994). In 1932, to induce more large-scale investments from Japan, the government general in Korea took control of hydroelectric power generation. Power generation was to be developed privately by the Noguchi group while transmission and distribution were to be government controlled. To promote development of power generation and other industries, the government adopted different forms of subsidy, and these typically were conditional on adherence to price controls. "Under these government policies, the nature of colonial industry was transformed remarkably in this period" (Park 1985, p. 50). Thus, conditionality of one sort, at least, made its appearance in Korea early on, in addition to the early appearance of diversified business groups and government economic intervention.

By 1940 industrial production nearly equaled agricultural production in value. Heavy and light industry attained roughly equal proportions in manufacturing output. Industries related both directly and indirectly to war expanded at phenomenal rates, including large-scale flour mills, breweries, textile mills, and synthetic fiber installations. In addition to a large chemical complex in northern Korea, a metal working complex arose in the south, in the Kyongson-Inchon area near Seoul, that specialized in the production of machine tools and machinery for mining, heavy vehicles, electrical equipment, and aerospace. A large cluster of subcontractors for machine parts was established in the Yongsan area centering around the Yongsan Engineering works. Workers engaged in the heavy industries increased from about one-quarter of the total workforce in 1931 to almost 38 percent in 1936 (Park 1985). By 1943, over 360,000 workers in Korea were estimated to be engaged in factory work (Park 1985). While most of the capital for expansion came from Japan, and most Korean-owned factories remained small, even Korean factories began to modernize. The Toyoda automatic loom, for example, invented in Japan and reputed to be the best of its kind in the world (patent rights were sold to Platt Brothers U.K. in 1929), began to be imported into Korea in large numbers (Izumi 1979, table II).

Trade provides another indicator of progress in Korean industrialization, and high prewar trade coefficients (imports and exports as a share of GDP) were yet another harbinger of a future trend. Whereas Korea's exports (almost all to Japan) were overwhelmingly agricultural at the time of annexation in 1910, the share of agriculture had fallen to around 50 percent by the 1940s. At the same time, the composition of imports had changed, and producer goods (capital goods plus construction materials) rose from 13.6 percent in 1914 to 31.4 percent in 1940. "We can infer that industrialization . . . during this period was high" (Hori 1994, p. 10). Even in international terms, Korea was becoming a producer or exporter of some significance. For example, in 1939 Korea ranked eleventh out of twenty-nine among the world's leading exporters of cigarettes; a year earlier it ranked fifteenth among the world's twenty-six largest producers of cotton fabrics (Woytinsky and Woytinsky 1953).

Koreans worked in various skilled and managerial capacities in Japanese-owned firms, not just in manufacturing but in services, including financial services (by 1943, Korea's *total* workforce in paid employment was estimated at 1.75 million). Despite racial prejudice and discrimination, "significant numbers of Korean workers were in fact able to rise to factory positions of skill and responsibility, especially during the latter half of the colonial period," when wartime scarcities of Japanese workers created opportunities for promotion of Koreans (Eckert 1996, p. 19). The colonial government began to invest more in Korean education, from the primary level to the professional level, and Japanese firms (such as the Onada Cement Company)[9] invested more in training in-house. A 1943 report on engineers engaged in design, construction feasibility studies and inspection, machine and tool work, medical treatment, hygiene, and research enumerated a total of 20,000 employees, over 32 percent of whom were Koreans (Eckert 1996). Thus, "that Chosen (Korea) was virtually bereft of native entrepreneurial or managerial talent when colonial rule came to an end in 1945" is "a common misconception" (Eckert 1996, p. 22).

Koreans even penetrated the ranks of large-scale capitalists. Wealthy Koreans had little difficulty investing in Japanese companies, examples being the men who were later to become founders of the Samsung and LG (Lucky-

Goldstar) groups, two of Korea's big four *chaebol*. Business directories for the 1930s show numerous Koreans identified as company officers or major stockholders in Japanese companies, especially in provincial towns and cities where capital investments were smaller than in Seoul. Moreover, by 1941 over 40 percent of the number of industrial enterprises were run by Koreans. In some industries, such as beverages, pharmaceuticals, and rice mills, Korean firms represented over 50 percent of the total, and even in war-related industries such as metalworking, chemicals, and textiles, they accounted respectively for roughly 28 percent, 30 percent and 39 percent of the total, not counting small-scale firms, most of which were Korean owned (Eckert 1996, p. 23).

In commerce and finance, Koreans had been active in founding small- and medium-size trading companies and banks since the turn of the century, a number that rose steeply as business in Manchuria boomed. White collar Korean managers filled the ranks of the government general's ministries and semiofficial institutions such as development banks. Even before war mobilization, one-third of the managerial staff of the Chosen Industrial Bank was accounted for by Koreans, and Korean quotas for higher positions rose to almost 45 percent as war conscription of Japanese managers increased. By the end of the war, Koreans had entirely replaced the Japanese staff in some departments (Moskowitz 1979). Koreans even became high officials outside Korea, in other parts of Japan's empire. Thus, "as a result of their experience with wartime economic mobilization and planning, the postwar bureaucratic and business elites in both Taiwan and Korea learned the importance of public institutions and central planning in large-scale endeavors to promote industrialization" (Kobayashi 1996, p. 327).

The division of manufacturing industry between northern Korea and southern Korea was such that by 1939–40, the north had the advantage, but only by a factor of 1.2 (Suh 1978). The chemical industry was mostly in the North, but the textile and metalworking industries were mostly in the South. In the case of textiles, which was to become Korea's "leading sector" in the 1960s, factories in 1939 numbered 608 and workers totaled 47,000, with a high concentration in large scale firms (large firms accounted for 67 percent of the total work force and 86 percent of all production). "Despite having been completely under the domination and financial control of Japan since the 1930s, the spinning and weaving industry made great strides toward becoming a modern factory-manufacturing industry" (Choi 1982, p. 257).

Korea had thus accumulated by the war's end considerable manufacturing experience in the form of a workforce accustomed to paid labor (under very disciplined conditions), a managerial elite with production capabilities in a wide range of industries and government bureaucracies, as well as a small cadre of entrepreneurs with project execution skills, both in private and public enterprise (as well as in the military). Korea's leading sector in the 1960s, textiles, was obviously "not something that suddenly sprang into existence as a result of the Park regime's much celebrated five-year development plans. On the contrary, it represented the culmination of a process of development that had begun during World War I and blossomed in the 1930s after the Manchurian Incident" (Eckert 1996, p. 37).

The elements of "manufacturing experience" that may be said to have been important are as follows:

1. *A labor force*
2. *Salaried management*, although mostly employed in foreign-owned rather than nationally owned firms
3. *Production know-how*
4. *Project execution skills* (in both the private *and* public sectors)

Taiwan

Taiwan's manufacturing experience before *the 1960s* was possibly as extensive as Korea's, although with different timing and weights attached to different elements, given the crucial fact that Taiwan benefited not only from Japanese mentoring but also from an influx in the 1950s of large numbers of experienced workers, managers, and entrepreneurs from the Chinese mainland. Heavy industry progressed further in Korea (especially in the northern part of the peninsula) while small-scale firms were more important in Taiwan—another harbinger of a future trend. The early importance of small-scale firms in Taiwan may be gleaned from the following: Taiwan's population in 1930 was only one-third as large as Korea's (4.5 million versus 13.5 million, as shown in table 1.6); its population density was higher by a factor of 4.7 (in 1938); but the number of Taiwanese-owned factories was 7.5 times greater than the number of Korean-owned factories (Hori 1994, p. 19).

Close parallels between prewar industrialization in Korea and Taiwan existed in trade (fast growth and high export coefficients [Hori 1994]), extensive government semiofficial enterprise (especially in mining and mineral exploitation [Ho 1984]), and government promotion of industry starting in the 1930s to create a bridgehead for Tokyo's expansionism (Korea into China and Taiwan into Southeast Asia). But due to different natural resources (especially the minerals and hydroelectric power in northern Korea that Taiwan did not have, and the long growing season and milder climate in Taiwan agriculture that Korea did not have), industrialization in Taiwan did not go as far as in Korea in terms of diversification and the development of basic industry. Taiwan's manufacturing sector remained overwhelmingly dominated by food processing (especially sugar refining). In the 1920s, food processing in Taiwan accounted for about 70 percent of manufacturing gross value (providing the basis for big business groups in the 1950s, noted in chapter 8), and "between 1926–1928 and 1938–1940 the output composition of Taiwan's manufacturing sector changed only slightly" (Ho 1984, p. 367).

Even the large-scale, modern spinning and weaving industry is estimated to have developed little by the war's end. According to one account: "Back in 1945, when Taiwan was restored to Nationalist China after 51 years of Japanese occupation, there existed on the island only two cotton mills, two jute plants and one woolen mill" (Far Eastern Economic Review 1962, p. 103).[10] The relative underdevelopment of textiles in prewar Taiwan is also suggested by the fact that they were a major import item, often from the coastal areas of China: "Cotton textile was imported to clothe the local population" (Ho 1978, pp. 30).

By 1954, however, imports as a percentage of supply were only 3.8 percent, indicating a remarkable import substitution in less than a decade (Ho 1978, p. 190). Rapid postwar progress was due partly to government policy. When Taiwan could no longer import textiles from communist China, and imports from Japan began to eat up foreign exchange, the Taiwan government heavily promoted the import substitution of textiles by offering various types of assistance to encourage investment by local entrepreneurs; investors practically enjoyed guaranteed profits (Lin 1973; San and Kuo 1991). Furthermore, rapid progress was made possible despite relatively weak prewar manufacturing experience by the large inflow into Taiwan of Chinese mainlanders, some with long experience in manufacturing textiles in Shanghai and other major Chinese areas (Shandong), which were centers before wartime of modern Japanese-owned spinning and weaving mills (see chapter 4). Thus, "the good quality and relatively low-cost labour force, combined with experienced textile entrepreneurs who had fled from mainland China in 1949, constituted a very strong base for Taiwanese industry. Beginning in the late 1960s, textiles became the country's largest export item" (San and Kuo 1991, p. 14). Textile entrepreneurs became the founders of large business groups, such as Far Eastern, Tai-yuen, and Chung-hsing. Whereas heavy industry was often the core of the chaebol in Korea, 33 of the top 106 business groups in Taiwan in 1976 had a textile firm as their flagship (Gold 1988).

Not just textiles but other industries as well, such as flour milling and machine tools, benefited from the experience (and sometimes capital and even equipment) brought to Taiwan by Chinese émigrés (for machine tools, see Amsden 1977). Thus, whatever experience Taiwan industry lacked from Japanese colonialism, it (partially) compensated for with experience from China. By the 1960s manufacturing experience in Taiwan was arguably as advanced as in Korea, but with a greater emphasis on small business and a lesser emphasis on heavy industry. The labor force, the managerial elites, the production capabilities and the project execution skills in both the private and especially public sectors were all in place, however insecurely. After World War II, therefore, Taiwan became an ideal locale for foreign "original equipment manufacturers" to source their parts and components and later, for local entrepreneurs to enter high-tech industry (Amsden and Chu 2003).

Neither Peddlers nor Princes: Indonesia

In the 1950s a renowned American anthropologist identified the absence of the modern firm as a major obstacle to Indonesia's economic development, finding no evidence of modern firm formation in either of Indonesia's two major economic formations, one related to the peddlers who dominated commerce and the other to the princes who lorded over agriculture. "What they lack is the power to mobilize their capital and channel their drive in such a way as to exploit the existing market possibilities. They lack the capacity to form efficient economic institutions; they are entrepreneurs without enterprises" (Geertz 1963, p. 28).

One formation comprised towns with thousands of traders engaged in a bazaar economy, in which "the total flow of commerce is fragmented into a very great number of unrelated person-to-person transactions" in response to the opportunities being created by commercialized agriculture but in opposition to the growth of big business (Geertz 1963, p. 28). The other formation comprised displaced aristocratic landlords and their peasant laborers, bound together by traditional ties and mutual obligations that inhibited profit maximization and that were only just beginning to weaken. Geertz despaired that either formation could provide the fertile soil for further industrialization, but he astutely observed that a modern economy cannot arise "*ex nihilo* out of an almost wholly traditional culture." Whatever their shortcomings, the traders, landlords, and laborers of awakening Indonesia "are what the Indonesian government has to work with" (Geertz 1963, p. 80).

While Geertz was right that modern Indonesian industry could not and did not arise ex nihilo, and that the changes underpinning a rise in commerce and a loosening of traditional agrarian ties were necessary for economic growth (discussed below), neither did modern Indonesian industry arise directly out of the two formations he studied. Instead, it emerged largely out of colonial investment and Chinese émigré manufacturing activity, which Geertz largely ignored. "Export-led economic expansion turned Southeast Asia into an exceptionally attractive investment outlet for private capital from the metropolitan world. *This region was probably more favoured among investors than were Africa or Latin America*" (Lindblad 1998, p. 15, emphasis added). As indicated in table 5.1, Indonesia accounted for half or more of the colonial investment flowing into the Southeast Asian region in 1914 and 1937.

While most colonial investments were in nonmanufacturing, some manufacturing investments began to arise. Between 1870 and 1914, Indonesian

Table 5.1. Foreign Direct Investment in Southeast Asia, 1914 and 1937

	1914 (mil $)	1914 (%)	1937 (mil $)	1937 (%)	Per Capita (1937 $)
Indonesia	675	61	1261	52	19
Malaya	150	14	372	14	69
Thailand	25	2	90	3	6
Other	250	23	845	31	—
Total	1100	100	2568	100	—

Sources: Adapted from Lindblad (1998), based on data from H. G. Callis, *Foreign Capital in Southeast Asia* (New York: Institute of Pacific Relations, 1942).

manufacturing was dominated by sugar refining. World War I stimulated industrial development as Western imports were temporarily disrupted. New industries included chemicals, petroleum, coal, and rubber products; food, beverages, and tobacco (including the acquisition of an existing plant by British American Tobacco); basic metals, machinery, and equipment; and ceramics. The period 1920–29 even witnessed the formation of an assembly plant for cars by General Motors (1927).

As the supply of electricity expanded during the 1920s, the number of factories grew. Nevertheless, most of the new factories were oriented toward the domestic market and were small. As competition from the North Atlantic resumed and transport costs fell, liquidations exceeded start-ups. Over two-fifths of the 10,343 industrial establishments recorded in 1921 were Indonesian, but 81 percent of these employed five or fewer workers. Overseas exporting of processed sugar and petroleum, as well as inter-island exporting of a wide variety of products, remained more important than foreign-dominated import substitution. Still, the use of steam boilers in metalworking increased, and "for the first time industry in the Netherlands Indies was able to prove that it was capable of more than just the repair of machinery" (Segers 1987, p. 23).

As the Great Depression abated and the likelihood of Pacific war increased, investments in Indonesian manufacturing escalated in importance. Investments were abetted by colonial measures to protect local industry. An embargo on capital exports created liquidity for the finance of manufacturing. Import quotas for cement, cooking utensils, tires for cars and motor cycles were supportive of import substitution. Quotas for artificial fertilizers, electric light bulbs, cotton blankets and bath towels were introduced to protect local Dutch manufacturing industry. All in all, a boost was given to so-called foreign oversea-plants (subsidiaries of foreign firms serving the local market or other Southeast Asian markets) in industries such as beer, biscuits, weaving, soap, paint, tires, bicycles, paper, footwear, cotton yarns, and cement. The decreasing importance of manufactured imports was a stimulus for various trading houses to enter into manufacturing. A big Dutch trading company (Internationale Credieten Handelsvereeniging Rotterdam) began to manufacture paper, phosphates, ceramics, and foodstuffs. Other large trading houses entered into metalworking. Chinese investors also began to contribute to an expansion of manufacturing after 1930, in such industries as woven goods, biscuits, electric light bulbs, buttons, soap, inner tubes for bicycles, and crown corks. "There are also indications that Indonesian capital was invested in manufacturing companies . . . active in the production of textiles, leather, the preparation of rubber, essential oils, soap and clove cigarettes" (Segers 1987, p. 34). Most of all, the textile sector expanded, especially modern weaving mills.

By 1940 the number of Indonesian factory workers was estimated at around 300,000, roughly double the number that existed four years earlier. For the first time, moreover, the number of factory workers in manufacturing exceeded the number of factory workers in mines or production units attached to plantations (Segers 1987, p. 29). Thus, in terms of the elements of manufacturing experience listed earlier, Indonesia had accumulated a factory labor force in prewar years. While that labor force was mostly concentrated in food processing, textiles, and woodworking, employment in other industries, including machinery, had risen, although not on a par found in Korea or even Taiwan. Whereas the modern labor force/population share around 1930 was very roughly 0.75 percent in Korea and 2.6 percent in Japan (as noted earlier), it was only about 0.5 percent in Indonesia (using population estimates from 1930). Stated otherwise, whereas factory workers circa 1940 totaled 300,000 in Indonesia with a population circa 1930 of 60.5 million, they totaled 360,000 in Korea with a population of only 13.5 million. Moreover, while detailed studies appear to be lacking on the localization of managerial positions in modern industries, it is almost certain that lower-rank positions were occupied by Indonesians. Localization, however, is unlikely to have gone as far in Indonesia as in Korea or Taiwan if only because local Dutch employees were not in short supply at the time of war to the same extent that Japanese employees were. Furthermore, it is almost certain that Indonesia did not acquire project execution capabilities comparable to those acquired by Korea and Taiwan because neither the Dutch government nor Dutch multinational firms mobilized resources for war on a par with mobilization in Japan's colonies. Still, when the Indonesians finally won their war of Independence against Dutch occupation, and Dutch properties were nationalized in December 1957 and early 1958, Indonesians acquired a rich bounty—489 Dutch corporations, including 216 plantations, 161 mining and industrial establishments, 40 trading firms, and 16 insurance companies (Creutzberg 1977). However out-of-date and in imperfect working order, these business enterprises existed in significant numbers and were more organizationally advanced than what Indonesia's own peddlers and princes had been able endogenously to create.

Malaya[11] and Thailand

Using Indonesia as a benchmark, prewar manufacturing experience, in the direct sense of the formation of firms and managerial and production skills, was probably higher in Malaya and lower in Thailand, as suggested by per capita foreign direct investment in 1937 (see table 5.1). As in Indonesia, Malayan manufacturing activity under British colonialism (and émigré Chinese) was initially a spin-off from mining (of tin and rubber) and plantation agriculture (of copra oil, palm oil, and pineapples). Such activities also constituted the core of the business groups (agency houses) that were to become major owners of manufacturing activity in postwar Malaysia (in 1965, for example, five leading houses, Harrisons & Crosfield, Guthrie, Boustead-Buttery, the Borneo Company, and R.E.A.-Cumberbatch controlled 220 manufacturing firms [Lindblad 1998]). Additionally, Malaya benefited from the arrival in 1881 of United Engineers, which started building small crafts and repairing ships (Allen and Donnithorne 1957) and then diversified into the construction of dredges and rubber machinery, the production of iron and steel, and the manufacture of parts, components, machinery, and boilers. This large job shop served as a training ground for local workers (mainly Chinese) whose skills were then utilized in independent enterprises or in subcontractual arrangements with United Engineers (Thoburn 1977). In the 1930s Malaya experienced the same boom as Indonesia in the import substitution of consumer goods. Ford, for example, established an assembly plant in 1932 (GM's assembly plant in Indonesia was started in 1927) and Bata Shoe began operations in 1937. Ten years later approximately 126,160 workers were estimated to be employed in manufacturing. Of these, 17 percent were engaged in food processing, 15 percent in textiles, 17 percent in wood working, and 19 percent in metalworking and machinery building. By the 1950s local producers were already exporting rubber manufactures, food, beverages, and machinery to Southeast Asia (Rasiah 1995, p. 67).

Without direct colonial intervention, Thailand's prewar manufacturing investments were less extensive than in Indonesia, but with minor compensatory factors. Thailand's abundance of arable land created an agrarian economy with a high level of market activity (Ingram 1971). This activity was conducive to the growth of trade, out of which emerged a precocious banking sector, controlled by both Thais and Chinese. Out of this banking sector emerged many of the diversified business groups that provided a head start to the Thai postwar textile industry (the Saha Union and Thai Blanket Industry, for example [Doner and Ramsay 1993]), the rudiments for national enterprise in basic industry, and partners for the many joint ventures formed with foreign firms in Thailand starting in the 1960s. Moreover, entrepreneurship for modern manufacturing did, in fact, come from princes, in the form of Thailand's Crown Properties Office, which established Thailand's largest business groups, Siam Cement (founded in 1909 with the participation of Danish capital and management) and Siam Motors (see chapter 8). The Thai military also played a leading role in stimulating manufacturing in the 1930s, forming alliances with Chinese capitalists and nationalizing foreign holdings in the cigarette, beer, cement, and sugar industries (including British-American Tobacco) (Suehiro 1985).

In short, among countries in "the rest," industrialization was probably most backward in Thailand, if only because Thailand had the fewest types of prewar manufacturing experience (see table 5.1). Thai industry suffered from a small domestic market, little capital, and negligible technological skills. Nevertheless, when World War II erupted, Thailand was no stranger to modern industry.

The Coming of Peace: The Limits of Experience

By the time war ended and peace arrived, industrialization had progressed everywhere in "the rest," although unevenly. Assuming data on the share of manufacturing in GDP are comparable across countries (despite differences in the coverage of small-scale firms), then the émigré North Atlantic form of manufacturing experience turned in the best performance, except in Turkey. Manufacturing output as a share of GDP in the 1950s ranged from around 20 to 30 percent in Argentina, Brazil, Chile, and Mexico, all of which had acquired their know-how from North Atlantic émigrés, and from only around 5 to 15 percent in other countries (see table 5.2). Differences in per capita income followed the same general pattern (see table 1.3). Manufacturing activity in countries whose economies had been weakened by war or transformed by decolonization (especially Korea, Taiwan, India, Indonesia, and Malaysia, not to mention China) was probably greater than statistics indicated. Still, whatever the source of manufacturing experience, all countries in "the rest" suffered in the 1950s from two shortcomings: no obvious modern manufacturing industries that could compete at world prices in international markets, including East Asia's cotton textile industry; and no obvious set of modern, well-managed firms to lead the diversification charge.

Ultimately, petrochemicals became Latin America's "leading sector" in the sense that in the 1970s or earlier, it became a magnet for investment, firm

Table 5.2. Distribution of Manufacturing by Industry, 1953–1990.

Industry	Percentage of Total Manufacturing		
	1963[1]	1975	1990
Argentina			
Food	23.6	22.8	19.6
Textiles	22.5	12.9	9.7
Wood	4.7	2.6	1.6
Paper	5.0	5.0	5.0
Chemicals	13.2	17.9	34.1
Nonmineral	4.6	5.0	4.4
Metals	24.3	14.0	11.9
Machinery	na	19.2	13.3
Other	2.1	0.6	0.3
Total	100	100	100
Mfg. output/GDP[2]	31	32	22
Brazil			
Food	22.5	15.5	12.2
Textiles	23.1	10.6	12.9
Wood	6.7	4.5	1.9
Paper	6.5	6.3	5.4
Chemicals	13.6	18.9	23.9
Nonmineral	7.3	6.2	4.3
Metals	17.9	13.1	13.4
Machinery	na	23.4	24.9
Other	2.4	1.4	1.1
Total	100	100	100
Mfg. output/GDP	24	29	26
Chile			
Food	26.6	21.8	21.7
Textiles	28.2	8.4	7.5
Wood	3.8	2.0	4.1
Paper	6.8	5.8	9.6
Chemicals	12.0	19.3	17.3
Nonmineral	6.0	2.8	3.2
Metals	16.1	28.3	31.9
Machinery	na	11.4	4.7
Other	0.6	0.4	0.2
Total	100	100	100
Mfg. output/GDP	23.0	21.0	22.0
India			
Food	19.7	10.8	11.5
Textiles	36.3	19.5	12.3
Wood	0.6	0.7	0.4
Paper	3.8	4.9	3.2

Table 5.2. (*continued*)

Industry	Percentage of Total Manufacturing		
	1963[1]	1975	1990
India (*cont.*)			
Chemicals	12.6	20.2	26.8
Nonmineral	3.5	3.9	4.7
Metals	16.5	16.3	13.1
Machinery	na	23.3	27.3
Other	7.0	0.5	0.6
Total	100	100	100
Mfg. output/GDP	12	16	19
Indonesia			
Food	38.0	33.4	20.1
Textiles	8.0	13.7	13.7
Wood	2.0	3.1	10.2
Paper	1.0	2.9	3.4
Chemicals	12.0	30.8	28.3
Nonmineral	4.0	4.3	2.6
Metals	11.0	3.8	11.7
Machinery	na	7.9	9.4
Other	24.0	0.2	0.5
Total	100	100	100
Mfg. output/GDP	8	9	20
Korea			
Food	21.0	17.8	11.3
Textiles	29.2	22.6	13.2
Wood	5.0	2.7	1.6
Paper	7.2	4.0	4.6
Chemicals	11.9	22.3	17.6
Nonmineral	8.9	5.7	4.6
Metals	14.7	8.9	12.8
Machinery	na	14.2	32.2
Other	2.2	1.9	2.1
Total	100	100	100
Mfg. output/GDP	9	27	31
Malaysia			
Food	36.6	27.0	15.6
Textiles	na	7.2	6.3
Wood	17.8	11.1	6.8
Paper	8.2	5.3	4.7
Chemicals	14.4	21.0	23.5
Nonmineral	6.3	4.2	6.4
Metals	4.5	6.7	7.6
Machinery	6.9	16.9	28.1
Other	5.2	0.6	1.0
Total	100	100	100
Mfg. output/GDP	9	18	24

Table 5.2. (*continued*)

Industry	Percentage of Total Manufacturing		
	1963[1]	1975	1990
Mexico			
Food	30.0	29.0	22.2
Textiles	18.0	14.1	9.0
Wood	5.0	3.1	2.5
Paper	4.0	4.9	5.8
Chemicals	11.0	18.0	28.6
Nonmineral	4.0	5.6	3.7
Metals	27.0	9.9	9.9
Machinery	0.0	14.2	16.6
Other	1.0	1.3	1.8
Total	100	100	100
Mfg. output/GDP	24	23.0	23.0
Taiwan			
Food	41.8	22.1	11.4
Textiles	16.3	17.4	12.5
Wood	4.1	2.5	1.6
Paper	5.6	2.8	5.1
Chemicals	12.7	18.7	21.7
Nonmineral	5.9	5.5	3.9
Metals	12.2	10.2	11.8
Machinery	na	18.2	22.5
Other	1.3	2.8	9.6
Total	100	100	100
Mfg. output/GDP	14	29[3]	36
Thailand			
Food	53.9	41.0	31.3
Textiles	9.5	15.4	25.5
Wood	8.1	4.4	2.9
Paper	3.0	3.0	2.2
Chemicals	5.6	14.4	10.5
Nonmineral	7.1	2.9	4.2
Metals	5.4	5.7	4.3
Machinery	6.2	9.6	11.8
Other	1.3	3.6	7.3
Total	100	100	100
Mfg. output/GDP	12	18	26
Turkey			
Food	35.6	22.0	16.0
Textiles	33.5	14.0	14.0
Wood	1.1	1.0	1.0
Paper	3.0	4.0	3.0
Chemicals	8.1	27.0	27.0
Nonmineral	3.7	5.0	7.0
Metals	14.7	12.0	14.0

Table 5.2. (*continued*)

Industry	Percentage of Total Manufacturing		
	1963[1]	1975	1990
Turkey (*cont.*)			
Machinery	na	14.0	17.0
Other	0.4	0.0	0.0
Total	100	100	100
Mfg. output/GDP	11	20	24
Italy			
Food	19.5	8.9	8.4
Textiles	14.6	11.8	12.9
Wood	5.3	2.7	3.1
Paper	5.2	5.3	6.9
Chemicals	16.8	17.6	13.2
Nonmineral	4.4	6.0	6.1
Metals	32.8	15.5	12.4
Machinery	na	31.3	35.7
Other	1.5	0.8	1.3
Total	100	100	100
Mfg. output/GDP	48	n/a	23
Japan			
Food	9.6	10.0	8.9
Textiles	16.0	7.9	4.7
Wood	4.4	4.2	2.5
Paper	9.7	8.2	7.9
Chemicals	16.2	14.7	15.0
Nonmineral	5.5	5.1	4.3
Metals	36.0	15.3	13.8
Machinery	na	32.9	41.4
Other	2.5	1.7	1.5
Total	100	100	100
Mfg. output/GDP			28
United Kingdom			
Food	10.3	12.9	13.4
Textiles	14.3	8.2	5.3
Wood	2.6	3.1	3.0
Paper	7.0	7.8	10.9
Chemicals	10.7	15.4	17.9
Nonmineral	4.0	4.4	4.9
Metals	48.4	14.2	10.2
Machinery	na	32.8	33.4
Other	2.6	1.2	1.1
Total	100	100	100
Mfg. output/GDP	56		23

Table 5.2. (*continued*)

Industry	Percentage of Total Manufacturing		
	1963[1]	1975	1990
United States			
Food	12.4	11.8	12.4
Textiles	9.9	6.9	4.9
Wood	4.2	2.9	2.9
Paper	9.3	9.7	12.1
Chemicals	12.0	15.8	17.6
Nonmineral	3.3	3.4	2.7
Metals	44.9	13.6	9.0
Machinery	na	34.4	36.9
Other	4.0	1.6	1.4
Total	100	100	100
Mfg. output/GDP			18

Notes:

1. 1953 data for Argentina, Brazil, Chile, India, Turkey, Italy, and Japan; 1958 data for Indonesia and Korea; 1959 data for Malaysia; 1950 data for Mexico; 1954 data for Taiwan, United Kingdom, and United States; 1963 data for Thailand.
2. For Manufacturing output/GDP, 1953 column is 1955 data.
3. 1970

UN and UNIDO Categories:
Food = food, beverages, tobacco (1–3)
Textiles = textiles, wearing apparel, leather and fur products, footwear (4–7)
Wood = wood products, furniture and fixtures (8–9)
Chemicals = industrial chemicals, other chemicals, petroleum refineries, coal and petroleum products, plastic, rubber (12–17)
Nonmineral = pottery/china/earthenware, glass products, other nonmineral (18–20)
Metals = iron/steel, nonferrous metals, metal products (21–24)
Machinery = electrical machinery, nonelectrical machinery, transport equipment, professional and scientific equipment (25–28)
Other = other (29)

Sources: United Nations (various years) and UNIDO (various years [b]).

formation, and international trade. It was emblematic of Latin America's primary product-based industrialization. Multinational investments in the Latin American oil industry had been extensive before World War II, but they were limited with respect to backward linkages. Typically, they were restricted to oil exploration, extraction, and refining. The share of the chemical industry in manufacturing output in the 1950s was no higher in Latin America than elsewhere in "the rest;" with the exceptions of Thailand and Turkey, the share in all countries hovered around 13 percent (see table 5.2). Pemex in Mexico was established after the nationalization of foreign oil holdings in 1938 but began producing petrochemicals only in the late 1950s. Similarly in the case of fertilizers, a large scale producer, Guanamex, was only founded as late as

1943 when the Mexican government assumed the entrepreneurial role. In Brazil, oil and gas production began to be undertaken on a large scale by state-owned Petrobras, formed in 1954. In turn, Petrobras created Petroquisa, responsible for undertaking investments in petrochemicals, as late as 1968. In Argentina, although Yacimientos Petrolíferos Fiscales (YPF) had been founded as a public enterprise in the 1920s, it did not establish its first petrochemical plant until 1943 (Cortes and Bocock 1984).

The ability to compete in the petrochemical industry, in subsectors ranging from synthetic fibers to fertilizers, depended chiefly on building plants of minimum efficient scale. This, in turn, depended on timing and mobilizing downstream investments to provide demand for upstream feedstocks. In terms of difficulties in timing (as experienced in Korea): "when less developed countries build plants, many internationally competitive firms of advanced countries often engage in dumping practices in the international market. For example, the competitive price of methanol was more than $70/T before Korea constructed a methanol plant. However, the price of methanol on the international market dropped to $40/T when Korea started to produce it" (O 1973, pp. 276–77). Moreover, as plants in "the rest" were being constructed, efficient scale was increasing due to technological change. In the case of the synthetic fiber industry,

> in the early years . . . the quantity of domestic demand was 1.5 to 1.6 tons per day. In spite of the existence of a number of potential competitors, only one (Korean) corporation was given a business permit. It was consequently expanded to the scale of 30 tons per day, which was the minimum unit for international competition at that time. When the scale of 30 tons was achieved, the government then transformed the industry into a competitive system by increasing the number of competitors. Meanwhile, however, the minimum unit for international competition had grown to 100 tons. The government then stopped increasing the number of competing enterprises and sought to expand existing factories to the scale of over 100 tons in keeping with the new international conditions. (O 1995, p. 355).

"Efficient scale," therefore, was not a static engineering concept but a dynamic policy problem. To raise domestic demand for petrochemicals and enable minimum efficient scales to be reached, governments everywhere in "the rest" intervened to create downstream users (see chapter 6). In the 1950s, despite lengthy manufacturing experience, Latin America's construction of a petrochemical sector was still in its infancy.

In the case of the textile industry, Asia's relative strength, Japan's neighbors first had to build modern capacity, which required raising foreign capital with government guarantees. Then they had to worry about increasing productivity and lowering costs. In the early 1960s labor productivity (units monitored per worker) was roughly 3.3 times greater in Japan than in Taiwan. Measured as machines tended per worker, Japan's productivity was

Table 5.3. Production Cost of Unbleached Cotton Sheeting (U.S. Cents per Linear Yard), United States, Japan, and Hong Kong*

	U.S. costs (%)	Japan costs (%)	Hong Kong costs (%)
Total cost	14.6 (100)	11.4 (100)	14.0 (100)
Cotton	8.4 (57.5)	7.8 (68.6)	7.0 (50)
Labor	3.9 (26.8)	1.7 (15.1)	2.1 (15)
Other	2.3 (15.7)	1.9 (26.3)	4.9 (35)

*United States and Japan, 1960; Hong Kong, 1963.

Sources: Adapted from United States, Department of Commerce (1961, table 8, p. 21) and GATT (1966) as cited in Young (1969).

roughly seven times greater (Lin 1969). Taiwan's advantage of lower wages, therefore, was offset by Japan's higher productivity, as suggested in figure 1.1.[12]

There are no available data for the early 1960s on the cost disadvantages of textile producers in "the rest" vis-à-vis Japan, but the cost factor may be inferred from data available for Hong Kong, which operated with a relatively market-determined exchange rate. If Hong Kong, with the "right prices," could not compete openly against Japan, it is dubious that other East Asian countries could have competed against it simply by "getting the prices right."[13] Table 5.3 presents a cost comparison for the early 1960s for un-bleached cotton sheeting (the bottom, least-skilled segment of the market) in the United States, Japan, and Hong Kong. It indicates that total costs per yard were *lowest in Japan*. They were higher in Hong Kong than in Japan by a factor of 1.3: $0.14 per linear yard in Hong Kong versus $.0.11 in Japan. Labor costs in Japan and Hong Kong both accounted for the same share in total costs, suggesting that Japan's productivity advantage and Hong Kong's wage advantage offset one another.

The American textile industry, with higher costs than those of Japan, survived Japanese competition after World War II by introducing "voluntary export restraints" (the first "gentlemen's agreement" between the two countries had been signed in the 1930s to restrict Japan's exports to the Philippines, a U.S. colony [Peattie 1996]). By contrast, Hong Kong survived Japanese competition by virtue of its membership in the British Commonwealth, which shielded it from competition against non-Commonwealth members, and its large export quotas under a 1962 textile agreement, which cartelized access to the textile markets of advanced countries.[14] Taiwan and Korea, on the other hand, relied heavily on subsidized credit, tariff protection, and restrictions on foreign investment to build capacity in modern spinning and weaving. Depending on how Taiwan's tariffs are measured, they at least doubled during 1949–55 (see table 5.4). They again either increased or remained

Table 5.4. Taiwan's Tariffs on Cotton Yarn and Cloth, 1949–1968

Year	Nominal Tariff		Actual Tariff	
	Cotton Yarn	Cotton Cloth	Cotton Yarn	Cotton Cloth
1949	5.0	20.0–30.0	8.4	26.4–38.4
1955	17.0	40.0	44.8	70.4
1959	25.0	42.5–45.0	39.6	64.8–68.4
1968	25.0	42.5–45.0	43.5	70.8–74.7

Notes: Nominal tariffs are marginally different in Scott (1979), but both measures show a small increase in tariffs between the 1960s and 1970s. Actual tariffs include not just nominal tariffs but also quantitative restrictions on both final manufactures and imported inputs. With a mark-up of 10 percent, the adjusted tariff rate for a "controlled" commodity with a nominal tariff rate of 40 percent was estimated to be 68.1 percent (Lee and Liang 1982).

Source: Taiwan custom import tariff schedules.

high in 1955–68, a period of supposed "liberalization." In terms of the trade-off suggested in figure 1.1 between cutting real wages (depreciating the exchange rate) or subsidizing learning, Taiwan did both in order to compete.

The Fate of Foreign Investment

Besides the failure of manufacturing experience to bequeath ready-made, modern industries capable of competing at world prices, an additional failure centered on the scarcity of professionally managed, *nationally owned* firms. If large-scale, professionally managed firms existed, they tended to be *foreign-owned*. Latin American countries with émigré manufacturing experience probably had the largest stock of such investment by World War II, but foreign direct investment (FDI) in Southeast Asia was nontrivial (see table 5.1), and Japanese investment in Korea and Taiwan had been extremely large, as noted above. What differed most among countries in "the rest," divided along lines of émigré and colonial history, was the fate in the period from, say, 1940 to 1960 of foreign investments.

The immediate postwar years were turbulent times for all countries in "the rest" in terms of foreign ownership. Almost everywhere the value of foreign ownership fell (however measured). Deliberate steps were also taken to transfer ownership and control of foreign properties to national owners (private and public) by means of nationalization or expropriation. Even before war had begun, Mexico had nationalized its oil industry. After hostilities had ended, Mexico acquired British-owned utilities. To finance its own war effort, Great Britain had liquidated many of its investments in Latin America. In the case of electric utilities, they tended to become Mexican properties (Wionczek 1964). British utilities passed to American hands and then to national hands in Argentina, which also expropriated Axis properties (Lewis 1990).

Nevertheless, the acquisition of foreign properties and the obliteration of a foreign presence in key manufacturing industries went furthest in countries that won political independence after World War II from colonial rule. Korea and Taiwan inherited farmlands and a functional banking system from Japan that was kept securely in state hands at least through the 1980s (under U.S. pressure, Korea had privatized banks in the 1950s but had renationalized them in 1961). Korean big business groups got their start on the basis of Japanese industrial properties that the Korean government first nationalized and then privatized. Taiwan acquired a vast state-owned enterprise complex from Japan (and the Chinese nationalist government) that by 2000 had not yet been privatized.[15] Indonesia nationalized all Dutch properties in December 1957 and early 1958. Nationalizations affected 489 Dutch corporations, as noted earlier, including 216 plantations, which provided the basis for diversification of national business groups into food processing, 161 mining and industrial establishments, 40 trading companies, and 16 insurance brokerages (Lindblad 1998; Thee 1996). In Thailand, a nationalist military government in the 1930s nationalized British properties (Suehiro 1985). In India, because most foreign business before 1914 was based around the procurement, processing, and shipping of primary export products—raw jute and jute manufactures, wheat, tea, and hides, to mention a few—these foreign businesses declined as the Indian economy shifted toward manufacturing. By independence in 1947, many agency houses had divested their holdings (Agarwala 1986). The new industries that developed in the 1930s and 1940s under tariff protection, such as electrical engineering, machinery and metal manufactures, food, tobacco and household goods, industrial chemicals and pharmaceuticals, rubber goods, and paints and varnishes, had attracted some foreign capital in the form of subsidiary manufacturing plants of multinational companies. Continuity was such that "more than half the British subsidiary manufacturing companies that were prominent in India in the early 1970s had already made sizable investments before Independence" (Tomlinson 1993, p. 143). All the same, investment by private Indian firms was much more aggressive and provided "more than 60 per cent of the total employment in large-scale industry by 1937, and over 80 per cent by 1944. Such firms also made the bulk of new private investment in the interwar period, especially in the 1930s" (Tomlinson 1993, p. 143). In Eastern India, foreign capital was routed by Indian capital (Tomlinson 1981). What thus appeared to contribute to the decline of expatriate capital in India was not expropriation wrought by decolonization. Instead, in contrast to the situation in Latin America, the political uncertainty introduced by decolonization discouraged foreign expansion.

The acquisition or marginalization of foreign manufacturing properties cleared the decks for the emergence of nationally owned businesses. It was a matter of history rather than theory that this happened most in countries with colonial backgrounds. Nevertheless, to the extent that an émigré background created an ambiguity about national identity, it is a matter of theory that after the immediate postwar years, émigré countries in Latin America, whether by default or design, gave greater encouragement than former colonies to additional foreign investment, as noted in chapter 8.

Conclusion

Prewar manufacturing experience emerges as a necessary condition for postwar industrial expansion given that no successful latecomer country managed to industrialize without it. Whatever the source of technology transfer (premodern, colonial, or émigré), it took time to build the production capabilities, project execution skills, and business organizations necessary to compete in world markets.

A big deficit in prewar manufacturing experience was the absence of nationally owned modern business enterprises. These may be regarded as a "benchmark of development" and "a miniature social system specialized to perform economic functions and integrated in terms of economic values" (Geertz 1963, p. 137). Not even the most advanced economies in "the rest" in the prewar period, those in Latin America, had created hierarchically managed national firms that undertook investments in plants with minimum efficient scale, technological capabilities, and related channels of distribution. The most modern firms were foreign-owned.

A major difference that emerged in the aftermath of war among countries in "the rest" concerned the durability of foreign ownership. Due to the dislocations of decolonization, the durability of foreign ownership was least in countries with colonial ties that explosively ruptured. In these countries—especially China, India, Korea, Taiwan, and Indonesia—the way was open wider in the postwar years to create nationally owned big businesses. Thus, while all countries in "the rest" after World War II retook the domestic market from foreign *exporters*, only some retook the terrain of big business from foreign *owners*.

The jewel in the crown of prewar manufacturing experience was a new elite of managers and engineers. In conjunction with investments in tertiary education, a cadre of experienced *tecnicos* emerged. Some were lost temporarily to brain drain. Others became the leaders in business and government who took the initiative to promote industrial development. It is to their efforts that attention is now turned.

II

SNEAKING AHEAD, CIRCA 1950–

6

Speeding Up

The developmental state was predicated on performing four functions: development banking; local-content management; "selective seclusion" (opening some markets to foreign transactions and keeping others closed); and national firm formation. As a consequence of these functions (the first two are examined in this chapter), "the rest" finally made the requisite three-pronged investment to enter basic industry—in large-scale plants, in hierarchical managements-cum-technological skills, and in distribution and marketing networks (Chandler Jr 1990). Two principles guided developmentalism: to make manufacturing profitable enough to attract private enterprise through the allocation of subsidies and to induce such enterprises to be results-oriented and to redistribute their monopoly profits to the population at large.

Step-by-step, governments groped toward a new control mechanism that replaced the invisible hand. The new mechanism ultimately shared credit with private initiative for a Golden Age of industrial expansion.

Development Banking

Like the North Atlantic, "the rest" was plagued after World War II by old and technologically obsolete capital equipment.[1] Unlike Europe, however, "the rest" had no Marshall Plan to guide and finance it.[2] Unlike Japan, it had no established Reconstruction Finance Bank.[3] Therefore, the development bank,[4] in conjunction with the development plan, filled the void.[5] For a very short time, until balance of payments problems emerged, "the rest" was cash-rich from wartime profits and forced savings. As wealth began to vanish with imports, developmental banks went into action to build local industry.[6]

Infrastructure was the first major target of postwar development banks. Unlike prewar railroad building, infrastructure projects such as electrification, highway construction, irrigation, sanitation, and airports created substantial demand for locally made inputs (many of Brazil's heavy capital goods producers, for example, were spin-offs from public infrastructure projects). Business groups were strengthened by participating in such projects (among Brazil's top fifteen business groups, five had their core competency in construction services, as shown in chapter 8). Development banks sharpened their own teeth on such projects by learning techniques related to project appraisal, bidding, and procurement of equipment and raw materials.

Table 6.1 gives a breakdown of infrastructure disbursements as a percentage of total lending by the development banks of Mexico, Brazil, India, and Korea. The types of infrastructure handled by each bank differed, but in all cases except India, the share of infrastructure in total lending began relatively high. It then tapered off over time as infrastructure demands were more fully met. Infrastructure expenditure as a share of lending was by far the lowest in India, no matter what the time period. In part, this reflected the fact that other institutions in India undertook infrastructure spending, including development banks at the state level. In part, it also reflected the fact that India seriously underinvested in infrastructure.[7]

With respect to rates of *total* investment, by 1960–64 there was a remarkable similarity among countries in "the rest." The share of gross domestic investment in GDP ranged narrowly, from a low of approximately 14.0 percent in Argentina, Chile, Indonesia, and Korea to a high of 21.2 percent in Thailand. The coefficient of variation in these years was a mere 15.4 percent (see table 1.12).

Nor was such capital formation driven by direct foreign investment. Foreign investment in total gross domestic investment was relatively small, possibly even smaller than in the prewar period due to a change in the ownership and finance of infrastructure (less direct foreign ownership in the postwar period). Direct foreign investment after the war was important in certain manufacturing industries, and critical in certain countries, as discussed in the next chapter, but it was minor in total capital formation (see table 1.14). For the seven countries in "the rest" for which data are available for 1960–64, direct foreign investment accounted for less than 5 percent. In the next period it became more important only in Brazil, with rich raw materials and a large domestic market, and Malaysia, with exceptionally rich raw materials.[8] In the 1990s, it became more important in almost all countries (discussed in chapter 9). Thus, since the nineteenth century, direct foreign investment in "the rest" tended to lag rather than lead economic development—it blossomed late, after national investment boomed (see chapter 3).

Instead, the big player in investment became the public sector. Public investment as a share of gross domestic investment in the period 1960–64

Table 6.1. Infrastructure* Disbursements as a Percentage of Total Lending by Development Banks, 1948–1991

Years	Infrastructure Disbursements (%)	Years	Infrastructure Disbursements (%)
Mexico		India	
1948–49	44.7	1949–61	1.5
1950–59	34.1	1962–69	3.6
1960–69	40.0	1970–79	4.2
1970–79	33.9	1980–89	7.8
1980–89	27.5	1990–94	7.5
1990–91	13.8		
		Korea	
Brazil		1954–61	27.7
1953–59	74.0	1962–71	17.9
1960–69	25.0	1972–79	23.9
1970–79	27.0	1980–89	11.0
1980–89	31.0	1990–94	12.5
1990–91	na		

*Infrastructure as defined by development bank reports. Infrastructure includes the following categories for the countries given— Mexico: electricity generation, transportation, irrigation, communication; Brazil: electric power, rail, road, water, other; India: electricity generation, waterworks; Korea: electricity generation, waterworks.

Sources: National development banks.

ranged from a high of 58 percent in Mexico to a low of 25 percent in Brazil (see table 1.13). These shares were higher than in the North Atlantic before and after the turn of the century.[9] Over time, the importance of the public sector in "the rest's" capital formation tended to decline (except in Taiwan), but for most of the postwar era, the developmental state was by far the single most important player in capital formation.

The state's agent for financing investment was the development bank. From the viewpoint of long-term capital supply for public *and private* investment, development banks throughout "the rest" were of overwhelming importance. Mexico's Nacional Financiera (NAFINSA) accounted for about twice the value of long-term loans of all private credit institutions in 1961, 8,114 versus 4,706 (in million pesos). It also accounted for over 60 percent of the total of stocks held by private credit institutions (see table 6.2).[10] Nor was NAFINSA's position atypical. In India, it was estimated by the late 1960s that more than one-fifth of total private investment in industry was financed through development banks; "the share of development banks in medium- and long-term loans would, of course, be much higher" (Goldsmith 1983, p. 187). The Industrial Development Bank of India financed both public and private ventures, but by 1985, cumulative assistance to private and joint

Table 6.2. Distribution of Manufacturing Lending by NAFINSA, 1948–1989
(Annual Averages in %)

Industry	1948–59	1960–69	1970–79	1980–89
Iron/steel	26.1	20.4	35.7	45.0[1]
Cement & other construction materials	2.7	1.3	1.0	na
Non-ferrous metals	1.0	3.0	5.5	1.5[2]
Food products	14.3	13.6	6.8	4.3
Textiles	11.0	6.9	6.1	6.5
Wood products	0.4	0.2	0.7	0.7
Paper/products	9.7	8.5	4.5	6.5
Fertilizers & other chem.	14.0	15.2	7.5	5.2
Metal & elec. prod./mach.	6.6	3.0	2.3	30.5
Transportation equip.	9.0	22.8	20.7	na
Other	5.2	5.5	9.1	na
Mfg. Total[3]	100.0	100.3	100.0	100.2
Total mfg. lending as % of mfg. GFCF[4]	na	na	35.5	17.5

1. Includes other metal products.
2. Nonmetallic mineral products
3. Does not include "petroleum and coal." Annual reports are unclear as to the extent to which this includes manufacturing.
4. Figures are for 1970 and 1980, respectively. Gross fixed capital formation.

Source: NAFINSA

private/public ventures accounted for 83 percent of total assistance (India, 1984–85). In Chile, between 1961 and 1970 the fixed investment of targeted projects by CORFO[11] in the industrial sector was scheduled at 55 percent of all fixed investment in industry, including artisan industry (CORFO 1961; Alvarez 1993). CORFO is estimated to have controlled over 30 percent of investment in machinery and equipment, more than one-fourth of public investment, and close to 20 percent of gross domestic investment (Mamalakis 1969). In 1957 the Korea Development Bank (KDB) accounted for 45 percent of total bank lending to all industries. After a military takeover in 1961, which resulted in the renationalization of commercial banks, "the next step in the financial reform program of the Military Government was revision of the KDB's charter to increase its capital, to authorize it to borrow funds from abroad and to guarantee foreign loans obtained by Korean enterprises" (Cole and Park 1983, p. 57). When only long-term ("capital fund") loans are considered, as early as 1969 the Korea Development Bank accounted for 53 percent of the total, "still maintaining its important role in financing the nation's industrial development" (Korea Development Bank 1969, p. 14). In the 1970s the National Investment Fund, used for the promotion of heavy and chemical industries, was partially funneled through the KDB. Later, when the brunt of lending shifted to commercial banks, preferential lending continued.[12] In Brazil, for forty years "no major undertaking involving private Brazilian capital was implemented without BNDES[13] support" (Banco Nacional de Desenvolvomento Econonico e Social [BNDES] 1992, p. 20). There was no real, alternative source for long-term capital in Brazil other than BNDES (Monteiro Filha 1994). Even in high-tech, BNDES was in the lead and created a special working group to explore the possibility of building a local computer industry. The "First Basic Plan for Science and Technology" emerged in 1973–74 from BNDES (Evans 1995). Regarding the Indonesian Development Bank (Bapindo), it was "the only significant bank specializing in long term lending" (McLeod 1984, p. 69). But in addition to Bapindo, there existed a large state-owned commercial banking sector and a national bank, Bank Indonesia, which also gave direct concessionary credit to major government enterprises, including Pertamina, Indonesia's giant oil company, and Krakatau Steel (Nasution 1983, p. 63).

The government's role in long-run credit allocation was substantial even in parts of "the rest" where development banks were of relatively minor importance (Malaysia, Thailand, Taiwan, and Turkey). When necessary, the whole banking sector in these countries was mobilized to steer long-term credit to targeted industries, acting as a surrogate development bank. Taiwan (like South Korea) inherited a well-functioning commercial banking system from Japan, as noted in the previous chapter. Excluding curb market institutions, this inheritance was government-owned and responsible for over 90 percent of long-term credit (Shea and Yang 1994; Wade 1990). According to the 1973 *Annual Report* (p. 10) of the Bank of Communications (a quasi-development bank), "The government has directed the different banking institutions to provide special credit facilities for different industries." As late as 1978 as much as 63.4 percent of domestic bank loans in Taiwan went to public enterprises (Lee 1990, p. 60).

The insignificance of development banking in Malaysia and Thailand owed to the fact that their major incentives to businesses in the early postwar period were tax rebates rather than credit concessions.[14] Still, four development banks existed in Malaysia devoted to the economic development of the Malay (Bumiputra) majority. There was also plenty of concessionary credit to government-supported projects beginning in the 1970s, and these were financed by a banking system that was heavily state-owned. By 1980 domestic banks accounted for 62.0 percent of the banking system's total assets. Bank Bumiputra Malaysia Berhad was the largest commercial bank and was wholly government-owned. The government was also a major shareholder in two other large banks (Malayan Banking Berhad and United Malayan Banking Corporation) (Akhtar Aziz 1984). In Thailand, most domestic banks were established by Thai-Chinese trading houses and became parts of diversified business groups. But the government owned more than a 90 percent share in two major banks (Krung Thai Bank and Bank for Agriculture and Agriculture Cooperatives) and minor shares in all other major banks (the Crown

Property Bureau was also a major shareholder in the Siam Commercial Bank). Krung Thai Bank, in turn, held the largest share in the Industrial Finance Corporation of Thailand, a development bank. Thailand's developmental state lodged most of its promotional activities in a Board of Investment (see chapter 1), which acted like a development bank to the extent that it targeted special industries (and firms) for support, which sometimes included concessionary credit, arranged through the Ministry of Finance.

Turkey had two important prewar development banks, the Sümerbank (1933) and the Etibank (1935), which invested in mining and steel (among other sectors) and various private enterprises. Owing to global politics, attempts were made to privatize these banks in the 1950s and a private Industrial Development Bank (IDB) was established with World Bank funding. Although privatization was halted for want of buyers, and the IDB remained inconsequential, state-owned enterprises executed various public policies, and commercial banks were heavily influenced by the state in their lending to specific industries (Hale 1981). In 1968 the State Planning Organization began issuing "certificates of encouragement" for investment. Similar to the Board of Investment's "promotion certificates" in Thailand, these certificates of encouragement entitled companies to favorable tax rates, duty exemptions, and subsidized credit. In the early 1990s such certificates again grew in importance (Barkey 1990; UNIDO 1995).

Theoretically, the importance of development banks in financing manufacturing industry can be measured either by their share in manufacturing *loans*, as just done, or by their share in manufacturing *investment*. The share of investment accounted for by manufacturing is itself of interest. Therefore, the available data are presented in table 6.3. The data are not especially illuminating because they do not show any clear-cut pattern among latecomers. Nevertheless, they do show a clear trend vis-à-vis that of the North Atlantic. "The rest's" share of manufacturing in total investment first matches and then exceeds the North Atlantic's share, which presumably falls with the rise of services. Given the share of manufacturing in total investment, table 6.4 shows the spending by development institutions as a percentage of total manufacturing investment in 1970, 1980, and 1990 (the countries shown are those with the two requisite data sets). The data for the Board of Investment (BOI) in Thailand represent the investment expenditures undertaken by the BOI's client firms. The data in table 6.4 are also not especially well-behaved because they are sensitive to the phase of large-scale investment projects and cyclical fluctuations in investment (such as a sharp economic downturn in Korea in 1980). Still, in the last year for which data are available, 1990, all four countries showed a substantial role for development banks, considering that manufacturing investment included not just long-term capital formation, the bread and butter of such banks, but also short-

Table 6.3. Manufacturing Gross Fixed Capital Formation as a Share of Total Gross Fixed Capital Formation 1950–1990 (%)

Country	1950	1960	1970	1980	1990
Brazil	13.0	8.1	19.7	13.8	13.5
Chile	na	na	9.9	11.8	10.3
Hong Kong	na	na	14.8	15.4	8.0
India	11.6	27.8	27.5	12.5	10.4
Indonesia	na	na	8.2	4.8	6.1
Korea	13.6	15.0	17.0	28.3	32.3
Malaysia	na	na	26.8	na	23.9
Mexico	na	na	37.6	39.5	39.7
Singapore	na	na	22.5	18.3	17.9
Taiwan	19.5	23.5	36.1	29.0	25.7
Thailand	25.4	25.7	na	na	48.8
Turkey	na	na	13.2	9.9	18.0
U.K.	27.3	25.0	18.1	16.9	14.2
U.S.	16.4	19.3	9.3	12.5	10.9
Italy	25.9	22.0	17.1	10.3	12.3
Denmark	13.7	16.3	9.2	10.3	10.6
Norway	18.5	17.3	8.8	11.6	10.5
Japan	na	na	20.1	9.5	10.8

Sources: Manufacturing GFCF: United Nations (1963) and UNIDO (various years). Brazil: Brazil (various years [b]). India: Chandhok (1996). Mexico: Mexico (1994). Total GFCF: International Monetary Fund (1995).

Table 6.4. Share of Development Banks in Total Manufacturing Investment, 1970–1990 (%)

Country	1970	1980	1990
Thailand (Board of Investment)	na	na	45.9
Brazil (BNDES)	11.0	18.7	18.1
Turkey (TSKB, Ind. Dev. Bank of Turkey)	6.7	na	na
India (All Development Banks)	7.6	16.8	26.0
Korea (Korea Development Bank)	44.7	10.1	15.3
Mexico (NAFINSA)	35.5	11.4	na

Notes
Brazil: 1970, 1980, and 1992
India: 1969–74 avg., 1979–80, and 1984–85
Korea: 1970, 1980, and 1990
Mexico: 1970 and 1990
Thailand: 1990. Represents % of manufacturing investment accounted for by BOI firms in 1990.
Turkey: Figure for TSKB lending represents 1968–69. This is divided by total manufacturing investment for 1969–70. Matching years were unavailable.

Sources: National development banks.

term working capital expenditures and investment financed by personal savings and retained earnings.

We may conclude, then, that the institution of the state-owned development bank transformed the financial arrangements of the prewar period, when long-term finance for industry came mainly in the form of private joint stock ownership (see chapter 4). The development bank (or its equivalent) accounted for a high proportion of postwar long-term lending to industry and infrastructure in all countries in "the rest" except Argentina. As discussed later, Argentina's development bank imploded as early as the 1940s owing to corruption and mismanagement (Lewis 1990).

Bureaucratic Fiscal Empowerment

Development banks raised capital at home or abroad and then used it either to buy equity in private or public firms or to lend to such firms at below-market interest rates.[15] Thus, in 1969, at the early stage of postwar industrial development, equity participation involved 86.7 percent of the Korea Development Bank's capital outflow (Korea Development Bank, 1969). Likewise, Mexico's development bank in its formative years frequently went into partnership with local companies; it "helped to organize business firms and maintained a significant voice in many of those in which it had equity investment" (Blair 1964, p. 198). Brazil's development bank was active in establishing a stock market. The functions of India's development bank over its life span is indicated by a breakdown of its direct finance (cumulative to March 1993): it made local currency loans (78 percent) and foreign currency loans (10 percent); it engaged in underwriting and made direct subscriptions (7 percent); it sold guarantees[16] for loans and offered facilities for deferred payments (4 percent); it engaged in venture capital, including seed capital assistance (0.5 percent); and it undertook equipment leasing (0.5 percent) (Industrial Development Bank of India, 1992–93).

Lending terms of development banks were almost always concessionary. A typical case was the Industrial Finance Corporation of Thailand: "special rates are provided for government sponsored projects, and are made possible through a concessional refinancing facility provided by the Bank of Thailand" (Skully 1984, p. 327). In addition, Thailand had negative real interest rates for the majority of quarters in the period 1970 to 1982 (Hanson and Neal 1984). Interest rates again turned negative in 1988. Likewise in Taiwan, government-owned banks targeted credit to specific industries and firms at concessionary terms (Shea and Yang 1994; Wade 1990).

The degree of subvention everywhere depended not just on the nominal interest rate on a loan but obviously also on inflation and the foreign exchange rate. In Brazil, rapid inflation in the 1970s led to indexation (of prices to the inflation rate), so if loans were not indexed, interest rates tended to fall below inflation. "Pressure for exemption from indexing came from the industrial sector. The public criticisms against growth of government and multinational enterprises to the detriment of the Brazilian private sector resulted in the reduction of the index burden of loans by the government development bank (BNDE). This amounted, in effect, to massive subsidy through indexation exemption" (Baer 1995, p. 86). Due to inflation and exchange rate overvaluation in South Korea, the real cost of getting a foreign loan with a guarantee from the Korea Development Bank was negative for the entire period 1966 through 1980, during the buildup of Korea's heavy industries (-3.1 percent in 1966–70, -3.0 percent in 1971–75 and -2.7 percent in 1976–80) (Park 1985).

The sources of funding for development banks spanned a wide spectrum. Foreign loans to finance Mexico's development banking rose from zero in 1941 to 57.7 percent of total resources in 1961 (Blair 1964). Brazil financed the BNDES through forced savings by workers, using their provident funds as capital (Monteiro Filha 1995). In 1969 the Korea Development Bank financed its activities by issuing industrial finance debentures (bought mainly by other state banks), inducing foreign capital, and attracting savings deposits (Korea Development Bank 1969). The Malaysian Industrial Development Finance Berhad (MIDF) was initially financed by an interest-free, long-term loan from the central government, which financed its own investments with tax revenues and foreign and domestic borrowing (Malaysia 1989). The Industrial Finance Corporation of Thailand borrowed long-term from the World Bank and other international sources. By 1992–93, the Industrial Development Bank of India was generating 60 percent of its funds internally (Industrial Development Bank of India, 1992–93, p. 124).

The public finance behind "the rest's" development banking (and other dimensions of industrial policy) was often "off-budget" and related to nontax revenues. It derived from foreign sources, deposits in government-owned banks, post office savings accounts, and pension funds (as in Brazil). In East Asia especially, these transactions typically occurred outside the general government budget and parliamentary political process.[17] "Off-budget" items were under the control of the bureaucracy rather than the legislature, even if the legislature was popularly elected. This greatly strengthened the hand of professional bureaucrats in the ministries responsible for planning, finance, and industry.

This so-called fiscalization of finance entailed different accounting systems across countries, making comparisons of fiscal rectitude difficult to measure. The system of the International Monetary Fund (IMF) was uniform, but it included only transactions involving wholly owned government funds (International Monetary Fund 1986). In "the rest," however, it was the grey area of public-cum-private money, and jointly owned or controlled private and public financial resources, that created the arena for industrial policy. International Monetary Fund accounts, therefore, tended to understate the extent of a country's expenditures on these policies.[18]

This is evident from an examination of the budgets of Japan and Korea (see tables 6.5 and 6.6).[19] When their "second budget" is fully accounted for, their public spending is substantially greater than what their IMF budget suggests. According to IMF data, the spending of Japan's central government as a share of GDP ranged from between 15 percent and 20 percent in the 1970s and 1980s. When a broader definition of central government, plus

Table 6.5. Japan's Government Spending and Deficit/Surplus as a Percentage of GDP[1]

Years	General Government (A)	Fiscal Invest. Loan Prog. (B)	Total: (A) + (B)	IMF[2]	Central Government
Spending					
1956–60	28.90	3.67	32.32	na	21.75
1961–65	26.53	4.59	30.90	na	19.20
1966–70	26.20	5.13	31.20	na	18.85
1971–75	29.43	6.48	35.84	13.07	19.92
1976–80	38.25	6.98	45.21	16.97	27.04
1981–85	41.86	7.00	48.85	18.11	30.36
1986–90	39.34	7.63	46.95	16.48	27.91
1991–93	40.41	9.74	50.13	22.04	27.45
Deficit/Surplus					
1956–60	−0.77	−0.58	na	na	−0.09
1961–65	−0.91	−0.91	na	na	−0.22
1966–70	−2.08	−1.06	na	na	−1.25
1971–75	−3.97	−0.48	na	−1.71	−2.32
1976–80	−8.37	−0.60	na	−6.64	−6.14
1981–85	−6.63	−0.88	na	−5.99	−4.88
1986–90	−4.07	−0.59	na	−3.02	−2.53
1991–93	−5.40	−0.43	na	0.15	−3.20

1. General government equals central government plus local government minus duplication between general account of central government and local government. Central government equals general account of central government plus special account of central government minus duplication between both accounts. "Total" equals central government plus Fiscal Investment Loan Program (FILP) minus FILP funding through the Industrial Investment Special Account. Deficit/surplus of FILP equals FILP funding through government guaranteed bonds and government guaranteed borrowings. Deficit/Surplus of central government equals net increase in the central government debt outstanding except short term (financing) bills.
2. International Monetary Fund, *Government Finance Statistics*. After 1991 there was a change in classification. Other data from the Japanese Ministry of Finance and Statistics Bureau.

Sources: World Bank (1994b); Ministry of Finance, Japan (1995); Ministry of Finance, Japan (1978); Ministry of Finance, Japan (various); Ministry of Finance, Japan (1975); Statistics Bureau, Japan (1996) and Suzuki (1987).

Table 6.6. Korea's Government Spending and Deficit/Surplus as Percentage of GDP[1]

Years	General Government (A)	Policy Loans (B)	Total (approx.): (A) + (B)	IMF[2]	Central Government
Spending					
1962–65	18.62	10.62	29.24	na	16.16
1966–70	22.09	10.97	33.05	na	19.08
1971–75	18.52	18.47	36.98	15.98	18.20
1976–80	22.24	20.08	42.33	18.66	19.16
1981–85	23.77	28.97	52.74	19.61	18.67
1986–90	20.99	25.08	46.06	16.86	17.08
1991–92	24.59	26.42	51.00	18.70	19.28
Deficit/Surplus					
1962–65	−9.80	−0.88	na	na	−0.66
1966–70	−8.82	−1.89	na	na	−4.12
1971–75	−1.56	−6.64	na	−1.85	−2.55
1976–80	−1.56	−6.22	na	−1.70	−0.04
1981–85	−2.06	−10.34	na	−2.01	−0.29
1986–90	1.02	−10.39	na	0.29	1.07
1991–92	−0.50	−10.85	na	−1.07	−0.55

1. General government equals central government plus local government minus duplication where possible. Policy loans are defined as policy loans through deposit money banks plus total loans from Korea Development Bank and Export-Import Bank of Korea. "Total" equals general government plus policy loans minus duplication where possible. Deficit/Surplus of policy loans equals borrowing from Bank of Korea in deposit money banks plus government guaranteed bonds of Korean Development Bank and Export-Import Bank of Korea.
2. International Monetary Fund, *Government Finance Statistics.*

Sources: Bank of Korea (1993), (1995a), and (1995b); Bahl, et al. (1986); Cho and Kim (1995); Lee (1994) and Won (1995).

local government, plus "off budget" Fiscal Investment and Loans (FILS) is included, government's share rises to between 35 percent and over 45 percent of GDP.[20] In Korea's case, too, off-budget policy loans nearly doubled the share of government spending in GDP. Such loans substantially increased the deficit/GDP ratio as well, from only 1 percent to over 11 percent. All countries in Asia (including China) whose fiscal accounting system was influenced by Japan tended to spend more than suggested by IMF reckoning.

Governments in "the rest" also controlled nontax related sources of funding, such as foreign borrowing (through loan "guarantees"), ownership of financial institutions, and the disposal of private savings. Development banking and foreign borrowing abroad were thus closely related, however indirectly. The major weakness of development banks, therefore, was not to spend on the wrong industries but to spend *too much overall* (see chapter 9).

Picking Winners

Broad-ranging investment criteria guided the industries to which development banks allocated their capital, reflecting the fact that initially development bank lending was targeted to a wide range of industries; a shotgun rather than rifle approach prevailed to kick-start industrialization (see the case of Thailand in chapter 1). Possibly the only obvious investment criterion that did *not* figure explicitly in credit allocation was 'comparative advantage'— industries with static comparative advantage already tended to exist while industries with *dynamic* comparative advantage could not be identified as such *ex ante*. Whatever the criteria or country, in Latin America or Asia, import substitution was the dominant form of investment, as inferred from the specific industries that received the largest share of credit. But development banks also funded export activity per se, the ease with which exports were extracted from import substitution industries depending on performance standards and the export-promotion infrastructure in which such standards were embedded (see chapter 7).

The criteria for Brazil's development banking emerged out of historical circumstance: "The second administration of President Getulio Vargas, begun in 1950, inherited from the previous administration a nation anxious for change. The favorable balance of trade was being weakened by the importation of heavy industrial products and equipment, the rise in post-war consumption and international fuel prices. Given such a dilemma, the nationalistic middle class emphatically called for funds for development of basic industries" (Banco Nacional de Desenvolvimento Economico e Social [BNDES] 1992, p. 9). None of this precluded the goal of raising exports: "Between 1958 and 1967, fully one half of BNDES's funds went to steel making, transforming Brazil, at the first stage, into a self-sufficient steel producer and, later, into a major exporter of steel products." Moreover, the policies of the BNDES changed over time: "Beginning in 1974, with the oil crisis that suddenly hit Brazil's balance of payments hard, the government decided to intensify its import substitution program, as set out in the second National Development Plan." BNDES began to finance "principally two major sectors: capital goods and basic raw materials, consisting of minerals and ores, steel and non-ferrous metal products, chemical and petrochemical products, fertilizers, cement, pulpwood and paper" (Banco Nacional de Desenvolvimento Economico e Social [BNDES] 1992, pp. 18–19).

Taiwan's heavy industries were targeted as early as 1961–64, during the Third Plan: "Heavy industry holds the key to industrialization as it produces capital goods. We must develop heavy industry so as to support the long-term steady growth of the economy" (Ministry of Economic Affairs, as cited by Wade 1990, p. 87). At the same time, exportables such as watches and other electronic products were promoted. After most heavy industries were, in fact, developed (steel, shipbuilding, petrochemicals, machinery), and the second energy crisis occurred (1979), goals changed. In 1982, the Taiwan government began to promote "strategic industries" (machinery, automobile parts, electrical machinery, and information technology) based on six criteria: large linkage effects; high market potential; high technology intensity; high value-added; low energy intensity; and low pollution (Shea and Yang 1994).

Selection of promoted industries in Thailand, as stated in the 1950s, also had multiple criteria. First, they had to save a lot of foreign exchange. Second, they had to have strong linkages to other industries. Third, they had to utilize domestic raw materials. Yet another reason for promotion, according to the Ministry of Industry, was to gain technological knowledge: "Hopefully, the industries to be promoted such as automobiles, chemicals, shipbuilding, and so forth will transfer technological knowledge from developed countries" (Patcharee 1985).[21]

India's development plans listed objectives that were broader and more political than those of other countries: (1) a faster expansion of basic industry than light industry, small firms than large firms, and the public sector than the private sector, (2) protection and promotion of small industries, (3) reduction in disparities in regional location of industry, and (4) prevention of economic power in private hands (Sandesara 1992).

According to Turkey's Second Five-Year Plan (1968–72), it was important to promote manufacturing because it was the sector that would "pull" the economy ahead in the future. Industry priorities were chemicals, commercial fertilizers, iron, steel and metallurgy, paper, petroleum, cement, and vehicle tires. "Intensified investments in these sectors will create to a large extent import substitution effects and lay the necessary foundations for industrialization in the long-run" (Türkiye Is Bankasi A.S. 1967, p. 45). At the same time, Turkey's Plan set targets for a large increase in exports, and the textile industry was heavily promoted.

In the case of Mexico's development bank, the principles that guided it in the early 1960s were to assist those industrial enterprises whose production could improve the balance of payments, achieve a better industrial integration, induce savings, or increase the level of employment. By the late 1980s, after a debt crisis, the principles were to "promote the restructuring, modernization and financial rehabilitation of companies as a way of achieving better efficiency and production, which is necessary in order to increase exports and substitute for imports permanently, thereby reaching a level of international competitiveness" (Nacional Financiera, S.A various years).

According to the 1969 *Annual Report* of the Korea Development Bank (KDB), top priority in lending was given to export industries and industries designated in a Bank Act that "improved the industrial structure and balance of payments." These included "import substitute industries." Import substitution and export promotion were not seen as antagonistic; both involved large, long-term capital investments. By 1979, the end of Korea's heavy industry drive, the following factors were emphasized in financial commitments: the economic benefits to the nation; the technical and financial feasibility of a project; its profitability; and the quality of an applicant's management (Korea Development Bank 1979).

The "hot" industries of development banking—industries that received the largest and second largest shares of credit in various decades—are shown in table 6.7. Basic metals (mostly iron and steel), chemicals (primarily petrochemicals), machinery (electrical and nonelectrical), transportation equipment (ships, automobiles, and automobile parts), and textiles are the most important borrowers.[22] These industries are broadly defined and comprise a variety of products. While the subbranches of such industries varied across countries, all of "the rest" (data exist for seven countries) targeted more or less the same basic industries for postwar growth.

Because light industries consumed less capital per project than heavy industries, they received a relatively small share of total bank lending, although a large number of projects tended to gain support. In South Korea, textiles (including clothing and footwear) was one of the most heavily subsidized sectors in the 1960s.[23] By 1974–79, however, textiles accounted for only 6.4 percent of the Korea Development Bank's new loans and manufacturing investments, supplanted by basic manufactures (Korea Development Bank various years). In 1950–62, textiles accounted for 21.1 percent of the new loan approvals of the Industrial Development Bank of Turkey. By 1990, the emphasis of the bank had shifted to clothing, which received 19 percent of new loan approvals (Bankasi, T. S. K. various years). The Development Bank of India allocated the textile industry on average 13.5 percent of its yearly support between 1949 and 1995; even in 1994–95 textiles accounted for as much as 14.1 percent of total loan value (Industrial Development Bank of India, various years).

Insofar as most of the "hot industries" targeted by development banks for support turned out to be relatively successful (discussed later), industry-level targeting *in the context of late industrialization* turned out to be a relatively straightforward task. For one, while targeted industries faced market uncertainty, they did not face the technological unknown, which complicated the targeting of science-based industries in advanced countries. For another, even market uncertainty was reduced by the historical road maps provided by already industrialized countries. Instead of presenting insuperable problems of choice, targeting facilitated the identification of potentially profitable investment industries which, in fact, *had* been an insuperable problem before the war, as discussed in earlier chapters.

Table 6.7. Hot Industries, Selected Country by Decade

Country	Decade[1]				
	1950s	1960s	1970s	1980s	1990s
Brazil (BNDES)	chemicals, basic metals & prod.	basic metals & prod., basic metals & prod.	basic metals & prod., chemicals	basic metals & prod., chemicals	pulp & paper, chemicals
India (AIFIs), 1949	food products, textiles	chemicals, textiles	chemicals, machinery	chemicals, textiles	chemicals, basic metals & prod.
Indonesia (CICB), 1952	na	na	chemicals, textiles	chemicals, textiles	chemicals, textiles
Korea (KDB)	na	textiles[3], ceramics	machinery, basic metals & prod.	machinery, basic metals & prod.	chemicals, basic metals & prod.
Malaysia (MIDF)	chemicals[2]	basic metals & prod., wood & wood prod.	food products, textiles	basic metals & prod., food products	basic metals & prod., non-met. min. prod.
Mexico (NAFINSA)	basic metals & prod., food products	transportation equip., basic metals & prod.	transportation equip., basic metals & prod.	basic metals & prod., machinery	basic metals & prod., machinery
Turkey (TSKB)	textiles, food products	ceramics, textiles	transportation equip., textiles	transportation equip., textiles	na

1. The two main manufacturing industries for each decade receiving the largest share of credit (largest listed first). Industry definitions vary by country.
2. This is the only category (besides "other") listed for these years by the source cited.
3. 1969 only

Chemicals: This category may include petrochemicals, chemical products, and fertilisers. For Korea in the 1990s, "chemicals" also includes rubber, plastic, and petroleum products.
Basic metals and products: Sometimes this category is broadly defined and includes "metallurgy" or "metalworking." More often, it is more narrowly defined and includes only "steel" or "iron and steel."
Textiles: Sometimes this category includes "clothing and apparel."
Machinery: This category may or may not include electrical machinery.
Transportation equipment: Sometimes this category is listed as "transportation vehicles." It is always listed separately from "transportation," which generally includes infrastructure projects.
Ceramics: This category may also include stoneware, glassware, and ceramic products.
Wood and wood products: This category is broadly defined to include all lumber and wood products.
Non-metallic mineral prod: This category includes all non-metallic mineral products.

Sources: Bank Indonesia (1996); Industrial Development Bank of India (various years); TSKB (various years); Banco Nacional de Desenvolvimento Economico e Social (various years); Korea Development Bank (various years); Bank Negara Malaysia (various years).

Sources of Efficiency

Development banks influenced the efficiency of their clients by subjecting them to *performance standards* related to firm-level management practices (*techno-standards*) and national policy goals (*policy standards*). Among other goals, policy standards included (1) exporting; (2) localizing the production of parts and components (typically in the automobile and electronics industries); (3) pricing; (4) building (not building) "national leaders" by concentrating (diffusing) resources in a few (many) firms; and (5) strengthening technological capabilities. Reciprocal-type discipline was necessary because, given a small endowment of skills and a large supply of "intermediate assets," conventional forms of competition were either *too weak or too strong* to induce good performance.

Latecomer Forms of Competition

Development banks tried to improve their clients' performance through means other than conventional competition. In theory and practice, the nature of competition varied historically. The competition of the First Industrial Revolution was defined by perfectly competitive markets and free trade. By the Second Industrial Revolution, the nature of competition had shifted to rivalry among capital-intensive, oligopolistic firms. By the last quarter of the twentieth century, its locus had switched from product to capital markets, the latter putting publicly traded firms on their best behavior with threats of hostile takeover [Hikino, 1997].

These forms of competition may have made the North Atlantic rich, but they were fundamentally dysfunctional in "the rest" for most of the half century after World War II. If the free-market form of competition was unleashed too early, it stunted an industry's growth, as prewar history amply demonstrated (see chapters 2–5). Exporting was possibly the best disciplinarian, but it took time to materialize in "the rest's" new industries (see chapter 7). If competition awaited either "gales of creative destruction" or hostile takeovers, the wait would be endless. Before 2000, "the rest's" monopolies were not threatened by innovation at the world technological frontier, which was too distant, and its capital markets were both immature and nearly irrelevant in disciplining the dominant forms of big business operating locally—family-owned firms, state-owned enterprises and the affiliates of multinational companies, none of whose equity was publicly traded on local stock markets.[24]

The lack of conventional categories to describe the type of discipline to which "the rest's" leading enterprises *were* subject is indicated by the tortuous explanation given for the success of Korea's automobile industry by the first president of Korea's most prestigious economic think-tank, the Korea Development Institute: "It is true that the success of the Korean automobile industry was achieved by private initiatives. But it is also true that the success could hardly be attributed to market competition per se. Korean automobiles faced severe competition in the export frontiers. However, it was not market competition that simulated the industry to grow strong enough to venture into the world market. I am not arguing that market competition was useless. Rather, *I would like to point out that the environment was provided in which the private sectors' creativity and responsibility could be maximized*" (Kim 1997, pp. 39–40).

The environment to which Mahn-Je Kim refers is that of the reciprocal control mechanism, with its conditionalities and performance standards. The Korean automobile industry did not export for roughly twenty years after it first began to assemble trucks and cars. But the obligation to export ultimately was built into its capacity designs and attempts to develop a network of local parts and components manufacturers. The immediate negative effects of duopoly were kept in check by threats of new entry (which began in the 1980s) and price surveillance.

It is to performance standards, first techno-standards in the case of Brazil, that attention is now turned.

Techno-Standards: The Brazilian Miracle

The techno-standards of Brazil's development bank, BNDES, were stipulated in clients' contracts. The contracts discussed below cover the following sample:[25]

Machinery	23 companies, 116 contracts, 1973–89;
Petrochemical	28 companies, 30 contracts, 1969–91;
Pulp and paper	9 companies, 56 contracts, 1970–90;
Steel	15 companies, 117 contracts, 1969–89.

Techno-standards are classified according to finance, administration, environment, raw materials, national equipment, technology, and miscellaneous.

Finance-related standards tended to be the same across companies and sectors. BNDES's clients were required to reach a certain debt/equity ratio and liquidity ratio. The debt/equity ratio was based on American banking standards, possibly because the United States had been an early lender to BNDES, and was low by East Asian standards—*typically debt could not exceed 60 percent of total assets*. Hence, "large" Brazilian companies tended to be small by East Asian standards (see chapter 8). Clients were also prohibited from distributing their profits to stockholders of a controlling company. Companies were not allowed to make new investments of their own or change their fixed capital without BNDES approval. In the case of a company that required financial restructuring, it was forced by BNDES to divest itself of nonproduction related assets.

The raw material requirement also tended to be similar across industries and firms. In the case of pulp and paper producers, BNDES made it mandatory for them to have a guaranteed source of local raw materials to minimize the need to import. They were also ordered to reforest a certain number of acres within a specified time period. In the iron and steel sector, a repeated contractual requirement was that clients had to provide the bank with details about reforestation projects as well as figures on sales over time of pig iron in the domestic and foreign markets. If the bank did not accept a company's pig iron selling patterns, the company was obliged to renegotiate a contract with the bank. There were also instructions about meeting vegetable carbon pollution standards.

Loan conditions concerning administration, national equipment, technology, and other subjects tended to be firm-specific. The conditions were often detailed, intrusive, and formulated in such a way that *a client had to comply before it received a loan.* Among the bank's primary concerns were that firms be managed efficiently; that family-owned firms hire professionals in top administrative positions who were independent and not family retainers; that ownership of a firm not change during a loan period; that companies develop their own technology; and that firms source their engineers and machinery locally, whenever possible.

Pulp and paper

1. A leading pulp and paper manufacturer with eighteen contracts with BNDES, 1970s:

   • With respect to technology, the company must prove that it has hired a Brazilian engineering company to do the detailed design for an expansion; BNDES has to approve the company's general plans to establish an R&D Department; the company must have its technology contracts registered with the appropriate Brazilian organization, INPI (which scrutinized technology contracts to insure that Brazilian companies were not overpaying for foreign technology). The company has to hire two consultants (one Swedish, one Finnish) and these consultants have to approve the company's choice of technology. BNDES has to approve the company's contracts with the consultants.
   • The company must make its best efforts to buy national equipment (although in this case BNDES made no specific requirement).
   • The company must build a harbor in the (backward) region in which it is planning to locate (more clauses follow on the nature of the harbor).
   • The company must provide workers with social services (health, education, cafeteria) given the absence of services in the region.

2. Another large pulp and paper manufacturer (1987)

- Present plans for investing in R&D with detailed discussion of projected costs for seven years. Prove to BNDES at the end of each year that company applied the plan.

3. A third large pulp and paper manufacturer (1979)

- BNDES asked the company to commit to buying 63 percent of its equipment locally.
- The company had to follow an environmental standard and dispose of the ash from its coal-burning in a specified way. The company had to show BNDES the plan of its board of directors for the handling and disposal of certain toxic acids it was using to avoid accidents.

Capital goods

1. A leading capital goods manufacturer (1983 and 1986: two loans for financial strengthening).

- (1983) In 60 days the company had to present an administrative program for the reduction of operating costs. In 120 days it had to present a plan for divesting itself of one operating unit.
- (1986) The company had to show BNDES a plan for relocation of certain production capacity, improvement of productivity, and strengthening of financial variables. As part of the reorganization program, the company had to hire a controller and implement an information system that was modern and that widened the scope of data processing. The company also had to modernize its cost system and improve its planning and control of production (within so many days). In 240 days the company had to present a strategic plan for long-run objectives. It also had to hire a vice-president for general administration who would sit on the board of directors. The company had to convince BNDES that this person had adequate qualifications and that the duties of the job were clearly specified.

2. A leading capital goods manufacturer (1975)

- To qualify for a loan to expand production capacity, the company had to show BNDES detailed investment plans for a three-year minimum.

3. A capital goods manufacturer (1979)

- To qualify for a loan for capacity expansion, the company had to show BNDES in 30 days that it had hired a consultant to analyze the company's administration. In 120 days, the company had to present BNDES the consultant's report. In 180 days, the company had to demonstrate to BNDES that its detailed reorganization plan was based on the consultant's recommendation.

4. A capital goods manufacturer (1975)

 • To qualify for a loan for capacity expansion, the company had to use
   equipment with a nationalization index of 60 percent or more.

5. A capital goods manufacturer (1975)

 • As part of a loan for modernization, the company had to restructure
   its financial department so that there would be more executive control
   over loans and accounts receivable. The company was also required to
   hire a financial director.

Iron and Steel

1. A leading state-owned iron and steel manufacturer with thirty-three
   contracts with BNDES, (1960s–80s)

 • As part of a loan for expansion, the company had to modernize its
   management system, including a revision of its marketing and distribution function for domestic and foreign sales. Its cost system had to
   be up-graded with a view toward reducing its number of personnel as
   well as inventory, according to prespecified benchmarks. The other aspects of management that had to be reformed concerned maintenance,
   technology, and data processing, with the bank providing details concerning the problems that restructuring had to address.
 • When the company bought a new system of equipment with machinery from multiple sources, it had to make sure that a single supplier
   accepted responsibility for the installation and operation of that equipment.

2. A small steel manufacturer with four contracts with BNDES (1970s–
   1980s)

 • The company had to hire a professional technical expert in a top management position, and the name of the expert had to be approved by
   BNDES before the person could be hired.
 • The company had to present plans for training people with the objective of absorbing foreign technology and then diffusing this know-how
   within the organization, to other personnel.

3. A steel manufacturer with eight contracts with BNDES (1970s)

 • The company had to introduce a new management information system
   to insure that it had adequate written reports for each level of administration, with different information contained in financial and output
   reporting.
 • The company had to present to BNDES a program for technology development with special emphasis on how the company proposed to
   develop new products and become independent of third-party technical
   assistance.

4. A state-owned steel manufacturer with ten contracts with BNDES (1970s)

- The company had to receive technical assistance from BNDES' other state-owned steel mill in order to improve its own cost accounting system (there follows several conditions to achieve this).
- The company must present a detailed technology development plan, indicating how it is going to develop basic engineering skills in the company.

Monitoring

As development banks imposed techno-standards on their clients, they themselves tightened their own monitoring skills and procedures. Monitoring was increasingly built into lending arrangements such that compliance at one stage was made contingent on further loan disbursement.

Regarding the Korea Development Bank, in 1970 it "strengthened review of loan proposals and thoroughly checked up on overdue loans to prevent capital from being tied up. Business analyses and managerial assistance to clients were conducted on a broader scale." For clients financed with foreign capital and, therefore, enjoying a sovereign guarantee from the KDB, "appropriate measures were worked out to strengthen KDB's administration of them. The Bank called for the submission of sales and financial plans by such enterprises. According to these plans, clients were required to deposit the equivalent sum in advance of the date on which repayments were due, either in the form of savings deposits or purchase of Industrial Finance Debentures. The Bank charged an extra 20 percent over the regular guarantee fee to those who failed to fulfill the requirement." In 1979 the KDB introduced a new procedure to tighten control over lending. "In order to ensure that loan funds are utilized according to their prescribed purpose, disbursements of loan proceeds are not made immediately upon commitment. Instead, loan funds are transferred into a Credit Control Account in the name of the borrower and the money may be withdrawn only for actual expenditures. The Bank is therefore able to monitor closely the progress of each project." For most of its history the KDB also maintained a ceiling ratio of loan commitment which, *in principle*, was set at 65 percent of total project cost. The idea of sharing the costs of a project with a client was designed to make the client more performance-conscious (Korea Development Bank, 1969, 1970, 1971, 1979).[26]

Development banks in "the rest" undertook careful appraisals of prospective clients, examining their managerial and financial status, past performance, and the merits of their proposed project. In India, "Appraisal Notes" included conditionalities. For every loan, the Industrial Development Bank of India (IDBI) insisted on the right to nominate a director to a company's board. This practice was comparable to that of the big German banks, but the purpose of the IDBI was not to gain control of its clients' strategic decisions. Rather, it was to gain information about them with a view toward exerting discipline over their operations. Other conditionalities in "Appraisal Notes" varied by loan. For example, in a loan to a large steel pipe manufacturer that represented 10 percent of IDBI's net worth, a condition of lending was that the firm form a Project Management Committee to the satisfaction of IDBI for the purpose of supervising and monitoring the progress of the project's implementation. Thailand's Board of Investment appraised and monitored clients thoroughly, and if a company failed to meet BOI terms (stipulated in a promotion certificate), its certificate was withdrawn (see chapter 1). Between January and December 1988, 748 firms received certificates for new projects, of which 37 certificates were withdrawn. In the case of Thai firms, 24 out of 312 certificates, or 8 percent, were withdrawn (see table 6.8).

Where the capabilities of borrowers—*and lenders*—were poor, the quality of development banking also suffered (as it tended to do in "the remainder"). In the case of Malaysia's development banks, which were designed to lend to local Malays in order to raise their relatively backward economic position vis-à-vis Malaysian Chinese entrepreneurs, operations were hampered by "the poor performance of many debtors." A failure rate on loans of about 30 percent was reported due in part to a shortage of viable projects. But even viable projects did not properly prepare their business proposals (Salleh and Meyananthan 1997). The exception that proves the rule was the Bank Industri, which "has a thorough research team on which it relies heavily. It has adopted a target market approach, and the research staff plays the key role in identifying and evaluating new areas of the economy for the bank to

Table 6.8. Thailand's Promotional Process

| | End of 1987 | January–December 1988 | |
		Certificate Issued	Certificate Withdrawn
Total no. of projects	2463	912	40
Total no. of firms	1992	748	37
Thai firms	1010	312	24
Foreign firms	72	91	1
Joint venture firms	910	345	12
Total regist. cap (mil US$)	51547.46	29574.23	1017.48
Thai (mil US$)	35484.44	14629.28	862.21
Foreign (mil US$)	16063.03	14944.95	155.28
Total investment (mil US$)	255625.16	87017.58	2665.50

Source: Board of Investment

penetrate. The researchers undertake very detailed industry studies, looking at all aspects of a potential project in order to gain familiarity with its strengths and weaknesses." Once a project has been approved, the Bank Industri "insists on being an active partner. It stays jointly involved in the financial management with its partner, often operating joint bank accounts with its clients, which requires the bank to countersign all checks for payment of expenses. Bank Industri is vigilant in monitoring the progress of its clients, frequently visiting business sites, and is quick to provide financial management advice" (Asian Development Bank 1990) (as cited in Salleh and Meyananthan 1997).[27]

In sum, the efficiency of development banking depended on discipline and performance standards, and the monitoring of techno-performance standards depended on bureaucratic capabilities. The extent of bureaucratic capabilities may be said to have varied with the degree to which a country was industrialized; the greater industrial experience, the greater capabilities on the part of both lender and borrower.

Generally, development banks were successful in creating a managerial culture in their clients because they themselves were managerial, often representing the most elite bureaucracy of the early postwar years.

In the case of Mexico's development bank, NAFINSA, its *técnicos* became "a respected voice in the councils of government. . . . Its influence has been diffused throughout the Mexican economy. Over the years (it was founded in 1934) the institution has been the training ground for numbers of bright and active men [sic] whose technical and political expertise has moved them into important government positions" (Blair 1964, p. 199).[28] With respect to the BNDES of Brazil, it had "a strong sense of institutional mission, a respected 'administrative ideology' and a cohesive *esprit de corps*" (Willis 1990, p. 17). According to two executives of Dow Chemicals Latin America, interviewed three years before the Pinochet military coup, the National Development Corporation in Chile (CORFO) excelled for its "organization and thoroughness of planning, . . . which sets Chile apart from some of the other countries that have engaged in similar activities. . . . The management of key Chilean Government agencies . . . are outstanding professionals who do not automatically change with each succeeding political regime" (Oreffice and Baker 1970, pp. 122 and 126).

Argentina was the exception. Its Banco Industrial and related institutions, such as a state trading company (Argentine Institute for Production and Trade, IAPI), were run by a crook, Miguel Miranda. "Not only was Miguel Miranda coming under attack for his mishandling of the economy, but his use of the IAPI to enrich himself was becoming scandalous. The army had removed all of its military purchases from IAPI's jurisdiction after it learned that Miranda got a $2 million kickback from a company that was awarded a contract to build a steel mill for Fabricaciones Militares. It turned out that the company in question was not even the lowest bidder" (Lewis 1990, p. 195).) An air force company producing engines and vehicles tried to become "a substitute for the Industrial Bank in promoting new enterprises," but with very limited results (Lewis 1990, p. 268). In general, Peronist political machinery "crowded out" fresh developmental machinery (see Sourrouille 1967; Diaz Alejandro 1971; and Mallon and Sourrouille 1975, for the absence of developmental machinery). Argentina thus failed to invest in mid-technology industries (and later in high-technology industries): "If industries such as steel, oil extraction, petrochemicals, and so on had received priority over light consumer goods industries producing for the domestic market," then Argentina might have become a leading exporter of advanced manufactures (Diaz Alejandro 1967, p. 23, as cited by Lewis 1990, p. 185).

Policy Standards

Performance standards with respect to policy goals were specified at the highest political levels; bureaucrats only implemented them and development banks may or may not have been the primary executor. Implementation, however, was an art, and bureaucracies exercised substantial power over the substance and impact of some policy goals. Export expansion, local-content, and price stability were three major policy goals that were coupled with performance standards in the postwar years (policy goals with respect to firm and skill formation are discussed in later chapters).

Exports

The intermediate assets that developmental states tied to export-oriented performance standards typically went beyond merely "creating a level playing field" (equalizing profitability between selling at home or abroad).[29] Firms that committed themselves to exporting were not only given access to working capital, tax breaks and duty drawbacks on imports, the typical package of *measured* export incentives. Besides these corrections for so-called market imperfections, they were also given something much more valuable: privileged access to *long-term subsidized capital*. Long-term capital subsidies, however, are excluded from estimates of export promotion.[30] This omission derives from the fact that long-term investment credits cannot be uniquely allocated to either export activity or import substitution—a firm can use its capital to produce for both domestic and foreign markets simultaneously. Because long-term loans cannot be uniquely allocated, they are simply ignored as a form of export incentive. Nevertheless, this omission seriously underestimates the role of performance standards in export activity. Even if subsidized capital is also used by a firm to produce for domestic consumers, the fact that exporting at some agreed-upon date is made a long-run condition for receiving subsidized investment capital makes the reciprocal control mechanism a more important institution in export planning and promotion than measured indices of export promotion suggest.

The most general export-oriented performance standard after World War II operated in the context of export processing zones, or free trade enclaves that enabled participating firms to acquire their imported inputs duty free in exchange for an obligation to export *all* their output (see chapter 1). Such enclaves may have created few backward linkages or technological spillovers, but they created employment, which was of critical sociopolitical and economic importance in densely populated countries with unlimited labor supplies after World War II.[31] Rising employment, in turn, helped to create a much-needed domestic market for other manufactures. Rising wages from fuller employment also provided a long-run incentive to invest in R&D (see chapter 8). Thus, considering both direct and indirect effects, the performance standard that defined such zones—duty-free imports in exchange for *100 percent* exports—may have impacted positively on a wide range of domestic manufactures. Export processing zones spread quickly from Korea and Taiwan to Malaysia, Indonesia, Thailand, and China.[32]

South Korea, with the highest growth rate of exports in "the rest" (see table 6.9), induced firms to become more export-oriented by making their subsidies contingent on achieving export targets, which were negotiated jointly by business and government and aired at high-level monthly meetings. These meetings were attended regularly by Korea's president, Park Chung Hee, and were designed to enable bureaucrats to learn and lessen the problems that prevented business from exporting more, information that was likely to have contributed further to export activity (Rhee et al. 1984). Reciprocity involved long-term lending by the Korea Development Bank. Starting in 1971, at the commencement of Korea's heavy industrialization drive, the KDB began to offer credit "to export enterprises recommended by the Ministry of Commerce and Industry" (Korea Development Bank 1971). The more a company exported, the more likely it was to receive cheap, long-term loans (as well as tariff protection for its sales in the domestic market). After 1975 the government made a lucrative license to form a general trading company contingent on big businesses reaching a certain level and diversity of exports. These qualifications unleashed fierce competition among Korea's big business groups at a time when the emergence of heavy industries was dampening competition at the industry level (Amsden 1997a). If a targeted firm in Korea proved itself to be a poor performer, it ceased being subsidized—as evidenced by the high turnover among Korea's top ten companies between 1965–85 (Kim 1993).[33]

The reciprocity principle in Korea operated in almost every industry. In electronics, for example, "the question could be asked why the chaebol-

Table 6.9. Total Exports: Growth Rate and Structure, Selected Countries, 1970–1995

Country	Annual Avg. Export Growth Rate, 1950–95	Main categories of exports (Total = 100%)		
		Manufactures	Chemicals	Machinery
Korea	26.3			
1970		76.5	1.4	7.2
1995		93.3	7.3	51.6
Taiwan	20.3			
1970		75.8	2.4	16.7
1995		92.7	6.5	47.7
Thailand	12.9			
1970		4.7	0.2	0.1
1995		73.1	3.8	31.5
China	11.8			
1970*		41.8	4.6	1.5
1995		84.0	6.1	19.5
Mexico	12.8			
1970		32.5	8.1	10.6
1995		77.7	4.9	51.4
Indonesia	11.5			
1970		1.2	0.5	0.3
1995		50.6	3.3	6.8
Turkey	11.4			
1970		8.9	1.6	0.4
1995		74.4	4.1	11.0
Malaysia	11.0			
1970		6.5	0.7	1.6
1995		3.0	50.0	
Brazil	10.2			
1970		13.2	1.6	3.5
1995		53.5	6.7	19.1
Chile	8.9			
1970		4.3	1.3	0.8
1995		13.5	3.5	1.8
India	7.9			
1970		51.7	3.3	4.7
1995		76.2	8.5	7.1
Argentina	7.5			
1970		13.9	3.1	3.8
1995		33.9	6.3	10.8
Japan	15.8			
1970		92.5	6.4	40.5
1995		95.2	6.6	67.3
Italy	13.3			
1970		82.9	6.9	36.8
1995		89.2	7.6	37.5
U.S.	10.0			
1970		66.7	9	42
1995		77.3	11.2	47.9
U.K.	9.2			
1970		80.1	9.7	40.9
1995		81.6	13.6	42.7

Note: Nominal U.S. dollars.
* Data are for 1975.

Source: Adapted from UNCTAD (1993).

affiliated enterprises did not confine their business to the domestic market where they could make large profits without difficulty. The primary reason was that the government did not permit it. An important Korean industrial policy for electronics was protecting the domestic market. In return for protection of the domestic market, the government required the enterprises to export a part of their production" (Sato 1997, p. 413).

Taiwan, with the second highest growth rate of exports (see table 6.9) also tied subsidies to exporting. In the case of the cotton textile, steel products, pulp and paper, rubber products, cement, and woolen textile industries, all formed industry associations and agreements to restrict domestic competition and subsidize exports (Wade 1990). Permission to sell in Taiwan's highly protected domestic market was made conditional on a certain share of production being sold overseas (Chu 1997; Lin 1973). In the "strategic Promotion Period" of Taiwan's automobile industry, 1977–84, the Ministry of Economic Affairs required new entrants into the industry to export at least 50 percent of their output (Wang 1989).

Other countries in "the rest" also connected subsidies with exporting, only in different ways and with different degrees of success (see chapter 7). Thailand's Board of Investment changed its policy toward the textile industry after the first energy crisis in 1973. Overnight it required textile firms (whether foreign, local, or joint venture) to export at least half their output to quality for continued BOI support (see chapter 1).

In Indonesia, "counter-purchase regulations" stipulated that foreign companies that were awarded government contracts, and that imported their intermediate inputs and capital goods, had to export Indonesian products to nontraditional markets of equal value to the imports they brought into Indonesia. In the case of timber, concessionaires were required to export processed wood rather than raw timber; in the mid-1980s plywood accounted for about one-half of Indonesia's manufactured exports (Poot et al. 1990). Moreover, joint venture banks and branches of foreign banks were required to allocate at least 50 percent of their total loans, and 80 percent of their offshore funds, to export activity (Cole and Slade 1996).

Turkey tried to promote exports starting in the 1960s, making them a condition for capacity expansion by foreign firms. In the case of a joint venture between a Turkish development bank, Sümerbank, and a German multinational, Mannesmann, "both the Turkish and German managing directors were of the opinion that the Turkish Government was constantly willing to help the company in its operations." Nevertheless, one point irritated foreign investors. Any capital increase required the consent of the Turkish government. It also became a policy of the Turkish government "to agree only to a capital increase by forcing companies to take on export commitments. The government maintained that, in general, any profit transfers abroad had to be covered by exchanges through exports. Since Turkish industry (steel pipes in the case of the Sümerbank-Mannesmann joint venture) could not yet compete at world market prices, export sales did not cover costs, so exports caused losses" (Friedmann and Beguin 1971, pp. 209–10). Gradually, Turkey established a functional export promotion system, one that gave firms incentives to cut costs and were generous enough to export at a profit (Baysan and Blitzer 1990; Senses 1990).

In the case of Mexico's oil company, Pemex, in the late 1970s it guaranteed private petrochemical producers a ten-year price discount of 30 percent on their feedstock in exchange for their willingness to export at least 25 percent of their installed capacity and maintain permanent employment (the debt crisis of 1981–82, however, led to the cancellation of this plan) (Mattar 1994).

In Brazil, a BEFIEX program authorized duty-free imports in exchange for export commitments. The Brazilian government established the BEFIEX program in early 1970, after negotiations with the Ford Motor Company's introduction of the Maverick model. This program allowed for increases in import content and tax exemptions against export performance commitments and "was in tune with Brazil's export promotion policies since the late 1960s." The turning point came during the first energy crisis, when the Brazilian government "forced a swing in the automobile industry's negative balance" by withdrawing all subsidies other than those under BEFIEX. "This led to a healthy rise not only in exports of vehicles but also in exports of engines and parts made at the terminals or by associated firms" (Fritsch and Franco 1991, p. 115). In the case of other industries, Brazil's export incentives included a standard package of duty drawbacks and other tax rebates. In addition, firms could negotiate their own customized incentive package in return for a specific commitment to export a certain proportion of their output (Baumann and Moreira 1987). The transport equipment industry especially was helped by this reciprocal arrangement (Lucke 1990). By 1990 it is estimated that 50 percent of Brazil's total exports were covered by BEFIEX incentives (Shapiro 1997).

India made exporting a condition for subsidies and privileges of various sorts but usually the terms of the agreement were unworkable. In the textile industry, for example, in the 1960s the government agreed to waive restrictions on firm's restructuring if they agreed to export 50 percent of their output—but few did because they lacked the capital to restructure (Nayyar 1973). In 1970 export obligations were introduced for various industries; industries or firms were required to export up to 10 percent of their output. But "the government was seldom able to enforce export requirements" except possibly in industries (software, for instance) that were already export-oriented (Verma 1996, p. 24). As India liberalized in the 1990s, however, trade balancing conditionalities appear to have become *more* workable. Even foreign investments that were given "automatic clearance" were to be subject to central bank scrutiny for foreign exchange details. Scrutiny "will generally require that the investing company not take out more hard currency than it brings in" (Gardner 2000, p. 9).

By way of conclusion, export-oriented performance standards, starting with export processing zones, became pervasive throughout "the rest" and probably strongest in Korea and Taiwan. These countries were extreme outliers in export performance, even with respect to other East Asian countries. Their conditionality distinguished itself for the tight relationship it created between exporting and accessing long-term investment capital. With tight coupling, exporting became wired into a firm's long-term strategic plans (see chapter 7). This was an ideal, but performance standards everywhere, sooner or later, at least became export-friendly.

Local-Content

Performance standards in the form of "local-content" requirements were focused on the automobile industry. They were designed to induce automobile assemblers (foreign or national) to "source" their parts and components from domestic suppliers in exchange for granting them tariff protection from finished vehicles, limits on entry by new assemblers, and financial subsidies.[34] The government's policy objective was to build national firms, enrich technological capabilities, and save or earn foreign exchange. The premise was that local content rules squeezed assemblers' profit margins, which gave them an incentive to train their local parts suppliers, whose greater efficiency would reduce their overall costs.

Localization requirements were among the most difficult performance standards to execute and evaluate. A high level of expertise was required on the part of government bureaucrats to choose specific parts and components correctly for sequential localization. The automobile industry was characterized by product differentiation, scale economies (in both assembly and parts manufacture) and high skill requirements. It was, therefore, vulnerable to control by politically and economically powerful multinational firms. Yet laissez-faire was out of the question. As industrialization expanded and as per capita incomes rose, demand for automobiles soared, and automobile imports destablilized a country's balance of payments. The kneejerk reaction was to strengthen tariffs on assembled automobiles, but tariffs only succeeded in increasing imports of "kits" of knocked-down or semi-knock down parts and components. Early local content rules were an attempt to induce assemblers to manufacture selected parts and components locally, with Brazil blazing the trail:

> assemblers had to meet an extremely ambitious domestic-content schedule to be eligible for the full range of financial subsidies. Each year their vehicles

had to contain an increased percentage of domestically purchased components. By July 1, 1960, trucks and utility vehicles were to contain 90 percent domestic content and jeeps and cars, 95 percent. . . . By offering the financial incentives for only a limited period, the plan would put laggardly entrants at a competitive disadvantage. (Shapiro 1994, pp. 81–83)

Firms that failed to meet Brazil's local-content schedule were threatened with a withholding of foreign exchange and a withdrawal of subsidies. (The larger the size of the domestic market, the more credible the government's threat. For their part, foreign assemblers, and sometimes national "first tier" parts suppliers, pressured latecomer governments for lower requirements using threats of "exit." The greater employment and the more obsolete the existing production capacity of an assembler, the more credible the assembler's threat.)

The goals of local content rules—easing balance of payments constraints, strengthening national firms, and enhancing technological skills—were variously met. Over time, localization rose almost everywhere (see Veloso et al. 1998, for Mexico, Taiwan, and Thailand). At least three countries also succeeded in transforming their automobile industry into a "leading sector" in terms of foreign exchange. Table 6.10 shows that by the early 1990s, a positive trade balance in assembled vehicles and parts had been achieved by Brazil, Korea, and Mexico. Imports and exports were more or less balanced in India, while China's automobile industry was still too immature to tell.

The policy objectives of strengthening nationally owned firms and deepening local capabilities were harder to attain and more difficult to measure. Suffice it to say here, in the absence of robust data, that local content requirements became a lightning rod for criticism under new World Trade Organization law in the late 1990s. Foreign assemblers saw it in their growing interest to source their parts and components globally. Therefore, in countries where the ownership of automobile assembly operations was mostly foreign (Argentina, Brazil, and Mexico), the ownership of key parts suppliers also tended to become de-nationalized (for Brazil, see Mesquita Moreira 1999). Still, even in these countries, the learning effects of local content laws appear to have been great, certainly warranting further study.[35] Whereas efficient, technologically advanced small- and medium-size enterprises largely failed to emerge in "the rest" before World War II, they appeared to arise in the postwar years on the heels of local content rules.

Price Controls

From the perspective of an *industrial* policy maker, price controls were typically imposed exogenously by a *macroeconomic* policy maker, whose objective was price stability and social peace rather than industrialization. Price controls had no long-term developmental rationale. Nor were they necessarily

Table 6.10. Trade Deficits in Autos and Auto Parts, 5-year Totals, 1970–1994

	Deficit or Surplus (mil 1990 US$)				
	1970–74	1975–79	1980–84	1985–89	1990–94
Argentina	−480	−212	−2,384	−853	−6,541
Brazil	−959	2,495	7,209	11,089	4,383
Chile	−1,325	−1,583	−2,023	−2,086	−4,904
China	na	na	−1,191	−7,952	−13,225
India	−322	222	743	−455	1,588
Indonesia	−2,506	−5,143	−6,436	−5,133	−8,668
Korea	−1,019	−1,915	584	11,273	10,011
Malaysia	−2,737	−3,824	−4,780	−3,021	−6,773
Mexico	−4,291	−7,305	−4,966	9,075	4,494
Taiwan	−1,246	−1,606	698	1,128	−6,358
Thailand	−2,561	−4,309	−3,746	−5,480	−14,372
Turkey	−1,831	−2,965	−1,563	−2,361	−5,930
France	22,219	40,060	24,987	20,721	30,095
Japan	59,911	136,171	206,155	325,403	369,070
U.K.	24,735	12,170	−8,302	−41,480	−27,224
U.S.	−45,029	−47,921	−107,909	−280,487	−229,257

Notes:
Negative numbers indicate deficits.
Data adjusted into real dollars using U.S. WPI. Taiwan data for autos and parts includes all transportation equipment. All China data is for 1983 and after. Chile did not report export figure for 1982–1989.
The UN Standard Classification of industries has been adjusted through the years. The old standard classification (Rev. 1) listed the following categories for autos and parts: 713—internal combustion piston engines (where printed, air & marine piston engines were subtracted), 7132—automotive piston engines, 7139—piston engine parts, 7783—automotive electronics, and 732—road vehicles (includes motor vehicle parts). The newer standard classification (Rev. 2) listed the following categories: 7115—nonair piston engines, 7294—automotive electronics, and 78—road vehicles (includes motor vehicle parts). The data are not strictly comparable from year to year or across countries as countries switched from Rev. 1 to Rev. 2 at various times.

Source: UNIDO (1997 and various years [a]); UNCTAD (various years [b]); International Monetary Fund (1997); Republic of China (1997).

reciprocal in nature. Their result, therefore, was as anticipated: sometimes they aided industry and sometimes they harmed it.

Their effects appeared to be most harmful in the the steel industry, whose price movements permeated the rest of the manufacturing sector. In Mexico, there was a price freeze on steel from March 1957 to the end of 1974 in order to contain inflation. "Throughout this period most of the firms in the Mexican steel market faced financial difficulties which hindered their modernization and expansion" (Perez and Jose de Jesus Perez y Peniche 1987, p. 185).[36] The postwar Indian steel industry, comprised of privately owned and publicly owned mills, was covered by a system of "retention prices" recommended by India's prestigious prewar Tariff Commission. The selling price of steel was higher than the retention price paid to producers, and the difference was used by the government to underwrite development projects (not necessarily in the steel industry). Nevertheless, production costs at the newer public sector mills were necessarily higher than at the older private mills because capital costs were relatively cheaper before the war, when private plants were built, and in the postwar period "the World Bank refused to finance government-owned industrial units as a matter of policy" (Johnson 1966, p. 38). Hence, investments that were private tended to cost less than those that were public. Because government plants received the same retention prices as private plants, they incurred substantial losses and could not finance their own modernization. The costs of this price system were described as "incalculable," as were the costs of the price controls governing the Indian cement industry (Lall 1987).

In Korea, the government was tampering with steel prices as late as 1996, but for no obvious developmental reason: "Foreign exporters normally had difficulty competing in the Korean market with POSCO (one of the world's most efficient steel makers) because transport costs and import tariffs made their products more expensive. . . . Domestic prices did not necessarily move directly with international prices or domestic supply and demand due to government controls" (Financial Times, 15 March, 1996, as cited in (Nolan 1996, p. 22).[37] In Brazil, by contrast, the government "passed a decree in 1965 giving firms certain tax advantages if they would not raise their prices by more than 10 percent a year. Government-controlled steel firms were forced to join this commitment, and so also were private firms, since most of them relied on government credit for their expansion programs, *but the tax break gave firms an incentive to hold down their costs and prices*" (Baer 1969, pp. 131–32, emphasis added).

Even in the same country, price controls failed in one industry but were protective of consumers and highly developmental in another, almost by chance. In India, price controls harmed the steel industry but helped the pharmaceutical industry. "India's system of normative ceiling prices . . . forced pharmaceutical firms (numbering around 28,000) to engage in process innovation . . . and made exports more profitable than domestic sales, thus pushing local drug firms to become exporters" (price controls, however, acted as a disincentive to improve quality and produce the cheapest controlled drugs). India's pharmaceutical exports rose from 46 in 1980–81 to 2,337 in 1995–96 (rupees crore), a fifty-fold rise. Innovativeness was encouraged because those local firms that manufactured new drugs (using indigenous technologies) were exempted from price controls for five years. Small firms in rural areas were exempted altogether from price controls, so multinationals began to subcontract to them, thereby diffusing technology and facilitating a supply of medicines to remote regions (Mourshed 1999, p. 107). All this, however, was fortuitous: "Just as the Indian government did not wittingly impose price controls to encourage process innovation, it also did not conceive of price control as a mechanism for motivating local drug firms to become world-class exporters" (Mourshed 1999, p. 110).

In the case of the automobile industry in Korea, prices were surveilled by the Ministry of Finance to bolster price stability.[38] Because assemblers could not initially compete internationally at world market prices (owing to their small production scale), they were allowed to set domestic prices high enough to offset losses in export markets.[39] If assemblers exported, the government allowed them to produce high-margin luxury cars equipped with six cylinder engines for the domestic market. When a new model was first introduced, Korean assemblers were also allowed to overcharge customers (by world standards), but then were pressured to reduce prices over time. This policy inadvertently helped assemblers recoup their initial investment costs and also forced them to increase productivity to remain profitable (Amsden and Kang 1995). In Taiwan, the price of a domestically made car was allowed to exceed that of a comparable foreign car. But "if the domestic price of a car was higher than its international market price by more than 15 percent, then foreign cars were automatically allowed to be imported." It was difficult for the Taiwan government to decide exactly how much the difference in domestic and international prices should be, but the concept was helpful in pushing domestic producers "toward efficient production and management" (Min 1982, p. 105).

The behavior of price controls in "the rest" illustrates a general principle about performance standards. A policy-related performance standard works "best"—advances a developmental goal—where the goal *is* developmental and clear-cut. Where the developmentalism of a goal is fuzzy, as in price controls, the outcome is likely to be fortuitous.

In India, "the rest's" second worst performer after Argentina in terms of manufacturing output growth, performance standards tended to have conflicting multiple goals. Unlike other countries in "the rest," the criteria India used to target industries included sociopolitical objectives: public enterprise over private enterprise and small firms over large ones. In fact, large firms grew faster than small firms and the public sector's expansion (from 4 percent of manufacturing in 1960–61 to 18 percent in 1984–85) was offset by restrictions on foreign investment, which buttressed national private big business (Sandesara 1992). But distributional objectives interfered with efficiency, as is evident from two of India's most awkward policy instruments, controlling prices and reserving market segments for small-scale firms (see chapter 9 on market reservation). Conflict in objectives abounds in the history of almost every strategic industry in which India lost ground. The Indian cotton textile industry suffered from obsolete plant and equipment in the 1950s, but the Indian government was reluctant to undertake full-scale mechanization because of shortages of foreign exchange and the fact that "in a labour abundant economy which already has a very high level of un-employment, any policy aimed at such modernisation requires careful consideration in view of its welfare implications" (Nayyar 1973, p, 9). The expansion of the Indian clothing industry, being very labor intensive, might have reduced the Indian government's anxiety about the unemployment effects of modernization in weaving. But the Indian clothing industry also stagnated in the 1970s: "The failure of the government to ensure the existence of an adequate supply of inputs, especially fabric, to this industry was the single most important effect of government policy on this sector. The government aimed to expand the handloom sector *by discouraging the growth of the larger textile mills*. The expansion of weaving capacity in mills was not permitted *unless textile producers undertook to sell a large proportion of their output at controlled prices, which were very low*" (Kumar 1988, p. 122, emphasis added).

As argued in chapter 8, an equal income distribution is a very valuable asset in industrialization. Nevertheless, the pursuit of distributional goals by means of industrialization policies may advance neither.

Performance

The performance of "hot" industries may now be assessed by the criteria of changing market share in total manufacturing output and exports. The share of "hot" industries in "the rest's" prewar manufacturing sector was generally small, so a rise in this share may be taken as evidence that development planning met its major goal.

Chemicals, machinery, or basic metals tend to appear as the target of every development bank represented in table 6.7. These are also the sectors that performed the strongest in postwar years. Chemicals increased their importance as a share of total manufacturing output in every country, typically by a wide margin (see figure 6.1). The same is true of machinery (except for Argentina and Chile) (see figure 6.2). Between the beginning and end of the 1970s, iron and steel production increased 17.1 times in Korea, 11.3 times in Taiwan, and by 2.1 times in China (UNIDO 1986). Heavy industry progressed the furthest in populous countries where prewar manufacturing experience tended to be longest and where postwar policy gave heavy industry the biggest push—Brazil, India, Korea, Mexico, and China. The industrial structures of these countries began to resemble those of the North Atlantic and Japan (see table 5.2).

The share of manufactures in "the rest's" total exports also soared (see table 6.8). The rise was spectacular in Brazil, Indonesia, Thailand, Malaysia, and Turkey. Between 1970 and 1995, the manufactured share in total exports rose from 1.2 to 50.6 percent in Indonesia, 4.7 to 73.1 percent in

CHEMICALS

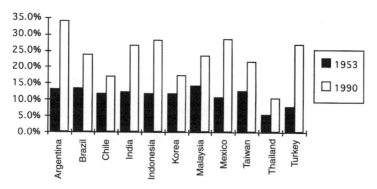

Figure 6.1. Share of chemicals in manufacturing value added, 1953–1990. The term "chemicals" encompasses the following industrial classifications: industrial chemicals, other chemicals, petroleum refining, petroleum and coal products, plastic and plastic products, and rubber and rubber products. Data for the following countries are given for the following years, rather than for 1953: India, 1958; Korea, 1958; Malaysia, 1959; Taiwan, 1954; Thailand, 1963; Indonesia, 1958; Mexico, 1960. *Sources:* United Nations (various years), UNIDO (various years [b]).

MACHINERY

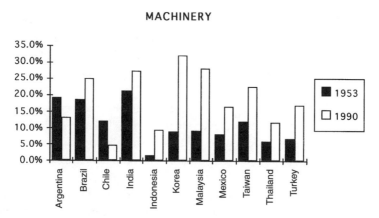

Figure 6.2. Share of machinery in manufacturing value added, 1953–1990. The term "machinery" encompasses the following industrial classifications: electrical machinery, nonelectrical machinery, transport equipment, and professional and scientific equipment. Data for the following countries are given for the following years, rather than for 1953: India, 1958; Korea, 1958; Malaysia, 1959; Taiwan, 1954; Thailand, 1963; Indonesia, 1960; Argentina, 1975; Mexico, 1960. *Sources:* United Nations (various years), UNIDO (various years [b]).

Thailand, 8.9 to 74.4 percent in Turkey, 6.5 to 74.4 percent in Malaysia, and 13.2 to 53.5 percent in Brazil. Machinery exports included light manufactures (such as consumer electronics), but also nonelectrical machinery and transportation equipment. Chemical industries produced intermediate inputs for final export products, thus finding their way into exports, but only indirectly. Taiwan's industrial strategy, for example, was predicated on state-owned "upstream" enterprises producing intermediate inputs for "downstream" small-scale private exporters (Chu and Tsai 1992; Chu 1994 and 1996). In Japan and Italy, which may be taken as benchmarks, the share of chemicals in 1992 in total exports equaled 5.5 percent and 7.1 percent respectively. Roughly, the same chemical export shares existed in 1992 in Korea, China, Mexico, Brazil, India, and Argentina. As for iron and steel, by the early 1990s, it became one of the top ten exports of Argentina, Brazil, Korea, and Turkey (United Nations Conference on Trade and Development 1993).

A new era had dawned.

Conclusion

After a century of failing to industrialize, "the rest" succeeded in diversifying its manufacturing base and in generating manufactured exports under a reciprocal control mechanism. Subsidies were conditional on the fulfillment of performance standards, which were widespread both by industry and country. Techno-standards transformed the family-owned firm by professionalizing its key management functions, as suggested by the case of Brazil. Policy standards raised the local content of fabrication and assembly industries, especially automobiles, thereby promoting national small-scale firms. Trade-oriented standards, as discussed in the next chapter, became export-friendly and an integral part of long-term capital formation in the best cases, Korea and Taiwan.

Despite challenges related to large scale economies and heavy capital requirements, development banks oversaw the rise of "the rest's" basic industries. "Hot industries" targeted for subsidies generally increased their share of manufacturing output and total exports, and manufacturing growth rates soared.

Late industrialization thus became an institutionally grounded growth process. The weakest performers, measured by manufacturing output growth, may be understood in terms of these institutions: Argentina never developed them and India overdeveloped them.

7

Selective Seclusion

Countries in "the rest" all allocated subsidies to the same set of mid-technology industries, and in almost all cases, these industries started as import substitutes. What differed among countries was how vigorously and rapidly exportables were extracted from a sequentially rising number of import substitution sectors. The wide variation among countries in export coefficient—share of exports (manufactured and nonmanufactured) in GDP—depended on structural characteristics (population size and density), investment rates, and price distortions. Even controlling for these variables, however, some countries in "the rest" became overexporters while others remained underexporters. The reasons behind this disparity—rather than its importance for growth—are explored below.

The role of history was such that not only manufacturing experience mattered and not only manufacturing experience that was colonial mattered (for national ownership)—manufacturing experience from Japan is what mattered most for rapid growth in foreign trade.

Deviations from predicted levels of exporting may be attributed to trading institutions. In turn, the trading institutions of latecomers were influenced by those of earlier industrializers, sometimes fortuitously and sometimes deliberately. North and South American trade patterns became similar. Japan's trade regime was an object of conscious emulation by its East Asian neighbors: An institutionally grounded and popularly promoted trade regime was created to mobilize exports, at the heart of which was a policy to allocate long-term investment capital to those import substitution industries that were expected—and equipped with the necessary inputs—to export at some future date. Thus, export activity became an integral part of import substitution activity.

This connection escaped conventional measures of export promotion because long-term subsidized credit can be used to produce for any market, domestic or foreign. Therefore, investment credit cannot be allocated uniquely to either import substitution or exporting, as noted in chapter 6, and cannot be counted as an export incentive per se.

Differences in "Economic Openness"

Export growth was fast *in all countries* in "the rest" for almost fifty years, 1950 to 1995; it was slightly above the world average (see table 7.1, which measures total exports, manufactured *and nonmanufactured*, in nominal dollars). Even in Argentina, with the lowest rate, it averaged 7.5 percent. This

Table 7.1. Growth Rate of Exports, 1950–1995 (%)

Country	1950–60	1960–70	1970–80	1980–90	1990–95	1950–95
Argentina	0.3	4.8	18.0	2.1	11.9	7.5
Brazil	2.1	7.2	21.8	5.1	5.3	10.2
Chile	3.7	10.0	15.9	8.1	15.0	8.9
China	18.8	1.3	20.0	12.9	19.4	11.8
India	0.4	3.7	17.3	7.3	11.7	7.9
Indonesia	−1.1	1.6	35.3	−0.3	12.1	11.5
Korea	1.3	39.8	37.2	15.0	14.3	26.3
Malaysia	0.6	4.2	24.2	8.6	20.3	11.0
Mexico	3.1	6.1	24.8	8.2	14.6	12.8
Taiwan	6.5	23.2	28.6	14.8	10.8	20.3
Thailand	1.7	5.9	24.7	14.0	19.7	12.9
Turkey	0.0	6.0	16.2	14.0	11.0	11.4
Standard deviation	5.3	11.1	7.1	5.1	4.4	5.4
Mean	3.1	10.5	23.7	10.2	13.8	12.7
Coefficient of variation	171.2	117.3	210.9	56.0	31.6	42.5
Italy	10.5	13.9	20.0	8.7	6.7	13.3
Japan	15.9	17.5	20.8	8.9	10.1	15.8
U.K.	4.7	5.9	18.5	5.8	4.4	10.2
U.S.	5.5	8.1	18.5	5.7	8.3	10.0
USSR	10.8	8.3	20.6	4.2	na	11.9
World	6.4	10.2	20.4	6.1	8.1	11.1
Developed	7.0	10.0	19.0	7.6	7.2	11.3
Developing	3.6	6.7	25.8	3.2	11.4	11.0
N. Africa	1.9	13.9	23.7	−3.8	−1.4	10.8
Other Africa	4.8	7.3	19.9	−1.3	−0.5	7.9
Asia	4.1	6.5	29.8	4.5	13.4	12.5
Latin America	2.4	5.0	20.8	2.1	10.1	8.7

Notes: Nominal U.S. dollars. USSR data are for 1950–1980.

Sources: UNCTAD (1996), except USSR; USSR, UNCTAD (1990).

was well below the world average but not inconsequential in absolute terms. Exports grew annually at almost identical double digit rates in China, Indonesia, Malaysia, Thailand, Mexico, and Turkey despite different degrees of protection. The share of manufactures in exports also soared (least of all in Argentina and Chile) (see table 6.9). Thus, "the rest's" postwar trade history is one of fast growth almost everywhere and spectacularly fast growth in two cases, Korea and Taiwan. Their average annual export growth in nominal dollars exceeded 20 percent for nearly half a century (see table 7.1).

What differed sharply among countries in "the rest" were *export shares in GDP*, a coefficient that crudely measures how exposed an economy is to international competition, how easily it can exploit economies of scale, how readily it can create employment for its "unlimited supplies of labor," and how adroitly it can overcome domestic market recessions.[2] In some countries, this coefficient started low and stayed low. In other countries, it rose rapidly after World War II from a low or high starting point to a level that was possibly unprecedented in world trade history. By 1990 exports in GDP varied from single digit figures in some large countries, Brazil and India, to almost 50 percent in Taiwan and almost 80 percent in Malaysia (see table 7.2).

By way of explanation, if a firm operates in a large domestic market, it is more likely than otherwise to develop its products with a view toward selling at home, and given large international differences in per capita income, tastes overseas and at home may be expected to differ. A large domestic market is a valuable asset, so a larger country may be expected to be more protectionist than a smaller country (*cet.par.*). Given sunk costs of product development and assuming that home tariffs discourage exporting (ignoring other interventions), then the larger the country (measured by population), the smaller the export coefficient, by virtue of both size and protectionism.

Population density (people per unit of land) is also likely to affect exporting because resource scarcity (the essence of "density") limits domestic income and purchasing power. Population density affects the supply of labor and hence real wages—the greater population density, the greater the labor supply relative to resources and the greater the downward pressure on wages. Both pressures, if great, make the production of exports relatively cheap.[3] Thus, in terms of involuntary structural characteristics (those over which a country has no control), the greater population size, the smaller the export coefficient, and the greater population density, the greater the tendency to export.

Investment in new plant and equipment may be considered a determinant of trade because it influences the supply of technologically up-to-date products for overseas sale. Therefore, the greater a country's rate of investment, the higher its export share is likely to be. If access to long-term preferential investment credit is made conditional on exporting, then the relationship between investing and exporting may be expected to be even stronger. Never-

Table 7.2. Share of Exports in GDP, Selected Countries

Year	Exports in GDP (%)	Year	Exports in GDP (%)
Argentina		Korea	
1910	24	1910	7
1970	6	1938	33
1980	5	1961	5
1990	10	1970	14
1995	7	1980	34
		1990	30
Brazil		1995	36
1910	16		
1970	7	Malaysia	
1980	9	1960	56
1990	8	1970	42
1995	8	1980	57
		1990	77
Chile		1995	90
1910	30		
1970	15	Mexico	
1980	23	1910	12
1990	34	1960	5
1995	28	1970	6
		1980	11
China		1990	16
		1995	13
1910	6		
1932	5		
1955	6	Taiwan	
1970	3	1910	32
1980	10	1938	34
1990	19	1960	12
1994	24	1970	30
		1980	53
India		1990	48
1910	11	1995	44
1960	5		
1970	4	Thailand	
1980	7	1960	17
1990	8	1970	15
1995	12	1980	24
		1990	34
Indonesia		1995	39
1964	14		
1970	13	Turkey	
1980	33	1910	14
1990	27	1963	9
1995	25	1970	6
		1980	6
		1990	13
		1995	21

Table 7.2. (*continued*)

Year	Exports in GDP (%)	Year	Exports in GDP (%)
United States		Russia	
1879–88	7	1910	8
1904–13	6	1959	3
1924–28	5	1965	3
1960	5	1970	4
1970	6	1980	5
1980	6	1989	5
1990	10	1994	4
1995	11		
Japan			
1878–87	5		
1908–13	15		
1918–27	18		
1965	11		
1970	11		
1980	14		
1990	11		
1995	9		

Sources: Unless otherwise noted, all data taken from UNCTAD (various years [b]). Data for 1960 represent exports/GDP and are taken from International Monetary Fund (various years). Data for the USSR represent exports/GNP and are taken from Steinberg (1990). The GNP estimates are Steinberg's. Data for 1994 also represent exports/GNP, are for the Russian federation only, and are taken from World Bank (1996). Data for the United States for 1879–1928 taken from United States (various years). Data for Japan for 1878–1927 from United States (various years). Unless otherwise noted below, data for 1930 taken from Hori (1994). United States (1819–1913) from Kravis (1972), and United States (1920s) from Kuznets (1967). Assumes imports and exports are equal. For 1970–1990, UNCTAD (1995). Data for "the rest" for 1910, Hanson (1986). "Data" are based on expert opinion. Russian figure (1910) is based on country statistics. China (1955) from Eckstein (1964). Russia (1959) from Kindleberger (1962). Mexico (1960) from Reynolds (1970). Turkey (1963–64) from Pamugoklu (1990). Korea and Taiwan (1938) and China (1932) from Hori (1994).

theless, because high rates of investment in infrastructure may be *domestic* market-oriented, the effect of investment on export shares is unpredicatable.

Finally, prices, especially of foreign exchange, may be expected to influence exporting to the extent that they make selling at home more profitable than selling aborad. If prices are neutral (undistorted), then they should have no influence on exporting.

To test these hypotheses, we estimate two regression equations using 1990 data for countries in "the rest," the North Atlantic and Japan (see table 7.3).[4] In general, the percentage of intercountry variability in export shares that is explained in these tests is large—the R^2 statistic for all independent variables reaches as much as 0.68 in a cross-section equation (regression 2). Even when only population size and population density are considered (regression

Table 7.3. Regression for Export Coefficient (Share of Exports in GDP), 1990

| | | Export Coefficient as Function of . . . | | | |
Regression	Constant	Log of Population	Log of Pop. Density	Log of Investment's Contribution to Growth	Log of Distortion
1. Involuntary	0.77	−0.28	0.17	—	—
(R-square = 0.59)		(−6.67)	(3.60)		
2. General	6.40	−0.32	0.15	0.14	−1.00
(R-square = 0.68)		(−7.73)	(3.24)	(1.85)	(−2.43)

Notes: Dependent variable: Export coefficient, 1990. Figures in parentheses are t-statistics. Investment's contribution to growth is the average for 1981–1990. The figure for each year is calculated by dividing the absolute growth in investment over the course of a given year by the overall level of GDP in the given year. The measure of distortion is based on a composite index derived by David Dollar that includes distortions introduced by trade barriers and exchange rate movements. Countries include: "The rest," Japan, the North Atlantic, Australia, New Zealand, South Africa, and Israel.

Sources: Distortion data from Dollar (1992); investment data from World Bank (1994); all other data from UNCTAD (1995).

1), the R^2 statistic is high——0.59. As expected, the sign on the coefficient of population size is negative (the greater the population, the lower the export share) while that of population density is positive (the higher the population density, the higher the export share). Thus, almost 60 percent of the variability in export shares among industrialized and semi-industrialized economies is attributable to *involuntary structural characteristics*. The unexplained residual of regression 1 is reduced somewhat by adding the variables "investment" and "exchange rate distortion" (shown in regression 2). As expected, the sign on investment is positive and that on exchange rate distortion is negative. But neither variable alone, nor the two together, adds much extra explanatory power.[5]

Given a country's population size and density, along with its investment rate and trade distortions, the difference between its *actual* export share in 1990 and its *predicted* export share (using regression [2] estimates) is shown in table 7.4. Underexporters were Brazil, India, and especially Argentina and Turkey. Overexporters were Chile, Indonesia, Taiwan, and Thailand.[6] Given our previous analyis of knowledge-based assets, we may expect the over-achievers to exhibit the following characteristics: (1) relatively high prewar experience in *exporting manufactures* and (2) reciprocity between access to long-term capital and export targets. The more exporting is wired into capital formation, the easier it is for a firm to invest in the skills and production capacity necessary to export, and the greater the discipline over the firm's use of preferential loans.

Table 7.4. Differences between the Actual Export Coefficient and the Predicted Export Coefficient, 1990 (%)*

	Rc (actual 1990)	Rc (actual 1995)	Rc (predicted)	Residual
Argentina	10.0	7.0	17.4	−7.4
Brazil	8.0	8.0	12.1	−4.1
Chile	34.0	28.0	24.0	10.0
China	na	24.0	na	na
India	8.0	12.0	11.8	−3.8
Indonesia	27.0	25.0	15.3	11.7
Korea	30.0	36.0	30.1	−0.1
Malaysia	77.0	90.0	26.7	50.3
Mexico	16.0	13.0	16.6	−0.6
Taiwan	48.0	44.0	38.8	10.2
Thailand	34.0	31.0	22.0	12.0
Turkey	13.0	21.0	20.3	−7.3
Japan	11.0	10.0	21.3	−10.3
Russia	na	27.0	na	na
United States	10.0	11.0	11.2	−1.2
Australia	18.0	18.0	15.6	2.4
Canada	25.0	34.0	14.2	10.8
Israel	31.0	31.0	49.6	−18.6
New Zealand	27.0	31.0	33.4	−6.4
South Africa	26.0	24.0	19.7	6.3
Average, Europe	38.6	28.0	37.4	1.2

*Predicted by Regression 2 in Table 7.3.

By way of example, export promotion by Argentina, an underachiever, was strongly encouraged in a report by Raul Prebisch, the chief economist of the United Nations Economic Commission for Latin America (CEPAL), to the Argentine Provisional Government *as early as 1956*.[7] The Prebisch doctrine, promulgated immediately after World War II, was held responsible by Washington for Latin America's export pessimism and "inward"-orientation and was bitterly criticized.[8] Nevertheless, CEPAL's "inward-oriented" orthodoxy lasted only a decade, as indicated by the date of Prebisch's strongly worded advice to Argentina in favor of export promotion. Argentina soon adopted export promotion measures, which included export credits, exemptions for exporters from payment of sales taxes, refunds of duties paid on imported inputs (drawbacks), and ad valorem export rebates (in the 1970s an even wider set of instruments was employed). "Judging by . . . the rapid growth (in nontraditional manufactured) exports, it would appear that the incentive system was quite effective" (Mallon and Sourrouille 1975, p. 81). According to regression analysis at the time, the real effective exchange rate (adjusted for export subsidies) did not have a statistically significant impact on Argentina's export behavior. Instead, the important explanatory variables turned out to be domestic productive capacity (the lower capacity utilization, the higher exports) and trade concessions connected with the newly formed Latin America Free Trade Association (LAFTA). Of Argentina's more than sevenfold increase in nontraditional exports between 1962 and 1968, over half was accounted for by LAFTA trade (Felix 1971). Not least of all, the growth of Argentina's nontraditional manufactured exports was found to be responsive to technological upgrading of import substitution industries. Nevertheless, nothing much happened in the way of exporting afterward; there were no attempts on the part of the Argentine government to coordinate investing and exporting, and no new dynamic industries arose (see chapter 6). In the

Table 7.5. Imports (%) of Capital Goods by Country of Origin, 1970 and 1990

	U.S.	Japan	Europe	World
1970				
Argentina	31.7	2.8	56.7	100
Brazil	32.2	7.5	53.6	100
Chile	45.1	4.0	44.5	100
China	na	na	na	na
India	17.5	6.0	42.9	100
Indonesia	15.8	30.0	39.6	100
Korea	24.4	43.6	30.8	100
Malaysia	18.1	27.7	43.1	100
Mexico	59.1	4.5	33.6	100
Taiwan	19.2	59.8	19.3	100
Thailand	15.7	43.0	35.1	100
Turkey	15.3	6.6	62.5	100
1990				
Argentina	22.9	8.7	35.5	100
Brazil	30.6	19.9	33.0	100
Chile	25.7	9.1	28.7	100
China	10.2	18.3	27.4	100
India	15.9	17.5	40.9	100
Indonesia	11.5	33.1	27.0	100
Korea	25.2	46.4	17.2	100
Malaysia	22.2	31.2	13.7	100
Mexico	63.6	6.6	17.7	100
Taiwan	na	na	na	na
Thailand	14.0	43.5	17.1	100
Turkey	7.7	9.9	61.6	100

Notes: 1970 includes categories 7.1 (nonelectrical machinery) and 7.2 (electrical machinery). 1990 includes categories 7.1 (power generating machines), 7.2 (special industrial machinery), 7.3 (metal working machines), 7.4 (general industrial machinery), 7.5 (office machines, ADP Mach), 7.6 (telecommunications sound equipment, etc.), and 7.7 (electrical machinery, apparatus, parts).

Source: UNCTAD (various years [a]).

long run, therefore, Argentina's poor export performance appears to have been heavily influenced by its failure to establish the skill- and capital-intensive industries necessary for a high-wage country to compete in world manufacturing markets. The same case can be made for Turkey's under-achievement (see the discussion on high-tech industry in chapter 8).

In terms of overachievers, most were East Asian, with strong historical links to Japan. Strong postwar links in general are suggested by flows of capital goods. A capital good is a potential transmitter of know-how because it embodies technology. A seller of a capital good may also provide a buyer with long-term technical assistance. As indicated in table 7.5, in either 1970, 1990, or both years, Japan was the major supplier of capital goods to Indonesia, Korea, Malaysia, Taiwan, and Thailand.[9]

Japan itself had become an underachiever by 1990—its predicted export coefficient was above its actual export coefficient (see table 7.4). Nevertheless, Japan's export coefficient was high historically relative to that of its major market and later rival, the United States.[10] Circa 1927, the Japanese coefficient was more than three times the American coefficient (see table 7.2). Japan's postwar share, moreover, tended to be understated.[11] In key mid-technology industries, Japan's export coefficient was extremely high.

We now examine the effects on exporting of prewar trade history and the institutions governing the extraction of exports from import substitutes.

Prewar Trade History

Japan and its neighbors were involved in an exchange of *manufactures* even before World War II (Hori 1994). A "colonial" division of labor, by contrast, characterized Latin America and the North Atlantic (O'Brien 1997).

Beginning in the 1880s intra-Asian trade grew faster than world trade and was possibly unique: "Intra-regional trade . . . certainly did not develop in other non-Western regions, at any rate to such a significant degree. For instance, the Argentine's trade with the West grew just as fast as Japan's trade with the West, and Brazil's trade with the West also grew fairly rapidly, but there was no great development of trade between the Argentine and Brazil.[12] Neither did it occur in Africa, for instance, between South Africa and West Africa" (Sugihara 1986, p. 710).[13] Intra-Asian trade flows took many forms, depending on the year. In 1913, India exported raw jute, oil seeds, raw cotton, jute cloth, tea, wheat, hides, and skins; Southeast Asia exported rice and tin; and China and Japan exported raw silk. In addition, Japan exported cotton yarn to China and India, and India exported cotton yarn to China. While Southeast Asia mainly exported raw materials, it also exported a wide variety of processed foods: seaweed, dried, boiled, or salted fish and shellfish, isinglass, mandarins, dried vegetables and fruits, eggs, small red and white beans, soya beans, millet, wheat flour, wheat bran, sago, jawar and bajra, salt, ghi, spices such as betel nuts, cloves, ginger, arcenuts, black and white pepper and chilies, tobacco, cigars and cigarettes, tea, and sake. The amount of this trade was greater than total Asian imports of processed food from the West, although in 1913, processed foods accounted for 21 percent of the exports of the United States to Asia (Sugihara 1986; Eysenback 1976).

As Japan's militarism in the 1930s engulfed Korea and Taiwan, which became loci for Japan's manufacturing production (see chapter 5), their trade in manufactures expanded as well. In 1938 Korea's export/GDP ratio is estimated to have been 32.5 percent, up from 8.3 percent in 1912. Taiwan's ratio is estimated to have been 34.4 percent, up from 27.4 percent (see table 7.2). These trade shares are comparable to postwar levels and are very high, as noted earlier. Moreover, in 1939 manufactures accounted for 58.3 percent of total exports from Korea and 60–90 percent of total exports from Taiwan (Hori 1994).[14] This manufacturing content in trade is also extremely high for the time. Taiwan's manufactured exports were mostly (but not exclusively) processed foods (as in the 1950s), but Korea's manufactured exports were diverse. In 1935 Korea was among the world's top five exporters of raw silk (International Labour Office 1937, p. 65). Korea had more looms for cotton cloth manufacture in 1936 than Argentina or Manchuria. As noted in chapter 5, it manufactured more cigarettes in 1939 than Spain, or the Scandinavian countries combined (Norway, Sweden, and Denmark) (Woytinsky and Woytinsky 1953). Thus, "the pattern of external relations (of Korea and Taiwan) formed between the two World Wars was similar to the one formed after World War II" (Hori 1994).

The impetus to trade was also spread throughout Asia by Japan indirectly, as in the case of Indonesia in the 1930s: "Japanese economic penetration and foreign protectionism forced the (Netherlands) Government to adopt an active trade policy." On the one hand, import substitution increased for a wide array of products. On the other hand, exports increased, primarily from Java to the Outer Islands, involving such goods as beer, soap, car tires, bicycles, and woven textile products (Segers 1987, p. 67).

By World War II, trade had engaged both Asian countries with long histories of foreign exchange (Taiwan) and Asian countries with almost no trade histories at all (Korea). New patterns had been established and old nineteenth-century patterns had been left behind (such as the opium trade). In part, therefore, one could argue that *the manufactured exports of East Asia grew fast after the war because they continued an earlier trend of rapid expansion before the war.*

While the exports of primary products from Argentina, Brazil, and Mexico may have grown quickly before the war as well, these Latin countries had little experience in exporting manufactures. Of total world manufactured exports in 1937, Latin America accounted for 0.5 percent and Asia for 11.8 percent. In the same year, manufactures represented only 1.7 percent of Latin America's total exports while they represented 27.2 percent of Asia's total exports (Yates 1959). The inclusion in "Asia" of Japan and India creates the appearance of Asia's greater development relative to Latin America's. But still, as noted above, the trade nexus that included Japan and India also included the manufactured exports of other Asian countries, even if exports took the form of processed foods. Assuming intergenerational learning, trade history favored a faster expansion of manufactured exports after the war within the Asian trade nexus compared with the Latin American–North Atlantic trade nexus.

Import Substitution

Import substitution industrialization preceded exporting in almost all industries, whatever the average bias at the aggregate level between exporting or selling at home. Plants in continuous process industries were initially scaled for the home market; internationally efficient scale minima influenced how many domestic plants would be licensed to operate. Exporting in fabrication/assembly industries (typically machinery-building or automobile manufacture) awaited greater skill formation. Import substitution was the mother of export growth.

The Early Precedence of Import Substitution

In Japan, "unit costs were reduced by increased domestic demand and mass production before the export-production ratio in growing industries began to be boosted" (Shinohara 1982, p. 144; Krugman 1984).[15] Similarly in Brazil, in the period 1960–1980 "exports resulted not only from further processing of natural resources, . . . which . . . enjoyed a comparative advantage, but also from manufactures that firms learned to produce during the import-substitution phase" (Edwards and Teitel 1986, p. 425; Teitel and Thuomi 1986).[16] In fact, "export performance after the 1960s would not have been possible without the industrialization effort which preceded it as export growth was largely based on sectors established through ISI in the 1950s" (Abreu et al. 1997, p. 21). Later, "import substitution policies created the capacity to export; the dominant export sectors of the 1980s and 1990s were the auto industry and those intermediate and heavy industries targeted for import substitution in the wake of the 1973 oil shock" (Shapiro 1997, p. 8). In Mexico, the chemical, automobile, and metalworking industries were targeted for import substitution in the 1970s and began exporting 10–15 percent of their output in the 1980s (Casar 1994).[17] "Much of the rise in non-oil exports during 1983–88 came from some of the most protected industries" (Lustig and Ros 1993, p. 124). Regarding the Chilean economy and its ability to adjust to an abrupt change in policy in 1973, "a portion of this response capacity, especially in the export sector, was based on the industrial development which had been achieved earlier through import-substitution policies" (Ffrench-Davis et al. 1992, p. 97). In Korea, "the shift to an export-oriented policy in the mid-1960s did not mean the discarding of import-substitution. Indeed, the latter went on along with the export-led strategy. Export expansion and import substitution were not contradictory activities but complemented each other" (Lim 1999). In electronics, "the initial ISI phase of the 1960s was critical to the development of the manufacturing skills that enabled (the chaebol) to become the efficient consumer electronics and components assemblers of the 1970s. Indeed, ISI in consumer electronics parts and components continued in the 1970s after domestic demand from export production justified it" (Sridharan 1996, p. 50). By 1984 heavy industry had become Korea's new leading export sector, exceeding light industry in value, and virtually all of Korea's heavy industries had come out of import substitution, just as textiles had done in the 1950s and 1960s (Amsden 1989). In Taiwan "in the first half of the 1960s, most of the exports came from the import substitution industries. Protection from foreign competition was NOT lifted. Getting subsidies to export was extra" (Chu 1997). In Taiwan's electronics industry,

> there is no clear-cut distinction between an import substitution phase and an export promotion phase. Even though the export of electronics products speeded up since the early 1970s, the domestic market for electronics products was still heavily protected through high import tariffs. Whether protection was necessary for the development of local electronics firms is controversial. However, we do observe that the protection of consumer electronics products did force Japanese electronics firms to set up joint ventures with local entrepreneurs and to transfer technologies to local people which helped to expand their exporting capabilities. (San and Kuo 1991, p. 23)

Taiwan's home market for electronics *consumption* was the largest in Asia outside Japan (about 38 percent of the Asian total). The ACER Group, Taiwan's most successful national electronics leader (discussed in the next chapter), got its start at home by operating "as a distributor of electronic products within Taiwan" (Harvard Business School 1993, p. 2).[18] In Thailand, approximately 50 percent of exports (excluding processed foods) in 1985 emerged out of import substitution (Thailand Development Research Institute 1987, pp. 4–23; Wiboonchutikula et al. 1989, p. 61). In the case of Turkey in the 1980s, "it is important to recognize that the growth in manufactured exports did not stem from the establishment of new export industries, but from existing capacity in industries that before had been producing mostly for the domestic market (that is, industries which had originally been established from import substitution)" (Baysan and Blitzer 1990, p. 25).

Some exports did not come out of the import substitution process directly but were produced by *firms* that emerged out of it. The managerial and technological expertise of import-substituting firms in Asia gained them a business reputation and contracts with American contractors of original equipment manufacturers (OEM) in search of a lower wage locale than Japan to produce their parts and components. The details have yet to be written of this hand-me-down from Japan to Korea and Taiwan in such diverse industries as bicycles and consumer electronics. Clearly, however, American companies that had first subcontracted to Japan were attracted to Korea and Taiwan for their low wages and manufacturing experience, which was gained through import substitution (see chapter 5).[19]

Policies to Promote Import Substitution

Successful industrial diversification through import substitution awaited the formation of a reciprocal control mechanism to establish development banking (discussed in chapter 6) and to *rationalize tariff and nontariff trade barriers.* Before reciprocity, a motley set of trade policies had arisen in knee-jerk response to balance of payments crises (Bruton, 1998). "The rest's" rationalization of protectionism first occurred pari passu with its mobilization of five-year plans and developmental machinery—around the late 1950s and early 1960s. Trade reform, however, proved to be a recurrent process.[20]

Sometimes reforms were *more* liberal—currency devaluations, for example, occurred around the late 1950s and early 1960s in countries ranging from Korea, Taiwan, and Thailand to India, Brazil, and Mexico. Sometimes reforms were *less* liberal—protection rose for leading sectors, as in the Korean and Taiwanese textile industries (see table 5.4). Mid-technology industries in general became and remained heavily protected at least through the 1980s, whether continuous process (steel, rubber, pulp and paper, and petrochemicals) or fabrication and assembly (machinery and transportation equipment) (Balassa Bela and Associates 1982) Thus, as new industries emerged, new trade regimes emerged to support them. Import substitution industrialization thus provided the impetus for trade reform as well as the products to supply to world markets.

Export promotion was as old as mercantilism, but it became a centerpiece of "the rest's" trade policies, operating side-by-side with measures to promote import substitution. Anti-export biases still existed in many countries in the 1970s, but were reduced "much more by export subsidies . . . than by (periodic) changes in the overall import regime" (Helleiner 1995, p. 16). In some countries, exporting became the core of a long-term growth strategy. It is to variations in export promotion regimes that attention is now turned.

Japan and Its Emulators

The linkage between import substitution and export activity in Japan began to be forged soon after the Meiji restoration. All modern industries were started as import substitutes, but exporting became concentrated in a small number of products and began almost at once. Tea, raw silk and fabrics, and cotton yarn and fabrics accounted for as much as 63 percent of total exports in 1873–77 and 59 percent of total exports in 1928–32.[21] In 1913, the *production-export ratio* was 77 percent for raw silk, 25 percent for cotton fabrics, and 30 percent for cotton yarn (Shinohara 1964). Persistently high production-export ratios signal an orientation on the part of producers that trade is not just a "vent-for-surplus" or a means to dispose of inventory that cannot be sold in the domestic market. Instead, *exports are built into import substitutes through long-range capacity planning.* Even after World War II, Japan's exports remained concentrated, and around 1970 production-export ratios for selected products remained high: 25 percent for iron and steel and synthetic rubber, 33 percent for motor vehicles, 39 percent for synthetic fibers, and 60 percent for ships (Hollerman 1975).

Entering export markets early in an industry's evolution, using a mass-volume leading sector like silk or cotton textiles, and cultivating import substitution industries with high production-export ratios was a pattern that proved relatively easy to emulate. In terms of export concentration, countries in "the rest" with silk reeling experience also had high specializations in textiles in their early exports:[22] China, 28.8 percent; Korea, 41.1 percent; Taiwan, 21.0 percent; and Turkey, 35.4 percent (UNCTAD 1995). Notwithstanding the fact that textiles are heterogeneous and international marketing requires a sophisticated understanding of consumer tastes and quality standards, this heavy concentration in a single family of products made exporting easier, especially since marketing was often handled by Japanese trading companies.[23] Even in Asian countries without textiles as a leading sector, concentration in the early stage of exporting manufactures tended to be high. Indonesia's largest three manufactures accounted for 68 percent of its total exports in 1982 (Hill 1996).

Japan's tariff (and its variance) rose between 1893 and 1938, but overall remained "moderate"—only 24 percent at its peak in 1931 compared to a peak of 50–60 percent in the United States (Minami 1994, pp. 193–94) (see also table 7.6).

Furthermore, Japan's exchange rate tended to be stable or deliberately undervalued, which also helped exporting. Between 1874–95, Japan was on

Table 7.6. Indicators of Tariff Levels in 1913, Selected Countries

Country	Tariffs 1908–12 (%)[1]	Tariffs[2] on Manufactures (%)
U.S.	0.21	44
Argentina	0.22	28[4]
Brazil	0.37	50–70[4]
Mexico	0.34	40–50[4]
Japan	0.09	25–30
China	0.03	4–5
Thailand[3]	0.03	3–4
Australia	0.12	—
Canada	0.19	—
New Zealand	0.17	15–20

1. Import duties as a percentage of special total imports.
2. Approximate average level of import duties on manufactured imports.
3. Siam.
4. Mainly levied on textiles.

Source: Adapted from Bairoch (1989, p. 139).

the silver standard, and since the price of silver declined relative to the price of gold, silver-based currencies (including many in "the rest") depreciated (Nugent 1973). When Japan went onto the gold standard, it adopted the lowest price rung, keeping its currency cheap. It abandoned the gold standard in 1931, so the yen again depreciated (Minami 1994).

Notwithstanding an otherwise liberal trade regime, export support by the Meiji government included help at critical turning points in the silk and cotton textile industries, including the establishment of "model" factories (see chapter 4). Promotion also included trouble shooting: "As European competition revived in the world market after World War I, Japan's exports staggered and export promotion became more important in her trade policy. Export promotion of various types was pursued in the 1920s and 1930s. One was to establish a quality control system for traditional industries. . . . Another was to encourage the penetration of new markets such as Latin America, the Middle East, and Australia by giving government guarantees to the bank acceptance of export bills to these markets," not to mention providing markets "for the emerging exports of heavy manufactures (metals, chemicals, and machineries) in colonies like Manchuria and Kwantung Province" (Yamazawa 1975, p. 58).

The Japanese government's commitment to exporting became more serious after World War II. Import substitution and exporting were deliberately connected in ways that were highly visible to the naked eye of Japan's students: the idea was that "MITI should promote *both* exports and domestic sales" (Johnson 1982, pp. 229–30).[24] To do this, it formed a Supreme Export Council composed of the prime minister; ministers of MITI, finance, and agriculture; the governor of the Bank of Japan; the president of the Export-Import Bank; and several top business leaders. "Its highly public function was to set export targets for the coming year and to publicize at the highest level of government the need to promote exports by all possible means." To implement the decisions of the Supreme Export Council, "the Japanese government provided specific policies to cover specific needs, thereby making the scale of each measure small" and difficult to measure (Okita 1975, p. 228). Typical of the incentives "the rest" eventually introduced, Japan also gave exporters generous tax breaks because the United States objected to outright subsidies (Okita 1975, p. 223). In the 1960s, *Korea established an organization that was almost identical to Japan's Supreme Export Council,* with the same functions and the same urgent commitment to expand export activity (Rhee et al. 1984). In the 1980s China did likewise (discussed below).

During the early process of economic development, Japan more than the United States relied on Southern markets for its exports. Between 1899 and 1929, about half of Japan's total exports were sent to developing countries (the comparable average for the United States was only around 25 percent). Between 1937 and 1957, about two-thirds of Japan's exports went "South" (compared with around 50 percent for the United States). If *manufactured* exports only are considered, both Japan and the United States had higher South-bound percentages than for their total exports, but more so in the case of Japan than the United States (Maizels 1963).

Profile of Overachievement

Key characteristics of Japan's trade history thus included a relatively high export propensity based on early entry into export markets, concentration on a few export products, a leading sector that generated employment and entrepreneurial opportunities (silk and cotton textiles), relatively low tariffs, aggressive exchange rate devaluations, a highly directive export promotion regime (especially after World War II), and trade diversification that exploited regional markets (the infamous prewar "Greater East Asia Co-Prosperity Sphere"). Overexporters, as defined earlier, deviated from this pattern in crucial respects. Typically, they did not go as far as engineeering aggressive exchange rate devaluations. They also went further than Japan in tying the right to import or sell domestically to an obligation to export. Overall, however, an approach akin to Japan's is evident in all five countries whose actual export shares in GDP surpassed their predicted shares, even Chile(!), whose case, along with Indonesia's and China's, is examined below.

Chile's Traditional Exports   After a coup d'état in 1973 which dismantled the developmental state, Chile continued to rely on its state-owned copper industry for exports. It also groped painfully toward a new trade model. This model resembled that of Japan in two respects. It relied on new techniques to produce traditional products, and these few products comprised a large share of total exports. Roughly 90 percent of Chile's exports at the end of the twentieth century came directly or indirectly from four sectors: forestry, mining, fisheries, and fruits and vegetables. Mining was subject to significant technological improvement by foreign concessionaires, although mine ownership remained public (Duhart 1993). In the other sectors, high quality products were developed for North Atlantic markets using scientific methods of farming and food processing (Perez-Aleman 1997; Gwynne 1993). These exports benefited from state-sponsored *long-term* investments in agro-industry before the start of the Pinochet dictatorship in 1973: "the growth in Chile's exports of fresh fruits requires an explanation that takes into account a long historical process to increase both planted acreage and technical capacity" (Pietrobelli 1993, p. 303). Chile's agricultural exports benefited from vigorous export promotion, which even after Pinochet seized power, ranged from tax incentives to aggressive trade-related services (Ffrench-Davis et al. 1992; Ffrench-Davis et al. 1997).

Indonesia   Indonesia's plywood industry, a leading sector, had only two mills in operation in 1973, but within less than two decades Indonesia controlled 43.3 percent of world exports of plywood and plywood accounted for about one-fifth of Indonesia's total exports. The basis for the increase was a performance standard placed on forest concessionaires by the Indonesian government to the effect that in exchange for the right to exploit Indonesia's rich forest reserves, exports of wood had to be processed at least to the stage of plywood, the objective being to create employment and manufacturing experience. Forest concession-holders were obliged to develop their own processing facilities. At first a ban was placed on raw wood exports. After objections from GATT,[25] prohibitive taxes were substituted for the ban. Criticisms of the program by economists were legion, ranging from allegations of corruption to the inefficiency of Indonesian plywood mills (see, for example, Hill 1996 and Repetto and Gillis 1988). In the 1960s, however, raw wood *from Indonesia* was processed in Korea and Taiwan and then exported as plywood, so there was a respectable model of processing to follow.

The plywood export marketing policies of the Indonesian government resembled those of Taiwan which, in turn, shared much in common with those of Japan (depending on the industry).[26] To support Indonesia's entry into international markets, the government encouraged foresters-cum-plywood makers to form a producer and exporter association, APKINDO. When plywood prices began to fall in 1986, APKINDO acted as a cartel and adopted a policy to control supplies and export quotas. Firms were also encouraged to form export clubs in order to coordinate sales to the same overseas region.

To avoid cutthroat competition among Indonesian sellers, exporters were required to obtain approval for overseas sales from a Joint Marketing Board, under government control. As expected, Indonesia's success in plywood exports encouraged new entrants from Malaysia and the Philippines, which kindled competition. The issue of using more advanced technology to sustain Indonesia's position in the plywood industry, therefore, came on APKINDO's agenda (Messi and Basri 1997).

China   After introducing Japanese-style export promotion measures, China's export coefficient soared from 10 percent in 1980 to 24 percent in 1994 (see table 7.2).

China's trade policy after 1978 included exchange rate devaluations as well as retention of import tariffs and other trade barriers. The Chinese government treated its industrial base like a giant infant industry and quantitative restrictions and high tariffs were maintained to encourage import substitution.[27] Exports were promoted simultaneously:

> A wide variety of mercantilist measures were introduced to stimulate exports. Priority export sectors retained a large share of foreign exchange earnings which were highly valued for their importance in capital expansion and technology acquisition. Exporting firms were given rebates of industrial and commercial taxes, and direct rewards. Large exporting firms were given preferential access to imported technology. Targeted export industries were given cheap credit for technical upgrading, and priority access to low price power and raw materials. Chinese exporters enjoyed access to land at negligible prices by world standards. (Nolan 1996)

Textiles and clothing became China's leading sector, accounting for almost one-third of its total exports in 1990, as noted earlier. The province whose exports grew the fastest was Guangdong. "While it would be tempting to attribute Guangdong's success entirely to its proximity to Hong Kong and its large share of China's foreign-invested enterprises," in fact, "half the growth between 1985 and 1990 was due to expanded international sales by indigenous firms in the region" (Lardy 1992, p. 711). A careful study of reforms in Guangdong observed, "state-owned enterprises led export growth, accounting for 83% of provincial exports in 1987" (Vogel 1989, p. 374–75). Thus, trade reforms were overlaid on an existing firm structure, although not all firms or structures survived; foreign trade organizations, for example, were gradually stripped of their monopoly powers.

In practice, a Sino-Japanese strategy meant

1. Targeting specific industries for export at the highest possible political level (equivalent to Japan's Supreme Export Council) and then implementing top decisions bureaucratically to insure that no barrier, including long-term investment finance, stood in the way of export expansion;

2. Continuing to protect import substitution industries while promoting exports (including repeated devaluations of the yuan), in order to insure a stream of new export products coming to market;
3. Setting export targets in exchange for exporters being allowed to gain access to valuable assets (especially foreign exchange); and
4. Establishing export processing zones with subsidized infrastructure to enable foreign firms to access duty free imports in exchange for a commitment to export 100 percent of their output (or otherwise to negotiate alternative performance standards for the right to sell in the domestic Chinese market). In 1996, of Asia's 225 export processing zones, as many as 124 were in China (UNCTAD 1998a).

In short, "China's strategy recalls that of Japan in the 1950s and 1960s" (Nolan 1996, p. 9).

The United States and Its Emulators

Being latecomers to exporting manufactures, the trade patterns of "the rest" typically resembled the trade patterns of one or another earlier industrializer, as we have just seen in the case of Japan. Given similar structural characteristics (especially low population densities and rich raw materials), the postwar trade patterns of Argentina and Brazil, both underexporters, tended to resemble the prewar trade patterns of the United States. The export coefficients of all three countries was low (see table 7.2). For various reasons, however, following the American trade-route to riches appears to have been harder than following the Japanese style.

First, the United States pattern was devoid of a "leading sector" on a par with cotton textiles. The United States entered world trade late in its industrial history. In 1883 it accounted for only 3.4 percent of total world trade, not much more than the 2.4 percent that India accounted for in the 1940s (Verma 1996). Initially, U.S. exports were overwhelmingly agricultural and even manufactures tended to be raw material-based.[28] Light manufactured exports were negligible. Despite the innovativeness of the American textile industry, of total U.S. exports, cotton textiles accounted for less than 1 percent in 1872 and only 1.8 percent in 1900 (Eysenback 1976). Like the United States, Latin America's most industrialized economies were not internationally competitive in textiles before or after World War II (see chapter 2).[29] Argentina, Brazil, and Mexico, therefore, were at a great disadvantage compared to Asia in lacking a leading export sector with high opportunities to expand manufacturing employment and promote entrepreneurship among small-scale firms.

Second, the United States was a hard act to follow because it was a pioneer in the exploitation of nonreproducible natural resource industries. Including petroleum, resource related exports accounted for about half of all American manufactured exports before World War I (Wright 1990). By the 1960s–70s, Brazil (and Mexico) was also investing heavily in the resource-based industries in which U.S. exports had once been concentrated, such as iron and steel and pulp and paper. But even if Latin America's natural resources were as rich as those of the United States a century earlier, they faced greater competition after World War II due to more global commercial development (Wright 1990). Countries no longer required their own domestic supplies of raw materials to become internationally competitive in raw material-based industries, as demonstrated by Japanese and Korean steel makers.

Third, the United States did not have a few high-volume exports that could easily be "targeted" for promotion. "Iron and steel" allegedly accounted for 37 percent of total U.S. exports in 1929, but this category actually comprised heterogenous products with diverse steel contents: the 37 percent figure was divided among iron and steel products (5.4 percent), machinery (16.4 percent), and automobiles and parts (15.7 percent) (Wright 1990). Latin America couldn't possibly replicate the product composition of the United States even roughly and thus had to improvise its own export basket. This was more difficult than following a ready-made path, such as the one Japan left for its followers.

Fourth, both resource-intensive and other manufactured exports of the United States were *driven by advanced technological capabilities* in the hands of "national leaders": "among such leading industrial firms as those making Kodak cameras and Singer sewing machines, constant attention to improved technology and new products secured more markets for American manufacturers and kept American producers in advance of their potential foreign competitors in key industries" (Becker 1982, p. 50).[30] Latin America, however, lacked the technological capabilities that made American exporting dynamic. Without such skills, Latin America was handicapped by relatively high costs of capital and labor and an absence of obvious products to promote.

Fifth, export promotion in American history was largely restricted to information-gathering by diplomatic consuls, extensive technical assistance for agriculture, and military expenditures to develop defense-related products. Aircraft became the single most important postwar U.S. manufactured export. Military aid was tied almost entirely to the procurement of U.S.-manufactured goods. These supports apart, American export promotion was virtually nil: "Foreign sales (in 1893–1921) were achieved for the most part without assistance from the US government" (Becker 1982, p. 50). This was mainly because American exports began to be undertaken primarily by big businesses on the basis of innovative technologies. Therefore, U.S. exporters required little government help and the United States became a poor model for export promotion.

In one critical—-and ironical—-respect the American pattern *was* very easy to follow: *it had high tariffs.* In its early stage of development, the United States adopted tariffs that were among the world's highest. In 1913, the United States average was almost twice that of Japan (see table 7.6).[31]

In 1913 Argentina's tariff level (import duties as a percentage of special total imports) was almost identical to that of the United States—21.6 percent and 21.4 percent respectively (table 7.6).[32] The system in force in Argentina just before World War II "could be described as a form of protectionism half-way between the moderate protectionism for the Western European countries and the strict protectionism of the United States" (Bairoch 1989, p. 152). Argentina's average (nominal) tariff rate was as much as 148.8 percent in 1960–65. Thereafter, however, nominal tariffs in Argentina settled down to slightly below 40 percent, the American "McKinley" rate.

Brazil emulated American tariff behavior starting in the nineteenth century.[33] After the American Congress passed the McKinley Bill of 1890, which called for a large 40 percent protective tariff regime, the Brazilians passed a similar bill. Thereafter "the ultra-protectionist Brazilian tariff of 1897 . . . *encouraged the imitation of the United States model"* (Teixeira Vieira 1951, p. 248, emphasis added).[34] In 1913 Brazil's average level of import duties on manufactures ranged between 50–70 percent (table 7.6). Measured in terms of average tariff rates, it was 42 percent. In fact, tariffs were largely restricted to textiles (Versiani 1980). After the war, however, Brazil's average tariff rate spiked in 1960–65 to as much as 85 percent and covered a wide range of products. It then quickly settled down in nominal terms to around 40 percent, precisely the "McKinley" rate (see table 2.4).[35]

Even before the first energy crisis in 1973, Brazil, along with other countries in "the rest," became much more aggressive in promoting exports. Import substitution industries such as steel, chemicals, and later automobiles and machinery began to supply products to markets overseas. Export growth in the 1980s had more to do with the rising competitiveness of Brazilian industry than changes in world demand (Bonelli 1992). The government's signal of its interest in raising national exports created business confidence in the sustainability of export-friendly policies and made exports less a reflex of domestic demand conditions.[36] "By undertaking a host of measures to stimulate manufactured exports the government reduced the risk attendant in export activities, as perceived by potential exporters. . . . Increasingly the Brazilian government committed itself to export expansion, and this commitment in itself had a beneficial effect on exports" (Tyler 1976, p. 269).[37] In addition to regular mini-devaluations that prevented gross overvaluation of the cruzeiro, various tax rebates, duty drawbacks, and export financing were put into effect. The most aggressive Brazilian export incentive was the "BEFIEX," as discussed in chapter 6, a program whereby mostly large firms could negotiate a package of incentives with the government, including the ability to import capital goods under free trade conditions in exchange for a commitment to export over what was usually a ten-year period (Fritsch and Franco 1991).

Generally, the effects of Brazil's export incentives were positive. "Available estimates of static efficiency indicate that these exports were not excessively costly forms of earning foreign exchange" (Edwards and Teitel 1986, p. 426). In terms of dynamic efficiency, it was estimated that "an export subsidy in Brazil is likely to have positive effects on national welfare through externalities and dynamic benefits" (Arantes Savasini 1978, p. 51). Nevertheless, Brazil scrapped its export promotion policies under pressure from the United States in the late 1980s. Although exports in the early 1990s grew fast in constant cruzeiros, their growth in U.S. dollars was modest (see table 7.1). Export growth was also associated with stagnant domestic demand—exports thus remained in the nature of a "vent for surplus" (Shapiro 1991). Thus, however energetic Brazil's export drive, and however beneficial its mini-devaluations, it was only with great difficulty and moderate success that Brazil broke out of the mold of a large country, rich in natural resources but poor in manufactured products that enjoyed high export-production coefficients (the paper and shoe industries apart). Brazil may or may not have taken longer than the United States to create an export mentality among its leading firms, but protection of the domestic market without American technological mastery, without a leading sector that could generate jobs, without a small number of manufactured export products that could be targeted, without a "first-mover" advantage in exploiting nonreproducible raw materials, and without a demonstration effect of how to promote exports did not necessarily constitute a recipe for dynamic expansion.

Late Traders and Role Models

The United States and Japan did not exhaust historical trade patterns. Europe was a major trading partner of Latin America and exhibited its own unique pattern, one of high-end, skilled and precision-engeneering goods. "Free trade" was another model, and the most compelling one of all theoretically.

Looking first at the European pattern, a striking characteristic of European trade was its *dense network of intra-regional exchange* (and relatively high export coefficients) (United Nations Conference on Trade and Development, various years). By 1830, 67.6 percent of Europe's trade was estimated to have been internal (Bairoch 1989; Woodruff 1966). By 1990 that figure had risen further to 79.5 percent.[38] Between 1970 and 1995 the European pattern became more evident in "the rest." Almost every country began to export more to regional neigbors (see tables 7.7–7.9).[39] In 1970 Indonesia, Malaysia, Tai-

Table 7.7. Direction of Trade, Latin America

Year	Exports to			Imports from		
	United States	Europe	Local*	United States	Europe	Local*
Argentina						
1970	10.3	55.5	21.1	27.6	39.2	22.9
1980	10.5	31.9	24.5	23.6	34.5	21.4
1995	9.0	22.5	47.2	22.3	31.4	21.3
Brazil						
1970	26.2	43.5	11.7	34.7	35.6	12
1980	18.6	32.2	18.1	22.5	11.3	12.5
1995	11.8	27.9	23.3	26.0	30.4	21.2
Chile						
1970	14.4	30.9	11.5	38.2	31.7	21.6
1980	11.5	41.7	24.7	27.1	20.4	28.6
1995	13.2	27.0	19.9	27.6	21.2	27.8
Mexico						
1970	71.2	11.1	10.5	65.7	22.1	3.7
1980	66.0	16.2	6.9	68.0	17.1	5.8
1995	86.2	5.0	6.1	76.2	10.5	2.8

*"Local" is defined (according to UNCTAD classifications) as "developing America" for Argentina, Brazil, Chile, and Mexico.

Source: UNCTAD (1996).

Table 7.8. Direction of Trade, India and Turkey

Year	Exports to			Imports from		
	Eastern Europe	Europe	Local*	Eastern Europe	Europe	Local*
India						
1970	20.4	20.1	10.0	14.9	110.8	10.8
1980	20.3	25.3	10.7	5.8	20.7	32.9
1995	0.5	21.1	20.9	0.6	28.3	21.2
Turkey						
1970	14.2	60.3	10.4	13	53.8	11.1
1980	16.9	51.7	31.8	10	37.7	66.0
1995	4.9	52.7	17.7	3.0	41.7	16.1

*"Local" is defined (according to UNCTAD classifications) as Asia for India and as OPEC plus West Asia for Turkey.

Source: UNCTAD (1996).

Table 7.9. Direction of Trade, East Asia

Country	Exports to			Imports from		
	Japan	United States	Local*	Japan	United States	Local*
Indonesia						
1970	33.3	14.1	29.4	29.5	18.1	20.1
1980	41.3	11.8	16.7	31.5	13.9	22.7
1995	27.1	14.7	33.5	22.7	13.7	26.8
Korea						
1970	27.7	41.4	7.0	40.8	30.6	10.1
1980	17.3	28.4	14.7	26.2	23.6	8.9
1995	13.7	21.5	34.3	24.6	24.7	16.7
Malaysia						
1970	18.3	20.9	33.1	17.5	10.7	34.9
1980	22.8	18.0	33.3	23.0	16.1	25.7
1995	12.7	14.2	44.4	28.1	17.1	32.1
Taiwan						
1970	15.1	46.4	20.3	42.8	25	10.4
1980	11.0	36.6	17.7	27.2	25.0	10.2
1995	11.8	25.0	40.7	29.5	21.4	11.9
Thailand						
1970	26.3	13.6	30.7	37.6	15.7	8.4
1980	15.3	13.2	26.9	20.7	18.0	22.2
1995	16.8	19.0	35.5	30.7	12.7	26.8

*"Local" is defined (according to UNCTAD classifications) as "other Asia" for Indonesia, Korea, Malaysia, Taiwan, and Thailand.

Source: UNCTAD (1996).

wan, and Thailand exported 20–30 percent of their total exports to other Asian countries. By the 1990s, although nothing close to European levels of intratrade were reached, the average for East Asia rose to 30–40 percent. After economic reforms, between 40 and 50 percent of China's total exports were sent to other Asian countries (intra-Asian trade for India also increased) (UNCTAD 1995). The reasons behind this explosion in intra-Asian trade were diverse. In part, rapid growth rates of manufacturing output were the driving force. In part, trade and direct foreign investment complemented one another (see, for example, Van Hoesel 1997).

With the exception of Mexico, which was and remained heavily oriented toward trade with the United States, Latin American countries began trading more with each other as well, spurred by the formation of MERCOSUR, a free-trade area in the Southern Cone. Latin American intraregional trade became of critical importance in at least two industries, automobiles and steel, but intraregional trade was typically higher among Asian than among Latin American countries.

Free Trade

As a catch-up strategy, free trade appears to have been limited to Switzerland and Hong Kong. That is, whatever the historical time period, these are the only two obvious "countries" that managed to achieve high per capita incomes without tariff protection or export promotion. Therefore, despite free trade's appeal in terms of administrative simplicity, and despite its theoretical claim to "pareto optimality" (assuming perfect knowledge), its practical significance for latecomers was relatively small. The question then becomes, *if free trade has so much to recommend it, why were its adherents so few?*

To the extent that vested interests are held responsible for protectionism, then the absence of vested interests ought to mitigate in favor of free trade (see, for example, Bhagwati 1988). But one fails to perceive any compelling evidence showing that Switzerland and Hong Kong were devoid of vested interests. Probably Switzerland and Hong Kong *had* vested interests like any other economy, but these interests favored free trade. Given Switzerland's and Hong Kong's diminutive size, competing on the basis of the domestic market was out of the question. Both economies, therefore, simply had to brace the full force of free markets in order to develop.

The question then becomes, how *did* they brace the full force of free markets, especially when their neighbors behaved as though their own survival depended on protectionism? By way of an answer, *both Switzerland and Hong Kong enjoyed extraordinary assets by neighboring country standards*, rendering protectionism and other forms of government support unnecessary.

Switzerland's wealth lay in its rich human resources combined with its exceptionally cheap labor: "Switzerland is an interesting example of industrial progress under free trade conditions, but at the price of successive and sometimes painful adaptations and of extremely low wages for labour" (Crouzet 1972, p. 103). Behind its economic success in the early nineteenth century was "freedom from a parasitic landed nobility (a "vested interest") and from its power to legislate in favour of agrarian interests; social mobility and urban self-government; the Calvinist-Protestant religion and the high level of education achieved; and associated with all of these, an active, innovative class of entrepreneurs, managers and engineers" (Pollard 1990, p. 27). Thus, "in comparison with the rest of Europe, the degree of literacy in Switzerland was remarkably high: *there can hardly be any doubt that human capital was the mainstay and the most important stimulating factor of the economic growth"* (Fritzsche 1996, pp. 137–38, emphasis added).

However remarkable Switzerland's educational standards were, its applied engineering skills were equally outstanding. *"Swiss engineering ingenuity was most remarkable.* Possibly the precision work required in watch making may have contributed to this. Steam power came late, but it was in textile machinery that the early engineers showed their skill and innovative abilities" (Pollard 1990, p. 28, emphasis added). In the early part of the nineteenth century, engineering genius was centered on the individual: "One reason why technologically oriented entrepreneurs in Switzerland were getting ahead of the British was Johann George Bodmer, a Swiss-born mechanical genius. . . . He not only gave Swiss compatriots free access to his inventions, which they sometimes could use before they had won a British patent, but also trained young Swiss mechanics in his shop" (Fischer 1991, p. 145). By the 1850s, machinery exports greatly exceeded imports, and *tariffs in neighboring countries were circumvented by exporting to North America, Latin America, the Levant, and Far East.* During the Second Industrial Revolution, Switzerland managed to stay in the vanguard of technological and institutional developments, and grew some of the world's largest businesses (Daems 1986).[40] Swiss national leaders included Ciba, Geigy (the two later merged), Roche, and Sandoz in pharmaceuticals; Nestle, Maggi, and Suchard in processed foods; and Escher-Wyss, Sulzer (the two later merged), Oerlikon-Buhrle, and Schindler in machinery (Schroter 1997).

After World War II, Switzerland continued to maintain its international reputation as a manufacturer even as its financial sector expanded. The share of manufacturing in GDP, although declining, was still as high as 26 percent in the mid 1990s (UNIDO various years [b], 1990 dollars). The international competitiveness of many Swiss specialties continued. As reliable, inexpensive electronic watches appeared in world markets, often made in Hong Kong, Swiss watchmakers struck back with the Swatch watch, a Swiss-made design also using an electronic movement. In 1990–91, watches and clocks were still Switzerland's largest single export, accounting for 7.6 percent of total exports. Next in importance came high-end exports of pharmaceuticals, machine tools, and machinery for the textile and specialty industries (UNCTAD 1995).

Hong Kong's specializations starting in the 1950s were virtually identical to those of Switzerland (ignoring shipping and chemicals): textiles, watches, and banking. But Hong Kong's *knowledge-based assets* were not nearly as rich as Switzerland's, particularly its engineering capabilities. By the end of the twentieth century, when Hong Kong manufacturers could no longer compete on the basis of low wages, Hong Kong all but deindustrialized. Whereas manufacturing once accounted for roughly one-third of Hong Kong's GDP, by the end of the century it barely accounted for one-tenth, and reexports were of greater importance than exports (Amsden 1997b).

Hong Kong transformed itself into a service economy, transferring virtually all manufacturing activity to China, where wages were barely one-tenth of those in Hong Kong (Amsden 1997b). Hong Kong could thrive as a provider of services owing to extraordinary assets: its prime location and its long-established commercial activity. National leaders comparable to Switzerland's multinationals existed in Hong Kong in the form of trading companies, such as Jardine Matheson. Few, if any, late-industrializing countries had comparable assets to sustain the loss of their manufacturing sector and to support themselves on the basis of finance, tourism, and the "China trade."

In fact, with fewer assets than Switzerland, Hong Kong was not as purely free market. Land was Hong Kong's most scarce resource, and the government owned and controlled all land (Hong 1995). The government leased unused land in small quantities each year partly for purposes of earning public revenue. Owing to land ownership, the government never had a real budget deficit, and built Hong Kong's highly competitive infrastructre, including housing. Worker's housing typically received a 50 percent state subsidy (World Bank 1993). Moreover, when Hong Kong's stock market teetered on the verge of collapse in 1997 after a region-wide financial crash, the government intervened heavily to bolster prices.

Hong Kong's manufacturing economy in the early postwar period also deviated from free trade. It was built on cotton textiles and clothing, with know-how of spinning and weaving transferred by Chinese textile entrepreneurs from prewar Shanghai. Despite higher costs of cotton sheeting in Hong Kong than Japan in 1960 (see table 5.4), Hong Kong's textile industry, unlike those of Korea and Taiwan, was able to survive without tariffs because it enjoyed Commonwealth preferences, and Commonwealth members had a common tariff against the exports of other countries, including Japan (see chapter 5). Later, Hong Kong switched to exporting its cotton goods almost exclusively in the form of clothing, and benefited from the relatively high-end American fashion houses that chose Hong Kong as a locus for their production owing to Hong Kong's stable colonial government and excellent communications infrastructure, which enabled fashions to get to market quickly. Among developing countries, Hong Kong enjoyed a *first-mover advantage in apparel*. Hence, in the global managed trade of the textile industry, Hong Kong was assigned higher export quotas than any other developing country.[41] In 1975, 51 percent of Hong Kong's exports consisted of textiles (of which clothing accounted for 42.6 percent). Other important export products were toys, telecommunications equipment (mainly plastic telephone boxes), and clocks and watches (using imported Japanese mechanisms) (UNCTAD 1979).

Arguably, then, free trade as a "catch-up" strategy was restricted to only two countries, Switzerland and Hong Kong, because only these two countries had the requisite assets to build their industries without being overwhelmed by imports or unable to export. In the absence of comparable assets, other latecomers had to, and did, rely on institutions other than free markets to grow.

Conclusion

Countries that were late to industrialize were also late to export manufactures. Therefore, when such countries finally succeeded in entering world manufacturing markets, their exporting tended to follow one or another established trading norm. One such pattern was defined by the United States, a large country with a low population density, rich raw materials, and a low export coefficient. Another such pattern was defined by Japan, a somewhat smaller country with a high population density, poor raw materials, and a relatively high export coefficient. The American pattern involved late entry into export markets, a wide range of "high-tech" specializations (that followers could not easily emulate), protection of the domestic market, and minimal institution building. The Japanese pattern involved early entry into export markets, concentration on a few products with high export/production ratios, relatively low tariffs (ignoring "structural impediments,") and a set of institutions that made exporting an integral part of capital formation.

Whatever the country, capital formation and exporting were intermediated by import substitution. Virtually every manufactured export, save the most labor-intensive (apparel and software), emerged out of an import substitution industry. The superprofits earned through selling in the protected domestic market helped to finance the learning and scale economies necessary to export. At a moment in time the trade regime of a whole country might be biased toward exporting or import substitution (depending on some price aggregation). Individual industries, however, shifted over time from one mode to the other, making any general characterization of them problematic.

Despite the ubiquity of import substitution, the timing and scope of exporting differed among latecomers, depending on their role model—American, Japanese, European or Russian. The European model, of high-skilled, high-end specializations, was possibly the hardest to reproduce. The Russian model—of quasi-autarchy (depending on politics)—was influential in Turkey (in the 1930s) and in India and China (in the 1950s). East Asia's spectacular entry into world markets followed Japan's lead insofar as exporting was made a performance standard for import substitution industries to receive long-term subsidized capital.

The influence of industrialized economies on "the rest's" trading patterns thus suggests that a "role model" is a knowledge-based asset of a sort that can impact positively or negatively on profits. Whatever the history of cooperation and conflict between a teacher and a student, whatever the mixture of love and hate, a role model may provide intimate insights into how a world-class economy works. Foreign ideas and practices are heavily filtered, and the *selectivity* of a country's seclusion (the term is Henry Rosovsky's) rather than simple openness becomes the key to success.

8

National Firm Leaders

<hr/>

After floundering for a century, "the rest" succeeded in creating professionally managed, large-scale, national firms. Their importance, however, varied by country. The mix of a country's business structures by size and ownership (private or public, foreign or national) influenced the level of its investment in skills. The long-term strategic "make"-or-"buy" technology choice was a function of firm composition.

The process whereby a latecomer succeeds or fails to create a corps of "national leaders" is the subject of this chapter. A national leader may be understood as a nationally owned and controlled firm that is "targeted" by government (it receives a disproportionate share of subsidies, which allows it to become a dominant player in its "competitive base" (domestic market), in exchange for which it is obliged to invest heavily in proprietary knowledge-based assets. These assets, in turn, allow it to globalize through exporting or outward foreign direct investment. Despite its bad press in the service sector, the state-owned enterprise (SOE) emerged in "the rest" after World War II as a national leader in the petrochemical and steel industries. In the private sector, small-scale national leaders were found mostly in the Indian software industry and the early Taiwan information technology hardware industry. Private large-scale national leaders took the ubiquitous form of the "diversified business group." Without specialized knowledge-based assets, big business in "the rest" diversified widely into technologically unrelated industries (Hikino and Amsden 1994).

Despite a similar group structure, private large-scale national enterprise differed among countries along three dimensions: market share (depending on the presence of foreign-owned firms); absolute size (depending on whether government policy concentrated or diffused intermediate assets among a small number of large firms or a large number of small firms); and core competence (depending on income distribution in the primary sector and, hence, on the importance of primary products in a firm's investment portfolio). In countries where the foreign-owned firm arrived early in time, achieved "first-mover" advantage in industries subject to scale economies, and experienced no discontinuity in control, it tended to "crowd-out" the private large-scale national firm, as in Latin America.

In theory, the advantages that a host country derives from the presence of an experienced multinational firm (compared with an inexperienced national firm) are short-term efficiencies and potential long-term "spillovers." The chief disadvantages lie at the root of accumulation: the inability to acquire full-set entrepreneurial skills and hence full-set entrepreneurial rents, assuming that a foreign firm invests less in knowledge-based assets overseas than at home. In practice, by the year 2000 foreign firms operating in "the rest" had invested *almost nothing* in innovation insofar as their local expenditures on R&D were virtually nil.[1] If, therefore, a latecomer wished to build its own state-of-the-art proprietary knowledge-based assets, it had to grow its own national firms, large or small.

In North Atlantic history, economic nationalism is identified with mercantilism and autarchy. In "the rest's" postwar history, it is identified with ownership and control: whether leading firms were owned by nationals or foreigners, and whether skills were "made" by nationals or were bought from sources overseas. Despite an initial heavy reliance everywhere on foreign technology transfer, by 2000 only China, India, Korea, and Taiwan had invested substantially in their own knowledge-based assets. China and India were the world's two most populous countries. China, Korea, and Taiwan had among the world's highest export/GDP ratios. *All* four countries, however, shared two fundamental traits: *all* had colonial manufacturing experience and, hence, a disruption in the pattern of foreign ownership after decolonization (see chapter 5); and *all* had equal income distributions. Income distribution (by class, race, region and ethnicity) influenced the allocation of subsidies and, hence, the nature of the firm. The less divided an economy by inequalities, the greater the concerted effort to create national leaders and proprietary skills, as argued below.

To begin to understand "the rest's" postwar process of firm formation, we first present some information on its salaried management and family ownership, firm size, competitive base, and government targeting. This provides the building blocks for further analysis.

The Firm in Late Industrialization

The long-standing difficulty in "the rest" of forming firms in which professionals (salaried employees) manage and coordinate complex, large-scale operating units partially stemmed from the difficulties of juxtaposing salaried management with family ownership, the predominant form of business enterprise in "the rest" as late as 2000 (for Argentina and Korea, see Chandler Jr. et al. 1997). Professional management allows the advantages of family ownership to exceed the disadvantages. In general, the strengths of family ownership include loyalty based on blood ties, freedom from outside interference in decision making, and the ability to groom the next generation of top managers early and systematically. The weaknesses include limited access to equity funds owing to the avoidance of capital from outside the family; a conservative policy of eschewing new, risky enterprises in order to meet the company's highest obligation, preservation of the family fortune; a tendency for the founding family to lose the ability and desire to engage in strategic management; a loss of drive on the part of salaried managers owing to the monopolization of top management posts by family members; and—especially important in "the rest"—a tendency for the private interests of the family to get in the way of rational management. "The Japanese zaibatsu were among the first to minimize these weaknesses by taking a long view of profits, being flexible and progressive, and *offering top management posts to non-family salaried managers*" (Morikawa 1992, p. 246).

There is no direct evidence that the professionalization of management was resisted in "the rest" after World War II. Nonetheless, it is a fact that even by 2000, *top* management posts in large family owned firms tended to remain in the hands of family members; supply became large enough to enable families to recruit salaried managers without having to give them top management posts. Even firms whose shares were publicly traded tended to remain under family control. In the typical case of Argentina's forty-three biggest groups, seventeen had at least one affiliate listed on the Buenos Aires stock exchange. In all seventeen cases, a family maintained controlling interest of no less than 50 percent of total capital as late as 1995 (Schvarzer 1995). The situation in Korea (Amsden 1997a) and India (Agarwala 1986) was similar. In the postwar period, however, all countries in "the rest" had at least succeeded in establishing family owned firms with salaried managers reaching *almost* to the top of the managerial hierarchy, especially at the plant level, where foreign technology had to be absorbed, adapted, and improved.

The Competitive Base

The industrial history of a latecomer first revolved around its competitive base: as we saw in chapter 7, most industries started as import substitutes and the home base facilitated learning and the realization of scale economies.[2] The intention of the developmental state was to woo national firms with subsidies in order to seize *"first mover" advantage* in import substitution industries subject to economies of scale.[3] The retaking of the domestic market in East Asia benefited from Japan's wartime disintegration (see chapter 5). Korea and Taiwan temporarily lost their fiercest foreign competitor and also inherited Japan's banking and manufacturing properties, however disabled. Indonesia expropriated Dutch assets in the 1950s. Malaysia began to indigenize British agency houses soon thereafter (as discussed below). Many British agency houses in India had divested their holdings following independence in 1947, and Indian investors triumphed over foreign investors frightened by political change. The retaking of the domestic market in Latin America benefited from Britain's wartime dislocations, but Latin America also confronted a powerful Northern neighbor strengthened politically and economically by war. Not only did Latin America not experience the same breakdown in foreign ownership that Asia experienced, but denationalization actually occurred in Latin America to the extent that existing national enterprises were acquired by new foreign firms. In Mexico, for example, about 50 percent of foreign investments in the early postwar years are estimated to have taken the form of takeovers of national firms (Whiting 1992; Bennett and Sharpe 1985). Thus, whereas all countries in "the rest" succeeded for the most part in retaking the home market from foreign *exporters*, the record of retaking the home market from foreign *investors* was mixed. Hence, the latitude for national leaders to arise also varied.

Targeting

National leaders in "the rest," private or public, all shared one characteristic: *they tended to be a product of government promotion ("targeting")*. In the case of the private leader, it tended to be either an affiliate of a *diversified business group* with a history of government patronage,[4] or a *"state spin-off."* A state spin-off could take one of several forms, entailing more or less government support: a joint venture between the government and a foreign technology leader (such as Maruti Motors in India's automobile industry and USIMINAS in Brazil's steel industry); a "model factory" with a mixture of state, foreign, and private national ownership (such as the Taiwan Semiconductor Manufacturing Corporation, the world's largest producer of foundry chips); a defense-related contractor that benefited from dual-use technology transfers (such as the systems engineering division of India's Wipro Infotech Ltd.); a privately owned enterprise "crowded in" by a SOE (as observed throughout "the rest" in downstream petrochemical industries such as synthetic fibers); or a "small" firm hatched and husbanded by a public research institute (such as Hsinchu Science Park's prize pupil, Taiwan's Acer Computers, with sales of over $8 billion in 1999).

Industry targeting and firm targeting involved the same control mechanism—subsidies were made conditional on performance standards. Performance standards related to firm targeting, however, differed from those related to industry targeting. At the firm level, performance standards that stipulated ceilings on debt equity ratios influenced *firm size*. Standards that entailed conditions related to equity and profit repatriation affected *foreign ownership*. Standards that concerned intrafirm profit distribution influenced *firm structure*. In addition, firm targeting involved restrictive *industrial licensing*—all major capacity additions and expansions in "the rest" usually required government approval, the rationale being the avoidance of costly duplication and excess capacity. Thus, licensing empowered governments to determine a firm's market structure while performance standards enabled it to influence its size, organization, and nationality.

In high-technology industries, firm-level targeting was typically transacted through public research institutes or "science parks." Even when admission into such parks depended on a competitive process, "picking winners" was inherent in this process. Otherwise, given the benefits of park residence, all firms would want to operate in such a setting. To qualify for the benefits of a science park, a firm had to meet prescreening criteria.[5] Admission into Taiwan's Hsinchu Science Park depended on the evaluation of a committee that consisted of representatives from government, industry, and academia. The major criterion for admission was the nature of the technology a firm was developing. Tainan Science Industrial Park (TSIP), approved by Taiwan's legislature in 1995, was designed to attract firms in the microelectronics, precision machinery, semiconductor, and agricultural bio-technology industries. Benefits for Park companies included grants of up to 50 percent of necessary funds from government programs, tax exemptions, low interest loans, as well as special educational facilities. In exchange, companies seeking admission into TSIP had to meet criteria related to operating objectives, product technology, marketing strategy, pollution prevention, and management (Tainan Science-Based Industrial Park 1996).

The principles of science parks throughout "the rest" were similar to those in Taiwan. Thus, as late as the year 2000, government support of science and technology was not simply generic (skill-specific); it was also targeted (firm-specific).

Firm Size

All national leaders in "the rest" tended to be small by North Atlantic or Japanese standards. Among *Fortune's* 500 leading global industrial enterprises, the number from late-industrializing countries rose over time (except in the 1990s) but remained modest: 4 in 1962, 33 in 1992, and 25 in 1999.[6] Among the world's top 100 transnational corporations, not one was from outside the North Atlantic or Japan (UNCTAD 1998). By "the rest's" standards, however, some national leaders started small whereas others started large in terms of capitalization. The ultimate size of both types of firms depended on the nature of the market—whether it was *mass production* or *niche*, and subject mainly to scale economies in production or scale economies in product development (ignoring distribution). Given the importance of scale economies in product development (design), small national leaders were not firms of "small" or even "medium" size as typically defined in developing countries (circa 2000); that is, firms with, say, annual sales of less than one hundred thousand dollars (or even one million dollars). Instead, "small" national leaders had sales in the hundreds of millions of dollars.

Examples of "small" firms from Taiwan in the year 1998 included: Lite-On Technology, a member of the Lite-On Group and the world's fourth largest computer monitor manufacturer, with annual sales of $820 million; Winbond, the world's tenth largest producer of memory ICs, with sales of $457 million; Delta Electronics, the flagship of the Delta Group and the world's leading producer of switching power supplies (SPS) with sales of $399 million; Macronix, the world's seventh leading maker of nonvolatile memory products, with sales of $370 million; Primax Electronics, the world's leading producer of hand-held scanners, with sales of $337 million; and Siliconware Precision Industries, the world's third largest independent IC packager (after Anam Industrial of South Korea), with sales of $268 million.[7]

Large national leaders with big initial capital outlays tended to predate small national leaders due to "the rest's" sequence of diversification. Targeting was first aimed at establishing firms in "hot" industries with large fixed capital requirements (see chapter 6). Because "hot" industries had large scale economies in production, the first entrants into them were strategically positioned to capture "first-mover" advantages. Where possible, therefore, the opening of such industries and the organization of large, nationally owned firms went hand in hand.

The diversification path of "the rest" after World War II is shown in figure 8.1. The figure is constructed on the assumption that "the rest" took the average composition of the manufacturing sectors of the North Atlantic and Japan—indexed at zero—as its benchmark; their manufacturing structure, on average, became "the rest's" ideal. In the time period in question (1980–95), labor-intensive industries such as textiles, footwear, and food, as well as early import substitution industries with big scale economies in production such as petroleum refining, steel, and industrial chemicals, exhibited shares in total domestic manufacturing output that were greater in "the rest" than in the North Atlantic and Japan. The reverse occurred in other capital-intensive and more skill-intensive industries. The share in total manufacturing output of ceramics, fine chemicals, electrical and nonelectrical machinery, and transportation equipment was smaller, on average, in "the rest" than in the North

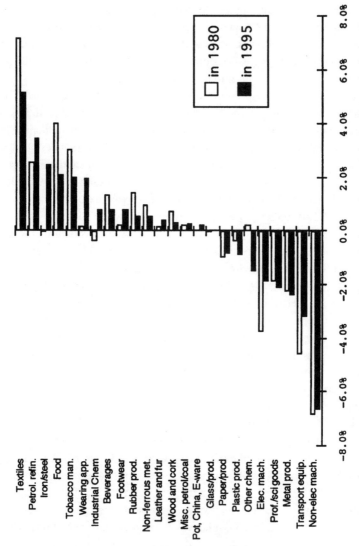

Figure 8.1. Distribution of manufacturing value added: Difference between the average of ''the Rest'' and the average of the North Atlantic, 1980 and 1995. North Atlantic shares are indexed at zero. *Source:* UNIDO (1997).

Atlantic and Japan, whether in 1980 or 1995. The object of "the rest" was to enter and expand in these industries, creating national leaders in order to reach minimum efficient scale and attain "first-mover" advantage.[8]

The diversified business group tended to be the initial agent of diversification in late industrialization and the incubator of large national leaders. Leading firms diversified widely because they lacked a proprietary core competence in any single technology family. Diversification created opportunities for them to expand without the high risk of hitting a technology ceiling. The initial absence of proprietary know-how and the group form of business thus went hand in hand (Hikino 1994). Among "the rest's" fifty largest enterprises, groups numbered as many as thirty-one. National specialized firms numbered only four, with the remaining fifteen firms accounted for by state-owned enterprises (SOEs) and multinational firms (see tables 8.1 and 8.2). Through multiple entries into unrelated industries, business groups could acquire *generic project execution skills*. The ability to diversify quickly and at minimum cost became an asset subject to *economies of scope*. The generic skills involved in diversifying included conducting feasibility studies, arranging finance, identifying sources of technology, supervising construction, procuring machinery, starting-up operations and trouble-shooting (see table 1.2). In light of its assets, the diversified business group soon became the single most important organization in "the rest" to develop basic industry and the crucible for national leaders (see table 8.1, as well as the summaries of data presented in table 8.2a–b).

The rise to world prominence of small firms in global niche markets was relatively slow because crossing the line between a cost-efficient "original equipment manufacturer" (OEM) to an "original design manufacturer" (ODM) to an "original brand manufacturer" (OBM) required heavy investments in product development and distribution. To recover prototyping, tooling, and development expenses, firms had to manufacture a large volume of a product. Thus, even small high-tech niche manufacturers were subject to scale economies. Scale economies in innovation are evident from observing the Taiwan information technology (IT) hardware industry in the late 1990s, one of Taiwan's largest exporters (*the* largest in 1996), the world's third largest production site for IT hardware after the United States and Japan, and an industry that grew in Taiwan between 1988 and 1998 at a compound annual rate of 20.3 percent.[9] The reputation of Taiwan's IT hardware industry was one of intense competition.[10] Yet domestic output concentration was high. It was especially high in more technologically complex market segments of the IT industry, suggesting economies of learning: in product lines where development costs were greatest, volume production was most critical and market concentration tended to be highest.

Table 8.1. Top 50 Manufacturing Enterprises,[1] Ranked by Sales, 1993, Selected Countries

Name	Sales (mil US$)	Type	Activities	Country
1. Hyundai	74,142	group	diversified	Korea
2. Samsung	66,845	group	diversified	Korea
3. LG	51,679	group	diversified	Korea
4. Daewoo	37,303	group	diversified	Korea
5. Samsung Co. Ltd.	24,819	affiliate/g	electronics	Korea
6. Sunkyoung	22,210	group	diversified	Korea
7. Petroleo Brasileiro	21,023	public	petroleum	Brazil
8. Samsung Electronics	20,869	affiliate/g	electronics	Korea
9. Petroleos Mexicanos	20,270	public	petroleum	Mexico
10. Daewoo	19,367	affiliate/g	electronics	Korea
11. Ssangyong	19,155	group	diversified	Korea
12. Hyundai Corporation	14,238	affiliate/g	diversified	Korea
13. LG International	13,467	affiliate/g	textiles	Korea
14. Hyundai Motor Co. Ltd.	13,328	affiliate/g	autos	Korea
15. Kia[3]	12,096	group	auto industry	Korea
16. Chinese Petroleum	11,836	public	petroleum	Taiwan
17. Hanjin	10,053	group	diversified	Korea
18. Autolatina Brasil S.A.[4]	9,660	mn	autos	Brazil
19. Hanwha	9,440	group	diversified	Korea
20. Salim	8,531	group	diversified	Indonesia
21. Yukong Ltd.	8,499	affiliate/g	petroleum	Korea
22. LG Electronics	8,497	group	holding co.	Korea
23. Lotte	8,272	group	diversified	Korea
24. Indian Oil Corporation	8,077	public	petroleum	India
25. Petrobras Distrib.	6,821	public	petroleum	Brazil
26. Hyosung	6,424	group	diversified	Korea
27. TATA	6,415	group	diversified	India
28. Fiat Automoveis S.A.	6,100	mn	autos	Brazil
29. Hyundai Motor Service	6,072	group	autos	Korea
30. Pertamina	5,924	public	petroleum	Indonesia
31. General Motors Brasil	5,873	mn	autos	Brazil
32. Goldstar Co. Ltd.	5,572	affiliate/g	electronics	Korea
33. Formosa Plastics Corp	5,346	group	diversified	Taiwan
34. Halla[5]	5,323	group	diversified	Korea
35. Lucky Goldstar Int.	5,292	group	diversified	Korea
36. Shell Brasil S.A.	5,261	mn	petroleum	Brazil
37. Doosan	5,202	group	diversified	Korea
38. Kumho	4,993	group	diversified	Korea
39. Kolon	4,811	group	textile congl	Korea
40. Siam Cement Group	4,470	group	diversified	Thailand
41. Comp. de Cigarros SC	4,290	spec-priv	tobacco	Brazil
42. Vitro S.A.	4,195	group	diversified	Mexico
43. Yacimientos Petroliferos	4,192	spec-priv	petroleum	Argentina
44. Steel Authority Limited	4,021	public	iron & steel	India
45. Shinkon Syn. Fibers	4,021	spec-priv	syn. fibers	Taiwan
46. Chrysler de Mexico	4,002	mn	autos	Mexico
47. Wei-Chuan Food Co.	3,872	spec-priv	food proc.	Taiwan

Table 8.1. (*continued*)

Name	Sales (mil US$)	Type	Activities	Country
48. Ford Motor Company	3,870	mn	autos	Mexico
49. Taiwan Tobacco & Wine	3,865	public	tobacco	Taiwan
50. General Motors Mexico	3,772	mn	autos	Mexico

1. Includes all types of manufacturing enterprises: public, multinational (mn), specialized-private (spec-priv), and private business groups. Sometimes groups are consolidated and sometimes large affiliates are listed separately, a reflection of the accounting procedures followed by each group. Separately listed group affiliates are denoted "affiliate/g." Enterprises that were *exclusively* involved in construction, mining, agriculture, finance, or public utilities (such as electric power and telephone companies) are excluded. All "petroleum" companies are included under the assumption that these enterprises were involved in the manufacture of petroleum products. Business groups that had operations in nonmanufacturing fields were included only if they also had significant operations in some manufacturing field.
2. All sales figures are for 1993 except for the following: Argentine groups, 1992; Korean groups, 1995; Taiwan groups, 1994; Brazilian groups, 1992; and all private and public specialized companies for Argentina, Brazil, and Mexico, 1994.
3. Absorbed by Hyundai group.
4. Since disbanded.
5. Bankrupted.

Sources: Moody's (1996), Kyang-Hoe, (1996), PT. Kompass Indonesia (1995), *Business Standard* (1995), Khanna (1997), Arokiasamy (1996), C.C.I.S. (various years), Gallegos (1997), Jomo (1993), Bank Indonesia (1996), Hill (1996).

The most technologically complex products produced in Taiwan's IT industry in 1998 were the notebook PC, the video card, the sound card, and the desktop PC (which was already relatively mature). These were the products that tended to have the highest concentration ratios (see table 8.3). Only three firms, for example, accounted for 84 percent of Taiwan's total output of desktop PCs. In order to lower the costs of making the video cards and sound cards that went into personal computers (as well as making personal computers themselves), manufacturers designed customized integrated circuits (ICs). Custom chips were like printing—all the money was in the design and set-up fees. Once production started, it was cheap to produce a long run, which mitigated toward scale. In contrast, the least technologically complex products—the case, monitor, and motherboard, for example—had much lower concentration ratios; anybody with a high volume plastic or metal working shop could make a computer case, so there were few barriers to entry (the top two firms making cases in Taiwan, however, still had a market share of 40 percent). Thus, market concentration and high investments in learning tended to go hand in hand, from which the importance of scale economies in learning and a firm's competitive base may be inferred.

Table 8.2a. Distribution of Top 50 Manufacturing Groups and Top 50 Manufacturing Enterprises, by Country

	No. of Manufacturing Groups	(No. of Other Groups)*	Total Enterprises
Argentina	1	***	1
Brazil	0	(13)	7
India	2	***	3
Indonesia	4	***	2
Korea	21	(1)	26
Malaysia	2	***	0
Mexico	7	(1)	5
Taiwan	10	(1)	5
Thailand	3	***	1
Total	50	16	50

*These include those groups that were originally included in the top 50 but were subsequently eliminated because their primary activities were nonmanufacturing (construction, finance, etc.).

The following 16 groups were those eliminated:

		Sales	Activities	Country
1.	Bradesco	19,351	finance	Brazil
2.	Itausa	18,418	finance	Brazil
3.	Bamerindus	11,494	finance	Brazil
4.	Real	9,092	finance	Brazil
5.	Economico	8,183	finance	Brazil
6.	Lin Yuan construction	6,119	construction	Taiwan
7.	Odebrecht	5,007	construction	Brazil
8.	Fenicia	4,798	finance	Brazil
9.	Grupo Cifra	4,582	commercial	Mexico
10.	Dong-Ah	4,260	construction	Korea
11.	Camargo Correa	4,158	construction	Brazil
12.	Andrade Gutierrez	3,706	construction	Brazil
13.	Multiplic	2,918	finance	Brazil
14.	Bandeirantes	2,591	finance	Brazil
15.	Mercantil Finasa	2,544	finance	Brazil
16.	CR Almeida	2,456	finance	Brazil

Table 8.2b. Distribution to Top 50 Enterprises, by Type

Type	No. of Enterprises
Groups & affiliates	31
Specialized-private	4
Public	8
Multinational	7

Note: Table 8.2b represents a summary of tables 8.1 and 8.5. Sources and additional notes are provided in those tables.

Table 8.3. Market Power in Taiwan's IT Hardware Products Industry, 1998

Product	Industry Output Concentration[1] (%)	Global Market Share (%)	Offshore Taiwan Production (%)	OEM Proportion (%)
Video card	95 (4)	40	18	48
Sound card	87 (2)	49	67	62
Desktop PC	84 (3)	na	89	65
SPS[2]	83 (5)	65	91	98
Notebook PC	74 (5)	39	0	85
CD Rom	72 (5)	33	59	30
Keyboard	64 (3)	65	91	75
Mouse	62 (3)	60	90	75
Scanner	57 (5)	85	38	48
Motherboard	55 (5)	66	37	28
Monitor	45 (5)	58	71	65
Graphics card	40 (5)	na	65	28
Case	40 (2)	75	75	63
UPS[3]	33 (5)	40	25	75

1. Numbers in parentheses refer to top firms with respect to their share of output. The data are for the second half of 1998.
2. SPS refers to switching power supply.
3. UPS refers to uninterruptible power source.

Sources: Market Intelligence Center, Institute for Information Industry, Taiwan, and Wang (1999).

Income Distribution

If, for the moment, we equate national leaders with the largest firms—which implies that (a) the largest firms got to the top by merit, and (b) small leaders succeeded in growing large—then what is striking about "the rest's" largest firms is how unevenly distributed they are among countries (see table 8.4). *Some countries had many national leaders and others had few.* In 1985, Taiwan had more entries among "the rest's" top 200 firms (the last reliable data point for such a comparison) than more populous Argentina or Mexico. It had as many entries among the top 200 as Brazil, with a population seventimes greater. (Korea had twice Taiwan's population size and twice as many national leaders). The poor showing of Argentina and Mexico is especially striking in high-tech: neither country had *any* top ranking firm in this category.

The country of origin of *niche* national leaders is not known in any systematic fashion—the population of such leaders is difficult to identify unambiguously. Appearances, however, suggest that many small national leaders originated in Taiwan. But, as just suggested, *Taiwan also ranked high in its share of big businesses.* Among the top fifty business groups in "the rest," Korea had twenty-one, Taiwan had ten, Argentina had one, and Brazil had none

Table 8.4. Distribution of the 200 Largest Industrial Enterprises[1] in Late Industrializing Countries, 1985 by Country and Industry[2]

Country	High-Tech	Mid-Tech	Low-Tech	Petroleum	Total
Argentina	0	4	6	2	12
Brazil	3	5	7	3	18
Chile	0	3	1	1	5
India	7	15	10	7	39
Korea	11	13	11	0	35
Malaysia	0	2	3	1	6
Mexico	0	2	3	1	6
Taiwan	5	7	5	1	18
Turkey	1	2	2	1	6
Asia	23	40	36	19	118
Latin America	4	15	20	12	51
Middle East and Africa	2	5	12	12	31
Total	29	60	68	43	200

1. Enterprises included are those owned and controlled by nationals (public or private) of late-industrializing countries. Rankings are by sales. Enterprises are operating units. Data for China not included.

2. Given the usually poor quality of data, the industry classification is sometimes arbitrary. "High"-tech may be exaggerated and relate mainly to electronic assembly operations and bulk pharmaceutical production.

High-tech: chemicals, pharamaceuticals, computers, electrical and electronic products, aircraft and aerospace, and professional and scientific equipment.

Mid-tech: rubber products; stone, clay and glass products; primary and fabricated metals; general machinery; and automobile and transportation equipment excluding aerospace.

Low-tech: food, textiles and apparel, lumber and paper, and miscellaneous manufactures.

Sources: Compiled and reclassified from "South 600," *South*, August 1987, pp. 14–24, and checked against other available sources such as *Moody's International*. As cited in and adapted from Hikino and Amsden (1994, p. 302).

(see table 8.5). Mexico had seven, but not all were as focused on manufacturing as the groups in Korea and Taiwan.[11] Among the top fifty manufacturing *enterprises* in "the rest" of *all types*—private firms, private groups, state-owned enterprises and multinationals—as many as twenty-six were from Korea. The few entries in this listing from Latin America comprise either foreign-owned or state-owned firms (see tables 8.1 and 8.2). Other data sources, for both manufacturing and non-manufacturing, tell roughly the same story. Of the *Financial Times*'s top 500 global companies in 2000 (ranked by market capitalization) twenty-four were from Asia (excluding Japan, Australia, and China) and only three were from Latin America (*Finiancial Times* 2000). Latin America's poor showing among large-scale firms contrasts with its more advanced industrialization than East Asia at the end of World War II (measured by the share of manufacturing in GNP, as shown in table 5.2).

Exporting enabled Taiwan and Korea to overcome their relatively small market size and sustain big businesses. But countries with large domestic

Table 8.5. Top 50 Private Business Groups in Manufacturing,[1] Ranked by Sales, 1993,[2] Selected Countries

Group	Sales (mil US$)	Activities	Affiliates	Established	Country
1. Hyundai	74,142	diversified	26	1947	Korea
2. Samsung	66,845	diversified	28	1938	Korea
3. LG	51,679	diversified	43	1947	Korea
4. Daewoo	37,303	diversified	14	1967	Korea
5. Sunkyoung	22,210	diversified	14	1953	Korea
6. Ssangyong	19,155	diversified	23	1939	Korea
7. Kia[3]	12,096	autos	7	1944	Korea
8. Hanjin	10,053	diversified	12	1945	Korea
9. Hanwha	9,440	diversified	22	1952	Korea
10. Salim	8,531	diversified	429	na	Indonesia
11. Lotte	8,272	diversified	24	1967	Korea
12. Hyosung	6,424	diversified	21	1957	Korea
13. TATA	6,415	diversified	37	1907	India
14. Formosa Plastics Corp.	5,346	diversified	na	na	Taiwan
15. Doosan	5,202	diversified	21	1896	Korea
16. Kumho	4,993	diversified	14	1948	Korea
17. Kolon	4,811	diversified	16	1953	Korea
18. Siam Cement Group	4,470	diversified	21	1913	Thailand
19. Daelim	4,345	diversified	13	1939	Korea
20. Shinkon Syn. Fibers	4,021	syn. fibers	na	na	Taiwan
21. Wei-Chuan Food Corp.	3,872	food proc.	na	na	Taiwan
22. Dong Kuk Steel	3,823	diversified	13	1949	Korea
23. Dongbu	3,822	diversified	13	1969	Korea
24. Hanbo[2]	3,774	diversified	na	na	Korea
25. Sime Darby Bhd	3,700	diversified	60	1910	Malaysia
26. Vitro, S.A.	3,518	diversified	106	1909	Mexico
27. Haitai	3,338	diversified	16	1945	Korea
28. Grupo Carso	3,169	diversified	16	1980	Mexico
29. Yuelong Motor Corp	3,036	diversified	na	na	Taiwan
30. Siam Motors Group	3,017	autos	34	1956	Thailand
31. Ching Feng	2,982	diversified	na	na	Taiwan
32. Grupo Cemex	2,975	cement	410	1920	Mexico
33. Kohap	2,973	diversified	6	1966	Korea
34. President Enterprises	2,859	diversified	na	na	Taiwan
35. Astra	2,791	diversified	149	1957	Indonesia
36. Grupo Gigante, S.A.	2,531	diversified	9	1983	Mexico
37. Grupo Industrial Alfa	2,495	diversified	26	1974	Mexico
38. Grupo FEMSA	2,426	industrial dev.	12	1986	Mexico
39. Perlis Plantations Bhd	2,405	diversified	na	1974	Malaysia
40. BK/AV/Kumar Birla	2,344	diversified	13	1947	India
41. Far Eastern Textile	2,332	diversified	na	na	Taiwan
42. Lippo	2,251	diversified	84	1967	Indonesia
43. Sinar Mas	2,251	diversified	121	1962	Indonesia
44. Sammi	2,201	diversified	10	1954	Korea
45. Her Hsing Group	2,090	diversified	na	na	Taiwan
46. Tatung Co.	1,983	diversified	na	na	Taiwan
47. Grupo ICA	1,949	diversified	89	1979	Mexico
48. Evergreen Group	1,900	diversified	na	na	Taiwan

Table 8.5. (*continued*)

Group	Sales (mil US$)	Activities	Affiliates	Established	Country
49. Boon Rawd Group	1,861	agrobusiness	9	1934	Thailand
50. SOCMA	1,853	diversified	na	na	Argentina

1. Sometimes groups are consolidated and sometimes large affiliates are listed separately, a reflection of the accounting procedures followed by each group. Enterprises that were *exclusively* involved in construction, mining, agriculture, finance, or public utilities (such as electric power and telephone companies) are excluded. All "petroleum" companies are included under the assumption that these enterprises were involved in the manufacture of petroleum products. Business groups that had operations in nonmanufacturing fields were included only if they also had significant operations in some manufacturing field.
2. All sales figures are for 1993 except for the following: Argentine groups, 1992; Korean groups, 1995; Taiwan groups, 1994; and all private and public specialized companies for Argentina and Mexico, 1994.
3. Since disbanded.

Sources: Moody's (1996), Kyang-Hoe (1996), P. Kompass Indonesia (1995), *Business Standard* (1995), Khanna (1997), Arokiasamy (1996), C.C.I.S. (various years), Gallegos (1997), Jomo (1993), Bank Indonesia (1996), Hill (1996).

markets should have been able to sustain big businesses as well. Moreover, even in highly export-oriented industries firm size was relatively small in some large countries. Pulp and paper, for example, was a heavily targeted Brazilian industry whose comparative advantage rested on exceptionally rich forest reserves. It was also export-oriented. In 1990, however, Brazil's largest pulp and paper company, Klabin, had only one-quarter the sales of the seventeenth world-ranking pulp and paper company, Jefferson Smurfit of the United States (UNIDO 1992). The petrochemical industry everywhere in "the rest" was also export-oriented (directly or indirectly) and had at its apex a state-owned enterprise that produced the feedstocks which downstream private petrochemical producers required. Private downstream producers, however, tended to be larger in East Asia than in Latin America (Cortes and Bocock 1984), as discussed shortly.

Besides exporting, outward foreign investment also allowed nationally owned companies to augment their size, and if a country's exchange rate was biased against exporting, by definition it was biased in favor of outward foreign investment. Yet Latin American companies, even if they did not export, did not augment their relative size either by globalizing their operations to the same extent as East Asia.[12] In relative terms, their outward foreign investments were small (see table 8.6). By 1997, the outward foreign investments of Korea, Taiwan, Malaysia, and Indonesia were roughly twice or three times as great as those of Brazil, Chile, and Mexico. Those of Argentina (as well as Turkey and India) were minuscule. Moreover, many of the 50 most outward-oriented Latin American transnational companies were not specialized in manufacturing; they were in construction or trade (UNCTAD 1998a,

Table 8.6. Outward Foreign Direct Investment (mil US$), 1986–1997, All Sectors

Country	Average, 1986–91	1995	1996	1997
Argentina	18	155	206	28
Brazil	443	1,559	(−)77	1,569
Chile	27	696	1079	1,949
Mexico	146	(−)482	(−)319	1,037
Turkey	3	113	110	116
India	3	117	239	100
China	745	2,000	2,114	2,500
Korea	923	3,552	4,670	4,287
Taiwan	3,191	2,983	3,843	5,222
Malaysia	311	2,575	3,700	3,100
Indonesia	7	3,552	4,670	4,287
Thailand	923	886	931	500

Source: Adapted from UNCTAD (1998b).

table 2.9). The outward investments of Latin American enterprises that were specialized in manufacturing tended not to be in high-tech fields and were limited to neighboring countries. Of 21 instances of outward foreign investment by Chilean groups as of 1993, 17 were in Argentina, one was in Colombia, and one was in Peru (Sanchez and Paredes 1994). Of the 105 cumulative foreign manufacturing investments (beginning in 1928) of 11 of Argentina's largest groups, only 21 were outside Latin America (ignoring sales outlets) (Bisang 1996). Of 49 reported cases of outward foreign investment in manufacturing from Mexico, only two were outside North or South America (Valdes Ugalde 1997). At least 60 percent of Brazil's outward investments in 1996 were in Latin America or the Caribbean; its major outward investments were in Argentina (Lopes 1999).[13]

Simply stated, Latin America had relatively small scale firms before World War II and continued to operate thereafter with relatively few private large-scale national firms dedicated to manufacturing. The reasons for this relative scarcity of large-scale national enterprises are twofold. First, because of historical reasons, inertia, sectional interests and pressure from Washington, private national leaders were "crowded out" by multinational firms. Second, for reasons directly related to income distribution, *performance standards inhibited the growth of national leaders*. Latin American national leaders were mainly to be found in the metallurgical and petrochemical industries, where they were state-owned.

We may now state the relationship between the distribution of income and the incidence of national leaders in the general case. We make three assumptions. First, an unequal income distribution exacerbates political unrest and uncertainty (real or imagined), which induces a "short-term horizon" among firms and government officials with respect to "make" versus "buy" decisions. Second, an unequal income distribution creates a reluctance on government's part to worsen income distribution further; less concentration of assets is preferred over more concentration of assets. Third, if income inequality is rooted outside the manufacturing sector, and if the skewed concentration of assets in nonmanufacturing creates either quasi-rents or a higher than otherwise capacity to absorb family members productively, then the core competency of leading national enterprises will be outside the manufacturing sector as well.

Short-termism may be hypothesized to favor all types of "buy" over "make" decisions—industrial licensing will favor multinational firms over national firms, and firms themselves will choose to expand more through acquisitions of existing enterprises than through organic development of new business units. Thus, a preference for "buying" over "making" limits national organization building and skill formation. A fear of worsening income distribution may be hypothesized to bias policy makers against firm-level "targeting"—concentrating resources in a few hands. Instead, there is a preference for a larger rather than a smaller number of entrants into an industry; a preference for state-owned enterprise over private enterprise in industries with large scale economies; a preference for specialized firms over diversified firms; and a preference for smaller firms over larger firms. Diversification is discouraged by performance standards that oppose the holding company and group form of business. Large firm size is discouraged by performance standards that place a ceiling on debt-equity ratios. Industrialization policies thus tend to *diffuse* rather than *concentrate* resources.

On the other side of the coin, an existing equal income distribution may be hypothesized to favor long-termism and, paradoxically, a greater tolerance for rising concentration. To offset the social costs of rising concentration, targeted firms are subject to performance standards. Over time, the most important standard involves heavy expenditures on R&D and other forms of learning.

We now turn to the empirical evidence for or against these hypotheses to explain the two divergent development models that emerged in "the rest." In one model, that of *independence*, leading enterprises are nationally owned (or majority joint ventures), the "make" technology choice is paramount, and relations with foreign firms largely involve competition. In the other model, that of *integration*, leading enterprises are foreign owned (or minority joint ventures), the "buy" technology choice is paramount, and relations with foreign firms largely involve integration. There is much overlap between the two models, and globalization in all countries has increased. Nonetheless, income equality in the nonmanufacturing sector tends to characterize latecomer countries following the former model, whereas income inequality in the nonmanufacturing sector tends to characterize countries following the latter.

The Multinational:
Crowding "In" or "Out"?

Like other large-scale firms, the multinational helped diffuse state-of-the art management practices in "the rest" after World War II. Indian business groups, for instance, emulated multinational companies such as Imperial Tobacco, Imperial Chemicals, Dunlop, Lever, Union Carbide, and Firestone, "who began to hire professionally qualified managers when import substitution on a massive scale led to expansion and diversification" (Agarwala 1986). The multinationals were also a benchmark for production skills, especially from American oil and chemical companies in the 1960s and from Japanese electronics and automobile manufacturers in the 1980s.[14] The operations of multinationals in consumer electronics (Malaysia), software (India), and other branches of informatics (Taiwan) also served as an important source of local technological dynamism.[15] Nevertheless, the multinationals did not accumulate or diffuse project execution know-how related to diversification because they were specialized and did not diversify widely. Nor, in the absence of government incentives and systematic coordination, does it appear that multinational enterprises invested locally, especially outside the North Atlantic, in the same types of advanced skills that they invested in at home. Over time, it may have become cheaper for the multinational to hire the same quality of researchers in "the rest" than at home, but *the limited evidence suggests that by the 1990s, the location of R&D activity was still overwhelmingly at home.*[16]

The R&D undertaken by multinational firms in "the rest" appears to have been minuscule, even though the definition of "R&D" in these countries may be broader than in advanced countries. The share of foreign firms in total R&D expenditure in Taiwan in 1995, for example, was estimated to be only *0.0009 percent* (Republic of China 1996, p. 22). In Korea, it was roughly 0.1 percent in 1991 and 1997 (Ministry of Science and Technology, [Korea] 1998). In Brazil, Chile, and Mexico, it was estimated to be nil while in Argentina (in 1992) it approximated merely 2 percent (Alcorta and Peres 1998). In Malaysia, where multinationals dominated in the electronics sector, Malaysia's major export industry, they conducted "little or no long-term R&D into new materials, novel product designs, production technologies or advanced software" (although "most firms carried out substantial innovative activity related to near-term production process improvements") (Hobday 1999). In the Brazilian electronics industry, "what is significant is that all R&D efforts have come from state enterprises, institutions, and national firms, and only later from multinational corporations under policy pressure" (Sridharan 1996, p. 89). Even if multinationals invested in local learning in order to adapt the products they sold domestically to suit consumer tastes (as in Proctor & Gambols' customization of Pampers for hot, low-income climates), and even if they transferred advanced production skills, as in the Mexican automobile industry, research for entirely new products or processes at or near the world frontier was rare.

Simple correlation coefficients for "the rest" in the 1990s, between a country's (a) foreign direct investment (FDI) (foreign firms' share in capital formation) and (b) stocks of a country's investments in science and technology were generally *negative*.[17] FDI was correlated negatively with:

R&D (− 0.45)
Patents (− 0.45)
Scientific publications (− 0.42)
Scientists and engineers engaged in R&D (per million population) (− 0.22).

These correlations are for a limited number of countries over a limited time period; they are essentially cross-sectional in nature and do not explore the possibilities of spillovers from foreign investment over time (see chapter 9). As expected, however, they suggest that countries with relatively *limited* foreign investments tend to invest more in their own national skills.

The inference to be drawn from all this is that the multinational's contribution to "the rest's" learning depended on the *timing* of its arrival and on whether it *crowded-in or crowded-out* nationally owned firms. In industry segments with low entry costs, such as the processing of imported inputs in pharmaceuticals or certain forms of electronic assembly, the early arrival of multinationals did not constitute an entry barrier to nationally owned firms and probably involved a transfer of knowledge, as in the Taiwan electronics industry, where initially foreign firms, including overseas Chinese, accounted for around 65 percent of output (data are for 1974) (Schive 1978). Most midtechnology industries, however, had high capital entry costs and, therefore, *large first mover advantages*. In such cases, the *later* the arrival of the multinational firm, the less the crowding-out effect and the better the prospects for a national leader to germinate.

In addition to government policies toward FDI, discussed later, and the effects of decolonization on foreign investment (see Chapter 5), the timing in the arrival of multinational firms depended in "the rest" on geography and history. Because manufacturing investment by multinationals in less developed countries tended to be influenced by distance—the United States invested mostly in Latin America and Japan invested mostly in Asia—and because U.S. manufacturing firms in general invested overseas much earlier than Japanese manufacturers (Wilkins 1970; Hikino 1994), *the arrival of foreign investment in manufacturing started earlier in Latin America than in Asia*.[18] Probably the émigré form of learning characteristic of Latin America, itself foreign in nature, was also more welcoming of foreign investment than premodern or colonial types of learning, although hard evidence for this assertion is lacking. In any event, the share of U.S. investment in Latin America's total manufacturing output was roughly as much as 20 percent by 1977 (see table 8.7). It was almost 65 percent in transportation equipment and 31 percent in electrical machinery. By contrast, in 1982 (the closest comparable year) Japanese investment in Asia accounted for no more than 5.8 percent of total manufacturing output and 19 percent of transportation equipment output. Moreover, whereas over time the share in manufacturing output of U.S. foreign investment fell in Latin America, the output share of American and

Table 8.7. Timing of Foreign Direct Investment (FDI)* in Latin America and Asia, 1977–1989 (% Share of Foreign Affiliates in Local Output)

	1977	1982	1989
U.S. FDI, Latin America			
Non-elec. machinery	22.6	13.5	31.4
Elec. machinery	31.4	22.6	15.6
Transport equip.	64.5	52.2	38.9
All mfg.	20.0	18.2	15.3
U.S. FDI, Developing Asia			
Non-elec. machinery	3.0	na	na
Elec. machinery	na	6.2	9.8
Transport equip.	na	na	8.5
All mfg.	3.6	2.2	4.5
Japanese FDI, Latin America			
Non-elec. machinery	na	0.6	1.8
Elec. machinery	na	2.2	5.4
Transport equip.	na	4.1	1.1
All mfg.	na	0.8	0.9
Japanese FDI, Developing Asia			
Non-elec. machinery	na	4.5	6.0
Elec. machinery	na	8.4	12.9
Transport equip.	na	18.7	29.1
All mfg.	na	5.8	7.8

*European OECD investments were negligible and, therefore, were ignored. Data for Japanese foreign affiliates include affiliates for all those companies in which Japanese ownership is 10 percent or more. Data for U.S. foreign affiliates include only thoese companies in which U.S. ownership is at least 50 percent. Figures for the United States, Japan, and OECD were not aggregated due to missing U.S. observations.

Sources: Adapted from United States, Department of Commerce (various years), Mortimore (1993), OECD (1996c).

Japanese foreign investment rose over time in Asia, the desirable pattern for host countries to extract the maximum technological know-how with the minimum crowding out. Because the definition of foreign investment used in table 8.7 is less restrictive for the United States than Japan, the U.S. share of output is also relatively *understated*, meaning that the early domination of Latin America's manufacturing sector by U.S. multinationals was probably greater than indicated (and probably greater still in key industries in the bigger Latin American countries).

Multinational investment tended to crowd in domestic investment under complementary production conditions (e.g., subcontracting) and crowd out such investment under substitutive conditions (competition in the same market segment).[19] Ex post, foreign and national producers in "the rest" usually operated in different market segments. In Argentina, for example, of the fifty largest industrial enterprises in 1975, those that were foreign clustered in transportation equipment, machinery, and tobacco while those that were national clustered in food processing and primary metals (steel) (Ines Barbero 1997). The same disparate clustering occurred in India with, for example, foreign firms specializing in jute textiles and national firms specializing in cotton textiles (Bagchi 1972). In Indonesia as well, "foreign investment and domestic investment have been complementary rather than competitive" (Hill 1989, p. 40).[20] In Malaysia, local firms were usually subcontractors to foreign firms rather than prime contractors themselves (Rasiah 1995).

One reason for such exclusivism is that multinationals were altogether uninterested in investing in some sectors. In other cases, exclusivism was idiosyncratic. Union Carbide, for example, retreated for strategic reasons from a market segment in India and sold a chemical plant to Ambani, one of India's fastest-growing postwar groups, with a core competency in chemicals (Herdeck and Piramal 1985). Sometimes joint ventures collapsed and the field was left open for local investors, as when Bechtel Corporation (U.S.) withdrew from a joint venture with Engineers India Ltd. once it discovered that the market for engineering services in petrochemical products and oil refining was smaller than anticipated (Lall 1987). Or multinationals arrived too late, after a local company had already gotten a foothold, as in South Korea's automobile assembly and Taiwan's second-tier petrochemical business. In the latter case:

> The real reasons remain unclear why the Formosa Plastics Group generally utilizes no direct foreign investment and as a rule enters only into short-term technological assistance contracts. . . . It is possible to assume that during the years preceding (the Chairman's) daring business expansion and investment strategy, there was probably no foreign investor on the scene who was willing to take on the risks involved at the time; and when foreign capitalists were more than willing to take the plunge into Formosa's enter-

prises, the Formosa Plastics Group had already become strong enough to stand on its own managerial strength (Taniura 1989, p. 78).

Another reason why local and foreign production tended to be complementary ex post was that *local firms could not survive direct competition ex ante.* Apart from foreign takeovers of national enterprises (the Mexican case was noted earlier), some sectors experienced wholesale denationalization as a consequence of foreign investment, such as the Latin American automobile industry (Evans 1971; Kronish and Mericle 1984; and Newfarmer 1985). To maximize competition in the automobile industry under conditions of high tariff protection (the simple arithmetic mean tariff on transport equipment in 1960 was 167 in Argentina, 40 in Brazil, and 50 in Chile), Argentina, Brazil, Mexico and Chile licensed as many entrants as possible to encourage competition (Macario 1964). In the case of Brazil's Executive Group for the Automobile Industry (GEIA), "one of GEIA's rationales for allowing so many firms to enter the market was the expectation that some would not survive and the industry would consolidate. There was in fact a shakeup in the mid-1960s, but it did not occur in the way GEIA had predicted." The weaker national firms did not survive the difficult years. In the end, only those companies controlled by transnational capital remained (Shapiro 1991, pp. 933–34). In Argentina, GM and Ford began assembling cars after World War I, and in 1954 the Henry Kaiser Corporation founded a joint venture with an Argentine company. Then in 1958 SIAM Di Tella, Argentina's largest metalworking firm, decided to move into automaking, raising hopes that Argentina would be able to grow its own world-class assembler. However, SIAM's entry coincided with a "new official policy to court foreign capital." By 1960 SIAM was only one of twenty-four automobile companies competing for a small domestic market. When a severe recession hit in 1962–63, SIAM retreated from the automobile business and eventually the whole SIAM group went bankrupt (Lewis 1990, p. 337). Chile's high-cost automobile industry was derided by economists because of the unlikelihood that it could ever become efficient given Chile's tiny domestic market. About twenty automobile assemblers located in Chile in the early 1960s, each assembling a "handful" of cars.

> The government considered restricting entry to only a few firms, so that each could operate at higher, more economic levels of output. But the government was not able to formulate acceptable criteria by which companies could initially be selected. The decision was therefore made to let any firm enter, so long as it was willing and able to meet the general conditions of operation. Some observers hoped that in the struggle of survival many firms would eventually be forced to close, leaving the field to a few of the strongest. (Johnson 1967)

The weeding out, however, did not happen quickly, and ultimately the whole industry collapsed. In Mexico, after a number of national assemblers went bankrupt, the government proposed a merger among existing national firms. The Ford Motor Company, however, feared the creation of a "Mexican superfirm," and the merger talks collapsed, leaving multinationals fully in control of automobile assembly (Whiting 1992, p. 215).

By contrast, a local assembler in the Korean automobile industry, Hyundai Motors, triumphed over a joint venture involving the Daewoo group and General Motors (Hattori 1989; Kim 1997). By the year 2000 Hyundai controlled about 85 percent of the Korean automobile market compared with Daewoo's 15 percent, and out-distanced Daewoo in exporting. In Taiwan, too, despite a domestic market not that much larger than Chile's, automobile assembly was dominated by joint ventures, which sourced their parts and components from local suppliers (Lai 1992; Veloso et al. 1998).

Success or failure in creating a national leader in automobile assembly[21] and other mid-technology industries depended not only on geography and historical timing. Among other determinants, the nature of government subsidies and performance standards figured prominently. In India,[22] Indonesia,[23] Korea,[24] Turkey,[25] and Taiwan,[26] *performance standards were deliberately made stringent enough to deter foreign investors from becoming dominant players in all but special sectors* (those that could not otherwise obtain technology or that were targeted to earn foreign currency). Multinationals had to conform with conditions related to profit repatriation, balance of payments, foreign ownership ceilings, and level of monopoly power, which discouraged their entry. Where they were not effectively banned, they were required to form joint ventures as a condition for entry, as in Indonesia. Foreigners in Malaysia were allowed to own from 30 to 100 percent of their investment depending on its conformance with development goals. In Latin America, by contrast, postwar controls on multinational firms were weak or erratic. Brazil promoted "triple alliances" between state, private, and multinational enterprise in certain heavy industries, but did not impose ceilings on individual foreign investments (see Evans 1979).[27]

Before the 1990s, no country in "the rest" had lost as much control over its manufacturing sector to nonnational firms as Canada, where as much as 51 percent of manufacturing output was foreign-controlled (compared with 25 percent for France; 7 percent for the United States; and 5 percent for Japan). Although definitions of foreign ownership varied by country (Korea, for example, used a lax definition that inflated the perceived importance of foreign capital), they did not vary enough to overturn the finding that foreigners' share of "the rest's" manufacturing output in the period 1976–84 was below Canada's: 39.8 percent in Malaysia; 32 percent in Brazil; 29.4 percent in Argentina; 27 percent in Mexico; 27 percent in Indonesia; 19.3 percent in Korea; 18 percent in Thailand; 8 percent in Turkey; and 7 percent in India (Dunning and Cantwell 1987).

Nevertheless, Latin countries in "the rest" had a relatively large stock of foreign manufacturing investment with an early arrival date and a tendency to crowd out local firms in both mid-tech and high-tech sectors, not least of all automobile assembly. Among "the rest's" top fifty manufacturing enterprises of all types in 1993 (see table 8.1), only seven were multinational (defined as having at least 50 percent foreign equity ownership). But of these seven, all operated in Latin America. Automobile assembly was a platform for national firm formation in Taiwan (Yuelong); in Thailand (Siam Motors); in Malaysia (Proton Motors); in Indonesia (a national car initiative that was opposed by the WTO and derailed by financial crisis in 1997); in China (the First Auto Works and two major joint ventures with Volkswagen); in India (Telco, Maruti Motors); in Korea (Hyundai Motors and Daewoo Motors, a joint venture at one time or another with General Motors); and in Turkey (seven joint ventures). In Latin America, by contrast, the multinationals dominated the assembly stage of production and even the first tier of parts manufacture. Brazil had a total of seven entries in "the rest's" top fifty firms, but of these, two were state-owned enterprises and as many as five were multinationals, among which were four automobile assemblers. Three foreign automobile assemblers figured among Mexico's four entries in "the rest's" top fifty firms. Private national firms in Latin America, moreover, were still losing ground to multinationals in the 1990s. Between 1990 and 1996, the share of national firms in the sales of Latin America's 100 largest industrial enterprises fell from 46 percent to 40 percent while the share of multinationals rose from 46 to 57 percent (Garrido and Peres 1998).

In summary, the prevalence of foreign investment in Latin America was due to historical circumstance, proximity to the United States (one of the world's earliest, largest, and most politically powerful foreign investors), an émigré form of manufacturing experience that was quintessentially foreign, and performance standards that did not deter foreign investment to the same extent as in East Asia, India, and even Turkey. As argued later, the nature of these standards was influenced by pervasive income inequalities.[28]

State Venture Capitalism

The state-owned enterprise (SOE), much maligned in the 1980s and 1990s for its "soft budget constraint" compared with the privately owned enterprise, operated in "the rest" mainly outside the manufacturing sector—in communications, transportation, and other service industries that provided social overhead.[29] Whatever the validity of its tarnished reputation in social services, its performance in manufacturing cannot be generalized.[30] In manufacturing, SOEs were concentrated in heavy industry. Among "the rest's" top fifteen public industrial enterprises in 1993, thirteen were either in petroleum or metallurgy, mainly iron and steel (see table 8.8).[31] Although the politicization of SOEs was a problem of unknown proportions in every sector, SOEs in petrochemicals and steel frequently became showcase "national leaders," and crowded in national firms. SOEs in petrochemicals and steel created the organizations necessary to coordinate and rationalize industry-wide growth. They undertook exemplary technology transfers, strengthened professional management, invested in R&D, and became a training ground for technical staff and entrepreneurs who later entered private industry.[32] However limited the number of industries and nongeneralizable the conditions, national leadership in "the rest" in key sectors after the war was assumed by the state-owned firm.

The basic industries in which SOEs specialized were characterized by high fixed capital requirements and high costs of error. To succeed, such industries initially depended on foreign finance and technology; usually the first plant to be constructed was completely engineered by a foreign firm (called a "turnkey transfer"). Therefore, the early success of SOEs in these sectors depended mainly on the quality of domestic *and foreign* management and relations between the two. With respect to management in India, when public enterprises were being established in the 1950s, the government tried to

Table 8.8. Top 15 Public Enterprises in Manufacturing, Ranked by Sales, 1993,[1] Selected Countries

Name	Sales (mil US$)	Country	Activities
1. Petroleo Brasileiro, S.A.	21,023	Brazil	petroleum
2. Petroleos Mexicanos	20,270	Mexico	petroleum
3. Chinese Petroleum Corp.	11,836	Taiwan	petroleum
4. Pohang Iron & Steel	9,900	Korea	iron and steel
5. Indian Oil Corp.	8,077	India	petroleum
6. Vale do Rio Doce	6,833	Brazil	minerals, metals, paper
7. Petrobras Distrbuidora	6,821	Brazil	petroleum
8. Pertamina	5,924	Indonesia	petroleum
9. Steel Authority Ltd.	4,021	India	iron and steel
10. Taiwan Tobacco & Wine	3,865	Taiwan	tobacco and spirits
11. Oil and Natural Gas Corp.	3,207	India	petroleum
12. Hindustan Petroleum	3,002	India	petroleum
13. PETRONAS Bhd	2,490	Malaysia	petroleum
14. Bharat Petroleum	2,126	India	petroleum
15. Bharat Heavy Elec. Ltd.	1,201	India	diversified

1. Some entries are for different years.

Sources: Moody's (1996), Kyang-Hoe (1996), PT. Kompass Indonesia (1995), *Business Standard* (1995), Khanna (1997), Arokiasamy (1996), C.C.I.S. (various years), Gallegos (1997), Jomo (1993), Bank Indonesia (1996), Hill (1996).

fill senior positions with professional managers, "but the very strong opposition of entrenched civil servants and bureaucrats managed to strangle this venture at birth" (a reliance on handpicked managers, however, might have led to cronyism) (Agarwala 1986, p. 252). In Brazil, performance differed radically among three Brazilian state-owned steel mills, all operating with roughly the same production capacity, 3.5 million tons/year. In the best case (USIMINAS), employment was 14,700. In the most politicized case (CSN), employment was 22,200, a reflection of "the featherbedding that resulted from political pressure" (Baer and Villila 1994, p. 6). Thus, given a dependence on organizational skills, performance could be expected to differ among SOEs operating within the same industry in the same country.[33]

A pathology of organizational failure is illustrated by India's Bokaro steel mill. As elsewhere, India's source of technology was dictated by its source of finance. In the case of Korea, luckily both came from Japan, the world's premier steel maker in the 1970s. In the case of India, both came from the Soviet Union. Russian-designed plants were turnkey with initially "practically no indigenous design or equipment content" despite the fact that by the late 1960s, two Indian engineering consulting companies, Dastur (private) and MECON (public), had the capabilities to engineer a complete integrated steel plant. "In 1971, the Russians insisted that their new aid-financed mill at Bokaro would be completely engineered by them." They rejected a detailed project report made earlier by Dastur, an evaluation by Dastur that suggested $150 million savings, and recommendations for more modern technology in the steel shop and finishing operations. "The Bokaro project was ill-fated from the start," with time delays and cost overruns. A very high proportion of equipment was eventually ordered from HEC, a state-owned Indian machinery builder established with Russian technology, but despite massive underutilized capacity, HEC delivered equipment *years* late (this compares with another state-owned Indian heavy equipment builder, Bharat Heavy Electricals, which evolved into a national leader after a management reorganization).[34] Thus, Bokaro stumbled due to incompetent foreign partners, an absence of local participation in the technology transfer process as well as to bureaucratic delays on the Indian side, too great a reliance on HEC, and "a general slackness in SAIL management" (Lall 1987, pp. 81–84; see also Desai 1972).

In Mexico, its state-owned steel company, Altos Hornos, suffered from technical troubles at the outset of operations. Secondhand technology was transferred to Altos Hornos by the American Rolling Mill Co. starting in 1942, but the installation of most pieces of equipment was delayed, and it was said that "the whole project had been erected on an unsound base . . . Altos Hornos became a source of embarrassment to the government and especially to the public investment bank, Nacional Financiera" (Mosk 1950, 143–44). By the 1980s Altos Hornos was still not functioning properly. The founder and director of the company used to say that "if the sun were not visible through the steel sheets, they could be sold." Engineering records were not kept, and plant operational and maintenance staff had scarce information about the likely impact of their engineering efforts on productivity, profitability, or performance (Perez and Jose de Jesus Perez y Peniche 1987, p. 191).

By contrast, performance tended to be outstanding in the steel mills that involved Shin Nippon Steel, one of the world's most efficient producers and itself a former Japanese state-owned enterprise. Relations between Shin Nippon and its (majority) joint venture partners (or its technical assistance partners, such as China Steel of Taiwan) were generally good, and high standards of efficiency and quality were established.

USIMINAS, Brazil's second integrated steel mill (after CSN at Volta Redondo, discussed in chapter 4), was created as a joint venture between a Japanese consortium headed by Shin Nippon, which initially held 40 percent of capital, and Brazil's development bank, BNDE (later BNDES), which held 25 percent (plus additional state investors). BNDE's share later rose to almost 40 percent and Japan's share fell to 20 percent due to unanticipated cost overruns during construction. USIMINAS was managed competently by Amaro Lanari Jr., who had nineteen years prior experience working at one of Brazil's small, private steel mills (Belgo-Mineiro, a Belgian-Brazilian joint venture). According to Lanari,[35] although BNDE was a major shareholder, and BNDE's president was Lanari's cousin, and although BNDE insisted on seeing all papers that crossed the controller's desk, the real influence in USIMINAS was the Japan group. It instilled a sense of purpose and hard work and kept the military government at bay, whereas the military interfered in two other public steel mills, CSN and COSIPAs.[36] The Japan group, however, also created a problem of overemployment. In the 1950s Shin Nippon regarded USIMINAS as an international showcase for its equipment. Therefore, to insure that a piece of equipment worked well, it threw labor at it. Lanari, therefore, went to Booz Allen (U.S.) and developed a management control system that differed from Shin Nippon's. This achieved almost a doubling in productivity. It also helped in the formation of an efficient managerial hierarchy responsible for future productivity gains and belatedly (given rapidly rising domestic demand) exports.[37]

Like USIMINAS, Korea's first integrated steel mill, POSCO, had Shin Nippon for a teacher and a brilliant technology transfer (costs of construction overran in USIMINAS but underran in POSCO). POSCO also had a very strong and inspirational leader, Park Taejun, a former military general. At the root of POSCO's independence was a strategic decision—similar to one undertaken by Shin Nippon early in its own development—to export roughly 30 percent of its output *despite excess domestic demand* to earn foreign exchange and, therefore, maintain more independence from the government (Amsden 1989).

Another Shin Nippon baby was the Bao Steel Company of China. Bao was profitable every year after beginning operations in 1985 and productivity (in tons of crude steel per person) rose from 15 in 1985 to 438 in 1994. Moreover, "every year Bao Steel sold 10% of its output abroad, especially to Japan, the pickiest country, to test the quality of its products" (Zhou 1996, p. 10).

Whereas before the war technology transfer usually took the form of foreign experts coming to "the rest" to teach (see chapter 3), after the war a mass exodus of managers went overseas to study. In USIMINAS, between 1966 and 1976, 380 specialists (243 of higher level, 137 of middle level) were sent abroad for traineeships or courses lasting between three and twenty-four months. In addition, numerous technical visits were made and various technical congresses were attended. This represented 6.5 percent of total investments in technology (Dahlman and Fonseca 1987). In POSCO, "two years before construction began (1971), the first trainees, armed with a list of guidelines for the most beneficial utilization of their sojourn, were sent to gain experience in the Japanese steel industry. Training records were kept in diary form, the contents of which were later distributed to employees back in Korea. Emphasis was laid on the accumulation of practical experience and familiarization with machinery" (Juhn 1991, p. 281; see also Amsden 1989). In China, Bao Steel also sent a large number of its personnel for overseas training; among them, 1,477 persons to learn engineering planning; 749 persons to learn construction, installation and start-up; and 1,899 persons to learn operations, maintenance, supervision and management (Zhou 1996).[38]

In petrochemicals, governments in "the rest" typically created a new state-owned entity to oversee sectoral development: Pemex in Mexico, Petrobras in Brazil, the China Petroleum Company in Taiwan, Companía de Petróleos in Chile, Sinopec in China, Pertamina in Indonesia, the Indian Petrochemicals Corporation in India, Petronas in Malaysia, and the Petroleum Authority of Thailand (PTT).[39] These apex organizations were responsible for oil refining and investments in naphtha crackers to produce feedstocks in the form of ethylene and propylene for processing at a second tier, by private chemical companies. Second-tier producers supplied products such as plastics and synthetic fibers to downstream third-tier producers, whose output included relatively low-value plastics, rubber products, and synthetic textiles for direct sale to consumers. Given this hierarchy, organizations at the top exercised considerable power over all levels of industrial transformation and facilitated technology transfer among them.[40] In Brazil, Petrobras "was known in the industry as a 'school for petrochemical management' " (Evans 1979, p. 237). In Taiwan, "the state played the role of entrepreneur, investor, and organizer in the initial stage of development," so it is not surprising that the state-owned China Petroleum Company, producer of ethylene and propylene (among other products), also played a major part in choosing foreign technology and overseeing the transfer process throughout the production chain (Chu 1994, p. 785). Nor is it surprising that China Petroleum Company itself diffused know-how. "The government-owned petrochemical giant, though producing mainly oil-based products other than petrochemical materials, proved to be a training ground for the human capital needed to manage the second tier operation" (Chu 1994, p. 785).

The oldest enterprise from "the rest" in petrochemicals was Pemex, formed in 1938 following Mexico's oil nationalization. After acquiring extensive experience in oil refining, Pemex began producing petrochemicals in the late 1950s. It used its position to promote local capabilities in the fields of detail and basic engineering and equipment manufacture for petrochemical plants. In 1973 local equipment made up about 75 percent of Pemex's procurement (although the percentage varied by type of project). Out of necessity, Pemex developed its own project management capabilities when the "seven sister" oil companies organized a boycott against it following nationalization. Pemex then contracted to the state-owned Instituto Mexicano de Petroleos (IMP) for its design work. By the early 1970s, IMP was capable of doing some basic design; in 1974 it even established two Pemex refineries in the United States (Cortes and Bocock 1984).

In the case of South Korea, its first oil refinery (Korean Oil Corporation) was established in 1964 as a 50:50 joint venture between the Korean government and Gulf Oil (U.S.). The joint venture was a major supplier of human resources to later petrochemical installations. Because of capital shortages, *all* Korean petrochemical plants were 50:50 joint ventures, with foreign investors supplying the (tied) technology and retaining many of the processes as proprietary knowledge. Still, the Korean partners were pro-active in absorbing know-how—the technology acquisition process in early state joint ventures became a model for the private sector, as in synthetic fibers.[41] The activism of the Korean government influenced not just the flow of funds but also the flow of information: "All in all, the role of the Korean government has been crucial and beneficial" (Enos 1988, pp. 73–74, 100).[42]

An advantage of state ownership was *state power*. It could be used to discipline a foreign partner or generally to promote national goals. In Brazil, the participation of Petroquisa (an off-shoot of Petrobras) in a project "gave partners confidence that the other private partners would not give up in the face of difficulties, leaving them without complementary plants and others to share the overhead. *The state was seen as a potential disciplinarian.* As one participant put it, 'If you have a policeman for a partner, he may only have 3% of the equity but he has a gun' " (Evans 1979, pp. 237, 240; see also Clemente de Oliveira 1994). The government in Korea invited the Fluor Corporation and

A. D. Little to make a feasibility study for its first petrochemical installation (the choice of American firms was dictated by tied U.S. aid). The reports indicated that the local market was "far too small to support plants capable of producing at low unit costs." The Korean government, however, did its own feasibility study that projected a higher growth rate of demand and showed that a petrochemical complex for 66,000 metric tons of ethylene would be efficient. The Korean government then insisted on an even more ambitious petrochemical program for inclusion in its next five-year plan, which was borne out by future demand behavior (Enos 1988, pp. 47–48). POSCO, Korea's first integrated steel mill and now one of the world's most efficient and profitable steel makers, got better finance through political channels than it could have gotten on the open market (or through the World Bank, which refused finance under U.S. pressure on the grounds that the world steel market already suffered from excess capacity). The Korean government extracted war reparations from the Japanese government to finance a larger steel mill than private financial markets would consider (Amsden 1989). In the case of a manufacturer of fertilizers in India that took the form of a joint venture between the Indian government, a foreign oil and chemical company (Chevron and the International Materials and Chemical Corporation, respectively), and Parry's (a private Indian firm), the board of directors took an active interest in the operations of the firm. "The Indian shareholders, who have a majority of the capital, are no more passive than the shareholders of any large US or European corporation. Actually, the Industrial Development Bank of India . . . (and other banks) are very active through their representatives on the Board" (Friedmann and Beguin 1971, pp. 190–91).

SOEs in the petrochemical industry tended to *crowd-in* second-tier private investors (we examine crowding-out by SOEs in countries with racial economic imbalances in the next section). The share of petrochemicals in total manufacturing output in "the rest" typically rose from 1975 to 1990, and ranged from a low of around 15 percent to as much as 30 percent depending on the country (see table 5.2). Even in Taiwan, where state-owned enterprise was relatively pervasive and hence, where private big business groups were small relative to those in Korea, the China Petroleum Company and Formosa Plastics, Taiwan's largest business group and one with a focus in petrochemicals, evolved side by side.[43] In Korea, the third largest *chaebol*, the LG group (formerly Lucky-Goldstar) had petrochemicals as one of its core competencies (Taniura 1993). Privatization of Korea's early petrochemical ventures was designed deliberately to create a national leader, which, after acquiring a state property (Yukong Oil), became the fifth-ranking Sunkyung group (see table 8.5). In Indonesia, alongside its state oil company, Pertamina, the Salim business group, Indonesia's largest, developed a specialization in petrochemicals;

it globalized downstream by investing in Singapore (alcohol ethoxylate), the Philippines (alkyl-benzene), Vietnam (synthetic detergent), Australia (surfactants, phosphates), the former Soviet Union (palm-oil refining), the former East and West Germany (fatty alcohol, sorbitol, alkyl-benzene, sodium lauryl sulphase, ether sulphate), and China (palm-oil refining) (Sato 1993). In Brazil, the Ipiranga group had a specialization in petrochemicals and ranked among Brazil's top ten groups by 1997 (Lopes 1999). Synthetic fibers, a petrochemical derivative, also became the core of big businesses: Kolon Nylon in Korea, Shinkon Synthetic Fibers in Taiwan, and the Alfa group in Mexico, for example.

In all of these cases, the private national manufacturers which were crowded-in by SOEs ranked among "the rest's" top fifty enterprises (see table 8.1). Nevertheless, besides the Alfa and Ipiringa groups, only one other petrochemical company from Latin America had a ranking at the top, and it was a multinational (Shell Brasil S.A.). Pemex, Petrobras, and YPL all crowded-in private downstream petrochemical companies (among Brazil's top ten groups, five produced chemicals), but such companies tended to be relatively small.

In response to pressures to privatize in the 1980s and 1990s, public national leaders in petrochemicals and steel restructured along similar lines: in one way or another, they retained their national identity.[44] The least nationalistic (and distinguished) was Malaysia's oil company, Petronas, which became a minority (40 percent) joint venture with BASF of Germany in 1997. The most nationalistic (and distinguished), such as POSCO, USIMINAS, and Vale do Río Doce, (Brazil's premier metallurgical company), were privatized in such a way that no single owner emerged and the government retained a stake.[45] Usiminas' voting shares were distributed among pension funds (26.8 percent); financial organizations (23 percent); Compania Vale do Rio Doce, which was itself sold to multiple owners (15 percent); Nippon Usiminas (13.8 percent), an original owner of Usiminas that was owned by Shin Nippon Steel; employees and employee pension funds (11.1 percent); and steel distributors (4.4 percent) (Usiminas 1993). Of twenty-four major Brazilian properties auctioned in 1991–93, only twelve had a single major buyer (Banco Nacional de Desenvolvimento Economico e Social [BNDES] 1993). POSCO, too, was sold publicly, to small shareholders. To avert a hostile takeover, it also arranged an equity deal with its old teacher, Shin Nippon of Japan.

Thus, firm-level performance varied in the same industry in both the public and private sectors, but probably more so in the public sector due to different responses to political constraints. In the best cases, found in both the steel and petrochemical industries, state-owned enterprises created de novo organizations, accumulated high levels of both managerial and technological capabilities, and diffused those capabilities to private enterprise.

The Spin-Off Model: Electronics

As in early heavy industries such as petrochemicals and steel, so, too in high-technology industries such as informatics (computers), semiconductors, and telecommunications, the state, in the best cases, acted as a venture capital-ist.[46] Where possible, it crowded-in private national firms. In some countries, a state-owned enterprise fulfilled the function of pioneer. In others, the government's entrepreneurial role was assumed by its research institutes, ministries, or science parks.[47] The principle of incubation, however, was the same even if the exact model differed (as in China). Nevertheless, as we shall see, performance among countries differed in high-technology industries.

In the Brazilian telecommunications industry, a newly formed ministry of communications established TELEBRAS, a financial holding company that adopted nationalist policies starting in 1974, raised Brazilian control over time, and redirected the behavior of multinational firms to conform with national goals. TELEBRAS induced progressive local manufacture of electronic exchanges and greater local R&D. In computers, COBRA, a state enterprise, set the pace under a market "reserve" policy that favored national firms (and that ultimately failed).[48] In India,

> one of the government's most important policy initiatives, right from the outset, was the creation of 'national champion'-type public sector electronics firms to pioneer local production"—the Electronics Corporation of India in mini- and large computers, televisions and instrumentation; ITI in telecommunications equipment; BEL in defense electronics; CMC in software and systems engineering; and Semiconductor Complex Ltd. in IC designs and wafers. By 1987, the private sector's share of electronics production had reached 68%, and jumped further after liberalization in the 1990s. (Sridharan 1996, p. 113)[49]

Side by side with state investment went private investment.

In Taiwan, the public Industrial Technology Research Institute (ITRI) formulated objectives for up-scaling the electronics sector (Amsden and Chu 2003). In the early 1970s, it founded an Electronics Research and Service Organization (ERSO) with a strategy to develop Taiwan's integrated circuit (IC) industry by borrowing foreign technology (from RCA), establishing a demonstration factory, and then diffusing know-how to the private sector (1976–77). To become technologically self-reliant, and to get first-mover advantage over foreign firms in scale and the best personnel, ERSO founded the United Microelectronics Corporation to manufacture ICs. Then, with a view toward increasing Taiwan's IC design houses, ERSO invested $400 million (U.S. dollars) jointly with Phillips of Holland to build a high-precision IC manufacturing facility, Taiwan Semiconductor Manufacturing Corporation. In personal computers (PCs), "ERSO usually takes the lead in developing the crucial technologies, and then transfers these to the PC enterprises" (Chang 1992, p. 208). In defense electronics, the Guomindang party of the government maintained its own research as well as production base.[50]

Korea was the exception that proved the rule. Its climb up the ladder of technological complexity in the electronics industry was led not by the state but by large diversified business groups; where the latter existed, state leadership was less critical. Still, the Korean government was instrumental in promoting the telecommunications industry. It also encouraged R&D at an early date (discussed later) through its electronics research institutes, one in telecommunications, one in semiconductors and computers, and one in basic research. The first two institutes were merged in 1984[51] and became instrumental in developing technology jointly with the chaebol.

Therefore, in terms of laying the groundwork for both *organization-building* and *capabilities-building*, the state played a major role in "the rest's" most important high-technology industry, electronics. This was true of all countries except Argentina and Chile, where high-technology husbanding by the state was minimal (Adler 1987), and Malaysia, Indonesia, and Thailand, the least industrialized economies, where policies to promote national electronic leaders were not as comprehensive by 2000 as elsewhere.[52] In countries where multinational firms had initially dominated the electronics industry—India, Taiwan, Korea, Mexico, and especially Brazil, all of whose electronics manufacture was begun by IBM or other North Atlantic electronics leaders—the government started the race to regain the national market and then to globalize (with long lags between the two in Brazil).

Nevertheless, despite this common groundwork, by the 1990s it was obvious that performance among countries in "the rest" in the electronics industry sharply differed. A country could be expected to specialize in some high-tech market segments while satisfying demand with imports in other high-tech market segments. But, in reality, some latecomer countries failed to specialize in *any* high-tech sectors that were growing rapidly by world standards. As indicated in table 8.4, Argentina, Chile, Malaysia, and Mexico had no entries in high-tech among "the rest's" 200 largest national enterprises. A neglect of high-tech industry is also evident from a comparison of the share of high-tech industries in manufacturing value added (table 8.9) and the trade balance of the electronics industry (table 8.10). By these criteria, performance was *worst* in Argentina, Chile, and Mexico. In terms of market share in the machinery sector (both electrical and nonelectrical), it was very small, whether in 1980 or 1995. The trade deficit in electronics of Argentina, Chile, and Mexico was also large and rising over time. In part, Argentina's large trade deficit in electronics in 1990–94 was due to economic recovery, but over time the deficit was persistent and the share of electronics in value added fell from 1980 to 1995. Mexico as well was weak in electronics

Table 8.9. Percentage of Manufacturing Value Added in High-Tech Industries, 1980 and 1995

Country	Other Chemicals	Non-elec. Machinery	Elec. Machinery	Transport. Equip.	Prof./Sci. Goods	Total
1995						
Argentina	3.5	3.1	3.0	7.4	0.4	17.4
Brazil	10.1	7.5	8.0	10.4	0.8	36.8
Chile	8.0	1.8	1.5	2.0	0.2	13.3
China	1.9	11.1	9.9	6.3	1.1	30.2
India	7.9	8.3	8.4	8.5	0.7	33.7
Indonesia	3.6	1.0	3.1	8.9	0.1	16.6
Korea	4.7	8.4	14.4	10.7	0.8	39.1
Malaysia	2.2	5.0	27.4	4.7	1.2	40.5
Mexico	7.2	3.3	3.2	10.1	1.7	25.6
Taiwan	2.7	5.2	17.3	7.4	1.0	33.6
Thailand	2.5	3.3	5.5	5.2	0.9	17.3
Turkey	4.7	4.5	6.0	6.7	0.3	22.3
"Rest" avg.	4.9	5.2	9.0	7.4	0.8	27.2
Japan	5.8	12.1	14.7	10.6	1.3	44.4
France	6.1	7.0	10.0	10.9	1.5	35.6
U.K.	7.0	11.3	8.4	10.4	1.6	38.8
U.S.	6.8	10.5	9.6	11.6	5.8	44.3
1980						
Argentina	4.9	5.5	3.7	9.3	0.4	23.8
Brazil	4.9	10.0	6.3	7.8	0.6	29.8
Chile	6.5	1.9	1.8	2.5	0.1	12.9
China	3.3	15.1	3.6	3.4	9.2	34.6
India	8.1	8.6	8.1	8.3	0.7	33.9
Indonesia	7.1	1.6	5.3	6.4	0.1	20.4
Korea	5.2	3.4	8.1	5.9	1.1	23.8
Malaysia	3.2	3.2	12.3	4.2	0.7	23.6
Mexico	5.2	4.8	4.4	6.9	0.7	22.1
Taiwan	1.0	1.9	7.0	2.5	0.9	13.4
Thailand	2.7	1.9	3.8	3.7	0.3	12.4
Turkey	3.6	4.7	4.3	5.0	0.1	17.6
"Rest" avg.	4.7	5.2	5.7	5.5	1.2	22.3
Japan	4.6	11.6	11.5	9.5	1.7	38.7
France	3.9	10.1	8.9	11.0	1.4	35.2
U.K.	4.6	13.0	9.3	10.7	1.3	38.9
U.S.	4.6	13.3	9.7	10.6	3.6	41.9

Source: Adapted from UNIDO (1997).

Table 8.10. Trade Balance in Electronics, Five-Year Totals for Selected Countries, 1970–1994

Country	Deficit or Surplus (mil 1990 US$)				
	1970–74	1975–79	1980–84	1985–89	1990–94
Argentina	−1,558	−1,769	−4,793	−2,789	−10,281
Brazil	−5,102	−7,368	−3,876	−2,782	−9,131
Chile	−1,021	−1,510	−2,332	−2,071	−5,004
China	na	na	−2,846	−17,633	−6,253
India	−1,474	−1,206	−1,630	−4,394	−3,579
Indonesia	−1,692	−4,964	−,763	−4,906	−5,885
Korea	−1,046	−1,386	2,154	23,953	46,413
Malaysia	−1,424	−1,728	−2,743	5,837	18,406
Mexico	−3,539	−3,712	−3,676	−6,187	−10,254
Taiwan	987	5,805	13,325	35,738	52,168
Thailand	−1,567	−1,887	−2,755	−4,108	−2,941
Turkey	−1,610	−2,519	−2,043	−5,225	−8,136
France	3,236	9,881	−3,512	−18,629	−21,924
Japan	43,427	95,776	172,362	320,664	405,530
U.K.	5,169	9,273	−11,391	−30,617	−30,336
U.S.	10,441	16,638	−8,172	−114,728	−131,121

Notes: Negative numbers represent deficits. This table refers to electronics as a share of total manufactured imports.

All China data is for 1983 and after.

Data adjusted into real dollars using U.S. WPI.

Chile did not report export figures for 1982–1989.

The UN Standard Classification of industries has been adjusted through the years. The old standard classification (Rev. 1) listed only one category for electric machinery (72, electrical machinery). The newer standard classification (Rev. 2) listed the following categories: 75—office machines, ADP equipment; 76—telecommunications and sound equipment; and 77—electric machinery, NES, etc. The data are not strictly comparable from year to year or across countries as countries switched from Rev. 1 to Rev. 2 at various times.

Sources: Adapted from UNIDO (1997) and (various years [a]); UNCTAD (various years [b]); International Monetary Fund (1997); Republic of China (1997).

and other types of machinery; its high-tech shares were up to "the rest's" average only in "other" (nonindustrial) chemicals and transportation equipment industries largely dominated by foreign firms, as noted earlier. Mexico, therefore, also had a large and rising trade deficit in electronics.

The stars in the electronics industry were Taiwan, Korea, and Malaysia, all with high shares of electrical machinery in manufacturing value added (MVA) and rising trade surpluses in electronics over time. Some electronics production, particularly in Malaysia, was not really high-tech; it was more in the nature of assembly operations (Rasiah 1995). This exaggeration of high-tech activity is suggested by comparing the shares of electrical *and* non-electrical machinery in the advanced economies on the one hand (Japan,

France, the United Kingdom, and the United States), and in "the rest" on the other hand (Malaysia, Korea, and Taiwan). If both the electrical and nonelectrical machinery industries in "the rest" were high-tech, then one would expect their shares in MVA to resemble those in the North Atlantic. But East Asia had higher shares of electrical machinery and lower shares of nonelectrical machinery, suggesting that the former comprised more than high-tech products. Still, the upward trend in electrical machinery–building in Korea and Taiwan was impressive.

The performance of Brazil, China, India, and Turkey lay somewhere in between the best and worst cases. In Brazil, the share of electrical machinery in manufacturing value added almost met the level of the North Atlantic, but the share was falling and Brazil's trade deficit in electronics was rising. The reverse was true of China: the share of electronics was rising and the trade deficit was falling. In India, both a (high) share and a (low) trade deficit were stable.

To begin to understand these cross-country discrepancies, we analyze government policies and income distribution.

Government Targeting and Income Distribution

By means of industrial licensing, subsidy allocation and performance standards, governments in "the rest" influenced firm structure—and hence industry performance. Government policies were constrained principally by the politics of income distribution. During periods in which racial or ethnic conflict was pronounced in Malaysia, Indonesia, Thailand, and Taiwan, governments were politically motivated to avoid concentrating resources in the hands of Chinese-owned companies (Taiwanese-owned companies in the case of Taiwan). SOEs rather than private enterprises were formed to encourage social harmony. In Argentina, Brazil, Chile, Mexico, and India, where class conflict was latent or severe (India experienced antagonism between small- and large-size firms), governments were politically motivated to avoid concentrating resources in the hands of only a few private national firms. Big, private national leaders oriented toward manufacturing, therefore, were constrained in their growth (as in Mexico) or failed to evolve altogether (as in Argentina, Brazil, and Chile). Over time, crowding-out in countries with racial or ethnic divisions tended to weaken as these divisions themselves weakened. But class divisions did not weaken, and in countries with skewed income distributions, the crowding-out of national leaders persisted, with negative effects on the formation of high-tech industries and the deepening of skills.

Class Divisions

Brazil represented one extreme where business group size was restrained in the interests of not worsening income distribution, given an income distribution that historically was highly unequal (see table 1.9). Brazil's development bank, BNDES, attached conditionalities to its loans in the form of *low debt/equity ratio ceilings* that constrained the size of national firms.[53] These ceilings may have arisen in the interests of financial prudence, but they constituted a *diffusionist* approach to resource allocation. BNDES required its clients to operate with debt/equity ratios that were less than 1:1. They did not on average exceed much more than 60 percent, a level typical of North American businesses but far below what characterized large Japanese and Korean companies (both Brazil and Korea succumbed to debt crises). Between 1973 and 1982, the average annual debt/equity ratio of BNDES' clients in major targeted industries was (in percent):

Steel	53.2
Petrochemicals[54]	64.3
Paper and pulp	72.3
Mechanical equipment	53.6
Electrical equipment	70.4
Transportation equipment	62.3

These compared with an average debt/equity ratio in all Korean manufacturing over the same ten year period of 373 percent, about six times greater than in Brazil (Bank of Korea various).

Low debt/equity ratio ceilings constrained the expansion of family-owned firms, the typical form of national private ownership in "the rest" after World War II. To finance expenditures on equipment and machinery without extensive recourse to borrowing, a family firm has to dilute its equity to a degree that might discourage entrepreneurship or encourage joint-venturing with a foreign firm. Those Brazilian business groups that grew large, therefore, tended to grow mainly *outside manufacturing* and outside the sphere of BNDES; the top five groups (Bradesco, Itausa, Bamerindus, Real, and Economico), all had *finance* as their primary economic activity, and the banks at their core tended to predate the BNDES (see table 8.2a–b).[55]

In Brazil's informatics industry, six of the ten largest national firms belonged to economic groups rooted mainly in banking. The advantage of bank ownership in computers was that user and producer of electronic data processing equipment were one and could therefore coordinate better (Sridharan 1996). The disadvantage was that banking groups knew less about manufacturing than industrial groups and had fewer scope economies among affiliates related to executing manufacturing projects. Moreover, because banks entered the computer industry via their demand-side connection, they were less likely to become agents of diversification into other high-tech industries. Each time the Brazilian government opened a new industry for expansion, it had to search for new market entrants rather than rely on experienced diversified groups.

Limitations on the growth rate of firms inherent in Brazil's low debt/equity ceilings were to some extent offset by the equity participation of BNDES in its clients' assets. Nevertheless, loans and loan guarantees were BNDES's major form of financial support, and BNDES's equity stake in its clients was low, averaging in 1978–82 less than 10 percent in steel, petrochemicals, and electrical equipment; less than 15 percent in mechanical and transportation equipment; and less than 20 percent in pulp and paper.

Nor did Brazil impose prohibitive performance standards on foreign firms to discourage their operations (as did India, Indonesia, Korea, Taiwan, and Turkey, as noted earlier). Of Brazil's seven entries among "the rest's" top fifty enterprises, as many as four were multinationals, (see table 8.1). Brazil's mobilization of state-owned enterprises was also intense: three of "the rest's" top fifteen SOEs in 1993 were Brazilian (see table 8.8).[56] Such crowding out, in addition to low debt/equity ratio ceilings, contributed to the fact that private national firms in targeted industries tended to be relatively small despite Brazil's large domestic market.

A stated goal of the BNDES was to prevent economic concentration from rising. Between 1973 and 1989 only in the steel industry was there a rise in *capital concentration*. The Gini index for the capital assets of producers in petrochemicals, pulp and paper, and mechanical, electrical, and transportation equipment either did not rise or actually fell (Monteiro Filha 1995).[57] Brazil thus met its goal of not worsening income distribution, but at the cost of not creating national manufacturing leaders.[58]

Exceeding Brazil in lack of support for large industrial groups was Argentina, with a Gini coefficient in land distribution of 0.86 in 1960, indicating slightly greater inequality than in Brazil (see table 1.9). Given Argentina's failure to establish an effective development bank or a functioning reciprocal control mechanism, support-cum-discipline of business of *any* type was tepid, but support of big national business was especially weak. In the 1940s and the beginning of the 1950s, government policy favored state enterprises and small- and medium-size firms.[59] Then, under the American-backed Frondizi administration, policy favored multinational companies.[60] Only after 1976 "did state policies favor economic groups" (Ines Barbero 1997, p. 387). By then, however, the energy crisis had paralyzed government spending altogether and the Argentine economy was deindustrializing,[61] so the period of government support to private big business was extremely short, and the expansion of Argentine groups was relatively small (Schvarzer 1978).[62] Only one group from Argentina, SOCMA, figured among "the rest's" top fifty groups (it ranked fiftieth and was largely involved in the production of au-

Table 8.11. Ten Largest Groups,[1] 1993,[2] by Country

Group	Sales (mil US$)	Principal Activities	Affiliates	Founded
Argentina				
1. SOCMA	1,852.8	autos, constr.	na	na
2. Techint	1,802.7	steel, constr., comm.	na	na
3. Bunge Y Born	1,752.6	food prod., trade	na	na
4. COFAL	1,285.6	autos	na	na
5. Perez Compano	918.9	energy, comm., agro.	22	1947
6. Comercial del Plata	738.6	energy, comm.	na	na
7. Bemberg	651.3	beverages, food prod.	na	na
8. Mastellone Hnos. SA	639.5	dairy	na	na
9. Arcor	619.0	food prod., agro.	na	na
10. Acindar	540.0	steel, services	4	1940
Brazil				
Bradesco	19,350.9	livestock, paper	na	na
2. Itausa	18,418.0	paper, telecomm., chem.	13	1965
3. Bamerindus	11,493.9	paper, livestock, wood	14	1964
4. Real	9,091.5	metals, food prod., transp.	na	na
5. Economico	8,182.7	agro., chem., food prod.	na	na
6. Odebrecht	5,006.8	constr., chem., minerals	10	na
7. Fenicia	4,797.9	finance, food prod.	na	na
8. Camargo Correa	4,157.5	metals, text., elec.	na	na
9. Andrade Gutierrez	3,705.6	constr., minerals, chem.	na	na
10. Multiplic	2,918.1	finance, chem.	na	na
India				
1. TATA	6,415.2	diversified	37	1907
2. BK/AV/Kumar Birla	2,343.5	diversified	13	1947
3. Ambani	1,799.2	diversified	2	1973
4. Unilever	1,727.2	diversified	6	1933
5. R P Goenka	1,193.8	power gen., rubber	16	na
6. ITC/BAT	1,026.8	tobacco, printing	5	1910
7. Larsen & Toubro	968.8	engineering, constr. equip.	1	1946
8. Bajaj-Mukand	968.8	autos, metals	5	1945
9. Thapar	893.6	diversified	4	1985
10. Mahindra	646.9	autos	4	1945
Indonesia				
1. Salim	8,530.8	diversified	429	na
2. Astra	2,791.5	diversified	149	1957
3. Lippo	2,251.2	diversified	84	1967
4. Sinar Mas	2,251.2	diversified	121	1962
5. Gudang Garam	1,706.2	cigarettes	3	1958
6. Barito Pacific	1,445.5	diversified	141	1979
7. Bimantra	1,421.8	diversified	49	na
8. Argo Manunggal	1,393.4	text., steel	35	na
9. Dharmala	1,199.1	agro., real estate, elec.	43	1971
10. Djarum	1,118.5	cigarettes	11	na

Table 8.11. (*continued*)

Group	Sales (mil US$)	Principal Activities	Affiliates	Founded
Korea				
1. Hyundai	74,142.2	diversified	26	1947
2. Samsung	66,845.2	diversified	28	1938
3. LG	51,679.4	diversified	43	1947
4. Daewoo	37,303.5	diversified	14	1967
5. Sunkyoung	22,209.9	diversified	14	1953
6. Ssangyong	19,154.5	diversified	23	1939
7. Kia[3]	12,096.3	autos	7	1944
8. Hanjin	10,052.9	diversified	12	1945
9. Hanwha	9,439.8	diversified	22	1952
10. Lotte	8,271.6	diversified	24	1967
Malaysia				
1. Sime Darby Bhd	3,700	diversified	60	1910
2. Perlis Plantations	2,405	diversified	na	1974
3. Amsteel Corp. Bhd	1,622	diversified	na	1920
4. Berjaya Group Bhd	1,298	diversified	118	1967
5. UMW Holdings Bhd	1,152	diversified	na	1976
6. Multi-Purp. Hold.	1,132	diversified	125	1975
7. Tanjong	426.5	na	65	na
8. Hong Leong Ind.	379.1	diversified	62	na
9. Antah Holdings	261.6	diversified	46	1976
10. Technology Res. Ind.	249.0	telecomm.	3	1966
Mexico				
1. Grupo Cifra	4,581.8	commercial	7	1965
2. Vitro, S.A.	3,518.0	industrial/glass	106	1909
3. Grupo Carso	3,169.1	diversified	16	1980
4. Grupo Cemex	2,975.1	cement	410	1920
5. Grupo Gigante, S.A.	2,530.9	commercial	9	1983
6. Grupo Ind. Alfa	2,495.2	diversified	26	1974
7. Grupo FEMSA	2,425.6	development	12	1986
8. Grupo ICA	1,948.5	diversified	89	1979
9. Grupo Televis, S.A.	1,925.8	TV stations	13	1972
10. Grupo Desc	1,706.4	chem., plastics	116	1973
Taiwan				
1. Formosa Plastics	5,346	plastics	na	na
2. Shinkon Syn. Fibers	4,021	text.	na	na
3. Wei-Chuan	3,872	food prod.	na	na
4. Yuelong Motor Corp.	3,036	autos	na	na
5. Ching Feng	2,982	diversified	na	na
6. President Enterp.	2,859	diversified	na	na
7. Far Eastern Textile	2,332	text.	na	na
8. Kao Hsing Group	2,090	diversified	na	na
9. Tatung Co.	1,983	diversified	na	na
10. Evergreen Group	1,900	diversified	na	na

Table 8.11. (*continued*)

Group	Sales (mil US$)	Principal Activities	Affiliates	Founded
Thailand				
1. Siam Cement Group	4,470	cement, steel, mach.	21	1913
2. Siam Motors Group	3,017	autos	34	1956
3. Boon Rawd Group	1,861	agro	9	1934
4. CP Group	1,808	agro	49	1951
5. SPI Group	875	diversified	31	1942
6. Osothsapha Group	838	pharmaceuticals	28	1899
7. Saha Union Group	748	text., shoes	33	1968
8. Hong Yiah Seng	704	agro	21	1947
9. Central Department	618	retail, garments	27	1952
10. Soon Hua Seng Group	544	agro	18	1945

1. Sometimes groups are consolidated and sometimes large affiliates are listed separately, a reflection of the accounting procedures followed by each group. Enterprises that were *exclusively* involved in construction, mining, agriculture, finance, or public utilities (such as electric power and telephone companies) are excluded. All "petroleum" companies are included under the assumption that these enterprises were involved in the manufacture of petroleum products. Business groups that had operations in nonmanufacturing fields were included only if they also had significant operations in some manufacturing field.
2. All sales figures are for 1993 except for the following: Argentine groups, 1992; Brazilian groups, 1992; Korean groups, 1995; Taiwan groups, 1994; and all private and public specialized companies for Argentina, Brazil, and Mexico, 1994.
3. Acquired by Hyundai group.

Sources: Moody's (1996), Kyang-Hoe (1996), PT. Kompass Indonesia (1995), *Business Standard* (1995), Khanna (1997), Arokiasamy (1996), C.C.I.S. (various years), Gallegos (1997), Jomo (1993), Bank Indonesia (1996), Hill (1996).

tomobile parts, energy and gas, and construction services). Other Argentine groups were concentrated in food processing and steel (see table 8.11).[63] Even in the steel industry, prior to consolidation, no Argentine company in 1990 ranked among the world's top forty steel producers. POSCO (Korea) ranked third, SAIL (India) ranked 11th, China Steel (Taiwan) ranked seventeenth, and USIMINAS and CSN (Brazil) ranked twenty-third and thirty-fourth, respectively (UNIDO 1992). Argentina had one of the oldest machine tool industries in "the rest," yet no Argentine company ranked among the world's top twenty-five producers (for 1989, see UNIDO 1992).[64] The Argentine pharmaceutical industry had the distinction of having seven national firms among its top ten producers, but the sales of the two largest enterprises (Roemmers and Bago), both leaders of "strong, local pharmaceutical conglomerates," were only about 8 percent as much as those of the world's fifteenth ranking pharmaceutical company, Upjohn, with sales of $1.6 billion in 1989 (Katz 1995; UNIDO 1991). The *foreign* share of domestic drug consumption, moreover, was higher in Argentina than in India, with only half of Argentina's market size.[65] However outstanding Argentina's pharmaceutical industry was, moreover, the share of "other" chemicals (including pharmaceuticals) in Argentina's manufacturing value added fell over time, from 4.9 percent in 1980 to only 3.5 percent in 1995 (see table 8.9).

In Mexico, government also constrained the size and manufacturing orientation of national big businesses. The Echeverría regime (1970–76) was known to be in intense conflict with private capital over the issue of income distribution (in response to a bloody encounter between students and police during the 1969 Mexico City Olympics), but it was also nationalistic. Industrial promotion policies, demanded by the old economic groups centered in Monterrey, "put a brake on the activities of foreign companies, while stimulating the growth of Mexico's indigenous groups, and as a result the latter grew faster than foreign companies" (Hoshino 1990, p. 30). The Salinas administration (1987–91) reopened the doors to foreign investment wider than ever. But it also strengthened national groups through privatization. Although foreign capital played some role in privatization, as much as 93 percent of privatized public enterprises were absorbed by Mexican big business (Rogozinski 1993).[66] This restructuring "brought about greater industrial concentration within Mexico's private sector" (Hoshino 1996, p. 59).[67] Mexico's fifty-nine biggest groups increased their share of GDP, from 11.9 to 14.7 percent (Garrido 1994).

This share of GDP, however, was extremely small by other countries' standards. In 1998, Taiwan's top 100 business groups accounted for as much as 54.0 percent of GNP (see table 8.12). In the same year, Korea's top thirty groups alone accounted for almost 40 percent of *manufacturing* shipments (Lee 1998). Instead of high concentration, the guiding principle of Mexico's dynastic political party (like Argentina's Peronist party) was to spread resources among as many Mexican businesses as possible (for relations between business and government in Mexico, see Valdes Ugalde 1997).

Table 8.12. Taiwan: Top 100 Business Groups, 1970–1996

Year	Sales (% of GNP)
1973	32.3
1986*	28.7
1990	38.3
1996	42.9
1998	54.0

*Data available for only 97 groups.

Sources: Adapted from C.C.I.S. (various years), as cited in Amsden and Chu (2003).

The performance standards that Mexico's development bank, NAFINSA, attached to its loans mitigated against the rapid expansion through debt of large national manufacturers, as in Brazil. Due to a low ceiling, the debt-equity ratios of the clients of NAFINSA were only slightly above those of BNDES. From 1947 to 1997, *the average never fell below 85 percent and never exceeded 95 percent.*[68] National leaders in Mexico, therefore, tended to be limited to old groups that were established around the turn of the *nineteenth* century (see chapter 3). Vitro (Mexico's second-ranking group), founded in 1909 with a core competence in glass manufacture, and Cemex (its fourth-ranking group), founded in 1920 with a specialization in cement, date from the first wave of modern industrialization in the 1890s to 1930s (Haber 1989; Cordero et al. 1985). The Alfa group, which ranked sixth, was established in 1974 by inheriting a number of iron and paper companies when a (now extinct) group, Cuauhtemoc-HYLSA split into two (Hoshino 1990). These three groups had recourse to finance from their retained earnings and the Mexican stock exchange. Therefore, they were less constrained in their expansion than new groups. By contrast, with the exception of Grupo Desc, which had its core competency in manufacturing and became a leader in Mexican R&D, no new group that ranked among Mexico's top ten in the early 1990s had a specialization in manufacturing (see table 8.11). Grupos Cifra, Carso, Gigante, Femsa, ICA, and Televis all had core competencies outside manufacturing (Garrido 1999). Some, such as grupo Carso, had grown through acquisition on the Mexican stock exchange. The owner of Carso was known in Mexico as the "genius of takeovers" (rather than the genius of manufacturing skills) (Hoshino 1990).

Like Brazilian groups, Mexican groups were crowded out both by performance standards attached to preferential credit and by foreign investment. Given Mexico's physical proximity to the United States, and given its history of acquiring manufacturing experience through North Atlantic émigrés, foreign investors were regarded ambivalently. Of Mexico's five entries in "the rest's" top fifty business enterprises of all types, one was PEMEX, another was the Vitro group, and the three others were multinationals—Chrysler, Ford, and General Motors, as noted above (see table 8.1). In the case of electronics, whose share in Mexican manufacturing value added was extremely small (see table 8.9), "to analyze the large enterprises in the electronics sector is equivalent to analyzing the transnationals that have located [there]" (Warman 1994, p. 415, trans).

Conflict over Firm Size

Given India's premodern manufacturing experience and traditional artisan enterprise (most conspicuously its handloom weavers), the Indian government adopted anti–big business policies in favor of small-scale firms. This bias, however, was partially offset by strong anti-foreign investor policies. More so than in Latin America, nationalism gave wide latitude to domestic groups to expand, a process that accelerated during World War II:

> The larger Indian industrial houses, which had set up the sugar, paper, and cement industries in the wake of tariff protection, reaped a rich bonanza during World War II and the immediate postwar years. Wartime profits and the phenomenal stock exchange boom of 1943–46 helped them consolidate the hold of their combines and paved the way for their mammoth expansion and diversification in the post-independence years. This was greatly facilitated by easy access to bank credit and the life insurance funds controlled by the groups. (Agarwala 1986, p. 242)

A 1969 restrictive trade practices act, however, hampered the growth of large industrial enterprises. Banks were nationalized and were required to lend at least 40 percent of their credit to firms below a minimum threshold (in the 1980s Korea had a similar policy with a threshold of 30 percent). Whole industry segments were reserved for small-scale firms. In some cases, such as pharmaceuticals, market reservation policies worked well; small and not so small national firms coexisted in tight subcontracting networks and jointly increased their market share vis-à-vis multinationals (see chapter 6). Alembic, India's seventh largest pharmaceutical firm in 1996, was part of a large Indian group (Amin). One of the world's leading producers of vitamin B12 was an Indian firm partially owned by the Tata group. Given an effective incentive system introduced by the government, national pharmaceutical firms of all sizes were energetic in cutting costs and introducing "new" products to the Indian market (Mourshed 1999). In other industries, however, the Indian government's market reserve policies were "a disaster." In electronics, big Indian groups were marginalized because the production of telecommunications and electronic equipment was reserved for state-owned enterprises (as noted earlier) and the production of consumer electronics and components was reserved for small-scale firms. These firms were judged to be "generally inefficient" with operations at "sub optimal scales" (Sridharan 1996, p. 142).

Nevertheless, large diversified groups in general were promoted by the government. Indian business houses needed government licenses to import foreign technology and capital goods. "In 1956, on the eve of the Second Plan and India's first decade of sustained industrial growth, Indian business houses cornered two-fifths of all foreign technology licenses granted by the government." The two largest groups, Tata and Birla (before dividing), received over one-tenth of all new government approvals to collaborate with multinationals. The top seventy-three groups received three-fifths of all permissions between 1956 and 1966 to import machinery (Encarnation 1989, p. 86). Even later, a new group, Reliance, with one focus on chemicals and another on textiles, took advantage of government export-promotion incentives as well as "access to key politicians and bureaucrats" to rise from rags to riches (Harvard Business School 1992, p. 12).

Thus, in spite of the Indian government's market reservation policies, throughout much of the postwar period large industry grew at a faster rate than small industry, modern small industries grew faster than traditional small industries, and large modern factories grew faster than small modern factories (Sandesara 1992). While only two Indian groups (Tata and Birla) figured among "the rest's" top fifty (see table 8.5), this small representation arose partially because the Monopolies and Restrictive Trade Practices Act (MRTPA) of 1969 imposed a ceiling on group size, and this ceiling prompted groups to subdivide in order to disguise their true proportions. For example, in the case of the Goenkas (India's fifth-ranking group in table 8.11), which "emerged as the largest takeover group, the real decision making powers rest with R. P Goenka, who . . . acquired control of the Ceat, Dunlop Tyre, and Bayer operations in India as well as 20 other foreign affiliates, along with his brothers, K. P. and J. P., who like the Mafatlals . . . (became) independent entities to overcome government regulation" (Agarwala 1986). From their early founding date to the early 1990s, not only were India's groups relatively large, they were also firmly rooted in manufacturing (see table 8.11). Excluding consumer electronics, where the government's reservation policies were strong, groups had a major presence in almost all basic industries, including automobiles and semiconductors.

Liberalization, begun in 1991, weakened market reserve policies and increased the entry of foreign firms. By that time, however, Indian groups were sufficiently strong to present themselves as desirable joint venture partners. Symbolic of change was the return to India of IBM, the American computer leader, which had left in 1978 after the government refused to allow it 100 percent equity ownership. In the late 1990s, IBM returned to form a joint venture with the Tata group. IBM's stake was in the minority.

Racial and Ethnic Conflict

In countries where a racial or ethnic majority suffered economic deprivation relative to a richer minority, governments sought to redress this imbalance by establishing state-owned firms. Foreign firms also came to be viewed as a counterweight to a privileged minority. Hence, they became welcomed. The Boards of Investment of Malaysia, Indonesia, and Thailand (the Thai board is examined in chapter 1) all gave equal preferential support to national *and foreign* firms (for Malaysia, see Capenelli 1997).[69] Taiwan actively recruited foreign investments for geopolitical reasons after the United States gave diplomatic recognition to mainland China in 1972 in the belief that the presence of foreign firms would improve foreign diplomatic relations (Gold 1988).

To de-alienize the Thai economy (of Chinese influence) in the 1950s, the government created over 100 state-owned enterprises, thirty-seven of which were in manufacturing (Choonhavan 1984). The race riots that erupted in Malaysia in May 1969 led to a radical restructuring of government policies away from poverty alleviation of a Malay population majority to the promotion of Malay business (Jomo 1988). Toward this end, Malaysia's state sector dramatically expanded. Between 1969 and 1972, sixty-seven new public enterprises were created, a number that rose to over 100 in the next few years (Ling 1993). In Indonesia, to promote the economic interests of a relatively impoverished Bumiputra majority, state-owned enterprises came to play "a more significant role than in any other developing market economy of East and South-East Asia" (Hill 1989, p. 22). In fact, the scope of state enterprise and state involvement in the economy in Taiwan possibly topped that in Indonesia. The occupation of Taiwan in 1947 by the mainland Guomindang army, and its bloody repression of a rebellion by Taiwanese nationalists, created antagonism between these two ethnic Chinese groups. This antagonism was seen to lie behind a big buildup of state enterprise owned and managed directly by the Guomindang, and the maintenance and strengthening of Taiwan's large inheritance of state-owned firms from Japan. Taiwan was probably unique in having four layers of state-owned enterprise:

1. Those inherited by the government from the defeated Japanese, such as major commercial banks, Taiwan Fertilizer, Taiwan Sugar, Taiwan Aluminum, Taiwan Machinery, Taiwan Cement, and Taiwan Paper Corporations (Taiwan Cement was privatized in the 1950s under pressure from U.S. Aid)
2. Those that came from the mainland, having followed Chiang Kai-shek's retreat to Taiwan, such as banks, the Chinese Textile Corporation, and the Chinese Chemical Engineering Corporation
3. Those that comprised a large network of production facilities under the military
4. Those that had been mismanaged companies and were restructured as state property, such as China Petrochemical, China Steel, and China Shipbuilding Corporations (Numazaki 1997; Fields 1995).

In Malaysia, racial conflict hastened the nationalization of British agency houses. As late as 1965, five leading British firms, Harrisons & Crosfield, Guthrie, Boustead-Buttery, the Borneo Company (later Inchcape) and R.E.A.-Cumberbatch controlled 220 Malaysian manufacturing firms alone. Malaysia's national capital corporation, Permodalan Nasional Berhad (PNB), then got a controlling interest in several groups. A joint venture was established between Harrisons & Crosfield and the Malaysian state (Lindblad 1998). Malaysia's largest private group, Sime Darby, was founded in 1910 as a British company to exploit Malaysia's rubber resources. When the demand for rubber slowed in the 1960s, Sime pioneered the formation of plantations in cocoa and palm oil. The company became a takeover target by the Malaysian government to improve the welfare of Malay *bumiputras* by enabling them to own shares in publicly traded companies. The government purchased enough shares on the London Stock Exchange to become Sime's largest owner, replaced the mostly Anglo majority on the board of directors with Asians, and moved company headquarters back to Kuala Lumpur (Harvard Business School 1996).

Adversarialism between racial and ethnic groups softened over time in both Thailand and Taiwan. Thais and Chinese intermarried, and mainlanders and Taiwanese banded together against retrocession by China. Synchronously, the crowding-out of large national capital declined and economic concentration rose. In Thailand, Chinese business groups gained in strength, buttressed by their commercial banking activities: among Thailand's biggest 100 manufacturing firms, by the 1990s fifty allegedly belonged to the sixteen groups that collectively controlled 90 percent of the total assets of all Thai firms (Rock 1995). These groups became sufficiently strong to provide "a significant part of domestic corporate investment in modern industry, and have been a principal channel through which joint ventures with overseas firms have developed" (Falkus 1995, p. 28). In Taiwan, it is unclear if the relatively small size and market share of business groups (*guanxigiye*) in the early postwar period owed itself to Chinese culture (Redding 1990) or government discrimination. Taiwan's financial institutions, banking and non-banking, were entirely in government hands (Wade 1990; Shea 1994). With power over the purse and control over industrial licensing, the government could influence the size and market share of private business as much as (and probably much more than) the development banks of Brazil and Mexico could influence them through control over long-term lending and debt/equity ratio ceilings. What is clear is that as antagonism between Taiwanese and mainlander abated, market concentration rose (see table 8.12).

Even in Malaysia and Indonesia, where racial conflict between bumiputras and a Chinese minority did not vanish, it is questionable whether or not private national big business was ever crowded-out by government policy (as opposed to being crowded-out by multinational competition). In Malaysia, Chinese-owned business groups flourished. Their core competence was largely in the processing of primary products. Two large groups that were built around sugar and flour (Perlis Plantations and Federal Flour Mills), for example, were part of the empire of Robert Kuok, an aristocratic Malaysian Chinese who also owned a regional hotel chain, a property development company, a trading house, and overseas joint ventures in partnership with Indonesian-Chinese (Heng 1994). The concentration of Chinese-owned groups in the processing of primary products may have been their choice, given Malaysia's rich natural resources, rather than the effect of government discrimination. Big groups elsewhere in "the rest" typically clustered initially in heavy industry, but such industry in Malaysia was small.[70] Outside processed foods, Malaysia's manufacturing sector was comprised primarily of labor-intensive industries such as electronic assembly, which, in turn, were dominated by multinational firms. Of all countries in "the rest," Malaysia had the highest share historically of foreign capital in gross domestic capital formation (see table 1.11).

In Indonesia as well, Chinese business groups flourished despite "crowding-out" by state-owned firms. Of "the rest's" top fifty groups, Indonesia accounted for four, including the largest non-Korean group, Salim (see table 8.5). Indonesian business groups under Chinese family ownership played "an integral part in Indonesia's economy, responsible for perhaps as much as 70 percent of all private economic activity. Their companies have contributed mightily to the rejuvenation of Indonesia's economy in recent years" (Schwarz 1994, p. 99). Racial inequalities in Indonesia mostly drove government promotion of Chinese business groups underground.

Thus, whereas inequalities by social class in Latin America severely crowded-out private national enterprise, inequalities by race and ethnicity in East Asia appear to have had much less of an exclusionary impact.

Homogeneity and Big Business

The country with the fewest economic divisions, whether by class, race, or ethnicity, was Korea. It was also the country with the largest private business groups and the greatest number of national leaders.[71] Among "the rest's" fifty top enterprises, those from Korea totaled twenty-six, all of them private and nationally owned (see table 8.1). Among "the rest's" top manufacturing groups, those from Korea totaled twenty-one (see table 8.5).

A bias toward biggness was deliberate on the Korean government's part, which held the Japanese zaibatsu as its model and believed in the importance of economies of scale and scope.[72] The Korean president who was instrumental in promoting national leaders and who masterminded Korean industrialization, Park Chung Hee (1961–79), was articulate in expressing the importance for economic development of both big business and its discipline:[73]

> Mammoth enterprise—considered indispensable, at the moment, to our country—plays not only a decisive role in the economic development and elevation of living standards, but further, brings about changes in the structure of society and the economy. . . . Where the appalling power of mammoth enterprise is concerned . . . there is no free competition. . . . Therefore, the key problems facing a free economic policy are coordination and supervisory guidance, by the state, of mammoth economic strength. (Park 1962, pp. 228–229)

Throughout most of the postwar period, the Korean government neither enforced a ceiling on groups' debt/equity ratios nor prevented their cross-subsidization of subsidiaries. In the 1970s the allocation of lucrative licenses for general trading companies in exchange for compliance with tough export targets simultaneously strengthened groups and Korea's export drive (Amsden 1997). In the 1980s promotion of private national businesses was made contingent on investing heavily in R&D (discussed below). In the 1990s when euphoria and financial market liberalization led to overexpansion and financial crash, the Korean government responded to greater international competition by trying to force the biggest businesses to merge and acquire each other's subsidiaries, the effect of which was to increase economic concentration even further (see chapter 9).

The chaebol came under heavy fire for not specializing and for not being transparent in their financial dealings. Yet no other major form of business in "the rest"—big or small—exhibited financial transparency either: multinationals did not publish financial statements for individual subsidiaries; the costs of state-owned enterprises' were soft and so profitability was difficult to assess; and private national businesses, publicly or non–publicly traded, tended to remain family controlled and selective in their financial disclosures. The trouble with Korean big business was less economic than social: it contravened Korean principles of egalitarianism. Only Korea, which started from a highly egalitarian base after land reform and civil war, could indulge in such antiegalitarian policies.[74]

From "Buying" to "Making" Technology: R&D

All countries in "the rest" initially "bought" rather than "made" technology. Contrary to prewar practice, they also invested heavily in higher education. Nevertheless, even before a debt crisis severely constrained skill-formation in Latin America, Latin American countries with a "diffusionist" approach to resource allocation tended to invest only modestly in their own technological capabilities, especially R&D. Whatever little R&D occurred, almost none of it was undertaken by private firms.

The technology flows that soared after World War II made late industrialization possible; before the 1990s at the earliest, it is difficult to identify any major industry that developed in "the rest" without foreign know-how. Measured as (1) total world receipts of royalties and fees (mostly for foreign licenses); (2) plus developed countries' exports of capital goods; (3) plus technical assistance to developing countries, technology transactions rose from roughly $27 billion in 1962 to $356 billion in 1982. This was a thirteenfold increase compared with only a threefold rise in the unit value index of all manufactures exported by developed countries over the same time period. Royalties and fees alone tripled in value in the single decade between 1972 and 1982, the heyday of "the rest's" investments in heavy industry (UNCTAD 1987, p. 88).

Small- and medium-size firms "bought" their technology at "zero price" through copying ("reverse engineering"). Large national firms obtained their technology through *"apprenticing"*: they bought licenses from (or paid royalties to) leading foreign technology suppliers (Kim 1997). Once large-scale firms acquired foreign know-how, they diffused it to small firms.[75] Diversified business groups diffused best-practice foreign techniques to their affiliates and sub-contractors in different industries without the legal barriers that existed in joint ventures.[76]

Government's role in skill formation during this early period was mainly oriented toward getting the best terms for technology transfers, spending heavily on formal education, and slowly increasing investments in R&D.[77] Following Japan, both Korea and Taiwan (as well as Brazil) strengthened the bargaining position of individual firms by placing national limits on admissible licensing fees and royalties (for Japan, see Ozawa [1974]). India went the furthest in limiting technology inflows, but probably with negative effects on learning (Lall 1987).

The most educated populations were to be found in Argentina, Chile, Korea, and Taiwan. In 1950 these countries had the highest mean years of schooling (see table 3.2). In 1960 their populations had the highest percentage of people with high school education (see table 1.9). Thirty years later, these same four countries had the highest rates of tertiary enrollments and engineering enrollments among tertiary students (see figures 8.2 and

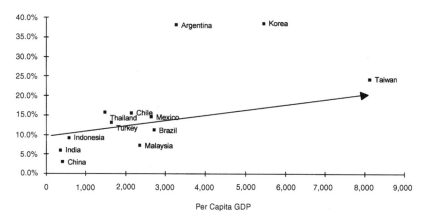

Figure 8.2. Per capita GDP and tertiary enrollment. The tertiary enrollment ratio represents the percentage of the school-age population (at the tertiary level) enrolled in third-level institutions. *Sources:* UNESCO (various years), World Bank (1976, 1994).

Table 8.13. Factor Increases in Primary, Secondary, Tertiary and Engineering Education,[1] 1960–1990

	Population	Primary	Secondary	Tertiary	Engineering
Argentina	1.6	1.2	4.0	6.0	5.5
Brazil	2.1	7.3	11.5	16.1	12.8
Chile	1.8	2.5	4.1	12.9	16.1
India	2.0	0.8	10.2	3.9	2.8
Indonesia	1.9	3.0	5.8	40.1	111.4
Korea	1.8	0.7	13.7	17.1	19.6
Malaysia	1.8	2.8	5.3	9.7	12.4
Mexico	2.5	4.1	23.2	17.0	14.4
Thailand	2.2	2.4	3.7	25.2	57.7
Turkey	2.0	2.4	3.7	12.4	15.3
Average	2.0	1.9	9.1	15.1	16.3
"Remainder"	2.4	2.5	3.5	9.0	9.1
North Atlantic	1.3	0.6	2.5	4.7	3.4
Japan	1.3	1.0	3.0	4.1	5.0

1. Primary and secondary education refer to the total population age 15 and higher (except where otherwise noted) with some primary or some secondary education. Tertiary education refers to the total number of students enrolled at the tertiary level. Engineering education refers to the tertiary students enrolled in engineering programs.

Primary and secondary: Argentina 1960–1991, Brazil 1950–1989 (1950 population 10+), India 1961–1981, Indonesia 1961–1980, Malaysia 1957–1980 (1957 population is West Malaysia only, 1980 population is 25+), Thailand 1960–1980, Turkey 1950–1980, Thailand 1950–1980, Japan population is 25+.

"Remainder" and North Atlantic include only those countries for which consistent 15+ data were available.

Source: UNESCO (various years)

8.3). Both China and India did not rank at the top in educational attainments, but nonetheless had large absolute numbers of highly educated people. Elsewhere in "the rest," especially Mexico, Indonesia and Thailand, gains in higher education were major. On average, "the rest's" factor increase for school enrollment between 1960 and 1990 was 1.9 for primary, 9.1 for secondary, 15.1 for tertiary, and 16.3 for tertiary engineering students (see table 8.13). The share of tertiary students enrolled in engineering tended to be high, especially in Taiwan and China (see table 8.14). Late industrialization was not just a process of learning in general, but a process of concentrating on building engineering skills.

What began to differ sharply *among* countries in "the rest" was the "make" technology decision related to R&D. While all countries continued to buy foreign technology, and continued to invest in production capabilities and possibly project execution skills, leading firms in some countries— the "independents"—also began to develop new technology, a necessary condition for sustainable national enterprise.

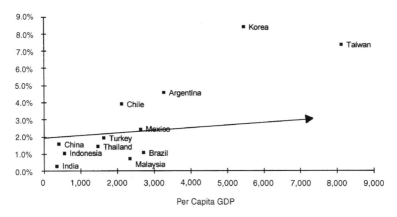

Figure 8.3. Per capita GDP and engineering enrollment, 1990. The engineering enrollment ratio represents the percentage of the school-age population (at the tertiary level) enrolled as engineering students. It is calculated by multiplying the tertiary enrollment ratio by the percentage of tertiary students in engineering. *Sources*: UNESCO (various years), World Bank (1976, 1994).

Differences in R&D spending, which may for the moment be taken as a proxy for spending on science and technology (S&T) in general, are indicated in table 8.15.[78] Korea and Taiwan were the big R&D spenders. The share of R&D in their GNP became comparable by the 1990s to that of North Atlantic countries and Japan. Then came India, Chile (whose R&D spending was almost totally natural resource-oriented), Brazil, Turkey, and China. The R&D expenditures of India and China were modest but still impressive in light of the vast size of their agricultural sector (a large component of GNP but a small source of R&D spending). Malaysia, Indonesia, and Thailand were in a class of their own; their manufacturing activity was still relatively underdeveloped and thus their R&D spending was small. The low spenders on the totem pole were Argentina and Mexico. Despite their relatively advanced manufacturing sectors at the time of World War II, nearly fifty years later their investments in R&D were practically nil.

Even before the 1980s, when a debt crisis struck and macroeconomic policy became contractionary, Argentina and Mexico spent almost nothing on science and technology. A law in Mexico to promote and develop a national science and technology system was passed only in 1984 (*Ley para Coordinar y Promover el Desarrollo Científico y Tecnológico*), two years *after* the start of Mexico's debt crisis. CONACYT, Mexico's major public science and technology agency, had its budget increased substantially starting only in 1989 (a specific entry for science and technology was included in the federal budget only in 1990). As for skill formation in the private sector, its share in R&D

Table 8.14. Engineers: Share in Total Tertiary
Students (%)

Country	Share in	
	1960	1990
"Rest" (w/o China or India)	13.8	14.7
Decreasing Countries		
Mexico	20.0	16.9
Brazil	12.0	9.6
India	7.0	5.0
Argentina	13.0	12.0
Increasing Countries		
Malaysia	8.0	10.2
Korea	19.0	21.7
Turkey	12.0	14.8
Thailand	4.0	9.2
Indonesia	4.0	10.4
Taiwan	19.8	30.2
Chile	20.0	25.0
China	40.9	53.9
Regions		
"Remainder"	12.1	12.3
North Atlantic	13.7	10.0
USSR, Eastern Europe, Cuba	40.6	29.7
Japan	14.0	16.9

Source: UNESCO (various years)

(including the share of foreign firms) was insignificant: the first estimate, for 1984, put the share of private industrial spending in total national spending on science and technology at 15 percent, with total national spending on science and technology itself less than half of one percent of GNP (0.42 percent). By 1991 Mexican private industry still accounted for only 23.1 percent of total spending on S&T (OECD 1994, pp. 58 and 61), and the share of R&D in national income had fallen to nil (see table 8.15). Although a few private firms were dynamic,[79] of all Mexican engineers and scientists dedicated to R&D in 1991, *only 4 percent were estimated to be in business firms, public or private* (Parra Moreno 1992). Some critics argued that not even imported technology was subjected to small, incremental improvements (Jaime 1995).

Table 8.15. Research and
Development (R&D) Expenditure,
Selected Countries, 1985[1] and
1995[2]

Country	R&D Expenditure (% of GNP)	
	1985	1995
Korea	1.8	2.8
Taiwan	1.2	1.8
India	0.9	0.8
Chile	0.5	0.7
Brazil	0.7	0.6
Turkey	0.6	0.6
China	na	0.5
Argentina	0.4	0.4
Malaysia	na	0.4
Indonesia	0.3	0.1
Thailand	0.3	0.1
Mexico	0.2	0.0

1. India, Korea 1994; Malaysia, 1992; Mexico,
1993
2. Brazil, Korea, Mexico, Turkey 1987; Chile,
Taiwan, 1988; India, Indonesia 1986

Sources: All countries except Taiwan: UNESCO
(various years); Taiwan: Taiwan, Republic of
China National Science Council (1996).

In Argentina, R&D expenditures as a share of GNP were only 0.4 percent and stagnant between 1985 and 1995 (see table 8.15). This was notwithstanding Argentina's impressive tertiary school enrollments and training of engineers (see figures 8.2 and 8.3). Early data on private sector Argentine R&D are scarce, but the insignificance of R&D spending before (and
after) the 1980s is suggested by data on patenting. In 1995 the cumulative
number of U.S. registered design and utility patents was lower in Argentina
(32) than in Brazil (60), Korea (1240), or Taiwan (2087), and the growth
rate of patents between 1980 and 1995 was lower in Argentina than in
any other country in "the rest" except Mexico (Amsden and Mourshed
1997).

Given the high costs of R&D and the challenge a firm faces to commercialize new technologies, the cost-effectiveness of R&D depends, at minimum,
on managerial capabilities. Argentina, however, was possibly furthest behind
all countries in "the rest" in building managerial skills. Before the war, even
the premier SIAM group "was held together by Di Tella (the owner) in person.

He would walk through the factory at least two or three times a week, talking with the chiefs and foremen and settling problems on the spot. . . . This highly personalized control was more suited to a small *taller* than a big factory." Di Tella was persuaded by a Westinghouse executive to hire an industrial engineer to design a more efficient organization. An engineer arrived from Westinghouse and designed a hierarchical organization. After months, he admitted that "results have only in part been obtained" (Cochran 1962, pp. 186–87). This leading Argentine business group went bankrupt as a consequence of its ill-fated automobile operations, as noted earlier. Productivity studies showed that SIAM took twice as long as its competitors (mostly foreign firms) to turn out vehicles (Lewis 1990). Even after the war, many groups in Argentina still operated along the same lines as the defunct SIAM group. In a survey in the early 1990s of 271 large enterprises, it was found that 117 groups had no organizational chart that was technically acceptable; barely 79 had a manual containing organizational procedures (Schvarzer 1995, p. 147). Without managerial expertise, investing in R&D was a waste of money.

Although Brazil's R&D expenditures amounted to a higher share of GDP than those of either Argentina or Mexico, private firms were little involved. Twenty-five of the biggest business groups were estimated to have undertaken only 17.4 percent of total R&D in the early 1980s, with as much as 62.6 percent accounted for by the state. By the 1990s the private sector's share had shriveled to insignificance—less than 10 percent of the total, and a core of only 366 firms was considered to be R&D active (Dahlman and Frischtak 1993). In Brazil's computer industry, whose import-substitution was based on the controversial principle of backward integration, such a policy required, among other things, "a corresponding investment in research and development, *which in the Brazilian case did not exist*. The weakness of the research effort is one reason why the Brazilian policy for the computer industry came under severe criticism" (Schwartzman 1994, p. 188, emphasis added).

In terms of the high R&D spenders, the efforts of Korea and Taiwan started early and then rapidly gained momentum. *The initial form was quite coercive.* As early as 1973, the Korean government introduced a reserve fund system that "require(d) firms to keep a certain proportion of income for R&D investment" (coverage included firms in manufacturing, construction, mining, computer processing, military supply, and machine engineering). If the amount set aside was spent on R&D (broadly defined) within a given time period, a loss could be deducted from taxable corporate income. If not used, the amount set aside had to be declared as profits and subject to taxation (OECD 1996, p. 99). The Taiwan government, fearful of the limited effort of small firms to invest in R&D, required *all firms* to spend a stipulated share of their sales revenues on R&D (the exact percentage depending on firm size and industry) or to remit an equivalent sum to finance government R&D (OECD 1990).

Soon, however, both Korea and Taiwan dropped an across-the-board R&D requirement in favor of *a targeted approach*. In 1979 the Korean government designed performance standards such that long-term credit and tax exemptions were made contingent on firms establishing central R&D laboratories, which many large groups began to do like clockwork (Amsden 1989). Simultaneously, it introduced a series of National R&D Projects whereby government agencies collaborated with the most advanced national firms in a given industry to gain technological mastery for purposes of global market expansion. That the initiative to engage in R&D lay with the Korean government is indicated by the timing in R&D expenditures. In the earliest period, the government accounted for roughly 80 percent of the total, with private national industry accounting for the rest. By the 1990s these proportions had been reversed. Nevertheless, as much as 65 percent of private R&D spending was financed at one time or another by state-subsidized credit (Kim 1997; Lim 1999).

In Taiwan, the government became more discriminating in its support of R&D through the establishment of government R&D institutes and science parks, where business and hand-picked private firms became involved in joint or independent research. In 1995, firms in the Hsinchu Science Park accounted for only 4.2 percent of manufacturing output but 17.5 percent of total R&D.[80] Moreover, the government's direct share of R&D expenditures remained high, at around 40 percent (Taiwan (Republic of China National Science Council) 1996). The dimension of the government's continuing R&D efforts is suggested by its second major science park, Tainan Science-Based Industrial Park (TSIP). As noted earlier, TSIP was founded in 1996 to build technological capabilities in the microelectronics, precision machinery, semiconductor, and agricultural bio-technology industries. The park was designed to provide high-quality residential and recreational facilities for as many as 110,000 people. By 2005 employment was anticipated to be roughly 21,000 and sales of $16 billion (U.S. dollars) were expected (probably over-optimistically) (Tainan Science-Based Industrial Park 1996).

Labor Cost Incentive

The earliest incentives that provoked Korea and Taiwan to start building institutions and raising finance for R&D were fears that foreign firms would refuse to sell them advanced technology, and that rapidly rising domestic wages would price unskilled industries out of world markets. Annual growth rates of manufacturing earnings for 1969 to 1990 are presented in table 8.16. The sharp differences between wage behavior in Korea and Taiwan on the one hand and Argentina and Mexico on the other are striking. Wages in the

Table 8.16. Annual Growth Rates of Real Manufacturing Earnings per Employee, Selected Countries, 1969–1990

Country	5-Year Averages (%)				
	1969–74	1975–79	1980–84	1985–90	1969–90
Argentina	7.3	−5.1	8.3	−9.3	−0.1
Brazil	13.8	3.2	−1.7	7.0	5.6
Chile	−1.8	11.8	3.8	0.2	4.2
China	na	1.3	3.7	3.2	3.1
India	−0.3	3.6	3.1	2.4	2.2
Indonesia	−1.8	4.7	6.6	6.6	5.1
Korea	7.2	13.0	2.7	8.2	7.8
Malaysia	−1.9	4.5	5.6	0.4	2.1
Mexico	0.9	1.4	−6.0	0.6	−0.8
Taiwan*	—	11.5	5.4	8.7	8.5
Thailand	−6.3	2.4	2.7	5.1	2.4
Turkey	4.5	8.4	−5.8	2.5	2.4
Japan	7.5	1.3	1.0	2.1	3.0
U.S.	0.3	0.2	0.0	0.6	0.3
U.K.	3.1	1.2	2.0	2.4	2.2
Italy	7.0	4.0	1.2	1.3	3.4

*Average for 1975–1990 only. Taiwan data may not be strictly comparable with other country data.

Sources: World Bank (various years [b]), except for Taiwan. CEPD (various years).

former rose on the order of 8 percent per annum while those in the latter *fell* slightly.

By the early 1970s the five-year development plans of both Korea and Taiwan had begun to note the long-term implications for competitiveness of rapid real wage increases. The response, first on the part of the government and then on the part of large private firms, was to increase domestic R&D activity and *to globalize*. One of the most important forms of globalization was to bring experienced Korean-Americans and Chinese-Americans back home. The exact dimensions of this technically qualified "reverse brain-drain" are unclear, but the potential supply was enormous. Nonreturn rates for students from "the rest" were not as high for Korea and Taiwan as for Argentina and Mexico (see table 1.10), but the absolute numbers of Korean and Taiwanese nationals studying abroad was larger, and the proportions were greater in relation to the size of Korea's and Taiwan's populations. The manifestation of reverse brain-drain for national innovation was everywhere.[81] Many R&D laboratories in Korea and Taiwan were started by Asian-Americans. In the second operating year of Hsinchu Science Park, 1988, 7 percent of paid-in capital came from overseas Chinese (Taiwan 1996). Government measures to accelerate reverse brain-drain included overseas recruitment, the provision of financial subsidies, and the offer of challenging, prestigious work. Attention to detail is indicated by the services provided to repatriates by science parks. Housing was designed to approximate conditions abroad and language training included the teaching of Chinese.

Argentina and Mexico did not have the incentive of sustained rising real wages to increase investment in R&D; to the contrary, declining wages contributed to maintaining the status quo. Without investments in science and technology, the demand-side for reverse brain-drain did not deepen. Without reverse brain-drain, the chances of successfully diversifying into high-tech industries on the basis of "national" capital became more remote. Yet given a slowdown in global demand for Argentina's and Mexico's leading sector, petrochemicals, high-tech industries were the best hope that a new leading sector would emerge, and one that was relatively labor-intensive. Nevertheless, as wages stagnated, as diversification into high-technology stalled, as North American pressures mounted for market liberalization, and as social cohesion became more fragile, the chance of creating national leaders fell.

In 1975 manufacturing value added in Latin America, mostly in Argentina, Brazil and Mexico, had accounted for 55 percent of total manufacturing value added for developing countries, both "the rest" and "the remainder." By 1994 Latin America's share had fallen to 35.9 percent. Meanwhile, the share of manufacturing output accounted for by south and east Asia had skyrocketed, from only 26.4 percent in 1975 to 47.9 percent only twenty years later (see table 8.17). Whereas East Asia had started the last half of the twentieth century behind Latin America, by 2000 it was pulling ahead.

Table 8.17. Distribution of Manufacturing Value Added (MVA) and Population, Selected Groups of Developing Countries, Selected Years (%)

	1975	1980	1985	1990	1994
MVA					
Africa	6.5	6.1	6.7	6.2	5.6
Latin America	55.1	51.2	43.5	37.2	35.9
S. Asia & E. Asia	26.4	29.0	34.9	43.3	47.9
W. Asia & Europe	12.0	13.7	14.9	13.3	10.6
Developing	100	100	100	100	100
Population					
Africa	19.2	19.6	20.1	20.8	21.4
Latin America	16.3	16.2	16.0	15.7	15.5
S. Asia & E. Asia	59.3	58.9	58.6	58.1	57.7
W. Asia & Europe	5.2	5.3	5.3	5.4	5.4
Developing	100	100	100	100	100

Sources: Adapted from UNIDO (1995a) and (1997).

Conclusion

De novo firms in newly established industries must be able to manufacture products, bring them to market, and manage enterprises of increasing complexity and scale. Given state support, all countries in "the rest" succeeded in establishing such enterprises by virtue of undertaking a three-pronged investment. After this step, however, heterogeneity arose. The share of foreign firms in manufacturing output differed sharply across countries. The degree to which national firms, small and large, were targeted for government support differed. In tandem with these distinctions, national efforts to invest in proprietary knowledge-based assets followed divergent paths.

In the next chapter, we continue our examination of divergence under the strain of debt crises and the dawn of a more liberal global economic order. Both put the developmental state on the defensive. Both, however, tended to reinforce existing trends in firm ownership and skill formation.

III

SQUARING OFF, CIRCA 1980–

9

From Mechanisms of Control to Mechanisms of Resistance

The expansionist tendencies inherent in developmental policies became overexpansionist when, by virtue of success itself, access to foreign capital eased. Two foreign debt crises ensued, one in Latin America starting in 1982 and the other in East Asia starting in 1997. The economic and political costs of financial disequilibria were enormous, involving prolonged falls in output and wages in Latin America (see tables 1.5 and 8.16) and greater foreign political intervention throughout the developing world. This chapter examines how the institutions centered around the developmental state absorbed external shock and adapted to a more advanced stage of development internally.

Freer trade confirmed the general healthiness of "the rest's" import substitution industries, as argued below. But aggressive foreign competition exposed the frailty of its nationally owned firms. In Brazil, it is estimated that between 1980 and 1995 foreign firms (with at least 10 percent foreign equity) increased their share of total output from 33 to 72 percent in the informatics industry, from 30 to 57 percent in the electrical machinery industry, from 41 to 64 percent in the non-electrical machinery industry, and from 46 to 68 percent in the chemical industry (Mesquita Moreira 1999). Continuity was such that the more/less a country had amassed skills and had concentrated resources in national leaders *before* stumbling from overborrowing, the more/less its high-technology industries were likely to expand and its mid-technology industries were likely to avert foreign takeover. A "neo-developmental state" lived or died in this new, more liberal world order depending on its success in building knowledge-based assets.

All economies in "the rest" groped towards "mechanisms of resistance": they introduced policies that upheld the letter but not the spirit of new WTO law. All became more global: they interlinked with the North Atlantic and

Japan, formed joint ventures and alliances with multinational firms, and established overseas manufacturing ventures. But only a handful of countries, the "independents," had the hubris to harbor ambitions to join the ranks of world class innovators, and to base their expansion in high-tech sectors on national firms and investments in R&D. The "integrationists," by contrast, depended for their long-run growth on technical licenses and economic collaboration with foreign firms. Each long-term strategy was rational, each held different implications for institutional change, and each faced enormous challenges.

Overexpansion

The dynamic between expansion and overexpansion is present under free-market conditions, but under the special conditions of industrializing late, and under the extraspecial conditions of industrializing late by dint of a developmental state, it is particularly intense. Overexpansion is defined as an excess of supply over demand due to erroneous supply or demand projections.

That conditions of "lateness" are inherently conducive to overexpansion is suggested by the fact that when a debt crisis occurs, it almost always occurs in a latecomer country. This is because, first, diversification in the presence of already well-established global industries involves moving from labor-intensive to capital-intensive sectors characterized by economies of scale. In order to reach minimum efficient scale, new entrants into capital-intensive industries initially maximize profits by maximizing sales. Korean companies in the 1990s, for example, were criticized for their strategy of maximizing global market share rather than profits, but given the large scale economies in their specializations (automobiles, semiconductors, and consumer electronics, for example), this strategy was rational. It also tended to be expansionary.

Second, as latecomers expand, the international division of labor changes. Incumbents from highly industrialized economies increasingly specialize in supplying services. This creates pressure on latecomers to liberalize their markets for such services, especially financial. Financial markets in latecomer countries tend to be closed when pressures for liberalization are applied, and decision making after markets are opened falls on inexperienced shoulders, private and public. Lobbying in Washington by American financial service providers for easier access to foreign financial markets intensified in the 1980s as financial services acquired a larger share of American GNP and required global operating scales to minimize costs.[2] "The rest's" repeal of its capital controls under American pressure fueled overexpansion.[3]

Third, given rapid structural change in tandem with greater financial market opening, information about late-industrializing countries becomes more imperfect. This makes it more difficult to forecast supply and demand accurately. In the absence of accurate forecasts, tendencies toward overexpansion increase. This is apparent as excess capacity appears and the chances improve for a financial panic. The volatile conditions which imperfect information creates tend to induce speculation ("hot money"). Speculation has a particularly destabilizing effect in small countries with shallow financial markets (Minsky, 1986). Small size and imperfect information confound attempts to anticipate and guard against exogenous macroeconomic shocks, which further complicate accurate demand and supply projections. For example, according to an activist in the Latin American debt drama, the CEO of Citicorp and a member of the Federal Reserve's Advisory Council, Walter Wriston, lending to Latin America went awry because of a sudden policy shift in 1979 at the Federal Reserve: "the Fed's tight money caused the debt problem" (Neikirk 1987, p. 176).

Late industrialization under the developmental state, with its singular objective of growth, entails still more expansionary tendencies. The dynamic of expansion involves using subsidies to make manufacturing activity more profitable than it would be under market forces, as analyzed earlier. To the extent that inflated profits activate "idle balances" or direct resources to activities with increasing returns, expansionary tendencies snowball. The emergence of greater profit-making opportunities in manufacturing leads to higher investment rates and greater demand for savings, national and foreign. Results-oriented and redistributive performance standards create a chain reaction that puts additional upward pressure on investment.

The debt crisis in Latin America in 1982 and in East Asia in 1997 were both preceded by a *surge in investment* (see table 1.12). In 1975–79, gross domestic investment as a share of GDP was at a peak in Argentina, Brazil, and Mexico. In Asia, the share of investment in GDP in 1990–95 compared to the previous five-year period was up, in absolute terms, by roughly 4 percentage points in Indonesia, 7 percentage points in Korea, 8 percentage points in Malaysia, and 10 percentage points in Thailand, where the Asian financial crisis began.

The countertendencies to expansionism in a developmental policy regime are relatively weak. They take the form of controls over capacity expansion (industrial licensing) and controls over foreign borrowing (financial repression). The politics of "lateness," however, become increasingly hostile to both controls.[4] Incumbents from the North Atlantic want access to "the rest's" markets. Industrialists from "the rest" want freedom from licensing restrictions and access to cheap North Atlantic credit. In general, performance standards are a cost. As industrialization proceeds and the benefits which the developmental state is able to offer industrialists decrease relative to the costs of performance standards, such standards become the object of political opposition.

Even in the absence of political opposition to controls, the "controller" of last resort is the government, and there is no way to check the government's own foreign borrowing. Such borrowing in the case of Mexico was unbridled and became overextended.[5] By contrast, the three countries in "the rest" that averted financial meltdown by the year 2000 were all statist: China, India, and Taiwan. The government's share in gross domestic capital formation in these countries was among the highest (for India and Taiwan, see table 1.13), and financial markets were liberalized only gingerly and partially. The only sure check on foreign borrowing by a latecomer state is restraint on the part of *lenders*. But when profit-making opportunities in a latecomer expand, this restraint on lenders' part tends to erode. Easier access to available foreign credit, owing to financial market liberalization and the greater willingness of foreign bankers to lend, becomes the necessary condition for a financial crash.

A surge in foreign borrowing after liberalization, as well as a surge in investment, was apparent in "the rest's" two worst postwar debt debacles.[6] In a very short time space, from the end of 1978 to the end of 1982, total foreign debt in Mexico, the epicenter of the Latin crisis, increased by a factor of 2.4, exceeded only by the increase of foreign indebtedness of Argentina (see table 9.1). Between the end of 1993 and the end of 1997, total foreign debt in Korea, the epicenter of the Asian crisis, rose by a factor of 3.3, the highest rise in East Asia, whose average rate of increase was high nonetheless (see table 9.2).

Given expansionist tendencies, it is thus arguable that in the most imme-diate sense, "the rest's" worst debt crises were *provoked by the "imperial state"* representing its financial services sector, and *not prevented by the developmental*

Table 9.1. Foreign Debt: Total and Short Term, Latin America, 1978 and 1982

Foreign Debt	Argentina	Brazil	Chile	Mexico
End of 1978				
Total (bil US$)	13.3	53.4	7.3	35.7
Short term (bil US$)	3.4	7.1	1.1	4.9
End of 1982				
Total (bil US$)	43.6	91.0	17.4	86.8
Short term (bil US$)	16.5	17.5	3.3	3.3
Change, 1978–82				
Total (bil US$)	(+3.3)	(+1.7)	(+2.4)	(+2.4)
Short term (bil US$)	(+4.8)	(+2.5)	(+3.0)	(+5.4)

Source: Adapted from World Bank (various years [a])

Table 9.2. Foreign Debt: Total and Short Term, East Asia, 1993 and 1997

Foreign Debt	Korea	China	Indonesia	Malaysia	Taiwan	Thailand
End of 1993						
Total (bil US$)	47.2	84.2	89.5	23.3	15.2	45.8
Short term (bil US$)	12.2	13.6	18.0	6.9	2.3	19.7
End of 1997						
Total (bil US$)	154.0	138.0	137.9	39.8[1]	26.2	90.8[1]
Short term (bil US$)	68.4	31.7	16.3	11.1	21.4	37.6
Change, 1993–97						
Total (bil US$)	(+3.3)	(+1.6)	(+1.5)	(+1.7)	(+1.7)	(+2.0)
Short term (bil US$)	(+5.6)	(+2.3)	(+0.9)	(+1.6)	(+9.3)	(+1.9)

1. End of 1996. In 1992, Malaysia's total debt was US$20.0 billion, and its short-term debt was US$3.6 billion. Comparable data from 1992 for Thailand were US$39.6 billion and US$3.6 billion.

Sources: Adapted from World Bank (various years [a]), except Taiwan. For Taiwan: Bank for International Settlement data.

state representing its manufacturing sector. Beyond immediate causes, "fundamentals" were responsible for the *duration* of crisis. Only three years after disaster struck in East Asia, rapid economic growth had resumed.[7] Latin America's economies, by contrast, *still* appeared to be ailing from their financial upheaval two decades earlier. Differences in allocative efficiency may be hypothesized to have influenced differential rates of recovery. Resource allocation, moreover, was squarely under the developmental state's control for most of the postwar years. Thus, in analyzing the efficiency of resource allocation, one is also indirectly analyzing the performance of the developmental state, which sustained a severe blow to its prestige on account of both debt debacles.[8]

One test of misallocation is to examine whether those industries targeted by the developmental state survived freer trade. If they did, there are grounds for arguing that the disparagement of the developmental state was exaggerated and that the prolonged economic stagnation of Latin America owed itself to causes other than allocative inefficiency. It is to resource allocation in the context of trade liberalization that attention is now turned.

The "Imperialism of Free Trade"

After benign neglect,[9] the United States adopted an international economic policy regime in the 1980s similar to that of Britain over a century earlier, a regime that had been accused of perpetrating "imperialism of free trade" (Gallagher and Robinson 1953). The advice of a British commission investigating Turkey's debt problem *in the 1860s* was almost identical to the advice of the International Monetary Fund investigating Turkey's debt problem *in the 1980s.* "All the programmes (for all latecomers) recommend the government to reduce budget deficits, restrict monetary growth, and ensure real devaluation for short-term stability; and to deregulate markets, curtail the role of the state, and liberalize foreign trade and foreign capital inflows for long-term growth" (Kiray 1990, pp. 254–55). As countries with the greatest knowledge-based assets at the time, both the United Kingdom and United States promoted their own industries by adopting an offensive rather than defensive strategy. Instead of simply domestic protection—the recourse of learners—they also pried open the markets of weaker economies:

> It is vital to the long-term prosperity and prestige of the United States . . . to take full advantage of our strong global position and *continue to push our trading partners for even more open markets and economic liberalization.* If we abdicate our strength, we risk missing a prime opportunity to advance those policies and values that have been so instrumental in making our economy the strongest and most efficient in the world. (United States Trade Representative 1998, p. 11, emphasis added)

Instead of "the rest," Japan was originally the major challenge to American economic hegemony. Hence, it became the prime target of market opening (Bhagwati and Patrick 1990). Japan's share of world manufacturing value added (MVA) more than doubled between 1975 and 1993, from 10.5 to 22 percent (see table 9.3). East Asia (excluding Japan) also saw its share in MVA rise steeply, from 1.8 to 6.1 percent. But Japan's share was larger in absolute terms and far larger relative to its share of world population. Moreover, Japan bore primary responsibility in the 1980s for the United States' deteriorating trade balance. Japan's alleged "non-tariff administrative trade barriers" (also called "structural impediments") were regarded in Washington as the root of the problem (Krugman 1991). The American trade balance was positive in 1980 and 1981. It then turned sharply negative as Japan's trade surplus with the United States ballooned (see table 9.4).

"The rest" initially was more of a political irritant to the United States than a serious economic challenge based on proprietary knowledge and skills. It represented a threat to American jobs. The developing world's share of global employment (table 9.5) and global exports (table 9.6) rose steeply, initially on the basis of manufacturing experience plus low wages and economies of scale. Employment and export shares both increased from the 1970s to the 1990s by at least ten percentage points. "The rest" gained ground in almost all industries, including chemicals, transportation equipment, and ma-

Table 9.3. World Shares by Region* in Manufacturing Value Added (MVA), 1975–1993

Region	MVA (%)				
	1975	1980	1985	1990	1993
Developed	89.3	87.2	85.9	86.6	84.7
North America	35.2	32.4	39.3	30.5	30.4
Japan	10.5	13.3	15.1	18.9	22.0
W. Europe (industrialized)	39.6	38.8	29.3	34.7	29.9
W. Europe (south)	0.7	0.7	0.6	0.7	0.7
Other Developded	2.2	2.0	1.6	1.8	1.6
Developing	10.7	12.8	14.1	13.4	15.3
E. Asia (exporters of mfrs.)	1.8	2.6	3.3	4.9	6.1
Africa	0.9	0.8	0.9	0.7	0.7
West Asia	1.0	1.1	1.4	2.1	1.2
Indian subcontinent	0.8	0.7	0.8	0.7	0.6
Latin America	6.2	7.5	7.5	5.0	6.7

Note: Current U.S. dollars.
*Regional classifcations are those used by UNIDO. Regions contain data for all available countries. Excluding China, the former USSR, and Eastern Europe.

Sources: Adapted from UNIDO (1986a and 1995a).

Table 9.4 U.S. Manufacturing Net* Trade Deficits (bil US$), by Country, 1980–1989

Country/ Region	1980	1981	1982	1983	1984	1985	1986	1987	1988	1989
World	21.9	15.4	(2.8)	(30.0)	(78.2)	(101.7)	(128.9)	(137.7)	(119.1)	(92.4)
Developed	(6.0)	(12.6)	(25.1)	(31.4)	(64.1)	(84.7)	(100.6)	(97.9)	(83.3)	(60.8)
Developing	(2.2)	28.4	22.7	1.9	(13.0)	(16.9)	(26.4)	(36.4)	(30.9)	(22.8)
S. America	10.6	10.0	8.2	2.1	0.5	1.2	2.3	2.8	2.9	3.2
Asia	(5.9)	(10.5)	(10.5)	(17.1)	(27.3)	(30.6)	(37.1)	(46.8)	(43.5)	(38.2)
Canada	6.9	7.2	0.7	2.0	(2.6)	(2.2)	(2.0)	0.2	1.9	3.6
Japan	(23.6)	(29.4)	(29.5)	(32.3)	(47.6)	(59.3)	(67.9)	(71.0)	(70.5)	(65.9)
W. Europe	7.9	4.2	(0.7)	(4.4)	(17.3)	(27.2)	(34.2)	(31.4)	(20.7)	(5.8)
Argentina	2.1	1.6	0.6	0.4	0.3	0.2	0.4	0.3	0.0	0.2
Brazil	1.8	0.8	0.6	(1.0)	(2.8)	(2.4)	(1.7)	(1.9)	(2.6)	(1.4)
Chile	0.6	0.7	0.2	(0.2)	0.1	0.1	0.3	0.2	0.3	0.5
India	0.4	0.2	0.2	(0.1)	(0.3)	(0.2)	(0.4)	(0.8)	(0.7)	(0.6)
Indonesia	0.9	0.6	1.2	0.5	0.1	(0.1)	(0.1)	(0.6)	(0.4)	(0.4)
Korea	(2.1)	(2.9)	(2.8)	(4.2)	(6.4)	(6.9)	(9.2)	(12.6)	(13.6)	(10.6)
Malaysia	(0.2)	0.0	0.0	(0.2)	(0.6)	(0.5)	(0.4)	(0.8)	(1.2)	(1.4)
Mexico	7.3	9.2	3.9	0.2	0.8	1.7	(0.2)	(1.6)	(0.4)	0.9
Taiwan	(4.3)	(5.7)	(6.4)	(8.9)	(42.8)	(14.4)	(17.1)	(20.6)	(16.6)	(15.7)
Thailand	0.5	0.3	0.1	0.2	(0.1)	(0.3)	(0.4)	(0.3)	(0.8)	(1.3)
Turkey	0.4	0.5	0.6	0.5	0.6	0.8	0.4	0.5	0.8	0.5
China	0.4	(0.1)	(0.5)	(0.4)	(0.2)	0.6	(1.1)	(2.6)	(3.9)	(6.8)

*Surpluses are net of deficits, and deficits are net of surpluses. Therefore, columns may not add up to U.S. deficit (surplus).

Source: Adapted from United States, Department of Commerce (various years).

Table 9.5. World Shares by Region* in Manufacturing Employment,
1975–1993

Region	Manufacturing Employment (%)				
	1975	1980	1985	1990	1993
Developed	72.6	67.3	62.0	64.4	61.2
North America	20.3	20.6	18.9	19.6	19.0
Japan	10.4	10.0	10.9	10.9	10.0
W. Europe (industrialized)	36.6	32.5	28.3	29.8	27.4
W. Europe (south)	1.4	1.3	1.2	1.3	1.3
Other Developed	3.0	2.8	2.7	2.8	2.6
Developing	7.4	32.7	38.0	35.6	38.8
E. Asia (exporters of mfrs.)	7.2	8.3	12.0	10.2	10.0
Africa	1.9	2.7	3.5	3.1	3.7
West Asia	1.6	1.7	2.0	2.0	2.1
Indian subcontinent	7.2	7.9	9.0	8.1	10.1
Latin America	9.5	12.2	10.5	12.3	12.0

Note: Current U.S. dollars.
*Regional classifications are those used by UNIDO (various years). Regions contain data for all available countries. Excluding China, the former USSR, and Eastern Europe.

Sources: Adapted from UNIDO (1986a) and (1995a).

chinery, both electrical and nonelectrical (see table 9.7). But its gains in global market share were greatest in labor-intensive industries such as footwear and textiles, and in capital-intensive industries with large labor requirements, such as iron and steel. By 1989, *all* Asian countries in "the rest"—India, Indonesia, Korea, Malaysia, Taiwan, and Thailand—enjoyed trade surpluses with the United States, as did Brazil (see table 9.4). Moreover, "the rest's" expansionism was highly visible. Among the top ten suppliers of U.S. imports, the number of countries *outside* the North Atlantic rose from four in 1980 to six in 1996 (see table 9.8).

There followed intense efforts, unilateral[10] and multilateral, to pry open the markets of "the rest" by way of liberalizing imports.

Table 9.6. Distribution of World* Manufactured Exports, 1975–1990 (%)

Year	W. Europe	N. America	Japan	Developing
1975	55.2	16.9	10.5	7.5
1980	54.0	15.7	10.3	10.5
1985	46.8	16.4	14.3	14.4
1990	52.1	14.5	10.4	17.9

* Excluding China.

Source: Adapted from UNIDO (1992, p. 43).

Table 9.7. Industry Shares and Gains (Losses) of Developing Countries, 1975–1995

10% or more gain	0–9% Gain	Loss
Footwear (43.8)	Pottery/china/earthenware	Plastic products
Iron and steel (28.3)	(25.7)	n.e.c. (12.8)
Textiles (36.4)	Rubber prod. (21.5)	Printing and pub-
Nonferrous metals (20.8)	Industrial chemicals (16.7)	lishing (7.6)
Wearing apparel (29.2)	Glass and glass prod. (17.8)	Tobacco mfg.
Leather/fur prod. (34.0)	Beverages (27.3)	(30.2)
Petroleum refineries (36.7)	Electrical machinery (14.1)	
Misc. petrol./coal prod. (24.0)	Transport equip. (12.6)	
Other non-metallic, mineral	Metal prod., excluding	
prod. (26.2)	machinery (15.0)	
	Non-elec. machinery (9.6)	
	Paper and paper prod. (13.5)	
	Furniture and fixtures (13.6)	
	Food (18.6)	
	Prof. and sci. goods (6.2)	
	Wood/cork prod. (15.5)	
	Other chem. prod. (19)	

Notes: Parentheses indicate developing world share (%) in total world output of that category, 1995, excluding China.
   Industries within categories are ranked in descending order from largest gains (or losses) to smallest.
   n.e.c. = not elsewhere classified.

Source: Adapted from UNIDO (1995a, p. 6).

Table 9.8. Top 25 Suppliers of U.S. Imports, 1980 and 1996

Supplier	Value of Imports (mil US$)	Supplier	Value of Imports (mil US$)
1980		1996	
1. Japan	35,257	1. Canada	120,444
2. Canada	27,652	2. Japan	114,503
3. W. Germany	11,857	3. Mexico	60,966
4. U.K.	7,358	4. China	49,928
5. Taiwan	7,106	5. Germany	37,901
6. HongKong	4,944	6. Taiwan	29,517
7. France	4,772	7. U.K.	24,862
8. Mexico	4,407	8. Korea	22,275
9. Korea	4,294	9. Singapore	20,093
10. Italy	4,045	10. Malaysia	17,265

Source: Adapted from United States, Department of Commerce (various years).

Trade Liberalization

The so-called Washington consensus (comprising the United States, the World Bank, and the IMF) argued strenuously that "getting the prices 'wrong' " had led to a misallocation of resources in the form of inefficient import-substitution industries that only survived behind high tariff walls.[11] Liberalization was intended to tear down those walls, redirect resources from less to more efficient industries ("structural adjustment"), and thereby stimulate economic growth.[12]

By way of a test, if a massive contraction of import substitution industries and a reallocation of resources to other sectors results from lower tariffs, then this would provide some supporting evidence for a misallocation of resources under the developmental state. To estimate the actual amount of industrial restructuring that occurred, we use a *structural change index*, S, that is calculated as follows:

$$S = \frac{\{|si(t) - si(t-5)|\}}{i \qquad 2},$$

where si(t) is the share of the i-th branch in total manufacturing value added in year t.[13] The right-hand side of the equation is the sum of the absolute values of sectoral changes in the share of total manufacturing across all sectors over five year intervals (divided by 2). A value of 100 means a complete transformation of the industrial structure. A value of 50 means that exactly half of all industries have changed their rank in terms of how much value added they produce. Given data limitations, the index could only be estimated for the period 1980–1994, before the East Asian debt crisis. But this earlier period is precisely when markets were being liberalized and alleged inefficiencies were being exposed.

The results of estimating this index are shown in table 9.9. *Generally structural change at the industry level is extremely low.* Given a maximum index value of 100, and given only a modest change in the estimated index value between the beginning and end of the measured restructuring period (1980–1994), the average for "the rest," 11.6 in 1980 and 11.2 in 1994, is not indicative of a great contraction of inefficient industries in response to market forces. In fact, the supposedly least efficient economies, Argentina and Mexico, had among the lowest restructuring rates; the highest restructuring rates were found in the least *industrialized* countries that were still in the process of diversifying (Indonesia, Malaysia, and Thailand). Restructuring, therefore, at least during this time period, largely emerges as an expansionary rather than contractionary phenomenon.

The structural change indicator used above is not a perfect measure of interindustry shifts. It may not be sufficiently sensitive to shifts *within* a

Table 9.9. Structural Change Indicators and Manufacturing-Value-Added (MVA) Growth Rate per Structural Change, 1980 and 1994

Country	Structural Change Indicator (max. = 100)		MVA Growth Rate per Structural Change[1] (%)	
	1980[2]	1994[3]	1980	1994
Argentina	5.8	7.7	2.2	−0.5
Brazil	8.0	10.9	9.9	−0.1
Chile	17.6	10.7	0.2	3.7
China	5.0	10.6	4.1	5.0
India	6.5	8.4	2.5	4.3
Indonesia	20.7	17.1	4.3	6.0
Korea	12.6	10.2	7.3	7.9
Malaysia	14.0	14.6	6.2	5.5
Mexico	5.1	6.8	7.3	1.2
Taiwan	12.5	8.5	4.1	3.5
Thailand	9.3	16.0	5.6	4.7
Turkey	10.3	10.7	3.9	4.9
Average[4]	10.6	10.2	4.8	3.8
France	4.7	5.3	2.2	1.0
Japan	6.0	5.3	3.1	2.6
U.K.	5.1	5.0	0.3	1.1
U.S.	4.6	6.4	3.2	2.0

1. The "MVA growth rate per structural change" is the growth rate of real value added for every percentage point of structural change in the five-year period.

2. 1980 measure is over previous 5 years.

3. 1994 measure is over previous 14 years, a weighted average of the UNIDO measures for 1985, 1990, and 1994

4. Average represents an average of the index numbers, not a measure of the average distribution. The structural change index, S, is measured as

$$S = \frac{\{|\ si(t) - \frac{si(t-5)|\}}{2}}{i},$$

where si(t) is the share of the i-th branch in total MVA in year t. S is the sum of the absolute values of sectoral changes in the share of total manufacturing value over a five-year period across all sectors, divided by 2. A value of 100 percent means complete reversal of this structure; a value of 50 percent means that exactly half of the industry has relocated in terms of MVA

Source: Adapted from UNIDO (various years [a]).

broadly defined industry; in any given industry, some *market segments* may be contracting while others are expanding due to freer trade. Nevertheless, the data used to estimate the above structural change indicator are fairly finely disaggregated (at the four digit level). The structural change indicator also fails to address the issue of deindustrialization: a decline in the share of total manufacturing industry in GDP. A misallocation of resources may have contributed to such a decline. Between 1980 and 1995, the share of total manufacturing in GDP fell in Argentina, Brazil, China, Korea, Mexico, Taiwan and Thailand, as shown below. In Argentina, deindustrialization was such that industry's share in GNP fell from 29.5 percent in 1980 to 21.2 percent in 1995 (see table 9.11). Nevertheless, a decline in this share does not necessarily indicate a misallocation of resources; it may simply indicate a growth in the importance of services, a function of economic maturity. In fact, the rise of foreign investment throughout "the rest" had a large service component. Based on the structural change indicator, therefore, one cannot dismiss the hypothesis that the industrial sector established by the developmental state was efficient. It largely withstood the test of freer trade.[14]

To gain still more insight into the bearing of trade liberalization on the developmental state's resource allocation, it is worth following a slightly different tack and examining precisely which industries exhibited expanding or contracting market shares. If those industries whose share was increasing were those that had been targeted by the developmental state, and if such industries were dynamic (in terms of skill formation), then one might infer that the developmental state had succeeded in creating leading sectors for future expansion. We first look at the average performance of an industry for all countries in "the rest." Later we look at how different industries fared in individual countries. We standardize for whether or not an industry was growing quickly or slowly worldwide: other things being equal, a slow-growing industry globally cannot be expected to grow exceptionally fast in "the rest." We do this by comparing an industry's share of manufacturing value added in "the rest" and in the North Atlantic and Japan. We thus take the North Atlantic and Japan as a benchmark for the ideal industrial structure at the world technological frontier (as we did in figure 8.1).[15] We also aggregate similar industries into relatively broad sectors for purposes of discussion.

The results are shown in table 9.10, which classifies sectors into one of four categories: dynamic advantage (*dis*advantage) and static advantage (*dis*advantage). If a sector's share in "the rest" starts in 1980 behind that of the North Atlantic and Japan and then rises (falls) over time, the sector is defined as experiencing *dynamic* comparative advantage (disadvantage). If, by comparison, a sector's share starts in 1980 ahead of that of the North Atlantic and Japan and then rises (falls) over time, the sector is defined as experiencing *static* comparative advantage (disadvantage). The results are quite positive. *Sectors in "the rest" that exhibit dynamic comparative advantage are electrical and nonelectrical machinery and transportation equipment.* These are among the most challenging sectors to develop because competing in them depends on scale, skills, brand name recognition, and reputation.[16] These sectors were also heavily targeted by the developmental state. Thus, on average, the skill-based industries that the developmental state targeted were precisely the industries that by world norms expanded the fastest.

For individual countries, by contrast, the same estimation procedure reveals substantial variation in the industries that exhibited dynamic compar-

Table 9.10. Change in the Composition of Manufacturing Value Added (MVA), the Average of "The Rest" vs. the Average of the North Atlantic and Japan, 1980–1995

DYNAMIC COMPARATIVE ADVANTAGE (DCA)	DYNAMIC COMPARATIVE DISADVANTAGE (DCD)
Non-elec. machinery	Prof./sci. goods
Transport. equip.	Metal products
Elec. machinery	Other chemicals

STATIC COMPARATIVE ADVANTAGE (SCA)	STATIC COMPARATIVE DISADVANTAGE (SCD)
Iron and steel	Rubber
Petroleum refining	Food
Wearing apparel	Beverages
	Tobacco
	Textiles

Notes: The classifications are organized according to the difference between the average of "the Rest" and the average of North Atlantic countries and Japan. The difference, D, is defined as follows:

$$D_{94} = \{X_{w,i}/MVA_w\}_{94} - \{X_{c,i}/MVA_c\}_{94}$$
$$D_{80} = \{X_{w,i}/MVA_w\}_{80} - \{X_{c,i}/MVA_c\}_{80}$$

Where:

$X_{w,i}$ = average MVA in ith industry for the world,

$X_{c,i}$ = average MVA in ith industry for a country,

MVA_w = average world MVA, and

MVA_c = total country MVA.

Dynamic comparative advantage: Industry's share in "the rest" starts behind the average share of the North Atlantic and Japan and, over time, gains ground.

Dynamic comparative disadvantage: Industry's share starts behind the average share of the North Atlantic and Japan and, over time, loses ground. In the static case, industries' initial shares start ahead of those of the North Atlantic and Japan. Note that only those industries were selected in which either $D_{94} > 1\%$ or $D_{80} > 1\%$.

Source: UNIDO (1997).

ative advantage. The most skill-intensive industries, machinery and transportation equipment, do not necessarily register any gain in share in some countries (see table 9.11). The industries in these countries that do show a gain are not necessarily skill-intensive. Only Korea, Malaysia, Thailand, and Turkey enjoyed dynamic comparative advantage *in all three* skill-intensive sectors (that is, the share of electrical machinery, nonelectrical machinery, and transportation equipment in their MVA were converging over time with that of the North Atlantic and Japan). Only two sectors in Taiwan were converging with the benchmark, but only because the third (electrical machinery) already had a higher share in 1980 than the norm; it therefore exhibited static advantage. Other countries where *two* of the three sectors in question exhibited dynamic comparative advantage were Brazil, China, and Indonesia. Only *one* sector exhibited dynamic advantage in Chile (nonelectrical machinery) and Mexico (transportation equipment). *None* of the three sectors in question exhibited dynamic comparative advantage in Argentina (Argentina's weak performance conforms with evidence presented earlier on

Table 9.11. Change in the Composition of Manufacturing Value Added,
Country Comparisons with the North Atlantic Average, 1980–1995

1995			
DCA	SCA	DCD	SCD

Argentina (mfg./GDP: 21.2% [1995], 29.5% [1980])

indust. chemicals	petroleum	non-elec. machinery	beverages
iron/steel		transport. equip.	food
tobacco		prof./sci. goods	textiles
		elec. machinery	
		plastics	
		wood/cork	

Brazil (mfg./GDP: 23.3% [1995], 31.3% [1980])

transport. equip.	indust. chemicals	non-elec. machinery	petroleum refining
elec. machinery	footwear	wood/cork	textiles
iron/steel	food	prof./sci. goods	
		plastic prod.	
		other chemicals	
		metal prod.	

Chile (mfg./GDP: 22.4% [1995], 21.4% [1980])

non-elec. machinery	paper prod.	transport. equip.	other chemicals
metal prod.	wood/cork	prof./sci. goods	nonferrous metals
indust. chemicals	footwear	elec. machinery	beverages
iron/steel	petroleum		tobacco
plastic prod.	food prod.		textiles

China (mfg./GDP: 37.6% [1995], 41.6% [1980])

transport. equip.	leather/fur	prof./sci. goods	textiles
wearing apparel	iron/steel	other chemicals	petroleum refining
elec. machinery	tobacco	rubber	indust. chemicals
wood/cork		non-elec. machinery	
food		metal prod.	
		plastic prod.	
		paper	

India (mfg./GDP: 18.5% [1995], 17.7% [1980])

wood/cork prod.	indust. chemicals	transport. equip.	other chemicals
non-ferrous metals		prof./sci. goods	iron/steel
beverages		elec. machinery	textiles
food		metal prod.	
wearing apparel		plastic prod.	
petroleum		paper prod.	
		non-elec. machinery	

Table 9.11. (*continued*)

	1995		
DCA	SCA	DCD	SCD

Indonesia (mfg./GDP: 24.3% [1995], 13.0% [1980])

DCA	SCA	DCD	SCD
non-elec. machinery	wood/cork	prof./sci. goods	rubber prod.
transport. equip.	footwear	elec. machinery	tobacco prod.
metal prod.	textiles	other chemicals	petroleum prod.
paper prod.		beverages	
wearing apparel		food prod.	
iron/steel		plastic prod.	
nonferrous metals			
indust. chemicals			

Korea (mfg./GDP: 26.1% [1995], 28.6% [1980])

DCA	SCA	DCD	SCD
non-elec. machinery	iron/steel	prof./sci. goods	tobacco prod.
transport. equip.		other chemicals	wearing apparel
elec. machinery		indust. chemicals	textiles
metal prod.		food	
plastic prod.		rubber prod.	
paper prod.		beverages	

Malaysia (mfg./GDP: 32.5% [1995], 21.2% [1980])

DCA	SCA	DCD	SCD
non-elec. machinery	elec. machinery	other chemicals	wood/cork
metal prod.		beverages	textiles
paper		food	rubber prod.
indust. chemicals		tobacco	
wearing apparel			
iron/steel			
transport. equip.			
prof./sci. goods			

Mexico (mfg./GDP: 18.3% [1995], 21.9% [1980])

DCA	SCA	DCD	SCD
transport. equip.	indust. chemicals	non-elec. machinery	footwear
prof./sci. goods	beverages	elec. machinery	food
iron/steel	petroleum	metal prod.	textiles
		plastic prod.	

Taiwan (mfg./GDP: 27.3% [1995], 36.2% [1980])

DCA	SCA	DCD	SCD
non-elec. machinery	elec. machinery	prof./sci. goods	plastic prod.
transport. equip.	iron/steel	other chemicals	tobacco
metal prod.	petroleum	paper prod.	textiles
	wearing apparel	food	indust. chemicals
		wood/cork prod.	

265

Table 9.11. (*continued*)

		1995	
DCA	SCA	DCD	SCD

Thailand (mfg./GDP: 27.3% [1995], 36.2% [1980])

non-elec. machinery	rubber	indust. chemicals	beverages
transport. equip.	wearing apparel	other chemicals	food
prof./sci. goods	textiles	plastic prod.	tobacco
metal prod.	petroleum	paper prod.	
iron/steel			
elec. machinery			

Turkey (mfg./GDP: 18.9% [1995], 17.2% [1980])

non-elec. machinery	pottery, earthen-	prof./sci. goods	textiles
transport. equip.	ware	metal prod	food
elec. machinery	iron/steel	plastic	beverages
wearing apparel	petroleum	paper prod.	tobacco
		indust. chemicals	
		wood/cork	

Notes: DCA = Dynamic Comparative Advantage; SCA = Static Comparative Advantage; DCD = Dynamic Comparative Disadvantage; SCD = Static Comparative Disadvantage.

Dynamic comparative advantage: Industry's share in "the rest" starts behind the average share of the North Atlantic and Japan and, over time, gains ground.

Dynamic comparative disadvantage: Industry's share starts behind the average share of the North Atlantic and Japan and, over time, loses ground. In the static case, industries' initial shares start ahead of those of the North Atlantic and Japan. Note that only those industries were selected in which either $D_{94} > 1\%$ or $D_{80} > 1\%$.

Source: UNIDO (1997).

deindustrialization and a shift from high to low manufacturing value added) or India (whose exports also allegedly suffer from low value added [Lall 1999]).

The classification scheme in tables 9.10 and 9.11 is biased against countries that started in 1980 with large machinery and transportation equipment sectors (see table 8.9). The fact that these industries started ahead means that their rate of increase is likely to be relatively slow. This was the case with India. These ambiguities aside, it is clear overall that some countries succeeded more than others in establishing dynamic "leading sectors."

By way of conclusion, on the basis of the selective evidence just provided, the resource allocation of the developmental state appears to have been efficient enough to withstand the market test. In general, *freer trade did not lead to massive restructuring in the form of a sharp contraction or expansion of different industries in total manufacturing value added.*[17] Market

Table 9.12. Tariffs before and after Liberalization (Pre- and Post-Uruguay Round)

Country	Trade-Weighted Tariff Averages (%)	
	Pre-Uruguay	Post-Uruguay
Argentina	38.2	30.9
Brazil	40.7	27.0
Chile	34.9	24.9
India	71.4	32.4
Indonesia	20.4	36.9
Korea	18.0	8.3
Malaysia	10.0	10.1
Mexico	46.1	33.7
Thailand	37.3	28.0
Turkey	25.1	22.3
European Union	5.7	3.6
Japan	3.9	1.7
United States	5.4	3.5

Notes: The pre-Uruguay duties refer to 1994 bound duties or, for unbound tariff lines, to duties applicable as of September 1986. The post-Uruguay duties refer to the concessions listed in the schedules annexed to the Uruguay Round Protocol to the GATT 1994. Import statistics refer in general to 1988, so trade weighted duties using post-Uruguay import data may be slightly different. The data are preliminary and may be revised to reflect the final schedules annexed to the Final Act of the Uruguay Round, although as of April 1999 no changes were registered except for Thailand. The changes for Thailand appear above.

Sources: GATT Secretariat, as cited in Hoda (1994).

forces tended to leave the existing structure of industries unchanged. In general, the developmental state also succeeded in creating dynamic "leading sectors" for future expansion. The machinery industries (electrical and nonelectrical) and the transportation equipment industry (mainly automobiles and ships) gained market share vis-à vis the North Atlantic and Japan. Nevertheless, performance varied by country. Argentina and Chile registered the weakest performance in terms of establishing leading sectors with high-skill content. Mexican industry also suffered in this regard until its automobile industry modernized in the 1990s. Thus, it is quite possible that one of the reasons why these countries suffered so long from financial shock is that *they lacked a sector dynamic enough to act as an engine of growth*.

We have thus far assumed that between 1980 and 1994 trade was liberalized. The assumption of freer (although not free) trade appears to be warranted. Tariffs (and nontariff barriers) came down in this period, sometimes unilaterally.[18] Table 9.12 compares trade weighted average tariffs before and after the formation of the WTO ("pre-Uruguay" and post-Uruguay").[19] These are *maximum* tariffs that parties to the GATT (General Agreement on Tariffs and Trade) and the WTO (World Trade Organization) committed themselves to upholding (the GATT was the WTO's predecessor). Actual *tariffs were almost certainly lower.* As observed, maximum average tariffs fell over time in all countries except Indonesia and Malaysia, although, with the exception of India and Mexico, trade barriers in the form of tariffs were not *that* high even before liberalization.

Mechanisms of Resistance

Developmental states in the 1990s were disparaged and demoralized, whether in slow-growing Latin America or fast-growing East Asia, but they were drawn nonetheless into a new set of problems. Instead of deindustrialization at the industry level, the major threat became *denationalization* at the firm level. This threat arose from greater foreign direct investment, actual or anticipated. A new element was cross-border mergers and acquisitions (M&As), which increased the likelihood of foreign takeover of national enterprise.[20] The policy questions became *if and how* to strengthen national companies and high-tech industries, and *whether or not* to balance the economic power of foreign and national firms.

To face this threat in a more liberal world milieu, old mechanisms of control were replaced with new *mechanisms of resistance.* A resistance mechanism may be defined as a policy that upholds the letter of the law but not necessarily its spirit. The letter, as written by a new World Trade Organization, supposedly abolished subsidies, freed trade, and deregulated competition. In fact, new WTO rules were not rigid and absolute. They were flexible insofar as they left ample room for contingent protection and selective subsidization; otherwise, the recruitment of members by the WTO would probably have stalled (OECD 1994). It was within the relatively gray area of safeguards and selective subsidies that the neo-developmental state nested its new policy regime.

The Illusion of Free Trade

The WTO, like the GATT, enabled members to protect themselves from two types of foreign import competition: competition from aggregate imports that destabilized their balance of payments (Article XVIII); and competition that threatened their individual industries, due either to an import surge (Article XIX on temporary safeguards) or to an unfair trade practice (Article VI on antidumping and countervailing duties). But GATT placed no formal limits on the duration of a safeguard whereas the WTO limited their duration to eight years and improved their transparency.

Under GATT, "voluntary export restraints" were the premier safeguard. While they had been used most prevalently by North Atlantic countries, they had also been relied upon by "the rest" to protect strategic industries. Korea, for example, used a form of VER to ban imports of automobiles and electronics from Japan, its most serious competitor. This "agreement" (to which Japan was not even a consenting party) began to function in the 1980s and remained in effect until 1999, long enough to allow these industries to build up their knowledge-based assets (Taiwan and China were neither GATT members nor early signatories to the WTO and thus, could—and did—protect these and other industries more openly, the electronics industry in Taiwan being a case in point). VERS were banned under the new WTO because they were discriminatory: their effect varied by country. The advantage of eliminating VERs was that they were nontransparent. The disadvantage was that they served a useful purpose, and "unless a superior means of serving that purpose is provided, then countries will find ways of their own to do it, and those ways are likely to be even worse" (Deardorff 1994, p. 57).

As predicted, countries in "the rest" raised tariffs in lieu of VERs or other cumbersome safeguards. Despite the fact that the level of tariffs fell after the Uruguay round of trade negotiations, developing countries had "bound" many of their tariffs at fairly high levels (or had left them altogether unbound) as the starting point for their entry into the WTO. In the event of an import threat, they could raise their tariffs to these high levels and keep them there for at least eight years:

> While developing countries have committed to a significant increase in their tariff bindings in the Uruguay Round (albeit at levels generally well above currently applied rates), they are still unlikely to invoke Article XIX (on safeguards) because they have both the unfettered right to raise tariffs to their bound levels and virtual *carte blanche* authority to impose new tariffs or quotas for balance of payments reasons. (Schott 1994, p. 113)

Raising tariffs in an emergency became the recourse even of countries whose policy regime had become avowedly neo-liberal. For example, when a new "free-trade" Mexico confronted stiff foreign competition in 1995, "tariffs were increased from the prevailing rates of 20 per cent or less to 35 per cent on clothing, footwear and manufactured leather products on imports from non-preferential sources. *These sectors were already protected to a certain degree through anti-dumping duties and a relatively restrictive use of marking and origin requirements*"(OECD 1996, p. 106, emphasis added).

Marking and origin requirements are forms of nontariff measures (NTMs) that restrict trade. In the Uruguay round of negotiations, moreover, "achievements in the area of NTMs had been less than had been expected" (Raby,

1994). Mexico's affiliation to NAFTA, a free trade agreement, was itself a form of managed trade that violated orthodox free-market principles. Members of free-trade agreements can protect themselves against all other countries except one another, and unlike members of a customs union, need not have common external tariffs. Of 100 or so regional trade agreements notified to the WTO, only one was approved by 2000 (that between the Czech Republic and Slovakia). But the others, such as NAFTA, were not forbidden; simply WTO members agreed not to take action on them.

Antidumping duties emerged as another way to protect trade in an emergency, supposedly when competitors engaged in dumping, or selling below costs. In the late 1980s, the United States, the European Union, Australia, and Canada accounted for about four-fifths of all antidumping cases. By 1998 they accounted for barely one-third of the 225 cases opened in that year. Instead, the developing countries were leaders in antidumping initiatives, especially India (which also maintained almost permanent import surcharges to protect its balance of payments), Brazil, and Mexico. As other types of trade barriers decreased, antidumping suits rose in importance. Thus Argentina's steel industry, a showcase of restructuring, cut tariffs unilaterally to a "mere" 0 to 24 percent. But when Brazilian steel started to flood the Argentine market in 1992, a tax on imports was temporarily increased by almost fourfold, as noted earlier (Toulan and Guillen 1996).[21]

In response to U.S. pressure, the Uruguay round of negotiations was extended to trade in services, which included foreign investment. The results of the Uruguay round on trade-related investment measures (TRIMs), however, were "relatively modest" (Startup 1994, p. 189).[22] As a consequence of limited agreement in the area of TRIMs, developing countries were able to maintain, temporarily, local content requirements. They could also retain ad infinitum trade balancing stipulations and the 100 percent export requirement of export processing zones, forms of export promotion (see chapter 7). In 1995, for example, Brazil hammered out an agreement with the countries representing its major automobile assemblers. All consented to export cars whose value equaled the imports of parts and components assemblers were bringing into Brazil.[23]

Thus, safeguards of various sorts enabled countries to buttress their balance of payments and sustain an industry under siege. Safeguards could also be used to protect an infant industry; eight years of protection were virtually guaranteed. The major risk was triggering unilateral trade sanctions under Section 301 of the U.S. Omnibus Trade Act, but not until an American industry was actually threatened by foreign competition were sanctions likely to be invoked (Low 1993).

Subsidies also received relatively permissive treatment under WTO law. They fell into three categories. Some were prohibited (for exports and for domestic rather than imported inputs); others were "actionable" (they could be punished subject to proof of injury); and three were permissible (all heavily utilized in the North Atlantic). Permissible subsidies included those to promote *R&D*, *regional development*, and *environmentalism*. Any high-tech industry, therefore, could receive unbounded subsidies for the purpose of strengthening S&T.

All in all, the liberal bark of the WTO appeared to be worse than its bite.

Nevertheless, it remained unclear in the 1990s how frequently trade-related mechanisms of resistance were invoked. Certainly they were no longer being used as part of a strategy to lure shy investors into manufacturing; this strategy was past history. Instead, beyond a common resort to protectionism, when necessary, "integrationist" countries opened the doors wider to foreign investment. They sought to discipline domestic economic activity by obeying foreign behavioral norms, as exemplified by Mexico's allegiance to NAFTA.[24] "Independent" countries, by contrast, used resistance mechanisms aggressively to promote science and technology and to buttress the market power of their national leaders, as discussed next.

The "Buy" Decision and Foreign Direct Investment

Foreign direct investment in the 1990s rose rapidly everywhere in "the rest" (see table 1.14). Nevertheless, in those countries where the inflow of direct foreign investment remained especially high, domestic skill formation remained low. The empirics of this association are shown in table 9.13. They include data on R&D on the one hand, and foreign investment on the other hand, including cross-border *mergers and acquisitions* (M&As).[26] Mergers and acquisitions were a relatively new global phenomenon in the 1990s, and a new perceived threat to national ownership in "the rest."

Countries that rely heavily on "buying" technology may be expected to exhibit relatively high levels of sales of productive assets to foreign buyers; hence, a high absolute value of cross-border M&As (column A). Given any level of M&As, "buying" is also likely to be associated with a relatively large share of foreign *majority* ownership (column B). That is, if a cross-border M&A sale occurs in a country that is not trying to strengthen its own innovative resources, that country may be assumed to prefer a majority foreign holding over a minority one.[27] Additionally, a "buy" strategy may be expected to go hand-in-hand with a high level of foreign direct investment in gross fixed capital formation (columns C and D). The presumption is that foreign investment is coveted for its supply of both capital and technology.

Most of these hypotheses are borne out by the data, with the proviso that the data are relatively weak.[28] It is clear that the absolute value of mergers

Table 9.13. "Make" or "Buy" Linked Characteristics, 1990s

	M&A		FDI/GFCF		
Country	A. Total, 1990–97 (bil US$)	B. Majority/ Total Average, 1990–97 (%)	C. Average (%) 1986–91	D. Average (%) 1992–96	E. R&D (% GNP), 1995
"Make"					
Korea	3.40	na	1.30	0.80	2.8
Taiwan	6.20	15	3.60	2.40	1.8
China	82.20	4	2.90	13.80	0.5
India	15.20	8	0.30	1.60	0.8
"Buy"					
Argentina	21.50	59	5.60	8.10	0.4
Brazil	22.90	73	1.60	3.50	0.6
Chile	10.10	44	14.10	12.80	0.7
Mexico	21.90	36	8.30	12.10	0.0
Turkey	3.50	30	1.80	1.70	0.6
Indonesia	22.40	8	2.30	5.40	0.1
Malaysia	11.60	13	14.70	16.70	0.4
Thailand	10.20	8	5.50	3.30	0.1

Notes:
M&A = cross-border mergers and acquisitions from the seller's country
FDI = inward foreign direct investment
GFCF = gross fixed capital formation
R&D = research and development (see table 8.15)
Majority refers to foreign control.

Source: For M&A, FDI, GFCF, UNCTAD 1998b).

and acquisitions and the extent of foreign majority ownership tend to be much higher in "buy" countries than in "make" countries: in Argentina, Brazil, Chile, Mexico, and Turkey, the majority share in M&As all equal at least 30 percent, whereas in Taiwan, China, and India, it equals 15 percent or less (M&As were altogether unimportant in Korea before 1997). China is the exception, but its absolute size warrants a high value of M&As.[29] Otherwise, as expected, M&As and majority ownership are greatest among countries whose technology comes mainly from abroad. The data for the share of foreign investment in total fixed capital formation (columns C and D) are somewhat less clear-cut. Overall, however, the behavior of this share is quite similar to that of mergers and acquisitions. Generally, countries intent on building their own stock of knowledge-based assets, as suggested by their high expenditure on R&D, have relatively little foreign participation in their economies, whether in the form of mergers and acquisitions, especially foreign majority share holding, or fixed capital formation.

The Scramble for Scale and Scope

In the postwar years, a big cost advantage of foreign firms derived from their sheer overall size. Their scale advantage may be imagined by comparing the size of their national markets with those of "the rest" (see table 9.14). In 1990 Korea's GDP was $32 billion (in constant 1995 U.S. dollars) whereas the Netherlands' GDP was *larger*, at $36 billion. The GDP of the Netherlands was three times larger than that of Indonesia although the population and land mass of the Netherlands were a mere fraction of those of its former colony. Countries in "the rest"—and firms in "the rest"—were still extremely small compared with foreign competitors: as noted in chapter 8, only thirty-three entries from "the rest" in 1992 were included among Fortune's 500 leading international firms.

To compete against foreign firms in more open markets, firms in "the rest" took various measures to enlarge their own scale. In the case of integration-ists, cross-border mergers and acquisitions became relatively important, as we have just seen. In the case of independents, in addition to globalization, local mergers and acquisitions gained momentum. Vertical integration, horizontal integration and diversification into unrelated industries all appear to have

Table 9.14. Gross Domestic Product, 1990 Market Prices (Constant 1995 US$)

Country	1990 GDP (bil US$)
Argentina	21.1
Brazil	60.3
Chile	3.9
China	39.8
India	25.9
Indonesia	13.9
Korea	31.8
Malaysia	5.8
Mexico	26.5
Thailand	11.1
Turkey	14.5
France	145.4
Germany*	228.6
Japan	478.2
Netherlands	35.8
Norway	12.2
U.S.	634.3
U.K.	103.8

* 1991

Source: United Nations (1998).

accelerated in "the rest" beginning in the 1980s. Thus, in addition to reorganizing and investing more in R&D, independents attempted to create more "orderly" domestic markets.

Restructuring in Taiwan involved a movement towards greater diversification on the part of business groups. An example of diversification is provided by the medium-size Pacific Electric Wire and Cable group, PEWC, which was established in 1950. PEWC had entered into a technical collaboration agreement with Sumitomo Electric Industries Ltd. of Japan in 1960, invested in a Singapore cable company in 1967 and a Thai cable company in 1971, established an R&D Laboratory and began to manufacture aluminum wire and cable in 1977, and was the first in Taiwan to manufacture core optical fiber cable in 1983 (the year in which PEWC founded the Pacific Laser Electric Optics Company). After 1986 internationalization and diversification went even further with the appointment of a salaried president (Pacific Electric Wire and Cable 1995). PEWC founded a joint venture in 1987 with Sumitomo Electric (Sumi-Pac Electro-Chemical Corporation); founded the Pacific Yoshida Engineering Company in 1988, a joint venture with Japanese engineering companies to make machinery to manufacture cable; founded Pacific Securities with other local companies, the Greenbay Entertainment Company and the Pacific Southwest Bank in Texas, all in 1988; established a construction company with Sumitomo Electric in 1989; founded the Hotel Conrad Hong Kong with Swire Properties and Hilton Hotel in 1989; moved an old plant in Taiwan to another site to build an "intelligent" high-tech industrial community in 1989; established additional joint ventures to produce electric wire and cable in Thailand and Hong Kong; reinvested in the Winbond Electronics Corporation in 1990 (Taiwan's 67th ranking company in 1997); founded Taiwan Aerospace Corporation with other local enterprises and invested in Taiwan Cogeneration Corporation with Taiwan Power Company and Communication Bank in 1991; established Fubon Life Insurance with the Fubon group and established Chung-Tai Telecommunication Corporation with Walsin, Hua Eng, and the Tatung group in 1992; established Open Systems Software as a joint venture with Hewlett Packard Delaware Corporation also in 1992; established an investment company with Sumitomo Electric, signed an agreement with U.S.-based Motorola and Iridium for joining "Global System-Iridiium Project" in 1993 (a project that failed); founded the subsidiary Pacific Iridium a year later; formed a joint venture with Raychem International Manufacturing of the United States to manufacture electric cables especially for use in aerospace, marine transport, telecommunications, and rapid transit systems in 1994; and in the same year invested in Mosel Vitelic, a U.S.-based specialized semiconductor producer in Taiwan.

Throughout this later period, PEWC's assets and return on sales both rose, driven by diversification into telecommunication services, a "strategic" industry (Pacific Electric Wire and Cable 1994). Despite all these diversifications, moreover, PEWC was nowhere near the top in group size. Diversification on the part of Taiwan's business groups increased their overall share in GNP. The share in GNP of the top 100 business groups rose between 1986 and 1998 from 28.7 percent to almost 54 percent (see table 8.12).

In China, the diversified business group became a deliberate model to emulate.[30] The Fifteenth Congress of the Chinese Communist Party in 1997 adopted a policy to propel three to five Chinese firms into the ranks of *Fortune's* 500 largest enterprises by the year 2000 and to promote *zaibatsu-like* groups in strategic sectors. The State Council began to back fifty-seven groups immediately while at the provincial level, fifty-four groups in Shanghai were being targeted and seventy large SOEs were being restructured into business groups in Guangdong (Smythe 2000).

Greater concentration was to occur through *domestic* merger and reorganization. In 1997 alone, 3000 enterprises were merged and 15.5 billion yuan in state assets were reallocated. The biggest mergers occurred in the petrochemical, steel, and automobile industries. China had established more than 120 motor vehicle assemblers in the mid-to-late 1980s. By the 1990s these manufacturers had been amalgamated into four automotive groups (in addition to four groups at the provincial-level). Other large enterprises were established in aerospace and electrical household appliances. In March 1998 four trading companies were merged to form the China General Technology Group, with the idea of systematizing the acquisition of foreign technology (Smythe 2000).

The tendency toward greater concentration was even apparent in consumer goods industries, which became targeted over heavy industries in the late 1970s in order to satisfy consumer demand.[31] Access to resources and conversion of some heavy industry-capacity into light industry-capacity swelled supply. By the early 1980s a problem of overcapacity had manifested itself, as in the bicycle industry. Local governments had been "extremely keen" to promote local bicycle production due to previous shortages and labor-intensive production techniques. Investment mostly financed new factories rather than existing capacity expansions despite evident economies of scale. The four factories with an annual output of over 100,000 bicycles had unit costs (in yuan) of 66–87, compared with the seventy factories with annual output of 2,000–5,000 bicycles, which had unit costs of 116–179. Unit costs fell as output rose over the entire spectrum of firm sizes; overexpansion was partly due to the efforts of small firms to produce more in order to drive down unit costs (Zhang 1991). In 1984 the Chinese central government placed all the existing 116 bicycle factories under the aegis of the Ministry of Light Industry in an attempt (not always successful in other industries) to reimpose central control over total supply. Twenty-five of the smallest factories were forced to close (with some waste of fixed assets) and a production licensing system was reintroduced. Measures were also taken to increase the supply of the three most important bicycle brands in China. The three producers of these brands were encouraged to form joint ventures and associations with other bicycle manufacturers, which then manufactured under their brand name for a fee. The total number of bicycle factories involved in manufacturing the three brands rose to twenty in 1987 and accounted for about 40 percent of national output. Simultaneously, leading enterprises improved their marketing skills and product quality (Zhang 1993).

In India, liberalization in 1991 entailed the abolition of industrial licensing and the loosening of controls on imports and foreign investment. In theory, the combination of freer imports and greater foreign investment was supposed to awaken India's sleepy oligopolies, not least of all in automobile assembly, which had failed to introduce any new models in the 1960s and 1970s (the government regarded automobiles as a luxury that did not deserve targeting). By importing parts and components from their established foreign suppliers, new assemblers in India were supposed to be able to overcome inadequate scale while exploiting expertise and brand name recognition. In fact, assemblers from the United States, Europe, Japan, and Korea invested in India, but were forced by domestic competition and fresh controls to cater to the limited demand for middle-size cars (D'Costa 1995; Narayanan 1998). The bulk of the passenger vehicle market continued to be dominated by Maruti Udyog Limited, a joint venture established in 1982 between the Indian government (with 60 percent equity) and a minor Japanese automobile manufacturer, Suzuki Motors. Maruti's localization rate had reached 96 percent by the 1990s and its market share after liberalization *increased* to 75 percent. Maruti's success (the company was personally championed by Indira Gandhi) owed itself to a strong yen, which had induced Suzuki to source components locally, and government insistence in the 1980s on high local content (in exchange for protection and cheap credit) (see chapter 6). New entrants in the 1990s "could hardly compete with the price of Maruti's small car, given their lower levels of localization and higher costs of imported components" (Okada 1999).[32] Cars and jeeps, as well as parts and components, also continued to be subject to high import duties, which were waived only in exchange for at least 50 percent local content.[33] The only credible threat to Maruti came from TELCO, an affiliate of the Tata group and a long-established Indian manufacturer of commercial vehicles. To cut costs, new assemblers encouraged mergers, acquisitions, and joint ventures among their suppliers (Okada 1999). Thus, market opening in the case of the automobile industry went hand-in-hand with greater concentration.

After financial markets crashed in 1997, the Korean government coerced the chaebol to merge, a strategy that became known as the "big deal."[34] In exchange for participating in "big deals," the chaebol received extensive tax benefits and financial support, such as debt-to-equity swaps, debt restructuring, and lower interest rates, akin to the intermediate assets they had once received in exchange for other performance standards. The political importance of "big deals" is indicated by the example of the Minister of Information and Communications, who was dismissed because of his "pessimistic remarks about the government-led big deals in the personal communications services sector" (PCS). According to the chairman of the Financial Supervisory Commission, "The government cannot leave overlapping investment in the PCS industry untouched any longer." As explained by a ruling party politician: "In order to prevent potential side effects that will be caused by excessive competition among local PCS companies, it is desirable that only three players out of five should survive" (Business Korea 1999, p. 32). The biggest prescribed deals involved Korea's four largest chaebol. Three of them (Hyundai, Daewoo, and Samsung) were forced to merge to strengthen the fledgling Korean aerospace industry. The government also ordered a merger in semiconductors between the affiliates of the Hyundai and LG groups, the purpose being to create a major player to stand against the Samsung group. The Samsung group was also ordered to swap its auto business for the electronics affiliate of the Daewoo group, the intent being to create two large players in the automobile industry, Hyundai Motors and Daewoo Motors, and two large players in consumer electronics, the Samsung and LG groups. In the automobile sector, Daewoo Motors had already acquired the bankrupt Ssangyong Motors and the Hyundai group had already purchased the defunct KIA Motors. Hyundai thereby increased its production capacity from 1.8 million to 2.85 million cars per year and its domestic market share from 39.8 to 60.7 percent, making it (only) the eleventh ranking producer of cars in the world (Korean Automobile Manufacturers' Association 1999).[35]

The "big deals" proposed at the end of the century mirrored the attempts by the Korean government to streamline major industries after a sharp economic contraction in 1980. The major opponents at the time were the companies to be merged and foreign partners. These were the same opponents to "big deals" almost twenty years later.[36] However big the *actual* deals (many failed), a trend toward higher concentration was apparent.

Nurturing Knowledge-Based Assets

By the 1990s the gap in expenditures on knowledge-based assets had widened further in "the rest" between "make" and "buy" countries. Even using a broader definition of learning than "R&D," Argentina, Brazil, Chile, and Mexico had generally fallen far behind Korea, Taiwan, China, and India in terms of patenting and publishing in scholarly journals (Amsden and Mourshed 1997), the share of GNP accounted for by science and technology, the share of R&D spending accounted for by the manufacturing sector, and the private sector's share in R&D activity (see table 9.15).[37] The private share of R&D spending generally fell below 30 percent in Latin America (one estimate for

Table 9.15. Expenditures on Science and
Technology and Research and Development
(R&D), 1995 or Late 1990s[1]

Country	% of GDP	Private Share of Total (%)
S&T		
Argentina	0.5	30
Brazil	1.2	31
Chile	0.6	15
Mexico	0.4	18
R&D		
Korea	2.8	74
Taiwan	1.8	55
India	0.8	41[2]
China	0.5	na
USA	2.5	73
Japan	2.8	70
Germany	2.3	66
France	2.3	62

1. The definition of science and technology (S&T) for Argentina, Brazil, Chile, and Mexico is broader than that of research and development (R&D) for other countries.
2. Share of private sector from Mani (1999).

Sources: Argentina, Brazil, Chile and Mexico adapted from Republica Argentina (1998); United States, Japan, Germany, and France adapted from OECD, (various years); Korea adapted from Ministry of Science and Technology, Korea (1998); Taiwan adapted from Taiwan, Republic of China National Science Council (1996).

Argentina in 1992 was as low as 8 percent ([Alcorta and Peres 1998]), whereas the share for Asia, including India, was over 40 percent. The overwhelming consensus was that Latin America's innovation systems "have developed into weak entities. . . . [its] innovative performance in high-tech products is not only not improving but seems to be worsening. . . . [T]he causes for the poor international competitiveness of the region . . . have not been the exclusive result of macroeconomic maladies or low investment" (Alcorta and Peres 1998, p. 878).

Even India, whose nationalist innovation system was behind that of China, Korea, and Taiwan in terms of an industrial orientation, pulled ahead of Argentina, Brazil, Chile, and Mexico in this regard. "Centers of excellence" in India helped to sustain national leaders in strategic sectors, such as TELCO's R&D laboratory in the automobile industry (Bowonder 1998). Government legislation in the 1990s was oriented toward improving both private incentives for R&D, public commercialization of R&D results, and partnering between public and private institutes (Sikka 1998; Katrak 1998). Industrial spillovers from government defense and health-related R&D laboratories were high, providing the basis for firm-level expertise in the manufacture of heavy electrical equipment and pharmaceuticals (Mani 1999; Ramamurti 1987; Sridharan 1996). By 1990 only one-quarter of R&D spending in India was focused on industry compared with three-quarters in Korea. Nevertheless, *the industrial focus of Latin America was even lower:* "By the mid-1980s, only 12% of total R&D expenditure by Brazil was in the manufacturing sector, while 55% was in natural resources and agriculture, and 33% in services. For Argentina in the late-1980s, R&D expenditure in manufacturing was only 4%, while in natural resources and agriculture and in services it amounted to 64% and 33% respectively" (Alcorta and Peres 1998, pp. 866–87). Much nonmanufacturing R&D was academic rather than commercial in nature.

In addition to rising concentration, the 1990s were a period in which the "independents" rationalized rather than reduced government promotion of high-tech. In India, private R&D institutes handpicked by the Department of Science and Technology were given permission to take equity positions in enterprises that used their technology, analogous to "science and technology enterprises" in China (discussed below) (Katrak 1998). In Korea, interministerial competition and duplication of R&D efforts were streamlined under a national master R&D plan. In Taiwan, science parks were expanded, and the conditionality imposed on their residents was tightened. According to the Hsinchu Park Administration, "an existing company would be asked to leave if it changed to labour-intensive operations and no longer met the evaluation criteria (which the Park Administration specified)" (Xue 1997, pp. 750–51).

Research and development expanded in Korea with a plan for Highly Advanced National Projects (HAN), or "G7 projects" as Koreans called them, in recognition of their aim to propel Korea into the ranks of the world's top group of seven countries.[38] Similar to Taiwan's science park administrations, Korea's G7 Planning Committee selected projects according to the criterion of how well they advanced "strategic industries," which were themselves selected at the highest political level of decision-making. By involving large-scale projects, however, the Korean approach also tended to involve participation by large-scale firms.

National projects in the 1990s were specifically designed to increase the competitiveness of national leaders in the global marketplace. In the North Atlantic, by contrast, the immediate goal of national projects typically involved defense, health or welfare, with the enhancement of private sector competitiveness taking the form of a spillover.[39] This difference is evident by comparing one HAN project, related to next-generation vehicle technology, with one "historic" U.S. project, the Partnership for a New Generation of Vehicles (PNGV). The PNGV was promoted by the Clinton administration with a proposed ten-year budget starting in fiscal year 2000 of $263 million (the Korean vehicle project had a proposed budget for 1992 through 2001 of around $50 million—depending on the exchange rate). The Korean vehicle project was designed to help Korea's major auto makers keep up with the world technological frontier; to the extent that keeping up with the frontier meant building a more environment-friendly car (as defined by the PNGV project), then technologies were to be developed to meet this goal (low pollution, maximum safety, and electric power). The PNGV project, by contrast, had the foremost goal of national defense. According to the White House, "the research and commercial applications resulting from PNGV will yield long-term benefits for the nation in increased energy security, a cleaner environment, and enhanced economic well-being" (White House 1999). It may be expected that R&D in cutting-edge countries whose explicit objective is national security, and R&D in latecomer countries whose explicit objective is firm-level competitiveness, will diverge over time with respect to the government's role.

By the 1990s, China had also moved away from the defense-centric national innovation systems of the United States and USSR toward a firm-focused system that emphasized industrial competitiveness.[40] The transition had come in 1985, when the Central Committee of the Chinese Communist party and the national State Council had decreed that "economic construction should rely on science and technology," which was far richer in China than in equally poor developing countries, and "science and technology research should serve the needs of economic development" (Lu 1997, p. 17). To modernize S&T, China combined science parks and national R&D projects, tax breaks and subsidized credit playing a large role in both. The Beijing city government, for example, established a leading-edge R&D testing zone dubbed "Beijing's Silicon Valley" with exports in 1998 of $267 million (expected to reach $1 billion by 2000). "In the enterprise zone, the government adopted institutional devices nested in the taxation process and investment process that redistributed resources to strategic sectors." Targeted industries were given tax breaks, special loans from state banks with below-market interest rates, and permission to exceed normal debt-equity ratio ceilings (Lu 1997, p. 234). On the other hand, the Chinese government also emphasized national R&D projects and the formation of "science and technology enterprises" that were neither state-owned nor private. The State Planning Commission announced a policy to build approximately 100 national key laboratories (analogous to corporate central R&D laboratories) in selected fields of basic science in which Chinese capabilities already excelled. "S&T enterprises" were spun-off by city, provincial, or national governments to commercialize the knowledge of public labs (see, for example, the annual report of Stone Electronic Technology, one of China's most successful S&T enterprises). Although these enterprises were nominally independent, "in granting S&T enterprises a special legal status, the government obliged them to meet certain requirements (analogous to performance standards under a reciprocal control mechanism). These requirements included the percentage of technology personnel employed, the percentage of sales contributed by new products, the percentage of products exported, the allocation of retained earnings, etc." (Lu 1997, p. 235).

Thus, to a greater or lesser degree, the neo-developmental state retained its conditionality-based form of subsidy allocation in the high-tech phase of industrial transformation. By comparison with the "national innovation systems" of the North Atlantic, those of the "independents" were "national*ist* innovation systems." Their primary purpose was to target knowledge-based asset formation in nationally owned firms.

Conclusion

By 2000 two distinct sets of countries within "the rest" were competing with one another for resources and global market share, as well as for leadership in providing a model for still later industrializers. In one set, embracing China, India, Korea, and Taiwan, call them the "independents" (with the understanding that all latecomers had become more global since World War II), long-term growth was premised on the "make" technology decision, which was synonymous with the build-up of national capabilities and national firms. In another set, embracing Argentina, Brazil, Chile, Mexico, and Turkey, call them the "integrationists" (with the understanding that no country in "the rest" had completely relinquished its economic or political autonomy), long-term growth was premised on the "buy" technology decision, and a reliance on both foreign rules of conduct to discipline business (as provided by membership in NAFTA and the EU), and spillovers from foreign investment and technology transfer to generate wealth.[41]

Given this divergence, the question of how the late-industrializing model reacted to exogenous shocks, a more hostile global environment, and internal maturation (political and economic) receives a clear answer. Change was radical insofar as a single model metamorphosed into two different species.

In the beginning stages of postwar late industrialization, roughly from the 1950s through the mid-1980s, all countries in "the rest" (except Argentina) shared to an extraordinary degree the same set of developmental institutions, defined by a reciprocal control mechanism. At the same moment in history, with the same set of major actors, operating with the same prerequisite of manufacturing experience, confronting the same trade-off of decreasing wages or increasing productivity, and facing the same external macroeconomic and political environment, an otherwise highly diverse set of learners all relied on subsidies buffered by results-oriented performance standards to establish the same set of basic industries. As in the Second Industrial Revolution of the

North Atlantic, the late industrialization of "the rest" amounted to a germination of the same seed (first developed in Japan) in different clay pots (Pollard 1973). Some flowers became less beautiful and hearty than others depending on the quality of the clay. In the case of Argentina, it never even planted the same seed as other latecomers. It failed altogether to introduce a reciprocal control mechanism. In the case of India, which grew more hearty over time, it at first overwatered by using its reciprocal control mechanism to attain conflicting goals.

Only at a later stage of economic development, beginning in the mid-1980s, did the seed responsible for the rise of "the rest" divide into two distinct strains, one of which retained fewer characteristics of the original plant than the other strain. The cause of the division centered around the competitive skills, capabilities and knowledge-based assets that we have argued lie at the root of staying behind or catching up. When, before the 1980s, the capabilities required for industrialization were limited simply to borrowing foreign technology and mastering production engineering and project execution skills, the institutions supporting a reciprocal control mechanism were robust enough to get the job done regardless of intercountry differences. When, however, the capabilities required to expand further demanded technology that was more implicit and proprietary, a profound choice had to be made—either to deepen relations with foreign firms or invest more in national firm-formation and R&D. Then inter-country differences predominated. The most critical differences among countries that governed this choice related to income distribution and history. The more equal income distribution and the more discontinuous direct foreign investment before and after World War II, the more likely a latecomer is to build its own national firms and proprietary knowledge-based assets.

Two implications for "the remainder" follow from the fact that "the rest" initially had a singular development model that only later underwent mitosis.

One, the herd or crowd effect, of a large number of latecomers all industrializing at once, probably made it easier for each to confront the North Atlantic's political and economic power. Synchronous development created more permissive conditions to deviate from the North Atlantic's market-driven model. Trade rules under the GATT implicitly acknowledged the right of poor countries to be more protectionist than rich countries. Moreover, synchronous industrialization enabled latecomers to learn from each other, and not just from the North Atlantic and Japan. This implies that it will be easier for new latecomers to accelerate development if they manage to expand together, assuming that the institutional apparatus they adopt to do so also deviates from free market norms.

Two, countries in "the rest" adopted the same model to industrialize because none had sufficient knowledge-based assets to compete in modern industry at world prices. Government intervention arose everywhere in response to this lack of competitiveness rather than to simple cronyism, or the need to "coordinate" investment decisions, or the desire to capture "external economies," or some other typical textbook explanation for government intervention. The exception proves the rule: the government of Hong Kong (and Switzerland, in the case of Europe) intervened less than its neighbors because Hong Kong enjoyed greater competitive assets, and thus government intervention was not necessary. Unless later industrializers have enough assets to compete in modern industry at world prices, their governments are also likely to intervene. Whether their interventions can be expected to exceed that of "the rest" we consider in a final chapter.

10

"The Rest" Will Rise Again

O ne of the most controversial aspects of "the rest's" rise was the role played by the government. As we see it, governments in "the rest" all intervened in markets in a deliberate and deep way because their economies had too few knowledge-based assets to compete at world market prices even in modern labor-intensive industries. But government failures were institutionally bounded. The set of institutions that framed the whole process of late industrialization was specifically designed to minimize the ill-effects of interventionist policies.

In this chapter we connect the controversy over the role of the state with the rise of "the rest." First we look at Alexander Gerschenkron's theory. Then we state the underlying assumptions of our own assets approach. Next we summarize what it means for market theory and its policy prescription of laissez-faire to drop the assumption of perfect knowledge. Finally we make a few remarks about countries that have stumbled back and those (possibly) at the forefront in "the remainder."

Gerschenkron Revisited

According to Alexander Gerschenkron, the most eminent expert on the process of catching up, the later a country industrializes in chronological history, the greater the economic interventions of its government. Interventions increase because production methods allegedly become more capital-intensive ("round-about"). Bigger absolute capital requirements over time bring forth new institutional arrangements that entail a larger role for the state (Gerschenkron 1962).

As predicted, "the rest" devised an innovative and state-centric institution to mobilize capital, the development bank, which became the flagship of the developmental state. Nevertheless, it is unclear if government intervention was as minimal in earlier industrializations as Gerschenkron suggests. Nor is it obvious that as newer and newer attempts to industrialize get underway, government intervention will continue to rise.

From a latecomer's viewpoint, early industrializers intervened plenty to promote their own self-interests. At whatever stage in their development, whether early or late, stronger economies opened the markets of weaker economies and decreed global economic rules:

> For more than a century, when the British economy was on its way to maturity as the workshop of the world, its governments were not particularly liberal nor wedded ideologically to laissez-faire. Like the proverbial hedgehog of Aeschalus, the Hanoverian Governments [1688–1815] knew some big things, namely that security, trade, Empire and military power really mattered. In fruitful (if uneasy) partnership with bourgeois merchants and industrialists they poured millions into strategic objectives which we can see (with hindsight) formed preconditions for the market economy and night-watchman state of Victorian England, as well as the British world order which flourished under British hegemony from 1846 to 1914. *By that time men of the pen, especially the pens of the political economy, had forgotten, and did not wish to be reminded, what the first industrial nation owed to men of the sword.* (Emphasis added).[1]

Contrary to Gerschenkron, then, government intervention may not be any greater the later the industrialization. It may simply be *different.*

It may not even be different to the extent that the interventions of "men of the sword" create market distortions similar to those created by "men of the pen." The two interventions become comparable—both create market distortions—under certain likely conditions: the usual definition of a distortion applies (it creates an inequality between marginal cost and price); a state of *disequilibrium* is possible wherein a firm is operating at the top rather than bottom of its learning curve; and intervention by the sword in the form of forced market opening prematurely subjects the learner to competitive forces that bankrupt it. Under these conditions, intervention by the sword reduces global competition. Hence, it is distortionary in the same way that the developmental state's use of subsidies to rig prices is distortionary. Both reduce market competition.

It is also unlikely that government intervention will increase ad infinitum in sequentially later industrializations *if* an alternative actor to promote industrialization presents itself. An alternative is desirable if the costs of subsidization rise as the world technological frontier shifts outward (or as production techniques become more capital-intensive, as Gerschenkron imagined). Costs are likely to rise assuming that an outward movement of the frontier means greater knowledge-based assets on the part of incumbent firms and, hence, greater entry barriers against newcomers. As the costs of subsidization rise in the face of stiffer foreign competition, and as national firms themselves feel the pinch on their profits of greater foreign competition, the perceived benefits of more foreign direct investment rise relative to those of more domestic government intervention. Whether in the case of Latin America in the 1990s (Brazil and especially Argentina, Chile and Mexico) or of Eastern Europe after its 1989 reforms, more intense foreign competition made the alternative of greater foreign direct investment appealing.

The distance from the world technological frontier and the degree of government intervention, therefore, do not necessarily move in unison in a latecomer. Instead, as the distance from the frontier rises, what probably does increase is *the role of the foreign firm.*

The aphorism of Alexander Gerschenkron, therefore, may be restated as follows, taking for granted his major original insight, that the chronological order of industrialization matters: *the later a country industrializes in chronological history, the greater the probability that its major manufacturing firms will be foreign-owned.*

The Assets Approach to Industrial Development

The assets approach to industrialization developed in previous chapters makes two strong assumptions but not a third. First, secure property rights are taken as given; they are a necessary but an insufficient condition for industrializing late. According to "new" institutionalist theories of development (see the pioneering work of North 1990), secure property rights and perfect information create zero "transactions costs," and as transactions costs fall, economies develop. Secure property rights and perfect information thus emerge as a sufficient condition for growth. They may not be sufficient, however, because even if "information" (publicly accessible facts) is perfect, imperfect "knowledge" (proprietary concepts) may create production costs in learners that exceed those in incumbents.

The transactions approach and assets approach to industrialization are thus both institutionally grounded. But they are analytically distinct. In the former, *given the division of labor,* what matters most for catching up are property rights and low transactions costs (however measured). In the latter, *given secure property rights,* what matters most are knowledge-based assets and low production costs (which include costs of distribution). Two different trajectories thus characterize economic development. One trajectory runs from incomplete markets to increasingly perfect markets in which transactions costs approach zero. In the early stages of development, institutions in the form of markets are rudimentary, and the formation of secure property rights is part of the evolution toward deeper and more perfect market structures. Another trajectory runs from achieving competitiveness in markets characterized by perfect competition to achieving competitiveness in global oligopolistic markets defended by incumbents with proprietary skills. Economic development is thus also a process of creating firm-specific proprietary skills that are distortionary (price exceeds marginal cost) because they confer market power. *Industrialization involves moving from one set of distortions that is related to the rigidities of underdevelopment and primary product production to another set of distortions that is knowledge-based.*

The creation of market institutions in latecomer countries accelerated before World War I under direct or indirect colonial rule. Generally, it was in the interests of North Atlantic states to extend the institutions of markets into new terrain, and thus the creation of markets, including secure property rights, appears to have been less fraught with difficulties in "the rest" than in the North Atlantic. Property rights did not necessarily have to be private to be secure, and security was relative—-adequate to support long-term investment. By contrast, the acquisition of proprietary skills by new competitors typically *conflicts* with the interests of foreign incumbents. In the case of "latecomers" (which, by definition, industrialize in the presence of incumbents and in the absence of cutting edge skills), there was more resistance to competing in global oligopolistic industries on the basis of knowledge-based assets than creating viable markets.

Second, whereas most development theories implicitly assume that firm size and structure don't matter, we have tried to argue theoretically and empirically that for industrial diversification, they do matter. Late industrialization awaited the formation of *"large-scale firms,"* or firms that are professionally managed with plants of minimum efficient scale. Small-scale firms in "the rest" were neither innovative nor the agent of industrial diversification, whether before World War II or throughout most of the postwar period. They dominated prewar industry but were generally noted for inefficiency. In the famous case of handloom weavers, they hung on only by reducing their own rate of return (see chapter 2). Relatively large-scale firms in the form of hierarchically managed national companies, state-owned enterprises, and multinational firms were the "first movers" in postwar industries ranging from integrated cotton spinning and weaving (Asia's leading sector), petrochemicals (Latin America's leading sector), iron and steel, ships, and automobiles. The principle of mass production rather than artisan production typically characterized "the rest's" modern industries; the mass production model was the one that latecomers imitated.

Dynamic small-scale firms in "the rest" were pivotal in certain segments of the heterogeneous machinery and transportation equipment sectors, as we saw earlier. Capital goods industries based on small-scale firms had emerged in the 1930s in Brazil, China, India, and Korea. Owing to the mass migration after the Chinese Communist Revolution in 1948 of mainland entrepreneurs, a dynamic capital goods sector also emerged rapidly in Taiwan. By the 1960s Taiwan's bicycle industry had attracted American "original equipment manufacturers" in search of lower labor costs than those prevailing in Japan (Chu 1997). Other metalworking industries flourished interconnectedly with bicycle and machine tool production, and Taiwan became an industrialization model initially based on small- and medium-size enterprises.

Nonetheless, the Taiwan "model" was tightly integrated institutionally with the developmental state, whose scope of operations was conceivably greater in Taiwan than anywhere else in "the rest." Well into the 1990s, the government's share of total gross fixed capital formation was largest in Taiwan (at around 50 percent) (see table 1.13). Taiwan had the biggest complex of state-owned enterprises; those inherited from colonial Japan were not privatized in the 1950s as were those in Korea. State-owned science parks were the incubators of private small-scale national leaders that pioneered in establishing high-tech electronics industries. Thus, the state venture capital model of Taiwan deviated from the conventional market model of small-scale entrepreneurship (Amsden and Chu 2003).

Third, it is assumed in the assets approach that macroeconomic policies with respect to savings, the exchange rate, the budget, and the money supply do not matter in *the very long run*—the time horizon that frames preceding chapters. The relatively poor economic performance of Argentina and Mexico, for example, was cast in terms of knowledge-based assets rather than macroeconomic policies. Nevertheless, macroeconomic instability can seriously slow the development process. A neglect of macroeconomic policy also tends to inflate the positive bearing on industrialization of the developmental state, with one arm in industry and the other arm in the macro economy.

To ignore the determinants of saving is to assume implicitly that investment opportunities determine the saving rate—exciting investment projects secure the savings necessary to finance them, which may only be partially true, if at all (see chapter 4). Causality may also run in the opposite direction: the rate of saving may be the decisive variable in industrialization insofar as it gives the developmental state a certain margin of error in which to manage its industrialization policies. India's slower growth relative to China's in the 1980s and 1990s, for example, may derive from the fact that India's saving rate was only about half of China's. If savings behavior is determined outside the industrial sphere, then the influence of industrialization policies on relative growth rates may be less than implied.

Performance standards, the centerpiece of "the rest's" reciprocal control mechanism, may also weaken or strengthen the effect of relative prices on economic behavior, not least of all the effect of the exchange rate on exporting. If a firm must export to receive subsidized long-term credit, which is not calculated as part of export subsidies, then this quid pro quo may override price incentives in influencing export expansion. A sensible exchange rate is widely believed to have hastened and smoothened "the rest's" rate of economic growth. Given any exchange rate, performance standards strengthened the incentive to export to the extent that they made exporting conditional on the receipt of subsidies. From the perspective of industrialization policies, the developmental state was export-friendly. From the perspective of macroeconomic policies, it may have "gotten the exchange rate 'wrong.' "

In general, by ignoring the macroeconomic side of developmentalism, the behavior of the developmental state may appear more glorious then it actually was. Nevertheless, given some set of prices determined either by market forces, technocrats, or politicians, the industrial managers of the developmental state were able to build an industrialized economy around prevailing prices, whatever they happened to be. Wildly wrong prices made their job more difficult. But the "right" prices were not a precondition for industrialization; ironically, they were a constraint.

Pareto Optimality and Perfect Knowledge

The implications for economic development theory of dropping the assumption of perfect knowledge are radical but have barely begun to be explored.

If knowledge is not perfect, then productivity and quality may vary among firms in the same industry in different countries. Consequently, simply allowing the market mechanism to determine the price level ("getting the prices 'right' ") may be insufficient to enable countries to compete internationally in industries in which they may be expected to enjoy a comparative advantage (labor-using industries in the case of labor-abundant countries, raw material-using industries in the case of raw material-abundant countries, and so forth). The price of labor, for example, may have to become negative before a labor-abundant country becomes internationally competitive in the most labor-using industry, holding productivity and quality constant, because the proprietary knowledge-based assets of a higher-wage competitor may earn it lower unit costs—as we saw in the case of the Japanese textile industry vis-à-vis both the prewar Indian and Chinese textile industries and the postwar Taiwanese and Korean textile industries.

Under conditions of imperfect knowledge, moreover, even if "getting *positive* prices 'right' " does create international competitiveness (by means of, say, devaluing the exchange rate or, equivalently, lowering wages), this is not a "Pareto optimal" solution, defined as a *single best* policy whereby no economic actor can be made better off without making another economic actor worse off. Neither the market nor the institutional approach is on higher moral or theoretical ground. As we saw in "the rest," it may be more growth-enhancing (and faster—about which theory can say nothing) to raise productivity by institutional engineering than to lower costs by cutting wages.

In the absence of perfect knowledge, then, how to resolve the problem of high production costs becomes an empirical rather than a theoretical question.

To drop the assumption of perfect knowledge is also to open the door wider to the possibility of constructing inductive theories of economic development. Models that are inductive use concrete cases of industrial expansion rather than abstract hypotheses to explain growth and guide policy making. Two inferences from the experience of "the rest" are relevant in this regard.

First, inductive role models may influence economic policy making more than (or as much as) deductive abstract theories. The influence of a role model was striking in the case of East Asia's highly successful export promotion policies, which extracted exports from import substitution industries based on Japan's past trade regime (policies and institutions). With a larger number of successful (and unsuccessful) late industrializers, inductive models provide as rich a learning resource for "the remainder" as deductive theories.

Second, "government failures" can no longer be taken for granted if governments do use institutional mechanisms to raise productivity and jump-start industrial growth. Government failures may be inevitable in the absence of systematic machinery to prevent them, but not necessarily in the presence of such machinery, as we saw in the case of "the rest." The reciprocal control mechanism of "the rest" was hardly perfect. But it illustrated the possibilities of minimizing government failures even in economies plagued by "moral hazard" and corruption (but enjoying manufacturing experience).

There has not thus far been widespread recognition of the systematic machinery that countries in "the rest" put in place, implemented, and monitored to avoid government failure and to pursue developmental goals. Yet "getting the control mechanism 'right,' " whether or not prevailing prices were "right," was central to the postwar process of catching up.

Stumbling Back

The institution-building necessary to create a functional control mechanism is the starting point to identify winners and explain losers. Among the latter, Argentina stands out as a country that stumbled back. Within "the rest," it had the lowest growth rate of manufacturing value added, real wages, and exports for nearly fifty years, having started the postwar period with the highest level of literacy and per capita income and nearly the longest manufacturing experience.

In terms of "getting the control mechanism "right" or "wrong," neither applies to Argentina. Simply Argentina never developed *any* functional control mechanism, as we saw earlier. It had no development bank comparable in elitism and esprit de corps to the BNDES in Brazil or NAFINSA in Mexico; a Peronist development bank in the 1940s was dysfunctionally corrupt. Argentina had no bureaucracy responsible for industrial promotion comparable to, say Thailand's Board of Investment. Instead, old Peronist machinery "crowded-out" new developmental machinery. Consequently, despite a well-educated population, a high-wage economy, and a long history of manufacturing, Argentine industry never made a three-pronged investment. As late as the 1990s, many companies had not professionalized their managements; few had well-defined organizational charts or chains of command. Investments in R&D were negligible, so high-paid workers were not employed in high-technology ventures. Even plants with minimum efficient scale were few and far between. With notable exceptions (the steel and pharmaceutical industries, for example), the center of gravity in the Argentine economy again became the countryside, which was characterized by one of the world's most unequal income distributions. In 1960 land was more unequally distributed in Argentina than in any major North Atlantic country or any other country in "the rest" (for which data are available). Given the opportunities provided by resource concentration to earn quasi-rents, the opportunity costs of investing in manufacturing were high. The Argentine economy, therefore, faced a choice: it could either tighten the rules or try something else. For all practical purposes, its choice in the 1990s was to return to the land.

Chile as well abandoned a growth strategy based on manufacturing, and did so as early as 1973. Instead, it disciplined its work force with martial law, continued to exploit state-owned copper reserves, and pioneered "gourmet farming," exporting high-value fruits to Northern markets counterseasonally. In historical terms, the refocus of the Argentine and Chilean economies on primary product production was rational. Both countries were rich in natural resources and, like other regions of recent settlement, had enjoyed a Golden Age of prosperity based on primary products before World War I.

Nevertheless, if post-1973 economic performance is compared in Chile and Taiwan, another small country with a prosperous agriculture, then Chile fares rather poorly. As is evident from table 1.4, by 1995 Chile's per capita income was only a fraction of Taiwan's (68 percent as much), whereas in 1973 Taiwan's per capita income had been only a fraction of Chile's (73 percent)— and population growth in this period was relatively fast in Taiwan. The strategy of Taiwan was to specialize in manufactures while the strategy of Chile was to specialize in mining and agro-industry. The share of manufactures in total exports in 1995 was 93 percent in Taiwan and only 14 percent in Chile.

In the nineteenth century, a focus on primary products generated growth rates of per capita income as high as those generated by a focus on manufactures. In the twenty-first century, when wealth is more likely than ever to derive from knowledge-based assets rather than primary product-based assets, whether or not the preponderance of Chileans can grow rich on the basis of exploiting primary products remains to be seen.

The Remainder

The countries in "the remainder" that are most likely to follow in the immediate footsteps of "the rest" are those with (1) manufacturing experience and (2) the ability to construct a reciprocal control mechanism that subsidizes learning (if prevailing production costs are above world costs) while giving nothing away for free. In light of the constraints imposed by the WTO, performance standards will have to become less export-oriented and more "R&D"-oriented than they were in the early postwar years. Tariff protection of up to eight years is still permissible for industries not yet able to compete internationally, and other types of trade restraints are legal as well (see chapter 9). Given the constraint on promoting exports, and the dangers of import protection without export promotion, and given the legality of promoting science and technology and regional development, any developmental strategy will have to revolve around regionalism and R&D, broadly defined.

Equating manufacturing experience with past real annual average growth rates of manufacturing output, table 10.1 presents the countries in "the remainder" with the fastest growing manufacturing sectors for the last forty-five years (1950–95). The table is misleading insofar as it excludes countries without the requisite data; Vietnam, for example, *may* have experienced rapid manufacturing growth but does not appear. Using the growth rate of manufacturing output also biases results in favor of countries with the least developed manufacturing sectors in 1950 (it would have been better to examine manufacturing output per worker, but cross-country employment data were not generally available). Bearing these limitations in mind, the table includes both countries that obviously "stumbled back" (the Philippines and Venezuela) and countries that "sneaked ahead" (Egypt and Tunisia). Among all these countries, the ones most likely to establish sustainable national enterprises based on proprietary skills are those with the most equal income distributions, late arrival times of foreign firms, and sensible role models, the last of critical importance for helping a country position itself in the world economy.

It is noteworthy that among the ten countries listed in table 10.1, only one is in Asia. Four are in Africa, including two in Northern Africa, whose logical role model is Europe, a neglected teacher in the case of "the rest." "The remainder," moreover, has the advantage of being able to choose among "the rest" for a mentor. Here two submodels promise to vie for global market

Table 10.1. Real Annual Average Growth Rates of GDP in the Manufacturing Sector, Top Ten "Remainder," 1950–1995

Country	1950–60	1960–70	1970–80	1980–90	1990–95	1950–95 (Mean)
Egypt	8.90	4.80	9.70	na	8.30	7.90
Tunisia	4.70	7.80	11.90	6.80	5.60	7.60
Pakistan	6.90	9.40	8.40	2.20	6.40	6.70
Philippines	10.20	6.70	7.00	1.10	9.50	6.60
Nigeria	6.10	9.10	14.80	(−)8.8	14.80	6.40
Venezuela	9.70	6.40	5.20	1.10	7.10	5.80
Colombia	6.50	5.70	5.70	3.00	9.10	5.70
Ecuador	4.70	4.90	9.60	0.50	11.70	5.70
Kenya	na	6.50	5.70	4.80	2.40	5.20
Honduras	7.00	4.50	5.70	3.00	3.40	4.90
Mean	8.20	9.40	8.40	6.10	10.90	8.40

Notes: Statistics for each column represent averages of real annual growth rates for all available years. An entry was labeled as not available (na) if growth rates were unavailable for 7 of 10 possible years. Growth rates calculated using inflation-adjusted current market prices. Comparability is not insured because sometimes "manufacturing" includes some combination of mining, construction, and/or utilities. The definition of "manufacturing" may also vary across countries, depending on the coverage of firms below a minimum employment level.

Sources: 1950–60 data adapted from United Nations (1965 and 1967). 1990–95 data adapted from UNIDO (1997) and earlier years from UNIDO (various years [b]). All other data adapted from World Bank (various years [b]).

share and mentoring in the next ten to twenty years: the "independent" approach of China, India, Korea and Taiwan and the "integrationist" approach of Argentina, Chile and especially Mexico (and Turkey, to the extent that it is joining the European Union).

These two approaches are not mutually exclusive; all countries in "the rest" have become more global since the early postwar years, as suggested by the rising share in foreign investment of joint ventures. Moreover, even the success of the "integrationist" approach depends strongly on the level of local capabilities; the weaker the capabilities, the fewer the "spillovers" from foreign firms. Nevertheless, the independent model emphasizes "getting the institutions 'right' " and building skills, while the integrationist model emphasizes "getting the prices 'right' " and buying skills. From the viewpoint of knowledge-based assets, the two approaches are very distinct and, as suggested in previous chapters, not necessarily of equal promise.

Notes

Chapter 1

1. This conception of technology derives from the work of Nelson (1987), Rosenberg (1976), and ultimately Schumpeter (1942).

2. See, for example, Clark (1909), Pearse (1929), Clark (1987), and Wilkins (1987).

3. For the equivalence under reasonable assumptions of a depreciation of the exchange rate and a decline in real wages, see Krugman and Taylor (1978).

4. By the 1930s even Finland, Sweden's erstwhile colony, supplemented its technology borrowing with innovation: "As original solutions [to technical problems] can be mentioned sawmill equipment produced by the Ahlström works, the grinding machines developed by Tampereen Pellava ja Rautatehdas, the electrical drive systems for grinders created by the leading domestic electrical engineering company Strömberg as well as some new processes in the bleaching of pulp" (Raumolin 1992, p. 332).

5. Italy managed to retain its market share in silk exports after 1900 owing to innovations in silk-weaving machinery by Northern Italian engineers (Federico 1994).

6. The concept of a control mechanism was first applied to the animal and the machine and adapted to cybernetics by a physicist (Wiener 1948). It also became an integral part of modern corporate management techniques (Merchant 1985).

7. All control mechanisms share these four elements (Anthony and Govinda-rajan 1995).

8. Attempts to measure corruption suffer from one-sidedness: they assume that government officials rather than business officials (the information source of such attempts) initiate bribery. They also fail to include corruption in the form of what may be called "constituentism," or demands on a government by private business officials to intervene on their behalf to influence the policies of another government. Hence, attempts to measure corruption also fail to differentiate different degrees of corruption. See, for example, the discussion in Ades and Tella (1999).

9. The standard we use for 'manufacturing experience' is that by 1955 industry account for at least 10 percent of GDP; that no more than 40 percent of industrial output occur in a single industrial branch; and that at least half of all industrial output occur in branches not directly related to the processing of petroleum or other raw materials. The primary data source was the United Nations (1963, 1965), supplemented where possible by country information.

10. We exclude the city states of Hong Kong and Singapore from "the rest" because it seemed unreasonable to make them an equivalent data point to Brazil and China, for example. Their diminutive size and avoidance of the need to shift economic activity from agriculture to industry during industrialization made them aberrant cases. We discuss Hong Kong in the context of free trade in chapter 7. The former Soviet bloc countries are also excluded because their historical links to Europe and postwar experience under a noncapitalist system put them in a different analytical category from other economically backward countries. China is included because its adherence to principles of central planning was relatively short, from 1948 to 1978.

11. In the Ottoman Empire, many artisan skills had become extinct before modern industry arose (Keyder 1994). In Mexico, not a single modern textile mill could trace its origins to the woolen *obrajes* that flourished in the sixteenth century in the Pueblo region of central Mexico (Glade 1982). Still, it may not have been coincidental that modern textile manufacture flourished on and off in Turkey in the nineteenth century, especially silk manufacture in the Western region near Bursa, and Mexico established the most precocious modern cotton textile industry in "the rest" in the 1830s (along with the first development bank) (see chapters 3 and 4).

12. Kuznets (1955) argued that as an economy expands by diversifying into manufacturing, income distribution worsens because inequalities *within* the manufacturing sector (due to varying educational attainments) become greater than within the agricultural sector. Kuznets says relatively little about income distribution *within* agriculture per se.

13. For an analysis of the North Atlantic's interpretation of the Sukarno years, see Thee (1996). For Soeharto, see Robison (1986) and Hill (1996).

14. The "winds of change" was a term coined by Prime Minister Harold Macmillan of the U.K. with reference primarily to decolonization.

15. Information on Thailand is from interviews with Board of Investment officials, Bangkok: Deputy Secretary General Vanee Lertudumrikarn, July 1991 and August 1993; Deputy Secretary General Khun Chakchai, July 1991 and April 1996; and Deputy Secretary General Chakramon Phasukavanich, April 1996. Shorter quotes in the text from Board of Investment officials are from one or another of these people.

16. This contrasted with a more even incidence of university education in the public and private sectors in India, Brazil, and Mexico, whose industry was more advanced than Thailand's in the late 1950s and hence, more managerial. For the private sector, see CEPAL (1963), for Latin America and Agarwala (1986) for

India. For the bureaucracies responsible for economic policy in Brazil, see Willis (1990). For country examples, see Ross Schneider (1998).

17. For a comparable situation in Korea, see Amsden (1994).

Chapter 2

1. Finer counts were produced in England with spinning mules that made use of the extensive capabilities of the experienced British workforce. The coarser counts were produced in the United States using a new ring spinning technology that required fewer labor skills (Huberman 1991).

2. Compare Landes (1969) on France, Morris (1983) on India, and Haber (1989) on Mexico.

3. The revisionists questioned whether France had grown slowly relative to England (see Levy-Leboyer and Bourguignon 1986), whether it was more protected (see Nye 1991), and whether the size of French firms were relatively small (see Nye 1987). For growth in general, see Trebilcock (1981), the debate between Crafts (1995) and Landes (1995), and the review articles by Aldrich (1987) and Nardinelli (1988).

4. Heywood argues "in the light of modern international trade theory" protection was necessary for the French textile industry but was excessive and lasted too long (p. 556).

5. See the article by Morris (1968), who argues against imperial explanations for underdevelopment, and the responses by Chandra (1968), Matsui (1968), and Raychaudhuri (1968). See also the exchange between Bagchi (1976) and Vicziany (1979). Macpherson (1972) reviews the "facts," Robb (1981) points to the advantages of an empirical approach, while Tomlinson (1982 and 1988) provides an overview. Roy (1999) examines traditional industry under colonialism.

6. On the vices and virtues of foreign intervention in China, see the debate between Esherick (1972) and Nathan (1972) and a broad discussion of the Treaty ports in Murphey (1977) and Rawski (1970). For an analysis of the comprador as something less than a devil, see Hao (1970). The staying power of handicrafts has been investigated by Feuerwerker (1970) and Chao (1975). The acceleration of modern industrial growth was first analyzed by Rawski (1980), who influenced a revision by Feuerwerker (1977).

7. See, for instance, Quataert (1994), Keyder (1994), and Pamuk (1986) in contradistinction to Issawi (1980a and b).

8. For Argentina, see Diaz Alejandro (1970), Gallo (1970), Schvarzer (1981), Taylor (1998), and Villanueva (1972). For an overview see Ines Barbero (1995) and Karol and Hilda (1990). For Brazil, see Dean (1969), Fishlow (1972), Leff (1982), Versiani (1980) and Abreu et al. (1997), and for Mexico, see Haber (1989), Coatsworth (1995), and Thomson (1991). These and other Latin American countries are analyzed by Cardenas et al. (2000), Cortes Conde (1992), Ground (1988), and Thorp (1992 and 1984). Especially useful are the bibliographical essays by William Glade, Rosemary Thorp, and Colin M. Lewis (in Bethell 1995). Generally, the revisionists fault the poor scholarship of dependency

theorists—Frank (1967) comes in for especially heavy criticism—or ignore them altogether, as in the "new economic history" (Coatsworth and Taylor 1998). For a rejoinder, see Frank (1998). For cultural insights into some of the long-standing debates in economic development, see Landes (1998). For a non-cultural approach, see Cypher and Dietz (1997).

9. The most radical revisionist was possibly Lloyd Reynolds, who comes close to suggesting that past growth was so fast that even countries in "the remainder" were no longer really badly off: "If Sri Lanka [and similar countries] have really been developing for more than a century, how can it still rank so low in per capita income? . . . Simon Kuznets . . . [indicates] that conversion from local currencies to U.S. dollars at official exchange rates exaggerates the actual difference in consumption levels. . . . Adjustment to a purchasing-power basis suggests that the "official" per capita figures for the lowest-income countries should be two to three times their current levels to make them at all comparable with figures from the richest countries" (Reynolds 1985, pp. 39–40). In fact, Kuznets denies that using purchasing-power exchange rates substantially changes the gap in income between rich and poor countries: "Given a gap of over 30 to 1 between the United States and the poor, less-developed countries, or one of 20 to 1 between all developed countries and the poor, less-developed countries, reduction [using purchasing power comparisons] to 15 or even 10 for the former or to 10 or even 7 for the latter, still leaves us with a large gap" (Kuznets 1972, p. 275).

10. For the 50 percent estimate, see Twomey (1983); for the 75 percent estimate, see Chandavarkar (1994).

11. A comprador, however, was quoted as saying that in the second half of the nineteenth century in the treaty ports and the cities and towns of the interior, *only twenty or thirty percent of people wore native cloth.* This compares with the period before 1831 when England purchased more nankeens (cloth manufactured in the Nanking region) than it sold British manufactured cloth to China (Feuerwerker 1969). The comprador's estimate of domestic market share may be as reliable as the figure cited in table 2.1.

12. According to Feuerwerker (1970, pp. 374–75), "While the absolute amount of handicraft cloth woven increased, . . . this increment was not large enough to accommodate the labor made redundant by a . . . decline in the output of handspun yarn. . . . Nor yet, until the early 1920's, did the textile mills of the cities provide a very large outlet. . . . [Thus], the employment effects of the changes from 1871–1880 to 1901–1910 were negative".

13. In the case of the Ottoman Empire, "weavers frequently focused on making the non-Western clothing still beloved by so many of their customers" (Quataert 1994, p. 97).

14. (Reynolds 1975, p. 97) estimates that Chinese handloom cloth (particularly the lower end) experienced a fall in price of about 40 percent in the period 1875–1931, "but the fall was probably somewhat less than the fall in the price of imported yarn."

15. Another possibility is that handweavers were protected by the costs of transporting imported cloth from coastal cities to rural hinterlands. This natural

protection, however, may be expected to have eroded during the nineteenth century as transportation improved. Moreover, the distribution of imported cloth could be expected to piggyback on existing, widespread distribution channels for imported yarn, so natural protection due to transportation costs was probably minimal, as it is claimed to have been in China (Chao 1975, p. 189). In Mexico, cotton textile producers rallied against the construction of a railroad for fear that cheaper transporation would raise competition (Thomson 1991).

16. It was once believed that after an initial burst of creativity textile manufacturing experienced technological stagnation, but more recent evidence suggests that this was not the case. As noted first by Davis and Stettler (1966), and then David (1970) and Zevin (1971), there was a continual rise in productivity (output per spindle per year and output per worker per year).

17. (Schumpeter 1947) distinguishes between a "creative" and an "adaptive" response to economic change.

18. Mexico's *obrajes* did not contribute a single entrepreneur to modern textile manufacture, as noted earlier (Glade 1982).

19. An imaginative part of Mexico's precocious textile venture was the government's creation in the 1830s of a development bank, *El Banco de Avío*, which for a short time used revenues from duties on prohibited imports to subsidize private textile investments (Potash 1983). Only a small fraction of the capital required to finance modern textile capacity, however, came from this source. But the absence of conventional financial institutions did not seem to impede the rise of the mechanical textile industry. See Keremitsis (1973) and Muller (1978), as cited in Thomson (1989).

20. Of all countries in "the rest," poor transportation especially afflicted Mexico before the rise of railways starting in the 1870s (Coatsworth 1978 and 1981). Yet the modern textile industry in Mexico, whose precocious spurt in the 1830s and 1840s allegedly floundered at the hands of high prices of transportation and raw cotton, was hemorrhaging and still far below international best practice in the 1890s or 1910s (or even the 1930s and 1940s), long after the construction of railroads and the resolution through imports of too high raw cotton prices. Even in the 1830s and 1840s, while transportation in Mexico—inland and international—was allegedly abysmal, and crime on the highways was acute, contraband had no difficulty finding its way from overseas into Mexico's most remote markets. If contraband textiles could get into and around Mexico, it is unclear why Mexican textiles could not get around and out of Mexico.

21. This is evident from data presented in Walker (1986, table 4).

22. Many investors were *agiotistas*, or speculators holding diverse investment portfolios (Potash 1983).

23. Trade policies also discriminated against colonies. India faced tariffs in the early nineteenth century on its textile exports to Britain of 40–60 percent, whereas British textiles entered India virtually duty-free (subject to an ad valorem duty of only 3.5 percent). Meanwhile, within India local manufacturers and traders in Indian textiles had to pay anywhere from 6 to 18 percent ad valorem inland transit duties, duties from which British traders were exempt (Lamb 1955). English textiles also entered the Ottoman Empire almost duty free, and the terms of

the Anglo-Turkish Commercial Convention of 1838 also stipulated that a Belgian merchant pays 5 percent on goods sold in Turkey while a Turkish merchant pays 12 percent for exports or even for transport from one of the Ottoman states to another (Issawi 1966).

24. France was also one of the North Atlantic countries that used its commercial policy to deter "the rest" from competing against France, as in the 1714 kidnapping and expatriation by the French ambassador in Istanbul of a Saxon dye master who had been brought to transfer technology to the local woolen industry, a threat to France's own woolen handicraft sector! (Genc 1994).

25. Brazil's textile industry was *not* competitive at international prices either. Through the whole period 1860–1913, Brazil experienced "a steady and sharp decrease in the competitiveness of local production vis-à-vis imports—*in the absence of tariffs*" (Versiani 1980, p. 324).

26. Taussig's view was reexamined by David (1970), who tried to determine if, given the nature of incremental learning, tariffs were the best way to capture learning externalities. His answer was that they were inferior because learning took the form of diffusion from domestic best practice firms rather than "the acquisition of widespread, repetitive experience of the kind measured by cumulated aggregate output" (p. 599). Nevertheless, David did not directly consider whether or not American textile companies could actually compete against the British without tariffs.

27. Based on such inference, Bils (1984, p. 1045) argues that "removing protection would have eliminated the vast majority of value added in the cotton textile industry" which "constituted nearly two-thirds of value added in large-scale manufacturing in New England in the 1830s."

28. Wolcott (1997, p. 135) examines the interwar period and argues that because India's problems were "imbedded in the structure of the labor market, [they] were beyond the control of any government" and, hence, tariffs would have been redundant (see also Wolcott and Clark 1999). Nevertheless, regardless of whether or not protectionism would have helped the Indian textile industry, Wolcott infers the supreme importance of workers' unwillingness to work as the explanation for low Indian productivity. She does this by holding constant other factors that are equally likely to influence productivity, such as the quality of Indian management. Clark (1987) also argues that India's textile industry and those of "the rest" more generally lost in foreign competition from labor's lower work loads (seemingly a consequence of culture). While "the rest's" lower labor productivity is supported by much of the available evidence, whatever its reliability, Clark rules out other plausible explanations for higher costs. On the question of management's role in low productivity, see his debate with Wilkins (1987). The importance of management is suggested by productivity differences in Chinese-owned cotton mills and Japanese-owned cotton mills operating in China, analyzed below.

29. It has been estimated that the cost of erecting a spinning mill in Bombay in 1877 was about three times the cost in Lancashire (Morris 1983) while the estimated cost of erecting a cotton mill in Mexico in 1910 was $19.72 per spindle compared with $12.72 per spindle in Great Britain (Clark 1987).

30. By the time Japanese textile firms invested in China in the 1920s, however, such investments were meticulously planned and swiftly executed. In the case of the Mitsubishi *zaibatsu*, it first bought a bankrupt Chinese company in 1902 as a trial. Two years later, it bought another Chinese mill which it had trial-operated for one year on a lease basis (Chao 1975 and Kuwahara 1986).

31. Japan had invested in China when its exports to China were threatened. In the 1860s and 1870s, India had sold yarn to China. By 1892 Japan had exceeded India in value of exports to the Chinese market (Indian merchants involved in the China trade then turned to financing more Indian cotton mills). Soon Japan began threatening India in its own domestic market, which prompted Indian mills to produce more cloth and higher count yarns, thereby threatening Lancashire's exports to India. As Chinese cotton mills expanded, Japan worried about losing its export market in China. Therefore, beginning in the 1920s, Japan invested in China itself (Koh 1966).

32. The discussion that follows is based on (Kuwahara 1986 and 1992).

33. Royle (1851) as cited in Gadgil (1959, p. 31).

Chapter 3

1. Tacitness refers to the incomplete specification of technology because (a) its scientific properties are not fully understood so documentation is impossible; (b) its properties are proprietary; or (c) the nature of its properties are more art than science. The first two types of tacitness typically refer to production techniques and hardware—machinery and equipment. The last two types typically refer to software—organizational and managerial capabilties. See Katz (1987) on Latin America, Lall (1987) on India, Mourshed (1999) on the pharmaceutical industry (India and Egypt), Westphal et al. (1985) on Korea, as well as Rosenberg (1982) and David (1997) for a general discussion. Teece (1976) examines the costs that tacitness exacts in technology transfer. For an analysis of the transfer of process technology from an historical perspective, see von Tunzelmann (1997).

2. As observed by Cairncross (1962, p. 43, emphasis added), "While foreign investment undoubtedly speeded up the development of (poor) countries, it is more accurate to think of it as accompanying and reinforcing their growth than as preliminary to it. . . . *the foreign investor usually did not join in until comparatively late in the day, lagging behind rather than running in front.*" U.S. experience "strongly supports" this assessment (Kravis 1972, p. 404).

3. Circa the 1930s, textiles and apparel as a share of total manufacturing output were roughly: 26 percent in Brazil (Kuznets 1955), 23 percent in Chile (Weaver 1980), 30 percent in Mexico (Bulmer-Thomas 1994), and 40 percent in China (Rawski 1989). Although Argentina had a textile industry, it was relatively small, around 15 percent of manufacturing output (Weaver 1980). In 1936 spindles in place (thousands) equaled 159 in Argentina, 2,311 in Brazil, and 862 in Mexico. The corresponding figures for looms in place (thousands) were 1.8, 81.9, and 33.2 (International Labour Office 1937, p. 111).

4. Their location in "the rest" was influenced by the availability of raw materials. Cotton textiles tended to be produced in countries where raw cotton was grown locally (Japan before the Meiji restoration, Brazil, China, India, Turkey, and Mexico). Steel tended to be made in countries with rich iron ore and coal deposits (they included the above countries except Japan, which sourced its steel inputs from Manchuria, which Japan colonized in the 1930s).

5. As noted in the last chapter, the modern Mexican textile industry began in the 1830s, but the first large-scale mill (the Compañía Industriala de Orizaba, CIDOSA) was founded in 1889 (it was the only mill in 1895 large enough to pay a tax on sales) (Keremitsis 1987). Mills in Brazil's northeast existed in the 1840s, but accelerated development began in other regions in Brazil in the 1890s (Versiani 1980). India's first cotton mill, the Oriental, was established by the Parsi merchant, N. F. Davar in 1854. India's "jewel," the Tata family's Empress Mills, started to operate with ring spindles in 1877 (Tripathi and Mehta 1990; Tripathi 1982).

6. Continental European companies around 1913 had very few manufacturing affiliates in "the rest," an exception being the Mexican subsidiary of Metallgesellschaft (Germany) (Franko 1974).

7. Contrast the early experience of modern sugar refining in Brazil with that in England. In 1875 Henry Tate and Sons joined forces with a German engineer who held a patent for sugar cubes. Previously, grocers had to hack conical loaves into pieces for customers. Tate called on an experienced engineer and within twelve months a refinery had been built. All was not sugar and spice for Tate; he went through a rough financial period and had to withdraw his daughter from boarding school. But he prevailed, and soon the Tate cube became the standard for quotation for refined sugar in London—so great was the confidence in "the lasting nature of the product's quality" (Chalmin 1990, 77).

8. Foreign investment lagged rather than led industrialization in imperial Russia as well as in "the rest." Its contribution was said to have been "decidedly of a minor nature" before 1880. Starting in 1880, it accelerated substantially, and, therefore, it became an important factor earlier than it did in "the rest" (McKay 1974, p. 336).

9. See also (Ficker 1995).

10. For the minimalist role of foreign investors in China's early industrialization, see Dernberger (1975) and Murphey (1977, p. 126). The latter argues that as late as 1931, "the role played by foreign investment was marginal." Remer (1933) suggests the role of foreign firms in early manufacturing was substantial but provides little supporting evidence. Hou (1965) provides detailed information on foreign investments in China's early industrialization but does not specify whether domestic firms were also active in the same industries at the time. Feuerwerker (1964) describes early foreign investment in China as "miniscule" in size.

11. For Japan, see also Okita and Miki (1967).

12. Nanyang was still alive in 1998 despite a highly competitive Chinese domestic market for cigarettes: "The company's major product is well known among Chinese smokers and regarded as one of a dozen high-end domestic and foreign brand names in China" (Bankers Trust 1998, p. 70).

13. In fact, a German company was involved, Gutenhoff-nungshutte (GHH).

14. Clark (1973) as cited in Rawski (1975).

15. "All that glittered was not gold" even in the postwar period. In Brazil, a technology transfer by Union Carbide in the late 1960s, for a Wulff naphtha cracker to supply ethylene, resulted in a costly setback: "what had been considered 'start-up' difficulties wherever it had been tried (in countries other than Brazil) turned out to be fundamental flaws. Wulff crackers just did not work" (Evans 1979, p. 233). In India, a chemical explosion in 1984 at a Union Carbide plant in Bhopal resulted in at least 3,000 deaths and 300,000 injuries. The report on the tragedy by the Council of Industrial and Scientific Research attributed it to "failures in design, equipment, supplies, and operating procedures" (Shrivastava 1992, p. 46). In Mexico, the machinery and process technology for a BOF oxygen steel mill purchased from the German firm DEMAG had "a number of problems embodied in the original design, which not only did not correctly take into account the specific conditions of the local environment, but also carried unresolved technical problems of the original design" (Perez and Jose de Jesus Perez y Peniche 1987, p. 187). In Korea, a cement mill was chronically troubled with a technically faulty process supplied by Mitsubishi Heavy Industry. Kolon Nylon invited Chemtex, an American fiber company, to participate in equity and share technology. Production started in 1963 "but confronted many technical difficulties," whereupon Kolon sought technology from Japan (Tran 1988, p. 399). In cases where foreign firms stumbled, local firms sometimes got the upper hand.

16. A failure to invest in education was once held partially responsible for Britain's economic decline, only to be superseded by the belief that a scientific relationship between education and industrial productivity was not empirically established. But "the influence of education may have been too readily dismissed" (Roderick and Stephens 1978, p. 149). On whether education was generally important for growth in light of nineteenth century skill requirements, see Tortella (1990). Kawabe and Daito (1993) analyzes training in modern corporations and business education.

17. Technical training was much more advanced in the North Atlantic, and even in Russia: "Despite its relative backwardness, Russia was on the whole fairly well catered for as regards formal technical education even before Emancipation, when its universities and engineering schools were able by 1860 to provide a comprehensive and up-to-date training in the main branches of applied science and technology" (Kenwood and Lougheed 1982, p. 109).

18. See also Kenwood and Lougheed (1982) and Saul (1972).

19. Silk manufacture follows four basic steps: (1) the cultivation of mulberry trees; (2) the raising of silkworms (sericulture); (3) the reeling of silk fiber (raw silk) from cocoons, either by hand or by mechanical steam filatures; and (4) the weaving of silk fabrics. The third step, the focus of competition between China and Japan, is composed of four operations: (a) the drying of the cocoons; (b) the boiling of the cocoons; (c) the reeling of the silk threads from the cocoons; and (d) the re-reeling of them for finishing.

20. In Italy, silk accounted for two-thirds of exports during the Napoleonic Kingdom (Poni and Mori 1996). In the second half of the nineteenth century, silk was still Italy's biggest export and produced more value added than the chemical, engineering, and metal-working industries combined (Davis 1991).

21. Cited in Li (1981, p. 6).

22. Due to Northern Italy's technological capabilities, the Italian silk industry remained a major world producer until it ran out of cheap agricultural labor in the 1910s. Although a latecomer among North Atlantic countries, Italy took the high road in the silk industry by virtue of the innovativeness of its engineering sector—in this it was like the French cotton textile industry analyzed in the last chapter. Italy competed by producing the highest quality silk using advanced equipment. Three innovations were introduced in Italian plants. First, a dryer for silk cocoons was developed between 1885 and 1890 (in response to a contest sponsored by the Italian Ministry of Agriculture, Industry and Trade) which saved labor and capital and raised productivity. Second, a mechanical device to prepare cocoons was invented that saved skilled labor and increased productivity in reeling. Third, a device was developed that mechanically attached the edges of new cocoons to a moving thread, thereby saving time and increasing productivity. From an initial number of two or four reels per basin, by the 1930s the most productive Italian silk factories were handling sixteen to twenty reels per basin (Federico 1994). For some Japanese incremental improvements, see Ono (1986).

23. The silk industry was dominated by émigrés from France, Armenia, and other regions to the west. When these émigrés were driven out of Turkey as a result of war and revolution in the early nineteenth century, the silk industry of Bursa collapsed.

24. A conservative assessment of the learning contribution of Tomioka is given by McCallion (1989).

25. The most well-known and successful dozen or so silk manufacturers in twentieth-century China were all concurrently compradors and many also operated their own silk wholesale firms (Eng 1984).

26. At the Shanghai filatures, "complaints about the workers' lack of skill and discipline were frequently voiced. One observer said that, compared to the orderliness of Japanese filatures, the Chinese factories were utterly chaotic. Workers were lazy, sloppy, dirty (they combed their hair in the reeling room and boiled corn ears in the cocoon basins), and dishonest" (Li 1981, p. 174).

27. The separation of ownership and management in Shanghai's small plants at this time appears to have been general (Lieu 1936).

Chapter 4

1. Comparisons of growth rates in manufacturing output before and after the interwar period are impeded by a shortage of reliable data. Revisionist economists suggest convincingly that manufacturing growth before World War I was faster than previously acknowledged (see chapter 2). Still, it is unclear if such growth rates were faster than after World War I and even less clear if the manufacturing

industries being compared in the two time periods are the same with respect to product and firm size. The data of Hofman (1993), the most comprehensive available, indicate faster growth after World War II than before it even in Latin America.

2. Measuring assets by per capita income, the ratio of per capita income in "the rest" compared with the North Atlantic fell from an all-time high of 0.33 in 1870 to 0.24 in 1913 to 0.17 in 1950 (see table 1.4). Needless to say, the reliability of the data on which these estimates are based is uncertain and probably varies across countries and time periods.

3. For government's role in Brazil, see Topik (1980 and Topik 1987). The Chinese government, while doing nothing to help industrialization, allegedly harmed it (Perkins 1967). For China, see also Rawski (1989). For India, see Bagchi (1972), Lamb (1955), and Tomlinson (1993). For the Ottoman Empire, see Keyder (1994), Issawi (1980a), and Issawi (1980b). For Mexico, see Haber (1989).

4. For obsolescence and inefficiency in the relatively modern Latin American cotton textile industry, see UNECLA (1951). For Argentina in general, see Diaz Alejandro (1970).

5. For Sweden, see chapter one.

6. India's exports to China, its major customer, collapsed at the hands of Japan, as noted in chapter 2. India's exports of yarn in India's total production of yarn were 47.4 percent in 1899–99, 11.7 percent in 1918/19, and only 3.1 percent in 1927/28 (Koh 1966). This decline paralleled that of Japan, whose share of yarn exports in Japan's own domestic yarn production fell from 41 percent in 1893–97 to only 2.4 percent in 1928–32 (Shinohara 1964). This occurred because the supply of domestically produced yarn was consumed by domestic rather than foreign cloth manufacturers. But Japan's declining coefficient of yarn exports was compensated by a large increase in cloth exports, whereas India's decline in yarn exports was not compensated by anything; India's cloth exports first rose and then fell in absolute value.

7. In 1900 concentration in Brazil and Mexico was higher than in the United States (which, of course, was much larger): The four-firm concentration ratio was estimated to have been .22 in Brazil, .28 in Mexico, and only .07 in the United States (Haber 1991). Brazil's textile industry in 1910 was structured such that eight mills accounted for more than one-third of all spindles, slightly less than one-third of all looms, and about one-fifth of the cotton mill labor force (Stein 1957). In China by 1930, out of 127 mills, 61 were owned by 14 companies (Chao 1975). At the end of World War II in India, the 14 biggest companies together comprised nearly a fifth of total assets and the 6 biggest companies controlled about one-sixth (Mehta 1953, p. 184).

8. In part, firm size diverged across countries due to different responses to bankruptcy and mergers. Most defunct Indian- and Chinese-owned cotton mills formed the basis for a new company, not a merger or acquisition. Therefore, mills tended to be small by Japanese standards, where dissolutions often represented a merger or acquisition and, hence, became multiunit enterprises. Out of a total of

fifty-seven Chinese-owned mills in 1929, only eight were multiunit, as estimated from (Pearse 1929, p. 154–55).

9. A "scientific" approach to labor relations was also evident in India's best national firms. In the case of the Tata steel mill at Jamshedpur, "in order to carry on the Social Welfare Work on modern scientific lines, a Committee of distinguished sociologists," including the British trade unionists Beatrice and Sidney Webb, were invited to draw out a scheme "for scientific welfare work to be done at Jamshedpur" (Fraser 1919, p. 95).

10. According to (Goldsmith 1983), in the period 1860–1913, India's net capital formation as a share of GNP varied from 2 percent to 4 percent. Between 1898 and 1938 gross public saving was less than 2 percent of GNP.

11. The investment share for Korea and Taiwan in 1914–38 is likely to be abnormally high given Japan's military build-up during this period.

12. See also (Saxonhouse and Wright 1984).

13. The most extensive research on labor supply relates to India. See Morris (1965) and Chandavarkar (1994).

14. The contract labor system in China and the jobber system in India were similar. In the early days of factory employment when labor was scarce, unskilled and unaccustomed to factory ways, jobbers from the same social class and village as workers recruited them and taught them basic skills. Jobbers were also responsible for the discipline of workers (Chandavarkar 1994). As labor became abundant, and as skill requirements rose, the failure to reform substantially the jobber system "became one of the many great failures of industrial management in India," although labor relations varied by region, being better in Ahmedabad than Bombay. Excess supply over demand for labor created an inadequately trained workforce and an open invitation to graft and corruption, as workers were forced to bribe the jobber for employment. The effect was to undermine "the very vitals of honest internal administration" (Mehta 1953, pp. 68–69). In China, contractors "got the cheapest labour possible," preferably child labor, since they were paid a fixed amount for wages for every bale of cotton produced. The contractor system was almost dead in China by 1929 although child labor persisted (Pearse 1929, p. 171). The jobber system in India continued in effect until after World War II. In China, by the 1930s most cotton mills and flour mills had gone over to a "supervisor system" directly under management's control (Lieu 1928).

15. Beginning in 1929, wages were estimated to have risen in Shanghai by 80–100 percent over the previous ten year period (King and Lieu 1929). Wages in the Ottoman Empire showed a rising long-term trend in the period 1839–1913. Money wages jumped 20 percent in the aftermath of the Young Turk Revolution of 1908, when trade unions were briefly legalized, strikes erupted, and labor became scarce due to rising emigration abroad (Boratav et al. 1985).

16. In the nine years from 1918 to 1926, there were estimated to have been 1,232 strikes in China, 44 percent in the textile industry, which accounted for roughly 43 percent of industrial production (King and Lieu 1929; Chang 1967).

17. For Brazil, see Leff (1968). In China, "imitations of foreign looms, hosiery machines, welding machines, electric and gasoline motors, and cigarette machines

all sold for a fraction of the price commanded by the imported originals" (Rawski 1980, pp. 6–15).

18. The director of one of India's largest cotton mills stated in 1939 that there was an "enormous field" for textile machinery manufacture in India. The existing wire and steel industries could produce the whole requirement of wire heals for the Indian cotton mills. "It is very annoying to me personally to see most excellent equipment for high drafting, manufactured in China, being delivered to India" (Chandavarkar 1994, p. 242).

19. For the complex effects of the 1930s Depression on "the rest," see Diaz Alejandro (1984) and Latham (1981). For China, see Rawski (1989). For India, see Thomas (1935). For Latin America, see Chu (1972), Ground (1988), and Cardenas et al. (2000).

20. In Argentina, for example, at the time of World War II, railroads accounted for around 40 percent of the stock of foreign direct investment, with another 20 percent accounted for by other utilities (Lewis 1990).

21. For India, see Kerr (1995); for Mexico, see Ficker (1995) for Mexico and Brazil, see Summerhill, 1997.

22. For overcosting and corruption on railroads, see Wright (1974); for Argentina, Huenemann (1984); for China, Pletcher (1972); and Ficker (1995) for Mexico.

23. It is unclear how Japanee textile companies saved on raw cotton. See the discussion on Japan in Moser (1930).

24. Procuring local cotton was a big problem in China because cotton distributors tended to adulterate their product (Moser 1930). Buying locally was an even bigger problem in Brazil because initially cotton was considered a poor man's crop and, therefore, was supplied irregularly and in nonstandard qualities. In Mexico, local cotton was hard to grow and overpriced; the conflict between raw cotton growers and textile manufacturers concerned who would get a higher tariff from the government, industry or agriculture, with both ultimately succeeding in limiting imports (Keremitsis 1987). Over time, however, as Mexico's cotton cultivation shifted from the coastal region to the North, procuring raw cotton became less problematic (see chapter 2).

25. Argentina was an exception insofar as a large, diversified export company founded by Belgian immigrants in the early eighteenth century, Bunge y Born, operated out of Buenos Aires from the late nineteenth century (Schvarzer 1989).

26. The low cost of entry in India has been debated. According to one study, Rs. 500,000 amounted to a lot of money, and the fact that cotton and jute mills and tea companies required independent managements added to their financial burden (Rungta 1970). As for the cost of entry in other countries, Japanese mill entrepreneurs were usually rich farmers or local manufacturers of soy sauce or wine who entered textile manufacture "out of a sense of patriotic duty." However, "mill manufacture forced them into unexpectedly high expenditure." The amount required to start an enterprise was already at the limit of their ability (Nakaoka 1991, p. 293). In China (1904–8), some cotton mills were on the low end of the specturm of authorized capital (in taels), and some were in the middle. The most expensive investments tended to be railroads, mining and smelting, and modern-

type banks (Feuerwerker 1958, p. 3). On the other hand, by the early 1930s out of a total of twelve industries in Shanghai, cotton textiles was found to have had the highest average capitalization per factory (Lieu 1936). Per contra, the capital requirements of the First Industrial Revolution were modest; entry into mechanized textile spinning or weaving was supposedly within the grasp of a typical artisan (Mathias 1973).

27. China's "outpayments," however, were estimated to have exceeded "inpayments" from at least 1903–30 (Remer 1933, p. 206). Reliable balance of payments accounts are altogether unavailable for other countries in this period. For capital formation in China before 1936, see Rawski (1989, chapter 5).

28. Pomeranz (2000) argues that consumption in the eighteenth century was roughly equal in China and Europe.

29. The best data exist for Mexico (1902–38), and suggest that "underlying Mexico's concentrated industrial structure was a surprisingly low level of profitability" (Haber 1989, p. 103).

30. As in the North Atlantic, profits in "the rest" were high during wars and low during depressions. World War I and its immediate aftermath generated extremely high rates of return in India, China, and Latin America (Miller 1981). In Bombay, between 1917 and 1922 gross profits averaged 75.6 percent and net profits (after commissions and depreciation) averaged 60.5 percent (Morris 1983). It was estimated that from 1914 to 1919 the average annual profit for China's cotton spinning mills rose by 70 percent. The most important companies increased their profits twenty-fold, some even fifty-fold (Bergere 1983). The record for five mills between 1915 and 1922 shows average annual profit rates of 83 percent, 75 percent (for two mills), 140 percent, and 57.6 percent (Chao 1975, p. 139).

31. The biggest compradores in late nineteenth-century China were said to earn an annual profit rate of very roughly 30 percent. They, too, however, faced high risks and were routinely bankrupted (Chan 1977). Money lenders were said to earn between 30 and 50 percent on loans and pawnshops and native banks 15 to 25 percent (Dernberger 1975). If accurate, these data suggest that moneylending was more lucrative than manufacturing (see the sporadic rates of profit for cotton textiles in China calculated by Chao [1975]).

32. The year 1929 was not one of economic depression because China was on the silver standard and the depressed silver price in the world market amounted to a devaluation of China's currency. Prosperity endured in China until the second half of 1931. Output tended to hold steady throughout the Depression although profits fell (Lieu 1928).

33. In Mexico, 134 cotton textile mills operated in 1900 but only 84 operated in 1915 as a consequence of bankruptcy as well as mergers and acquisitions (Haber 1989, p. 125). In Brazil, of nine cotton mills founded by planters before 1900, seven had been sold to importers by 1917 (Dean 1969).

34. Reported industry-level profit rates depended on accounting procedures with respect to bankrupt firms. The exclusion of companies that went bankrupt raised profitability by as much as ten percentage points over estimates that included failures (Mehta 1953, p. 191).

35. During a recession in 1907–8, the rate of return on paid-up capital of the ten biggest Japanese spinning companies was generally around 20 percent because these companies had established oligopolies in the principal cotton yarn markets, and fluctuations at home or abroad had litle impact on them. By contrast, "the business performance of small-to-medium firms was far worse" (Kuwahara 1986, p. 120).

36. None of "the rest" had a banking system in the late nineteenth century or early twentieth century that was willing to lend long-term to manufacturers. See Rawski (1989) for China and Rungta (1970) for India. In part, the absence of banks resulted from a lack of demand. Family-owned enterprises were reluctant to borrow from banks because of the risk of having to share their equity with banks in case of default. On the supply side, modern banks were expensive to establish. Of the 227 Chinese companies that registered with the Ministry of Agriculture, Industry, and Commerce between 1904 and 1908, only twelve had authorized capital above 1,000,000 taels. Of the twelve, three were modern-type banks (and three were cotton spinning and weaving mills) (Feuerwerker 1958). Based on limited evidence, debt-equity ratios in Mexico are reported as having been "incredibly" low due to an absence of bank loans in firms' financial portfolios (Haber 1989, p. 66). See Chao (1975) for China.

37. The founders of twenty-six textile mills in China between 1890–1910 included thirteen senior officials, seven retired officials and members of the gentry, and seven compradors (Chan 1977, p. 61).

38. See Tripathi and Mehta (1990, p. 34f, 43), for references to the debate.

39. ". . . managing agents were the largest stockholders as well as directors of the companies of which they were nominated agents. (Since 1970 the agency houses have been reorganized as holding companies and continue to control their business groups.) Thus there was no separation of management control from ownership. Controlling a number of companies, each agency house formed a business group similar to that of the zaibatsu in Japan. Zaibatsu (business groups owned by families) differed from agency houses, however, in that they were in effect managed by salaried managers" (Yonekawa 1986)

40. Whereas mills in Lancashire were mainly proprietorships, in India they were mainly joint stock companies.

41. The entry on speculation (by Jean Tirole) in *The New Palgrave Dictionary of Money and Finance* reads as follows: "The concept of speculation has always fascinated academics and practitioners alike; this may be due to inconsistent definitions, occasional misunderstanding and genuine economic importance" (Tirole 1992, p. 513). According to the Oxford Universal Dictionary, speculation is "the action or practice of buying and selling goods, stocks and shares, etc., in order to profit by the rise or fall in the market value, as distinct from regular trading or investment."

42. It is unclear whether Indian cotton mills speculated in raw cotton. According to a 1927 study, "speculative purchases of either spot or futures cotton are rarely indulged in by Bombay mills," but it was added that speculators in the cotton trade subjected mills to speculative impulses (Rutnagur 1927, p. 350).

Rungta (1970, p. 215) argues that the mills themselves speculated in raw cotton.

43. Because Japan had no domestic spot market for raw cotton in the 1920s, it also had to buy cotton equal to three months' future consumption to assure steady production. The risk, however, was allegedly not as high as in China because many mills in Japan were affiliated to zaibatsu groups and so were relatively strong financially. Japanese mills were vertically integrated—the procurement of raw cotton and marketing of finished product were conducted by the same organization—so whenever the price of raw cotton was expected to fall, a firm could lower the prices of its finished products slightly to speed up sales. There would then be less loss on the products when their price was later brought down by the actual fall in the price of cotton (Chao 1975). The three large cotton dealers that handled cotton purchases were presumably skilled in this business and shared some of their speculative gains with their customers (Moser 1930).

44. That such speculation was not simply part of traditional Indian culture but rather a phenomenon of underdevelopment is suggested by the fact that early British entrepreneurs operating in India also speculated. The first attempt to produce steel in India was made by the Bengal Iron and Steel Company, which was incorporated in England in 1889. After examining the record, "we are left with a sense of the ramshackle character of the technical and financial proposals and the impression that plans were formulated and operations conducted in impulsive, speculative and unsystematic ways (particularly in contrast to the first Indian attempt to build a steel mill)" (Morris 1983, p. 588).

45. Countries that manufactured both textiles and steel tended to have the raw materials that both industries required, as noted elsewhere.

46. A troubled Brazilian company that produced iron and steel on a small scale formed a joint venture with a Belgian syndicate in 1921, ultimately becoming one of Brazil's largest steel mills through incremental growth, We did not choose this as Brazil's first integrated steel complex because of its step-by-step, disintegrated expansion.

47. The North Atlantic's catch-up in steel with England probably involved more technological unknowns than the above but a greater number of skills as well; therefore, catch-up was much faster. As early as the first half of the nineteenth century "in several important instances American iron and steel producers not only adopted new technologies quickly, but then surpassed European practice in short order" (Hyde 1991, p. 52). By the end of the nineteenth century, the American steel industry was responsible for introducing a long series of technological changes, including fast-driving, independent blowing, new blowing engines, mechanical charging, mechanical casting, and direct delivery of molten iron to steelworks (Temin 1964). In Germany, most of the technical improvements on the original plan of the Bessemer converter were invented and first applied in Britain and the United States, but these innovations "were implemented in Germany without any significant delay.... Concerning the major innovations in steelmaking, any noticeable lag toward Britain had been rectified as early as the 1860s" (Fremdling 1991, pp. 123, 132). Sweden, one of Europe's poorest and

tardiest industrializers, eased its way into steel manufacture through its experience in iron making. Sweden had long exported iron to England, but this important trade was being threatened by changes in England's demand patterns. Swedish metallurgists went to England to investigate and resolved a quality problem as early as the 1830s. Another difficulty arose, and in 1845 the invention by a Swede of a gas generator saved the day. All these innovations allowed iron to continue to be one of Sweden's major exports and "facilitated the transition from the mode of entrepreneurial organization peculiar to the early Swedish iron industry with its many scattered, often isolated works and its patriarchal relationship between ironmasters and their workers, to the present-day large-scale production based on the converter, and the open-hearth and electric furnaces" (Soderlund 1960, p. 64; see also Wohlert 1991, Ahlstrom 1993, and Jorberg 1969).

48. "Unfortunately Karabuk's reputation has not tended to be a good one, particularly among efficiency oriented foreign observers. In addition to the usual causes of high costs for state enterprises, such as an undue number of employees, political interference and management difficulties, the Works have generally been regarded as having been neither well located nor well designed" (Singer 1977, p. 31). Acording to one efficiency-oriented foreign observer, who visited Turkey to give advice to American foreign aid donors, "the question remains whether a great modern steel plant ought to have top priority in the industrial development of an economy which still, for the most part, is operated at levels characteristic of Europe in the Middle Ages" (Thornburg 1949, p. 111).

49. Despite technological prowess, both the American and German steel industries received substantial tariff protection. In Germany, advanced technology and tariffs were combined with cartels to pump up profits, and apparently without any negative effect on performance (Fremdling 1991).

50. A major delay in both India and Brazil concerned ore prospecting, but in each case the delay seemingly contributed to better planning. For the politics behind the delay of Volta Redonda, see Callaghan (1981).

51. Morris (1983) and Johnson (1966).

52. Except for providing tariff protection, the government's role in the steel industry in both the United States and Germany was small (Abe 1991). In Sweden it was virtually nonexistent.

53. The government was also very unsupportive in several respects. See Bagchi (1972).

Chapter 5

1. Under the terms of the Bowring Treaty (1855–1932), Thailand became a virtual colony of Britain; it lost control over its finances and tariffs, which were set at roughly 3 percent. By 1930 about 70 percent of Thai trade was with Britain and 95 percent of its modern economy was estimated to be owned by foreigners, mainly Britons (Ingram 1971).

2. The selection criterion for these twenty-nine developing countries was simply the availability of data.

3. The year 1994 is the last year for which data were available at the time the regression equations were estimated. Data for 1992 and 1994 yielded approximately similar results.

4. In the early 1930s, "the Netherlands East Indies government had passed the Crisis Import Ordnance designed to impose quotas on a whole range of Japanese goods, and, in the Philippines, Japan was forced by the United States to come to a gentleman's agreement limiting its cotton exports to that colony. Parallel measures were undertaken in all the insular colonies restricting foreign investment, export of strategic materials, immigration, and land-ownership, all of which were clearly aimed at the Japanese economic advance" (Peattie 1996, p. 203).

5. For a review of this early literature, see Hori (1994).

6. The empirical research at the industry and firm level was guided by Professor An Pyongjik at Seoul National University. The groundwork was laid by Park (1985, 1990, 1999). Major sources relied on below also include Choi (1982), Eckert (1996, 1991, 1990), and Hori (1994).

7. The original source for this estimate is Kawai Akitake, *The Current State of Korean Manufacturing* (in Japanese), Seoul, 1943.

8. For Japan's factory labor force, see Park (1985, p. 83). For population, see table 1.6.

9. According to personnel records, the percentage of Koreans receiving training (a three-year apprenticeship) exactly offset the percentage decline in Japanese workers receiving training (Park 1985).

10. Another account suggests that fourteen textile mills existed, but they were small and typically engaged in weaving. Total weaving machines, however, were fewer than 1,000 and total capacity for grey cloth in the mid-1940s was only two million yards per year (San and Kuo 1991).

11. Later Malaysia, which excludes Singapore.

12. In the case of the Thai textile industry in the 1950s, "Imported cotton yarn from Pakistan was by far cheaper than the domestically produced yarn. Imported cotton and synthetic fabrics from Japan were more popular in Thailand. In 1957 the domestic production of cotton fabric could meet only 25 percent of total local demand. The 1950s was a decade of trouble for the private capital who had no support of political leaders" (Suehiro 1985, p. 3–49).

13. Comparing Taiwan and Hong Kong, their costs in the textile industry around 1960 are likely to have been similar. Taiwan's wages (and rent) were possibly slightly lower than those in Hong Kong, but its capital and distribution costs are likely to have been higher. Hong Kong's cost of capital benefited from a parallel dollar-denominated free exchange market (Schenk 1994), and distribution costs benefited from a long-standing reexport trade. Productivity was also lower in Taiwan than in Hong Kong: in 1962 the ratio of kilograms of yarn production per spindle hour worked was .0237 in Hong Kong and only .0192 in Taiwan; the ratio of kilograms of cloth production per loom in place was 2,901 in Hong Kong compared to only 1,593 in Taiwan (GATT 1966, pp. 203; 209).

14. According to Ho and Lin (1991, p. 277), "Hong Kong possessed larger export quotas than Taiwan and South Korea, and especially other LDCs" because

Hong Kong already had a high volume of textile exports by 1962, when quotas were allocated on the basis of existing market shares.

15. For Korea, see Cole and Lyman (1971), Jones and Il (1980), Amsden (1989), and Fields (1995). For Taiwan, see Gold (1986), Wade (1990), and Fields (1995).

Chapter 6

1. In Latin America, "at the outbreak of the Second World War, a good share of the Latin American social overhead capital and industrial capacity was already stretched thin and at the verge of obsolescence; war shortages were to aggravate these conditions" (Diaz Alejandro 1984, p. 48). Conditions tended to be even worse in Asia (Indonesia and Malaysia, for example) due to wartime destruction.

2. The World Bank was supposed to finance third world development. Unlike the Marshall Plan, however, World Bank assistance included no grants, and loans were typically not oriented toward manufacturing. Turkey was a special case that proved the rule. It was covered by the Marshall Plan, but the idea was to develop Turkish agriculture (Pamugoklu 1990).

3. In the case of coal, iron and steel, fertilizers, electric power, and ocean shipping, the Reconstruction Finance Bank (1951) supplied 84 percent of the total funding for Japan's postwar capital investment. Its resources came from the government in the form of bonds and equity (Japan Development Bank and Institute 1994). Japan's first development bank was the Yokohama Specie Bank, which helped to finance the Japanese silk and cotton textile industries in the late nineteenth century (see chapter 3).

4. The postwar development bank in "the rest" appears to have been sui generis. Gerschenkron (1962) emphasized the importance of innovative institutions in catching up, but when he discussed his prime example, Russia, he mentioned only an aggressive fiscal policy before 1890 and then the emergence of a private banking system. He did not mention any institution resembling the postwar development bank. Mexico's development bank, Nacional Financiera, "had no counterpart in the United States unless it was a combination of the Reconstruction Finance Corporation (of the New Deal) and the old J. P. Morgan and Company" (Myers 1954, p. 588). A joint-stock bank created in 1822 by King Willem I in Belgium was endowed with state properties and was supposed to undertake investment projects (Cameron 1993). It failed, and many investment banks (*société general*) emerged thereafter, but they were private and did not support nor take equity positions in both private and public enterprises, nor did they impose performance standards on clients. For state involvement in the development of financial institutions, see Sylla et al. (1999).

5. For planning, see Hanson (1966), Streeten and Lipton (1968), and (Chakravarty 1991).

6. For immediate postwar macroeconomic history, see Diaz Alejandro (1970) for Argentina; Abreu et al. (1997), Baer (1965), Fishlow (1972), and Leff (1982 and 1982) for Brazil; Lieu (1948) for the three-year interval between the end of World War II and the communist takeover in China; Mamalakis and Reynolds

(1965) and Instituto de Economia, (1956, and 1963) for Chile; Bhagwati and Chakravarty (1969) and Vaidyanathan (1982) for India; Cole and Park (1983) for Korea; Lee (1974) for Malaysia; and Reynolds (1970) for Mexico.

7. The Industrial Finance Corporation of India, India's first development bank, was founded shortly after independence in 1948. Its initial activities were haphazard and funds tended to be provided on a "first come, first served basis." As a result, the early lending pattern of IFCI tended to represent the existing industrial structure in India rather than infrastructure needs, with the largest share of funds going to the food and textile industries (Saksena 1970). See also Ahluwalia (1985, p. 73) and Gulyani (1999).

8. For Malaysia, see Hoffmann and Tan Siew (1980), Peng (1983), and Rasiah (1995). For Brazil, see Evans (1979) and Newfarmer and Mueller (1975).

9. In Canada, government spending as a share of gross fixed capital formation (G/C) was estimated to have been only about 7 percent at the turn of the century and then rose and fell and rose again to about 10 percent in the late 1920s. For the United States, estimates of Simon Kuznets suggest that G/C was very low initially, and then no higher than 16.3 percent for 1929–55. For the United Kingdom, according to estimates of Charles Feinstein, G/C rose from under 10 percent in 1856–75 to around 28 percent in 1920–38. In Sweden, G/C was not above 10 percent before 1900 and then was about 20 percent in 1920–40. In Germany, the pattern differed somewhat from other countries: the public sector share started at around 30 percent in the 1850s, rose to a peak of 36 percent in 1875–79, and then fell to a range of 14 percent to 18 percent from 1885–1914. The peak coincided with a railroad boom (Reynolds 1971). Tanzi and Schuknecht (1998) compare forms of government spending in the North Atlantic other than investment before and after the war.

10. See also Nacional Financiera (1971).

11. Corporacion de Fomento de la Produccion.

12. Preferential loans were at least 50 percent of all bank loans even in the early 1980s (Ito 1984).

13. Banco Nacional de Desenvolvimento Economico e Social (the "Social" was added in 1982).

14. The weakness of development banking in Malaysia is indicated by the fact that the Malaysian Industrial Development Finance Berhad accounted in 1988 for only $292.5 million industrial loans (including short-term loans) compared with $9,391 million by commercial banks, $600.7 million by finance companies, and $895 million by merchant banks (Malaysia 1989).

15. Starting in the 1980s the International Monetary Fund prevented governments from using IMF loans to on-lend to state-owned enterprises; only private enterprises could be financed with IMF credit. For Brazil, see Monteiro Filha (1995).

16. Governments in "the rest" were typically required to give sovereign guarantees of repayment to induce private foreign lenders to provide credit to private or public domestic borrowers. Governments used such guarantees to gain control over foreign credit in order to allocate it to particular firms and industries.

17. Within Latin American governments, the distribution of public investment expenditures also heavily favored autonomous agencies and public enterprises over central, state, and municipal governments. In 1966 public enterprises and autonomous agencies accounted for 69.1 percent of government investment in Brazil, 71.4 percent in Chile, and 55.2 percent in Mexico (CEPAL 1968, as cited in Baer 1971).

18. From the viewpoint of an IMF director: ' "*cherchez le deficit.*" . . . If it is not in the central government accounts, it will be in the state-owned enterprise accounts. If not there, the central bank is likely to be running a large quasi-fiscal deficit, providing subsidized credit to farmers, or investors' (Fischer 1995, p. 24).

19. Compare these estimates of budgetary stance with those of Sachs (1989).

20. Postal savings (under the Trust Fund Bureau) accounted in the mid-1980s for around 100 percent of individual saving in deposit banks (Suzuki 1987, p. 290).

21. An industry-wide breakdown of expenditures by the Board of Investment in Thailand is not available until the 1990s.

22. In Japan, it was recognized that the type of export to be promoted should have a high income elasticity of demand by international standards and the comparative growth of technology had to be high. This led Japan to promote strongly the machinery industry, which ultimately achieved an unprecedented share of total exports by world standards (Shinohara 1982).

23. Between 1948–59 textiles each year in Mexico received around 10.7 percent of NAFINSA's total credit allocation. In the case of Malaysia, with extremely rich raw materials and a history of labor scarcity, textiles were not targeted at all. In Brazil, rather than supporting textiles, promotion went to footwear, which became a highly successful foreign exchange earner (Lücke 1990,).

24. Given that business groups in "the rest" typically did not compete against state-owned enterprises (each operated in different spheres) and could not compete head-on with multinationals (see chapter 8), domestic competition within "the rest" depended on how vigorously groups competed with one another. Intergroup competition, in turn, may be said to have depended on (1) how rapidly industry was expanding (the more rapid growth, the less need for collusion) (Amsden 1994) and (2) the ownership structure of business groups. Assuming a closed economy, the less groups held shares in one another ("cross-holdings") and the more they entered the same industries in order to maintain parity in their overall group size ("full-set" oligopoly) then the greater competition, as exemplified by the Japanese *zaibatsu* and the Korean *chaebol* (for the "full-set principle" see (Miyazaki 1980 [orig., 1965]). If all groups have mutual share holdings, and each network of groups has an affiliate in every industry, then there is less incentive for groups to pressure governments to open industries to new entrants and for a single group to diversify widely into all industries (since each group has a financial stake, however small, in every industry). Each group will also tend to be relatively small. Countries in which groups held equity ownership in each other included Argentina, Brazil, Chile, India, Indonesia, Malaysia, Mexico, Taiwan, and Thailand. In practice, full-setism may lead to oligopolistic collusion and overcapacity, as in the Japanese and Korean petrochemical and automobile industries (Hikino

1998), and cross-holdings may still be complementary with competition (in India, there was said to be "intense competition and rivalry not only among different groups to control the companies belonging to other groups, but also among the individual members of a group to control the companies of the same group. Often this competition was as ruthless as among the firms in the competitive markets" [Sandesara 1992, pp. 136–37]). Without comparative, cross-country information on industry-level market structure, the issue of domestic competition in "the rest" cannot be pursued much further. But for the 1990s, see Singh (2000) and Tybout (2000).

25. Data were collected and analyzed by Joana Behr Andrade and Dulce Correa Monteiro Filha, both of the BNDES.

26. The "own" capital requirement of a project was not always publicly known. In Korea, however, it is claimed that "entrepreneurs with little capital of their own were able to inaugurate new or expand businesses simply by applying for commercial loans and obtaining the Economic Planning Board minister's approval" (Hattori 1997, p. 464).

27. In the case of Indonesia, one of the least industrialized countries in "the rest," "the poor performance of state banks in channeling medium- and long-term credit to finance fixed investment in selected quick-yielding projects during the first two development plans showed their inexperience in this new field" (Nasution 1983, p. 67). No evidence is presented to support this presumption of technocratic inexperience, and capable technocrats existed, since those responsible for macroeconomic policies received lavish praise (Cole and Slade 1996; Hill 1996). But it is not surprising that there was incompetence if there was inexperience. For Indonesia's economic history generally, see Booth (1998).

28. See also Anderson (1963).

29. A fuller discussion of exporting appears in chapter 7.

30. See, for example, Krueger (1995), Nam (1995), and Rodrik (1995; 1996). The standard methodology of calculating export incentives was developed by Bhagwati (1972) as a way to determine whether firms faced a profitability bias in selling at home or abroad.

31. According to one Latin American assessment: "Employment effects are also insignificant—*they are generally confined to unqualified female labour [sic]*" (Fritsch and Franco 1991, p. 78, emphasis added). Some countries, however, wisely attached importance to the employment of such labor.

32. In 1996, Asia had 225 export processing zones while Latin America had only 41 (UNCTAD 1998a, p. 59).

33. The same turnover among business groups was evident in India. "Though the Tatas and Birlas have remained at the top, there has been a considerable reshuffling in the ranking of other groups in the context of the top 20 or top 75 or top any other number. Some new groups have entered, and some old groups have dropped from these numbers" (Sandesara 1992, p. 136).

34. Instead of protecting domestic parts and components production with a single omnibus tariff or quota, one that would allow final assemblers to choose which specific parts and components to source locally, local-content requirements typically specify the exact inputs that assemblers must produce domestic-

ally in order to fulfill development criteria, such as the maximization of national skills.

35. The theoretical framework used to evaluate local content rules tended to assume that performance standards by their very nature could lead to no outcome other than a distortion. Learning effects were ignored (see, for example, Grossman 1981).

36. For price controls on Mexican sugar (to keep down living costs), see Bennett and Sharpe (1982).

37. According to one study, "the price-aggressiveness of the South Koreans in international markets is attributable in significant part to Korean competitive strategy. Steel facilities are operated at a high rate of utilization, substantially reducing unit costs, while surpluses are exported at low prices with the assistance of government export promoting measures" (Howell et al. 1988).

38. Until 1987, the Korean government surveilled as many as 110 commodity prices to dampen inflation (Amsden 1989).

39. According to Korean antitrust law, monopolists and oligopolists had to hand in their cost data to the government. Then the government decided on a price. Automobiles were subject to this regulation. A Korean advisor to the government who taught at the Massachusetts Institute of Technology in Mechanical Engineering, advised the government in 1980: "Until there is reasonable competition the price of the vehicles should be regulated through tax incentives and other appropriate measures, allowing a sufficient profit margin for reinvestment and an adequate return on investment" (Suh 1980, p. 13).

Chapter 7

1. This chapter builds on an earlier examination of exporting in chapter 6.

2. To identify "openness" with the export coefficient (export share in GDP) is to take an *ex-post* approach: the actual incursion of foreign imports in domestic GNP is measured. To identify "openness" with the degree of price distortion is to take an *ex ante* approach: the potential for trade is measured if barriers come down. That potential may not be realized, as in an example provided by Edwards (1993) and Taylor (1998), to the effect that if trade barriers fall between two identical economies, trade will not increase despite greater liberalization. Ironically, Taylor (1998) uses this curious example to criticize the *ex-post* approach.

3. Instead of population density to capture the wage level effect, Kuznets (1966) uses per capita income.

4. To increase the sample size of industrialized countries, we also include data from Australia, New Zealand, South Africa, and Israel in our regressions.

5. Distortions alone accounted for only 28 percent of variability in export growth in an estimate of Dollar (1992). By contrast, they are all important in an estimate of Taylor (1998).

6. Because reexports inflated Malaysia's export share, we do not discuss Malaysia below.

7. Before export promotion was introduced in Argentina, its manufacturing sector barely exported—less than 5 percent of output, excluding meat packing

houses, sugar and flour mills, and vegetable oil producers (Katz and Kosacoff 1996).

8. "Growing 'pragmatism' at the operational level (of the World Bank) co-existed with a measure of continuing, underlying, pro-openness ideology. This was done, in part, by *caricaturizing and satanizing Prebisch and CEPAL*" (Webb 2000). For academic critiques of Prebisch's ideas, see Baer (1962), Di Marco (1972), and Flanders (1964).

9. In 1987, for example, 50 percent of imports of technology-intensive manufactures of Korea and Taiwan were obtained from Japan, compared with 40.5 percent in 1980 (Park and Park 1991).

10. In 1913, the ratio of merchandise trade to GDP was 12.5 percent in Japan and 6.1 percent in the United States (Feenstra 1998).

11. Japan had the highest percentage among North Atlantic countries of manufactures in its total exports. Intermediate manufactures that are used to produce final exports, however, are not counted in a country's export total. Assuming that inputs of intermediate manufactures tend to be greater in final manufactures than in raw material products, then the higher the percentage of manufactures in total exports, the more total exports are understated (Hollerman 1975). As late as 1990, the share of manufactures in total exports was 95 percent in Japan and only 77 percent in the United States (see table 6.9).

12. In the 1920s, "as an element of a network of international economic transactions, the Argentine Republic was positioned on the Atlantic, in-between the United States and Great Britain, *more than on the South American continent* (Fodor and A. O'Connell 1997, emphasis added, p. 9).

13. See also Latham and Kawakatsu (1994), Miller et al. (1998), and Sugiyama and Guerrero (1994).

14. For Taiwan, see also Hsiao and Hsiao (1995).

15. The progression from import substitution to export activity has been described as a "flying geese" formation (Akamatsu 1961 [1938]; Shinohara 1982).

16. It is argued that "protection provided during the 1950s and 1960s to metalworking and metallurgincal industries producing consumer durables, capital goods, and transportation equipment has been later reduced, and efficiency has evolved leading—sometimes in spite of significant antiexport policy biases—to a substantial volume of exports in the 1970s" (Teitel and Thuomi 1986, p. 486).

17. For an industry level example of import substitution generating exports, sometimes indirectly in the form of embodiment in exported final products (as discussed in chapter 8), see the chemical industry in Argentina (Chudnovsky 1994); in Brazil (Clemente de Oliveira 1994); in Korea (Enos 1988); and Taiwan (Chu 1996).

18. For the import substitution underpinnings of exporting in Taiwan's personal computer industry, see Chang (1992).

19. As relocation from high-wage countries reached Southeast Asia, the interconnections between import substitution and exporting within a single firm became even more complex. In the case of the Astra Group of Indonesia, for example, after a sharp decline in oil prices in 1983, the Indonesian government

shifted its economic policies from import substitution to exporting, and "the machinery segment of the Astra Group, which had been a typical import-substitution industry, commenced exports of certain parts, such as batteries and spark plugs, as well as (Toyota) engines and (Komatsu) forklift frames in 1988–89." Nevertheless, "the selection of export items, export volume, and destinations, generally depended on the global strategies of the Japanese principals that were the parent companies of the joint venture." As a consequence, "apart from these exports by the existing joint ventures, the Astra Group set up export-oriented machinery joint ventures with foreign companies that were newly coming into Indonesia as part of their relocation of production base." The relocations involved forging parts for heavy machinery from Japan, TV set assembly from Korea, and semiconductor assembly from Singapore (Sato 1996, p. 260).

20. For overviews of trade reforms at various different time periods, see among many others, Agosin and Tussie (1993), Bhagwati and Srinivasan (1975), Cardoso (1987), Edwards (1993), Helleiner (1995), *Journal of Developing Economies* (1994), Krueger (1995), Ocampo and Taylor (1997), Papageorgiou et al. (1991), Rodrik (1997), World Bank (1992), and Taylor (1993).

21. Concentration also characterized the manufactured exports of some North Atlantic countries before the First World War. In 1913 textiles accounted for as much as 48 percent of the United Kingdom's exports, 40 percent of France's and 49 percent of Italy's (Yates 1959).

22. Data are for 1970 except for China, whose data are for 1990.

23. No country in "the rest" came close to creating general trading companies on a par with Japan's *sogo shosha*. Korea came the closest, but even Korea's general trading companies handled mostly their own group's export business. They did not offer the diversified services offered by trading companies from Japan (Amsden 1997). "The rest" continued to struggle in the 1990s with other aspects of a trading system: administrative honesty at ports and at bureaucracies responsible for tariff rebates (duty drawbacks) and marketing in the case of small-scale firms. For Indonesia, see (Poot et al. 1990). For the role of Japanese general trading companies in Taiwan, see Chu (1989).

24. MITI refers to the Ministry of International Trade and Industry.

25. General Agreement on Tariffs and Trade.

26. When Korea and Taiwan were still protecting their cotton textile industries in the 1960s, they began promoting cotton textile exports (see chapter 6). *The right to sell in the protected domestic market, whose profitability was inflated from import barriers, was made contingent on exporting.* Taiwan used publicly regulated private cartels to enforce this, not just in cotton textiles but also in steel products, pulp and paper, rubber products, cement, woolen textiles, and later drilling machines and telephones (Wade 1990). Korea used export targets negotiated between business and government in the context of the Supreme Export Council mentioned above (Rhee et al. 1984).

27. "In many sectors, tariffs, quotas and other barriers still provided significant protection to Chinese import competing industries" (Lardy 1992, p. 710, fn. 46).

28. In 1879–81, manufactured and semimanufactured articles (excluding foodstuffs) amounted to only 16.2 percent of United States exports (Bairoch 1989).

29. Only during the war had Mexico and Brazil exported a small value of textiles to other Latin American countries (Wythe 1949).

30. Comparing exports in the United States and Brazil, "the United States, like Brazil, a large primary-product exporter with a favorable natural resource endowment, did not have a large discontinuity in its marginal comparative advantage in different export activities. By the last quarter of the nineteenth century, the United States had become a large exporter of manufactures. The key difference with Brazil seems to have been the United State's large stock of human capital, which was embodied in its industrial exports" (Leff 1982, fn. 73, p. 193).

31. Different measures of tariffs appear in (Little et al. 1970, p. 162), but the orders of magnitude are the same. See also (Minami 1994, pp. 193–94). Whatever the measure, the United States tends to have had among the world's highest tariff rates.

32. In the 1920s, "there are grounds to believe that the level of effective protection of manufacturing activities in Argentina was in fact much lower than in other 'new' countries with apparently comparable tariff height" (O'Connell 1984, p. 39).

33. In Mexico, by contrast, between 1939–61, duties as a percent of exports (11.1 percent) exceeded duties as a percent of imports (9.6 percent), showing Mexico's lack of enthusiasm for either import substitution or export promotion (Reynolds 1970). Mexico did not join the GATT until 1986 and, therefore, used nontariff barriers as well as tariffs to protect domestic industry and balance of payments. As much as 80 percent of imports after the war were estimated to have been covered by nontariff barriers (Reynolds 1970).

34. At the time, Brazil also imitated the American political model of loosely federated states (Callaghan 1981).

35. The McKinley Tariff also contained a limited reciprocity clause under which bilateral reciprocity agreements were negotiated with a number of Latin American governments. While such reciprocity laid the foundation for mutual reduction of tariffs, this experiment was short-lived because Democrats in the American Congress refused to extend the reciprocity clause a few years after. The average ad valorem equivalent of the rates of the McKinley Act "was a high 49 percent" (Dobson 1976, p. 19).

36. In Mexico, too, exports were found to be highly responsive to perceived government support for exporting (Maloney and Azvedo 1995).

37. See also Fasano-Filho et al. (1987). For export promotion policies, see Arantes Savasini (1978) and Shapiro (1997).

38. Includes the intratrade of the European Union (fifteen countries) and the European Free Trade Association (six countries) (UNCTAD 1995).

39. For South-South trade, see Amsden (1976 and 1986) and Beers (1991).

40. Laissez-faire in Switzerland did not always mean competition. "Switzerland surely belonged to the set of most cartelized states in Europe. In 1939 about 500 cartels were active in Switzerland" (Schroter 1997, p. 195).

41. As noted earlier, "Hong Kong possessed larger export quotas than Taiwan and South Korea, and especially other LDCs" (Ho and Lin 1991, p. 277).

Chapter 8

1. "Far from being irrelevant, what happens in home countries is still very important in the creation of global technological advantage for even these most internationalised firms. Little R and D occurs overseas" (Patel and Vega 1999, p. 145–55, esp. 154). Further discussion appears in a later section.

2. For the locational advantages of the home market from a business strategy and competitivness point of view, see Porter (1990).

3. This term was first used by Chandler Jr. (1990) in the context of the Second Industrial Revolution. It refers to the first entrant into an industry that is able to exploit economies of scale and scope.

4. Prewar support to nationally owned firms was negligible, but even the Tata group's affiliate in the Indian steel industry was saved from bankruptcy in the 1920s by the Raj (see chapter 4).

5. "Because of the attractive investment policies in Hsinchu Science Industrial Park, HSIP could easily be filled with companies from various kinds of industries. . . . Should that happen, however, HSIP would simply become another industrial park or Export Processing Zone. It would not be able to achieve its main objective of developing high-tech industry. To prevent this from happening, the Park Administration (under the auspices of the National Science Council) has played an active role as the 'gatekeeper' to make sure that only firms which fit the target industry list are considered" (Xue 1997, p. 750).

6. The data for 1962, 1992 and 1999 are not comparable because of changes in "industry" coverage. Figures for 1992 and 1999 include firms in airlines, banking, insurance, and other industries that earlier years do not include. Data are from various issues of *Fortune Magazine* (April). For the methodology used to compile data in 1962 and 1992, see Hikino and Amsden (1994, table 1).

7. The exchange rate of 32.13NT dollar was used to convert sales figures into U.S. dollars (Bankers Trust 1998). Acer Computers ranked tenth among desktop vendors in 1996 with sales of $4.5 billion dollars (Chandler Jr. 2000).

8. For the industries in which large firms in North Atlantic countries tend to cluster, see Chandler Jr. (1990). For comparable data for Korea, see Amsden (1989).

9. Information about Taiwan's IT industry is from Wang (1999).

10. According to one study, "All PC (personal computer) companies throughout the world face intense competition in the international markets, *but those in Taiwan have additional challenges arising from heated local rivalries*" (Chang 1992, p. 210, emphasis added).

11. Table 8.5 comprises groups with a primary, but not exclusive, focus on manufacturing.

12. The U.S. National Science Foundation estimated that in March 1992, the number of companies active in high-tech fields operating in the United States was 35 from Taiwan, 22 from Korea, 6 from India and 600 from Japan. No mention is made of firms from Latin America (United States National Science Foundation 1995). For outward foreign investments from Korea and Taiwan, and for the high incidence of business groups in this internationalization, see Van Hoesel (1997).

13. For outward investments from Argentina, Brazil, Chile, and Mexico in the late 1990s, see Chudnovsky et al. (1999).

14. For the influence of Japanese management practices on "the rest," see (Kaplinsky 1994 and 1997). For their influence on India, see Venkataramani (1990). For their influence on the Chinese automobile industry, see Lee (1995).

15. For an overview, see Lall (1993).

16. See Prasada Reddy (1993), Patel and Pavitt (1995), Doremius et al. (1998), Patel and Vega (1999), Archibugi and Michie (1997), Amsden et al. (2000), and OECD (1999).

17. Data were unavailable for China and Malaysia. Thus, only ten countries were sampled. Korea was an outlier, but in or out of the correlation estimates, the results were similar.

18. U.S. multinationals began investing in Latin America as early as the 1910s (see chapter 3). Japan also invested early in Asia, especially in the 1930s in its colonies, Korea and Taiwan (see chapter 5), but Japan lost these investments as a consequence of war, as discussed earlier.

19. In theory, multinationals had the *dis*advantage over local producers in distance from their home base, but the advantage of greater market-empowering assets (Hymer 1976) and multisite learning (Lessard and Amsden 1998).

20. Aggregate foreign ownership in Indonesia remained quite modest even after 1987, the start of a rush of foreign investors, but the aggregate data may be misleading because "most firms in the manufacturing sector have some kind of commercial involvement with foreign parties" (Hill 1996, p. 165).

21. In contrast to assembly operations, parts production almost everywhere in "the rest" was promoted by means of local content requirements (see chapter 6).

22. India's Foreign Exchange Regulation Act of 1973 defined foreign firms as those with over 40 percent foreign equity. Their entry (or expansion) into most industries was restricted, except for 100 percent export-oriented operations and cases where advanced technologies were transferred (Encarnation 1989). In India's automobile industry, localization requirements imposed by the Indian government led General Motors and Ford to pull out of India in the 1950s (Makoto Kojima, as cited by Okada 1999).

23. In Indonesia, foreign investors both before and after liberalization in 1986 faced stringent performance standards with respect to equity ownership (the formation of joint ventures was required to win government licensing), exporting, and local content. The energy sector (oil, natural gas, and coal), especially susceptible to corruption, and the banking sector, were covered by special procedures (Poot et al. 1990; Hill 1989).

24. In Korea, foreign investment laws were amalgamated into a new Foreign Investment Inducement Act in 1966, but

as the basic goals of the earlier laws were the quantitative expansion of foreign capital inducement and the introduction of advanced technology, they contained a large number of restrictive regulations. . . . The tenet of government policy in the 1970s was to induce more foreign capital, but to restrain FDI except that which was needed for the introduction of technology and know-how. Moreover, even when advanced technologies were introduced, joint ventures, technical cooperation, or royalty payments, rather than foreign direct investment, were encouraged. This is because *managerial control in key industries would be vulnerable to take-overs by foreigners in light of the size of the Korean economy.* (Lee 1998, p. 141, emphasis added)

25. In Turkey, in principle, virtually all economic sectors since 1954 were open to foreign investment. "However, a restrictive application of the relevant statutes, including controls over the transferability of profits, combined with overall economic and political instability in the late 1970's, brought direct investment flows to a trickle" (Kopits 1987, p. 11).

26. Taiwan was especially adept at using performance standards not only to obstruct the foreign investment it did not want but also to extract the best conditions from the multinational investments it did want, in terms of domestic linkages and training (Schive 1978); the semiconductor industry is discussed later in this chapter.

27. For statistics from the early 1980s on tie-ins between domestic and foreign capital, see Dunning and Cantwell (1987). For collaboration between local and foreign capital in Brazil, see also Fritsch and Franco (1991). For Mexico, see Whiting (1992). The Brazilian government reserved the production of mini- and microcomputers for national firms; otherwise, foreign companies were welcomed in the electronics industry (Sridharan 1996; Evans 1995). For the Mexican electronics industry, which was almost completely dominanted by foreign firms, see Warman (1994).

28. Income inequality may also have created a relatively large domestic market for foreign-produced luxury goods. For the effect of distribution on domestic demand, see, for example, Furtado (1963), Fishlow (1972), and Taylor and Bacha (1976). For the relationship between distribution and performance, see Bardhan et al. (2000).

29. A "soft budget constraint" refers to a SOE's ability to receive public revenues irrespective of performance (Kornai 1992).

30. Because state-owned enterprises do not necessarily aim to maximize profits, and because their costs are usually not market-determined, their performance is hard to measure. A balanced assessment of SOEs was made more difficult by ideological hostility toward them, which climaxed in the 1990s (World Bank 1994a) but began immediately after the war. In the 1950s, Washington used the leverage of foreign aid to pressure Korea and Taiwan to privatize the state-owned enterprises they had inherited from Japan. Korea briefly privatized its banking system but then reprivatized it in 1961 under President Park Chung Hee (Cole and Lyman 1971). Taiwan privatized even fewer enterprises in the 1950s than Korea, mostly a cement company (Amsden 1985).

31. The metallurgical sector in Brazil accounted for some two-thirds of the revenues and net worth and almost 90 percent of the net fixed assets of all manufacturing SOEs in 1990 (Pinheiro and Giambiagi 1994). See also Goldstein (1999).

32. Even outside heavy industry, mentoring by state enterprises was evident, as in the Indian pharmaceutical industry (Felker et al. 1997).

33. For careful comparisons of performance among SOEs in high-tech industries, see Ramamurti (1987).

34. The crucial role of good leadership in India "is illustrated by the public sector firms, especially Bharat Heavy Electricals Limited, which was 'turned around' from a sorry state of incompetence and confusion to dynamic growth by a reorganization and change in management" (Lall 1987, p. 190).

35. Interview, Belo Horizonte, October 1995.

36. Additionally, USIMINAS benefited from a first-rate technology transfer from Japan whereas COSIPAS suffered from a problematic technology transfer from Kaiser Steel Corporation (U.S.) (Taniura 1986).

37. For the economic performance of USIMINAS, and the very low costs of protection of the iron and steel industry in Brazil, see Taniura (1986).

38. By contrast, when the Wuhan Iron and Steel Company (WUSHIN) bought modern continuous casting machines from Germany in 1972, trial operation went smoothly but the machines did not attain rated capacity until 1985. This was partly due to the fact that there was no domestic steel mill with continuous casting equipment in which WUSHIN could learn, and it was not easy at that time to send engineers and technicians to study abroad (Zhou 1996, p. 19).

39. A case of "first-mover *dis*advantage" was the Argentine oil company, YPL. It was founded in the 1920s and over time became a victim of political patronage (Lewis 1990).

40. For an analysis of how the choice of second-tier firms was made in India, see Kapur (1994); for Brazil, see Clemente de Oliveira (1994) and Evans (1979).

41. See also Tran (1988).

42. For the petrochemical industry in China, see Wang and Nolan (1996). State involvement in the petrochemical industry in the North Atlantic typically confined itself to tariff protection. Tariff protection of petrochemicals was important in Japan (Hikino et al. 1998), as well as in the most precocious nineteenth-century learner, the United States, and the most backward, Russia. "For both countries (the United States and Russia) action to provide effective tariff protection was an essential precondition for a large chemical industry; without such duties western Europe would continue to supply their requirements." The difference between the two countries was simply that "Russia was above all a child of the tariff" while in the case of the American chemical industry, it was a child of "growing demand and the effects of technical change in a setting of buoyantly confident free enterprise, but further boosted by the imposition of duties" (Warren 1991, p. 158). State involvement in the petrochemical industry in "the rest" included tariff protection as well. But it also included other incentives and, as just indicated, a large organizational role due to government ownership of naphtha cracking facilities.

43. Formosa Plastics started with government help. It struggled later, however, to be given a government license to develop its own feedstocks (upstream production). See Taniura (1989).

44. The exception was YPL, but given its relatively poor performance (for the prewar years, see Lewis 1990), it was never a champion. By 2000 it was acquired by a Spanish energy company, Repos, SA.

45. Foreign investors bought only 3.4 percent of the shares of thirteen out of twenty-four Brazilian companies privatized in 1991–1993 (Banco Nactional de Desenvolvimento Economico e Social (BNDES) 1993). Later, this figure rose to around 30 percent (see chapter 9). See also Goldstein (1999).

46. For an original analysis of the *tripé* form of business (private, state, foreign), see Evans (1979).

47. In an empirical analysis of the key success factors in Taiwan's semiconductor industry, "the empirical results show that strategic industry planning and establishment of science-based industrial parks are the most important government policies that impact on the development of DRAM industry" (Yuan and Wang 1999, p. 107). For East Asia's semiconductor industries, see Mathews and Cho (2000).

48. For the Brazilian electronics industry, see Tigre (1983), Erber (1985), Adler (1987), Hobday (1990), Evans (1995), and Sridharan (1996). For foreign opposition to Brazilian policy, see Bastos (1994).

49. See also Evans (1995).

50. For Taiwan's electronics industry, see Wu (1992), Gee and Kuo (n.d.), Li (1988), Mathews (1997), Sato (1997), Schive (1995), and Wang (1999).

51. The new organization was called the Telecommunications Research Institute (ETRI). For Korea's electronics industry, see Lim (1999), Kim (1997), Ungson et al. (1997), OECD (1996a), Sridharan (1996), and Evans (1995).

52. The Malaysian strategy to catch up in electronics relied on joint ventures. In 1997, for example, three major cross-border acquisitions occurred, with American companies forming joint ventures with Malaysian companies, some already joint ventures with equity participation by Malaysia's Bank Industri. In the largest deal, at around $600 million, the American company VLSI Technologies Inc. formed a joint venture with Khazanah Nasional BHD, Bank Industri, and BI Walden International, another American company (UNCTAD 1998b).

53. Information on Brazil in this section is from Monteiro Filha (1994), unless otherwise indicated.

54. Camaçari complex only.

55. See also Lopes (1999).

56. Privatization was a means to strengthen business groups, and did so in the Brazilian steel industry. Four state-owned steel mills (Cimetal, Usiba, Cosinor, and Piratini) were sold to the Gerdau group, which allowed it to monopolize the non-flat steel market in north and northeast Brazil. Some other mills were bought by their competitors, which created a duopoly, as in Argentina (Baer and Villila 1994). Nevertheless, most privatized firms in Brazil after October 1991 did not fall into the hands of a single buyer with a manufacturing focus, as noted previously (see also Goldstein 1999).

57. Data on capital concentration by industry are unavailable for other countries to make a comparison. Nevertheless, the Korean evidence for the same period,

1973–89, while not strictly comparable, suggests that, over time, concentration at the industry level either did not rise or fell (measured by the share of output accounted for by the four largest firms) (Lee 1998). The concentration that differed the most between Brazil and Korea occurred at the *aggregate* level. Aggregate economic concentration almost certainly rose in Korea but not necessarily in Brazil.

58. In terms of brand-name recognition, Korea's top four groups were known internationally in industries ranging from automobiles to electronics (the Lotte foodstuffs brand of Korea's tenth ranking group, owned by a Japanese-Korean, was a household name in Japan) (see table 8.11). By comparison, arguably none of Brazil's top ten groups (with the exception of Embraer in aerospace) had gained global brand-name recognition in *any* manufacturing industry.

59. "... import constraints favored the rise of small and medium-sized firms of national capital. A research study based on industrial censuses indicates that between 1935 and 1954 a process of dispersion in the Argentine industry occurred, especially in the expanding sectors such as textiles, metallurgy, machinery, and electrical appliances (Goetz 1976). Industrial census data also show a diminishing share for stock companies: in 1935 stock companies accounted for 5.6 percent of all firms, but they controlled 53.8 percent of total production; in 1947 their share had decreased to 3.3 percent of all firms and to 45.2 percent of total production" (Ines Barbero 1997, p. 380).

60. The period 1953–68 has been called "a euphoric opening to foreign capital" (Schvarzer 1996, p. 221).

61. Between 1975 and 1982, industrial output fell more than 20 percent and 20 percent of the largest industrial plants closed (Azpiazu and Kossacoff 1989, as cited in Ines Barbero 1997).

62. For the history of business-government relations in Argentina, see Sabato (1988) and Lewis (1990). For a review of Latin American business history in Argentina and Brazil, see Lewis (1995).

63. Among a select group of Argentine business groups in 1992, energy and gas, food processing, steel, and automobile parts were found to be the major industries (Bisang 1996).

64. Comparing plant size of twenty-six select Argentine groups and other countries, in only three cases was Argentine plant size equal to or greater than foreign plant size (Bisang 1996).

65. In 1996, the foreign share (imports plus local production by multinational subsidiaries and affiliates) of domestic drug sales was 45 percent in Argentina, 57 percent in Brazil, 62 percent in Mexico, 49 percent in Korea (which started drug production much later than Argentina), and only 32 percent in India. Yet Argentina's domestic drug sales in 1996 were over twice those of India ($4.9 billion versus $2.2 billion) (Mourshed 1999).

66. Foreign participation (based on sales value) in privatization from 1988 through 1993 was roughly 10 percent in East Asia, 18 percent in Latin America, and nil in South Asia (Sader 1995).

67. A careful study of postprivatization performance in Mexico attributes a 24 percentage point increase in the ratio of operating income to sales to: higher prices

(10 percent); laid-off workers (33 percent), and a residual productivity (57 percent). (La Porta and Lopez-de-Silanes 1997). Part of the residual may include the gains a private firm within a group derives from access to capital and other assets within a group, including distribution outlets, shared skills, and so forth.

68. Data from NAFINSA were kindly supplied by Jorge Mario de Soto for 1935–97.

69. The BOI in Thailand constrained the growth of large-scale firms by denying breaks to firms that added capacity through acquiring existing firms or adding to the capacity of existing plants (see chapter 1).

70. According to one account of Malaysia's heavy industry:

the model for this attempted second stage of import-substituting industrialization was South Korea. . . . The emulation of South Korea was consistent with the 'Look East' strategy, which the Malaysian government adopted under the leadership of Prime Minister Mahathir Mohamad from the early 1980s. The government's objectives, *inter alia*, included the development of a capital goods sector. . . . In the Malaysian context, 'heavy industrialization' meant setting up a hot briquetted iron and steel billets plant, two additional cement plants, the Proton (state-owned) national car project, three motorcycle engine plants, a petroleum refining and petrochemical project, and a pulp and paper mill. (Jomo 1997, p. 101)

71. Korea's *chaebol* arose out of the rent seeking and business opportunities surrounding American aid allocation and distribution of Japanese-owned factories in the 1950s (Jones and Sakong 1980; Hattori 1997; Amsden 1997). The background of many groups in Taiwan was similar and involved "refugee capitalists" from the mainland, former Taiwanese landowners and Taiwanese merchants (Numazaki 1986). In Malaysia, early groups emerged out of the plantation and mining operations of British "agency houses" or merchant banks, such as Sime Darby (Hui 1981; Puthucheary 1979). In Indonesia, groups had *pribumi* (indigenous), military-bureaucratic and especially Chinese origins, stemming from trade, finance, and distribution (Kano 1989; Schwarz 1994). In Thailand, traditional business groups arose out of trade, rice milling, and commercial banking, while a new elite emerged in the 1960s in conjunction with import substitution (Suehiro 1985). Similarly in Turkey, big industrial groups (such as Koc and Sabanci) emerged out of import substitution (Onis 1993). In India, the British managing agency system (see chapter 4) proved to be "ideally suited to the Hindu joint family system in India," and provided the basis for the formation of modern diversified business groups by the middle of the nineteenth century, such as the Tatas and Birlas (Herdeck and Piramal 1985, p. 6; Yonekawa 1986). In Latin America the prewar group often took the form of familially unconnected merchant émigrés banding together and diversifying into many activities to reduce risk, as in Brazil, Chile, and Mexico. Over time such business associations often fell into the hands of a single family (see chapter 4). Argentina's groups evolved in two distinct periods, the first (1860–1930) associated with agro-exports (such as Bunge y Born) and the second (1930–60) associated with import-substitution (such as Siam di Tella) (Ines Barbero 1997). In Brazil, groups moved into industry

via commerce (Evans 1979, p. 108). Groups began to emerge in China after the onset of economic reforms in 1978, established by local governments (Walder 1995), the military (Nolan 1996), and SOEs (for the Shougang Capital Iron and Steel Company, see Steinfeld [1998]). For a treatise on groups in general, see Granovetter (1995). For "the rest," see Hikino and Amsden (1994).

72. For the views of an architect of Korea's heavy industrialization drive, see (O 1995).

73. (Park 1963) chose the Meiji fathers as his model over Sun Yat Sen, Kemal Pasha, and Gamel Abdul Nasser.

74. For the tension between egalitarianism and authoritarianism in Korean culture, see Brandt (1986). For studies of Korean income distribution, see Leipziger (1992) and the World Bank (1993). Over the half century after World War II, Korean income distribution supposedly did not become substantially more unequal. Aggregate economic concentration, however, certainly rose. Koreans also perceived large regional inequalities: the Taegu region was regarded as being politically privileged and the Cholla region was recognized as being relatively poor. In fact, regional income inequalities in Korea were very low compared with those in Argentina, Brazil, China, Mexico, and India (data, from national census estimates, are for the 1980s and 1990s and may be sensitive to the way a regions is defined).

75. For Taiwan, see Amsden (1991).

76. The Samsung group in Korea, for example, structured itself so as to maximize a flow of information among affiliates. Recruitment of managers occurred at the group level, where intensive training also occurred. Then new managers were assigned to different affiliates, insuring that no affiliate fell below a minimum managerial standard and that close ties were forged between managers of a certain age group, all of whom had gone through training together (Amsden 1989; Kang 1997).

77. For general studies of education in "the rest," see Ashton and Green (1996), Birdsall and Sabot (1993), Koike and Inoki (1990), McMahon (1999), Ranis et al. (2000), and Psacharopoulos (1994). For comparisons with earlier industrializations, see Tortella (1990).

78. Because firm-level and government R&D in "the rest" was initially oriented toward solving production problems, the early composition of R&D tended to be broader than in the North Atlantic. Hence, the legitimacy of generalizing from R&D to all of S&T. For the initial production-orientation of R&D in Japan, see Ozawa (1974).

79. There were reputed to be "important R&D expenditures" in a number of Mexican firms in areas such as petrochemicals, chemicals, consumer products, steel, and communications (TELMEX). Many of these firms were "part of a larger holding company or industrial group." The Grupo Desc, for example, which ranked tenth in table 8.11 and was one of the few Mexican groups with a core competency in manufacturing, allegedly invested 4.1 percent of its net sales in R&D (OECD 1994b, p. 117).

80. For a discussion of the (positive) effects of R&D incentives on R&D spending in Taiwan, see Wang and Tsai (1995) and San (1995).

81. To encourage reverse brain drain both Korea and Taiwan introduced aggressive government policies in the 1980s to woo well-educated scientists and engineers back home to work in both the public and private sectors. For Korea, see Hentges (1975), Yoon (1992), and Kim (1997).

Chapter 9

1. Thailand's and Indonesia's investments in tertiary and engineering education rose rapidly in the 1980s (see table 8.13). In the 1990s, however, Thailand's educational investments were evaluated as inadequate for a long-term "make" strategy (see Lall 1998). Malaysia had begun constructing a "multimedia corridor," a large government R&D initiative to promote the build-up of Malaysia's knowledge-based assets. It was designed along the same lines as Taiwan's Hsinchu Science Park but also contained a Multimedia University. Simultaneously, the private sector began to consider the founding of an engineering college with assistance from the Massachusetts Institute of Technology.

2. "The rest" became a direct target for financial market opening in the 1990s insofar as Japan's financial markets had been opened under pressure much earlier, in the 1970s (Suzuki 1987).

3. The shift in emphasis in American foreign economic policy, from free trade in manufactures to free trade in services, is suggested by the bilateral "Financial Policy Talks" held between the United States and Korea from the late 1980s to 1997, when Korea's financial markets crashed (Fall 1995). The talks began over Korea's large merchandise trade surplus with the United States. The U.S. Treasury became involved because American trade negotiators believed that the Korean currency, the won, was undervalued. In response to pressures to appreciate the won, the Korean government opened the door to financial market liberalization in the belief that more open financial markets might keep the won from becoming too strong, which was perceived as a threat to Korea's exports. As negotiations shifted to financial markets, U.S. demands for market opening extended beyond the Korean government's original intent. The United States also held bilateral financial policy talks with Taiwan and China, and, by law, regularly surveyed the openness of foreign financial markets to American financial institutions (see United States, Department of the Treasury 1994).

4. There is a rich literature on the politics of liberalization and structural adjustment. See, for example, Haggard and Webb (1994), Kahler (1995), and Stallings (1992).

5. See, for example, Fishlow (1991), Ros (1994), Sachs (1989), and Taylor (1988).

6. For liberalization in Latin America, see Diaz Alejandro (1985); for liberalization in East Asia, see Fry and Murinde (1998), UNCTAD (1998), Rodelet and Sachs (1998), Wade (1998), Chang (1998), and Patrick and Park (1994). For the case for capital controls, see Eatwell and Taylor (2000).

7. *The Economist* magazine's front cover as early as August 21–27, 1999, ran the headline "Asia's Astonishing Bounce-back."

8. For one of the harshest attacks on developmentalism, see (World Bank 1991). For greater tolerance on the part of the World Bank toward developmentalism in an earlier period, see Kim (1997) for Korea and Urzua (1997) for Mexico.

9. The North Atlantic powers pried open Japan's markets in the 1850s and 1860s, but then a period of benign neglect gave Japan a "breathing space" (Norman 1940, p. 46). The benign neglect enjoyed by "the rest" (except China) immediately after World War II derived from the preoccupation of the North Atlantic powers with first liberalizing each other's markets. Thus, "at the Inter-American Conference on Problems of War and Peace held in Mexico in 1945 (known as the Chapultepec Conference), the United States proposed a general approach to international trade problems, *embracing free trade in the broadest sense.*" Yet world opinion was such that developing countries could resist this call, even countries most closely tied to the United States economically. Mexico and other Latin American countries maintained "firm opposition" to the Chapultepec charter (Izquierdo 1964, p. 264, emphasis added). For the World Bank's early support of developmentalism, see Gwin (1997).

10. Under a "Super 301" trade clause, the American judicial system prosecuted countries suspected of trade infractions. Of 95 "Super 301" cases tried between 1975 and 1995, Korea accounted for nine; Taiwan, Argentina and Brazil each accounted for five (Low 1993).

11. See, for example, Corbo and Fischer (1995), Fischer (1995), Khan (1993), Krueger (1995), Little (1982), Thomas et al. (1991), and World Bank (1991). Williamson (1990) is credited with the term "Washington Consensus." Singh (1994) evaluates the World Bank's "market friendly" approach.

12. World Bank structural adjustment loans (with liberal conditionalities) were intended to support a country's balance of payments after its industries had been opened to foreign competition. Only a very small number of loans was designed to help a country actually restructure its industries to make them more competitive by reducing excess capacity and modernizing plant and equipment (Mosley, et al. 1991; Toye 1995). This restructuring was to be left to market forces.

13. The index was developed by the United Nations Industrial Development Organization. The usage here follows that of Moreno-Brid (1998).

14. For other studies that come down on the side of efficiency in latecomers' manufacturing sector, see Singh (2000) and Tybout (2000).

15. The benchmark is an average of industrial structures in the North Atlantic and Japan. Hopefully, this average (of roughly thirty countries) irons out intercountry differences in natural resources and other endowments that may be expected to influence the composition of manufacturing industry. We focus only on industries with major differences in shares between the North Atlantic and "the rest" and then see what type of change occurred between 1980 and 1995. The criteria for selection was a difference of one percentage point or greater between "the rest" and the North Atlantic in either 1980 or 1995.

16. "Electrical machinery," however, is a highly heterogeneous category and includes many low-tech assembly operations as well as high-tech market segments at the world technological frontier.

17. We have relied on measures of structural change rather than measures of total factor productivity growth in the belief that it is very difficult to estimate changes in capital, productivity, and even labor accurately at the aggregate level in countries where firm-level and even plant-level product composition and production techniques are rapidly changing. Possibly for this reason, even the most careful estimates of total factor productivity (TFP) growth sometimes contradict one another or are counterintuitive. For contradictory results (based on the same data), see, for example, World Bank (1993) and Kwon (1994). For a sample of sixty-six countries, the annual growth of total factor productivity between 1970–85 was highest in the unlikely cases of Egypt, Pakistan, Botswana, the Congo, and Malta. Countries with the lowest productivity growth, from the bottom up, were Switzerland, Fiji, Sri Lanka, Singapore, and India (Young 1994). For an overview of TFP studies in East Asia, see Felipe (1999).

18. Effective rates of protection are required in order to make accurate estimates of trade barriers, but are extremely time-consuming to measure. "The rest's" reputation before the mid-1980s for high *nominal tariffs*, at any rate, is probably exaggerated, based on a one-time set of estimates published in a landmark study (Little et al. 1970), immediately after which nominal tariffs appear to have come down sharply. In Argentina and Brazil, for example, average nominal tariffs in 1960–65 were estimated to be 148.8 percent and 85 percent, respectively. By 1967–70 they had come down to 36 percent and 37 percent, respectively (Ground 1988) (see table 3.3). Even effective tariffs, which presumably include nontariff barrier equivalents, were low for both Taiwan and Mexico: 27 percent in Mexico (1960) and 33 percent in Taiwan (1966) (Little et al. 1970).

19. The "Uruguay" round refers to the trade negotiations that gave rise to the World Trade Organization (WTO) in 1994.

20. Reforms in "the rest" in the 1990s were increasingly equated by the North Atlantic with foreign investment. A review in the *New York Times* of Korean reforms, for example, noted: "There are also signs that reforms are taking hold. Both Commerzbank of Germany and Goldman, Sachs have successfully invested in South Korean banks. Royal Philips Electronics of the Netherlands recently announced an investment equivalent to $1.6 billion, the largest ever by a foreign company in South Korea" (Strom 1999, p. C6).

21. The steel industry accounted for roughly 40 percent of all antidumping cases in 1998. Anti-dumping data were collected by the London law firm Row and Maw.

22. Trade-related aspects of intellectual property rights (TRIPs) were a whole other new area of regulation, designed to protect rather than liberalize access to proprietary know-how. The United States placed TRIPs on the WTO agenda: "Just before the Uruguay round an American *enquête* among industries cited intellectual property rights as the biggest problem when investing in other countries" (Knutrud 1994, p. 193). By 2000 the effect of TRIPs was still unknown, but much feared by developing countries, especially those with large pharmaceutical industries, which circumvented patents to produce and deliver drugs locally at below-world prices (see Mourshed 1999). There was also a movement afoot to regulate international business practices (Malaguti 1998).

23. After demonstrations in Seattle in December 1999 against a meeting of the WTO, further liberalization of foreign investment and trade was frustrated, if only temporarily.

24. Discipline from exogenous rules of behavior began to spread. Argentina (and then Ecuador) adopted a currency board which made the peso and dollar interchangeable currencies. Chile sought to join NAFTA and establish free-trade agreements with East Asia.

25. The stock of FDI in developing countries in the late 1990s was heavily concentrated in China, Mexico, Malaysia, Brazil, Argentina, Indonesia, Thailand, and Chile, in descending order of importance (OECD 1998). On a per capita basis (population data are for 1995 from table 1.6), these FDI stocks amounted to $1630 in Malaysia (population, 19,615 million), $710 in Chile, $648 in Argentina, $429 in Mexico, $237 in Thailand, $145 in Brazil, $130 in China, and $105 in Indonesia.

26. A foreign direct investment may take the form of a merger or an acquisition on the one hand, and a greenfield investment on the other. In the case of an M&A, foreign control can either be majority or minority. If the latter, it is considered a "portfolio investment" on the part of the buyer (UNCTAD 1998b).

27. Cross-country data for the 1990s appear to be unavailable on the percentage of joint ventures in total greenfield foreign investments, but country-specific data strongly suggest that joint ventures were on the rise in general.

28. The data exist for a very short time period and lack consistency across countries. All data points are not available for all countries in all categories. Nor in 1990 were all countries equally diversified. Hence, their capacity for mergers and acquisitions differed.

29. In 1990, China's population was almost eight times greater than Brazil's, its GNP (assuming it was correctly measured) was .66 times greater, and the value of its M&As was 3.5 times greater. The low value of M&As in Turkey may reflect the late start of such transactions.

30. A Chinese journal, *Economic Theory and Business Management*, stated in 1989 (January 28, pp. 44–49):

> Study and discussion of the development and present situation of Japan's enterprise groups is of very great theoretical and practical significance for the development of China's enterprise groups.... The development of Japan's enterprise groups has from beginning to end received policy and economic support and assistance from the Japanese government.... Now, China is facing a crucial period of economic system reform and economic takeoff, and enterprise groups should also play an enormous role in the development of China's economy.... Japan's experience in this area is worth using as a reference. There must also be specialized governmental departments to plan and formulate industrial policy, apply persuasion, and guide the industrial direction of enterprises (especially enterprise groups), as well as supervise and promote the implementation by enterprises of the state's economic policy. (Cited in Johnson 1996).

31. For some mergers in the knitwear and machine tool industries, see Yatsko (1996).

32. In the mid-1950s, General Motors and Ford closed down their operations in India (which had been established in the late 1920s and early 1930s, respectively) in response to government insistence on gradual localization of production, (Makoto Kojima, as cited by Okada 1999).

33. Although foreign investments (up to 51 percent ownership) were given automatic approval in thirty-four industries starting in 1991, by 1994 the Indian government announced that preference would be given to joint ventures. In 1995, however, the Foreign Investment Promotion Board approved a 100 percent Hyundai investment in exchange for a promise of 98 percent localization by 2000.

34. Ten industries were identified as having excess capacity or duplicative investments. Of these ten, seven priority industries were identified for downsizing: semiconductors, automobiles, aerospace, train car manufacturing, power plant equipment/vessel engines, and oil refining. Some of these industries, such as automobiles and power plant equipment, were also targeted for downsizing in 1980.

35. Ironically, banking was the first sector to become more concentrated partly as a consequence of IMF conditionalities requiring the liquidation of weaker banks. Mergers among seven large commercial banks created four mega-banks and triggered a merger wave among nonbanking financial institutions as well. Almost immediately after the collapse of the Korean won, five out of thirty-three banks had their licenses suspended and sixteen out of thirty merchant banks had their licenses revoked.

36. The Federation of Korean Industries (FKI), the association of big business, was "strongly opposed" to the government's reform policies in the late 1990s. It made "harsh comments" about the government's prohibition of the chaebols' mutual loan guarantee practices and government's targeting of a debt/equity ratio of 200 percent. The report of the FKI warned that high unemployment and another credit crunch would result (Yoo 1998).

37. For Argentina, see Katz and Bercovich (1993), Correa (1998) and Republica Argentina (1998); for Brazil, see Dahlman and Frischtak (1993) and Etzkowitz and Brisolla (1999); for Latin America in general, see Alcorta and Peres (1998).

38. Four HAN projects fell into the product technology category: new agrochemicals, broad band-integrated service digital networks, high definition television, and next-generation vehicle technology. Seven projects fell into the fundamental technology category: next-generation semiconductors, advanced manufacturing systems, new functional bio-materials, environmental technology, new energy technology, next-generation nuclear reactors, and advanced materials for information, electronics, and energy. In addition to these projects, S&T in Korea in the 1990s involved more centralized coordination (to avoid duplication by competing ministries), a 1997 law ("Special Law for the Promotion of S&T Innovation") to expedite R&D within a five-year period, and the internationalization of R&D activity (see Cho and Amsden 1999; Cho and Kim 1997; Kim and Yi 1997; Lim 1999; and OECD 1996a).

39. For U.S. S&T policy, see Center for Science and International Affairs (n.d.) and Mowery and Rosenberg (1993); for the United Kingdom, see Cunningham (1998); for Europe, see the entries in Lundvall (1992) and Nelson (1993).

40. For the old system, see Wang (1993) and Saich (1989), who also discusses reforms in the 1980s.

41. For spillovers, see Aitken et al. (1997), Blömstrom and Kokko (1998), Borensztein et al. (1998), Chan (1998), Chuang and Lin (1999), Cohen and Levinthal (1989), and Love and Lago-Hidalgo (1999).

Chapter 10

1. O'Brien (1991, p. 33), in his inaugural lecture at the University of London. He refers to the work of Silbner (1972).

References

Abe, M., and M. Kawakami (1997). "A Distributive Comparison of Enterprise Size in Korea and Taiwan." *The Developing Economies* 25(4): 382–400.

Abreu, M., et al. (1997). *Import Substitution and Growth in Brazil, 1890s–1970s.* Rio de Janeiro: Pontificia Universidade Catolica do Rio de Janeiro.

Ades, A., and R. Di Tella (1999). "Rents, Competition, and Corruption." *American Economic Review* 89(4): 982–993.

Adler, E. (1987). *The Power of Ideology: The Quest for Technological Autonomy in Argentina and Brazil.* Berkeley: University of California Press.

Agarwala, P. N. (1986). "The Development of Managerial Enterprises in India." In *Development of Managerial Enterprise.* Ed. K. Kobayashi and H. Morikawa. Tokyo: University of Tokyo Press. 12: 235–257.

Agosin, M., and D. Tussie, eds. (1993). *Trade Policy for Development in a Globalizing World.* Aldershot: Macmillan.

Ahlstrom, G. (1993). "Technical Competence and Industrial Performance: Sweden in the Nineteenth and Early Twentieth Centuries." In *Education and Training in the Development of Modern Corporations.* Ed. N. Kawabe and E. Daito. Tokyo: University of Tokyo Press. 19: 196–218.

Ahluwalia, I. J. (1985). *Industrial Growth in India: Stagnation since the Mid-Sixties.* Delhi: Oxford University Press.

Aitken, B., et al. (1997). "Spillovers, Foreign Investment and Export Behavior." *Journal of International Economics* 43: 103–32.

Akamatsu, K. (1961 [1938]). "A Theory of Unbalanced Growth in the World Economy." *Weltwirtschalftliches Archiv* 2.

Akhtar Aziz, Z. (1984). "Financial Institutions and Markets in Malaysia." In *Financial Insitutions and Markets in Southeast Asia.* Ed. M. T. Skully. London: Macmillan. 110–166.

Alcorta, L., and W. Peres (1998). "Innovation Systems and Technological Specialization in Latin America and the Caribbean." *Research Policy* 26: 857–881.

Allen, G. C., and A. G. Donnithorne (1954). *Western Enterprise in Far Eastern Economic Development: China and India.* New York: Macmillan.

——— (1957). *Western Enterprise in Indonesia and Malaya.* London: George Allen and Unwin.

Alvarez, C. (1993). "La Corporación de Fomento de la Producción y al Transformación de la Industria Manufacturera Chilena." In *La Transformación de la Producción en Chile: Cuatro Ensayos de Interpretacion.* Ed. CEPAL. Santiago, Chile: Naciones Unidas Comision Económica Para América Latina y el Caribe. 63–148.

Amsden, A. H. (1976). "Trade in Manufactures between Developing Countries." *Economic Journal* 86: 778–790.

——— (1977). "The Division of Labor Is Limited by the 'Type' of Market: The Taiwanese Machine Tool Industry." *World Development* (5): 217–234.

——— (1985). "Taiwan's State and Economic Development." In *Bringing the State Back In.* Ed. P. Evans, D. Rueschemeyer, and T. Skocpol. Cambridge: Cambridge University Press.

——— (1986). "The Direction of Trade—Past and Present—and the 'Learning Effects' of Exports to Different Directions." *Journal of Development Economics* 24: 282–286.

——— (1989). *Asia's Next Giant: South Korea and Late Industrialization.* Oxford: Oxford University Press.

——— (1991). "Big Business and Urban Congestion in Taiwan: The Origins of Small Enterprise and Regionally-Decentralized Industry (Respectively)." *World Development* 19(9): 1121–1135.

——— (1994). "The Spectre of Anglo-Saxonization Is Haunting South Korea." In *Korea's Political Economy: An Institutional Perspective.* Ed. L.-J. Cho and Y. H. Kim. Boulder, Colo: Westview. 87–125.

——— (1997a). "Korea: Enterprising Groups and Entrepreneurial Government." In *Big Business and the Wealth of Nations.* Ed. Alfred D. Chandler Jr., F. Amatori, and T. Hikino. New York: Cambridge University Press. 336–367.

——— (1997b). "Manufacturing Capabilities: Hong Kong's New Engine of Growth." In *Made by Hong Kong.* Ed. S. Berger and R. Lester. Hong Kong: Oxford University Press.

Amsden, A. H., and W.-W. Chu (2003). *Beyond Late Development: Taiwan's Upgrading Policies.* Cambridge, Mass.: MIT Press.

Amsden, A. H., and Y.-d. Euh (1995). "A Study on the Business Restructuring of Korean Firms." Seoul: Korea Economic Research Center.

Amsden, A. H., and T. Hikino (1994). "Project Execution Capability, Organizational Know-how and Conglomerate Corporate Growth in Late Industrialization." *Industrial and Corporate Change* 3(1): 111–147.

Amsden, A. H., and R. van der Hoeven (1996). "Manufacturing Output, Employment and Real Wages in the 1980s: Labour's Loss until the Century's End." *Journal of Development Studies* 32(4): 506–523.

Amsden, A. H., and J.-Y. Kang (1995). "Learning to Be Lean in an Emerging

Economy: The Case of South Korea." Cambridge, Massachusetts Institute of Technology, International Motor Vehicle Program.

Amsden, A. H., and L. Kim (1985). "A Comparative Analysis of Local and Transnational Corporations in the Korean Automobile Industry." In *Management behind Industrialization: Readings in Korean Business*. Ed. D.-K. Kim and L. Kim. Seoul: Korea University Press: 579–596.

Amsden, A. H., and M. Mourshed (1997). "Scientific Publications, Patents and Technological Capabilities in Late-Industrializing Countries." *Technology Analysis and Strategic Management* 9(3): 343–359.

Amsden, A. H., and A. Singh (1994). "The Optimal Degree of Competition and Dynamic Efficiency in Japan and Korea." *European Economic Review* 38(3/4): 941–951.

Amsden, A. H., et al. (2000). *The Measurable Properties of R&D: Classification of Activity for International Comparisons*. Tokyo: Asian Development Bank Institute.

Anderson, C. W. (1963). "Bankers As Revolutionaries." In *The Political Economy of Mexico*. Ed. W. P. J. Glade and C. W. Anderson. Madison: University of Wisconsin Press.

Anthony, R. N., and V. Govindarajan (1995). *Management Control Systems*. Chicago: Irwin.

Aoki, M., et al., eds. (1997). *The Role of Government in East Asian Economic Development*. Oxford: Clarendon Press.

Arantes Savasini, J. A. (1978). *Export Promotion: The Case of Brazil*. New York: Praeger.

Archibugi, D., and J. Michie, eds. (1997). *Technology, Globalisation and Economic Performance*. Cambridge: Cambridge University Press.

Asian Development Bank (1990). *Malaysia: Study on Small and Medium Enterprises with Special Reference to Technology Development*. Manila: Asian Development Bank.

Ashton, D., and F. Green (1996). *Education, Training and the Global Economy*. Cheltenham, U.K., Edward Elgar.

Azpiazu, D., and B. Kossacoff (1989). *La industria argentina. Desarrollo y cambios estructurales*. Buenos Aires: Centro Editor de América Latina.

Baer, W. (1962). "The Economics of Prebisch and ECLA." *Economic Development and Cultura Change* 10: 169–182.

——— (1965). *Industrialization and Economic Development in Brazil*. Homewood, Ill.: R. D. Irwin.

——— (1969). *The Development of the Brazilian Steel Industry*. Nashville, Tenn.: Vanderbilt University Press.

——— (1971). "The Role of Government Enterprises in Latin America's Industrialization." In *Fiscal Policy for Industrializaton and Development in Latin America*. D. T. Geithman. Gainesville, Fla.: University of Florida Book. 263–292.

——— (1995). *The Brazilian Economy: Growth and Development*. Westport: Praeger Publishers.

Baer, W., and A. V. Villila (1994). "Privatization and the Changing Role of the State in Brazil." In *Privatization in Latin America: New Roles for the Public and Private Sectors.* Ed. W. Baer and M. H. Birch. Westport, Conn.: Praeger: 1–19.

Bagchi, A. K. (1972). *Private Investment in India, 1900–1939.* Cambridge: Cambridge University Press.

——— (1976). "De-industrialisation in Gangetic Bihar, 1809–1901." In *Essays in Honour of Professor Susobhan Chandra Sarkar.* Ed. B. De. New Delhi: People's Publishing House: 499–522.

Bahl, R., et al. (1986). *Public Finance during the Korean Modernization Process.* Cambridge, Mass.: Harvard University Press.

Bairoch, P. (1989). "European Trade Policy, 1815–1914." In *The Cambridge History of Modern Europe.* Ed. P. Mathias and S. Pollard. New York: Cambridge University Press. 8: 1–160.

——— (1993). *Economics and World History: Myths and Paradoxes.* Chicago: University of Chicago Press.

Balassa Bela and Associates (1982). *The Structure of Protection in Developing Countries.* Baltimore, Md.: Johns Hopkins University Press.

Banco Nacional de Desenvolvimento Economico e Social (BNDES) (1992). *BNDES, 40 years. An Agent of Change.* Rio de Janeiro: BNDES.

——— (1993). *Brazilian Privatization Program.* Rio de Janeiro: BNDES.

——— (various years). *Estadísticas.* Rio de Janeiro: Banco Nacional de Desenvolvimento Economico e Social.

Banerjee, A. K. (1963). *India's Balance of Payments: Estimates of Current and Capital Accounts from 1921–22 to 1938–39.* Bombay: Asia Publishing House.

Bank Indonesia (1996). *Report for the Financial Year 1995/96.* Jakarta: Bank Indonesia.

Bank Negara Malaysia (various years). *Annual Report.* Kuala Lampur.

Bank of Korea (1993). *The Financial System of Korea.* Seoul.

——— (1995a). *Economic Statistics Yearbook.* Seoul.

——— (1995b). *Statistics of the Bank of Korea.* (Diskette). Seoul.

——— (various years). *Financial Statement Analysis.* Seoul.

Bankasi, T. S. K. (various years). *Annual report.* Ankara, Turkey: Turkiye Sinai Kalkinma Bankasi.

Bankers Trust (1998). "Taiwan Electronics Companies: Built to Withstand Adversity." *Asia Window* (October): 22–26.

Bardhan, P., et al. (2000). "Relationship between Economic Inequality and Economic Performance." In *Handbook of Income Distribution.* Ed. A. B. Atkinson and F. Bourguignon. Rotterdam: North-Holland.

Barkey, H. J. (1990). *The State and the Industrialization Crisis in Turkey.* Boulder, Colo.: Westview.

Bastos, M. I. (1994). "How International Sanctions Worked: Domestic and Foreign Political Constrains on the Brazilian Informatics Policy." *Journal of Development Studies* 30(2): 380–404.

Baumann, R., and H. C. Moreira (1987). "Os Incentivos as Exportacoes Brasileiras de Produtos Manufacturados—1969/85." *Pesquisa e Planejamento Economico* 17: 471–490.

Baysan, T., and C. Blitzer (1990). "Turkey's Trade Liberalization in the 1980s and Prospects for Its Sustainability." In *The Political Economy of Turkey.* Ed. T. Aricanli and D. Rodrik. Basingstoke, U.K.: Macmillan. 9–36.

Becker, W. H. (1982). *The Dynamics of Business-Government Relations: Industry and Exports, 1893–1921.* Chicago: University of Chicago.

Beers, C. V. (1991). *Exports of Developing Countries: Differences between South-South and South-North Trade and Their Implications for Economic Development.* Amsterdam: Tinbergen Institute.

Bennett, D., and K. Sharpe (1982). "The State as Banker and Entrepreneur: The Last Resort Character of the Mexican State's Economic Intervention, 1917–1970." In *Brazil and Mexico: Patterns in Late Development.* Ed. S. A. Hewlett and R. S. Weinert. Philadelphia: Institute for the Study of Human Issues. 169–211.

——— (1985). *Transnational Corporations versus the State: The Political Economy of the Mexican Auto Industry.* Princeton, N.J., Princeton University Press.

Bergere, M.-C. (1983). "The Chinese Bourgeoisie, 1911–37." In *The Cambridge History of China.* Ed. J. K. Fairbank. Cambridge: Cambridge University Press. Vol. 12, Republican China 1912–1949, part 1.

Bethell, L., ed. (1995). *The Cambridge History of Latin America.* Cambridge: Cambridge University Press.

Bhagwati, J. (1972). "Trade Policies for Development." In *The Gap Between Rich and Poor Nations: Proceedings of a Conference Held by the International Economic Association at Bled, Yugoslavia.* Ed. Gustav Ranis. London: Macmillan.

——— (1988). *Protectionism.* Cambridge, Mass.: MIT Press.

Bhagwati, J., and S. Chakravarty (1969). "Contribution to Indian Economic Analysis: A Survey." *American Economic Review* 59 (Supplement) (4, part 2): 1–73.

Bhagwati, J., and H. T. Patrick (1990). *Aggressive Unilateralism: America's 301 Trade Policy and the World Trading System.* New York: Harvester Wheatsheaf.

Bhagwati, J. N., and T. N. Srinivasan (1975). *Foreign Trade Regimes and Economic Development: India.* New York: National Bureau of Economic Research.

Bils, M. (1984). "Tariff Protection and Production in the Early U.S. Cotton Textile Industry." *Journal of Economic History* 44(4): 1033–1045.

Birchal, S. de Oliveira (1999). *Entrepreneurship in Nineteenth Century Brazil.* New York: St. Martin's.

Birdsall, N., and R. H. Sabot (1993). *Virtuous Circles: Human Capital Growth and Equity in East Asia: Background Paper for the East Asian Miracle.* Washington, D.C.: World Bank, Policy Research Department.

Bisang, R. (1996). "Perfil Tecno-Productivo de los Grupos Económìcos en la Industrial Argentina." In *Establization Macroeconómica, Reforma Estructural y Comportamiento Industrial.* Ed. J. M. Katz. Buenos Aires: Alianza Editorial for CEPAL/IDRC: 377–478.

Blair, C. P. (1964). "Nacional Financiera: Entrepreneurship in a Mixed Economy." In *Public Policy and Private Enterprise in Mexico*. Ed. R. Vernon. Cambridge, Mass.: Harvard University Press. 191–240.

Blömstrom M., and A. Kokko (1998). "Foreign Investment As a Vehicle for International Technology Transfer." In *Creation and Transfer of Knowledge: Institutions and Incentives*. Ed. G. Barba Navaretti, P. Dasgupta, K.-G. Maler, and D. Siniscalco. Berlin: Springer. 279–311.

Bonelli, R. (1992). "Fontes de Crescimento e Competitividade das Exportacoes Brasileiras na Decada de 80." *Revista Braseileira de Comercio Exterior* (April–June).

Booth, A. (1998). *The Indonesian Economy in the Nineteenth and Twentieth Centuries: A History of Missed Opportunities*. New York: St. Martin's.

Boratav, K., et al. (1985). "Ottoman Wages and the World-Economy, 1839–1913." *Review* 8(3): 379–406.

Borensztein, E., et al. (1998). "How Does Foreign Direct Investment Affect Economic Growth?" *Journal of International Economics* 45: 115–135.

Bowonder, B. (1998). "Competitive and Technology Management Strategy: A Case Study of TELCO." *International Journal of Technology Management* 15(6/7): 646–680.

Bowring, S. J. (1857). *The Kingdom and People of Siam*. London.

Brandt, V. (1986). Korea. *Ideology and Competitiveness: An Analysis of Nine Countries*. Ed. G. C. Lodge and E. F. Vogel. Boston: Harvard Business School Press.

Brazil, Government of (various years). *Anuario Estatistico Do Brasil*. Rio de Janeiro: Ministerio do Planejamento e Coordenacao Geral.

Bruland, K. (1989). *British Technology and European Industrialisation: The Norwegian Textile Industry in the Mid-nineteenth Century*. Cambridge: Cambridge University Press.

Bruton, H. J. (1998). "A Reconsideration of Import Substitution." *Journal of Economic Literature* 36(2): 903–936.

Bulmer-Thomas, V. (1994). *The Economic History of Latin America Since Independence*. Cambridge: Cambridge University Press.

Business Korea (1999). "Industry Refuses to Be Fixed." *Business Korea* (January): 32–33.

Business Standard (1995). "BS 1000." In *Business Standard*. Calcutta.

Cairncross, A. K. (1962). *Factors in Economic Development*. New York: Frederick A. Praeger.

Callaghan, W. (1981). "Obstacles to Industrialization: The Iron and Steel Industry in Brazil during the Old Republic." Ph.D. dissertation, University of Texas, Austin.

Cameron, R. (1993). *A Concise Economic History of the World*. Oxford: Oxford University Press.

Capanelli, G. (1997). "Industry-Wide Relocation and Technology Transfer by Japanese Electronic Firms: A Study on Buyer-Supplier Relations in Malaysia." Ph.D. dissertation, Graduate School of Economics, Hitotsubashi University, Tokyo.

Cardenas, E., et al., eds. (2000). *The Export Age: The Latin American Economies in the Late Nineteenth and Early Twentieth Centuries*. London: Macmillan.

Cardoso, E. A. (1987). *Inflation, Growth, and the Real Exchange Rate. Essays on Economic History in Brazil and Latin America*. New York: Garland Publishing.

Casar, J. I. (1994). *Un Balance de la Transformación Industrial en México*. Santiago: CEPAL (Comisión Económica Para América Latina).

C.C.I.S. (China Credit Information Service) (various years). *The Largest Corporations in the Republic of China*. Taipei: CCIS.

Center for Science and International Affairs (n.d.). *Core Policy Documents: Bibliography*. Cambridge, Mass.: John F. Kennedy School of Government Harvard University.

CEPAL (Comisión Económica Para América Latina) (1963). *El empresario industrial en América Latina (Documento preparado por la Secretaria Ejecutiva)*. Santiago, Chile: CEPAL.

——— (1968). *Estudio de América Latina 1968*. New York: United Nations.

CEPD (Council for Economic Planning and Development) (various years). *Taiwan Statistical Data Book*, Republic of China.

Chakravarty, S. (1991). "Development Planning: A Reappraisal." *Cambridge Journal of Economics* 15(1): 5–20.

Chalmin, P. (1990). *The Making of a Sugar Giant: Tate and Lyle, 1859–1989*. Chur, France: Harwood Academic Punlishers.

Chan, V.-L. (1998). *Economic Growth and Foreign Direct Investment in Taiwan's Manufacturing Industries*. Taipei: Academia Sinica.

Chan, W. K. K. (1977). *Merchants, Mandarins and Modern Enterprise in Late Ch'ing China*. Cambridge, Mass.: Harvard University Press for the East Asian Research Center.

Chand, M. (1949). "A Note on the Cotton Textile Industry in India." *Indian Journal of Economics* 30(116).

Chandavarkar, R. (1985). "Industrialization in India before 1947: Conventional Approaches and Alternative Perspectives." *Modern Asian Studies* 19(3): 623–668.

——— (1994). *The Bombay Cotton Textile Industry, 1900–1940*. Cambridge: Cambridge University Press.

Chandhok, H. L. (1996). *India Database—The Economy—Annual Time Series Data*. New Delhi: Living Media India.

Chandler Jr., A. D. (1977). *The Visible Hand: The Managerial Revolution in American Business*. Cambridge, Mass.: Harvard University Press.

——— (1990). *Scale and Scope: The Dynamics of Industrial Capitalism*. Cambridge, Mass.: Harvard University Press.

——— (2000). *Paths of Learning: The Evolution of High-Technology Industries*. New York: Free Press.

Chandler Jr., A. D., F. Amatori and T. Hikino, eds. (1997). *Big Business and the Wealth of Nations*. Cambridge: Cambridge University Press.

Chandra, B. (1968). "Reinterpretation of Nineteenth Century Indian Economic History." *Indian Economic and Social History Review* 5(1): 35–75.

Chang, C.-C. (1992). "The Development of Taiwan's Personal Computer Industry." In *Taiwan's Enterprises in Global Perspective*. Ed. N. T. Wang. Armonk, N.Y.: M. E. Sharpe: 193–214.

Chang, H. J. (1998). "Korea: The Misunderstood Crisis." *World Development* 26, no. 8.

Chang, J. K. (1967). "Industrial Development of Mainland China, 1912–1949." *Journal of Economic History* 27(1): 56–81.

Chang, K.-N. (1943). *China's Struggle for Railroad Development*. New York: John Day.

Chao, K. (1975). "The Growth of a Modern Textile Industry and the Competition with Handicrafts." In *China's Modern Economy in Historical Perspective*. Ed. D. H. Perkins. Stanford: Stanford University Press. 167–202.

——— (1977). *The Development of Cotton Textile Production in China*. Cambridge: Harvard University, East Asian Research Center.

Chaudhuri, M. R. (1964). *The Iron and Steel Industry of India*. Calcutta.

Cho, H.-D. and A. H. Amsden (1999). *Government Husbandry and Control Mechanisms for the Promotion of High-Tech Development*. Cambridge, Mass.: MIT, Materials Science Laboratory.

Cho, H. H., and J. S. Kim (1997). "Transition of the Government Role in Research and Development in Developing Countries: R&D and Human Capital." *International Journal of Technology Management, Special Issue on R&D Management* 13(7/8): 729–43.

Cho, Y. J., and J.-K. Kim (1995). *Credit Policies and the Industrialization of Korea*. Washington, D.C., World Bank.

Choi, J. T. (1982). "Business Climate and Industrialization in the Korean Fiber Industry." In *The Textile Industry and Its Business Climate*. Ed. A. Okochi and S.-I. Yonekawa. Tokyo: University of Tokyo Press. 8: 249–269.

Chokki, T. (1979). "Labor Management in the Cotton Spinning Industry." In *Labor and Management*. Ed. K. Nakagawa. Tokyo: University of Tokyo Press. 4: 143–167.

Chomchai, P. (1973). "Thailand's Industrial Development: Rationale, Strategy and Propsects." *Studies in Contemporary Thailand*. Ed. R. Ho and E. C. Chapman. Canberra: Australian National University. 67–85.

Choonhavan, K. (1984). "The Growth of Domestic Capital and Thai Industrialisation." *Journal of Contemporary Asia* 14(2): 135–146.

Chu, D. (1972). "The Great Depression and Industrialization in Latin America." In *Economics*. New Haven: Yale University Press.

——— (1989). *Japanese General Trading Companies in Taiwan*. Taipei: ISSP.

Chu, W.-W. (1994). "Import Substitution and Export-led Growth: A Study of Taiwan's Petrochemical Industry." *World Development* 22(5): 781–794.

——— (1996). *Demonstration Effects and Industrial Policy: The Birth of Taiwan's Petrochemical Industry*. Taipei: Acadmia Sinica.

——— (1997). *The OEM Model of Industrial Development*. Taipei: Academia Sinica.

——— (1997). "Causes of Growth: A Study of Taiwan's Bicycle Industry." *Cambridge Journal of Economics* 21(1): 55–72.

Chu, W.-W., and M. C. Tsai (1992). *Linkage and Uneven Growth: A Study of Taiwan's Man-Made Fiber Industry.* Taipei: Academia Sinica.

Chuang, Y.-C., and C.-M. Lin (1999). "Foreign Direct Investment, R&D and Spillover Efficiency: Evidence from Taiwan's Manufacturing Firms." *Journal of Development Studies* 35(4): 117–137.

Chudnovsky, D. (1994). *Del Capitalismo Asistido al Capitalismo Incierto: El Caso de la Industrial Petroquímica Argentina.* Santiago de Chile: CEPAL (Comisión Económica Para América Latina).

Chudnovsky, D., et al. (1999). *Las multinacioinales latinoamericanas: sus estrategias en un mundo globalizado.* Mexico: Fondo de Cultura Económica.

Church, R. (1994). "Enterprise and Management." In *The European Economy: 1750–1914.* Ed. D. H. Aldcroft and S. P. Ville. Manchester: Manchester University Press. 110–155.

Cipolla, C. (1969). *Literacy and Development in the West.* Baltimore: Penguin Books.

Clark, E. C. (1969). "The Emergence of Textile Manufacturing Entrepreneurs in Turkey, 1804–1968." Ph.D. dissertation, Princeton University, Princeton.

Clark, E. C. (1974). "The Ottoman Industrial Revolution." *International Journal of Middle East Studies* 5: 65–76.

Clark, G. (1987). "Why Isn't the Whole World Developed? Lessons from the Cotton Mills." *Journal Of Economic History* 47(1)(March 1987): 141–173.

Clark, M. G. (1973). *The Development of China's Steel Industry and Soviet Technical Aid.* Ithaca, N.Y.: Cornell University Press.

Clark, W. A. G. (1909). *Cotton Goods in Latin America.* Washington, D.C.: U.S. Government Printing Office.

——— (1914). *Cotton Goods in Japan.* Washington, D.C.: U.S. Government Printing Office.

Clemente de Oliveira, J. (1994). "Firma e Quase-Firma no Setor Industrial: O Caso da Petroquimica Brasileira." Ph.D. dissertation, Rio de Janeiro, Universidade Federal do Rio de Janeiro.

Coatsworth, J. H. (1978). "Obstacles to Economic Growth in Nineteenth Century Mexico." *American History Review* 83: 80–100.

——— (1981). *Growth Against Development: The Economic Impact of Railroads in Porfirian Mexico.* DeKalb: Northern Illinois University Press.

——— (1995). *Economic Retardation and Growth in Latin America and Southern Europe since 1700.* Cambridge, Mass.: Harvard University.

——— and A. M. Taylor, eds. (1998). *Latin America and the World Economy Since 1800.* Cambridge, Mass.: Harvard University Press.

Cochran, S. (1980). *Big Business in China: Sino-Foreign Rivalry in the Cigarette Industry, 1890–1930.* Cambridge, Mass.: Harvard University Press.

Cochran, T., and R. Ruben (1962). *Entrepreneurship in Argentine Culture.* Philadelphia: University of Pennsylvania Press.

Cochran, T. C. (1972). *Business in American Life: A History.* New York: McGraw-Hill.

Cohen, W. M., and D. A. Levinthal (1989). "Innovation and Learning: The Two Faces of R&D." *Economic Journal* 99 (397): 569–596.

Cole, D. C., and P. N. Lyman (1971). *Korean Development: The Interplay of Politics and Economics.* Cambridge, Mass.: Harvard University Press.

Cole, D. C., and Y. C. Park (1983). *Financial Development in Korea, 1945–1978.* Cambridge, Mass.: Harvard University Press for the Council on East Asian Studies.

Cole, D. C., and B. F. Slade (1996). *Building a Modern Financial System.* New York: Cambridge University Press.

Corbo, V., and S. Fischer (1995). "Structural Adjustment, Stabilization and Policy Reform: Domestic and International Finance." In *Handbook of Development Economics.* Ed. J. R. Behrman and T. N. Srinivasan. Amsterdam: North Holland. 3: 2846–2924.

Cordero, H., et al. (1985). *El Poder Empresarial en México.* Mexico: Editorial Terra Nova.

CORFO (Corporación de Fomento de la Producción). (1961). *Programa Nacional de Desarrollo Económico, 1961–1970.* Santiago, Chile: CORFO.

Correa, C. M. (1998). "Argentina's National Innovation System." *International Journal of Technology Management* 15(6/7): 721–760.

Cortes Conde, R. (1992). "Export-Led Growth in Latin America: 1870–1930." *Journal of Latin American Studies* 24: 163–169.

Cortes, M., and P. Bocock (1984). *North-South Technology Transfer: A Case Study of Petrochemicals in Latin America.* Baltimore, Md.: Johns Hopkins University Press for the World Bank.

Crafts, N. F. R. (1995). "Macroinventions, Economic Growth, and 'Industrial Revolution' in Britain and France." *Economic History Review* 48(3): 591–598.

Creutzberg, P. (1977). *Changing Economy in Indonesia.* The Hague: Nijhoff.

Crossley, J. C., and R. Greenhill (1977). "The River Plate Beef Trade." In *Business Imperialism, 1840–1930.* Ed. D. C. M. Platt. Oxford: Clarendon. 284–334.

Crouzet, F. (1972). "Western Europe and Great Britain: 'Catching Up' in the First Half of the Nineteenth Century." In *Economic Development in the Long Run.* Ed. A. J. Youngson. London: George Allen & Unwin. 98–125.

Cunningham, P. (1998). *Science and Technology in the United Kingdom.* London: Cartermill.

Cypher, J. M., and J. L. Dietz (1997). *Process of Economic Development.* London: Routledge.

D'Costa, A. P. (1995). "The Restructuring of the Indian Automobile Industry: Indian State and Japanese Capital." *World Development* 23(3): 1–18.

Daems, H. (1986). "Large Firms in Small Countries: Reflections on the Rise of Managerial Capitalism." In *Development of Managerial Capitalism.* Ed. K. Kobayashi and H. Morikawa. Tokyo: University of Tokyo Press. 12: 261–276.

Dahlman, C. J., and F. V. Fonseca (1987). "From Technological Dependence to Technological Development: The Case of Usiminas Steel Plant in Brazil." In *Technology Generation in Latin American Manufacturing Industries.* Ed. J. M. Katz. New York: St. Martin's. 154–182.

Dahlman, C. J., and C. R. Frischtak (1993). "National Systems Supporting Technical Advance in Industry: The Brazilian Experience." In *National Systems of Innovation.* Ed. R. R. Nelson. New York: Oxford University Press. 414–450.

Daito, E. (1986). "Recruitment and Training of Middle Managers in Japan, 1900–1930." In *Development of Managerial Enterprise.* Ed. K. Kobayashi and H. Morikawa. Tokyo: University of Tokyo Press. 151–179.

Das, N. (1962). *Industrial Enterprise in India.* Bombay: Orient Longmans.

David, P. A. (1970). "Learning By Doing and Tariff Protection: A Reconsideration of the Case of the Ante-Bellum United States Cotton Textile Industry." *Journal of Economic History* 30(3): 521–601.

––––– (1997). "Rethinking Technology Transfers: Incentives, Institutions and Knowledge-based Industrial Development." In *Chinese Technology Transfer in the 1990s: Current Experience, Historical Problems and International Perspectives.* Ed. C. Feinstein and C. Howe. Cheltenham: Edward Elgar. 13–37.

Davis, L., and R. Huttenback (1982). "The Political Economy of British Imperialism: Measures of Benefits and Support." *Journal of Economic History* 42 (1)(March 1982): 56–81.

––––– (1986). *Mammon and the Pursuit of Empire: The Political Economicy of British Imperialism, 1860–1912.* Cambridge: Cambridge University Press.

Davis, L., and H. L. Stettler (1966). *The New England Textile Industry, 1825–60: Trends and Fluctuations. Output, Employment and Productivity in the United States after 1800.* Princeton University Press.

Davis, M., Ed. (1991). "Innovation in an Industrial Latecomer: Italy in the Late Nineteenth Century." In *Innovation and Technology in Europe. From the Eighteenth Century to the Present Day.* Ed. P. Mathias and J. A. Davis. Cambridge, Mass.: Blackwell.

Dean, W. (1969). *The Industrialization of Sao Paulo, 1880–1945.* Austin, Tex.: University of Texas Press.

Deardorff, A. V. (1994). "Market Access." In *The New World Trading System: Readings.* Ed. Organization for Economic Cooperation and Development. Paris: OECD. 57–63.

Dernberger, R. F. (1975). "The Role of the Foreigner in China's Economic Development." In *The Growth of a Modern Textile Industry and the Competition with Handicrafts.* Ed. D. H. Perkins. Stanford, Calif.: Stanford University Press. 19–48.

Desai, P. (1972). *The Bokaro Steel Plant: A Study of Soviet Economic Assistance.* Amsterdam: North Holland.

Di Marco, L. E. (1972). "The Evolution of Prebisch's Economic Thought." In *International Economics and Development: Essays in Honor of Raul Prebisch.* Ed. L. E. Di Marco. New York: Academic Press. 3–13.

Diaz Alejandro, C. (1967). "An Interpretation of Argentine Economic Growth since 1930, Part I." *Journal of Development Studies* (October): 14–41.

––––– (1970). *Essays on the Economic History of the Argentine Republic.* New Haven: Yale University Press.

––––– (1971). "The Argentine State and Economic Growth: A Historical Review." In *Government and Economic Development.* Ed. G. Ranis. New Haven: Yale University Press. 216–249.

——— (1984a). "Latin America in the 1930s." In *Latin America in the 1930s: The Role of the Periphery in the World Crisis*. Ed. R. Thorp. New York: St. Martin's. 17–49.

——— (1984b). "No Less Than One Hundred Years of Argentine Economic History Plus Some Comparisons." In *Comparative Development Perspectives*. Ed. G. Ranis, R. L. West, M. W. Leiserson, and C. T. Morris. Boulder, Colo.: Westview Press. 328–361.

——— (1985). "Good-Bye Financial Repression, Hello Financial Crash." *Journal of Develoment Economics* 19(1–2).

Dobson, J. M. (1976). *Two Centuriees of Tariffs: The Background and Emergence of the U.S. International Trade Commission*. Washington, D.C., U.S. International Trade Commission, U.S. Government Printing Office.

Dollar, D. (1992). "Outward-Oriented Developing Economies Really Do Grow More Rapidly: Evidence from 95 LDCs, 1976–1985." *Economic Development and Cultural Change* 40(3): 523–544.

Doner, R. F. (1991). *Driving a Bargain: Automobile Industrialization and Japanese Firms in Southeast Asia*. Berkeley: University of California Press.

Doner, R. F., and A. Ramsay (1993). "Postimperialism and Development in Thailand." *World Development* 21(5): 691–704.

Doremius, P. N., et al. (1998). *The Myth of the Global Corporation*. Princeton, N.J.: Princeton University Press.

Dorfman, A. (1970). *Historia de la Industria Argentina*. Buenos Aires: Solar/ Hachette.

Duhart, J.-J. (1993). *Impacto Tecnológico y Productivo de la Minería Del Cobre en la Industria Chilena, 1955–1988*. Santiago de Chile: Naciones Unidas, Comisión Económica Para América Latina y el Caribe.

Dunning, J., and J. Cantwell (1987). *The Directory of Statistics of International Investment and Production*. New York City: New York University Press.

Eakin, M. C. (1989). *British Enterprise in Brazil: The St. John d'el Rey Mining Company and the Morro Velho Gold Mine, 1830–1960*. Durham: Duke University Press.

Eatwell, J., and L. Taylor, eds. (2000). *Global Finance at Risk: The Case for International Regulation*. New York: New Press.

Eatwell, J., et al., eds. (1989). *Allocation, Information and Markets*. The New Palgrave. London: Macmillan.

Eckert, C. (1990). "The South Korean Bourgeoisie: A Class in Search of Hegemony." *Journal of Korean Studies* 7: 115–148.

——— (1991). *Offspring of Empire: The Koch'ang Kims and the Colonial Origins of Korean Capitalism*. Seattle: University of Washington Press.

——— (1996). "Total War, Industrialization, and Social Change in Late Colonial Korea." In *The Japanese Wartime Empire, 1931–1945*. Ed. P. Duus, R. H. Myers, and M. R. Peattie. Princeton, N.J.: Princeton University Press. 3–39.

Eckstein, A. (1964). "Sino-Soviet Economic Relations: A Re-Appraisal." In *The Economic Development of South-East Asia*. Ed. C. D. Cowan. London: George, Allen, and Unwin. 128–159.

Edwards, S. (1993). "Openness, Trade Liberalization, and Growth in Developing Countries." *Journal of Economic Literature* 31: 1358–1393.

Edwards, S., and S. Teitel (1986). "Introduction to Growth, Reform, and Adjustment: Latin America's Trade and Macroeconomic Policies in the 1970s and 1980s." *Economic Development and Cultural Change* 34(3): 423–431.

Encarnation, D. J. (1989). *Dislodging Multinationals: India's Strategy in Comparative Perspective.* Ithaca: Cornell University Press.

Eng, R. Y. (1984). "Chinese Entrepreneurs, the Government, and the Foreign Sector: The Canton and Shanghai Silk-Reeling Enterprises, 1861–1932." *Modern Asian Studies* 18(3): 353–370.

Enos, J. L., and W. H. Park (1988). *The Adoption and Diffusion of Imported Technology. The Case of Korea.* London: Croom Helm.

Erber, F. S. (1985). "The Development of the Electronics Complex and Government Policies in Brazil." *World Development* 13(3): 293–309.

Esherick, J. (1972). "The Apologetics of Imperialism." *Bulletin of Concerned Asian Scholars* 4(4).

Etzkowitz, H., and S. N. Brisolla (1999). "Failure and Success: The Fate of Industrial Policy in Latin America and South East Asia." *Research Policy* 28: 337–350.

Evans, P. (1971). "Denationalization and Development: A Study of Industrialization in Brazil." Cambridge, Mass.: Harvard University.

———— (1995). *Embedded Autonomy: States and Industrial Transformation.* Princeton, N.J.: Princeton University Press.

———— (1979). *Dependent Development: The Alliance of Multinational, State, and Local Capital in Brazil.* Princeton, N.J.: Princeton University Press.

Evers, H. D., and T. H. Silcock (1967). "Elites and Selection." In *Thailand: Social and Economic Studies in Development.* Ed. T. H. Silcock. Durham, N.C.: Australian National University Press in Association with Duke University Press. 84–104.

Eysenback, M. L. (1976). *American Manufactured Exports, 1879–1914.* New York: Arno.

Falkus, M. (1995). "Thai Industrialization: An Overview." In *Thailand's Industrialization and its Consequences.* Ed. M. Krongkaew. Basingstoke, U.K.: Macmillan. 13–32.

Fall, J. H. I. (1995). "The US-Korea Financial Dialogue." In *The US-Korea Economic Partnership.* Ed. Y.-S. Kim and K.-S. Oh. Aldershot, U.K.: Avebury. 179–185.

Far Eastern Economic Review (1962). *Asian Textile Annual.* Hong Kong.

Farnie, D. A. (1991). "The Textile Machine-Making Industry and the World Market, 1870–1960." In *International Competition and Strategic Response in the Textile Industries since 1870.* Ed. M. B. Rose. London: Frank Cass. 150–170.

Faroqhi, A. (1994). "Labor Recruitment and Control in the Ottoman Empire (Sixteenth and Seventeenth Centuries)." In *Manufacturing in the Ottoman Empire and Turkey, 1500–1950.* Ed. D. Quataert. Albany, N.Y.: State University of New York Press. 13–57.

Fasano-Filho, U., et al. (1987). *On the Determinants of Brazil's Manufactured Exports: An Empirical Analysis.* Tubingen: J. C. B. Mohr.

Federico, G. (1994). *Il filo d'oro: L'industria mondiale della seta dalla restaurazione ala grande crisi*. Venice: Marsilio.

Feenstra, R. (1998). "Integration of Trade and Disintegration of Production in the Global Economy." *Journal of Economic Perspectives* 12(4): 31–50.

Felipe, J. (1999). "Total Factor Productivity Growth in East Asia: A Critical Survey." *Journal of Development Studies* 35(4): 1–41.

Felix, D. (1971). "Industrial Structure, Industrial Exporting, and Economic Policy: An Analysis of Recent Argentine Experience." In *Fiscal Policy for Industrialization and Development in Latin America*. Ed. D. T. Geithman. Gainesville, Fla.: University of Florida. 293–339.

Felker, G., et al. (1997). *The Pharmaceutical Industry in India and Hungary*. Washington, D.C.: World Bank.

Feuerwerker, A. (1958). *China's Early Industrialization: Sheng Hsuan-Huai (1844–1916) and Mandarin Enterprise*. Cambridge, Mass.: Harvard University Press.

———— (1964). "China's Nineteenth Century Industrialization: The Case of the Hanyeping Coal and Iron Company Ltd." In *The Economic Development of China and Japan: Studies in Economic History and Political Economy*. Ed. C. D. Cowan. London: George Allen & Unwin.

———— (1967). "Industrial Enterprise in Twentieth-Century China: The Chee Hsin Cement Co." In *Approaches to Modern Chinese History*. Ed. A. Feuerwerker, R. Murphey, and M. C. Wright. Berkeley, Calif.: University of California Press. 304–341.

———— (1969). *The Chinese Economy, ca. 1870–1911*. Ann Arbor: Center for Chinese Studies, University of Michigan.

———— (1970). "Handicraft and Manufactured Cotton Textiles in China, 1871–1910." *Journal of Economic History* 30(2): 338–378.

———— (1977). *Economic Trends in the Republic of China, 1912–1949*. Ann Arbor, Mich.: Center for Chinese Studies, University of Michigan.

Ficker, S. K. (1995). *Empresa Extranjera y Mercado Interno: El Ferrocarril Central Mexicano, 1880–1907*. Mexico: El Colegio de México.

Fields, K. J. (1995). *Enterprise and the State in Korea and Taiwan*. Ithaca: Cornell University Press.

Financial Times (2000). "FT500" [the *Financial Times*' annual list of the world's 500 largest companies]. *Financial Times* (London), May 4.

Fischer, S. (1995). "Structural Adjustment Lessons from the 1980s." *Structural Adjustment: Retrospect and Prospect*. Ed. D. M. Schydlowsky. Westport, Conn.: Praeger. 21–31.

Fischer, W. (1991). "The Choice of Technique: Entrepreneurial Decisions in the Nineteenth-Century European Cotton and Steel Industries." In *Favorites of Fortune: Technology, Growth, and Economic Development Since the Industrial Revolution*. Ed. P. Higonnet, D. S. Landes, and H. Rosovsky. Cambridge, Mass.: Harvard University Press. 142–158.

Fishlow, A. (1972). "Origins and Consequences of Import Substitution in Brazil." In *International Economics and Development: Essays in Honor of Raul Prebisch*. Ed. L. E. Di Marco. New York: Academic Press. 311–365.

————. (1991). "Liberalization in Latin America." In *Economic Liberalization: No Panacea.* Ed. T. Banuri. Oxford: Oxford University Press.

Flanders, J. M. (1964). "Prebisch on Protectionism: An Evaluation." *Economic Journal* 74: 305–326.

Fodor, J. G., and A. O'Connell (1997). "Argentina and the Atlantic Economy in the First Half of the 20th Century." Buenos Aires: Instituto Torcuato Di Tella, Centro de Investigaciones Económicas.

Frank, A. G. (1967). *Capitalism and Underdevelopment in Latin America.* New York: Monthly Review Press.

————. (1998). *ReOrient: Global Economy in the Asian Age.* Berkeley, University of California Press.

Franko, L. G. (1974). "The Origins of Multinational Manufacturing by Continental European Firms." *Business History Review* 48(3): 277–302.

Fraser, L. (1919). *Iron and Steel in India.* Bombay.

Fremdling, R. (1983). "Germany." In *Railways and the Economic Development of Western Europe, 1830–1914.* Ed. P. O'Brien. New York: St. Martin's Press. 121–147.

———— (1991). "The German Iron and Steel Industry in the 19th Century." In *Changing Patterns of International Rivalry.* Ed. E. Abe and Y. Suzuki. Tokyo: University of Tokyo Press. 17: 113–136.

French-Davis, R., et al. (1992). *Trade Liberalization in Chile.* Geneva: United Nations Conference on Trade and Development.

———— (1997). *La Industrialización Chilena Durante el Proteccionismo y Después (1940–95).* Washington, D.C.: Inter-American Development Bank.

Fridenson, P. (1997). "The Relatively Slow Development of Big Business in 20th Century France." In *Big Business and the Wealth of Nations.* Ed. A. D. J. Chandler, Jr., F. Amatori, and T. Hikino. Cambridge: Cambridge University Press. 207–245.

Friedmann, W. G., and J.-P. Beguin (1971). *Joint International Business Ventures in Developing Countries: Case Studies and Analysis of Recent Trends.* New York: Columbia University Press.

Fritsch, W., and G. Franco (1991). *Foreign Direct Investment in Brazil: Its Impact on Industrial Restructuring.* Paris: Development Centre of the Organisation for Economic Co-operation and Development.

Fritzsche, B. (1996). "Switzerland." In *The Industrial Revolution in National Context.* Ed. M. Teich and R. Porter. Cambridge: Cambridge University Press, 126–148.

Fry, M. J., and V. Murinde., eds. (1998). "International Financial Flows and Development: Special Issue." *World Development* 26(7): 1165–1368.

Furtado, C. (1963). *The Economic Growth of Brazil: A Survey from Colonial to Modern Times.* Berkeley: University of California Press.

Gadgil, D. R. (1959). *The Industrial Evolution of India in Recent Times.* London: Oxford University Press.

Gallagher, J. and R. Robinson (1953). "The Imperialism of Free Trade." *Economic History Review* 6(1): 1–15.

Gallo, E. (1970). *Agrarian Expansion and Industrial Development.* Buenos Aires: Instituto Di Tella.

Gardner, D. (2000). "India Liberalizes Inward Investment Regulations." *Financial Times* (London), February 3.

Garrido, C. (1994). "National Private Groups in Mexico, 1987–1993." *CEPAL Review* 53(August): 159–175.

——— (1999). "El Caso Mexicano." In *Las Multinacionales Latinoamericanas: Sus Estrategias en Un Mundo Globalizado*. Ed. D. Chudnovsky, B. Kosacoff, and A. Lopez. Mexico: Fondo de Cultura Económica. 166–300.

Garrido, C., and W. Peres (1998). "Las Grandes Empresas y Grupos Industriales Latinoamericanos en los Años Noventa." In *Grandes Empresas y Grupos Industriales Latinoamericanos*. Mexico: Siglo XXI-CEPAL.

GATT (1966). *A Study on Cotton Textiles*. Geneva: General Agreement on Tariffs and Trade.

Geertz, C. (1963). *Peddlers and Princes: Social Development and Economic Change in Two Indonesian Towns*. Chicago: University of Chicago Press.

Gelb, A., et al., eds. (1988). *Oil Windfalls: Blessing or Curse?* Washington, D.C.: World Bank.

Genc, M. (1994). "Ottoman Industry in the Eighteenth Century: General Framework, Characteristics, and Main Trends." In *Manufacturing in the Ottoman Empire and Turkey, 1500–1950*. Ed. D. Quataert. Albany: State University of New York. 59–86.

Gerschenkron, A. (1962). *Economic Backwardness in Historical Perspective: A Book of Essays*. Cambridge, Mass.: Harvard University Press.

Gibb, G. S. (1950). *The Saco Lowell Shops*. Cambridge, Mass.: Harvard University Press.

Glade, W. P. (1982). "Obrajes and the Industrialisation of Colonial Latin America." In *Economics in the Long View: Essays in Honour of W. W. Rostow*. Ed. C. P. Kindleberger and G. Di Tella. New York: New York University Press. 2: 25–43.

Glen, J. D., and M. A. Sumkinski. (1998). *Trends in Private Investment in Developing Countries*. Washington, D.C.: World Bank, International Finance Corporation.

Goetz, A. (1976). "Concentración y desconcentración en la industria argentina desde la década de 1930 a la de 1960." *Desarrollo Económico* 15(60): 510–521.

Gold, T. B. (1986). *State and Society in the Taiwan Miracle*. Armonk, N.Y.: M. E. Sharpe.

——— (1988). "Entrepreneurs, Multinationals, and the State." In *Contending Approaches to the Political Economy of Taiwan*. Ed. E. A. Winckler and S. Greenhalgh. Armonk, N.Y.: M. E. Sharpe. 175–205.

Goldsmith, R. W. (1983). *The Financial Development of India, 1860–1977*. New Haven: Yale University Press.

Goldstein, A. (1999). "Brazilian Privatization in International Perspective: The Rocky Road from State Capitalism to Regulatory Capitalism." *Industrial and Corporate Change* 8, no. 4: 673–709.

Graham, R. (1968). *Britain and the Onset of Modernization in Brazil 1850–1914*. Cambridge: Cambridge University Press.

Granovetter, M. (1995). "Coase Revisited: Business Groups in the Modern Economy." *Industrial and Corporate Change* 4, no. 1: 93–130.

Great Exhibition of the Works of All Nations, v. (London, 1851), III, pp. 1168–1169. (1968). *Documents of European Economic History.* Ed. S. Pollard and C. Holmes. New York, St. Martin's Press. Volume 1, *The Process of Industrialization, 1750–1870.* 347–350.

Grossman, G. M. (1981). "The Theory of Domestic Content Protection and Content Preference." *Quarterly Journal of Economics* 96(4): 583–603.

Ground, R. L. (1988). "The Great Depression and the Genesis of Import Substitution." *CEPAL Review* (34–36): 179–203.

Gulyani, S. (1999). "Innovating with Infrastructure: How India's Largest Carmaker Copes with Poor Electricity Supply." *World Development* 27(10): 1749–1768.

Gwin, C. (1997). "U.S. Relations with the World Bank, 1945–1992." In *The World Bank: Its First Half Century.* Ed. D. Kapur, J. P. Lewis, and R. Webb. Washinton, D.C.: Brookings Institution. 195–274.

Gwynne, R. N. (1993). "Non-Traditional Export Growth and Economic Development: The Chilean Forestry Sector Since 1974." *Bulletin of Latin American Research* 12(2).

Haber, S. H. (1989). *Industry and Underdevelopment: The Industrialization of Mexico, 1890–1940.* Stanford, Calif.: Stanford University Press.

——— (1991). "Industrial Concentration and the Capital Markets: A Comparative Study of Brazil, Mexico, and the United States, 1830–1930." *Journal of Economic History* 51, no. 3 (September 1991): 559–580.

Haggard, S., and S. B. Webb, eds. (1994). *Voting for Reform: Democracy, Political Liberalization, and Economic Adjustment.* Washington, D.C.: Oxford University Press for the World Bank.

Hale, W. (1981). *The Political and Economic Development of Modern Turkey.* London: Croom Helm.

Hanson, A. H. (1966). *The Process of Planning: A Study of India's Five Year Plans, 1950–1964.* Oxford: Oxford University Press.

Hanson, J., and C. Neal (1984). *A Review of Interest Rate Policies in Selected Developing Countries.* Washington, D.C.: World Bank Financial Unit, Industrial Department.

Hanson, J. R. II. (1986). "Export Shares in the European Periphery and the Third World Before World War I: Questionable Data, Facile Analogies." *Explorations in Economic History* 23, no. 1 (January): 85–99.

Hao, Y.-P. (1970). *The Comprador in Nineteenth Century China: Bridge between East And West.* Cambridge, Mass.: Harvard University Press.

Harley, C. K. (1992). "International Competitiveness of the Antebellum American Cotton Textile Industry." *Journal of Economic History* 52(3): 559–584.

Harvard Business School (1992). *The House of Tata.* Boston: Harvard Business School.

——— (1993). *Acer Incorporated.* Boston: Harvard Business School.

——— (1996). *Sime Darby Berhad, 1995.* Boston: Harvard Business School.

Hattori, T. (1989). "Hyundai Motor Company: The New Standard-Bearer of Korean Industrialization." *East Asian Cultural Studies* 28(1–4): 45–61.

—— (1997). "Chaebol-Style Enterprise Development in Korea." *Developing Economies* 35(4): 458–477.

Helleiner, G. K. (1995). *Trade, Trade Policy and Industrialization Reconsidered.* Helsinki: United Nations University, WIDER.

Hemmi, K. (1970). "Primary Product Exports and Economic Development: The Case of Silk." In *Agriculture and Economic Growth; Japan's Experience.* Ed. K. Ohkawa et al. Princeton: Princeton University Press. 303–323.

Heng, P. K. (1994). *Malaysia's Sino-Capitalist for All Seasons.* Toronto: University of Toronto—York University, Joint Centre for Asia Pacific Studies.

Hentges, H. A. (1975). *The Repatriation and Utilization of High-Level Manpower: A Case of the Korea Institute of Science and Technology.* Baltimore, Md.: John Hopkins University.

Herdeck, M., and G. Piramal (1985). *India's Industrialists.* Washington, D.C.: Three Continents Press.

Herrera Canales, I. (1977). *El comercio exterior de México, 1821–1875.* Mexico City: El Colegio de México.

Hershlag, Z. Y. (1968). *Turkey: The Challenge of Growth.* Leiden: E. J. Brill.

Heywood, C. (1977). *The Cotton Industry in France, 1750–1850.* Loughborough, U.K.: Loughborough University, Department of Economics.

—— (1981). "The Launching of an Infant Industry? The Cotton Industry of Troyes under Protectionism, 1792–1860." *Journal of European Economic History* 10: 553–581.

Hikino, T. (1997). "Managerial Control, Capital Markets, and the Wealth of Nations." In *Big Business and the Wealth of Nations.* Ed. A. D. Chandler Jr., F. Amatori, and T. Hikino. New York: Cambridge University Press. 480–496.

Hikino, T., et al. (1998). "The Japanese Puzzle: Rapid Catch-Up and Long Struggle." In *The Engines of Growth: The Chemical Industry.* Ed. A. Arora, R. Landau, and N. Rosenberg. New York: John Wiley. 415–457.

Hikino, T., and A. H. Amsden. (1994). "Staying Behind, Stumbling Back, Sneaking Up, Soaring Ahead: Late Industrialization in Historical Perspective." In *Convergence of Productivity: Cross-National Studies and Historical Evidence.* Ed. R. R. Nelson. William J. Baumol and Edward N. Wolff. New York: Oxford University Press: 285–315.

Hill, H. (1989). *Foreign Investment and Industrialization in Indonesia.* Singapore: Oxford University Press.

—— (1996). *The Indonesian Economy Since 1966.* Cambridge: Cambridge University Press.

Ho, S. P.-S. (1978). *Economic Development of Taiwan, 1860–1970.* New Haven: Yale University Press.

—— (1984). "Colonialism and Development: Korea, Taiwan, and Kwantung." In *The Japanese Colonial Empire, 1895–1945.* Ed. R. H. Myers and M. R. Peattie. Princeton: Princeton University Press: 347–398.

Ho, Y.-p. and T.-b. Lin (1991). "Structural Adjustment in a Free-Trade, Free Market Economy." In *Pacific Basin Industries in Distress: Structural Adjustment and Trade Policy in the Nine Industrialized Economies.* Ed. H. Patrick. New York: Columbia University Press. 257–310.

Hobday, M. (1990). *Telecommunications in Developing Countries: The Challenge from Brazil.* London: Routledge.

———— (1995). *Innovation in East Asia: The Challenge to Japan.* Aldershot, U.K.: Edward Elgar.

———— (1999). "East vs South East Asian Innovation Systems: Comparing OEM and TNC-led Growth in Electronics." In *Technological Learning and Economic Development.* Ed. L. Kim and R. R. Nelson. New York: Oxford University Press.

Hoda, A. (1994). "Trade Liberalisation." In *The New World Trading System: Readings.* Ed. Organization for Economic Co-operation and Development. Paris: OECD.

Hoffmann, L., and Tan Siew (1980). *Industrial Growth, Employment, and Foreign Investment in Peninsular Malaysia.* Kuala Lumpur: Oxford University Press.

Hofman, A. (1993). "Economic Development in Latin America in the 20th Century—A Comparative Perspective." In *Explaining Economic Growth: Essays in Honour of Angus Maddison.* Ed. A. Szirmai, B. V. Ark, and D. Pilat. Amsterdam: North-Holland. 241–267.

Hollerman, L. (1975). "Foreign Trade in Japan's Economic Transition." In *The Japanese Economy in International Perspective.* Ed. I. Frank. Baltimore: Johns Hopkins University Press. 168–206.

Hong, Y.-H. (1995). "Public Land Leasing in Hong Kong: Flexibility and Rigidity in Allocating the Surplus Land Value." Ph.D. dissertation, Massachusetts Institute of Technology, Cambridge, Mass.

Hori, K. (1994). "East Asia between the Two World Wars—Industrialization of Japan and Its Ex-Colonies." *Kyoto University Economic Review* 64(137): 1–22.

Hoshino, T. (1990). "Indigenous Corporate Groups in Mexico: High Growth and Qualitative Change in the 1970s to the Early 1980s." *The Developing Economies* 28(3): 302–328.

———— (1996). "Privatization of Mexico's Public Enterprises and the Restructuring of the Private Sector." *Developing Economies* 34(1): 34–60.

Hou, C.-m. (1965). *Foreign Investment and Economic Development in China.* Cambridge, Mass.: Harvard University Press.

Howell, T. R., et al. (1988). *Steel and the State: Government Intervention and Steel's Structural Crisis.* Boulder, Colo.: Westview.

Hsiao, F. S. T., and M.-C. W. Hsiao (1995). *Taiwanese Economic Development and Foreign Trade.* Cambridge, Mass.: Harvard University Fairbank Center Studies on Taiwan. Papers of the Taiwan Studies Workshop.

Hsiao, L.-l. (1974). *China's Foreign Trade Statistics, 1864–1949.* Cambridge, Mass.: Harvard University Press for the East Asian Research Center.

Hsu, M. C. (1915 [repr. 1968]). *Railway Problems in China.* New York: Ams Press.

Huberman, M. (1991). "How did Labor Markets Work in Lancashire? More Evidence on Prices and Quantities in Cotton Spinning, 1822–1852." *Explorations in Economic History* 28(January): 87–120.

Huenemann, R. W. (1984). *The Dragon and the Iron Horse: The Economics of Rail-*

roads in China, 1876–1937. Cambridge, Mass.: Harvard University Press for the Council on East Asian Studies.

Hughlett, L. J., ed. (1946). *Industrialization of Latin America*. New York: McGraw Hill.

Hui, L. M. (1981). *Ownership and Control of the One Hundred Largest Corporations in Malaysia*. Kuala Lumpur: Oxford University Press.

Hyde, C. K. (1991). "Iron and Steel Technologies Moving between Europe and the United States, before 1914." In *International Technology Transfer: Europe, Japan, and the USA, 1700–1914*. Ed. D. J. Jeremy. Aldershot: Edward Elgar. 51–73.

Hymer, S. (1976). *The International Operations of National Firms: A Study of Direct Foreign Investment*. Cambridge, Mass.: MIT Press.

ILO (International Labour Organization) (1970). *Yearbook of Labour Statistics*. Geneva: International Labour Organization.

IMF. *See* International Monetary Fund.

Inalcik, H. (1987). "When and How British Cotton Goods Invaded the Levant Markets." In *The Ottoman Empire and the World-Economy*. Ed. H. Islamoglu-Inan. Cambridge: Cambridge University Press.

Industrial Development Bank of India (1984–85). *Report on Industrial Development Banking in India*. Bombay: Industrial Development Bank of India.

——— (various years). *Report on Industrial Development Banking in India*. Bombay: Industrial Development Bank of India.

——— (1992–93). *Report on Industrial Development Banking in India*. Bombay: Industrial Development Bank of India.

Ines Barbero, M. (1990). "Grupos Empresarios, Intercambio Comercial e Inversiones Italianas en la Argentina: El Caso de Pirelli (1910–1920)." *Estudios Migratorios Latinoamericanos* 5 (15–16): 311–341.

——— (1997). "Argentina: Industrial Growth and Enterprise Organization, 1880s–1980s." In *Big Business and the Wealth of Nations*. Ed. A. D. Chandler Jr., F. Amatori, and T. Hikino. Cambridge: Cambridge University Press. 368–393.

Ingram, J. C. (1955). *Economic Change in Thailand Since 1850*. Stanford, Calif.: Stanford University Press.

——— (1971). *Economic Change in Thailand, 1850–1970*. Stanford, Calif.: Stanford University Press.

International Labour Office (1937). *The World Textile Industry*. Geneva: International Labour Office.

International Monetary Fund (1986). *A Manual on Government Finance Statistics*. Washington, D.C.: International Monetary Fund.

——— (1995). *International Financial Statistics Yearbook*. Washington, D.C.: International Monetary Fund.

——— (1997). *International Financial Statistics Yearbook*. Washington, D.C.: International Monetary Fund.

——— (various years). *International Financial Statistics Yearbook*. Washington, D.C.: International Monetary Fund.

Issawi, C., ed. (1966). *The Economic History of the Middle East, 1800–1914: A Book of Readings*. Chicago: University of Chicago Press.

———— (1980a). "De-Industrialization and Re-Industrialization in the Middle East Since 1800." *International Journal of Middle East Studies* 12(4): 469–479.

———— (1980b). *The Economic History of Turkey 1800–1914*. Chicago: University of Chicago Press.

Itami, H. (1987). *Mobilizing Invisible Assets*. Cambridge, Mass.: Harvard University Press.

Ito, K. (1984). "Development Finance and Commercial Banks in Korea." *The Developing Economies* 22(4): 453–475.

Izquierdo, R. (1964). "Protectionism in Mexico." In *Public Policy and Private Enterprise in Mexico*. Ed. R. Vernon. Cambridge, Mass.: Harvard University Press. 241–289.

Izumi, T. (1979). "The Cotton Industry." *Developing Economies* 17(4): 398–420.

Jaime, E. (1995). "Technología e Industria en el Futuro de México." In *México a la Hora del Cambio*. Ed. L. Rubio et al. Distrito Federal, Mexico: Cal y Arena. 193–222.

James, W. E., et al. (1987). *Asian Development: Economic Success and Policy Lessons*. Madison, Wis.: University of Wisconsin for the International Center for Economic Growth.

Japan Development Bank and Japan Economic Research Institute (1994). *Policy-Based Finance: The Experience of Postwar Japan*. Washington, D.C.: World Bank.

Johnson, C. (1982). *MITI and the Japanese Miracle: The Growth of Industrial Policy, 1925–1975*. Stanford, Calif.: Stanford University Press.

———— (1996). "Nationalism and the Market: China as a Superpower." *Japan Policy Research Unit* (No. 22).

Johnson, L. L. (1967). "Problems of Import Substitution: The Chilean Automobile Industry." *Economic Development and Cultural Change* 15: 202–216.

Johnson, W. A. (1966). *The Steel Industry of India*. Cambridge, Mass.: Harvard University Press.

Jomo, K. S. (1988). *A Question of Class*. Singapore: Oxford University Press.

————, ed. (1993). *Industrialising Malaysia: Policy, Performance, Prospects*. London: Routledge.

———— (1997). *Southeast Asia's Misunderstood Miracle: Industrial Policy and Economic Development in Thailand, Malaysia and Indonesia*. Boulder, Colo.: Westview.

Jones, L., and I. Sakong (1980). *Government, Business, and Entrepreneurship in Economic Development: The Korean Case*. Cambridge, Mass.: Harvard University Press for the Council on East Asian Studies.

Jorberg, L. (1969). "Structural Change and Economic Growth: Sweden in the Nineteenth Century." In *Essays in European Economic History 1789–1914*. Ed. F. Crouzet, W. H. Chaloner, and W. M. Stern. London: Edward Arnold.

Journal of Developing Economies (1994). "Trade Liberalization and Productivity Growth in Asia." *Journal of Developing Economies* 32(4): 363–524.

Juhn, S.-I. (1991). "Challenge of a Latecomer: The Case of the Korean Steel Industry with Specific Reference to POSCO." In *Changing Patterns of International Rivalry: Some Lessons from the Steel Industry*. Ed. E. Abe and Y. Suzuki. Tokyo: Tokyo University Press. 17: 269–293.

Kahler, M. (1995). *International Institutions and the Political Economy of Integration.* Washington, D.C.: Brookings.

Kang, C.-K. (1997). "Diversification Process and the Ownership Structure of Samsung Chaebol." In *Beyond the Firm: Business Groups in International and Historical Perspective.* Ed. T. Shiba and M. Simotani. Oxford: Oxford University Press. 31–58.

Kano, H. (1989). "Indonesia Business Groups and Their Leaders." *East Asian Cultural Studies* 28 (March): 145–172.

Kaplinsky, R. (1994). *Easternisation: The Spread of Japanese Management Techniques to Developing Countries.* Essex: Frank Cass.

——— (1997). "Technique and System: The Spread of Japanese Management Techniques to Developing Countries." *World Development* 25(5): 681–694.

Kapur, D. (1994). "On Industrial Performance: Technology, Policies and Institutions in the Indian Petrochemical Industry." Ph.D. dissertation, Woodrow Wilson School, Princeton University, Princeton, N.J.

Karol, J. C., and S. Hilda (1990). "Incomplete Industrialization: An Argentine Obsession." *Latin American Research Review* 25(1): 7–30.

Katrak, H. (1998). "Economic Analyses of Industrial Research Institutes in Developing Countries: The Indian Experience." *Research Policy* 27: 337–347.

Katz, J., (1987). *Technology Generation in Latin American Manufacturing Industries.* New York: St. Martin's.

——— (1995). *El Escenario Farmacéutico y Farmoquímico Latinamericano e International de la Década de los Años Noventa.* Santiago, Chile: CEPAL.

Katz, J., and N. A. Bercovich (1993). "National Systems of Innovation Supporting Technical Advance in Industry: The Case of Argentina." In *National Innovation Systems: A Comparative Analysis.* Ed. R. R. Nelson. New York: Oxford University Press.

Katz, J., and B. Kosacoff (1996). *Import Substitution Industrialization in Argentina in the Period 1940–1980: Its Achievements and Shortcomings.* Santiago de Chile: United Nationis Economic Commission for Latin America.

Kawabe, N., and E. Daito, eds. (1993). *Education and Training in the Development of Modern Corporations.* International Conference on Business History. Tokyo: University of Tokyo Press.

Kenwood, A. G., and A. L. Lougheed (1982). *Technological Diffusion and Industrialisation Before 1914.* London: Croom Helm.

Keremitsis, D. (1973). *La Industria Textil Mexicana en el Siglo xix.* Mexico City: Secretaria de Educación Pública.

——— (1987). *The Cotton Textile Industry in Porfiriato, Mexico, 1870–1910.* New York: Garland Publishing.

Kerr, I. J. (1995). *Building the Railways of the Raj, 1850–1900.* Delhi: Oxford University Press.

Keyder, C. (1987). *State and Class in Turkey: A Study in Capitalist Development.* London: Verso.

——— (1994). "Manufacturing in the Ottoman Empire and in Republican Turkey, ca. 1900–1950." In *Ottoman Industry in the Eighteenth Century: General*

Framework, Characteristics, and Main Trends. Ed. D. Quataert. Albany, N.Y.: State University of New York. 123–164.

Khan, A. R. (1993). *Structural Adjustment and Income Distribution: Issues and Experience.* Geneva: International Labour Organization.

Khanna, T. (1997). *Sime Darby Berhad, 1995.* Cambridge, Mass.: Harvard Business School.

Kim, L. (1993). "South Korea." In *National Systems of Innovation.* Ed. R. R. Nelson. New York: Oxford University Press.

—— (1997). *Imitation to Innovation: The Dynamics of Korea's Technological Learning.* Boston: Harvard Business School Press.

Kim, L., and G. Yi (1997). "The Dynamics of R&D in Industrial Development: Lessons from the Korean Experience." *Industry and Innovation* 4(2): 167–182.

Kim, M.-J. (1997). "The Republic of Korea's Successful Economic Development and the World Bank." In *The World Bank: Its First Half Century.* Ed. D. Kapur, J. P. Lewis, and R. Webb. Washington, D.C.: Brookings. 17–47.

Kindleberger, C. P. (1962). *Foreign Trade and the National Economy.* New Haven: Yale University Press.

King, S. T., and D. K. Lieu (1929). *China's Cotton Industry.* Shanghai: Chinese Mill Owners Association.

Kiray, E. (1990). "Turkish Debt and Conditionality in Historical Perspective: A Comparison of the 1980s with the 1860s." In *The Political Economy of Turkey: Debt, Adjustment and Sustainability.* Ed. T. Aricanli and D. Rodrik. London: Macmillan: 254–268.

Kiyokawa, Y. (1983). "Technical Adaptation and Managerial Resources in India: A Study of the Experience of the Cotton Textile Industry from a Comparative Viewpoint." *Developing Economies* 21: 97–133.

Knutrud, L.-H. (1994). "TRIPs in the Uruguay Round." In *The New World Trading System: Readings.* Ed. OECD. Paris: OECD. 193–195.

Kobayashi, H. (1996). "The Postwar Economic Legacy of Japan's Wartime Empire." In *The Japanese Wartime Empire, 1931–1945.* Ed. P. Duus, R. H. Myers, and M. R. Peattie. Princeton: Princeton University Press. 324–334.

Kobayashi, K., and H. Morikawa, eds. (1986). *Development of Managerial Enterprise.* Proceedings of the Fuji Conference on International Business History. Tokyo: University of Tokyo Press.

Kocka, J. (1978). "Entrepreneurs and Managers in German Industrializationi." In *The Cambridge Economic History of Europe.* Ed. P. Mathias and M. M. Postan. Cambridge: Cambridge University Press. Vol. 7, part 1.

Koh, S. J. (1966). *Stages of Industrial Development in Asia: A Comparative History of the Cotton Industry in Japan, India, China, and Korea.* Philadelphia: University of Pennsylvania Press.

Kohli, A. (1994). "Where Do High Growth Political Economies Come From? The Japanese Lineage of Korea's 'Developmental State'." *World Development* 22: 1269–1293.

Koike, K., and T. Inoki, eds. (1990). *Skill Formation in Japan and Southeast Asia.* Tokyo: University of Tokyo Press.

Kopits, G. (1987). *Structural Reform, Stabilization, and Growth in Turkey*. Washington, D.C.: International Monetary Fund.

Korea Development Bank (1969). *Annual Report*. Seoul: Korea Development Bank.

—— (1970). *Annual Report*. Seoul: Korea Development Bank.

—— (1971). *Annual Report*. Seoul: Korea Development Bank.

—— (1969). *Annual Report*. Seoul: Korea Development Bank.

—— (1979). *Annual Report*. Seoul: Korea Development Bank.

—— (1993). *Annual Report*. Seoul: Korea Development Bank.

—— (1995). *Annual Report*. Seoul: Korea Development Bank.

—— (various years). *Annual Report*. Seoul: Korea Development Bank.

Korean Automobile Manufacturers' Association (1999). *Output Data*. Seoul: Korean Automobile Manufacturers' Association.

Kornai, J. (1992). *The Socialist System: The Political Economy of Communism*. Princeton: Princeton University Press.

Kravis, I. B. (1972). "The Role of Exports in Nineteenth-Century United States Growth." *Economic Development and Cultural Change* 20(3): 387–405.

Kronish, R., and K. S. Mericle, eds. (1984). *The Political Economy of the Latin American Motor Vehicle Industry*. Cambridge, Mass.: MIT Press.

Krueger, A. O. (1995). "East Asian Experience and Endogenous Growth Theory." In *Growth Theories in Light of the East Asian Experience*. Ed. T. Ito and A. O. Krueger. Chicago: University of Chicago Press. 9–36.

—— (1995). *Trade Policies and Developing Nations*. Washington, D.C.: Brookings Institution.

Krugman, P. (1984). "Import Protection as Export Promotion: International Competition in the Presence of Oligopoly and Economies of Scale." In *Monopolistic Competition and International Trade*. Ed. H. Keirzkowski. Oxford: Oxford University Press.

Krugman, P., ed. (1991). *Trade with Japan: Has the Door Opened Wider?* Chicago: University of Chicago Press for the National Bureau of Economic Research.

Krugman, P., and L. Taylor (1978). "Contractionary Effects of Devaluation." *Journal of International Economics* 8: 445–456.

Kumar, A. (1988). *India's Manufactured Exports, 1957–1980*. Delhi: Oxford University Press.

Kuwahara, T. (1986). "The Establishment of Oligopoly in the Japanese Cotton-Spinning Industry and the Business Strategies of Latecomers: The Case of Naigaiwata & Co., Ltd." *Japanese Yearbook on Business History: 1986* 3: 103–134.

—— (1991). "The Local Competitiveness and Management of Japanese Cotton Spinning Mills in China in the Inter-war Years." In *The Transfer of International Technology: Europe, Japan and the USA in the Twentieth Century*. Ed. D. J. Jeremy. Aldershot, U.K.: Edward Elgar. 147–166.

Kuznets, S. (1955). "Economic Growth and Income Inequality." *American Economic Review* 45, no. 1 (March): 1–28.

—— (1966). *Modern Economic Growth: Rate, Structure, and Spread*. New Haven: Yale University Press.

—— (1967). "Quantitative Aspects of the Economic Growth of Nations: X. Level and Structure of Foreign Trade: Long-term Trends." *Economic Development and Cultural Change* 15, no. 2 (part II): 1–232.

——— (1972). "The Gap: Concept, Measurement, Trends." In *The Gap Between Rich and Poor Nations: Proceedings of a Conference Held by the International Economic Association at Bled, Yugoslavia.* Ed. Gustav Ranis. London: Macmillan.

Kuznets, S., Wilbert E. Moore, and Jospeh J. Spengler, eds. (1955). *Economic Growth: Brazil, India, Japan.* Durham, N.C.: Duke University Press.

Kwon, J. (1994). "The East Asia Challenge to Neoclassical Orthodoxy." *World Development* 22(4): 635–644.

La Porta, R., and F. Lopez-de-Silanes (1997). *"The Benefits of Privatization: Evidence from Mexico."* Cambridge, Mass.: National Bureau of Economic Research.

Lai, S.-B. (1992). "Strategy for Technology Development of Taiwan's Automobile Industry: A Case Study of Yeu-Tyan Machinery Company." In *Taiwan's Enterprises in Global perspective.* Ed. N. T. Wang. Armonk, N.Y.: M. E. Sharpe. 235–268.

Lal, D. (1988). *Hindu Equilibrium: Cultural Stability and Economic Stagnation, India, c[irca] 1500 BC–AD 1980.* Oxford: Clarendon Press.

Lall, S. (1987). *Learning to Industrialize: The Acquisition of Technological Capability by India.* Basingstoke: Macmillans.

———. (1993). "Multinationals and Technology Development in Host Countries." In *Transnational Corporations and Economic Development.* Ed. S. Lall. London: Routledge. 3: 237–250.

———. (1998). "Thailand's Manufacturing Competitiveness: An Overview." In *Competitiveness and Sustainable Economic Recovery in Thailand.* Ed. J. Witte and S. Koeberle. Bangkok: World Bank Thailand Office and the National Economic and Social Development Board. 211–234.

——— (1999). "India's Manufactured Exports: Comparative Structure and Prospects." *World Development* 27 (10): 1769–1786.

Lamb, H. B. (1955). "The "State" and Economic Development in India." In *Economic Growth: Brazil, India, Japan.* Ed. S. Kuznets, W. E. Moore, and J. J. Spengler. Durham, N.C.: Duke University Press.

Landes, D. (1969). *The Unbound Prometheus: Technological Change and Industrial Development in Western Europe from 1750 to the Present.* Cambridge: Cambridge University Press.

——— (1995). "Some Further Thoughts on Accident in History: A Reply to Professor Crafts." *Economic History Review* 48 (3): 599–601.

——— (1998). *The Wealth and Poverty of Nations: Why Some Are So Rich and Some So Poor.* New York: Norton.

Lardy, N. R. (1992). "Chinese Foreign Trade." *China Quarterly*: 691–720.

Latham, A. J. H. (1978). *The International Economy and the Undeveloped World, 1865–1914.* London: Croom Helm.

——— (1981). *The Depression and the Developing World, 1914–1939.* London: Croom Helm.

Latham, A. J. H., and H. Kawakatsu, eds. (1994). *Japanese Industrialisation and the Asian Economy.* London: Routledge.

Lee, C. (1995). "Adoption of the Ford System and Evolution of the Production System in the Chinese Automobile Industry, 1953–93." In *Fordism Transformed: The Development of Production Methods in the Automobile Industry*. Ed.H. Shiomi and K. Wada. New York: Oxford University Press. 298–314.

Lee, K. U. (1998). *Competition Policy, Deregulation and Economic Development: The Korean Experience*. Seoul: Korea Institute for Industrial Economics and Trade.

Lee, K. Y. (1994). *Policy Loans System—Performance, Effect, and Improvement Measure*. Seoul Korea Tax Institution.

Lee, S.-Y. (1990). *Money and Finance in the Economic Development of Taiwan*. Houndmills: Macmillan.

Lee, S. A. (1974). *Economic Growth and the Public Sector in Malaya and Singapore, 1948–1960*. Singapore: Oxford University Press.

Lee, T. H., and K.-s. Liang (1982). "Taiwan." In *Development Strategies in Semi-Industrial Economies*. Ed. Bela Balassa and associates. Baltimore: Johns Hopkins University Press for the World Bank. 310–350.

Leff, N. (1968a). *The Brazilian Capital Goods Industry, 1929–1964*. Cambridge, Mass.: Harvard University Press.

——— (1968b). *Economic Policy-Making and Development in Brazil, 1947–1964*. New York: John Wiley.

——— (1982). *Underdevelopment and Development in Brazil*. London: George, Allen, and Unwin.

Leipziger, D. (1992). *The Distribution of Income and Wealth in Korea*. Washington, D.C.: World Bank.

Lessard, D., and A. H. Amsden (1998). "The Multinational Enterprise as a Learning Organization." In *Proceedings of the International Economic Association*. New York: Macmillan.

Levy-Leboyer, M., and F. Bourguignon (1986). *L'economíe francaise au XIXe siecle: analyse macro-economique*. Paris: Economica.

Lewis, C. M. (1995). "Latin American Business History, c. 1870–1930: Recent Trends in the Argentinian and Brazilian Literature." *América Latina en la Historia Económica. Boletin de Fuentes* 4 (Julio–Diciembre): 89–109.

Lewis, P. H. (1990). *The Crisis of Argentine Capitalism*. Chapel Hill: University of North Carolina Press.

Lewis, W. A. (1949). *Economic Survey, 1919–1939*. London: Allen & Unwin.

——— (1954). "Economic Development with Unlimited Supplies of Labour." *Manchester School of Economics and Social Studies* 22(May): 139–191.

——— (1970). *Tropical Development, 1880–1913*. Evanston, Ill.: Northwestern University Press.

Li, K. T. (1988). *The Evolution of Policy behind Taiwan's Development Success*. New Haven: Yale University Press.

Li, L. M. (1981). *China's Silk Trade: Traditional Industry in the Modern World, 1842–1937*. Cambridge, Mass.: Harvard University Press for the Council on East Asian Studies.

Liao, K. (1994). *The Development of Small and Medium Sized Enterprises in the Republic of China*.

Lieu, D. K. (1928). *China's Industries and Finance*. Peking: Chinese Government Bureau of Economic Information.

—— (1936). *The Growth and Industrialization of Shanghai*. Shanghai: China Institute of Pacific Relations.

—— (1948). *China's Economic Stabilization and Reconstruction*. New Brunswick, N.J.: Rutgers University Press.

Lim, Y. (1999). *Public Policy for Upgrading Industrial Technology in Korea*. Boston: MIT Press.

Lin, B.-C. (1969). "The Study of Taiwan's Textile Industry Development." In *On Taiwan Industrial Development*. (In Chinese.)

Lin, C.-y. (1973). *Industrialization in Taiwan, 1946–72*. New York: Praeger.

Lindblad, J. T., Ed. (1996). *Historical Foundations of a National Economy in Indonesia, 1890s–1990s*. Amsterdam: North Holland.

—— (1998). *Foreign Investment in Southeast Asia in the Twentieth Century*. Canberra: Macmillan in Association with the Australian National University.

Ling, S. L. M. (1993). "The Transformation of Malaysian Business Groups." In *Southeast Asian Capitalists*. Ed. R. McVey. Ithaca, N.Y.: SEAP, Cornell University. 103–126.

Little, I., et al. (1970). *Industry and Trade in Some Developing Countries: A Comparative Study*. Paris: Oxford University Press for the OECD.

Little, I. M. D. (1982). *Economic Development: Theory, Policy, and International Relations*. New York: Basic Books.

Lopes, A. (1999). "El Caso Brasileño." In *Las Multinacionales Latinoamericanas: Sus Estrategias en Un Mundo Globalizado*. Ed. D. Chudnovsky, B. Kosacoff, and A. Lopez. Mexico: Fondo de Cultura Económica. 301–346.

Love, J. H., and F. Lago-Hidalgo (1999). "The Ownership Advantage in Latin American FDI: A Sectoral Study of U.S. Direct Investment in Mexico." *Journal of Development Studies* 35(5): 76–95.

Low, P. (1993). *The GATT and U.S. Trade Policy*. New York: Twentieth Century Fund Press.

Lu, Q. (1993). Industrial Organization and Underdevelopment: The Case of Chinese Textile Industry, 1890–1936. Cambridge, Mass.: Harvard University.

—— (1997). *Innovation and Organization: The Rise of New Science and Technology Enterprises in China*. Ph.D. dissertation, Harvard University, Cambridge, Mass.

Lücke, M. (1990). *Traditional Labour-Intensive Industries in Newly Industrializing Countries: The Case of Brazil*. Tubingen: J. C. B. Mohr.

Lundvall, B.-A., ed. (1992). *National Systems of Innovation: Towards a Theory of Innovation and Interactive Learning*. London: Pinter.

Lustig, N., and J. Ros (1993). "Mexico." In *The Rocky Road to Reform: Adjustment, Income Distribution and Growth in the Developing World*. Ed. L. Taylor. Cambridge, Mass.: MIT Press. 267–320.

Macario, S. (1964). "Protectionism and Industrialization in Latin America." *Economic Bulletin for Latin America* 9(1): 61–101.

Macpherson, W. J. (1955–1966). "Investment in Indian Railways, 1845–1875." *Economic History Review*, 2d series, vol. 8, nos.: 1,2, and 3 177–186.

——— (1972). "Economic Development in India under the British Crown, 1858–1947." In *Economic Development in the Long Run.* Ed. A. J. Youngson. London: George Allen & Unwin. 126–191.

Maddison, A. (1971). *Class Structure and Economic Growth: India and Pakistan Since the Moghuls.* New York: W. W. Norton.

——— (1991). *A Long Run Perspective on Saving.* Groningen: Institute of Research, Faculty of Economics, University of Grongingen.

——— (1995). *Monitoring the World Economy 1820–1992.* Paris: OECD.

Maizels, A. (1963). *Industrial Growth and World Trade.* Cambridge: Cambridge University Press for the National Institute of Economic and Social Research.

Malaguti, M.-C. (1998). "Restrictive Business Practices in International Trade and the Role of the World Trade Organization." *Journal of World Trade* 32(3): 117–152.

Malaysia, Bank Negara. (1989). *Money and Banking in Malaysia, 30th Anniversary Edition, 1959–1989.* Kuala Lumpur: Bank Negara Malaysia.

Malaysia, Government of (various years). *Economic Report.* Kuala Lumpur: Ministry of Finance.

Mallon, R. D., and W. J. V. Sourrouille (1975). *Economic Policymaking in a Conflict Society: The Argentine Case.* Cambridge, Mass.: Harvard University Press.

Maloney, W. F., and R. R. Azvedo (1995). "Trade Reform, Uncertainty and Export Promotion: Mexico 1982–88." *Journal of Developoment Economics* 48: 67–89.

Mamalakis, M. (1969). "An Analysis of the Financial and Investment Activities of the Chilean Development Corporation: 1939–1964." *Journal of Development Studies* 5(2): 118–137.

——— (1976). *The Growth and Structure of the Chilean Economy: From Independence to Allende.* New Haven: Yale University Press.

Mamalakis, M. J., and C. W. Reynolds (1965). *Essays on the Chilean Economy.* New Haven: Yale University Press.

Mandeville, B. (1714 [repr. 1924]). *The Fable of the Bees: or, Private Vices, Publick Benefits.* London: Oxford University Press.

Mani, S. (1999). *Government and the Organisation of Industrial Research and Development, An Examination of the Japanese, Korean and Indian Experiences.* Maastricht: United Nations University/Institute for New Technologies.

Markovitch, T. J. (1966). "L'Industrie francaise de 1789 a 1964—Analyse des faits (suire)." In *Histoire quantitative de l'economie francaise.* Paris. 5: tables, section 16.

Mathews, J. A., and D.-S. Cho (2000). *Tiger Technology: The Creation of a Semiconductor Industry in East Asia.* Cambridge: Cambridge University Press.

Mathews, J. K. (1997a). "The Development and Upgrading of Manufacturing Industries in Taiwan: Industrial Development Bureau, Ministry of Economic Affairs." *Industry and Innovation* 4(2): 277–302.

——— (1997b). "A Silicon Valley of the East: Creating Taiwan's Semiconductor Industry." *California Management Review* 39(4): 26–53.

Mathias, P. (1973). "Capital, Credit, and Enterprise in the Industrial Revolution." *Journal of European Economic History* 2: 121–143.

Matsui, T. (1968). "On the Nineteenth-Century Indian Economic History—A Review of a 'Reinterpretation'." *Indian Economic and Social History Review* 5, no. 1 (March 1968): 17–33.

Mattar, J. M. (1994). "La Competitividad de la Industria Química." In *La industrial mexicana en el mercado mundial: Elementos para una política industrial*. Ed. F. Clavijo and J. I. Casar. Mexico: Fondo de Cultura Económica. 159–312.

Mattoon, R. H. (1977). "Railroads, Coffee, and the Growth of Big Business in Sao Paulo, Brazil." *Hispanic American Historical Review* 57(2): 273–295.

McCallion, S. W. (1989). "Trial and Error: The Model Filature at Tomioka." In *Managing Industrial Enterprise: Cases from Japan's Prewar Experience*. Ed. W. D. Wray. Cambridge, Mass.: Harvard University Press. 87–120.

McKay, J. (1974). "Foreign Enterprise in Russia and Soviet Industry: A Long Term Perspective." *Business History Review* 48(3): 336–356.

McLeod, R. (1984). "Financial Institutions and Markets in Indonesia." In *Financial Institutions and Markets in Southeast Asia*. Ed. M. T. Skully. London: Macmillan: 49–109.

McMahon, W. W. (1999). *Education and Development: Measuring the Social Benefits*. New York: Oxford University Press.

Mehta, D. S. (1953). *The Indian Cotton Textile Industry: An Economic Analysis*. Bombay: G. K. Ved for the Textile Association.

Merchant, K. (1985). *Control in Business Organizations*. Marshfield, Mass.: Pitman.

Mesquita Moreira, M. (1995). *Industrialization, Trade and Market Failures: The Role of Government Intervention in Brazil and South Korea*. London: Macmillan.

———— (1999). *Estrangeiros Em Uma Economia Aberta: Impactos Recentes Sobre Productividade, Concentracao E Comercio Exterior*. Rio de Janeiro: Banco Nacional de Desenvolvimento Economico e Social (BNDES).

Messi, M. N., and F. H. Basri (1997). *The Development of Plywood Industry in Indonesia*. Tokyo: Foundation for Advanced Studies on International Development.

Mexico, Government of (1994). *Anuario Estadístico de los Estados Unidos Mexicanos*. Mexico City: Instituto Nacional de Estadística.

Miller, R. (1981). "Latin American Manufacturing and the First World War." *World Development* 9(8): 707–716.

Miller, S. M., et al., eds. (1998). *Studies in the Economic History of the Pacific Rim*. London: Routledge.

Min, S. (1982). "A Study of the Internationalization of the Korean Automobile Industry." M.S. thesis, Massachusetts Institute of Technology, Sloan School of Management, Cambridge, Mass.

Minami, R. (1994). *The Economic Development of Japan: A Quantitative Study*. New York: St. Martin's Press.

Ministry of Finance, Japan (1975). *History of Public Finance in Showa Years*. Tokyo: Ministry of Finance.

———— (1978). *Fiscal and Monetary Statistics Monthly: Fiscal Investments and Loan Program, Special Edition*. Tokyo: Ministry of Finance.

———— (1995). *Annual Report on National Accounts of 1995*. Tokyo.

———— (various years). *Fiscal Statistics Yearbook*. Tokyo: Ministry of Finance.

Ministry of Science and Technology, Korea (1998). *Science and Technology Annual*. Seoul: Ministry of Science and Technology.

Minsky, H. P. (1986). *Stabilizing an Unstable Economy*. New Haven, Conn.: Yale University Press.

Miyamoto, M. (1988). "The Products and Market Strategies of the Osaka Cotton Spinning company: 1883–1914." In *Japan Yearbook On Business History*. 117–159.

Miyazaki, Y. (1980 [orig. 1965]). "Excessive Competition and the Formation of Keiretsu." In *Industry and Business in Japan*. Ed. K. Sato. White Plains, N.Y.: M. E. Sharpe. 53–73.

Monteiro Filha, D. C. (1994). *A Aplicacao de Fundos Compulsorios Pelo BNDES na Formacao da Estrutura Setorial Da Industria Brasileira: 1952–1989*. Ph.D. dissertation, Instituto de Economia Industrial, Universidade Federal do Rio de Janeiro.

——— (1995). "A Contribuicao do BNDES para a Formacao da Estrutura Setorial da Industria Brasileira no Periodo 1952/89." *Revista do BNDES* 2(3): 151–166.

Moody's (1996). *Moody's International*. New York.

Moreno-Brid, J. C. (1998). *Reformas Macroeconómicas e Inversion Manufacturera en México*. Santiago, Chile: CEPAL.

Morikawa, H. (1986). "Prerequisites for the Development of Managerial Capitalism: Cases in Prewar Japan." In *Development of Managerial Enterprise*. Ed. K. Kobayashi and H. Morikawa. Tokyo: University of Tokyo Press. 12: 1–33.

——— (1992). *Zaibatsu: The Rise and Fall of Family Enterprise Groups in Japan*. Tokyo: University of Tokyo Press.

Morris, M. D. (1965). *The Emergence of an Industrial Labour Force in India: A Study of the Bombay Cotton Mills, 1854–1947*. Berkeley: University of California Press.

——— (1968). "Towards a Reinterpretation of Nineteenth Century Indian Economic History." *Indian Economic and Social History Review* 5: 1–15.

——— (1983). "The Growth of Large-Scale Industry to 1947." In *The Cambridge Economic History of India*. Ed. D. Kumar and M. Desai. Cambridge: Cambridge University Press. Vol. 2.

Mortimore, M. (1993). "Flying Geese or Sitting Ducks? Transnationals and Industry in Developing Countries." *CEPAL Review* 51(December): 15–34.

Moser, C. K. (1930). *The Cotton Textile Industry of Far Eastern Countries*. Boston: Pepperell Manufacturing Company.

Mosk, S. A. (1950). *Industrial Revolution in Mexico*. Berkeley: University of California Press.

Moskowitz, K. (1979). *Current Assets: The Employees of Japanese Banks in Colonial Korea*. Cambridge, Mass.: Harvard University.

Mosley, P., et al. (1991). *Aid and Power: The World Bank and Policy-Based Lending in the 1980s*. London: Routledge.

Mourshed, M. (1999). "Technology Transfer Dynamics: Lessons from the Egyptian and Indian Pharmaceutical Industries." Ph.D. dissertation, Massachusetts Institute of Technology, Cambridge, Mass.

Mowery, D., and N. Rosenberg (1993). "The U.S. National Innovation System." In *National Innovation Systems: A Comparative Analysis*. Ed. R. R. Nelson. New York: Oxford University Press. 29–75.

Muller, W. (1978). "El financiamiento de la industrializacion, el caso de la industrial textil poblana." *Comunicaciones* 15.

Murphey, R. (1977). *The Outsiders: The Western Experience in India and China*. Ann Arbor: University of Michigan Press.

Myers, M. G. (1954). "Mexico." In *Banking Systems*. Ed. B. H. Beckhart. New York: Columbia University Press. 573–607.

Myers, R. G. (1972). *Education and Emigration: Study Abroad and the Migration of Human Resources*. New York: David McKay Company.

Nacional Financiera, S. A. (1971). *La política industrial en el desarrollo económico de México*. Mexico: Nacional Financiera, S. A.

——— (various years). *Informe Annual*. Mexico: Nacional Financiera, S. A.

Nakaoka, T. (1991). "The Transfer of Cotton Manufacturing Technology from Britain to Japan." In *International Technology Transfer, Europe, Japan and the USA, 1700–1914*. Ed. D. J. Jeremy. Aldershot: Edward Elgar. 181–198.

Nam, C.-H. (1995). "The Role of Trade and Exchange Rate Policy in Korea's Growth." In *Growth Theories in Light of the East Asian Experience*. Ed. T. Ito and A. O. Krueger. Chicago: 153–180.

Narayanan, K. (1998). "Technology Acquisition, De-regulation and Competitiveness: A Study of Indian Automobile Industry." *Research Policy* 27: 215–228.

Nardinelli, C. (1988). "Productivity in Nineteenth Century France and Britain: A Note on the Comparisons." *Journal of European Economic History* 17(2): 427–434.

Narongchai, A., and J. Ajanant (1983). *Manufacturing Protection in Thailand: Issue and Empirical Studies*. Canberra: ASEAN-Australia Joint Research Project.

Nasution, A. (1983). *Financial Institutions and Policies in Indonesia*. Singapore: Institute of Southeast Asian Studies.

Nathan, A. (1972). "Imperialism's Effects on China." *Bulletin of Concerned Asian Scholars* 4, no. 4 (December).

Nayyar, D. (1973). "An Analysis of the Stagnation in India's Cotton Textile Exports during the 1960s." *Oxford Bulletin of Economics and Statistics* 35(1): 1–19.

Neikirk, W. R. (1987). *Volcker: Portrait of the Money Man*. New York: Congdon & Weed.

Nelson, R. R. (1987). "Innovation and Economic Development: Theoretical Retrospect and Prospect." In *Technology Generation in Latin American Manufacturing Industries*. Ed. J. M. Katz. New York: St. Martin's, 78–93.

———, ed. (1993). *National Innovation Systems: A Comparative Analysis*. New York: Oxford University Press.

Newfarmer, R., ed. (1985). *Profits, Progress and Poverty: Case Studies of International Industries in Latin America*. Notre Dame, Ind.: University of Notre Dame.

Newfarmer, R., and W. Mueller (1975). *MNCs in Brazil and Mexico: Structural Sources of Economic and Non-Economic Power*. Washington, D.C.: U.S. Senate.

Nolan, P. (1996a). *From State Factory to Modern Corporation? China's Shougang Iron and Steel Corporation Under Economic Reform*. Cambridge: University of Cambridge, Department of Applied Economics.

——— (1996b). "Large Firms and Industrial Reform in Former Planned Economies: The Case of China." *Cambridge Journal of Economics* 20: 1–29.

Nolan, P. and A. W. Xiaoqiang. (1996). *The Chinese Army's Firm in Business: The Sanjiu Group*. Cambridge: University of Cambridge, Department of Applied Economics.

Norman, E. H. (1940). *Japan's Emergence as a Modern State*. New York: Institute of Pacific Relations.

North, D. C. (1965). "Industrialization in the United States." In *The Cambridge Economic History of Europe*. Ed. H. J. Habakkuk and M. Postan. Cambridge: Cambridge University Press. Vol. 6. *The Industrial Revolution and After: Incomes, Population and Technological Change* (2): 673–705.

——— (1990). *Institutions, Institutional Change and Economic Performance*. Cambridge: Cambridge University Press.

Nugent, J. B. (1973). "Exchange Rate Movements and Economic Development in the Late Nineteenth Century." *Journal of Political Economy* 81, no. 5 (September/October): 1110–1135.

Numazaki, I. (1986). "Networks of Taiwanese Big Business." *Modern China* 12(4): 487–534.

——— (1997). "The Laoban-Led Development of Business Enterprises in Taiwan: An Analysis of the Chinese Entrepreneurship." *Developing Economies* 34(4): 485–508.

Nye, J. V. (1987). "Firm Size and Economic Backwardness: A New Look at the French Industrialization Debate." *Journal of Economic History* 47: 649–669.

——— (1991). "The Myth of Free Trade Britain and Fortress France in the Nineteenth Century." *Journal of Economic History* 51(1): 23–46.

O, Won Chul. (1995). "Korean-Type Economic Construction: An Analysis of the Engineering Approach." *The Pacific Review* 8(2): 345–357.

O'Brien, P. K. (1991). *Power with Profit: The State and the Economy, 1688–1815: An Inaugural Lecture Delivered in the University of London*. London: University of London.

——— (1997). "Intercontinental Trade and the Development of the Third World Since the Industrial Revolution." *Journal of World History* 8(1): 75–133.

O'Connell, A. (1984). "Free Trade in One (Primary Producing) Country: The Case of Argentina in the 1920's." Instituto Torcuato Di Tella, Buenos Aires.

Ocampo, J. A., and L. Taylor (1997). "Trade Liberalization in Developing Economies: Modest Benefits but Problems with Productivity Growth, Macro Prices, and Income Distribution." *Economic Journal* 108(450): 1523–1546.

Odell, R. M. (1916). *Cotton Goods in China*. Washington, D.C.: U.S. Department of Commerce.

OECD (Organisation for Economic Co-operation and Development) (1990). *Industrial Policy in OECD Countries Annual Review, 1990*. Paris: OECD.

————, ed. (1994a). *The New World Trading System: Readings*. OECD Documents. Paris, OECD.

———— (1994b). *Reviews of National Science and Technology Policy Mexico*. Paris: OECD.

———— (1996a). *Reviews of National Science and Technology Policy Korea*. Paris: OECD.

———— (1996b). *Trade Liberalization Policies in Mexico*. Paris, OECD.

———— (1996c). *International Direct Investment Statistics Yearbook*. Paris: OECD.

———— (1998). *Foreign Direct Investment and Economic Development: Lessons from Six Emerging Economies*. Paris: OECD.

———— (1999). *The Globalization of R&D Expenditures*. Paris: OECD.

Okada, A. (1999). "Skill Formation and Foreign Investment in India's Automobile Industry." Ph.D. dissertation, Massachusetts Institute of Technology, Cambridge, Mass.

Okita, S., and T. Miki (1967). "The Treatment of Foreign Capital—A Case Study for Japan." In *Capital Movements and Economic Development*. Ed. J. H. Adler. London: Macmillan. 139–174.

Okita, Y. (1975). "Foreign Trade in Japan's Economic Transition." In *The Japanese Economy in International Perspective*. Ed. I. Frank. Baltimore: Johns Hopkins University Press. 207–230.

Onis, Z. (1993). "Organization of Export-Oriented Industrialization: The Turkish Foreign Trade Companies in a Comparative Perspective." In *Politics and Economics of Turkish Liberalization*. Ed. T. Nas and M. Odeken. London: Associated University Press. 73–100.

Ono, A. (1986). "Technical Progress in Silk Industry in Prewar Japan: The Types of Borrowed Technology." *Hitotsubashi Journal of Economics* 27: 1–10.

Oreffice, P. F., and G. R. Baker (1970). "The Development of a Joint Petrochemical Venture in Chile—The Petrodow Project." In *Problems and Prospects of the Chemical Industries in the Less Developed Countries: Case Histories*. Ed. N. Beredjick. New York: American Chemical Society. 122–129.

Ozawa, T. (1974). *Japan's Technological Challenge to the West, 1950–1974: Motivation and Accomplishment*. Cambridge, Mass.: MIT Press.

Pacific Electric Wire and Cable (1994). *Annual Report 1994*. Taipei: Pacific Electric Wire and Cable.

———— (1995). *Annual Report 1995*. Taipei: Pacific Electric Wire and Cable.

Pamugoklu, G. (1990). "Import Substitution and Industrialization in Turkey." Ph.D. dissertation, Massachusetts Institute of Technology, Cambridge, Mass.

Pamuk, S. (1986). "The Decline and Resistance of Ottoman Cotton Textiles 1820–1913." *Explorations in Economic History* 23.

Papageorgiou, D., et al., eds. (1991). *Liberalizing Foreign Trade. Lessons of Experience in the Developing World*. Cambridge, Mass.: Basil Blackwell.

Park, C. H. (1962). *Our Nations Path: Ideology for Social Reconstruction*. Seoul: Dong-A.

———— (1963). *The Country, the Revolution and I*. Seoul.

Park, S. W. (1985). *The Emergence of a Factory Labor Force in Colonial Korea: A*

Case Study of the Onoda Cement Factory. Cambridge, Mass.: Harvard University Press.

———— (1990). "The First Generation of Korean Skilled Workers: The Onoda Cement Sunghori Factory." *Journal of Korean Studies* 7: 55–96.

———— (1999). *Colonial Industrialization and Labor in Korea: The Onoda Cement Factory*. Cambridge, Mass.: Harvard University Press.

Park, Y. C. (1985). "Korea's Experience with External Debt Management." In *International Debt and the Developing Countries*. Ed G. Smith and J. Cuddington. Baltimore: John Hopkins University.

Park, Y. C., and W.-A. Park (1991). "Changing Japanese Trade Patterns and the East Asian NICs." In *Trade With Japan: Has the Door Opened Wider?* Ed. P. Krugman. Chicago: University of Chicago Press for the National Bureau of Economic Research: 85–120.

Parra Moreno, J. (1992). "Mexico." In *Los Sistemas de Ciencia y Tecnologia en Iberoamerica*. Ed. L. A. Oro and J. Sebastian. Madrid: Secretaria General del Plan Nacional. 243–268.

Patcharee, T. (1985). *Patterns of Industrial Policymaking in Thailand: Japanese Multinationals and Domestic Actors in the Automobile and Electrical Industries*. Madison: University of Wisconsin.

Patel, P., and K. Pavitt (1995a). "The Localized Creation of Global Technological Advantage." In *Technological Innovation, Multinational Corporations and New International Competitiveness: The Case of Intermediate Countries*. Ed. J. Molero. Amsterdam: Harwood Academic Publishers. 59–74.

———— (1995b). "Patterns of Technological Activity: Their Measurement and Interpretation." In *Handbook of the Economics of Innovation and Technological Change*. Ed. P. Stoneman. Oxford: Blackwell.

Patel, P., and M. Vega (1999). "Patterns of Internationalisation of Corporate Technology: Location vs. Home Country Advantages." *Research Policy* 28: 145–155.

Patrick, H. T., and Y. C. Park, eds. (1994). *The Financial Development of Japan, Korea, and Taiwan: Growth, Repression and Liberalization*. New York: Oxford University Press.

Pearse, A. S. (1921). *Brazilian Cotton*. Manchester: International Federation of Cotton and Allied Textile Industries.

———— (1929). *The Cotton Industry of Japan and China*. Manchester: International Federation of Cotton and Allied Textile Industries.

Peattie, M. R. (1996). "Nanshin: The 'Southward Advance,' 1931–1941, as a Prelude to the Japanese Occupation of Southeast Asia." In *The Japanese Wartime Empire, 1931–1945*. Ed. P. Duus, R. H. Myers, and M. R. Peattie. Princeton: Princeton University Press.

Peng, K. K. (1983). *The Malaysian Economy*. Kuala Lumpur: Marican for the Institut Masyarakat.

Perez, L. A., and Jose de Jesus Perez y Peniche (1987). "A Summary of the Principal Findings of the Case-Study on the Technological Behavior of the Mexican Steel Firm Altos Hornos de Mexico." In *Technology Generation in Latin*

American Manufacturing Industries. Ed. J. M. Katz. New York: St. Martin's. 183–191.

Perez-Aleman, P. (1997). "Learning and Economic Development in Chile: The State and Transformations in Inter-Firm Relations." Ph.D. dissertation, Massachusetts Institute of Technology, Cambridge, Mass.

Perkins, D. H. (1967). "Government as an Obstacle to Industrialization: The Case of Nineteenth-Century China." *Journal of Economic History* 27(4): 478–492.

Phelps, D. M. (1936). *Migration of Industry to South America.* New York: Little Brown.

Pietrobelli, C. (1993). "El Proceso de Diversificación de Exportaciones en Chile." In *La Transformación de la Producción en Chile: Cuatro Ensayos de Interpretación.* Comisión Económica Para América Latina y el Caribe. Santiago de Chile: Comisión Económica Para América Latina y el Caribe.

Pinheiro, A. C., and F. Giambiagi (1994). "Brazilian Privatization in the 1990s." *World Development* 22(5): 737–753.

Piore, M., and C. Sabel (1984). *The Second Industrial Divide.* New York: Basic Books.

Platt, D. C. M. (1973). *Latin America and British Trade, 1806–1914.* New York: Harper and Row.

Pletcher, D. M. (1972). *Rails, Mines, and Progress: Seven American Promoters in Mexico, 1867–1911.* Port Washington, N.Y.: Kennikat Press.

Pollard, S. (1973). "Industrialisation and the European Economy." *Economic History Review* (2d. series) 26(4): 636–648.

——— (1981). *Peaceful Conquest: The Industrialization of Europe, 1760–1970.* Oxford: Oxford University Press.

——— (1990). *Typology of Industrialisation Processes in the Nineteenth Century.* Chur, Switzerland: Harwood Academic Publishers.

Pomeranz, K. (2000). *The Great Divergence.* Princeton, N.J.: Princeton University Press.

Poni, C., and G. Mori (1996). "Italy in the *longue duree*: The Return of an Old First-Comer." In *The Industrial Revolution in National Context.* Ed. M. Teich and R. Porter. Cambridge: Cambridge University Press. 149–183.

Poot, H., et al. (1990). *Industrialisation and Trade in Indonesia.* Yogyakarta: Gadjah Mada University Press.

Porter, M. (1990). *The Competitive Advantage of Nations.* London: Macmillan.

Potash, R. (1983). *Mexican Government and Industrial Development in the Early Republic: Banco de Avio.* Amherst, Mass: University of Massachusetts Press.

Prasada Reddy, A. S. (1993). "Emerging Patterns of Internationalization of Corporate R&D: Opportunities for Developing Countries?" In *New Technologies and Global Restructuring: The Third World at a Crossroads.* Ed. C. Brundenius and B. Goransson. London: Taylor Graham. 78–101.

Psacharopoulos, G. (1994). "Returns to Investment in Education: A Global Update." *World Development* 22(9): 1325–1344.

PT. Kompass Indonesia (1995). Top Companies and Big Groups in Indonesia. Jakarta.

Puthucheary, J. J. (1979). *Ownership and Control in the Malayan Economy.* Kuala Lumpur: University of Malaya Co-Operative Bookshop.

Quataert, D. (1983). "The Silk Industry of Bursa, 1880–1914." *Collection Turcica* 1: 481–505.

——— (1992). *Manufacturing and Technology Transfer in the Ottoman Empire, 1800–1914.* Istanbul-Strasbourg: The Isis Press.

———, ed. (1994a). *Manufacturing in the Ottoman Empire and Turkey, 1500–1950.* New York: State University of New York Press.

——— (1994b). "Ottoman Manufacturing in the Nineteenth Century." In *Manufacturing in the Ottoman Empire and Turkey, 1500–1950.* Ed. D. Quataert. Albany: State University of New York. 87–122.

Raby, G. (1994). Introduction to *The New World Trading System: Readings.* Paris: Organization for Economic Cooperation and Development. 13–25.

Radelet, S., and J. Sachs (1998). "The East Asian Financial Crisis: Diagnosis, Remedies and Prosepcts." *Brookings Papers on Economic Activity,* no. 1: 1–90.

Rady, D. E. (1973). *Volta Redonda: A Steel Mill Comes to a Brazilian Coffee Plantation.* Albuquerque, N.M.: University of Arizona Press.

Ramamurti, R. (1987). *State-Owned Enterprises in High Technology Industries: Studies in India and Brazil.* New York: Praeger.

Ramseyer, J. M., and F. M. Rosenbluth (1995). *The Politics of Oligarchy: Institutional Choice in Imperial Japan.* New York: Cambridge University Press.

Randall, L., ed. (1977). *An Economic History of Latin America in the Twentieth Century.* New York: Columbia University Press.

Ranis, G., et al. (2000). "Economic Growth and Human Development." *World Development* 28 (2): 197–220.

Rasiah, R. (1995). *Foreign Capital and Industrialization in Malaysia.* London: MacMillan.

Raumolin, J. (1992). "The Diffusion of Technology in the Forest and Mining Sector in Finalnd: The Shift From the Object to the Subject of Transfer of Technology." In *Mastering Technology Diffusion—the Finnish Experience.* Ed. S. Vuori and P. Yla-Anttila. Helsinki: Research Institute of the Finnish Economy. Series B. 82: 321–378.

Rawski, E. S. (1989). "Competetive Markets As an Obstacle to Economic Development." The Second Conference on Modern Chinese Economic History. Taipei: Institute of Economics, Academia Sinica.

Rawski, T. (1970). "Chinese Dominance of Treaty Port Commerce and Its Implications, 1860–1875." *Explorations in Economic History* 7(4): 451–473.

——— (1975). "The Growth of Producer Industries, 1900–1971." In *China's Modern Economy in Historical Perspective.* Ed. D. H. Perkins. Stanford, Calif.: Stanford University Press.

——— (1980). *China's Transition to Industrialism: Producer Goods and Economic Development in the Twentieth Century.* Ann Arbor: University of Michigan Press.

——— (1989a). "Economic Growth in China before World War II." Second Conference on Modern Chinese Economic History. Taipei: Institute of Economics, Academia Sinica.

———— (1989b). *Economic Growth in Prewar China*. Berkeley, Calif.: University of California Press.

Raychaudhuri, T. (1968). "A Re-Interpretation of Nineteenth Century Indian Economic History?" *Indian Economic and Social History Review* 68(1): 77–99.

Redding, S. G. (1990). *The Spirit of Chinese Capitalism*. Berlin: Walter de Gruyter.

Remer, C. F. (1933). *Foreign Investments in China*. New York: Macmillan.

Repetto, R. and M. Gillis, eds. (1988). *Public Policy and the Misuse of Forest Resources*. Cambridge: Cambridge University Press.

Republic of China (1996). Indicators of Science and Technology, Republic of China. Taipei: Republic of China.

———— (1997). *Taiwan Statistical Data Book 1996*. Taipei: Council for Economic Planning and Development.

———— (various years). Taiwan Statistical Data Book. Taipei.

República Argentina (1998). *Argentine Multiannual National Plan on Science and Technology, 1999–2001*. Buenos Aires: Presidencia de la Nación Gabinete Científico Tecnológico.

Reubens, E. P. (1955). "Foreign Capital and Domestic Development in Japan." In *Economic Growth: Brazil, India, Japan*. Ed. S. Kuznets, W. E. Moore, and J. J. Spengler. Durham, N.C. Duke University Press. 179–228.

Reynolds, B. L. (1975). "The Impact of Trade and Foreign Investment of Industrializtion: Chinese Textiles, 1875–1931." Ph.D. dissertation, University of Michigan, Ann Arbor.

Reynolds, C. W. (1970). *The Mexican Economy: Twentieth Century Structure and Growth*. New Haven: Yale University Press.

Reynolds, L. G. (1971). "Public Sector Saving and Capital Formation." In *Government and Economic Development*. Ed. G. Ranis. New Haven: Yale University Press. 516–551.

———— (1985). *Economic Growth in the Third World, 1850–1980*. New Haven: Yale University Press.

Rhee, Y. W., et al. (1984). *Korea's Competitive Edge: Managing the Entry into World Markets*. Baltimore: Published for the World Bank by the Johns Hopkins University Press.

Rippy, J. F. (1947). *Latin America and the Industrial Age*. Westport, Conn.: Greenwood.

Riskin, C. (1975). "Surplus and Stagnation in Modern China." In *China's Modern Economy in Historical Perspective*. Ed. D. H. Perkins. Stanford: Stanford University Press. 49–84.

Robb, P. (1981). "British Rule and Indian 'Improvement'." *The Economic History Review* 34, no. 4 (November 1981): 507–523.

Robinson, E. (1975). "The Transference of British Technology to Russia, 1760–1820: A Preliminary Survey." In *Great Britain and Her World 1750–1914*. Ed. B. M. Ratcliffe. Manchester: University of Manchester Press.

Robison, R. (1986). *The Rise of Capital*. Sydney: Allen & Unwin.

Rock, M. T. (1995). "Thai Industrial Policy: How Irrelevant Was It to Export Success?" *Journal of International Development* 7, no. 5: 745–759.

Roderick, G. W., and M. D. Stephens (1978). *Education and Industry in the Nineteenth Century*. London: Longman.

Rodrik, D. (1995). "Trade and Industrial Policy Reform." In *Handbook of Development Economics*. Ed. J. R. Behrman and T. N. Srinivasan. Amsterdam: North Holland. 3B: 2925–2982.

——— (1996). "Understanding Economic Policy Reform." *Journal of Economic Literature* 34(1): 9–41.

——— (1997). "Trade Strategy, Investment and Exports: Another Look at East Asia." *Pacific Economic Review* 2(1): 1–24.

Rogozinski, J. (1993). *La privatización de empresas paraestatales*. Mexico City: Fondo de Cultura Económica.

Ros, J. (1994). "Mexico's Trade and Industrialization Experience Since 1960." In *Trade Policy and Industrialization in Turbulent Times*. Ed. G. K. Helleiner. New York: Routledge.

Rosenberg, N. (1976). *Perspectives on Technology*. Cambridge: Cambridge University Press.

——— (1982). *Inside the Black Box: Technology and Economics*. Cambridge: Cambridge University Press.

Ross Schneider, B. (1998). "Elusive Synergy: Business-Government Relations and Development." *Comparative Politics* (October): 101–122.

Roy, T. (1999). *Traditional Industry in the Economy of Colonial India*. Cambridge: Cambridge University Press.

Royle, J. F. (1851). "Arts and Manufactures of India: Lectures on the Result of the Great Exhibition of 1851." In *Documents of European Economic History: The Process of Industrialization, 1750–1870*. Ed. S. Pollard and C. H. Holmes. New York: St. Martin's. 1: 347–350.

Rungta, R. S. (1970). *The Rise of Corporations in India, 1851–1900*. Cambridge: Cambridge University Press.

Rutnagur, S. M. (1927). *Bombay Industries: The Cotton Mills*. Bombay: Indian Textile Journal.

Sabato, J. F. (1988). *La Clase Dominante en la Argentina Moderna: Formación y Características*. Buenos Aires: CISEA.

Sachs, J. D., ed. (1989). *Developing Country Debt and the World Economy*. Chicago: University of Chicago Press for the National Bureau of Economic Research.

Sader, F. (1995). *Privatizing Public Enterprises and Foreign Investment in Developing Countries, 1988–93*. Washington, D.C.: International Finance Corporation, World Bank.

Saich, T. (1989). "Reforms of China's Science and Technology Organizational System." In *Science and Technology in Post-Mao China*. Ed. D. Simon and M. Goldman. Cambridge: Cambridge University Press. 69–88.

Saksena, R. M. (1970). *Development Banking in India*. Bombay: Vora & Co.

Salleh, I. M., and S. D. Meyananthan (1997). "Malaysia: Growth, Equity, and Structural Transformation." In *Lessons from East Asia*. Ed. D. M. Leipziger. Ann Arbor: University of Michigan Press. 279–343.

San, G. (1995). "An Overview of Policy: Priorities for Industrial Development in Taiwan." *Journal of Industry Studies* 2(1): 27–55.

San, G., and W.-J. Kuo (1991). *Export Success and Technological Capabilities: The Case of Textiles and Electronics in Taiwan Province of China.* Geneva: United Nations Conference on Trade and Development.

Sanchez, J. M., and R. M. Paredes (1994). *Grupos Economicos Y Desarrollo: El Caso de Chile.* Santago, Chile: CEPAL.

Sandesara, J. C. (1992). *Industrial Policy and Planning, 1947–91.* New Delhi: Sage Publications.

Sato, Y. (1993). "The Salim Group in Indonesia: The Development and Behavior of the Largest Conglomerate in Southeast Asia." *The Developing Economies* 31(4): 408–441.

——— (1996). "The Astra Group: A Pioneer of Management Modernization in Indonesia." *Developing Economies* 34(3): 247–280.

——— (1997). "Diverging Development Paths of the Electronics Industry in Korea and Taiwan." *The Developing Economies* 35(4): 401–421.

Saul, S. B. (1972). "The Nature and Diffusion of Technology." In *Economic Development in the Long Run.* A. J. Youngson. London: George Allen & Unwin. 36–61.

——— (1982). "The Economic Development of Small Nations: The Experience of North West Europe in the Nineteenth Century." In *Economics in the Long View.* Ed. C. P. Kindleberger and G. di Tella. New York: New York University Press. 2, Part 1: 111–131.

Saxonhouse, G., and G. Wright (1984). "Rings and Mules Around the World: A Comparative Study in Technological Choice." In *Technique, Spirit and Form in the Making of the Modern Economies: Essays in Honor of William N. Parker.* Ed. G. Saxonhouse and G. Wright. Greenwich, Conn.: Research in Economic History, Supplement 3.

Schenk, C. R. (1994). "Closing the Hong Kong Gap: The Hong Kong Free Dollar Market in the 1950s." *Economic History Review* 47, no. 2 (May): 335–353.

Schive, C. (1978). "Direct Foreign Investment, Technology Transfer and Linkage Effects: A Case Study of Taiwan." Ph.D. dissertation, Case Western Reserve University, Cleveland.

——— (1995). "Industrial Policies in a Maturing Taiwan Economy." *Journal of Industry Studies* 2, no. 1 (August): 5–26.

Schott, J. J. (1994). "Safeguards." In *The New World Trading System: Readings.* Ed. OECD Paris: OECD. 113–116.

Schroter, H. G. (1997). "Small European Nations: Cooperative Capitalism in the Twentieth Century." In *Big Business and the Wealth of Nations.* Ed. Alfred D. Chandler Jr., F. Amatori, and T. Hikino. New York: Cambridge University Press. 176–204.

Schumpeter, J. A. (1942). *Capitalism, Socialism and Democracy.* New York: Harper.

——— (1947). "The Creative Response in Economic History." *Journal of Economic History* 7(2): 149–159.

Schvarzer, J. (1978). "Estrategia Industrial Y Grandes Empresas: El Caso Argentino." *Desarrollo Económico* 18(71): 307–351.

——— (1981). *Los industriales.* Buenos Aires: Colección La vida de nuestro pueblo-CEAL.

————— (1989). *Bunge Y Born, Crecimiento y Diversificación de un Grupo Económico.* Buenos Aires: Grupo Editor Latinoamericano.

————— (1995). "Grandes Grupos Económicos en la Argentina: Formas de Propiedad y Lógicas de Expansión." In *Más Allá de la Estabilidad.* Ed. P. Bustos. Buenos Aires: R. Ebert. 133–157.

————— (1996). *La industria que supimos conseguir.* Buenos Aires: Planeta.

Schwartzman, S. (1994). "Brazil: Scientists and the State—Evolving Models and the 'Great Leap Forward'." In *Scientists and the State: Domestic Structures and the International Context.* Ed. E. Solingen. Ann Arbor: University of Michigan Press. 171–188.

Schwarz, A. (1994). *A Nation in Waiting: Indonesia in the 1990s.* Boulder, Colo.: Westview Press.

Scott, M. (1979). "Foreign Trade." In *Economic Growth and Structural Change in Taiwan.* Ed. W. Galenson. Ithaca: Cornell University Press.

Segal, A. (1993). *An Atlas of International Migration.* London: Hans Zell Publishers.

Segers, W. A. I. M. (1987). *Volume 8: Manufacturing Industry 1870–1942.* Amsterdam: Royal Tropical Institute.

Senses, F. (1990). "An Assessment of the Pattern of Turkish Manufactured Export Growth in the 1980s and Its Prospects." In *The Political Economy of Turkey: Debt, Adjustment and Sustainability.* Ed. T. Aricanli and D. Rodrik. Basingstoke: Macmillan. 60–77.

Shapiro, H. (1991). "Determinants of Firm Entry into the Brazilian Automobile Manufacturing Industry, 1956–1968." *Business History Review* 65(Winter): 876–947.

————— (1994). *Engines of Growth: The State and Transnational Auto Companies in Brazil.* Cambridge: Cambridge University Press.

————— (1997). *Review of Export Promotion Policies in Brazil.* Washington, D.C.: Inter-American Developmen Bank, Integration, Trade and Hemispheric Issues Division.

Shea, J.-D. (1994). "Taiwan: Development and Structural Change of the Financial System." In *The Financial Development of Japan, Korea, and Taiwan: Growth, Repression and Liberalization.* Ed. H. T. Patrick and Y. C. Park. New York: Oxford University Press. 222–287.

Shea, J.-D., and Y.-H. Yang (1994). "Taiwan's Financial System and the Allocation of Investment Funds." In *The Role of the State in Taiwan's Development.* Ed. J. D. Aberbach, D. Dollar, and K. L. Sokoloff. Armonk, N.Y.: M. E. Sharpe. 193–230.

Shepherd, P. (1989). "Transnational Corporations and the Denationalisation of the Latin American Cigarette Industry." In *Historical Studies in International Corporate Business.* Ed. A. Teichova, M. Levy-Leboyer, and H. Nussbaum. Cambridge: Cambridge University Press. 201–228.

Shinohara, M. (1964). "Economic Development and Foreign Trade in Pre-War Japan." In *The Economic Development of China and Japan: Studies in Economic History and Political Economy.* Ed. C. D. Cowan. London: George Allen & Unwin. 220–248.

———— (1982). *Industrial Growth, Trade, and Dynamic Patterns in the Japanese Economy*. Tokyo: University of Tokyo Press.

Showers, V. (1979). *World Facts and Figures*. New York: John Wiley and Sons.

Shrivastava, P. (1992). *Bhopal: Anatomy of a Crisis*. London: Paul Chapman.

Siamwalla, A. (1975). "Stability, Growth and Distribution in the Thai Econoomy: Essays in Honour of Khunying Suparb Yossundara." In *Finance, Trade and Economic Development in Thailand*. Ed. P. Sondysuvan. Bangkok: Sompong Press. 21–48.

Sikka, P. (1998). "Analysis of In-House R&D Centres of Innovative Firms in India." *Research Policy* 27: 429–433.

Silbner, E. (1972). *The Problem of War in Nineteenth Century Economic Thought*. Princeton: Princeton University Press.

Singer, M. (1977). *The Economic Advance of Turkey, 1938–1960*. Ankara: Ayyildiz Matbaasi.

Singh, A. (1994). "Openness and the Market Friendly Approach to Development: Learning the Right Lessons from the Development Experience." *World Development* 22, no. 12: 1811–1823.

———— (2000). *Competition, Corporate Governance, and Corporate Finance in Emerging Markets: Empirical Studies in the Light of the Asian Crisis*. Cambridge: Faculty of Economics, University of Cambridge.

Skully, M. T. (1984). "Financial Institutions and Markets in Thailand." In *Financial Institutions and Markets in Southeast Asia*. Ed. M. T. Skully. London: Macmillan. 296–378.

Smith, M. S. (1993). "The Beginnings of Big Business in France, 1880–1920: A Chandlerian Perspective." *Essays in Economic and Business History* 11: 1–24.

Smythe, R. (2000). "Should China Be Promoting Large-Scale Enterprise and Enterprise Groups?" *World Development* 28 (4): 721–737.

Soderlund, E. F. (1960). "The Impact of the British Industrial Revolution on the Swedish Iron Industry." In *Studies in the Industrial Revolution*. Ed. L. S. Pressnell. London: Athlone Press: 52–62.

Sourrouille, J. (1967). "Los Instrumentos de Promoción Industrial en la Postguerra." *Desarrollo Económico* 6(24).

Sridharan, E. (1996). *The Political Economy of Industrial Promotion: Indian, Brazilian, and Korean Electronics in Comparative Perspective, 1969–1994*. Westport, Conn.: Praeger.

Stallings, B. (1992). "International Influence on Economic Policy: Debt, Stabilization, and Structural Reform." In *The Politics of Economic Adjustment: International Constraints, Distributive Conflicts, and the State*. Ed. S. Haggard and R. R. Kaufman. Princeton: Princeton University Press.

Stanford University Graduate School of Business (1995). *Tata Consultancy Services: Globalization of Software Services*. Stanford: Stanford University, Graduate School of Business.

Startup, J. (1994). "An Agenda for International Investment." In *The New World Trading System: Readings*. Ed. OECD. Paris: OECD. 189–192.

Statistics Bureau, Japan. (1996). *Japan Statistical Yearbook*. Tokyo: Statistics Bureau.

Stein, S. J. (1955). "Brazilian Cotton Textile Industry, 1850–1950." In *Economic Growth: Brazil, India, Japan*. Ed. S. Kuznets, W. E. Moore, and J. J. Spengler. Durham, N.C.: Duke University Press. 430–447.

—— (1957). *The Brazilian Cotton Manufacture; Textile Enterprise in an Under-Developed Area, 1850–1950*. Cambridge, Mass.: Harvard University Press.

Steinberg, D. (1990). *The Soviet Economy, 1970–1990, A Statistical Analysis*. San Francisco, Calif.: International Trade Press.

Steinfeld, E. S. (1998). *Forging Reform in China: The Fate of State-Owned Industry*. Cambridge: Cambridge University Press.

Stiglitz, J. E. (1989). "Markets, Market Failures, and Development." *American Economic Review* 79(2): 196–203.

Streeten, P., and M. Lipton, eds. (1968). *The Crisis of Indian Planning: Economic Policy in the 1960s*. Oxford: Oxford University Press.

Strom, S. (1999). "Skepticism over Korean Reform." *New York Times*, July 30. C1, C6.

Suehiro, A. (1985). *Capital Accumulation and Industrial Development in Thailand*. Bangkok: Chulalongkorn University Social Research Institute.

—— (1993). "Capitalist Development in Postwar Thailand: Commercial Bankers, Industrial Elite, and Agribusiness Groups." In *Southeast Asian Capitalists*. Ed. R. McVey. Ithaca: Cornell University, Southeast Asia Program. 35–63.

Sugihara, K. (1986). "Patterns of Asia's Integration into the World Economy, 1880–1913." In *The Emergence of a World Economy, 1500–1914, Part II: 1850–1914*. Ed. W. Fischer, R. M. McInnis and J. Schneider. Weisbaden: Franz Steiner Verlag. 700–719.

Sugiyama, S., and M. C. Guerrero, eds. (1994). *International Commercial Rivalry in Southeast Asia in the Interwar Period*. Monograph, no. 39. New Haven: Yale Southeast Asia Studies.

Suh, N. P. (1980). "An Assessment of Critical Issues Confronting the Korean Machinery Industries." A preliminary report to the Economic Planning Board, Republic of Korea. Massachusetts Institute of Technology, Cambridge, Mass.

Suh, S.-C. (1978). *Growth and Structural Change in the Korean Economy, 1910–1940*. Cambridge, Mass.: Harvard University Press for the Council on East Asian Studies.

Summerhill, W. (1997). "Transport Improvements and Economic Growth in Brazil and Mexico." In *How Latin America Fell Behind: Essays on the Economic Histories of Brazil and Mexico*. Ed. S. Haber. Stanford, Calif.: Stanford University Press.

Suzuki, Y. E. (1987). *The Japanese Financial Systeem*. Oxford: Clarendon Press.

Sylla, R., et al., eds. (1999). *The State, the Financial System and Economic Modernization*. New York: Cambridge University Press.

Tainan Science-Based Industrial Park (1996). *Prospectus*. Tainan: Tainan Science-Based Industrial Park.

Taiwan, Republic of China National Science Council (1996). *Indicators of Science and Technology*. Taipei: National Science Council.

Takamura, N. (1982). "Japanese Cotton Spinning Industry during the Pre-World

War I Period." In *The Textile Industry and Its Business Climate*. Ed. A. Okochi and S.-I. Yonekawa. Tokyo: University of Tokyo. 8: 277–285.

Taniura, T. (1986). "Economic Development Effects of an Integrated Iron and Steel Works: A Case Study of Minas Gerais Steel in Brazil." *Developing Economies* 24(2): 169–93.

——— (1989). "Management in Taiwan: The Case of the Formosa Plastics Group." *East Asian Cultural Studies* 28(1–4): 63–90.

——— (1993). "The Lucky-Goldstar Group in the Republic of Korea." *Developing Economies* 31(4): 465–484.

Tanzi, V., and L. Schuknecht (1998). "The Growth of Government and the Reform of the State in Industrial Countries." In *Social Inequality: Values, Growth and the State*. Ed. A. Solimano. Ann Arbor: University of Michigan. 171–207.

Taussig, F. (1892). *The Tariff History of the United States*. New York: G. Putnam [repr. Augustus M. Kelley].

Taylor, A. M. (1998a). "Argentina and World Capital Markets: Saving, Investment, and International Capital Mobility in the Twentieth Century." *Journal of Development Economics* 57(1): 147–184.

——— (1998b). "On the Costs of Inward-Looking Development: Price Distortions, Growth and Divergence in Latin America." *Journal of Economic History* 58, no. 1: 1–29.

Taylor, L., ed. (1988). *Varieties of Stabilization Experience*. Oxford: Clarendon Press.

———, ed. (1993). *The Rocky Road to Reform: Ajustment, Income Distribution, and Growth in the Developing World*. Cambridge, Mass.: MIT Press.

Taylor, L., and E. L. Bacha (1976). "The Unequal Spiral: A First Growth Model for Belindia." *Quarterly Journal of Economics* 90: 197–218.

Taylor, P. (1998). "Software Exports." In *Financial Times* (London), December 2. 111.

Teece, D. J. (1976). *The Multinational Corporation and the Resource Cost of International Technology Transfer*. Cambridge, Mass.: Ballinger.

Teitel, S., and F. E. Thuomi (1986). "From Import Substitution to Exports: The Manufacturing Exports Experience of Argentina and Brazil." *Economic Development and Cultural Change* 34(3): 455–490.

Teixeira Vieira, D. (1951). "The Industrialization of Brazil." In *Brazil: Portrait of Half a Continent*. Ed. T. L. Smith and A. Marchant. New York: Dryden Press: 244–264.

Temin, P. (1964). *Iron and Steel in Nineteenth-Century America: An Economic Inquiry*. Cambridge, Mass.: MIT Press.

——— (1988). "Product Quality and Vertical Integration in the Early Cotton Textile Industry." *Journal of Economic History* 68 (4 December): 891–907.

Thailand, Government of (various years). *Thailand, Official Yearbook*. Bangkok: Government House Printing Office.

Thailand Development Research Institute (1987). *Productivity Changes and International Competitiveness of Thai Industries*. Bangkok: Thailand Development Research Institute.

Thee, K. W. (1996). "Economic Policies in Indonesia during the Period 1950–

1965, in Particular with Respect to Foreign Investment." In *Historical Foundations of a National Economy in Indonesia, 1890s-1990s.* Ed. J. T. Lindblad. Amsterdam: North Holland. 315–329.

Thoburn, J. T. (1977). *Primary Commodity Exports and Economic Development: Theory, Evidence and a Study of Malaysia.* London: John Wiley.

Thomas, P. J. (1935). "India in the World Depression." *Economic Journal* 45: 469–483.

Thomas, V., et al., eds. (1991). *Restructuring Economies in Distress: Policy Reform and the World Bank Washington, DC.* Washington, D.C.: Oxford University Press for the World Bank.

Thomson, G. P. C. (1989). *Puebla de Los Angeles: Industry and Society in a Mexican City, 1700–1850.* Boulder, Colo.: Westview Press.

——— (1991). "Continuity and Change in Mexican Manufacturing, 1800–1870." In *Between Development and Underdevelopment: The Precocious Attempts at Industrialization of the Periphery, 1800–1870.* Ed. J. Batou. Geneva: Librairie Droz. 255–302.

Thornburg, M. W. (1949). *Turkey, An Economic Appraisal.* New York: Twentieth Century Fund.

Thorp, R., ed. (1984). *Latin America in the 1930s: The Role of the Periphery in World Crisis.* London: Macmillan, in association with St. Antony's College, Oxford.

——— (1992). "A Reappraisal of the Origins of Import-Substituting Industrialisation, 1930–1950." *Journal of Latin American Studies* 24: 181–195.

Tigre, P. B. (1983). *Technology and Competition in the Brazilian Computer Industry.* New York: St. Martin's.

Tirole, J. (1992). "Speculation." *The New Palgrave Dictionary of Money and Finance.* Ed. P. Newman, M. Milgate, and J. Eatwell. London: Macmillan. 3: 513–515.

Togo, K. (1997). *Elements of the Development of the Japanese Raw Silk Industry.* Tokyo: Foundation for Advanced Studies on Internationial Development.

Tomlinson, B. R. (1981). "Colonial Firms and the Decline of Colonialism in Eastern India, 1914–47." *Modern Asian Studies* 15(3): 455–486.

——— (1982). "The Political Economy of the Raj: The Decline of Colonialism." *Journal of Economic History* 42, no. 1 (March): 133–137.

——— (1988). "The Historical Roots of Indian Poverty: Issues in the Economic and Social History of Modern South Asia: 1880–1960." *Modern Asian Studies* 22(1): 123–140.

——— (1993). *The Economy of Modern India, 1860–1970.* Cambridge: Cambridge University Press.

Topik, S. (1980). "State Intervention in a Liberal Regime: Brazil, 1889–1930." *Hispanic American Historical Review* 60(4): 593–616.

——— (1987). *The Political Economy of the Brazilian State, 1889–1930.* Austin: University of Texas.

Tortella, G., ed. (1990). *Education and Economic Development Since the Industrial Revolution.* Valencia: Generalitat Valenciana.

Toulan, O., and M. Guillen (1996). *Internationalization: Lessons from Mendoza.* Cambridge, Mass.: CIT/MIT.

Toye, J. (1995). *Structural Adjustment and Employment Policy: Issues and Experience.* Geneva: International Labour Organization.

Tran, V. T. (1988). "Foreign Capital and Technology in the Process of Catching Up by the Developing Countries: The Experience of the Synthetic Fiber Industry in the Republic of Korea." *The Developing Economies* 26 (4): 386–402.

Trebilcock, C. (1981). *The Industrialization of the Continental Powers 1780–1914.* London: Longman.

Tripathi, D. (1982). "Innovation in the Indian Textile Industry." In *The Textile Industry and Its Business Climate.* Ed. A. Okochi and S.-I. Yonekawa. Tokyo: University of Tokyo Press. 8: 175–197.

Tripathi, D., and M. Mehta (1990). *Business Houses in Western India: A Study of Entrepreneurial Responses, 1850–1956.* Columbia, Mo.: South Asia Publications.

TSKB (Industrial Development Bank of Turkey) (various years). *Annual Report.* Ankara.

Turkey, Government of (various years). *Statistical Yearbook of Turkey.* Ankara: State Institute of Statistics.

Türkiye Is Bankasi A. S. (1967). *Development Plan of Turkey, Second Five-Year (1968–1972).* Ankara: Economic Research Department, Türkiye Is Bankasi A. S.

Twomey, M. J. (1983). "Employment in Nineteenth Century Indian Textiles." *Explorations in Economic History* 20: 37–57.

Tybout, J. (2000). "Manufacturing Firms in Developing Countries." *Journal of Economic Literature* 37(1): 11–44.

Tyler, W. (1976). *Manufactured Export Expansion and Industrialization in Brazil.* Tubingen: Mohr.

U.S. Dept. of Commerce. *See* United States, Department of Commerce.

UNCTAD (United Nations Conference on Trade and Development) (1979). *Handbook of International Trade and Development Statistics.* Geneva: United Nations.

(1987). *Trade and Development Report, 1987.* Geneva: United Nations.

——— (1990). *Handbook of International Trade and Development Statistics.* Geneva: United Nations.

——— (1993). *Handbook of International Trade and Development Statistics.* Geneva: United Nations.

——— (1995). *Handbook of International Trade and Development Statistics.* Geneva: United Nations.

——— (1996). *Handbook of International Trade and Development Statistics.* Geneva: United Nations.

——— (1998a). *Trade and Development Report, 1998.* Geneva: United Nations.

——— (1998b). *World Investment Report.* Geneva: United Nations.

——— (various years [a]). *Commodity Trade Statistics.* Series D. Geneva: United Nations Conference on Trade and Development.

——— (various years [b]). *Handbook of International Trade and Development Statistics.* Geneva: United Nations Conference on Trade and Development.

UNESCO (United Nations Economic and Social Council) (1972). *Literacy, 1969–1971: Progress Achieved in Literacy Throughout the World.* New York: United Nations.

UNESCO (1993). *Statistical Yearbook.* Geneva: United Nations.

UNESCO (various years). *Statistical Yearbook.* Geneva: United Nations.

Ungson, G. R., et al. (1997). *Korean Enterprise: The Quest for Globalization.* Boston: Harvard Business School Press.

UNIDO (United Nations Industrial Development Organization) (1986a). *Industry and Development Global Report, 1985–1986.* Vienna: UNIDO.

———— (1986d). *Prelminary Analysis of the Iron and Steel Industry in the Developing ESCAP Regioin.* Bangkok: UNIDO.

———— (1991). *Industry and Development Global Report, 1991–1992.* Vienna: UNIDO.

———— (1992). *Industry and Development Global Report, 1992–1993.* Vienna: UNIDO.

———— (1995a). Industrial Development Global Report, 1995. Oxford: Oxford University Press.

———— (1995b). *International Yearbook of Industrial Statistics.* Vienna: Edward Elgar Publishing.

———— (1995c). *Policies for Competition and Competitiveness: The Case of Industrialization in Turkey.* Vienna: United Nations.

———— (1997). *International Yearbook of Industrial Statistics.* Vienna: Edward Elgar Publishing Limited.

———— (various years [a]). *Industrial Development Global Report.* Vienna: UNIDO.

———— (various years [b]). *International Yearbook of Industrial Statistics.* Geneva: United Nations.

United Nations (1963). *The Growth of World Industry, 1938–1961: National Tables.* New York: United Nations.

———— (1965). *The Growth of World Industry, 1938–1961: International Analyses and Tables.* New York: United Nations.

———— (1998). *National Accounts Statistics.* New York: United Nations.

United Nations, Department of International Economic and Social Affairs (1985). *Special Study, National Accounts Statistics: Compendium of Income Distribution Statistics.* New York: United Nations.

———— (various years). *Growth of World Industry.* Geneva: United Nations.

United States (various years). *Historical Statistics of the United States.* Washington, D.C.: Government Printing Office.

United States, Department of Commerce (1961). *Comparative Fabric Production Costs in the United States and Four Other Countries.* Washington, D.C.: U.S. Government Printing Office.

———— (various years). *U.S. Foreign Affiliates: Direct Investment Abroad.* Washington, D.C.: U.S. Government Printing Office.

United States, Department of the Treasury (1994). *National Treatment Study 1994.* Washington, D.C.: Department of the Treasury.

United States, National Science Foundation (Lawrence M. Rausch) (1995). *Asia's New High-Tech Competitors.* Washington, D.C.: USGPO.

United States, Trade Representative's Office (1998). *1998 Trade Policy Agenda and 1997 Annual Report of the President of the United States on the Trade Agreements Program.* Washington, D.C.: U.S. Government Printer.

Urzua, C. M. (1997). "Five Decades of Relations between the World Bank and Mexico." In *The World Bank: Its First Half Century.* Ed. D. Kapur, J. P. Lewis, and R. Webb. Washington, D.C.: Brookings. 49–108.

Usiminas (1993). *The Privatization Experience at Usiminas.* Belo Horizonte: Usinas Siderurgicas de Minas Gerais S. A.

Vaidyanathan, A. (1982). "The Indian Economy Since Independence, 1947–1970." In *Cambridge Economic History of India.* Cambridge: Cambridge University Press. 2.

Valdes Ugalde, F. (1997). *Autonomía y Legitimidad: Los Empresarios, La Política y el Estado en México.* Mexico: Siglo Veintiuno.

Van Hoesel, R. (1997). *Beyond Export-Led Growth: The Emergence of New Multinational Enterprises from Korea and Taiwan.* Amsterdam: Erasmus University Thesis Publisher.

Veloso, F., et al. (1998). "A Comparative Assessment of the Development of the Auto Parts Industry in Taiwan and Mexico: Policy Implications for Thailand." Cambridge, Mass.: Massachusetts Institute of Technology, Center for Technology Development, International Motor Vehicle Program.

Venkataramani, R. (1990). *Japan Enters Indian Industry.* New Delhi: Radiant.

Verma, S. (1996). "Liberalisation, Institutions and Export Growth: A Study of the Indian Garment and Software Industries." Ph.D. dissertation, New School for Social Research, New York.

Versiani, F. R. (1980). "Industrial Investment in an Export Economy: The Brazilian Experience Before 1914." *Journal of Development Economics* 7: 307–329.

Vicziany, M. (1979). "The Deindustrialization of India in the Nineteenth Century: A Methodological Critique of Amiya Kumar Bagchi." *Indian Economic and Social History Review* 16(2): 105–146.

Villanueva, J. (1972). "El Origen de la industrialización argentina." *Desarrollo Económico* 12, no. 47 (November–December): 451–476.

Vogel, E. (1989). *One Step Ahead in China.* Cambridge, Mass.: Harvard University Press.

von Tunzelmann, N. (1997). "The Transfer of Process Technologies in Comparative Perspective." In *Chinese Technology Transfer in the 1990s: Current Experience, Historical Problems and International Perspectives.* Ed. C. Feinstein and C. Howe. Cheltenham: Edward Elgar.

Wade, R. (1990). *Governing the Market: Economic Theory and the Role of the Government in East Asian Industrialization.* Princeton, N.J.: Princeton University Press.

——— (1998). "The Asian Debt and Development Crisis of 1997–?" *World Development* 26(8): 1535–1553.

Walder, A. G. (1995). "Local Governments as Industrial Firms: An Organizational Analysis of China's Transitional Economy." *American Journal of Sociology* (September): 263–301.

Walker, D. W. (1986). *Kinship, Business, and Politics: The Martinez del RIO Family in Mexico, 1824–1867.* Austin: University of Texas.

Wang, J.-C., and K.-H. Tsai (1995). "Taiwan's Industrial Technology: Policy Measures and an Evaluation of R&D Promotion Tools." *Journal of Industry Studies* 2(1): 69–82.

Wang, K. (1989). "Development Strategies for the Automobile and Parts Industry of the Republic of China." Cambridge, Mass.: Massachusetts Institute of Technology, International Motor Vehicle Program.

Wang, T.-P. (1999). "The Status of IT Industry in Taiwan." Taipei: Market Intelligence Center, Institute for Information Industry.

Wang, X., and P. Nolan (1996). "Where Is the Firm? The Shanghai Petrochemical Company under Economic Reform." Cambridge: Cambridge University, Department of Applied Economics.

Wang, Y.-F. (1993). *China's Science and Technology Policy: 1949–1989*. Aldershot: Avebury.

Ware, C. F. (1931). *The Early New England Cotton Manufacture: A Study in Industrial Beginnings*. Boston: Houghton Mifflin Company.

Warman, J. (1994). "La Competitividad de la Industria Electrónica: Situación Y Perspectivas." In *La Industria Mexicana en el Mercado Mundial*. Ed. F. Clavijo and J. I. Casar. Mexico: Fondo de Cultura Económica. 395–426.

Warren, K. (1991). "Technology Transfer in the Origins of the Heavy Chemicals Industry in the United States and the Russian Empire." In *International Technology Transfer, Europe, Japan and the USA, 1700–1914*. Ed. D. J. Jeremy. Aldershot: Edward Elgar. 153–177.

Weaver, F. S. (1980). *Class, State and Industrial Structure: The Historical Process of South American Industrial Growth*. Westport, Conn.: Greenwood Press.

Webb, R. (2000). "The Influence of the International Financial Institutions on ISI in the Period 1944–1980." In *Industrialisation and the State in Latin America: The Black Legend and the Postwar Years*. Ed. E. Cardenas, J. A. Ocampo, and R. Thorp. Oxford: Macmillan.

Wernerfelt, B. (1984). "A Resource-based View of the Firm." *Strategic Management Journal* 5(2): 171–180.

West, E. G. (1975). *Education and the Industrial Revolution*. New York: Harper and Row.

Westphal, L. E., et al. (1985). "Reflections on the Republic of Korea's Acquisition of Technological Capability." In *International Technology Transfer: Concepts, Measures, and Comparisons*. Ed. N. Rosenberg and C. Frischtak. New York: Praeger.

White House (1999). *President Proposes $23 Million Increase in Funding for PNGV*. Washington, D.C.: White House.

Whiting, V. R. J. (1992). *The Political Economy of Foreign Investment in Mexico: Nationalism, Liberalism, and Constraints on Choice*. Baltimore, Md.: Johns Hopkins University Press.

Wiboonchutikula, P., et al. (1989). "Thailand in the International Economic Community. In *The 1989 TDRI Year-end Conference*. Ed. TDRI. Bangkok: Thailand Development Research Institute.

Wiener, N. (1948). *Cybernetics: Or Control and Communication in the Animal and Machine*. New York: John Wiley.

Wilkie, J. (1970). *The Mexican Revolution: Federal Expenditure and Social Change Since 1910*. Berkeley, Calif.: University of California Press.

Wilkins, M. (1970). *The Emergence of Multinational Enterprise: American Business Abroad from the Colonial Era to 1914.* Cambridge, Mass.: Harvard University Press.

——— (1987). "Efficiency and Management: A Comment on Gregory Clark's 'Why Isn't the Whole World Developed?' " *Journal of Economic History* 67, no. 4 (December): 121–123.

Williamson, J. (1990). "What Washington Means by Policy Reform." In *Latin American Adjustment: How Much Has Happened?* Ed. J. Williamson. Washington, D.C.: Institute of International Economics.

Willis, E. J. (1990). *The Politicized Bureaucracy: Regimes, Presidents and Economic Policy in Brazil.* Boston, Mass.: Boston College.

Wionczek, M. S. (1964). "Electric Power: The Uneasy Partnership." In *Public Policy and Private Enterprise in Mexico.* Ed. R. Vernon. Cambridge, Mass.: Harvard University Press.

Wohlert, C. (1991). "The Introduction of the Bessemer Process in Sweden." In *Technology Transfer and Scandinavian Industrialisation.* Ed. K. Bruland. New York: Berg: 295–306.

Wolcott, S. (1997). "Did Imperial Policies Doom the Indian Textile Industry?" *Research in Econmic History* (17): 135–83.

Wolcott, S., and G. Clark (1999). "Why Nations Fail: Managerial Decisions and Performance in Indian Cotton Textiles, 1890–1938." *Journal of Economic History* 59, no. 2: 397–423.

Won, S.-Y. (1995). "A Study on the Persistency of the Policy Loans." KSESA. (In Korean.)

Woodruff, W. (1966). *Impact of Western Man: A Study of Europe's Role in the World Economy, 1750–1960.* New York: St. Martin's Press.

World Bank (1976, 1994). *World Tables.* Washington, D.C.

——— (1982). *World Development Report.* Washington, D.C.: World Bank.

——— (1985). *World Development Report.* Washington, D.C.: World Bank.

——— (1987). *World Development Report.* Washington, D.C.: World Bank.

——— (1991). *World Development Report: The Challenge of Development.* Washington, D.C.: World Bank.

——— (1992). *Trade Policy Reforms under Adjustment Programs.* Washington, D.C.: World Bank.

——— (1993). *East Asian Miracle: Economic Growth and Public Policy.* New York: Oxford University Press.

——— (1994a). *Bureaucrats in Business.* Washington, D.C.: World Bank.

——— (1994b). *World Tables.* Washington, D.C.

——— (1995). *World Development Report.* Washington, D.C.: World Bank.

——— (1996). *Statistical Handbook of the States of the Former USSR.* Washington, D.C.: World Bank.

——— (1998–99). *World Development Report: Knowledge for Development.* Washington, D.C.: World Bank.

——— (various years [a]). *World Debt Tables.* Washington D.C.: World Bank.

——— (various years [b]). *World Tables.* Washington, D.C.: World Bank.

——— (various years [c]). *World Development Report.* Washington, D.C.: World Bank.

Woytinsky, W. S., and E. S. Woytinsky (1953). *World Population and Production: Trends and Outlook*. New York: Twentieth Century Fund.

Wright, G. (1990). "The Origins of American Industrial Success." *American Economic Review* 80: 651–668.

Wright, S. F. (1966). *China's Struggle for Tariff Autonomy, 1843–1938*. Taipei: Ch'eng Wen Publishing.

Wright, W. R. (1974). *British-Owned Railways in Argentina: Their Effect on Economic Nationalism, 1854–1948*. Austin: University of Texas Press for the Institute of Latin American Studies.

Wu, S.-H. (1992). "The Dynamic Cooperation Between Government and Enterprise: The Development of Taiwan's Integrated Circuit Industry." In *Taiwan's Enterprises in Global Perspective*. Ed. N. T. Wang. Armonk, N.Y.: M. E. Sharpe. 171–192.

Wythe, G. (1949). *Industry in Latin America*. New York: Columbia University Press.

Wythe, G. (1955). "Brazil: Trends in Industrial Development." In *Economic Growth: Brazil, India, Japan*. Ed. S. Kuznets, Wilbert E. Moore, and Jospeh J. Spengler. Durham, N. C.: Duke University Press. 29–77.

Xue, L. (1997). "Promoting Industrial R&D and High-Tech Development through Science Parks: The Taiwan Experience and Its Implications for Developing Countries." *International Journal of Technology Management, Special Issue of R&D Management* 13(7–8): 744–761.

Yamazaki, H. (1988). "The Development of Large Enterprises in Japan: An Analysis of the Top 50 Enterprises in the Profit Ranking Table (1929–1984)." *Japanese Yearbook on Business History: 1988* 5: 12–55.

Yamazawa, I. (1975). "Industrial Growth and Trade Policy in Prewar Japan." *Developing Economies* 13, no. 1 (1 March): 38–65.

Yates, L. (1959). *Forty Years of Foreign Trade: A Statistical Handbook with Special Reference to Primary Products and Under Developed Countries*. London: George Allen and Unwin.

Yatsko, P. (1996). "Urge to Merge: China Pins Hopes on Mergers to Save State Firms." *Far Eastern Economic Review* (May 23): 56–59.

Yonekawa, S.-i. (1982). "The Growth of Cotton Spinning Firms: A Comparative Study." In *The Textile Industry and Its Business Climate*. Ed. A. Okochi and S.-I. Yonekawa. Tokyo: University of Tokyo Press. 1–44.

——— (1986). "Comment." In *Development of Managerial Enterprise*. Ed. K. Kobayashi and H. Morikawa. Tokyo: University of Tokyo Press. 12: 258–260.

Yonekura, S. (1994). *The Japanese Iron and Steel Industry, 1850–1990*. New York: St. Martin's.

Yoo, J.-H. (1998). *Korea's Four Major Reform Programs: Progress and Evalutaion*. Seoul: Ewha Women's University.

Yoon, B.-S. (1992). "Reverse Brain Drain in South Korea: State-Led Model." *Studies in Comparative International Development* 27(1): 4–26.

Young, A. (1994). "Lessons From the East Asian NICs: A Contrarian View." *European Economic Review* 38.

Young, S. C. (1969). "The Gatt's Long-Term Cotton Textile Arrangement and

Hong Kong's Cotton Textile Trade." Ph.D. dissertation, Washington State University.

Yuan, B. J. C., and M. Y. Wang (1999). "Analysis On the Key Factors Influencing Competitive Advantages of DRAM Industry in Taiwan." *International Journal of Technology Management* 18(1–2): 93–113.

Zevin, R. B. (1971). "The Growth of Cotton Textile Production After 1815." In *The Reinterpretation of American Economic History*. Ed. R. W. Fogel and S. L. Engerman. New York: Harper and Row.

Zhang, X.-H. (1991). *Enterprise Response to Market Reforms: The Case of the Chinese Bicycle Industry (1979–1988)*. Adelaide: University Of Adelaide.

——— (1993). *Enterprise Reforms in a Centrally Planned Economy: The Case of the Chinese Bicycle Industry*. Basingstoke: St. Martin's Press.

Zhou, G. X. Z. (1996). "Memorandum on Field Work in China, 1995." Cambridge, Mass.: Massachusetts Institute of Technology.

Index

Acer Computers, 193, 321n.7
ACER Group, 172
A. D. Little, 219
agriculture, 18, 107, 177, 291
Alemán, Miguel, 20
Alembic, 233
Alfa group, 220, 232
Altos Hornos, 215–16
Ambani, 210
America Fabril, 57
American Rolling Mill Company, 215
Amin, 233
Anaconda, 7
antidumping duties, 269, 270, 331n.21
Antuñano, Esteban de, 41, 42
APKINDO, 177, 178
Arbed, 7
Argentina, 11, 160, 281, 288, 293,
   327–28n.71, 332n.24
   antidumping initiatives, 270
   automobile industry, 154, 211
   class divisions, 225, 227, 230–31,
      326nn.59–61, 63, 64
   comparative advantage, 263, 266,
      267
   control mechanism, 282, 290–91
   deindustrialization, 261–62
   development banks, 132, 147–48,
      291
   education, 239
   electronics industry, 222
   exporting, 163, 166–70, 179,
      307n.25, 317–18nn.7, 12

family-owned firms, 192
foreign debt, 254
foreign investment by, 204
foreign investment in, 14, 16, 205,
   210, 272, 286, 332n.25
gross domestic investment, 126, 253
labor unrest, 79, 81
land distribution, 18, 291
literacy rates, 59
manufactures, 163
manufacturing experience, 1, 16
manufacturing output, 111
multinational enterprises in, 52–54,
   207, 210, 212
national firms, 119, 201
patents, 243, 277
petrochemicals industry, 117
pharmaceutical industry, 230–31,
   326n.65
railroads, 82, 83, 307n.20
research and development, 241, 243–
   44, 247, 277–79
restructuring rate, 260
small-scale firms, 72, 75
steel industry, 160, 230, 270
tariffs, 181, 320n.32, 331n.18
textile industry, 301n.3
wages, 81, 245–47
Arthur G. McKee and Company, 97
assessors, control mechanism, 9
assets, 19, 90, 206. *See also*
   intermediate assets; knowledge-
   based assets

387

assets approach theory, 284, 286–89
Astra Group, 318–19n.19
Australia, 220, 270
automobile industry, 7, 10, 157
  local-content requirements, 153–55,
    160, 322n.21
  See also under specific countries

Bago, 230
Banco Industrial, 147–48
Banco Nacional de Desenvolvomento
    Econonico e Social, 129, 133, 136,
    141–45, 147, 216, 226, 227, 291
Bank Bumiputra Malaysia Berhad, 129
Bank for Agriculture and Agriculture
    Cooperatives, 129
Bank Indonesia, 129
Bank Industri, 146–47, 325n.52
banking, 110, 129–30, 226–27,
    309n.36, 333n.35. *See also*
    development banks
Bank of Japan, 67
bankruptcy, 71, 88–89, 308nn.33, 34
Bao Steel Company of China, 217
BASF, 220
Bata Shoe, 110
Bayer, 7, 234
Bechtel Corporation, 210
BEFIEX program, 152, 181–82
BEL, 221
Belgium, 72, 313n.4
Bengal Iron and Steel Company, 95,
    310n.44
Bharat Heavy Electricals, 215, 324n.34
bicycle industry, 275–76, 288
Birla group, 233, 234, 327–28n.71
BI Walden International, 325n.52
BNDES. *See* Banco Nacional de
    Desenvolvomento Econonico e Social
Board of Investment (BOI; Thailand), 20,
    24–28, 130, 146, 151, 291,
    327n.69
Bodmer, Johann George, 186
Bokaro steel mill, 215
Booz Allen (U.S.), 216
Borneo Company, 110, 235
Boston Manufacturing Company, 39
Boustead-Buttery, 110, 235
Brazil, 51, 158, 160, 281, 315n.23,
    326–28nn.65, 71
  antidumping initiatives, 270

automobile industry, 152–54, 211,
    213, 270
class divisions, 225–27
comparative advantage, 263
deindustrialization, 261
development banks, 126, 128–29,
    132, 133, 136, 141–45, 147, 226,
    227, 291
electronics sector, 221, 225–27, 244,
    323n.27
exporting, 152, 163, 166, 169–71,
    173, 179–82, 270
foreign investment by, 204, 205
foreign investment in, 14, 16, 126,
    212, 272, 286, 332n.25
gross domestic investment, 127, 253
infrastructure projects, 126
institution-building, 20
labor unrest, 79
land distribution, 18
licensing fees and royalties, 239
loan interest rate indexation, 132–33
local-content requirements, 153–54
manufactures, 73
manufacturing experience, 1, 16
manufacturing output, 111
multinational enterprises in, 52–53,
    57, 207, 212, 221, 222, 227, 251
national firms, 201, 204, 326n.58
oil, gas, petrochemicals, 117, 217,
    218, 220
patents, 243, 277
privatization, 325nn.45, 56
railroads, 82–84
reciprocal control mechanisms, 10–11
research and development, 241, 244,
    277–79
small-scale firms, 72, 75, 288
state-owned enterprises, 215–18, 221,
    227, 323n.31
steel industry, 93–97, 136, 144–45,
    156, 160, 215, 216, 230, 310–
    11nn.46, 50, 324–25nn.36, 56
tariffs, 181, 331n.18
technology transfer, 53, 57, 58,
    303n.15
techno-standard imposition, 141–45
textile industry, 46, 47, 57, 58, 75,
    79, 86, 300–302nn.25, 3, 5,
    305n.7, 307–8nn.24, 33, 320n.29
trade issues, 173, 256

British American Tobacco, 53, 55, 56, 75, 85, 108, 111
British Commonwealth, 118, 187
business diversification. *See* diversification; diversified business groups

Canada, 212, 270, 314n.9
capital formation
  development bank criteria, 136
  domestic, 21, 22t., 78–79, 126–27, 253, 254
  as exporting factor, 166, 188
  foreign investment and, 21, 23t., 126
  government share of, 21, 23t.
  in silk industry, 67, 68
  three-pronged investment issues, 87–93
capital goods, 168t., 169, 287–88
capital investment, 71, 75–81, 163, 165, 166
Carso, 232
cement industry, 51, 88, 90
Cemex, 232
CEPAL. *See* United Nations Economic Commission for Latin America
certificates of encouragement, 130
chaebol. See under Korea
Chee Hsin Cement Company, 88, 90
chemical industry, 7, 116, 158–60. *See also* petrochemicals
Chemtex, 303n.15
Cheng Kuan-ying, 56
Chevron, 219
Chiang Kai-shek, 235
Chien Chao-nan, 55, 75, 77–78
Chile, 281, 291–93, 332n.24
  automobile industry, 211
  class divisions, 225
  comparative advantage, 263, 267
  development banks, 128, 147
  development strategy, 14
  education, 239
  electronics industry, 222
  exporting, 166, 172, 176–77, 291
  foreign investment by, 204, 205
  foreign investment in, 272, 286, 332n.25
  gross domestic investment, 126
  institution-building, 20
  land distribution, 18

manufactures, 163, 291
manufacturing experience, 1, 16
manufacturing output, 111
multinational enterprises in, 53, 207
railroads, 82, 84
research and development, 241, 277, 278
state-owned enterprises, 217
technology transfer, 58
textile industry, 301n.3
China, 32, 51, 160, 281, 293, 327–28n.71, 332n.30
  automobile industry, 154, 213, 275
  bicycle industry, 275–76
  cement industry, 88, 90
  cigarette industry, 55, 56, 75–78, 85, 302n.12
  comparative advantage, 263
  compradors, 33, 56, 88, 298n.11, 304n.25, 308n.31
  contract labor, 48, 306n.14
  deindustrialization, 261
  domestic capital formation, 254
  education, 240
  electronics sector, 225
  emigrants from, 15, 99, 105–7, 109, 110, 288
  exporting, 149, 162, 169, 174, 178–79, 184, 188, 319n.26
  finance issues, 88–90, 307–8nn.26–28, 31–32
  foreign investment in, 272, 302n.10, 332nn.25, 29
  income distribution, 18
  institution-building, 20
  kuan-tu shang-pan, 90
  land distribution, 18
  leading industries, 1931–1933, 66t.
  manufactures, 72–73
  manufacturing experience, 1, 15, 16
  manufacturing output, 111
  multinational enterprises in, 52–56, 220
  national firms, 14, 18, 121, 191
  railroads, 82–85, 88, 95
  reciprocal control mechanisms, 11
  research and development, 11, 241, 277, 280–81
  savings rate, 288
  silk production, 52, 53, 64–68, 304nn.25–27

China (*continued*)
  small-scale firms, 71–72, 75, 288
  state-owned enterprises, 217, 275
  steel industry, 62–63, 93–97, 158,
    217, 324n.38
  subcontracting of management, 79
  tariffs, 43, 46, 70, 178
  tea industry, 85
  technology transfer, 57–59, 61–63
  textile industry, 31, 33–39, 43, 46–
    50, 52–54, 56, 57, 81, 86, 89, 92–
    93, 174, 178, 298n.13, 301nn.30,
    31, 3, 305–9nn.7, 8, 16, 24, 26,
    37
  trade organizations, 269
  wages, 81, 306n.15
China General Technology Group,
  275
China Petroleum Company (Taiwan),
  217, 218, 219
China Steel of Taiwan, 216, 230, 235
Chosen Industrial Bank, 103
Chosen Rawsilk Thread Corporation,
  101
Chosen Textile Corporation, 101
Chosun Silk Mill, 101
Chrysler, 232
Chung-hsing group, 106
CIBA, 72, 186
Cifra, 232
cigarette industry, 53, 170
  China, 55, 56, 75–78, 85, 302n.12
class divisions, 225, 226–32
CMC, 221
COBRA, 221
Colombia, 205
colonialism, 287
  Japan and, 7, 15, 100–105, 119,
    120, 170
  manufacturing experience and, 99–
    105, 107–10, 119, 191
  See also decolonization
colonial manufacturing, 15, 16, 191
communication, technology transfer
  and, 52, 62
communications networks, control
  mechanism, 9
Companía de Petróleos, 217
Compania Vale do Río Doce, 220
comparative advantage, 5–6, 49–50,
  136, 262–67, 289

competition
  latecomer forms of, 140–41, 315–
    16n.24
  market theory, 287
competitive base, 192–93, 199
compradors. *See under* China
CONACYT, 241
Constancia, La (textile mill), 41, 42
contract labor, 48, 306n.14
control mechanism, 8–13, 125, 295n.6.
  See also reciprocal control
  mechanisms
CORFO. *See* National Development
  Corporation
Corning Glassworks, 54
corruption, 11, 290, 295n.8
  in Argentina, 147–48
  management agency system, 91–92
  in railway projects, 85
  in Thailand, 25
COSIPAS, 216, 324n.36
cotton gin, 7, 40
cotton textiles, 1, 10, 46–49, 50, 72–73
  Japan, 7, 52, 174, 310n.43
  Korea, 101
  Mexico, 40–42
  speculation in, 92–93, 309–10n.42
  Thailand, 26
counter-purchase regulations, 151
Cristalerías Rigolleau Company, 54
Crown Properties Office (Thailand), 111,
  129–30
CSN. *See* Volta Redonda
Cuauhtemoc-HYLSA, 232
Cuba, 15
currency, 74, 173, 175, 308n.32,
  332n.24
Curson, Viceroy, 59
Czech Republic, 270

Daewoo, 212, 213, 277
Danforth, A. W., 56, 57
Dastur, 215
Davar, N. F., 302n.5
debt, foreign, 254–55
debt crises, 1, 11, 251–55
debt-to-equity ratio, 19, 141, 194, 206,
  226
decolonization, 16, 20, 111, 120, 121,
  191, 208, 296n.14
defense-related contractors, 193

deindustrialization, 261–62
Delta Electronics, 195
DEMAG, 7, 303n.15
denationalization, 268
Denmark, 72
depreciation, budgeting for, 90
Development Bank of India, 138
development banks, 125–32, 160, 173,
  285, 291
  capital investment criteria, 136–39
  funding sources, 133–35
  loans from, 10–11, 93, 127, 132–33,
    141–46, 314n.16
  performance standard imposition, 140–
    58. *See also under specific countries*
distribution networks, 70, 85–87, 93,
  125
Di Tella (Argentine businessman), 243–
  44
diversification, 111, 195–97, 206, 252,
  273–75, 287
diversified business groups, 85, 190,
  193, 197, 222, 239, 274–75
divestments, 88–89
dividends, guaranteed, 90, 91
division of labor, 252, 286
Dow, 7
Dunlop, 7, 207, 234
DuPont, 7

East India Company, 84
Economía, La (textile mill), 42
economic development, 19, 290, 292
  institution-building and, 19–28, 284,
    290
  knowledge-based assets and, 2–8, 286–
    89
  overexpansion, 251–55
economies of scale, 117, 192–93, 195,
  197, 252, 273–77, 287
economies of scope, 197, 273–77
Ecuador, 332n.24
education, 3, 5, 238–40, 303nn.16–17,
  329n.1
  foreign student migration, 20, 21t.,
    246
  literacy, 59–61, 63, 185–86
  manager overseas study, 217
  reverse brain-drain, 246, 247,
    329n.81

See also learning; *under specific*
  countries
effectors, control mechanism, 9
efficient scale. *See* economies of scale
Egypt, 15, 292
Electronics Corporation of India, 221
electronics industry, 7, 10, 172, 221–
  27. *See also under specific countries*
Electronics Research and Service
  Organization, 221–22
émigré manufacturing, 15, 16, 213
Empress Mill, 46, 302n.5
engineers, 15, 121, 186, 240, 241f.,
  242t.
Engineers India Ltd., 210
England. *See* Great Britain
Escher-Wyss, 7, 72, 186
Esperança, 95
ethnic conflict, 225, 234–37
Etibank, 130
European Union, 270, 281, 293
exchange rates, 6, 10, 288–89
  exports and, 74, 166, 317n.5
  as interest rate factor, 132, 133
  silver standard, 74, 175
Executive Group for the Automobile
  Industry (Brazil), 211
EXIMBANK, 97
export processing zones, 10, 149, 270,
  316n.32. *See also* free trade zones
exports, 161–82, 288–90
  economic openness differences, 162–
    69, 317n.2
  global distribution, 256, 258t.
  growth rate, 150t., 162–63
  manufactures as, 72–74, 158, 160,
    163
  national firms and, 190, 202, 204
  policy standards, 148–53, 160
  pre-World War II trade history, 169–
    71
  quotas, 187, 320n.41
  reciprocal control mechanisms, 10–
    12, 149
  voluntary restraints, 118, 269
  See also import substitution; *under*
    specific countries

family ownership, 18, 85, 160, 192,
  226
Far Eastern group, 106

Federal Flour Mills, 236
Federal Reserve, U.S., 253
Federation of Korean Industries, 333n.36
Femsa, 232
Fiat, 7
finance, 87–93, 133–35, 141–42, 307–8n.26
financial markets, 1, 252, 254, 329n.2
Finland, 295n.4
Firestone, 7, 207
First Auto Works, 213
first mover advantage, 16, 192–93, 321n.3
fixed assets, 90
Fluor Corporation, 218–19
food processing, 1, 51, 105–6, 169–70, 186
Ford Motor Company, 7, 52, 110, 152, 211, 212, 232, 322n.22, 333n.32
foreign investment, 262, 282, 301n.2, 332nn.25–27
  capital formation, 21, 23t., 126
  as denationalization factor, 268
  development strategy and, 14
  Gerschenkron's theory, 286
  government policies toward, 208
  in Latin America, 119, 121, 208–10, 213, 231, 232, 286
  manufacturing experience and, 16, 119–21
  by multinational firms, 207–10
  national firms and, 190, 193, 204–5
  in railroads, 84, 85
  resistance mechanisms and, 271–72
  in Southeast Asia, 100, 108t., 119
  technology transfer and, 51–62, 69
  See also multinational enterprises
foreign trade. See trade
Formosa Plastics Group, 210–11, 219, 324n.43
France, 43, 79, 86
  textile industry, 7, 31–35, 43, 50, 65, 297nn.3, 4, 300n.24, 319n.21
free trade, 31, 182, 185–88, 255–71, 330nn.9, 10. See also North American Free Trade Agreement
free trade zones, 10, 149

Gandhi, Indira, 276
GATT. See General Agreement on Tariffs and Trade
GDP. See gross domestic product
Geertz, C., 107
Geigy, 72, 186
General Agreement on Tariffs and Trade, 177, 268–69, 282
General Electric, 7, 84
General Motors, 7, 108, 110, 211–13, 232, 322n.22, 333n.32
Gerdau group, 325n.56
Germany, 33, 83, 220, 314n.9
  steel industry, 54, 55, 63, 310–11nn.47, 49, 52
  technology transfer, 62, 63
  Turkey and, 96, 151–52
Gerschenkron, Alexander, 284–86, 313n.4
GFDI. See gross fixed domestic investment
Gigante, 232
glass industry, 74
globalization, 14–19, 190, 206, 246, 251–52, 273
GM. See General Motors
Goenkas group, 234
gold standard, 175
Goodyear, 7
government, 284–93
  development bank funding, 133–35, 285
  economic development and, 5, 6, 8, 70
  foreign debt, 254
  Gerschenkron's theory, 284–86
  gross investment levels, 21, 23t.
  in industrialization model, 282–83
  institution-building and, 19–28, 284
  national firms and, 190, 193–94, 212
  performance standards imposition, 212, 225
  silk industry role, 66–68
  steel industry and, 95–97
  subsidies, 8, 10–11, 19, 212, 225
  See also state-owned enterprises
Great Britain, 82, 86, 110, 285, 314n.9
  British Commonwealth, 118, 187
  foreign economic policy, 255–56
  Latin American investments, 119

India (*continued*)
  foreign investment in, 120, 210, 272, 333n.33
  gross fixed domestic investment, 79, 306n.10
  income distribution, 18
  infrastructure projects, 126
  institution-building, 20
  jobber system, 306n.14
  joint ventures, 234, 276
  land distribution, 18
  management agency system, 85, 91–93, 309n.39
  manufactures, 72–74
  manufacturing experience, 1, 15, 16
  manufacturing output, 111
  multinational enterprises in, 52, 54–56, 207, 210, 212, 222
  national firms, 14, 18, 121, 190, 191, 193, 321n.4
  performance standards, 157–58, 212, 322n.22
  pharmaceutical industry, 11, 156–57, 233, 326n.65
  price controls, 155–57
  railroads, 82–85
  reciprocal control mechanisms, 11, 282
  research and development, 241, 277–79
  savings rate, 288
  small-scale firms, 71, 75, 232–33, 288
  state-owned enterprises, 214–15, 217, 219, 221, 233, 324nn.32, 34
  steel industry, 54, 93–98, 155–56, 215, 230, 306n.9, 310–11nn.44, 50
  subcontracting of management, 79
  tariffs, 43, 46, 70, 268, 299–300n.23
  technology transfer, 57, 59, 61, 303n.15
  textile industry, 31, 33–39, 43, 46, 49, 50, 52, 55–57, 61, 71, 75, 78, 79, 81, 86, 88, 89, 93, 138, 152, 157–58, 299–302nn.23, 28, 29, 31, 5, 305–9nn.6–8, 26, 40, 42
  trade issues, 173, 256
  wages, 81
Indian Petrochemicals Corporation, 217
Indonesia, 158, 316n.27, 327–28n.71
  automobile industry, 213

  capital goods, 169
  colonial government, 100, 107–9
  comparative advantage, 263
  development banks, 129
  education, 240, 329n.1
  electronics industry, 222
  exporting, 149, 151, 162, 166, 170, 174, 177–78, 182, 318–19n.19
  foreign investment by, 204
  foreign investment in, 210, 332n.25
  gross domestic investment, 126, 253
  gross domestic product, 273
  institution-building, 20
  joint ventures, 318–19n.19
  manufacturing experience, 1, 15, 107–10
  manufacturing output, 111
  multinational firms in, 108, 110, 210, 212, 237, 322n.20
  national firms, 120, 121, 193
  performance standards, 212, 322n.23
  petrochemicals industry, 217, 219–20
  plywood industry, 178
  racial and ethnic conflict, 225, 234–37
  research and development, 241
  restructuring rate, 260
  state-owned enterprises, 217, 235
  tariffs, 268
  technology strategy, 14
  trade issues, 107, 108, 256
Indonesian Development Bank, 129
Industrial Development Bank (Turkey), 130, 138
Industrial Development Bank of India, 127, 133, 145–46, 219
Industrial Development Bureau (Taiwan), 20
Industrial Finance Corporation of India, 314n.7
Industrial Finance Corporation of Thailand, 25, 130, 132, 133
industrialization, 52, 70
  assets approach theory, 284, 286–89
  Gerschenkron's theory, 284–86
  globalization and national ownership, 14–19
  institution-building, 19–28, 284
  late-occurring, 1–8, 191–206, 252–53, 281–86

manufacturing experience and, 99–121

reciprocal control mechanisms, 8–13, 19–20, 23–28, 125, 141, 290

industrial policy, 9, 19

Industrial Technology Research Institute, 221

inflation, loan interest rates and, 132–33

information technology hardware industry, 190, 197, 199, 201t.

infrastructure projects, 126, 127t., 132

innovation capabilities, 3, 4t., 46

institution-building, 19–28, 284, 290

Instituto Mexicano de Petroleos, 218

integration development model, 14, 206, 252, 271, 273, 281, 293

interest rates, 85, 90, 132–33

intermediate assets, 8, 10, 15, 18–19, 125, 285, 289

as expansion factor, 253, 281

mid-technology industries, 161

national firms and, 190–94

See also subsidies

International Materials and Chemical Corporation, 219

International Monetary Fund, 133–35, 256, 260, 314–15nn.15, 18

investment. *See* capital investment; development banks; foreign investment; three-pronged investment

Ipiranga group, 220

iron and steel industry. *See* steel industry

Iron Mountain Company, 95

Italy, 52, 86, 160, 319n.21

silk production, 65, 295n.5, 304nn.20, 22

ITI, 221

Japan, 24, 160, 193, 256, 324n.42

colonialism, 7, 15, 100–105, 119, 120, 170

development banks, 89

distribution networks, 86–87

education initiatives, 59, 61

exporting, 161, 169–71, 174–76, 188, 269, 315n.22, 318nn.9–11

finance issues, 89, 307–8n.26

foreign investment by, 208–10, 322n.18

foreign trade, 161

government spending, 134–35

gross fixed domestic investment, 79

industrialization, 7, 51

joint ventures, 27–28, 216, 217, 274, 318–19n.19

land distribution, 18

manufactures, 72, 170, 318n.11

multinational enterprises, 54, 55

railroads, 83, 84

Reconstruction Finance Bank, 125, 313n.3

silk production, 7, 50–52, 64–65, 67, 68, 174

steel industry, 55, 56, 63, 95–97, 180, 215–17, 302n.4

as subcontractor, 173

technology transfer, 51–52, 55, 57–58, 63

textile industry, 7, 31, 47–52, 54, 57–58, 74, 75, 79, 86–87, 89, 92, 117–18, 174, 301nn.30–31, 305n.6, 307–10nn.26, 35, 43

trading companies, 319n.23

zaibatsu, 54, 85, 91, 101, 192, 237, 309n.39

Japanese Cotton Mills Association, 86

Japan Nitrogen Fertilizer Corporation, 102

Japan Steamship Company, 86

Jardine, Matheson and Company, 53, 187

Jefferson Smurfit, 204

jobber system, 79, 306n.14

John Deere, 7

joint-stock companies, 83, 89, 132

joint ventures, 14, 332n.27

India, 234, 276

Indonesia, 318–19n.19

Japan, 27–28, 216, 217, 274, 318–19n.19

multinational firms and, 210, 212, 213, 218, 252

state-owned enterprises and, 217–19

state spin-off model and, 193, 221–25

Thailand, 27–28, 111

Turkey, 151–52

Julian Kennedy, Sahlin and Company, 97

Kaiser Steel Corporation, 324n.36
Karabük (steel mill), 96, 311n.48
Katakura Silk Manufacturing Company, 67, 68
Khazanah Nasional BHD, 325n.52
KIA Motors, 277
Kim, Mahn-je, 141
Klabin, 204
knowledge-based assets, 2–8, 166, 269
  industrial development theory, 286
  multinational firms and, 191
  national firms and, 190
  nurturing of, 277–82
Kolon Nylon, 220, 303n.15
Korea, 160, 226, 233, 272, 281, 293, 326n.65, 331n.20
  automobile industry, 140–41, 154, 157, 212, 213, 277, 280, 317n.39
  big business emphasis, 237–38
  "big deal" strategy, 276–77, 333nn.34–36
  capital goods, 169, 288
  chaebol, 104, 219, 222, 237, 276–77, 327–28n.71
  comparative advantage, 263
  deindustrialization, 261
  development banks, 126, 128, 133, 133, 137–38, 145, 314n.12, 316n.26
  education, 103, 239, 312n.9
  electronics sector, 149, 151, 222, 224–25, 277
  exporting, 149, 151, 153, 160, 163, 170, 172–75, 202
  family-owned firms, 192
  financial markets, 329n.3
  foreign debt, 254
  foreign investment by, 204
  globalization, 246, 252, 329n.81
  government spending, 134–35
  gross domestic investments, 79, 126, 253, 306n.11
  gross domestic product, 273
  income distribution, 18, 328n.74
  infrastructure projects, 126
  institution-building, 20
  Japanese colonialism, 7, 15, 100–103, 119, 120, 170
  land distribution, 18
  licensing fees and royalties, 239

manufacturing experience, 1, 15, 16, 101–5
manufacturing output, 111
multinational firms in, 207, 210, 212, 222, 233
national firms, 14, 18, 121, 191, 193, 201, 202, 233, 237, 326n.58
patents, 243, 277
performance standards, 212, 245, 322–23n.24
petrochemicals industry, 117, 218–20
price controls, 156, 157, 317nn.37–39
reciprocal control mechanisms, 11, 141, 149, 151
research and development, 238, 241, 244–46, 277, 279–80, 325n.51, 333n.38
silk production, 101
state-owned enterprises, 218–19, 222, 323n.30
steel industry, 156, 158, 160, 180, 215–17, 219, 230
as subcontractor, 173
technology transfer, 63, 303n.15
textile industry, 101, 104–5, 118, 138, 170, 173, 174, 319n.26
trade issues, 103, 173, 256
trade unions, 8
trading companies, 319n.23
voluntary export restraints, 269
wages, 245–47
Korea Development Bank, 128, 132, 133, 138, 145, 149
Korean Nitrogen Fertilizer Corporation, 102
Korean Oil Corporation, 218
Krakatau Steel, 129
Krung Thai Bank, 129, 130
Krupp, 7, 96
kuan-li. See dividends, guaranteed
kuan-tu shang-pan, 90
Kubitschek, President, 20
Kungping Company, 53
Kuok, Robert, 236
Kyongsong Textile Corporation, 101

labor. See trade unions; workers
laissez-faire policy, 284, 320n.40
Lanari, Amaro, Jr., 216
land, distribution of, 17–18

managerial skills (*continued*)
  in state-owned enterprises, 214–15
  technology transfer and, 57, 82
  three-pronged investment and, 70, 82–85, 125
Manchuria, 7, 15, 100, 102, 104
Manchurian Incident (1931), 101, 105
Mannesmann, 151–52
manufactures
  as export share, 72–74, 158, 160, 163, 318n.11
  pre-World War II trade history, 169–71
manufacturing, 7, 18, 71
  deindustrialization, 261–62
  development bank investment, 130–32
  efficient scale. *See* economies of scale
  experience in, 1, 14–17, 99–121, 161, 292, 296n.9
  knowledge-based assets, 2–3
  localization of, 10, 153–54
  national firm leaders, 202, 203–4t., 205
  output, 1, 2t., 11–12, 51, 99–100, 111, 112–16t., 158–60, 195, 197, 212, 247, 251, 292, 304–5n.1
  reciprocal control mechanisms, 8–12
  scientific management, 76–77
  state-owned enterprises, 213–14
  See also specific industries
manufacturing value added, 222–25, 247, 256, 257t., 261t., 262–66
marketing, 7, 125
markets
  domestic, 163, 165, 190, 193
  niche, 195, 197
  selective seclusion of, 125, 161–89, 192–93, 317n.2
market theory, 284, 286–87
marking, 269
Martinez del Río family, 41, 42
Maruti Motors, 193, 213
Maruti Udyog Limited, 276
Marx, Karl, 34, 50
mass production, 31, 39–40, 195, 287
meat-packing industry, 53
MECON, 215
Mercedes Benz, 7
MERCOSUR, 185
mergers and acquisitions, 268, 271–73, 332n.26

Metallgesellschaft, 302n.6
metals, primary, 7, 158
Mexico, 51, 158, 160, 281, 288, 293, 326n.65
  antidumping initiatives, 270
  automobile industry, 154, 211–13, 267
  class divisions, 225, 231–32
  comparative advantage, 263, 267
  deindustrialization, 261
  development banks, 126–28, 132, 133, 137, 147, 232, 291, 299n.19, 313n.4
  education, 240
  electronics industry, 222, 224, 232
  exporting, 152, 162, 170–73, 179, 180, 184, 318n.16, 320n.36
  foreign debt, 254
  foreign investment by, 204, 205
  foreign investment in, 14, 16, 193, 231, 232, 272, 286, 332n.25
  glass industry, 74
  gross domestic investment, 127, 253
  infrastructure projects, 126
  institution-building, 20
  labor unrest, 79
  land distribution, 18
  manufactures, 72
  manufacturing experience, 1, 15, 16
  manufacturing output, 111
  multinational enterprises in, 52, 53, 55, 207, 208, 212, 222, 232
  national firms, 116–17, 119, 193, 201, 202
  North American Free Trade Agreement, 14, 270, 271
  oil and petrochemicals industry, 116–17, 119, 152, 217, 218, 220
  patents, 243, 277
  price controls, 155
  privatization, 231, 326–27n.67
  railroads, 82–84
  research and development, 241–42, 277, 278, 328n.79
  restructuring rate, 260
  state-owned enterprises, 215–18
  steel industry, 93–95, 155, 215–16
  tariffs, 42, 43, 46, 50, 268, 269, 320n.33, 331n.18
  technology transfer, 57, 303n.15

Ottoman Empire (*continued*)
  textile industry, 31, 33–39, 43, 46,
    49, 55, 296n.11, 298–300nn.13,
    23
  wages, 64, 306n.15
  See also Turkey
Ottoman Public Debt Administration,
  67
overexpansion, 251–55

Pacific Electric Wire and Cable, 274–75
Pakistan, 15
Pareto optimality, 185, 289–90
Park Chung Hee, 20, 149, 237,
  323n.30
Park Taejun, 216
Parry's, 219
Partnership for a New Generation of
  Vehicles, 279–80
Pasteur, Louis, 65
patents, 5, 11, 243, 277
pebrine (silkworm) disease, 65–66
Pemex, 116, 152, 217, 218, 220, 232
perfect knowledge, 3, 185, 284, 286,
  289–90
performance standards, 18, 93, 253,
  288–89
  debt-to-equity ratio, 19, 141, 194,
    206, 226
  development bank imposition of, 140–
    58
  government setting of, 212, 225,
    245, 322–23nn.22–26
  reciprocal control mechanisms, 8, 10–
    11, 141, 160
  in "remainder" countries, 292
  targeting of firms and, 193–94
  See also under specific countries
Perlis Plantations, 236
Permodalan Nasional Berhad, 235
Pertamina, 129, 217, 219
Peru, 205
Petrobras, 117, 217, 220
petrochemicals, 220, 324n.42
  Latin America, 111, 116–17, 152
  national firm leaders, 204, 214
  state-owned enterprises, 190, 214,
    217–19
Petroleum Authority of Thailand, 217
Petronas, 217, 220
Petroquisa, 117, 218

pharmaceutical industry
  Argentina, 230–31, 326n.65
  India, 11, 156–57, 233, 326n.65
  Switzerland, 186
Philippines, 178, 220, 292
Philips, 7, 72, 221
Pinochet, Augusto, 177
Pirelli, 7, 52
Pittsburgh Glass Company, 54
plywood industry, 177–78
Pohang Iron and Steel Mill, 63, 156,
  216–17, 219, 220, 230
policy standards, 140, 148–58, 160
population, 2t., 13t., 163, 165–66
POSCO. *See* Pohang Iron and Steel Mill
postal savings, 315n.20
Prebisch, Raul, 167, 318n.8
premodern manufacturing, 15, 87
prices, 5, 38–39, 111, 288–89
  controls on, 154–58
  as exporting factor, 165, 166
  reciprocal control mechanisms, 8–9
Prieto, Carlos, 94
Primax Electronics, 195
privatization, 220, 231, 323n.30, 325–
  26nn.45, 56, 66
Procter and Gamble, 207–8
production capabilities, 3, 4t., 18, 46,
  84, 207
production units, investment in, 70–75,
  125
productivity, 5–6, 10, 51, 289–90
  textile industry, 37–40, 47–48, 65,
    89, 117–18
profits, 5, 308nn.29, 30, 34
  distribution of, 19, 125
  inflation of, 90–92
  maximization of, 252
project execution capabilities, 3, 4t., 46,
  84–85, 197
promotion certificates, 130, 146
property rights, 286–87
proprietary innovations, 2, 282
proprietary skills, 14, 190, 191, 287
protectionism, 163, 173, 181, 185
  against Japanese exports, 100, 312n.4
  textile industry, 31, 43–46, 50, 70,
    173, 300n.28
Proton Motors, 213
public research institutes, 193, 194
pure learning, 2

quasi-rents, 18, 206, 291
quotas, export, 187, 320n.41

racial conflict, 225, 234–37
railroads, 81–85, 88, 95, 307n.20
raw materials, 142, 310n.45
R.E.A.-Cumberbatch, 110, 235
reciprocal control mechanisms, 8–13,
 141, 173, 281–82, 290
 exports and, 149, 151, 160
 institution-building, 19–20
 in "remainder" countries, 292
 See also under specific countries
Reconstruction Finance Bank, 125,
 313n.3
Reliance, 233–34
"remainder" countries, 1, 16, 292–93
rent seeking, 2, 15
Repos, SA, 325n.44
research and development, 149, 252,
 277–82, 321n.1, 328n.78
 foreign firm investments, 191, 207–8,
 271
 government support of, 221, 222,
 238–47
 performance standards, 11, 206
research institutes, 221, 222, 245, 279,
 325n.51
resistance mechanisms, 251–52, 268–
 81
resource allocation, 255, 260–66
resource scarcity, 163
reverse brain-drain, 246, 247, 329n.81
reverse engineering, 58, 239
Rio Flour Mills, 57
Roemmers, 230
Rosovsky, Henry, 189
Russia, 188, 220, 302–3nn.8, 17,
 324n.42. *See also* Soviet Union

Saha Union, 110
SAIL, 230
St. John del Rey company, 53
Salim business group, 219, 237
Samsung, 103–4, 277, 328n.76
Sandoz, 72, 186
savings rate, 288
scale economies. *See* economies of scale
science and technology enterprises, 11,
 280–81

science parks, 11, 193, 194, 221, 245,
 246, 279, 288, 321n.5, 325n.47
scientific management, 76–77
Second Industrial Revolution, 7, 75,
 140, 186, 281–82
Semiconductor Complex Ltd., 221
sensors, control mechanism, 9
Shanghai Cotton Cloth Mill, 46, 56, 57
Shell Brasil S.A., 220
Sheng Hsuan-Huai, 94
Shinkon Synthetic Fibers, 220
Shin Nippon Steel, 216–17, 220
shyness of capital, 71, 87
Siam Cement, 111
Siam Commercial Bank, 130
SIAM Di Tella, 211
SIAM group, 243–44
Siam Motors, 111, 213
Siemens, 7
Siliconware Precision Industries, 195
silk production, 1, 64–69, 92, 303n.19
 China, 52, 53, 64–68, 304nn.25–27
 Italy, 65, 295n.5, 304nn.20, 22
 Japan, 7, 50–52, 64–65, 67, 68,
 174
 Korea, 101
 Turkey, 66–67, 304n.23
silver standard, 74, 175, 308n.32
Sime Darby, 235–36
Singapore, 220, 296n.10
Sinopec, 217
skill deficits, 46–49, 51
Slater, Samuel, 39
slavery, 53
Slovakia, 270
small-scale firms, 71–72, 75, 105, 232–
 33, 287–88
SOCMA, 227, 230
Soeharto, General, 20
South Africa, 169
South Korea. *See* Korea
Soviet Union, 215, 220
speculation, 92–93, 253, 309–10nn.41,
 42, 44
spinning enterprises. *See* textile
 production
Ssangyong Motors, 277
state-owned enterprises, 287, 288,
 323nn.29, 30
 national firm leaders, 190, 197, 205,
 213–20

state-owned enterprises (*continued*)
  racial and ethnic conflict and, 234, 235
  spin-off model, 193, 221–25
  See also under specific countries
State Planning Office (Turkey), 20, 130
steel industry, 51, 180, 302n.4, 310–11n.47
  government role in, 70, 95
  national firm leaders, 214, 230
  performance increases, 158, 160
  price controls, 155–56
  railroads and, 84, 95
  state-owned enterprises, 190, 214–17, 220
  three-pronged investment in, 93–98
  See also under specific countries
Stone Electronic Technology, 280
strategic alliances, 14, 252
structural change index, 260–62, 330–31nn.15, 17
subcontracting, 79, 173, 210
subsidies, 8, 10–11, 19, 125, 160, 212, 225
  export-related, 148–49, 151, 152
  Gerschenkron's theory, 285–86
  long-term capital, 148–49, 153
  selective, 268
  WTO regulations, 270–71
sugar refining, 52–53, 108, 302n.7
Sukarno, President, 20
Sulzer, 72, 186
Sümer Development Bank, 96, 130, 151
Sumitomo Electric Industries Ltd., 274
Sunkyung group, 219
Super 301 trade clause (U.S.), 270, 330n.10
Supreme Export Council (Japan), 175–76
Suzuki Motors, 276
Swatch, 186
Sweden, 7, 72, 310–11nn.47, 52, 314n.9
Switzerland, 72, 185–88, 283, 320n.40

tacitness, of technology, 51, 301n.1
Tainan Science Industrial Park, 194, 245
Taiwan, 104, 160, 177, 281, 291, 293, 327–28n.71
  automobile industry, 157, 212, 213
  capital goods, 169, 288

comparative advantage, 263
deindustrialization, 261
development banking, 129, 132, 136–37
diversification, 274–75
domestic capital formation, 254
education, 239, 240
electronics sector, 221–22, 224–25
exporting, 163, 166, 170, 172–74, 182, 184, 202
export policy standards, 149, 151, 153, 160
foreign investment by, 204
foreign investment in, 234, 272, 322n.18
globalization, 246, 329n.81
gross domestic investment, 127, 306n.11
income distribution, 18
information technology hardware industry, 190, 197, 199, 201t., 321n.10
institution-building, 20
Japanese colonialism, 7, 15, 100, 105, 119, 120, 170
land distribution, 18
licensing fees and royalties, 239
manufacturing experience, 1, 15, 16, 105–7
manufacturing output, 111
multinational firms in, 207, 208, 210–11, 222
national firms, 14, 18, 121, 190, 191, 193, 195, 197, 201, 202
patents, 243, 277
performance standards, 212, 323n.26
petrochemicals industry, 217–20
price controls, 157
racial and ethnic conflict, 225, 234–36
reciprocal control mechanisms, 11
research and development, 11, 241, 244–46, 277
science parks, 11, 193, 194, 245, 279, 288, 321n.5, 325n.47
small-scale firms, 71, 105, 288
state-owned enterprises, 217–19, 221–22, 235, 288, 323n.30
steel industry, 158, 230
as subcontractor, 173
tariffs, 118–19, 331n.18

textile industry, 106, 117–19, 173, 174, 312nn.10, 13, 319n.26
top business groups, 1970–96, 231
trade issues, 105, 106, 173, 256, 269
trade unions, 8
wages, 245–47
Taiwan Semiconductor Machinery Corporation, 193
Taiwan Semiconductor Manufacturing Corporation, 221
Tai-yuen group, 106
tariffs, 70, 173, 260, 292, 299–300nn.23, 26
level indicators, 1913, 175t.
liberalization and, 267–68, 331n.18
petrochemical industry, 324n.42
protectionism and, 43–46, 50, 70, 163, 173
raising of, 269
See also under specific countries
Tata, Jamshedji, 63, 78
Tata group, 54, 63, 94, 96–98, 233, 234, 302n.5, 321n.4, 327–28n.71
Tata Sons and Company, 88, 94
Tate, Henry, 302n.6
Tatung group, 274
Taussig, Frank, 43
Taylor, Frederick Winslow, 77
tea industry, 85
technological capabilities, 3, 4t., 7, 70, 75–81, 180
technology
buying of, 14, 238–39, 271, 281
development strategy issues, 14, 16, 206
knowledge-based assets and, 3–5
science parks. See science parks
technology transfer, 5, 51–69, 82, 239, 303n.15. See also under specific countries
techno-standards, 140, 141–45, 147, 160
Telco, 213, 276, 278
TELEBRAS, 221
telecommunications industry, 221, 222
Televis, 232
textile production, 1, 31–51, 289, 298–302nn.9–31, 3–5
artisanship, 31–34, 39, 50
capital investment, 78, 79, 80t.
cotton gin and, 7, 40

development bank loans, 138
distribution networks, 86, 93
manufacturing experience issues, 117–19
protectionism, 31, 43–46, 50, 70, 173
skill deficits, 46–49
speculation in, 92–93, 309–10nn.41, 42
spinning firm sizes, 75, 76–77t.
subsidies, 10, 151, 152
See also cotton textiles; silk production; under specific countries
Thai Blanket Industry, 110–11
Thailand, 100, 116, 158, 160. 311n.1, 327–28n.71
automobile industry, 27, 213
Board of Investment, 20, 24–28, 130, 146, 151, 291, 327n.69
capital goods, 169
comparative advantage, 263
corruption in, 25
deindustrialization, 262
development banks, 129–30, 132, 133, 146
education, 24, 240, 329n.1
electronics industry, 222
exporting, 28, 149, 151, 162, 166, 172, 173, 184
foreign investment in, 332n.25
gross domestic investment, 126, 253
institution-building, 19–28
joint ventures, 27–28, 111
land distribution, 18
manufacturing experience, 1, 15, 110–11
multinational firms in, 25, 212, 236
national ownership, 111, 120
performance standards, 25–26
racial and ethnic conflict, 225, 234–36
reciprocal control mechanism, 23–28
research and development, 241
restructuring rate, 260
state-owned enterprises, 25, 217, 235
tariffs, 25–27
technology strategy, 14
textile industry, 110–11, 151, 312n.12
trade issues, 25–26, 173, 256
U.S. foreign aid, 24

three-pronged investment, 7, 68, 70–98, 125
    capital-related, 71, 75–81
    distribution, 70, 85–87, 125
    finance issues, 87–93
    iron and steel industries, 93–98
    management, 70, 82–85, 125
    production units, 70–75, 125
tire industry, 7
TISCO, 96–98
tobacco industry. *See* cigarette industry
Tomioka Filature, 67
Toppe, Mr., 55, 63
trade, 251
    antidumping duties, 269, 270, 331n.21
    direction of, 183–84t.
    free trade zones, 10, 149
    Heckscher-Ohlin-Samuelson theory, 3
    intra-Asian growth, 169–71, 184
    intraregional pattern of, 182–85
    Latin American growth, 170–71
    liberalization of, 260–68
    market seclusion, 125, 161–89
    nontariff measures, 269–70
    See also exports; free trade; imports; tariffs; *under specific countries*
trade-related intellectual property rights, 331n.22
trade-related investment measures, 270
trade unions, 8
trading companies, 53, 68, 187, 319n.23
transactions approach theory, 286
transportation, 52, 62, 95, 262–67, 287. *See also* automobile industry; railroads
TRIMs. *See* trade-related investment measures
TRIPs. *See* trade-related intellectual property rights
Tunisia, 292
Turkey, 116, 158, 160, 281, 293, 313n.2, 327–28n.71
    automobile industry, 213
    comparative advantage, 263
    debt problems, 256
    development banks, 130, 137, 138
    electronics sector, 225
    exporting, 162, 166, 169, 172–74, 188

export policy standards, 151–52
foreign investment by, 204
foreign investment in, 14, 16, 54, 272, 332n.26
institution-building, 20
joint ventures, 151–52
manufacturing experience, 1, 15, 16
manufacturing output, 111
multinational enterprises in, 52, 54, 212
performance standards, 212, 323n.25
research and development, 241
silk industry, 66–67, 304n.23
steel industry, 93, 95–97, 160, 311n.48
textile industry, 174, 296n.11, 299–300n.23
See also Ottoman Empire
turnkey transfers, 214

Union Carbide, 207, 210, 303n.15
United Engineers, 110
United Kingdom. *See* Great Britain
United Malayan Banking Corporation, 129
United Microelectronics Corporation, 221
United Nations Economic Commission for Latin America, 167, 318n.8
United States, 33, 252, 314n.9
    antidumping cases against, 270
    cotton gin impact, 7, 40
    exporting, 175, 179–81, 188, 318–20nn.10, 28, 30
    Federal Reserve, 253
    foreign economic policy, 255–58, 260, 329–30nn.3, 9, 10
    foreign investment by, 208–10, 322n.18
    imports to, 258, 259t.
    manufactures, 72
    multinational enterprises, 52, 53
    research and development projects, 279–80
    steel industry, 310–11nn.47, 49, 52
    subcontracting by, 173
    tariffs, 40, 43, 46, 49, 181, 311n.49, 320nn.31, 35, 324n.42
    textile industry, 31, 39–40, 43, 46, 49, 50, 65, 75, 118, 179, 297n.1, 305n.7
    Thailand and, 24

Upjohn, 230
USIMINAS, 193, 215–17, 220, 230, 324n.36

Vargas, Getulio, 136
Venezuela, 15, 292
vertical integration, 273–74
Vidriera Monterrey, 74
Vietnam, 220, 292
Vitro, SA, 74, 232
VLSI Technologies Inc., 325n.52
Volkswagen, 213
Volta Redonda, 94–97, 215, 216, 230
voluntary export restraints, 118, 269

wages
    as capital investment factor, 79, 81
    as comparative advantage, 5–6
    cuts in, 6, 8
    daily earnings, East Asia, 8t.
    exporting issues, 10, 163
    financial crises impact on, 251
    in post-World War II Japan, 7
    as R&D investment incentive, 149, 245–47
    technology transfer issues, 63–64
    textile industry, 39, 79, 81, 306n.15
Waltham system, textile production, 39
Washington consensus, 260
watch making, 186
Webb, Beatrice and Sidney, 306n.9
Westinghouse, 7, 244
Whitney, Eli, 7, 40

Winbond Electronics Corporation, 195, 274
Wipro Infotech Ltd., 193
workers, 316n.31
    capital investment issues, 79
    contract labor, 48, 306n.14
    development loan issues, 10–11
    female wage gap, 7
    global employment, 256, 258t.
    jobber system, 79, 306n.14
    supply of as exporting factor, 163
    textile industry, 37t.
    See also managerial skills
World Bank, 130, 133, 156, 219, 260, 313n.2, 330n.12
World Trade Organization, 154, 213, 251, 268–71, 292, 332n.23
World War I, 101, 105, 108
Wriston, Walter, 253
WTO. *See* World Trade Organization
Wuhan Iron and Steel Company, 324n.38

Yacimientos Petrolíferos Fiscales, 117, 220, 324n.39, 325n.44
Yawata Steel Works, 55, 56, 63, 96
Yokohama Specie Bank, 67, 313n.3
Yongsan Engineering, 102–3
YPL. *See* Yacimientos Petrolíferos Fiscales
Yuelong, 213

zaibatsu. See under Japan